THE WORKS OF JONATHAN EDWARDS

VOLUME 15

Harry S. Stout, General Editor

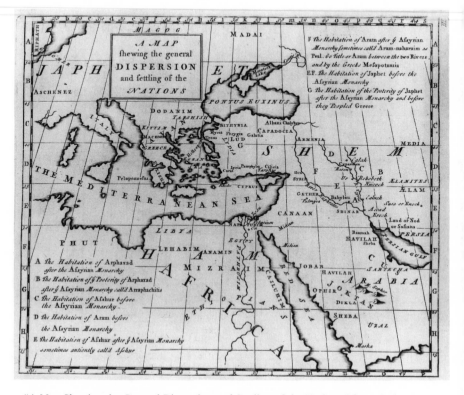

"A Map Shewing the General Dispersion and Settling of the Nations," from Arthur Bedford, *The Scripture Chronology Demonstrated by Astronomical Calculations* (London, 1730), Appendix.

JONATHAN EDWARDS

Notes on Scripture

EDITED BY
STEPHEN J. STEIN

CHANCELLORS' PROFESSOR OF RELIGIOUS STUDIES
INDIANA UNIVERSITY

New Haven and London

YALE UNIVERSITY PRESS, 1998

Funds for editing The Works of Jonathan Edwards
have been provided by The Pew Charitable Trusts, Lilly
Endowment, Inc., and The Henry Luce Foundation, Inc.

Published with assistance from The Exxon Education
Foundation.

Set in Baskerville type by The Composing Room
of Michigan, Inc., Grand Rapids, Michigan.

Printed in the United States of America by Vail-Ballou
Press, Binghamton, New York.

Library of Congress Cataloging-in-Publication Data

Edwards, Jonathan, 1703–1758.
  Notes on Scripture / Jonathan Edwards ; edited by
Stephen J. Stein.
    p.   cm. — (The works of Jonathan Edwards ; v. 15)
    Includes bibliographical references and indexes.
    ISBN 0–300–07198–1 (alk. paper)
    1. Bible—Commentaries—Early works to 1800.
I. Stein, Stephen J., 1940– . II. Title. III. Series:
Edwards, Jonathan, 1703–1758. Works. 1957; v. 15.
BX7117.E3 1957 vol. 15
[BS490]
285.8 s—dc21
[220.7]   97–25895
                                                  CIP

A catalogue record for this book is available from the
British Library.

The paper in this book meets the guidelines for permanence
and durability of the Committee on Production Guidelines
for Book Longevity of the Council on Library Resources.

10 9 8 7 6 5 4 3 2 1

EDITORIAL COMMITTEE FOR
THE WORKS OF JONATHAN EDWARDS

PREVIOUSLY PUBLISHED

CONTENTS

ILLUSTRATIONS

TABLES

NOTE TO THE READER

This is the first volume within *The Works of Jonathan Edwards* devoted solely to Edwards' exegetical notebooks. It is comprised of Edwards' four-volume manuscript notebook entitled "Notes on Scripture." Two more volumes of exegetical materials, containing Edwards' "Blank Bible" (although Edwards himself called these materials his "Miscellaneous Observations on Scripture"), are to follow.

Although some of these rich but understudied exegetical writings were published in various nineteenth-century editions of Edwards' works, volume 15 of the Yale Edition signals the inauguration of the first modern, critical, and comprehensive publication of these manuscript treasures. It is our hope that the Yale Edition of Edwards' biblical writings will raise new questions and provide important new materials for those interested in exploring the biblical groundwork of Edwards' thought. We anticipate a host of new studies connecting Edwards' biblical writings to the intellectual and cultural currents of the early modern West and to the growing scholarly literature dealing with the long and fruitful history of biblical exegesis in the context of the Judeo-Christian tradition.

Harry S. Stout
General Editor

Preparation of the Text

The text of Jonathan Edwards is reproduced in this Edition as he wrote it in manuscript, or, if he published it himself, as it was printed in the first edition. In order to present this text to modern readers as practically readable, several technical adjustments have been made. Those which can be addressed categorically are as follows:

1. All spelling is regularized and conformed to that of *Webster's Third New International Dictionary*, a step that does not involve much more than removing the "u" from "colour" or "k" from "publick" since Edwards was a good speller, used relatively modern spelling, and gen-

erally avoided "y" contractions. His orthographic contractions and abbreviations, such as ampersands, "call'd," and "thems." are spelled out, though pronounced contractions, such as "han't" and "ben't," are retained.

2. There is no regular punctuation in most of Edwards' manuscripts and where it does exist, as in the earliest sermons, it tends to be highly erratic. Editors take into account Edwards' example in punctuation and related matters, but all punctuation is necessarily that of the editor, including paragraph divisions (especially in some notebooks such as the "Miscellanies") and the emphasizing devices of italics and capitalization. In reference to capitalization, it should be noted that pronouns referring to the deity are lower case except in passages where Edwards confusingly mixes "he's" referring to God and man: here capitalization of pronouns referring to the deity sorts out the references for the reader.

3. Numbered heads designate important structures of argument in Edwards' sermons, notebooks, and treatises. Numbering, including spelled-out numbers, has been regularized and corrected where necessary. Particularly in the manuscript sermon texts, numbering has been clarified by the use of systematic schemes of heads and subheads in accordance with eighteenth-century homiletical form, a practice similar to modern analytical outline form. Thus the series of subordinated head number forms, 1, (1), *1*, a, (a), in the textual exegesis, and the series, I, *First*, 1, (1), *1*, a, (a), in Doctrine and Application divisions, make it possible to determine sermon head relationships at a glance.

4. Textual intervention to regularize Edwards' citation of Scripture includes the correction of erroneous citation, the regularizing of citation form (including the standardization of book abbreviations), and the completion of quotations which Edwards' textual markings indicate should be completed (as in preaching).

5. Omissions and lacunae in the manuscript text are filled by insertions in square brackets ([ ]); repeated phrases sometimes represented by Edwards with a long dash are inserted in curly brackets ({ }). In all cases of uncertain readings, annotation gives notice of the problem. Markings in the text designate whole word units even when only a few letters are at issue.

6. Minor slips of the pen or obvious typographical errors are corrected without annotation. Likewise, Edwards' corrections, deletions, and internal shifts of material are observed but not noted unless of substantive interest.

7. Quotations made by the editor from the Bible (AV) and other secondary sources are printed *verbatim ac literatim*. Edwards' quotations from such sources are often rather free but are not corrected and are not annotated as such unless significant omissions or distortions are involved.

Acknowledgments

When a research project extends over several years it is necessary to acknowledge a large number of individuals and institutions that have played a role in bringing it to completion. Among the institutions to whom I am most grateful are the Beinecke Rare Book and Manuscript Library at Yale University, the Lilly Rare Book and Manuscript Library at Indiana University, the libraries of Yale Divinity School, Yale University, Harvard University, and Harvard Divinity School, and the Interlibrary Loan Division of the Indiana University Library. Special thanks to Diana Hanson and Marty Sorury in the Microfilm Room at Indiana University Library for their patience and generous assistance over the past several years.

A number of individuals played significant roles in nurturing my early interest in Jonathan Edwards and in encouraging my continuing involvement with the Yale Edition. The late Sydney E. Ahlstrom exerted a shaping influence on my professional life. John E. Smith, the former General Editor of the Edition, made possible my initial participation as an editor. Harry S. Stout, the present General Editor, has been a friend and steady supporter. Conversations through the years with Wilson H. Kimnach, John F. Wilson, and Jon Butler have always proved valuable. As readers will discover, this volume, as well as several others in the Edition, rests firmly on the pioneering scholarship of Thomas A. Schafer, whom I also count a special friend. It would be impossible to imagine a more generous colleague. Several of these individuals have been kind enough to read early drafts of the Introduction to this volume. None of them, of course, is responsible for it.

Other individuals have played critical roles in the production of this volume as it moved from the earliest stages of transcription through the preparation of an edited text. Lauren Bryant's first pass at inputting a literal transcription provided an electronic foundation for the project as well as occasional light moments when Edwards' hand confounded her best efforts. Shane Blackman proved a reliable and creative research assistant, whose pursuit of specific sources included a successful trip to England. James S. Ackerman and David Brakke provided helpful critiques of the foreign-language insertions. Mark A. Noll and E. Brooks Holifield both read the Introduction at late stages and offered highly instructive suggestions. My present research assistant, Catharine Cookson, also contributed to this endeavor. Jenny Louis has solved technical computing problems and been steady with her secretarial assistance. The staff members at the central office of the Edition in New Haven, including Ava Chamberlain and Douglas A. Sweeney, have been consistently helpful. Special thanks to Executive Editor Kenneth P. Minkema for countless answers to specific questions, for savvy advice, for careful checking of my edited text, and for orchestrating the entire production process.

I have received financial assistance for the preparation of this volume from the Pew Charitable Trusts through the grant given to the Yale Edition of the *Works* and from Indiana University. My thanks to Morton Lowengrub, Dean of the College of Arts and Sciences at Indiana University, for making possible an extended leave in 1994–95 and for his continuing support of my department. Colleagues in the Department of Religious Studies provide constant intellectual stimulation and collegial encouragement.

My children, Beth and Stephen, now grown, have never known a time when the name of Jonathan Edwards was absent from family conversation. My wife Devonia bears the same burden more patiently than I deserve. This volume may be the first undertaking of my professional career that my deceased father, Frederick C. Stein, would have had a sustained interest in reading. His demands during my childhood stamped the language and phrasing of the King James Version deeply into my memory. For that reason, I dedicate this project to him.

Funding for this volume and for the Edition as a whole has been provided by the Pew Charitable Trusts, Lilly Endowment, Inc., and the Henry Luce Foundation, Inc.

Ayoung Jonathan Edwards (1703–58) penned the following private resolution in the closing months of 1722 while serving as a supply minister in New York City: "*Resolved*, To study the Scriptures so steadily, constantly and frequently, as that I may find, and plainly perceive myself to grow in the knowledge of the same."[1] Diary entries the following year document his persistence and the difficulties he encountered in pursuit of that goal. On January 14, for example, he experienced "spiritual insight" while reading Romans 8. On May 12, after returning to his home in East Windsor, Connecticut, he chided himself for having "lost that relish of the Scriptures" that he had known earlier.[2] Subsequent months witnessed renewed delight in biblical study and meditation, as well as continuing problems in maintaining his resolve. At the beginning of 1724, Edwards, now pastor of the congregation in Bolton, Connecticut, wrote a brief entry on Genesis 2:10–14, the first note in what was to become a lifelong exegetical series later entitled "Notes on Scripture."[3]

Fifteen years later, looking back on his early ministry, Edwards recollected: "I had then, and at other Times, the greatest Delight in the holy Scriptures, of any Book whatsoever."[4] "Notes on Scripture," a biblical commentary that includes more than five hundred numbered entries, is evidence of that continuing preoccupation. The last entry in the series, No. 507, written approximately two years before his death

---

1. "Resolutions," in Sereno E. Dwight, ed., *The Works of President Edwards: With a Memoir of His Life* (10 vols. New York, S. Converse, 1829–30 [hereafter Dwight ed.]), *1*, 70.

2. "Diary," Dwight ed., *1*, 80, 85.

3. For this date, see *The Works of Jonathan Edwards*, *13*, *The "Miscellanies," a–500*, ed. Thomas A. Schafer (New Haven, Yale Univ. Press, 1994), 94. (After the initial citation, individual volumes in the Yale Edition are referred to as *Works*, followed by a volume number.) "Notes on Scripture" is sometimes called "Notes on the Scriptures" and "Notes on the Scripture."

4. "Personal Narrative," in Samuel Hopkins, *The Life and Character of the Late Reverend Mr. Jonathan Edwards, President of the College of New-Jersey* (Boston, 1765), p. 31.

in 1758, is a lengthy comparison between Canticles and Psalm 45.[5]
Seven years after Edwards' death, Samuel Hopkins (1721–1803), his
close associate and first biographer, declared that his friend "had studied the Bible more than all other books."[6] This volume provides evidence of the fruits of that study.

"Notes on Scripture" is a private working notebook in which Edwards recorded exegetical ideas, took notes on his reading, and devel-
oped select theological themes. He did not intend to publish it. At
times his entries seem highly tentative. Edwards often changed his
mind on the choice of words. He frequently made mistakes on such
matters as the numbering of entries, the citation of biblical references,
and the grammatical structure of sentences. Sometimes he corrected
his errors; other times he did not. He was reading widely in the scholarly literature of his day; at times he cited it at length, paraphrased it,
or absorbed it into his own prose without acknowledgment.

At first glance, "Notes on Scripture" appears to have little organiza-
tional coherence or thematic integration. Edwards made no attempt
to survey all parts of Scripture; the entries move randomly among the
books of the Bible. Brief entries of a few lines alternate with notes that
fill several pages. Some comments hinge directly on the original language or the historical context; others use the biblical texts as a pretext
to launch exegetical excursuses. A number of entries derive from
publications Edwards was reading, including other commentaries.

Close examination of the seemingly random notes discloses the hermeneutic Edwards consistently employed throughout the series.
"Notes on Scripture" documents his consuming interest in typology, a
traditional method of biblical interpretation that links the Old and
New Testaments by means of correspondences between "types" in the
former and "antitypes" in the latter. Broadly defined, a type is a figure
or image that, in addition to its own historical significance, prefig-
ures a future reality, the antitype.[7] In Edwards' hands, typology's conven-

5. Here and elsewhere a capitalized "No." with numerals always refers to "Notes on
Scripture" entries; the lower case "no." is used for all citations in other MSS by JE.

6. Hopkins, *Life and Character*, p. 40.

7. Useful discussions of typology include Ursula Brumm, *American Thought and Religious
Typology* (New Brunswick, N.J., Rutgers Univ. Press, 1970); Sacvan Bercovitch ed., *Typology
and Early American Literature* (Amherst, Univ. of Massachusetts Press, 1972); Earl Miner, ed.,
Literary Uses of Typology: From the Late Middle Ages to the Present (Princeton, Princeton Univ.
Press, 1977); and Mason I. Lowance, Jr., *The Language of Canaan: Metaphor and Symbol in New
England from the Puritans to the Transcendentalists* (Cambridge, Harvard Univ. Press, 1980). See
also Janice Knight, "Learning the Language of God: Jonathan Edwards and the Typology of

tional limits were exceeded as he applied a typological reading not only to biblical material but also to extra-biblical historical events and natural phenomena. He found, for example, "the great destruction of the heathen" in Constantine's time to be a foreshadowing of a "vastly greater destruction of the wicked" in the future; similarly, he regarded the screams of an owl as a representation of the misery of devils dwelling in eternal darkness.[8] The collective result of his exegesis is a scriptural organon with the typological principle at its foundation, a system composed of biblical themes that Edwards regarded as central to Christianity and that he used in his public ministry as the basis for sermons, occasional writings, and major treatises.

"Notes on Scripture" represents only a portion of Edwards' extensive exegetical writings, for through the years he also wrote entries interpreting the Bible in several other manuscripts. Together, these entries form a loosely structured network of commentary. The links among his manuscripts are evident in "Notes on Scripture." For instance, numerous references point to Edwards' interleaved "Blank Bible." The latter, formally entitled "Miscellaneous Observations on the Holy Scriptures," is a large biblical commentary that he began writing in 1730.[9] Similarly, other references in the "Notes on Scripture" point to Edwards' "Miscellanies," a theological and philosophical series he began in late 1722 that also contains substantial exegetical materials, as well as to his smaller manuscripts, such as the "Images" and "Apocalypse" notebooks.[1]

Nature," *William and Mary Quarterly*, 3rd ser. 48 (1991), 531–51; *The Works of Jonathan Edwards, 11, Typological Writings*, eds. Wallace E. Anderson and Mason I. Lowance, Jr. (New Haven, Yale Univ. Press, 1993); and Stephen H. Daniel, *The Philosophy of Jonathan Edwards: A Study in Divine Semiotics* (Bloomington, Indiana Univ. Press, 1994), pp. 41–65.

8. "Images," nos. 166 and 204 (*Works, 11*, 113, 127). JE's liberal application of typology contrasts with that of other commentators who restricted types to biblical materials.

9. JE's "Blank Bible" is constructed of leaves of foolscap interleaved between the pages of an Old and New Testament. In this rebound volume JE wrote biblical commentary on all books of the Bible. This MS is in the Beinecke Rare Book and Manuscript Library, Yale University, New Haven, Conn. Throughout this volume it is assumed that all of JE's MSS are in the Beinecke Library unless otherwise indicated. Wilson H. Kimnach has pointed out that the interleaved Bible functioned as a reference center for JE. See *The Works of Jonathan Edwards, 10, Sermons and Discourses 1720–1723*, ed. Wilson H. Kimnach (New Haven, Yale Univ. Press, 1992), 102.

1. For these texts, see *The Works of Jonathan Edwards, 5, Apocalyptic Writings*, ed. Stephen J. Stein (New Haven, Yale Univ. Press, 1977); and *Works, 11* and *13*. The "Miscellanies" is JE's most important theological notebook, featuring doctrinal and apologetic entries; but it also contains considerable biblical commentary.

The text of "Notes on Scripture" appears in this edition for the first time in its entirety and in the order in which the entries occur in the manuscripts. The only previous edition was published by Sereno E. Dwight (1786–1850) in 1830.[2] Dwight omitted entries, imposed a canonical order on the series, and took great liberties in his editing. Here the complete text in its correct sequence allows the reader to follow Edwards' developing exegetical interests and interpretive patterns.

Edwards and the Commentarial Tradition

Commentaries and the commentarial mode of discourse have exercised an immense influence in Western culture, especially before the rise of modern critical thought. A commentary, defined in the most restricted sense, is a running gloss on a text; the task of the commentator, no matter what the text, is interpretation. Precritical commentators carried out the interpretation of sacred texts within the confines of dogmatic or systematic theological commitments. Modern critics adopted an alternative set of exegetical procedures by turning to the philological, historical, and scientific study of ancient texts. In the premodern period in the West—which lasted roughly until the full impact of such developments as the printing revolution, the expansion of the philological sciences, and the rise of modern science was felt in Europe—exegetes of sacred and classical texts wielded great power in literate circles and beyond because of the significance widely accorded to canonical writings. In no case was that truer than with Christian interpreters of the Bible.[3]

In a comparative study of commentarial traditions, both East and West, John B. Henderson has identified a body of common assumptions and strategies used by exegetes to interpret canonical texts, whether they be scriptural or classical. According to Henderson, "Commentary dominated much of the intellectual life of postclassical, premodern man not only by virtue of its importance as genre or form, but also through the habits of mind and modes of thought it fos-

2. "Notes on the Bible," Dwight ed., 9, 113–563.

3. John B. Henderson, *Scripture, Canon, and Commentary: A Comparison of Confucian and Western Exegesis* (Princeton, Princeton Univ. Press, 1991), pp. 200 ff. See also "The Exposition and Exegesis of Scripture," G. W. H. Lampe et alii, in *The Cambridge History of the Bible: The West from the Fathers to the Reformation*, ed. Lampe (Cambridge, Cambridge Univ. Press, 1969), pp. 155–279; and Frederick W. Danker, "Biblical Exegesis: Christian Views," *The Encyclopedia of Religion*, ed. Mircea Eliade (16 vols. New York, Macmillan Publishing Company, 1987), 2, 142–52.

tered."[4] In some traditions, in fact, a process of the canonization of commentaries occurred. Such was the case, for example, in the Western church before the Reformation, when the writings of church fathers rivaled the Bible in importance. In many traditions, therefore, the relation between canon and commentary was fluid and changing.

In the premodern period commentators traditionally wrote in defense of canonical texts. They accentuated the positive qualities of the texts, defended them against attacks, and sought suitable meanings in them. These commentaries often featured the inspired quality of the canon or its cosmic significance. Regardless of the tradition, commentators assumed that canonical texts were not contradictory, incoherent, superfluous, implausible, or inappropriate.[5]

This premodern commentarial way of thinking included many assumptions shared by Edwards, too. His core beliefs as an exegete of the Bible included a supernaturalism that affirmed a God revealed through sacred texts and a three-story universe inhabited by humans and spirits, both good and evil. For Edwards, the boundaries of the Christian canon were not debatable. He accepted the prevailing view that the biblical canon had been closed long ago and that there was no need to augment it.[6] He showed little patience with those in his day who claimed inspiration for new revelations. Premodern commentators also viewed the Bible as a comprehensive source of knowledge. Writing in late 1728 or early 1729, Edwards asserted that "the doctrines of the Word of God are the foundation of all useful and excellent knowledge. . . . Revelation is that light in the world from whence has beamed forth not only the knowledge of religion, but all valuable truth; 'tis the fountain of that light which has lightened the understandings of men with all sorts of knowledge."[7] In his judgment, the biblical canon was a coherent and ordered source of beneficial knowledge and historical truth as well as a revelation of God's plan of salvation.

4. Henderson, *Scripture, Canon, and Commentary*, p. 81.

5. Henderson's discussion of assumptions governing interpretation is based in part on Tzvetan Todorov's *Symbolism and Interpretation*, translated by Catherine Porter (Ithaca, Cornell Univ. Press, 1986). See *Scripture, Canon, and Commentary*, p. 136. Todorov speaks of "triggers" for exegesis that call forth the explanation of texts. Interpretation is triggered when "the immediately accessible meaning is insufficient" in some respect (p. 98).

6. See JE's sermon on I Cor. 13:8–13 (May 1748) with the following doctrine: "The extraordinary influences of the Spirit of God imparting immediate revelations to men were designed only for a temporary continuance while the church was in its minority and never were intended to be steadily upheld in the Christian church."

7. "Miscellanies," no. 350 (*Works, 13*, 425).

According to the commentarial tradition, the task of the exegete is to interpret sacred texts and to identify and reconcile conflicting elements within the canon. The commentator must clarify obscurities, find coherence in what may seem to be incoherent, harmonize elements that appear discordant, and propose moral possibilities where the text seems to approve of immoral actions. In his efforts to interpret the Bible, Edwards resorted to these same time-honored commentarial strategies. He found meaning in obscure passages by reading them against others, as when he interpreted the struggle of Jacob and Esau in their mother's womb (Gen. 25:22) as a reference to the war between the flesh and the spirit (Gal. 5:17).[8] He reconciled differences among parallel texts by resorting to linguistic and syntactical arguments, as in the case of the disparate accounts of Jesus' passage through Jericho (Matt. 20, Mark 10, and Luke 18).[9] He discovered virtue in the scatological when viewed from a spiritual perspective, for example, proposing a "mystical signification" of the severe penalty dealt to the woman who grabbed the genitals of her husband's opponent (Deut. 25:11–12).[1] He used multiple levels of meaning to rise above the offense of the literal, showing how the vow made by Jephthah the Gileadite need not result in the offering of his daughter in a burnt sacrifice (Judg. 11:30–40).[2] But at the same time Edwards refused to conflate or confuse his commentary with canon, affirming the Protestant principle that the Scripture alone is the authoritative source of Christian teaching. He recognized that interpreters, himself included, could err.

Edwards shared the assumptions and strategies of the Protestant commentarial tradition (including the principle of *sola scriptura*) with a distinguished line of exegetes who set out to explain and interpret the Bible for their own instruction as well as the edification and nurture of others.[3] He was heavily indebted to this Protestant tradition. Among the most significant predecessors to whom Edwards was beholden were the English commentators Matthew Poole (1624–79) and Mat-

8. "Notes on Scripture," No. 71, below, p. 69.

9. "Notes on Scripture," No. 233, below, pp. 182–84.

1. "Blank Bible," p. 162.

2. "Notes on Scripture," No. 223, below, pp. 160–69. See also Stephen J. Stein, "The Quest for the Spiritual Sense: The Biblical Hermeneutics of Jonathan Edwards," *Harvard Theological Review* 70 (1977), 99–113.

3. Roland H. Bainton, "The Bible in the Reformation," in *The Cambridge History of the Bible: The West from the Reformation to the Present Day*, ed. S.L. Greenslade (Cambridge, Cambridge Univ. Press, 1963), pp. 1–37.

thew Henry (1662–1714). Both were victims, directly or indirectly, of the Acts of Uniformity, which required the use of the Anglican Book of Common Prayer in worship and removed from their parishes all ministers who refused to conform; both also represented the zealously anti-Roman Catholic school of English Protestants. Poole's principal work was the five-volume *Synopsis Criticorum aliorumque Sacrae Scripturae Interpretum* (1669–76), in which he compiled and distilled the biblical exegesis of other commentators. His encyclopedic folios— books of the largest kind—were used widely in New England. Henry's six-volume *Exposition of the Old and New Testaments* (1708–10), completed by his friends following his death, combined scholarly and pastoral commentary. He was intent on the practical application of biblical truths to the Christian life. His folios also gained a sizable audience in America.[4] Edwards' combined exegetical output in the notebooks and other projects may well rival the scope and even the size of these massive publications.

Edwards' knowledge of biblical scholarship, however, went well beyond these two pivotal works. His "Catalogue" lists references to other general commentaries as well as to expositions of specific books in the Bible.[5] Included in the former category is *The Family Expositor,* by the Nonconformist divine Philip Doddridge (1702–51), and in the latter, volumes by the dissenting clergyman Moses Lowman (1680–1752) on the book of Revelation and by John Locke (1632–1704) on Galatians and II Corinthians, all of which Edwards cited in "Notes on Scripture." Edwards read widely in sources dealing with biblical history, chronology, and geography—perennial topics of interest that were enjoying expanding scholarly attention in the seventeenth and eighteenth centuries. In "Notes on Scripture," for example, he referred in one entry to William Reading's *History of Our Lord and Saviour Jesus Christ* (2nd

---

4. Poole, *Synopsis Criticorum aliorumque Sacrae Scripturae Interpretum* (4 pts. in 5 vols. London, 1669–76). Henry, *An Exposition of All the Books of the Old and New Testament; Wherein the Chapters are summ'd up in Contents; the Sacred Text inserted at large, in Paragraphs, or Verses; and each Paragraph, or Verse, reduc'd to its proper Heads; the Sense given, and largely illustrated, with Practical Remarks and Observations* (6 vols. London, 1708–10). For biographical information on both Poole and Henry as well as details concerning multiple editions of these works, see *Works,* 5, 59–63.

5. The "Catalogue" is a MS in which JE noted books and other items of interest. It defines his intellectual world as well as the range of his reading. He began this bibliographical notebook while in college and maintained it in one form or another throughout his lifetime. Some of JE's most commonly used books are not cited in the "Catalogue," however, perhaps because he owned them.

ed., 1717), and in other entries he quoted at length from Arthur Bedford's *Scripture Chronology Demonstrated by Astronomical Calculations* (1730) and Edward Wells' *Historical Geography of the Old Testament* (1711).[6]

Edwards was also familiar with a variety of publications that addressed specific hermeneutical questions, the kinds of issues that shaped the assumptions and strategies employed by commentators. In "Notes on Scripture" he cited the Welsh minister and biblical critic Jeremiah Jones (1693–1724) on canonical authority, the Anglican educator and bishop Thomas Sherlock (1678–1761) on the nature of prophecy, and the English-born nonconforming divine Samuel Mather (1626–71) on the interpretation of types.[7] He used other standard resources to assist with the task of exegesis, including lexicons, concordances, books on grammar, and general encyclopedias. Several publications mentioned in "Notes on Scripture" fall into this category: Johann Buxtorf's *Lexicon Hebraicum* (6th ed., 1646), Nathan Bailey's etymological dictionary (1736), and Ephraim Chambers' *Cyclopaedia* (2nd ed., 1738).[8]

6. Doddridge, *The Family Expositor: or, a Paraphrase and Version of the New Testament: with Critical Notes; and a Practical Improvement of each Section. Containing the Latter Part of the History of our Lord Jesus Christ, as recorded by the Four Evangelists, Disposed in the Order of an Harmony* (6 vols. London, 1739–56); Lowman, *A Paraphrase and Notes on the Revelation of St. John* (London, 1737); Locke, *A Paraphrase and Notes on the Epistle of St. Paul to the Galatians* (3rd ed., London, 1708), and *A Paraphrase and Notes on the Second Epistle of St. Paul to the Corinthians* (London, 1706); Reading, *The History of our Lord and Saviour Jesus Christ. In Three Parts with suitable Meditations and Prayers. To which are added the Lives of the Holy Apostles and Evangelists. To Which is Prefix'd the Life of the Blessed Virgin Mary, Mother of Our Lord* (2nd ed., London, 1717); Bedford, *The Scripture Chronology Demonstrated by Astronomical Calculations, and also by the Year of Jubilee, and the Sabbatical Year among the Jews: or, An Account of Time, from the Creation of the World, to the Destruction of Jerusalem; as it may be proved from the Writings of the Old and New Testament* (London, 1730); and Wells, *An Historical Geography of the Old Testament* (3 vols. London, 1711). For information on Lowman and Bedford, see *Works*, 5, 55–59, 64–66.

7. Jones, *A New and Full Method of Settling the Canonical Authority of the New Testament. Wherein All the antient Testimonies concerning this Argument are produced; the several Apocryphal books, which have been thought canonical by any Writers, collected, with an English Translation of each of them; together with a particular Proof that none of them were ever admitted into the Canon, and a full Answer to those, who have endeavoured to recommend them as such* (3 vols. London, 1726–27); Sherlock, *The Use and Intent of Prophecy, in the Several Ages of the World. In Six Discourses Delivered at the Temple-Church in April and May 1724* (3rd ed., London, 1732); and Mather, *The Figures or Types of the Old Testament, by which Christ and the Heavenly things of the Gospel were preached and shadowed to the People of God of old; Explained and improved in sundry Sermons* ([Dublin], 1683).

8. Buxtorf, *Lexicon Hebraicum et Chaldaicum* (6th ed., London, 1646); Bailey, *An Universal Etymological English Dictionary* (London, 1736); and Chambers, *Cyclopaedia: or, an Universal Dictionary of Arts and Sciences* (2 vols. 2nd ed., London, 1738).

Edwards constantly kept an eye out for new exegetical aids. The publication by the Scotsman Alexander Cruden (1701–70) of a concordance to the Bible is a case in point.[9] Edwards first learned of its publication from an advertisement in *The London Magazine* of 1737, where it was said to be "more useful than any book of this kind hitherto published." By late 1739 or 1740 he had gained access to the volume and immediately noted that Cruden's preface gave favorable mention to "Buxtorf's Hebrew Concordance," "Erasmus Schmidius' Greek Concordance to the New Testament," and "Abraham Trommius' Greek Concordance to the Old Testament in the Septuagint version."[1] These kinds of resources, in combination with the Hebrew text of the Old Testament and the Greek text of the New, were the basic tools of Edwards' trade as an exegete.[2]

Edwards' preoccupation with biblical typology, an interest that began before he wrote the first entry in the notebook, emerges as the unifying theme in "Notes on Scripture." On the night of August 28, 1723, for instance, he penned the following in his "Diary": "When I want books to read; yea, when I have not very good books, not to spend time in reading them, but in reading the scriptures, in perusing Resolutions, Reflexions, &c., in writing on Types of the Scripture, and

---

9. Cruden, *A Complete Concordance to the Scriptures of the Old and New Testament* (London, 1738).

1. JE, "Catalogue," pp. 8, 14.

2. JE's "Catalogue" contains two 1750 references to John Mill's *Novum Testamentum Graecum* (London, 1707) which was issued in numerous editions (pp. 24, 25). Mill's version, based on the text prepared by the Paris house of Stephanus, added some 30,000 variant readings from ancient manuscripts and the church fathers. Mill was joined by other scholars in the eighteenth century who also challenged or abandoned the Textus Receptus, including Edward Wells, Daniel Mace, and Johann Bengel (W. F. Howard, "The Greek Bible," in *The Bible in Its Ancient and English Versions*, ed. H. Wheeler Robinson [Oxford, Clarendon Press, 1940], pp. 75–76). Similarly, JE's "Catalogue" refers to a "new edition of the Hebrew Bible" by Charles Francois Houbigant entitled *Biblia Hebraic: Cum Notis Criticis et Versione Latina* published in 1753 (p. 30). Among the many editions of the Hebrew Bible available before this time are those of Johann Buxtorf, Joseph Athias, and E. Van der Hooght. In addition, several Polyglot Bibles were available, containing the Hebrew text, the Septuagint, and other ancient versions (H. Wheeler Robinson, "The Hebrew Bible," in Robinson, ed., *Bible*, pp. 21–23). It appears that JE's primary text for linguistic study was a large quarto version of the Hebrew Bible with the Apocrypha and the New Testament in Greek, the whole interlined in Latin. This version was based on the Antwerp Polyglot (1569–72) edited by Benedictus Arias Montanus. JE's Bible is now part of the Edwards Collection at Princeton University Library. In the margin at Gen. 30:17, he wrote, "see my other Hebrew Bible." The variety of biblical texts available in colonial America is illustrated in Arthur O. Norton, "Harvard Text-Books and Reference Books of the Seventeenth Century," *Publications of the Colonial Society of Massachusetts* 28 (1933), 388–93.

other things, in studying the Languages, and in spending more time in private duties."[3] He never abandoned his early resolve to write about types. He scattered comments about typology in a variety of locations, and those comments reveal his departure from the conservative hermeneutical tradition that found types and antitypes only within the pages of the Bible. In the "Miscellanies," for example, in an entry entitled "Types," he spoke of God's ordering natural things in creation so "that they livelily represent things divine and spiritual," and he asserted that "innumerable things in human affairs . . . are lively pictures of the things of the gospel."[4] In other words, Edwards saw connections between the natural and the spiritual worlds as well as between historical events and divine truths. About the same time, in his "Catalogue," under the heading "Books to be inquired for," he listed "The best upon the types of the Scripture."[5] Later in the "Miscellanies," when describing the relation between types and antitypes, he pointed out that "the inferior and shadowy parts" of God's creation "represent those things that are more real and excellent, spiritual and divine."[6] In his "Types" notebook he offered the summary judgment that the world is "a typical world" because every aspect of it can typify something.[7]

Edwards' most sustained reflections on typology appeared in the "Miscellanies" as no. 1069, entitled "Types of the Messiah." He wrote this essay, which fills more than seventy pages in the manuscript, in the mid-to-late 1740s.[8] In it he suggested that "human nature renders types a fit method of instruction" because, among other reasons, types are enlightening, instructive, and pleasurable in much the same way that art, poetry, metaphor, and drama are delightful.[9] For Edwards truth and pleasure were fit companions. In "Notes on Scripture" he also wrote about types in general. In No. 482, for example, he stated that "types are a sort of word; they are a language, or signs of things, God would reveal, point forth, and teach as well as vocal or written words, and they are called 'the word of the Lord.'"[1] The exegete's task

3. Dwight ed., *1*, 94.
4. "Miscellanies," no. 119 (*Works, 13*, 284).
5. "Catalogue," p. 1.
6. "Miscellanies," no. 362 (*Works, 13*, 434).
7. *Works, 11*, 146.
8. "Miscellanies," no. 1069, has been published separately in *Works, 11*, 187–328.
9. *Works, 11*, 191.
1. John Locke declared words to be "immediately the signs of men's ideas, and by that means the instruments whereby men communicate their conceptions" (*An Essay Concerning*

is to interpret these signs by which God communicates with human beings.

"Notes on Scripture" functions for Edwards as a collection point for his interpretations of biblical types.[2] The first appearance of the word "type" in the series is in No. 6, where he declares the temple in ancient Israel to be a "type of Christ." But already in the previous entry, No. 5, he had explained how the "monstrous births" described in Genesis 6:4 typify what happens when holy and wicked things are joined, producing hypocrites and enemies of religion. In No. 262 Edwards constructs an elaborate complex of associations around the "hidden manna" mentioned in Revelation 2:17, a reference that points backward to the "pot of manna" in the ark of the covenant and the "first fruits of the Spirit" on Pentecost and forward to "communion with Christ" and the "satisfying communications of the Holy Spirit." All of these Edwards regarded as "typical." Late in "Notes on Scripture," in No. 503, he links Moses' rod, the tabernacle, the ark of the covenant, and the cloud of glory accompanying Israel in the wilderness as "types and symbols" of Christ's presence. Scattered among these select examples from "Notes on Scripture" are scores of other entries featuring typological exegesis.

Practitioners of a precritical approach to the Bible, although they resorted to a variety of exegetical strategies, often employed typology in the effort to meet challenges to the premodern commentarial mindset. Edwards was no exception. For example, in "Notes on Scripture" he muted what had become by the eighteenth century the moral scandal of God's command that Abraham sacrifice his son Isaac by associating the "ram" typologically with Christ (No. 7). He rejected the suggestion that Canticles was "an ordinary love song" by treating the affection between the biblical lovers as a "shadow" of the "love, union, and communion" between Christ and the church (No. 147) and by linking typologically the spouse in the Song of Solomon and the "tents of Kedar" (Cant. 1:5) with the church (No. 458). He turned the discussion of the sun and the moon that stood still when Joshua fought the enemies of Israel (Josh. 10:12–14) away from questions of science by declaring the sun to be an "eminent type" of Christ, "the Sun of Righteousness and the Light of the world" (No. 207). These and many

---

Human Understanding, ed. Alexander Campbell Fraser [2 vols. New York, Dover Publications, 1959], 2, 11).

2. For additional background on JE's situation when he began "Notes on Scripture," see *Works*, *13*, 10–15.

other entries confirm the hermeneutical importance of typology for Edwards and its centrality in his biblical writings.

Edwards and the Challenge of Modern Criticism

The thirty-five years during which Edwards wrote and used "Notes on Scripture" were part of an era of change and accelerating controversy in the field of biblical exegesis. Hans Frei has described the eighteenth century as the time of the breakdown of precritical interpretation. Before this period Christian exegetes accepted a "single, unitary canon" embracing both the Old and New Testaments, which were tied together by figures or types. Prophecy, too, played a crucial role in linking the two testaments. Christian commentators commonly interpreted passages in the Hebrew Bible, or Old Testament, prophetically. Even Protestant exegetes, who after the Reformation increasingly emphasized the literal sense of the biblical text, adopted this approach. A precritical outlook also knew no division between the biblical world and contemporary experience: scriptural narrative reflected, indeed, made sense of, everyday life.[3]

The rising resistance to traditional orthodoxies, religious and cultural, launched by the Renaissance and carried to new heights by the Enlightenment, had immense implications for the study of the Bible. New knowledge about the nature of the universe, the geography of the earth, and the possibilities of scientific inquiry was combined with a commitment to the supremacy of reason to produce a series of questions that undermined standard assumptions based on the biblical cosmogony. In the seventeenth century the application of scientific rationalism, first in the hands of those professing orthodoxy and then by those willing to forgo ecclesiastical approval, raised doubts about the authority of Scripture. Increasingly, the view articulated by the Dutch Jewish philosopher Benedict de Spinoza (1632–77) and published anonymously in his *Tractatus Theologico-Politicus* (1670)— namely, that the Bible was to be studied in the same way as any other book—gained a following.[4]

3. Hans W. Frei, *The Eclipse of Biblical Narrative: A Study in Eighteenth and Nineteenth Century Hermeneutics* (New Haven, Yale Univ. Press, 1974), pp. 1–16.

4. See Robert Grant with David Tracy, *A Short History of the Interpretation of the Bible* (2nd ed., Minneapolis, Fortress Press, 1984), pp. 100–09; Paul Hazard, *The European Mind 1680– 1715* (Cleveland, The World Publishing Company, 1967), pp. 180–97; W. Neil, "The Criticism and Theological Use of the Bible, 1700–1950," in Greenslade, ed., *Cambridge History of the Bible*, pp. 238–93; Roy A. Harrisville and Walter Sundberg, *The Bible in Modern Culture:*

For many early Enlightenment thinkers, reason was not diametrically opposed to revelation; rather, to cite the nineteenth-century scholar Mark Pattison, many thought that reason should be a "habit of thought ruling all minds" by which "all alike consented to test their belief by the rational evidence for it."[5] John Locke, for example, spoke of the complementary relation between reason and revelation, asserting that "he that takes away reason to make way for revelation, puts out the light of both."[6] As increasing numbers of writers began to raise questions about the authority of the Bible, however, they focused their attacks on biblical mysteries, miracles, and prophecies. Figural readings of the text also suffered with the discrediting of precritical suppositions. In response, a host of apologists spanning a wide range of religious perspectives defended the necessity of revelation as well as the credibility, authority, and unity of the biblical text. Ironically, even the evangelicals, who, as Pattison pointed out, reacted against rationalism, often succumbed to its attraction by proposing "rational" accounts of Christianity.[7]

Edwards' "Catalogue" and the sources he cited in "Notes on Scripture" document his involvement with the new critical literature and his participation in the republic of letters that tied together the Atlantic community. Even the remote regions of the English colonies felt the effects of the rise of rationalism because of the increasing availability of European publications.[8] In the face of these changes, Edwards and

---

Theology and Historical-Critical Method from Spinoza to Käsemann (Grand Rapids, William B. Eerdmans Publishing Company, 1995), pp. 32–48; and Frei, *Eclipse*, pp. 42–46.

5. Mark Pattison, "Tendencies of Religious Thought in England, 1688–1750," in *Essays by the Late Mark Pattison Sometime Rector of Lincoln College*, ed. Henry Nettleship (2 vols. Oxford, Clarendon Press, 1889), 2, 45–46.

6. Locke, *An Essay*, 2, 431.

7. Pattison, *Essays*, p. 48. JE contemplated writing a treatise he proposed to title "A Rational Account of the Main Doctrines of the Christian Religion." For a time he also used "Rational Account" as an alternate name for the "Miscellanies." See *Works*, 6, 394, 396–97; and *13*, 6–7.

8. See Henry F. May's discussion of the availability of European publications in America, in *The Enlightenment in America* (New York, Oxford Univ. Press, 1976), pp. 26–41; and Norman Fiering's description of the transatlantic republic of letters, *Jonathan Edwards's Moral Thought and Its British Context* (Chapel Hill, Univ. of North Carolina Press, 1981), pp. 13–28. Evangelical literature also moved freely in both directions across the Atlantic. See Susan O'Brien, "Eighteenth-Century Publishing Networks in the First Years of Transatlantic Evangelicalism," in *Evangelicalism: Comparative Studies of Popular Protestantism in North America, the British Isles, and Beyond 1700–1790*, eds. Mark A. Noll, David W. Bebbington, and George A. Rawlyk (New York, Oxford Univ. Press, 1994), pp. 38–57; and Frank Lambert, *"Pedlar in Divinity": George Whitefield and the Transatlantic Revivals* (Princeton, Princeton Univ. Press, 1994).

like-minded others defended traditional exegetical perspectives at the same time they appropriated some of the new ways of thinking.

"Notes on Scripture" reflects the issues that divided exegetes in this transitional period. Much of the discussion and debate over these hermeneutical questions centered on the book of Genesis and the four gospels in the New Testament. It is no accident that the single book of the Bible most commented on by Edwards in "Notes on Scripture" is Genesis, with ninety entries, or nearly one-fifth of the total, devoted to it; similarly, the gospels collectively represent another seventy-seven notes, or more than 15 percent of the entries.[9] As the series progresses, Edwards' exegetical agenda increasingly reflects the critical issues raised by Enlightenment thinkers.

The longest single entry in the series, No. 416, entitled "Whether the PENTATEUCH was written by MOSES" (see fig. 1), joins the debate generated by the judgments of Thomas Hobbes (1588–1679) and others who attacked the Mosaic authorship of the first five books of the Hebrew Bible. In a chapter of *Leviathan* (1651) dealing with "the Number, Antiquity, Scope, Authority, and Interpreters of the Books of Holy SCRIPTURE," Hobbes argued that the conventional identification of the Pentateuch as "the five Books of *Moses*" did not automatically provide sufficient reason to conclude that he wrote them, for often the names of books mark content rather than authorship, as, for example, in the book of Ruth. On the basis of internal evidence, Hobbes concluded that "the five Books of *Moses* were written after his time," though when was not clear.[1]

Edwards' defense of Mosaic authorship included an argument based on the internal witness of Scripture. He assumed the correctness of the ancient testimony linking Moses with the writing of the precepts delivered on Mount Sinai. His task, however, was to establish that Moses wrote the balance of the Pentateuch. Edwards posited a necessary link between history and law in the Pentateuch. The history of God's dealings with ancient Israel served as an essential "preamble," or rationale, for the legal codes; Moses would not have trusted the memory of those events to oral tradition. Therefore he also recorded in writing the great acts of God. Furthermore, Edwards cited references throughout the Old Testament that he regarded as further confirma-

---

9. See the "Index of *Notes on Scripture* Entries."
1. Thomas Hobbes, *Leviathan, or the Matter, Forme & Power of a Commonwealth, Ecclesiasticall and Civill*, ed. A. R. Waller (Cambridge, Cambridge Univ. Press, 1904), pp. 275–76.

tion of Moses' authorship of the entire Pentateuch and as proof that a written record containing both precepts and history existed from the time of Moses. Such record-keeping, he pointed out, was common among ancient nations. The existence of the Book of the Law in the period before the Babylonian captivity was, in Edwards' judgment, further proof of the Pentateuch's antiquity and evidence against any notion of possible "forgery" by a later hand.[2]

Edwards turned his attention at several points in "Notes on Scripture" to alleged inconsistencies and other problems among the New Testament gospels. In this activity he was joining a long line of commentators, extending back to the second century, who attempted to harmonize the gospel accounts of Jesus' life.[3] The most explicit example of his efforts to create a unified narrative from disparate texts is No. 220, entitled "The accounts of the four evangelists concerning the resurrection of Christ reconciled." In it he wove contradictory details from the four gospels into an integrated story of the women and the disciples visiting the tomb after the resurrection. In No. 225 Edwards constructed a reasoned explanation for the conflicting details surrounding Jesus' prayer in the Garden of Gethsemane. In No. 446 he attempted to explain why it seemed "strange" that John the Baptist is reported not to have known Jesus (John 1:31)—strange because their mothers were cousins. His explanation strains to make that ignorance reasonable, citing the flight of the holy family into Egypt, the early deaths of John the Baptist's father and mother, and John's subsequent

2. JE also defended Mosaic authorship of the Pentateuch in an untitled MS notebook of 131 pages (Beinecke Library) filled with random observations. In the notebook he argued that it would have been impossible for the Jews to create a forgery or imposture because of widespread public knowledge concerning the law in ancient Israel. Schafer regards the notebook, which contains references to No. 416 under the title "Pent. Writ. by M.," as a "continuation" of No. 416 (*Works, 13*, 142n). JE referred to Moses' authorship of "the history of the creation and fall of man, and the history of the church from the creation" in "Miscellanies," no. 352 (*Works, 13*, 427).

3. See, for example, John Lightfoot, *The Harmony of the Foure Evangelists among Themselves, and with the Old Testament* (London, 1647); John Eliot, *The Harmony of the Gospels in the Holy History of the Humiliation and Sufferings of Jesus Christ from his Incarnation to his Death and Burial* (Boston, 1678); John Le Clerc, *The Harmony of the Evangelists* (London, 1701); *The Harmony of the Holy Gospels Digested into One History, According to the Order of Time* (London, 1705); and James McKnight, *A Harmony of the Four Gospels in which the Natural Order of Each is Preserved* (London, 1756). These efforts at harmonization of the gospels preceded later debates concerning the order of the composition of the synoptic gospels, the scholarly argument known as the Synoptic Problem. See Thomas Richmond, Willis Longstaff, and Page A. Thomas, eds., *The Synoptic Problem: A Bibliography, 1716–1988* (Macon, Ga., Mercer Univ. Press, 1988).

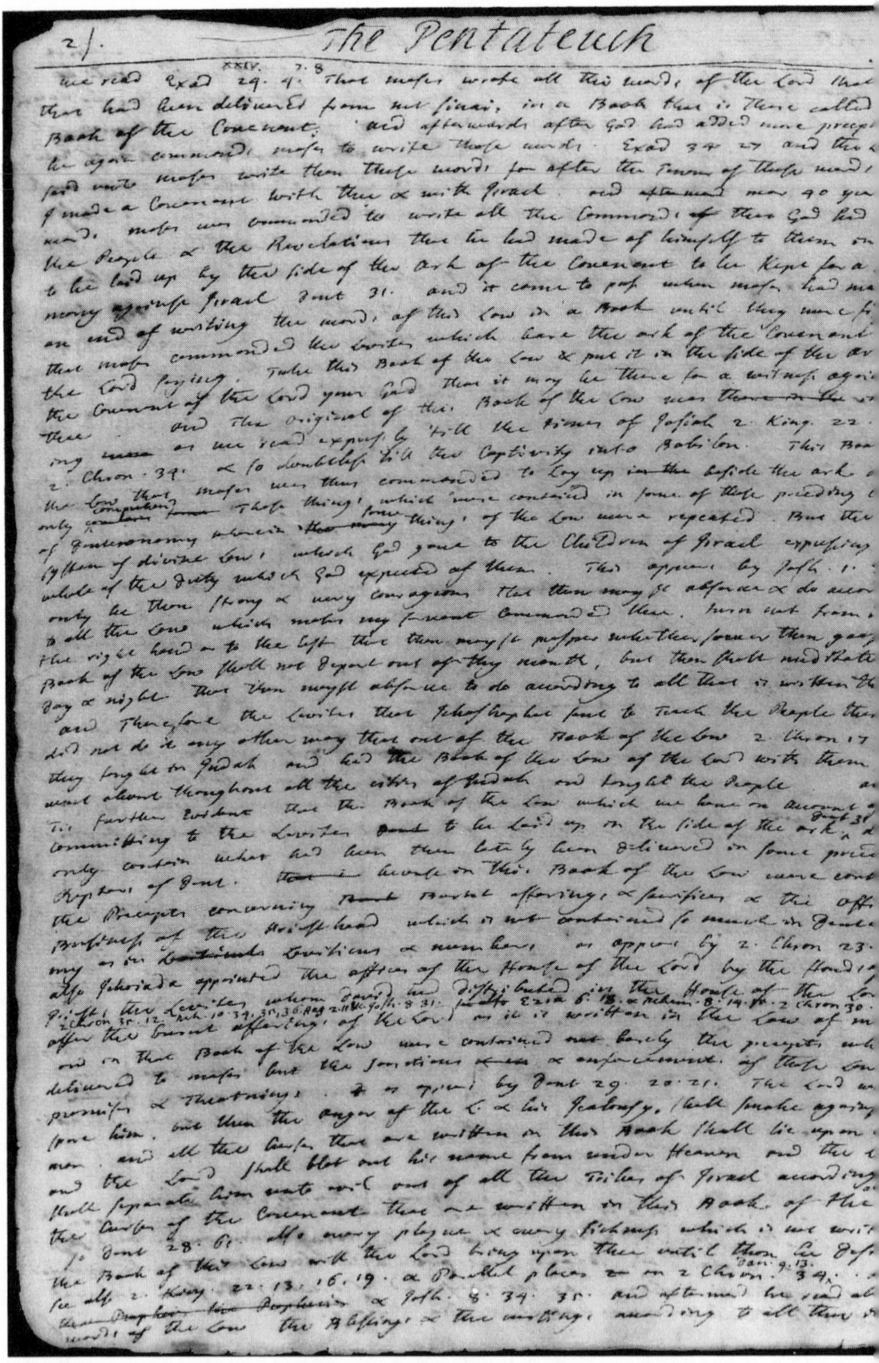

The Pentateuch

Fig. 1. Pages 2–3 in No. 416, with heading "The Pentateuch written by Moses." Courtesy of Beinecke Rare Book and Manuscript Library, Yale University.

in the Book of the Law. There was not a word of all these things Moses com
Ps. 105. 8. 9. 10. did which Joshua read not &c —   a you not only the Promise & threat
a were contained in this Book of the Law but also the Revelations that
were any way as tended to inforce it or any way related to it towards &
the Prophesies that were there contained of what should afterward,
on to the People on their sin or on their Repentance. This appear
hem.   8. 9. Remember I beseech thee the word that then common and diff
went Moses saying if ye transgress, I will scatter you abroad among the nati
But if ye turn unto me and keep my commandments & do them tho there
of you cast out unto the uttermost part of the Heaven yet will I gather
from thence and will bring them unto the place that I have chosen to
name there.   and besides we read of Moses being expressly commanded to
Histories of the acts of the Lord toward his People as well as the Revelation,
he made to them.   So he was commanded to write on account of them the
war with Amalek with its circumstances, that Posterity might see the Rea
of their perpetual war God had declared against Amalek. Exod 17. 9. And
I said unto Moses, write this for a memorial in a Book and rehearse it
Case of Joshua for I will utterly put out the Remembrance of Amalek
under Heaven.   now a full account could not be given of this affair without
my mind of the History of Israels preceding of it an as for an account
be given in the writing to what of the Reason and occasion of the Chil
of Israels coming to the Border of the Amalekites & where near the Confe
I depend & war there was between them & Israel which would take up
a part of the History of the Book of Exodus   & being Besides we are
by told that Moses wrote the Journeys of the Children of Israel by
command Num. 33. 2. & Moses wrote their going, out according to their
by the commandment of the Lord   and it is probably to be supposed
he would write these for the use of the Children of Israel in after Genera
& not write the Great & mighty acts of the Lord toward, this People
as at the Red Sea & don't not pass & the wilderness, which about
it was a then of an these should times were a thousand more now
of a record & to be kept in memory of being delivered down to posteri
a forward more forward of the Peoples progress in the wilder
without these mighty acts in every way incredible that Moses
are use as so often and expressly the he wrote God, commands, Revelations Prom
Promises & Revelations & Histories than he should not write these
acts of the Lord & commit a Record of them Leave a Record of them
the Congregation of Israel. Especially when it is evident in Text that he
so exceeding careful that they might not forget these Great acts of the God
tive Generation. Deut. 4. & 9. 10. 11. 12. Only take heed to thyself
a they pull diligently lest then forget the things, which thine Eyes have
& lest they depart from thine Heart all the Days of thy. Life but teach
they Sons & thy Sons Sons Specially the Day when then stood so before
and they Sad on Horeb. &c —— Here the way some orders are given
in keeping the acts of the Lord in memory the memory of Posterity &
reason for the keeping up the memory of the Precepts. Chap. 6. 7.
18. 19. for teaches of writing mention'd in a Book in a person man to keep
does from God to Moses. 31. 30 &. now gal write it before them in a Table and not in a Book, this it
a memory of them. Moses did not keep the Precepts of God only to
the time to come forever & ever. he was sensible these may only was not sufficient that be
Tradition we put a charge to the People to teach their Children & the memory

isolated life in the wilderness. These entries by Edwards demonstrate his confidence that the perceived inconsistencies in the gospels were not actual and that all such problems had a reasonable solution.[4] His commentary also reveals the ways he was influenced positively by the Enlightenment and likewise affirmed the authority of reason.[5]

The Enlightenment debate over revelation often took the form of questioning the credibility of the miracles recorded in the Bible. Science and reason seemed opposed to miracle, and attacks on the miraculous often used sarcasm and ridicule. For example, Thomas Woolston (1670–1733), a freethinker and advocate of the allegorical method of scriptural interpretation, branded Jesus' miracle of cursing the barren fig tree (Mark 11:14) "an absurd, foolish, and ridiculous, if not malicious and ill-natur'd, Act." Jesus ought to have used his power to make the barren tree fruitful, Woolston opined. Edwards rose to the defense of that miracle by citing one of the many vigorous responses to Woolston, an essay by the English Anglican divine Zachary Pearce (1690–1774).[6] In No. 226 Edwards' defense involved a linguistic argument hinging both on the particle "for" and information gleaned from Pearce about the seasons in which fig trees bore fruit in Palestine.[7]

4. In "Miscellanies," no. 139 (154), JE proposed "that there are many things in religion and the Scriptures that are made difficult on purpose to try men, and to exercise their faith and scrutiny, and to hinder the proud and self-sufficient" (*Works, 13,* 296–97).

5. D. W. Bebbington, who argues that the Evangelical movement must be viewed as "permeated by Enlightenment influences," perhaps overstates the case and fails to distinguish sufficiently between evangelicals oriented toward Calvinism and those of Arminian persuasion, most notably, JE and John Wesley respectively. See *Evangelicalism in Modern Britain: A History from the 1730s to the 1980s* (London, Unwin Hyman, 1989), especially pp. 20–74. For a useful discussion of JE's appropriation of the Enlightenment, see John E. Smith, "Puritanism and Enlightenment: Edwards and Franklin," in William M. Shea and Peter A. Huff eds., *Knowledge and Belief in America: Enlightenment Traditions and Modern Religious Thought* (Cambridge, Cambridge Univ. Press, 1995), pp.197–211. See also Knud Haakonssen ed., *Enlightenment and Religion: Rational Dissent in Eighteenth-Century Britain* (Cambridge, Cambridge Univ. Press, 1996).

6. Thomas Woolston, *Discourses on the Miracles of our Saviour* (In 6 pts. London, 1727–29); and [Zachary Pearce], *The Miracles of Jesus Vindicated. In Four Parts* (3rd ed., London, 1730). On Woolston, see John Redwood, *Reason, Ridicule and Religion: The Age of Enlightenment in England 1660–1750* (Cambridge, Harvard Univ. Press, 1976), pp. 147–50. On Pearce, see Wilfrid Semour Andrews, "The Life and Work of Bishop Zachary Pearce, 1690–1774" (Ph.D. diss., University of London, 1952). On the argument from miracles, see Leslie Stephen, *History of English Thought in the Eighteenth Century* (2 vols. New York, Harcourt, Brace & World, 1962), *1,* 192–213.

7. JE directed considerable attention to the miracles of Christ in the "Miscellanies." See his entry on "Miracles" in the "Table to the 'Miscellanies'" (*Works, 13,* 141).

Rising concern with the problems of authorship of the biblical books is further evidence of Edwards' engagement with the Enlightenment challenge to the credibility and authority of the Bible. In "Notes on Scripture" he wrote entries on the authorship of the Pentateuch, Job, the Psalms, Canticles, and Revelation. In all these cases he marshaled evidence in support of traditional opinions. His judgment about the "penman" of the book of Job in No. 202 is illustrative. Much of the entry is an extract drawn from Bedford's *Scripture Chronology* that argued, on the basis of a distinction between the names "Job" and "Jobab," the location of the "land of Uz" (called Ausitis in the Septuagint), and the presence of Arabic words and phrases in the text, that Elihu, one of Job's friends, was the likely author. Edwards concurred with Bedford, noting also that Elihu was esteemed a person of "eminent piety and wisdom." Edwards speculated with Bedford that Moses may have translated the book of Job into Hebrew for the children of Israel in Egypt during his stay in Midian.[8]

Nothing is more telling of Edwards' commitment to a traditional exegetical outlook than his understanding of prophecy. He believed that prophecies of the Old Testament, or Hebrew Bible, were fulfilled in the New Testament, a fulfillment that verified the divine inspiration of the prophets and the authority of the Bible. Against such attacks as those of the English Deist Anthony Collins (1676–1729), Edwards affirmed that the descriptions of "the affairs of the church of Israel" in the Old Testament "very exactly described the affairs of the gospel and the Christian church," and in that respect they were prophetic.[9] Elsewhere, he observed that it was "God's manner of old in the times of the Old Testament" to "prefigure future events" by inspired prophets, including especially matters relating to "the Messiah and his kingdom and salvation," which matters were fulfilled in the time of the New Testament.[1] By contrast, in *A Discourse of the Grounds and Reasons of the Christian Religion* (1724), Collins had severed the connection between the two testaments, arguing that the Old Testament prophecies, understood literally, could not be read as predictions fulfilled in the events of the New Testament. He maintained that only when such prophetic texts were interpreted "in a secondary, or typical, or mysti-

---

8. In "Miscellanies," no. 810, JE speculated "that Moses either wrote the book [of Job] in Midian, or brought it thence with him, written by another, to his own people in Egypt; or else it was brought to him in the wilderness by Jethro, or written by Moses there."

9. "Miscellanies," no. 251, "Prophecy of the Old Testament" (*Works, 13*, 363).

1. "Types" (*Works, 11*, 202–04).

cal, or allegorical, or enigmatical sense" could the claims of prophetic fulfillment be made. But in Collins' judgment, such a "secondary" sense was arbitrary and meaningless. His critique of prophecy was especially devastating because he acknowledged that Christianity stood or fell on the truthfulness of the prophetic link with Judaism—a link he flatly denied.[2]

For Edwards, however, the validity of prophecy was never in doubt. Prophecy was for him an integrating force in the Bible. In No. 357, commenting on Enoch's prophecy of the second coming of Christ in Jude 14, he writes:

> And this last coming of Christ, and what is accomplished by it, is in many respects the greatest of all events; and 'tis so in this respect, that 'tis what all that God has made, and all that Christ has done and suffered, and all the events of providence from the beginning of the world, and all that he has foretold, ultimately terminates in. Therefore with this does Scripture prophecy both begin and end. It begins in Enoch's prophecy, which is the first prophecy we have an account of in Scripture; and it ends with this in the last words of the last of the prophets, even John, in the conclusion of the Revelations.

In other words, Edwards regarded prophecy as a hermeneutical clue of primary significance in support of the unity of the testaments and the integrity of the entire Bible.

Edwards was no less intent on affirming the legitimacy of the concept of mystery in Christianity. He found "mystery," in the sense of that which is kept secret and not known, "everywhere in the Scripture." All of the principal particulars of Christianity might be called "mysteries": the Trinity and Christ's "birth, life, death, resurrection, ascension, and kingdom." Similarly, the Antichrist was a figure of mystery. All these were concealed until revealed.[3] But mystery was also a product of language, Edwards asserted, for the words of "our common affairs" often prove inadequate for the "high and abstracted

2. Collins, *A Discourse of the Grounds and Reasons of the Christian Religion* (London, 1724), pp. 39, 44. Collins stated that "if the proofs for christianity from the Old Testament be not valid; if the arguments founded on those books be not conclusive; and the *prophesies* cited from thence be not fulfill'd; then has christianity no just foundation: for the foundation on which Jesus and his apostles built it is then invalid and false" (p. 31). On Collins' challenge to the argument from prophecy, see Stephen, *History of English Thought, 1,* 179–92; and Frei, *Eclipse,* pp. 66–85.

3. "Apocalypse" (*Works, 5,* 118).

ideas" involved with divinity. "Therefore [does] religion [abound] with so many paradoxes and seeming contradictions."[4]

In another sense, mystery for Edwards was "something that is intricate and difficult in its own nature," and in this sense he shared the Enlightenment's discomfort with the mysterious.[5] He spent considerable time attempting to solve such biblical mysteries. In No. 148, for instance, he used parallel gospel accounts to understand Christ's promise of a reward to his disciples in Mark 10:29–30. In No. 215 he quoted Bedford's calculations in order to resolve "the seeming difference in the population of Israel when David numbered them in Samuel and in Chronicles." A similar mathematical puzzle confronted Edwards in II Chronicles 22:1–2. He acknowledged a "great difficulty" because Ahaziah the king appears to be "two years older than his father." Again he followed Bedford's mathematical calculations, and then he added his own judgment that the dating of kings in the Bible does not "always make the person's birth the epoch from whence the date is taken" (No. 222). Edwards was not content to leave mystery in this sense unresolved or to allow critics an opportunity to capitalize on such problems. But his discontent with one kind of mystery did not signal any reluctance to celebrate what he regarded as the true mysteries of the Christian religion.

In an era of changing patterns of biblical exegesis, Edwards remained steadfast in defense of the integrity of Scripture. He willingly pursued multiple meanings of the biblical text, using typology as the principal means to create a coherent interpretation consistent with his understanding of Protestant Christianity. He never doubted the credibility, authority, unity, or sufficiency of the Bible.

Edwards as an Exegete

"Notes on Scripture" adds to the increasingly complex picture of Edwards as an intellectual by documenting the centrality of the Bible in his activities. Previous literature has often failed to reckon sufficiently with the scriptural principle in his thought, despite the widespread presence of biblical language, citations, and discourse throughout his writings. Early estimations overstated Edwards' scientific and philosophical precociousness and contributed to the masking

4. "Miscellanies," no. 83, entitled "Theology" (*Works, 13*, 249).
5. "Apocalypse" (*Works, 5*, 118).

of this aspect of his thought. That oversight is not corrected by repeating Sereno Dwight's mistaken hagiographic judgments about the originality and genius of the "Notes on the Bible." On the contrary, the proper corrective calls for a more thorough examination of the biblical dimension of Edwards' study habits and his writings and a recognition of his selective appropriation of the work of others. In other words, we need not use the language of "genius" in order to understand and appreciate Edwards' creative approach to the interpretation of the biblical text.

As described above, Edwards' reading was a primary element in his method of study. In "Notes on Scripture" he cited forty different identifiable sources. More than a hundred entries include quoted or paraphrased materials for which Edwards listed a source. Furthermore, there is no way of knowing for certain how many additional unidentified citations or paraphrases are part of this series. Literary conventions of the time make it often difficult, if not impossible, to recognize such dependence. "Notes on Scripture" situates Edwards firmly in the exegetical world of the eighteenth century.

The variety of the sources in "Notes on Scripture" is instructive in other ways as well. For example, a few of the most frequently cited volumes are rather surprising, considering Edwards' theological views. Two deserve special comment. Edwards drew directly on *De veritate religionis christianae* (1622), by Hugo Grotius (1583–1645), for six successive entries in the series (Nos. 427–432). Grotius, a Dutch humanist of astonishing scholarly breadth, had sided with the liberal faction in the split between the strict Calvinists and the Arminians. *De veritate* went through multiple editions, including a translation with notes and additions by John Clarke (1682–1757), the dean of Salisbury, from which Edwards derived entries on Genesis and Exodus.[6] Grotius provided Edwards with linguistic, historical, and literary information from ancient sources. The citations in No. 428, for example, derive from Grotius's references to Homer, Plato, Ovid, and Seneca, as well as to Pliny and Josephus—to name but the most familiar authors. The subject matter of the six successive entries includes the proper translation of מְרַחֶפֶת, rendered as "moved" in the King James Version; archeological evidence for giants in Crete; an account

6. *The Truth of the Christian Religion in Six Books by Hugo Grotius, Corrected and Illustrated by Mr. Le Clerc. To which is added a Seventh Book Concerning this Question, What Christian Church we ought to join our selves to; By the said Mr. Le Clerc. The Second Edition with Additions. Done into English by John Clarke, D.D. and Chaplain in Ordinary to His Majesty* (London, 1719).

of the Scythian Deucalion from whom, in similar fashion to Noah, according to ancient Greek and Roman myths, the entire human race is said to have descended after a flood; testimony concerning the burning of Sodom; and references to Moses in non-Jewish literature.

Edwards drew on a similarly wide range of materials from *The Court of the Gentiles* by Theophilus Gale (1628–78), an English Nonconformist divine and scholar.[7] Gale's multivolume work argues for the Hebrew origin of other languages as well as of pagan religion, philosophy, and culture. Edwards took extensive notes from Gale on a number of topics: pagan gods, including Bacchus, Silenus, and Pan⁻(Nos. 400–401, 403–405); giants in the land of Canaan (No. 402); the advancement of Joseph in Egypt as related in Egyptian sources about Apis and Serapis (No. 407); ancient accounts of a flood and of the division of languages (Nos. 409–410); and heathen notions of a god with the name "I AM THAT I AM" (No. 412). His notes from both Grotius and Gale reveal a growing interest in what might be called comparative religions.

The sources Edwards used are impressive for the scope of their subject matter, the variety of the ancient references, and the sophistication of the linguistic arguments. They are filled with Latin, Greek, and Hebrew citations, many of which he entered into "Notes on Scripture." The debate about Edwards' facility in the ancient languages, especially Hebrew, will not be decided by this one notebook. His entries, however, do provide evidence of the uses to which he put the biblical languages.[8] In general, the scholarly side of Edwards' interests rather than the pastoral dominates this series.

In colonial America only one contemporary, or near contemporary, invites comparison with Edwards as an exegete—Cotton Mather (1663–1728), perhaps the most learned American of his generation,

---

7. Theophilus Gale, *The Court of the Gentiles: Or A Discourse touching the Original of Human Literature, both Philologie and Philosophie, From the Scripture & Jewish Church* (2nd ed., 4 vols in 2. Oxford, Thomas Gilbert, 1672–78).

8. In "Edwards as Hebraist" (unpublished paper, Edwards Conference, Bloomington, Ind., June 1994), Shalom Goldman disputes the judgment of Thomas H. Johnson concerning JE's facility in Hebrew. Johnson reduced JE's knowledge of Hebrew to "a negligible amount of marginalia and a few Hebrew idioms" ("Jonathan Edwards' Background of Reading," *Publications of the Colonial Society of Massachusetts* 28 [1931], 197). Goldman asserts that JE's "Hebrew knowledge has been underestimated" (p. 3). See JE's MS, "Hebrew Idioms." For background on the study of Hebrew and the growth of a tradition of American Hebraism, see Goldman, ed., *Hebrew and the Bible in America: The First Two Centuries* (Hanover, N. H., Univ. Press of New England, 1993).

certainly the most prolific.[9] Edwards and Mather were equally aware
of the changing circumstances of biblical exegesis in their day and of
the rising threat to traditional ideas of the authority and sufficiency of
the Bible. Both sought to assert themselves as defenders of the tradition but in doing so found themselves forced to become better acquainted with the new scholarship. Edwards and Mather both defended the use of typology as a hermeneutical strategy. They also
shared a consuming interest in eschatology, prophecy, and history. It is
mere accident, however, that the major exegetical efforts of both men
remained unpublished during their lifetimes. Mather was unsuccessful in securing a British publisher for the "Biblia Americana."[1] Edwards did not even contemplate publishing "Notes on Scripture" or
the "Blank Bible."[2]

As an exegete Edwards rarely followed any discernible order in his
biblical reflections. Only occasionally does "Notes on Scripture" show
him proceeding systematically through a particular book or section of
the Bible. Early in 1724, for example, he wrote eleven entries on the
gospel of Mark in which he followed the canonical order (Nos. 23–27,
29–34). In the latter half of 1729 Edwards wrote ten entries on the two
epistles to the Corinthians, although these notes do not follow the

9. On Mather, see Robert Middlekauff, *The Mathers: Three Generations of Puritan Intellec-
tuals, 1596–1728* (New York, Oxford Univ. Press, 1971); Sacvan Bercovitch, *The Puritan
Origins of the American Self* (New Haven, Yale Univ. Press, 1975); Richard F. Lovelace, *The
American Pietism of Cotton Mather* (Washington, D. C., Christian Univ. Press, 1979); and
Kenneth Silverman, *The Life and Times of Cotton Mather* (New York, Harper & Row, 1984). See
also Thomas J. Holmes, *Cotton Mather: A Bibliography of His Works* (3 vols. Cambridge, Har-
vard Univ. Press, 1940); and Winton U. Solberg's edition of Mather's *The Christian Philosopher*
(Urbana, Univ. of Illinois Press, 1994).

1. The "Biblia Americana," comprising six folio MSS, is at the Massachusetts Historical
Society in Boston. Mather described his plan for the MSS, which included commentary on
types, natural philosophy, chronology, sacred geography, history, and prophecy, in a letter to
John Woodward, Nov. 12, 1712 (Kenneth Silverman, ed., *Selected Letters of Cotton Mather*
[Baton Rouge, Louisiana State Univ. Press, 1971], pp. 110–12). On his unsuccessful efforts
to secure a publisher, see Silverman, *Life and Times*, pp. 257–59.

2. JE and Mather both made use of the works of Edward Wells (1667–1727), an English
mathematician, geographer, and Anglican divine. JE took the second longest entry in
"Notes on Scripture," No. 416, entitled "The Dispersion and First Settlement of the Nations," directly from Wells' *Historical Geography of the Old Testament*. No. 419 identifies the
locations to which the sons of Noah and their descendants scattered following the Flood and
the building of the Tower of Babel. Mather used the *Historical Geography* as a major source in
his treatise entitled "Triparadisus" (Reiner Smolinski, ed., *The Threefold Paradise of Cotton
Mather: An Edition of "Triparadisus"* [Athens, Ga., The Univ. of Georgia Press, 1995]). JE and
Mather both regarded Wells' account as confirmation of the Mosaic record of the earth's
geography.

progression of the scriptural text (Nos. 151–153, 155–158, 162, 164–165). In the early 1740s he worked his way through the book of Genesis, using Matthew Henry's *Exposition* (Nos. 342–348). Later in the same decade he wrote another cluster of entries on Genesis (Nos. 448, 450–456). And finally, late in the series he based twelve successive notes on Canticles on Poole's *Synopsis criticorum* (Nos. 486–497). But these five cases, plus the long entries on the Pentateuch, are the exceptions. In general, the series documents a free-ranging pattern of biblical study.

Edwards' ability to link unrelated biblical texts is one of the most remarkable features of "Notes on Scripture." His powers of association document a mastery of the biblical text achieved through regular study of the Bible. He often found imaginative ways to extract meaning from unrelated texts.[3] No. 62 is a striking case in point. In it Edwards associated the words of the Psalmist, "Mine ear hast thou opened" (Ps. 40:6), with the law in Exodus 21:6 concerning a manservant who had served his master the required six years and then wished to remain with his wife and children. Edwards linked the consequent ritual of boring the servant's ear "with an awl to the door" with Christ's "assumption of a body" when he assumed the "form of a servant" for his church—his wife and children. "Christ's ear is as it were bored thereby to the door of God's house (his church) forever." The "ear" Edwards further associated with hearing and obeying the "master's commands," the "door" with going "in and out in execution of them," where one "waits to know them." In this one short entry Edwards tied together a song of praise attributed to David, a legal statute from the Pentateuch, Christ's incarnation and his relation to the church, and the Christian's responsibility to hear, obey, and do the Master's will—all by means of his assumptions concerning typology and by his use of the literal as well as the secondary and tertiary senses of the text.

This creative side of Edwards' exegetical activity was especially useful to him in his role as a preacher. In the pulpit he faced the continual obligation of making biblical texts relevant to the lives of his parishioners. The weekly pressure of producing two or more sermons or preaching units was unrelenting.[4] In that respect the scholarly study

---

3. See Stein, "Quest for the Spiritual Sense"; and "The Spirit and the Word: Jonathan Edwards and Scriptural Exegesis," in *Jonathan Edwards and the American Experience*, eds. Nathan O. Hatch and Harry S. Stout (New York, Oxford Univ. Press, 1988), pp. 118–30.

4. For a study of JE's creative process, particularly as it relates to homiletics, see Wilson H. Kimnach's "Introduction" to *Works, 10*. Kimnach points out that JE "often composed ser-

and reflection documented in "Notes on Scripture" and the "Blank Bible" cannot be isolated from the practical side of Edwards' activities. The pastoral responsibility of applying and improving scriptural passages pulled Edwards in a different direction from the scholarly agenda that dominated many of the authorities he was reading. There was no place in his sermons for descriptions of Bacchus, stories about giants on the island of Crete, or Hebrew citation. There was, however, frequent occasion for him to make use of the types of Christ that filled his notebooks. They became the substance of meditation, reflection, and exhortation. Edwards' typological hermeneutic provided a means to connect virtually any text with Christ and his work of redemption. In that respect Edwards' scholarly and pastoral activities were closely linked with each other through his Christocentric emphasis.

Study and meditation—that is, examination of the text and reflection on its application—intersect throughout the series. Edwards used Jesus' statement that some sins are not "forgiven in this world" (Matt. 12:32), for example, to point out that sometimes the godly go to their graves before they receive the "joy and comfort" of forgiveness of their grievous sin (No. 22). In No. 87 he took a brief reference to the manner in which a victorious God is said to have spread forth his hands, namely, as one who swims (Is. 25:11), and linked it to "the posture that Christ was crucified in." The account of the sweetening of the waters at Marah by means of a tree (Ex. 15:25) became the occasion for a sentence-long meditation on Christ's incarnation, death, and union with his people (No. 130). Each of these brief entries might well have provided the germinal idea for a sermon. Wilson H. Kimnach has shown that Edwards often moved backward from ideas to the selection of a text for his sermons.[5] Study and meditation therefore constituted mutually sustaining processes for Edwards.

Sometimes the occasion for a particular entry in "Notes on Scripture" was an event in Edwards' own day. No. 365 is perhaps the clearest example of this. The entry appears to be a draft of exegetical reflections that became part of the expanded version of Edwards' sermon preached at the Yale College commencement on September 10, 1741, in New Haven. In that year New England was divided over what histo-

---

mons requiring two or more preaching sessions to complete" (p. 32, n. 6). See also John E. Smith's chapter entitled "Edwards as preacher and interpreter of Scripture," in *Jonathan Edwards: Puritan, Preacher, Philosopher* (Notre Dame, Univ. of Notre Dame Press, 1992), pp. 138–47.

5. Kimnach, "Jonathan Edwards's Pursuit of Reality," in Hatch and Stout, eds., *Jonathan Edwards*, p. 112.

rians have called the Great Awakening. Advocates and opponents debated the merits of the revivals and the authenticity of the conversions that were occurring. In this context, commenting on Romans 2:29, Edwards asserted that God alone is able to judge the inner workings of the heart, and therefore not even ministers should attempt to distinguish the sincere professor from the hypocrite. Such is the work of God on the day of judgment.[6]

Yet it is somewhat surprising how infrequently Edwards' personal circumstances and experiences show up in his biblical commentaries.[7] In "Notes on Scripture" Edwards drew explicitly on his own social context on only a few occasions. In one case, for example, when attempting to reconcile "the seeming inconsistence" in gospel accounts of Jesus' journey through Jericho on his way to Jerusalem (No. 233), Edwards concluded a lengthy semantic argument by proposing a contemporary analogy consistent with common ways of speaking in his own day. He compared Jesus' situation with that of a person traveling from Northampton to Hartford and then proposed a similar ambiguity in the potential descriptions of the two journeys.

Far more personally revealing, however, are two entries that suggest the impact of Edwards' domestic situation on his exegetical activity. In a typological exposition of Luke 1:35, Edwards links ministers in the church, who bring forth and nourish believers "at the breasts of ordinances" and by the means of grace, with the Virgin Mary, the mother of Christ, and also with the image of "a tender mother" who feeds and nourishes her infant (No. 314). Edwards then described maternal care in a manner that undoubtedly reflected his own household, for by that time (late 1738) he was the father of six young children.[8] In No. 314 he writes:

---

6. JE, *The Distinguishing Marks of a Work of the Spirit of God*, in *The Works of Jonathan Edwards, 4, The Great Awakening*, ed. C. C. Goen (New Haven, Yale Univ. Press, 1972), pp. 213–88. For more on the controversy surrounding the revivals, see Goen's analysis in ibid., pp. 52–65; and Edwin Scott Gaustad, *The Great Awakening in New England* (Chicago, Quadrangle Books, 1968), pp. 80–101. See also Timothy D. Hall, *Contested Boundaries: Itinerancy and the Reshaping of the Colonial American Religious World* (Durham, N. C., Duke Univ. Press, 1994).

7. The contrast with "Images of Divine Things" is striking. In that notebook JE commented on a variety of natural and human phenomena he had experienced personally (*Works, 11,* 49–142).

8. JE married Sarah Pierpont on July 28, 1727, in New Haven. By late 1738 their family included the following children: Sarah, Jerusha, Esther, Mary, Lucy, and Timothy. See Leonard I. Sweet's description of the Northampton parsonage in "The Laughter of One: Sweetness and Light in Franklin and Edwards," *Benjamin Franklin, Jonathan Edwards, and the Representation of American Culture*, eds. Barbara B. Oberg and Harry S. Stout (New York, Oxford Univ. Press, 1993), pp. 119–20.

'Tis a very constant care; the child must be continually looked after. It must be taken care of both day and night. When the mother wakes up in the night, she has her child to look after, and nourish at her breast; and it sleeps in her bosom, and it must be continually in the mother's bosom or arms, there to be upheld and cherished. It needs its food and nourishment much oftener than adult persons; it must be fed both day and night. It must be very frequently cleansed, for 'tis very often defiled. It must in everything be gratified and pleased. The mother must bear the burden of it as she goes to and fro.

In all likelihood, this description mirrored the reality in the Edwards' household. Another reference to young children occurs in No. 305, where he explains the phrase in I Corinthians 13:11 about putting away "childish things" as an equivalent to putting away "leading strings and gocarts"—devices used in early America to help young children learn to walk. At the time Edwards had a house full of young children, toddlers, and new babies every second year, all being cared for primarily by his wife, Sarah.[9]

But "Notes on Scripture" is not diarylike. It is a working notebook in which Edwards compiled exegetical materials for use elsewhere. To the extent that there are thematic continuities among the entries, they cluster around the concerns of the commentarial tradition, the challenges of the Enlightenment, the usefulness of typology, the subjects of his publications or planned publications, and the practical demands of the ministry. There is perhaps no better summary of those principal themes than the "Table" of the "Miscellanies."[1] Readers are advised to examine that index with care.

In sum, Edwards' exegetical efforts, scattered among his notebooks, sermons, and published works, constitute a complex network that cannot be outlined in any simple fashion. Although the Old and New Testaments formed a unity for Edwards, the connection was not one-directional. Prophecy pointed forward, but interpretation reached back for enrichment. Nor is it possible to argue for a limited core of

9. On one occasion when his wife Sarah was absent from home nursing an ill Colonel John Stoddard, JE arranged for a Mrs. Phelps to care for their youngest child, Elizabeth, who was thirteen months old. He also sought assistance for two older sick daughters. To Sarah he wrote, "We have been without you almost as long as we know how to" (Letter of June 22, 1748, in Iain H. Murray, *Jonathan Edwards: A New Biography* [Carlisle, Penn., Banner of Truth Trust, 1987], p. 313).

1. See *Works, 13*, 111–50.

biblical concepts on which all of Edwards' other ideas rest. What makes Edwards' scriptural commentary intriguing is its complexity, not its simplicity. No one notebook or document, including "Notes on Scripture," exhausts the exegetical possibilities of the biblical text for him. For that reason the concept of a scriptural organon provides a useful way to describe the architecture of his network of commentary. "Notes on Scripture" is only a part of the foundation on which his system of thought rests.

Edwards' Reputation as an Exegete

Edwards' reputation as an avid student of the Bible began during his lifetime; he himself had a hand in spreading word of it. In 1757 Edwards sketched for the Trustees of the College of New Jersey several projects he hoped to publish in the future, including a "*History of the Work of Redemption*" and a "*Harmony of the old and new Testament.*" The former was to present Christian theology as history in which all events in time would be considered "so far as the scriptures give any light."[2] The latter was to deal successively with prophecies of the Messiah, Old Testament types, and "the harmony of the old and new Testament." Of this second project, the "Harmony," Edwards wrote: "In the course of this work, I find there will be occasion for an explanation of a very great part of the holy scripture; which may, in such a view be explained in a method, which to me seems the most entertaining and profitable, best tending to lead the mind to a view of the true spirit, design, life and soul of the scriptures, as well as to their proper use and improvement."[3] Edwards' untimely death a year later kept him from fulfilling these plans.

Edwards' reputation as an exegete was first formulated biographically by Samuel Hopkins, who had access to his teacher's manuscripts after his death. In 1765 he declared Edwards to be "one of the *greatest of divines.*" Hopkins credited biblical study as a major reason for Edwards' acclaim as a theologian. When he detailed the reasons for his

2. Letter to the Trustees, Oct. 19, 1757, in Hopkins, *Life and Character*, p. 77. For a discussion of JE's "History" project, see the introduction of *The Works of Jonathan Edwards, 9, A History of the Work of Redemption*, ed. John F. Wilson (New Haven, Yale Univ. Press, 1989).

3. Hopkins, *Life and Character*, pp. 77–78. For a discussion of the "Harmony" project, see Kenneth P. Minkema, "The Other Unfinished 'Great Work': Jonathan Edwards, Messianic Prophecy, and 'The Harmony of the Old and New Testament,'" in *Jonathan Edwards's Writings: Text, Context, Interpretation*, ed. Stephen J. Stein (Bloomington, Indiana Univ. Press, 1996), pp. 52–65.

judgment, Hopkins described, among other things, Edwards' "study and knowledge of the Bible" and his emphasis on the importance of knowledge of the Scripture in his preaching and pastoral activities. He also spoke of Edwards' "unwearied study of God's word."[4] In the final section of the biography, which focused on Edwards' manuscripts, Hopkins wrote: "[Edwards] wrote a great deal on the Bible, in the same way, by opening his thoughts on particular passages of it, as they occur'd to him in reading or meditation; by which he has cast much light on many parts of the bible, which has escaped other interpreters. And by which his great and painful attention to the Bible, and making it the only rule of his faith, are manifest."[5] Hopkins' admiration for Edwards' method of biblical study is evident.

It took another sixty-five years after Hopkins' biography before the text of "Notes on Scripture" became available in published form. In 1830 Sereno Dwight's edition appeared under the title "Notes on the Bible" as part of his ten-volume edition of *The Works of President Edwards: With a Memoir of His Life*. In the biography accompanying the edition, Dwight underscored Edwards' "regular and diligent study of the Sacred Scriptures." Dwight emphasized his maternal great-grandfather's determination to deal with obscure and difficult passages, contradictions, and inconsistencies, in an effort "as far as possible" to possess the "true meaning" of the Bible. Edwards, Dwight noted, regarded "the sacred volume with the highest veneration" and was especially taken with the complementary qualities of the Old and New Testaments.[6]

Dwight also stressed the originality of Edwards' biblical commentary. "Perhaps no collection of Notes on the Scriptures," he wrote, "so entirely original, can be found." He spoke admiringly of the youthful age at which Edwards had undertaken the "plan" of explaining the difficulties of the Bible (while still in college). Dwight's admiration was misplaced, it turns out. In the same context Dwight acknowledged that his edition omitted a "few of the articles of an historical or mythological nature" that Edwards "marked as quotations from the writings of others." (In fact, Dwight omitted more than a few.) Later, Dwight explicitly laid out the basis for his principle of editorial selection, declaring that well before settlement in Northampton, Edwards "had already discovered, that much of what he found in Systems and Com-

4. Hopkins, *Life and Character*, Preface (np), and pp. 47, 51.
5. Ibid., p. 83.
6. Dwight ed., *1*, 57.

mentaries, was a mere mass of rubbish"; as a result, he had turned away from those sources to the direct study of the Bible. According to Dwight, Edwards continued that practice when he went to Northampton as the colleague of his grandfather Solomon Stoddard (1643–1729). This judgment, too, it turns out, was inaccurate. In support of his opinions, Dwight quoted from Hopkins' *Life* and pointed to his own edition of "Notes on the Bible."[7]

Hopkins and Dwight in combination established Edwards' reputation as an exegete. Their view of his work prevailed almost uncontested throughout the nineteenth century, especially among those committed to evangelical religion. Among New Divinity ministers in the late eighteenth and nineteenth centuries, "Edwards' reputation as a spokesman for true Christianity" reached "heroic proportions."[8] The reprinting of Dwight's edition of "Notes on the Bible" was the primary way that knowledge of Edwards' biblical commentary was disseminated among Edwardsians. Yet surprisingly little scholarly comment was given to the scriptural aspect of Edwards' thought. By the end of the nineteenth century, scholarship focused primarily on other concerns, including especially Edwards' philosophical idealism.[9]

The first half of the twentieth century witnessed little change in this situation. In 1940 Ola Elizabeth Winslow's award-winning biography paid almost no attention to the biblical side of Edwards' activities. Only in the context of his preaching does Winslow even treat his use of scriptural texts. Her description of "Notes on Scripture" incorrectly identifies it as three quarto manuscripts. Her reference to the "Blank Bible" virtually ignores the nine hundred pages of biblical commen-

7. Ibid., *1*, 57–58, 108, 110–12.

8. David W. Kling, *A Field of Divine Wonders: The New Divinity and Village Revivals in Northwestern Connecticut, 1792–1822* (University Park, Penn., Pennsylvania State Univ. Press, 1993), p. 80. See also William Breitenbach, "Piety *and* Moralism: Edwards and the New Divinity," in Hatch and Stout, eds., *Jonathan Edwards*, pp. 177–204; and Joseph A. Conforti, *Jonathan Edwards, Religious Tradition, & American Culture* (Chapel Hill, Univ. of North Carolina Press, 1995), pp. 11–61. These authors present an alternative to the earlier view of the New Divinity movement in Joseph Haroutunian, *Piety versus Moralism: The Passing of the New England Theology* (New York, Henry Holt & Co., 1932).

9. See Egbert C. Smyth, "Jonathan Edwards' Idealism with Special Reference to the Essay 'Of Being' and to Writings not in his Collected Works," *American Journal of Theology* 1 (1897), 950–64; and Harry N. Gardiner, "The Early Idealism of Jonathan Edwards," *Philosophical Review* 9 (1900), 573–96. The most significant exception to the lack of interest in JE's biblical writings is Alexander B. Grosart who published in Scotland a small number of biblical observations from the "Blank Bible" in a limited edition *(Selections from the Unpublished Writings of Jonathan Edwards of America* [Edinburgh, 1865]).

tary in favor of the three pages listing the financial accounts of Edwards' children.[1]

The negative attitude toward biblical scholarship expressed in Perry Miller's intellectual biography of Edwards later that same decade is even more telling. Miller misidentifies "Notes on Scripture" as "a King James version of the Bible belonging to Sarah's father" that Edwards interleaved, filled, and then supplemented with three more manuscripts.[2] But the problems with Miller's account do not stop with incorrect information. Miller had little interest in the biblical side of Edwards' thought and, correspondingly, little patience with it. On one occasion Miller characterized Edwards' use of the Bible as both "literalistic" and "unrewarding." In commenting on *A History of the Work of Redemption*, Miller wrote that it reads "like a story book for fundamentalists"; when measured against contemporary scholarship, "it is an absurd book, where it is not pathetic." It appears that for Miller commentary on the Bible was an unimportant, if not embarrassing, dimension of Edwards' thought.[3]

But scholarly opinion changed in the second half of the twentieth century. The revival of interest in Edwards, sparked in part by the Neo-Orthodox movement and the resurgence of evangelicalism, brought increased attention to the biblical side of his intellectual activity. The influence of Edwards on such figures as H. Richard Niebuhr is now common knowledge. Niebuhr's classic study of *The Kingdom of God in America*, for instance, contains extensive discussion of Edwards' evangelicalism, Calvinism, and millennialism.[4] Other scholars influ-

---

1. Ola Elizabeth Winslow, *Jonathan Edwards 1703–1758* (New York, Macmillan, 1940), pp. 128, 374. The children's accounts to which Winslow refers are in the "Blank Bible," pp. 902–04.

2. Perry Miller, *Jonathan Edwards* (New York, William Sloane Associates, 1949), p. 127. Miller mistakes the "Blank Bible" for "Notes on Scripture" and also errs regarding its origin. JE, in fact, inherited the "Blank Bible" from Sarah's brother, Benjamin Pierpont, who was an unsuccessful candidate for the ministry. See Stephen J. Stein, "The Biblical Notes of Benjamin Pierpont," *The Yale University Library Gazette* 50 (1976), 195–218.

3. Miller, *Jonathan Edwards*, pp. 297, 310. For an alternative critique of Miller's views and those of other contemporary scholars, see R. C. De Prospo, *Theism in the Discourse of Jonathan Edwards* (Newark, Univ. of Delaware Press, 1985).

4. See, for example, H. Richard Niebuhr, *The Kingdom of God in America* (Chicago, Willet, Clark & Co., 1937), pp. 101, 137–39. In 1962 Niebuhr identified JE's *Nature of True Virtue* as a shaping influence on his thought ("Ex Libris," *Christian Century* 79 [June 13], 754). Niebuhr was to have been the editor of the volume containing JE's ethical writings (*The Works of Jonathan Edwards, 8, Ethical Writings*, ed. Paul Ramsey [New Haven, Yale Univ. Press, 1989], p. 3). See also William Stacy Johnson ed., *H. Richard Niebuhr: Theology, History, and Culture* (New Haven, Yale Univ. Press, 1996), pp. xxix–xxx, 43–45. See Niebuhr's previously unpublished essay, "The Anachronism of Jonathan Edwards," in ibid., pp. 123–33.

enced by Niebuhr focused more directly on Edwards' use of the Bible. Conrad Cherry, for example, demonstrated the critical role the Bible played in much of Edwards' writing as a primary form of proof and evidence. The context for Edwards' theology was biblical—that is, it must be understood within the framework of the work of redemption.[5] Writing later in another venue, Cherry asserted that "Jonathan Edwards was preeminently a biblical theologian" and noted perceptively: "In giving his wholehearted attention, Puritan fashion, to biblical, and by extension to cosmic, typology, he anticipated our contemporary absorption with the meaning and function of religious symbolism."[6]

Intellectual and historical curiosity about Edwards drives some of the expanding interest in his biblical writings; shared religious convictions motivate other researchers. Even scholars fundamentally at odds with Edwards' religious outlook, like Peter Gay, have acknowledged that for the New England divine the "authority of the Bible" was absolute.[7] Alfred Owen Aldridge described "Notes on the Scriptures" as "an encyclopedic attempt to answer every objection to the Scriptures and explain every difficulty."[8] A few individuals have returned to the adulatory stance of Edwards' earliest biographers. Ralph G. Turnbull, for instance, was sufficiently instructed by Edwards' writings, including his biblical expositions, to publish a devotional collection.[9] Fred W. Beuttler has argued for greater appreciation of Edwards' commitment to the supernatural dimension of the principle of biblical

5. Conrad Cherry, *The Theology of Jonathan Edwards: A Reappraisal* (Garden City, N.Y., Doubleday, 1966) p. 201. H. Richard Niebuhr's influence on Cherry is explicit (pp. 68–69, 72–73).

6. Conrad Cherry, "Symbols of Spiritual Truth: Jonathan Edwards as Biblical Interpreter," *Interpretation: A Journal of Bible and Theology* 39 (1985), 263, 271. Examples of the contemporary interest in the broad application of typological interpretation include Northrop Frye, *The Great Code: The Bible and Literature* (London, Routledge & Kegan Paul, 1982); and Tibor Fabiny, *The Lion and the Lamb: Figuralism and Fulfilment in the Bible, Art and Literature* (New York, St. Martin's Press, 1992).

7. Peter Gay, *A Loss of Mastery: Puritan Historians in Colonial America* (Berkeley, Univ. of California Press, 1966), p. 97. In the same year that Gay published his study, Alan Heimert's magisterial study, *Religion and the American Mind: From the Great Awakening to the Revolution* (Cambridge, Harvard Univ. Press, 1996) appeared. Heimert's special focus on JE included considerable attention to topics relating to his biblical interests. See, for example, pp. 65–66.

8. Alfred Owen Aldridge, *Jonathan Edwards* (New York, Washington Square Press, 1964), p. 10.

9. Ralph C. Turnbull, "Jonathan Edwards—Bible Interpreter," *Interpretation: A Journal of Bible and Theology*, 6 (1952), 422–35; and *Devotions of Jonathan Edwards* (Grand Rapids, Baker Book House, 1959).

authority.[1] John H. Gerstner, in his massive volume celebrating Edwards' Calvinism, finds little in his commentaries and sermons that does not "enlighten and bless."[2]

The publication of the Yale Edition of the *Works* has further stimulated this expanding interest in and growing knowledge of Edwards' exegetical writings. Several volumes already published in the Edition shed considerable light on the scriptural side of his thought.[3] This volume will make possible more sophisticated study of his biblical exegesis. Future volumes promise to provide access to his other exegetical texts.

Dwight's Edition of "Notes on the Bible"

The only previous edition of "Notes on Scripture" was Dwight's "Notes on the Bible," part of his ten-volume *Works of President Edwards: With a Memoir of His Life* (1829–30).[4] His edition of "Notes on the Bible" was also included in the two-volume edition of *The Works of Jonathan Edwards, A.M.* issued by Edward Hickman in London in 1834 and reprinted perhaps nine times in London before 1865. In 1875 "Notes on the Bible" appeared again in *The Posthumous Works of President Edwards* (London). More recently, the Banner of Truth Trust in Carlisle, Pennsylvania, reprinted the Hickman two-volume edition five times between 1974 and 1992. "Notes on the Bible" did not appear, however, in the eight-volume Worcester edition or the four-volume Worcester revised edition, the two most widely circulated editions of Edwards' writings in America.[5]

"Notes on the Bible" is a seriously flawed edition of "Notes on Scripture." Dwight rearranged the entries, reordering them by canonical reference instead of retaining the chronological sequence in which

1. Fred W. Beuttler, "Jonathan Edwards and the Critical Assaults on the Bible" (M.A. thesis, Trinity Evangelical Divinity School, 1988).

2. John H. Gerstner, *The Rational Biblical Theology of Jonathan Edwards* (3 vols. Powhatan, Vir., Berea Publications, 1991), *1*, 3. Gerstner's volume is a labor of love presented in what he calls "the traditional orthodox theological form" (p. 2).

3. See especially *Apocalyptic Writings* (*Works*, 5), *A History of the Work of Redemption* (*Works*, 9), *Sermons and Discourses, 1720–1723* (*Works*, 10), *Typological Writings* (*Works*, 11), and *The "Miscellanies," a–500* (*Works*, 13).

4. Dwight ed., 9, 113–563.

5. This bibliographical information is, in part, from Thomas H. Johnson, *The Printed Writings of Jonathan Edwards* (Princeton, Princeton Univ. Press, 1940), pp. 118–24. See also *The Works of President Edwards* (8 vols. Worcester, 1808–09), and *The Works of President Edwards* (4 vols. New York, 1843).

they were written. He combined into one entry notes written on the same biblical text at different times without any indication that the constituent parts were not contemporary.[6] This rearrangement destroyed the possibility of following the chronological development of Edwards' ideas.

In line with nineteenth-century editorial practice, Dwight took great liberty with Edwards' text. He displayed no reluctance in correcting or improving the syntax, changing the sequence of words in sentences, substituting alternative terms for those he found objectionable, omitting sentences, or dropping entire entries without explanation. He frequently changed the singular to plural or vice versa in order to obtain a consistency in number that Edwards' text frequently does not possess. He often arbitrarily substituted his own words for those in the text: "customary" for "vulgar," "restraining" for "curbing," "putrid" for "stinking," and "Christians" for "saints."[7] Sometimes he added emphasis to the text; at other times he qualified its meaning. He added "literal" to the word "brethren," put "may represent" for "represents," and changed "in great measure" to "in a most important degree."[8] His personal scruples are evident in the persistent effort to remove sexually explicit language. In No. 232, on Ephesians 5:30–32, Dwight omitted references to the following: the Jewish church as a "womb" in which Christ was held, Isaac's taking Rebecca "into his mother's tent," and the New Testament church as Christ's wife, "whom he is joined to." In No. 314, which describes the Virgin Mary as a type of "every believing soul," Dwight dropped the phrase "with milk from her paps" when speaking of the nourishment she provided "her babe. . .from her breast." In No. 377, when discussing Samson's treacherous relationship with the "woman of Timnath," Dwight cut from his account the clause, "and he [Samson] never enjoyed her." Finally, and most significant, Dwight completely omitted forty-four entries from his edition, or approximately one out of every twelve.[9]

Dwight's edition has uncounted textual errors and numerous gross misreadings. Some of the latter lead to nonsense. For example, he reads "more charitable" for "merchantable" (No. 344), "individual"

---

6. For example, Dwight conflated Nos. 196 and 206 (Dwight ed., 9, 521–27), Nos. 223 and 290 (Ibid., 300–08), and Nos. 267 and 358 (Ibid., 271–74) without comment.

7. See Nos. 233, 267, 294, 316, and 365.

8. See Nos. 241, 368, and 381.

9. Nos. 1, 18, 20, 56, 58, 62, 123, 138, 153, 160, 190, 192, 193, 194, 212, 237, 248, 250a, 258, 262, 286, 300, 303, 308, 327, 334, 343, 345, 369, 386, 388, 401, 402, 409, 411, 420, 424, 429, 447, 449, 454, 455, 459, and 467.

for "executioner" (No. 360), "conscience" for "contrivance" (No. 390), "vest" for "veil" (No. 463), and "Son of man" for "sin of man" (No. 471). Yet every manuscript editor knows how close misreadings lurk, especially when the handwriting is as difficult as Edwards'. Therefore, in spite of the many problems associated with "Notes on the Bible," it must be acknowledged that on many occasions Dwight's edition has been helpful in establishing correct readings.[1]

Note on the Manuscripts

"Notes on Scripture" consists of four manuscript notebooks located in the Beinecke Rare Book and Manuscript Library of Yale University. Edwards commonly referred to the manuscripts as "Scripture" (abbreviated "SS"), Books 1–4.[2] The entries in the series are numbered consecutively throughout the four books from 1 through 507, following the present arrangement of the manuscripts, although there are gaps in the numbering and some doubling.[3]

"Notes on Scripture" Entries by Books

Book 1:	1–290
Book 2:	291–412
Book 3:	413–499
Book 4:	500–507

Book 1 is a quarto composed of nine double leaves of foolscap folded separately and arranged in a gathering, and four quires of double leaves, measuring approximately 15.5 × 19 cm. The cover, a bit larger and now broken apart, is stiff paper with heavy decorated oilcloth glued to the outside. Stenciled on the oilcloth and still visible are portions of an Anglo-Dutch coat of arms including the body parts of a lion and a scroll with the words "*Londra Serge De*" and "*Mon droit*" (see fig. 2). Splotches of red, blue, and green paint remain on the oilcloth, but they provide no hint of the manuscript's contents.[4] The nine dou-

1. Dwight's edition has been especially helpful for readings where the MS edges are broken off.
2. JE's "SS" should not be confused with "SSS," an abbreviation he frequently employed for Matthew Poole's *Synopsis Criticorum.*
3. The gaps in the series include Nos. 114, 180–187, 245, and 371–376. Doubles occur at Nos. 95, 138, 250, and 501.
4. The cover of Book 2 of the "Miscellanies" appears to be another piece of the same oilcloth (*Works, 13,* 154). "*Serge*" is a twilled fabric used for suits, coats, and dresses. Perhaps this cover came from wrapping for imported cloth.

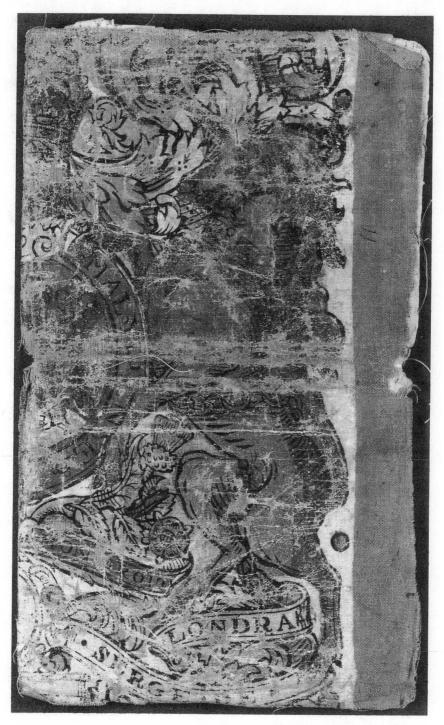

Fig. 2. The oilcloth cover of Book 1, showing the coat of arms, lion, scroll, etc. Courtesy of Beinecke Rare Book and Manuscript Library, Yale University.

ble leaves, once stitched together, now simply form a stack. The first quire consists of four infolded double leaves; the last three quires are composed of ten double leaves each. On page 1, after writing the initial entry on Genesis 2:10–14 across the entire page, Edwards then wrote Nos. 2–11 in two columns (see fig. 3), a practice he quickly abandoned with No. 12 at the top of page 2. He paginated the first twenty-four pages and wrote "SS" on the top of the first rectos of the first six double leaves.

Thomas A. Schafer has determined that in the fall of 1729 Edwards rearranged the double leaves that compose the opening pages of Book 1, infolding them into a quire, having already filled eight of them and a portion of the ninth.[5] Previously, they had simply constituted a gathering of folded double leaves stitched to one another. The numbers for the entries on these opening pages have also been changed by someone who wrote over the original numerals. Therefore, the present sequence of entries is not the precise order of Edwards' composition.

On the basis of ink, handwriting, and correlation with other manuscripts, Schafer has established that it was most likely Sereno Dwight who took apart the quire constructed by Edwards, reconstituted the half-sheets as a stack, and renumbered the entries, in effect returning the opening entries much closer to the order of original composition. Schafer has gone on to pinpoint the sequence in which Edwards wrote the entries in the gathering.

Original Order of Composition for Nos. 1–196

Nos. 1–63
Nos. 99–102
Nos. 77–88
Nos. 103–110
Nos. 89–98
Nos. 64–73
Nos. 111–141
Nos. 74–76
Nos. 142–196[6]

5. Thomas A. Schafer's unselfish sharing with others the results of his chronological investigations of JE's manuscripts is legendary. This observation appeared in an earlier draft of his Introduction for *Works, 13*.

6. See Schafer's "Table 2. The 'Miscellanies' and Chronological Parallels: May 1719–August 1731" (*Works, 13*, 91–109).

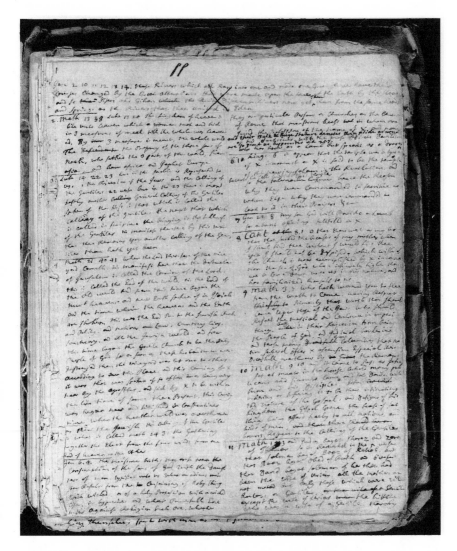

Fig. 3. The first page of "Notes on Scripture," Book 1, showing entry Nos. 1–11.
Courtesy of Beinecke Rare Book and Manuscript Library, Yale University.

Book 2 is a quarto of similar dimensions to Book 1, consisting of
four quires stitched separately and also sewn to a cover composed of
foolscap glued to an outer piece of stiff blue paper. Each of the four
quires contains twelve infolded double leaves. The front cover bears
the marking "II" in both ink and crayon. On the inside of the back
cover, which is detached from the manuscript, Edwards wrote the

following note to himself regarding the construction of future note-books:

> If I live to make another book of this sort, to observe to cut the gashes for the stitching in deeper and not so near to the joinings of the stitch, that the book may open more freely and fully. And let the sheets be divided into twice so small divisions, and starch no paper in a paper cover, for that makes it crack. And if that don't do, try next stitching the backs of all the divisions of sheets to a slip of leather, and sew the cover over the leather.[7]

In fact, the next manuscript in the series is constructed very differently from what Edwards wrote here and from Book 2.

Book 3, a folio-sized manuscript, consists of one quire of thirty infolded double leaves, and it measures approximately 20×31.5 cm. The cover, marked "III" and "SS," is similar to that of Book 2. It, too, has broken away from the manuscript. Book 4, a folio of the same size, has only eight infolded double leaves in one quire. This cover is also of similar construction, though greenish-gray in color. It has "IV" and "SS" on it. Ten pages following Edwards' last entry, No. 507, are blank. Six pages at the end of the manuscript contain an index arranged by canonical references and entry numbers.

In general, the manuscripts are in good condition even though the double leaves in the gathering of Book 1 have suffered from handling and rearrangement. The fourth double leaf has badly broken edges that interfere with a few readings. With the exception of the gathering in Book 1, which is composed of paper bearing diverse watermarks representing different batches purchased and used by Edwards, the quires in all four manuscripts are constructed from paper bearing London/GR watermarks.[8]

The ink and the handwriting throughout the series provide useful clues for establishing chronology as well as for identifying periods of concentrated study, revisions, and later additions. The most striking contrasts in ink are found in the gathering of Book 1, where numerous noticeable changes in color, intensity, and clarity occur within the space of a few entries. These changes and other data are the grounds for Schafer's dating of the earliest entries. The brown inks Edwards

---

7. This appears below in JE's text as the last note in No. 412.

8. See *Works*, *13*, 60–64 and 558–61, for Schafer's discussion of paper and watermarks, including illustrations of the latter.

used in the subsequent quires appear in general far more consistent to the naked eye and therefore are less useful for determining the times of composition, although contrasting inks often signal later additions, as in the case of the addendum at the end of No. 278. Brown inks of varying intensity continue throughout the series. The most obvious differences in the appearance of these inks involve other factors, namely, the texture of the ink, the sharpness of the quill, and the roughness of the paper. Fuzziness, for example, may result from various combinations of these elements.[9]

At times Edwards was very careful and deliberate in his writing, leaving the impression that he took his time in forming letters. At other times, however, it appears that he wrote in great haste, for his letters are carelessly shaped. The latter judgment is sometimes confirmed by the presence of numerous errors in the text, such as incorrect spellings, omitted words, and mistaken references.

Edwards began "Notes on Scripture" during a period of expanding creativity that saw him monitoring his own personal situation in the "Resolutions" and "Diary," tracking and targeting his reading in the "Catalogue," engaging in scientific observations in the "Natural Philosophy," launching a series of theological reflections in the "Miscellanies," and speculating about the meaning of the book of Revelation in the "Apocalypse." Schafer dates the first entry in "Notes on Scripture" as January–February 1724. He also concludes that Edwards made a conscious decision at that point to create a separate notebook for exegetical matters, especially for the study of types, which led directly to the inauguration of this series.[1] Edwards had written a number of scriptural notes before this date among the early entries in the "Miscellanies."[2]

By the end of 1724, when he left Bolton and assumed a tutorship at Yale College, Edwards had written forty-three entries in his new notebook. Over the course of the next year and a half, owing to his responsibilities as tutor and a period of sustained illness, he managed to write only fifteen additional notes (Nos. 44–58). From October 1726, when he went to Northampton to begin his ministerial relationship with his

---

9. The pioneering research of Schafer on these topics is summarized in *Works, 13,* 63, 65–68. In order to appreciate fully the value of his research, one must work carefully through his Introduction to the "Miscellanies."

1. *Works, 13,* 14 and 94. More than a year before he began "Notes on Scripture," JE wrote a short entry in the "Miscellanies," no. m, entitled "Types of the Scriptures" (ibid., 169).

2. See nos. e, g, k, m, ss, uu, ww, xx, and yy, in *Works, 13.*

grandfather Solomon Stoddard, until February 1729, when Stoddard died, Edwards wrote eighty entries in the notebook (Nos. 59–63, 99–102, 77–88, 103–110, 89–98, 64–73, 111–141). During the remainder of the year of Stoddard's death, after a period of several months in which all of his notebooks except the "Miscellanies" sat idle, he carried the series through No. 191 (Nos. 74–76, 142–191). That same autumn Edwards created the quire out of the initial gathering in Book 1. The following year, 1730, he entered only three additional notes (Nos. 192–194); this may be explained in part by the fact that it was the year in which he inaugurated his use of the "Blank Bible," which gave him another manuscript in which to write biblical commentary.[3]

As the series unfolds after 1730, it is possible to establish approximate dates for several specific entries by using the sources Edwards was reading. In each case, the entry could not have been written before the publication date of the source cited and may have been written later. For instance, the first quotation from Arthur Bedford's *Scripture Chronology* (1730) occurs in No. 199. Edwards cited Nathan Prince's *Essay* (1734) in No. 220, Moses Lowman's *Paraphrase and Notes* (1737) in No. 291, and the second edition of Ephraim Chambers' *Cyclopaedia* (1738) in No. 319. No. 485 contains a citation from the 1748 edition of James Hervey's *Meditations*. No successive entries could have been written earlier than these dates of publication, although preceding entries may have been written later than these publication dates. By contrast, No. 400 contains a late addition drawn from Ralph Cudworth's *True Intellectual System*, which, according to Wallace E. Anderson, Edwards was reading in 1757 during the last year of his ministry in Stockbridge, Massachusetts.[4]

"Notes on Scripture" includes several entries with dates or datable references in them. No. 459 refers to a letter of September 4, 1747, sent by Edwards to Thomas Gillespie (1708–74), a Scottish correspondent.[5] No. 462 contains an extract from the *Boston Evening-Post* of January 4, 1748, followed by a reference to a similar account in the *Boston Gazette* of January 27, 1748. No. 482 mentions *Notes on Scripture-Texts, No. 1*, by John Glas (1695–1773).[6] In a letter to John Erskine (1721–1803) in

---

3. This dating of the early entries in "Notes on Scripture" is summarized in Schafer's table of "Chronological Parallels" for JE's MSS (*Works*, *13*, 91–109).

4. *Works*, *11*, 46.

5. For the text of JE's letter to Gillespie, see Dwight ed., *1*, 232–42.

6. No copy of John Glas, *Notes on Scripture-Texts, No. 1*, has been located. For the text see *The Works of Mr. John Glas* (2nd ed., 5 vols. Perth, 1782–83), *3*, 21–22.

Scotland dated July 5, 1750, Edwards mentioned receipt of "Mr. Glass' Notes on Scripture Texts" in the winter of 1749–50.[7]

Numerous references to other manuscripts by Edwards occur in "Notes on Scripture," some of which provide additional chronological data. No. 324 contains a reference to "Images," no. 81, which Anderson dates in the six months following January 1739; Nos. 324 and 319 both deal with the same subject as no. 81.[8] In No. 331 the reference to "Apocalypse," no. 78, which has been dated in 1739, correlates with the content of the sermon series on the "History of Redemption" preached by Edwards in 1739.[9] No. 338 includes a reference to "Images," no. 94, dated by Anderson in late 1739.[1] No. 365 contains materials Edwards incorporated into the commencement address he delivered at Yale College on September 10, 1741.[2] No. 381 refers to "Miscellanies," no. 811, which contains a reference to Edwards' sermon on Romans 12:4–8 preached on August 19, 1739.[3]

In several other instances, the content of particular entries in "Notes on Scripture" is sufficiently similar to that in other writings by Edwards to warrant the establishment of approximate dates. For example, Edwards preached two sermons on II Peter 1:19 between August and November 1737 on the doctrine "Divine revelation is like a light that shines in a dark place," a theme he discussed at length in No. 265.[4] Nos. 304–305, which focus on I Corinthians 13, relate directly to his sermon series preached from April to October 1738, which was published posthumously in 1852 as *Charity and Its Fruits*.[5] His discussion of divine providence represented by the revolution of Ezekiel's wheels in No. 389 relates directly to a late reference in his sermons on the "History of Redemption" preached in 1739.[6] Edwards used No. 468 in writing the *Humble Inquiry,* which was published in mid-1749.[7] The content of No. 479 parallels that in "Miscellanies," nos. 1102, 1105, and 1114, which were written sometime after mid-1748. Edwards

7. JE's letter to Erskine is in Dwight ed., *1,* 405–13.
8. *Works, 11,* 42.
9. Ibid., *5,* 78; and *9,* 101.
1. Ibid., *11,* 43.
2. Ibid., *4,* 213–14.
3. MSS in the Yale collection.
4. Ibid.
5. *Works, 8,* 123–397.
6. *Works, 9,* 517, 519.
7. *The Works of Jonathan Edwards, 12, Ecclesiastical Writings,* ed. David D. Hall (New Haven, Yale Univ. Press, 1994), 199–201.

quoted from Thomas Goodwin's exposition of Ephesians in No. 504, a source he was also citing in "Miscellanies," nos. 1272 and 1274–1275.[8] "Miscellanies," no. 1277b, contains a dated reference to the *Monthly Review* of March 1754.

A final issue related to the dating of "Notes on Scripture" involves the question of Edwards' use of this series during the last years of his lifetime. Although he wrote additions to entries in the manuscripts in 1757, it seems clear that following his move to Stockbridge he turned away from writing many new notes in this series. He changed his pattern and increasingly used the "Blank Bible" for general biblical commentary. There are relatively few entries in "Notes on Scripture" from the Stockbridge period. During these years he was also occupied with preparing several major projects for the press.[9]

The following chronological table has been constructed principally from the data described above. This table indicates the tentative time frame for specific entries. Square brackets mark the earliest possible date, or a potential *terminus a quo*.

Dating of Select Entries in "Notes on Scripture"[1]

Nos. 1–43 1724
Nos. 44–58 February 1725–August 1726
Nos. 59–63, 99–102, 77–88 October 1726–October 1727
Nos. 103–110, 89–98 January–June 1728
Nos. 64–73, 111–141 August 1728–February 1729
Nos. 74–76, 142–191 June–December 1729
Nos. 192–194 January–August 1730
No. 199 [1730]
No. 220 [1734]
No. 265 August–November 1737
No. 291 [1737]
No. 304–305 April–October 1738

8. Thomas Goodwin, *An Exposition on the First Eleven Verses of the Second Chapter of the Epistle to the Ephesians*, in *The Works of Thomas Goodwin*, Vol. I, Pt. 2 (London, 1681).

9. In Stockbridge JE wrote and published *Misrepresentations Corrected, and Truth Vindicated* (*Works*, *12*, 349–503) and *Freedom of the Will* (*The Works of Jonathan Edwards*, *1*, ed. Paul Ramsey [New Haven, Yale Univ. Press, 1957]). JE also wrote *Original Sin* (*The Works of Jonathan Edwards*, *3*, ed. Clyde A. Holbrook [New Haven, Yale Univ. Press, 1970]) as well as *Concerning the End for which God Created the World* and *The Nature of True Virtue* (*Works*, *8*, 399–627), all of which were published posthumously.

1. The dates for Nos. 1–194 in this Table are drawn from Schafer's chronology (*Works*, *13*, 91–109).

No. 319 [1738]
Nos. 319 and 324 January 1739
No. 331 1739
No. 338 Late 1739
No. 365 Before September 1741
No. 381 After August 1739
No. 389 After August 1739
Nos. 400–412 Before May 1743[2]
No. 433 After October 1741
No. 430 Late Addition from Henry Winder, after 1746[3]
No. 459 [September 1747]
No. 462 [January 1748]
No. 468 Before Mid-1749
No. 479 After Mid-1748[4]
No. 482 After Winter 1749–1750
No. 485 [1748]
No. 504 Near March 1754
No. 270 Late Addition from Philip Doddridge, after 1756
No. 400 Late Addition from Ralph Cudworth, 1757

This table corroborates what Thomas Schafer discovered concerning the early entries in "Notes on Scripture," namely, that Edwards did not write at a uniform pace through the years. He had periods of activity as well as times of inactivity in writing the series. Furthermore, merely tracking the pace of entries without taking into account their length distorts the measure of his investment. Long entries, such as Nos. 416 and 419, required considerable time and effort. Edwards

2. No. 400 contains the first Theophilus Gale reference in "Notes on Scripture." In the "Miscellanies" the first reference to Gale occurs in no. 953 shortly after no. 951 where JE criticizes those who talk too much about religious experiences. In no. 951 he writes of a cloud and wind without rain, an image that also appears in his letter of May 12, 1743, to his Scottish correspondent William McCulloch (*Works*, *4*, 541).

3. JE's "Catalogue" contains numerous references to Henry Winder, *A Critical and Chronological History of the Rise, Progress, Declension, and Revival of Knowledge, Chiefly Religious. In Two Periods. I. The Period of Tradition from Adam to Moses. II. The Period of Letters from Moses to Christ* (2 vols. London, 1745–46). See pp. 14, 19, 27, and 39. JE's "Diary and Account Book" contains the following entry: "Lent Mr. Hopkins Dr. Winder on *Knowledge*, December 22, 1755." The late addition to No. 430 is therefore probably dated in the decade between 1746 and 1755.

4. The content of No. 479 is parallel to "Miscellanies," nos. 1102, 1105, and 1114. No. 1101 contains an integral reference to John Taylor, *A Paraphrase with Notes on the Epistle to the Romans. To which is Prefix'd a Key to the Apostolic Writings* (London, 1745). JE thanked John Erskine for sending this item in a letter of Aug. 31, 1748 (Dwight ed., *1*, 251).

wrote approximately the first two-fifths of all entries in less than seven years, but those first 194 notes constitute a much smaller fraction than two-fifths of the total contents of "Notes on Scripture." The 1730s and 1740s were the decades of his greatest activity in this series. Equally striking is the fact that this series figured only marginally in his activities after he left Northampton.

The text of "Notes on Scripture" that follows provides a fresh view of a critical component in the intellectual and theological world view of Edwards. Without this biblical element the writings of Jonathan Edwards make little sense.

NOTES ON SCRIPTURE

1. GENESIS 2:10–14. Those rivers, which all ran into one and made one great river, have their courses changed by the great alterations that were made upon the face of the earth by the flood. And so Pison and Gihon, though quite different rivers now, yet then[1] run from the same heads and springs as the rivers that then united in Eden.[2]

2. MATTHEW 13:33; LUKE 13:21. "The kingdom of heaven is like unto leaven, which a woman took and hid in three measures of meal, till the whole was leavened." By "three measures" is meant the whole world, the[3] progeny of the three sons of Noah, who settled the three parts of the world: Shem, Asia; and Ham, Africa; and Japheth, Europe.

3. LUKE 14:22–23. Here in this parable is represented to us, first, the rejection of the Jews and the calling of the Gentiles (v. 22); but in the twenty-third [verse], there is manifestly another general calling of the Gentiles spoken of. The first is that which is called "the calling of the Gentiles," the next that which is called in Scripture the bringing in "the fullness of the Gentiles" [Rom. 11:25]. 'Tis manifest therefore by this text that there remains yet another calling of the Gentiles than hath yet been.

4. MATTHEW 21:40–41. "When the lord therefore of the vineyard cometh." 'Tis manifest here that the destruction of Jerusalem is called the coming of the Lord. This is called the end of the world. 'Tis the end of the old world, and from this time began the new heavens and new earth spoken of in Is. 65:17, and the time wherein the heavens and the earth are shaken [Is. 13:13]. This was the end put to the Jewish church, and polity, and nation, and law, country, city, sanctuary, and all the Jewish world. And from this time began the Gentile church to be the

1. This word is a later interlineation.
2. JE marked this entry with a large "X."
3. JE deleted "descendants."

only people of God, for as soon as those husbandmen were destroyed, then the vineyard was let out to others, according to this place. And this coming of Christ, it was that [which] was spoken of so often as being very near by the apostles, and said by Christ to be within the lifetime of some there present [Matt. 24:34]. This coming was begun now and finished in Constantine's time, when the heathen world was overthrown, as then the Jewish. This calling of the Gentiles is what is called, Matt. 24:31, "the gathering together the elect from the four winds, from one end of heaven to the other."

5. GENESIS 6:4. The monstrous births that arose from the conjunction of the sons of God with the daughters of men, typifies unto us what an odious monster results from the conjoining of holy things with wicked, or of a holy profession with a wicked life in hypocrites, and what powerful enemies against religion such are, whether they are particular persons or churches, as the Church of Rome, that monstrous beast, in whom are joined the profession of the name of Christ and many of his doctrines with the most odious devilism, who has "horns as a lamb, but speaks as a dragon" [Rev. 13:11]. And their bulk and huge stature denotes their pride, as none are so proud as hypocrites.[4] See No. 257.

6. I KINGS 6. It appears that the temple was a type of Christ, inasmuch as Christ is said to be the temple of the New Jerusalem in the Revelation, because he calls himself this temple[5] [Rev. 21:22]; and so the tabernacle before. Hence the reason why they were commanded to sacrifice nowhere else, why they were commanded to look to it in their prayers, etc.

7. GENESIS 22:8. "My son, God will provide a lamb for a burnt offering." Fulfilled in Christ.

8. CANTICLES 8:1. "O that thou wert as my brother, that sucked the breasts of my mother! When I should find thee without, I would kiss thee; yea, I should not be despised." Which wish of the church is now accomplished by Christ's incarnation. The Son of God, who is infinitely higher than we, is come down unto us in our nature, and has familiarized himself to us.

4. JE interlined this sentence and the following cross-reference when he wrote No. 257.
5. This clause is a later interlineation.

9. MATTHEW 3:7. "Who hath warned you to flee from the wrath to come?" Having respect primarily to that wrath that should come upon those of the Jews who should reject the Messiah and continue in impenitency, both in their rejection from being the people of God and judicial hardening, and those many great calamities that nation suffered after Christ's ascension, especially[6] their dreadful overthrow by[7] the Romans.

10. MATTHEW 9:10. "And it came to pass as Jesus sat at meat in the house, behold, many publicans and sinners came and sat down with him and his disciples." Jesus' ordering or suffering it to be thus, intimating the nature of the gospel and designs of his kingdom, the gospel grace, the "feast of fat things" [Is. 25:6], being offered freely to all nations and kinds of men, having respect to the calling of the Gentiles.

11. MATTHEW 1:3. "And Judas begat Phares and Zara of Thamar." So 'tis remarked in the 5th verse, that "Salmon begat Booz of Rachab," and that "Booz begat Obed of Ruth"; and [in the] 6th verse, that "David begat Solomon of her that had been the wife of Urias." All the mothers are not noted, but only those which were either harlots or Gentiles, except the wife of Urias the Hittite, who was a wife of a Gentile. These are taken notice of because Christ's descending from several harlots and Gentiles intimates unto us that all that are saved by Christ were sinners, that the church of Christ is made up wholly of such as were once sinners, that is, spiritual harlots, or adulterers, and idolaters, thereby also typifying the calling of the Gentiles.

12. MATTHEW 8:25. "And his disciples came to him, and awoke him, saying, Lord, save us; we perish." This ship shadows to us the Christian church, which indeed it contained in it with its head. God commonly suffers his people to be just upon the very brink of destruction before he delivers them, as here the tempest arose so much that the ship was covered with waves. God seems to be asleep and to let them alone, as Christ was, and must be awaked by the earnest prayers and cries of his people before he will deliver them; and [they] say as in Ps. 44:23, "Awake, why sleepest thou, O Lord? Arise, cast us not off forever." [See also] Ps. 7:6, and 35:23, and 59:4–5. "Then will the Lord awake as one out of sleep, and like a mighty man that shouteth by reason of wine" [Ps. 78:65].

6. MS: "Especial."
7. JE deleted "Titus."

13. JEREMIAH 1:5. "Before I formed thee in the belly I knew thee; and before thou camest forth out of the womb I sanctified thee, and I ordained thee a prophet unto the nations." In the same sense as God is said to foreknow Jeremiah as a prophet before he was, whom he had elected to be such, so is he said to foreknow the elect as saints, and children, and heirs of life. Ex. 23:12, 17.[8]

14. JEREMIAH 2:32. "Can a maid forget her ornaments, or a bride her attire? Yet my people have forgotten me days without number." For our holiness is all the righteousness of God; all the beauty of the soul is wholly and only divine light reflected. All grace is nothing but the Holy Spirit dwelling in us; and all those graces and spiritual beauties, which are to the mind as attire, and ornament are to the body, are Christ in the soul, and nothing else. Wherefore we are commanded to put on Christ [Rom. 13:14].

15. ISAIAH 53:12. "Therefore will I divide him a portion with the great, and he shall divide the spoil with the strong." Intending at least partly that Christ's portion should be the most perfect and glorious kingdom of the earth, the most wise, opulent, and learned nations of the world. Ps. 45:12, "And the daughter of Tyre shall be there with a gift; even the rich among the people shall entreat thy favor." Is. 60:13, "The glory of Lebanon shall come unto thee, the fir tree, and pine tree, and the box together, to beautify the place of my sanctuary; and I will make the place of my feet glorious." Ps. 72:10, "The kings of Tarshish and of the isles shall bring presents: the kings of Sheba and Seba shall offer gifts."

16. PSALMS 48:7. "Thou breakest the ships of Tarshish with an east wind." 'Twas by the[9] gospel, which was as the light that cometh out of the east and shinest to the west [Matt. 24:27], whereby Satan's pagan kingdom in Europe was overthrown.

17. PSALMS 49:3–4. "My mouth shall speak of wisdom; and the meditation of my heart shall be of understanding. I will incline mine ear to a parable; I will open my dark saying upon the harp," being about to speak of a future state and the resurrection, which were great mysteries in Old Testament times. And perhaps a future state is here

8. These Exodus passages bear no perceivable relationship to this entry.
9. JE deleted "word of God."

more plainly spoken of than anywhere else in the Old Testament; the Psalmist really speaks right down plain about it, to the 14th verse. He speaks how impossible it is by strength, riches, or wisdom to avoid death; good and bad, and all, die. And [he] takes notice of the folly of men to set their hearts on riches; for, says he, "like sheep they are laid in the grave," etc., "and the upright shall have dominion over them in the morning," etc. [v. 14]. But he says, notwithstanding this certainty and unavoidableness of death, v. 15, "God will redeem my soul from the power of the grave, for he shall receive me"; and [he] goes on to the end of the psalm to show the misery of the wicked in comparison of the godly.

18. PHILIPPIANS 3:15. "Let therefore as many as be perfect, be thus minded; and if in anything ye be otherwise minded, God shall reveal even this unto you." The thing that is manifestly spoken of all along in this chapter is the rejection of legal works and ceremonies of the Mosaic dispensation, and to count them as loss and dung for the excellence of the knowledge of Christ Jesus, as in the 8th and 9th verses, which the Apostle urges from his own example, down to this verse; and now [he] manifestly exhorts them to be so minded, and tells them if they have yet scruples remaining about the law of Moses, whether it ought not to be observed, God would reveal even this to them, here as in the next verse, to walk according to what they had obtained, etc.

19. JEREMIAH 13:11. "For as a girdle cleaveth to the loins of a man, so have I caused to cleave unto me the whole house of Israel and the whole house of Judah." As the body of man is incomplete and defective without his garments, so doth Christ look on himself as incomplete without his church.

20. I CORINTHIANS 15:29. "Else what shall they do which are baptized for the dead, if the dead rise not at all? Why are they then baptized for the dead?" What folly is it to baptize for persons that are dead and not risen again, nor ever to rise! What folly is it to baptize in the name of such! But this is our case, if there is no resurrection of the dead; we are baptized in the name of a dead man. But who are we if he is not risen, nor to rise? [So][1] the foregoing verses, speaking of the resurrection of Christ, as from the 16th verse, "For if the dead rise not,

1. MS: "X is ~~here speaking~~."

then is not Christ raised: and if Christ be not raised, your faith is vain; ye are yet in your sins." And if so, surely our baptism is also vain, as in this verse; and why[2] stand we in jeopardy every hour, if Christ is yet dead and so to continue.

21. MATTHEW 26. These things seem to be intended to be shadowed by what is related in this chapter. First, that Christ is betrayed by his pretended disciples; these are those that deliver him up to his open enemies. So it has been all along. Antichrist is another Judas who, pretending to be the follower of Christ, are his worst enemies in the world, as Judas more incensed God's anger than his crucifiers. So hypocrites in all ages are the betrayers of Christ, who, by a seeming embracing religion, expose Christ to shame and mockery, as Judas with a kiss. And again, what should afterwards come to pass, that the clergy would be the chief persecutors of Christ, as the priests of the Jews are.

22. MATTHEW 12:32. "It shall not be forgiven him, neither in this world, nor in the world to come." Some sins may not be forgiven in this world, that yet are forgiven in the world [to come]. That is, God don't manifest his forgiveness in this world, but is provoked sometimes by the grievous falls of the godly in a great measure to hide his face as long as they live, so that ever after they shall go hanging down their heads, even to their graves. Sometimes [he] inflicts judgments that last as long as life, and their former joy and comfort is no more restored to its wonted degree, till they die.

23. MARK 4:5. "And immediately it sprang up, because it had no depth of earth." The vainest minds, and persons of the least solidity, soonest receive a thing that is new and externally plausible, and at first receive it with most lively emotions of their spirits, being guided by fancy only. But the more solid and substantial mind is more slow and deliberate, and weighs matters in an even balance, and comes to it by degrees; but when once it is fixed, it's lasting and immovable, and grows stronger and stronger, and brings forth substantial fruit.

24. MARK 4:25. "For he that hath, to him shall be given; and he that hath not, from him shall be taken away, even that which he hath." Spiritual and heavenly gifts are not given only in proportion to a

2. Conjecture for word broken at margin.

person's improvement of what he has; so that he that has but little, if he improves it as well in proportion to what he has, shall receive as great a reward as he that has a great deal.[3] For then the additional talent should with equal reason be given to him, who at first received the two talents, as to him who received five (Matt. 25:28); but it was not, and the reason is given in the 29th verse. "For to everyone that hath shall be given, and he shall have abundance; but from him that hath not shall be taken away, even that which he hath." It is[4] so with respect to advantages and privileges too: he that improves great advantages well shall receive a greater reward than he that improves small ones; otherwise there could be no advantage. Therefore "glory, honor, and peace is given to every man that worketh good, but to the Jew first" (Rom. 2:10).

25. MARK 4:26–28. "And he said, So is the kingdom of God, as if a man should cast seed into the ground, and should sleep, and rise night and day; and the seed should spring and grow up, he knoweth not how. For the earth bringeth forth fruit of herself; first the blade, then the ear, after that the full corn in the ear." So the kingdom of God comes without observation, without noise and tumult, but goes silently and calmly, but irresistibly, on. So it increased gradually from Christ's disciples, till in about three hundred years it filled the world, and yet grew nobody knew how, being promoted by an invisible hand, without war, noise, and clamor, by operating on men's understandings and wills. So the kingdom of God often in the same manner grows in men's hearts, being at first only as an invisible seed, but afterwards as the blade, then the ear, then the full corn.

26. MARK 6:44. "And they that did eat of the loaves were about five thousand men." Not that the multitude that was about him now was more numerous [than] that very frequently at other times, whereby we learn how publicly Christ's miracles were wrought.

27. MARK 6:52. "For they considered not the miracle of the loaves, for their heart was hardened." By hardness of heart here, and in other places, is intended so largely as to take in blindness of mind, and the depravation of the faculties of the mind in general, and the perversion of their exercises.

3. JE deleted "that grace or wisdom that a man has is a motive to co." He then failed to delete "for then he that received the two talents," the substance of which is repeated in what follows.
4. JE deleted "very commonly."

28. LUKE 11:44. "Woe unto you, scribes, Pharisees, hypocrites!" etc. The Jewish church was now in its apostatized state, being become an hypocritical, superstitious, corrupt, haughty, persecuting church, very much as the apostatized Christian church under Antichrist, only in a far less degree, but their crimes were exactly of the same nature. 'Tis called a "generation of vipers" [Matt. 12:34],[5] like as the Church of Rome, the dragon, the beast. Here it was that our Lord was crucified; and "the blood of all the prophets, which was shed from the foundation of the world, was required of this generation" (v. 50). So the Church of Rome is said to be the city "where our Lord was crucified" (Rev. 11:8), and that "in her was found the blood of prophets, and of saints, and of all that were slain upon the earth" [Rev. 18:24]. And in innumerable things did this apostatized church agree with the Church of Rome. Now the scribes and Pharisees were the teachers of the nation, and as their clergy, and were the haughtiest, most hypocritical, most covetous, deceitful, malicious, persecuting sort of men in the whole nation, their enormities, that are mentioned here and elsewhere, exactly to a wonder corresponding with those of the Romish clergy and the high church; their temper and behavior was just as theirs is.

29. MARK 9:29. "This kind can come forth by nothing, but by prayer and fasting." Wherefore fasting, that which is here so called, is acceptable to God now under the New Testament.

30. MARK 9:38–39. "And John answered him, saying, Master, we saw one casting out devils in thy name, and he followeth not us; and we forbad him, because he followeth not us. But Jesus said, Forbid him not." Hereby is the practice of many in these days condemned, who will not suffer others to do good, and use their endeavors to save men's souls, and dispossess Satan, because they follow not them.

31. MARK 9:42. "And whosoever shall offend one of these little ones that believe in me," etc. Christians are but babes and infants in this world; especially were Christ's disciples so at this time. And the primitive church was an infant; they are called by the apostle John "little children" [John 13:33]. Christians must become as little children in humility, innocency, tenderheartedness, etc. By "offend" in Scripture is intended "to cause to offend." We hereby learn how dangerous and

5. JE deleted "and a perverse generation oftentimes."

dreadful a sin it is to endeavor to make weak Christians go against their consciences.

32. MARK 12:7. "But those husbandmen said among themselves, This is the heir; come, let us kill him, and the inheritance shall be ours." This was really the case with the Pharisees; they were the teachers of this people, and they see that if Christ was followed, they should be neglected. This greatly startled them; they feared losing their credit, so that they should [not] be able to ride[6] that nation any longer. But if they could any way prevail to kill him, they doubted not but they should have quiet possession still.

33. MARK 12:24–25. "And Jesus answering said unto them, Do ye not therefore err, because ye know not the Scriptures, neither the power of God? For when they shall rise from the dead, they neither marry, nor are given in marriage, but are as the angels which are in heaven." We may conclude therefore that these doctrines of a future state and the resurrection are taught, and may be learned, in the Old Testament; yea, and in general the manner of it may be known by it.

34. MARK 13:22. "For false Christs and false prophets shall rise, and shall show signs and wonders, to seduce, if it were possible, even the elect." Let us explain election which way we will, and one of these two doctrines is established. If the election spoken of precedes their calling, then the doctrine of predestination is established; if it follows, and they are chosen for their Christianity, then the doctrine of perseverance is established, for 'tis impossible to seduce such, as is implied.

35. GENESIS 27:29. "Let the people serve thee, and nations bow down to thee. Be lord over thy brethren, and let thy mother's son bow down to thee," etc. Hence we learn that the prophets themselves may not understand their prophecies, for Jacob thought that this should be accomplished of Esau.

36. MATTHEW 6:13. "And lead us not into temptation." That is, trials brought upon [us] by God's providential hand, as well as the temptations of lust. God often leads his children into these, and always for their good; but yet we are to pray against it, with submission to God's will, because, simply considered, 'tis an evil.

6. Or "rule."

37. JEREMIAH 16:15. "But the Lord liveth, that brought up the children of Israel from the land of the north, and from all the lands whither he had driven them; and I will bring them again into their own land that I gave unto their fathers." This has not only, nor principally, a respect unto the return of the captivity of the Israelites from Babylon, but unto the gathering of the gospel church, the gathering "together the elect (the spiritual Israel) from the four winds, from one [end] of heaven to the other," into the church, their own land, from whence they were captivated by Satan (Matt. 24:31). This is one sense of all those prophecies of the Old Testament that speak of recalling of the Jews.

38. JEREMIAH 11:20. "Let me see thy vengeance on them, for unto thee have I revealed my cause." Also Jer. 18:21, "Therefore deliver up their children to the famine," etc. We hence learn that these imprecations that are to be found in Scripture, are not to be understood as expressions of a private desire of ill to their enemies contrary to the precepts of the gospel, for 'tis evident that Jeremiah did not hate his country, or desire or rejoice in its overthrow.

39. MATTHEW 15:21–22. "Then Jesus went thence, and departed into the coasts of Tyre and Sidon. And, behold, a woman of Canaan," etc. The casting out of the devil out of the daughter of this woman, in my opinion, figures forth the casting the devil out of the Gentile and antichristian world, Tyre frequently representing in the Scripture Satan's idolatrous kingdom.

40. LUKE 15:22–23. "And the father said to his servants, Bring forth the best robe, and put it on him; and put a ring on his hand, and shoes on his feet. And bring hither the fatted calf," etc. As Christ's eating with publicans and sinners was figurative of the calling[7] of the Gentiles, so are the parables of the lost sheep [vv. 3–7], piece of money [vv. 8–10], and prodigal son [vv. 11–32], especially the last, agreeing in all circumstances.

41. LUKE 17:20. "And when he was demanded of the Pharisees, when the kingdom of God should come, he answered and said, The kingdom of God cometh without observation." This clears up any difficulties that might be raised from any speeches of Christ or the

7. MS: "Called."

apostles, that seem to speak of a bodily descent of Christ from heaven to receive his kingdom in a very short time.

42. LUKE 17:30–37. "Even thus shall it be in the day when the Son of man is revealed." This and the following verses, especially the last, may convince us that the coming or revealing of Christ, so often spoken of by Christ and his apostles, that was to be so suddenly, was at the destruction of Jerusalem.

43. JOHN 12:47; 5:45; 8:15. "I judge him not, for I came not to judge the world, but to save the world." Men are not properly judged and condemned by the covenant of grace, but by the law, or covenant of works; that is the eternal rule of judgment. The covenant of grace is a deliverance from this judgment; those who are in Christ are delivered from the law, and escape the condemnation of it. The law has its force upon Christ, and can go no further; but the law has its full force upon unbelievers.

44. II SAMUEL 23:16. "And the three mighty men brake through the host of the Philistines, and drew water out of the well of Bethlehem, that was by the gate, and took it, and brought it to David; nevertheless, he would not drink thereof, but poured it out before the Lord." No doubt but this was ordered[8] for a type of[9] something evangelical; otherwise it is wonderful how and why it should happen that he should long for the water of that particular well, and for what reason he should esteem it unlawful for him to drink it. Bethlehem being the place of Christ's birth, the waters of it may signify the same as the water of the sanctuary, the water of the New Jerusalem, or the water of life. This was the price of the blood of those three mighty men; so is the water of life of the blood of the mighty Son of God. They obtained it by conquering Israel's enemies; so doth Christ, by the conquest of the enemies of his spiritual Israel. David would not drink it, but poured it out before the Lord; so we ought to give all the glory of our salvation unto God, as God gives it unto us by the blood of Christ; we ought to give it all back again unto God in praise.

45. MATTHEW 18:16. "And if he neglect to hear thee, then take with thee one or two more, that in the mouth of two or three witnesses every

8. MS: "order."
9. JE deleted "some gospel truth."

word may be established." 'Tis evident, by the next verse, that the end
of bringing these others is that he may hear them, and be convinced of
the evil of what he has done, and not to entrap him in his words. They
are come indeed as witnesses, that is, as witnesses of the evil of what he
has done (for "witnesses," in Scripture phrase, are not only of facts).
'Tis this only that is wanted. They are come because he will not hear
the first, that he may hear when the voice of two or three concur in the
matter. 'Tis this that wants to be established to the man; and the joint
voice of several has the same tendency to establish such a thing, when
they jointly bear testimony of the evil of a thing, as in bearing testimony to a fact. The end of their joining together, therefore, is that
every word of their admonition may be heard. This is evidently the
meaning of the place.

46. THE BOOK OF ESTHER. It appears to me very probable, that this
book of Esther is an history that is a shadow of gospel things and times,
by the agreement of it with events, and the agreeableness to the manner of other typical histories of the Old Testament. The great feast that
Ahasuerus made is the gospel feast. Christ's incarnation, life, and
death, and the benefits thereof, are frequently represented both in
Old Testament and New by the making of a feast. The feast is made
"both unto great and small" (Esther 1:5), agreeing [with] the universality of the gospel offer. 'Twas made in the king's palace, as the gospel
feast is made in the house of God. It was a rich and glorious feast (vv.
6–7), answering to the excellency of gospel benefits. None was compelled, but every man eat and drank according to his pleasure. So the
gospel benefits are offered to all, but everyone is left to his own choice;
none are compelled. Vashti the queen is the church, or God's people,
who is called "the queen in gold of Ophir" [Ps. 45:9], and is often
represented as being the wife of God, the great King. Vashti is sent for
to this feast, to appear before the king [1:11]; so when the gospel feast
was made, the call was made more especially to the Jews that has
hitherto been God's people. They were a long [time] urged to come,
and earnestly invited, before God left them and turned to the Gentiles.
Vashti, though she was the king's own wife, refused to come, for she
had a feast of her own. So the Jews, though God's peculiar people,
refused to come to the glorious feast he made, through their pride and
vanity, trusting in their own righteousness, in their own wisdom, being
foolishly fond and proud of their own ceremonies, temple, and superstition, being lifted up that they were Abraham's seed and God's pecu-

liar people, as Queen Vashti's high station made her too proud to obey the king. Upon this, Ahasuerus repudiates Vashti, and gives "her royal estate to another" [1:19]. So we find the rejecting of the Jews and calling the Gentiles compared to God's repudiating of his wife and taking another better than she. Esther was exceeding "fair and beautiful" [2:7], and the king delighted in her. So Christ's heart is ravished with the beauty of the queen. Mordecai is the gospel ministry; he nourished and brought up Esther, and was as a father to her (2:7). So the church is nourished by God's ministers. He brought her to Ahasuerus; so the gospel ministers present the church "as a chaste virgin to Christ" (II Cor. 11:2). Esther must be purified before she is married to the king, "six months with oil of myrrh, and six months with sweet odors" [2:12]. So God's people must be prepared and purified, sanctified with the sweet graces of God's Spirit, before they are admitted to the full enjoyment of God's love. So the Christian church was three centuries a-preparing before she had the royal crown put on her head in the time of Constantine the Great. When the king "set the royal crown upon her head, and made her queen instead of Vashti, then the king made a great [feast] unto all his princes and servants, even Esther's feast; and he made a release to the provinces, and gave gifts, according to the state of the king" (2:17–18). So when God's people are sufficiently prepared, they shall be admitted to that glory which is compared to a feast, and shall receive gifts, according to the state of the King of kings. Likewise in Constantine's time, 'twas a time of joy and rejoicing to Christians, as the time of a feast, and a time of glorious liberty. Mordecai used to sit in the gate of the king's palace [2:21]; so the place of God's ministers is in his house, which is the gate of heaven, which is God's palace.

After these things, God[1] promoted Haman, the grand enemy of God's people, above all others (3:1), who seems to typify Antichrist (as will appear probable by the agreement in many things), whom God in his providence advanced above all, and gave him[2] dominion over all the world. Haman was exceeding proud and of an haughty [spirit]; so Antichrist is the most remarkable son of pride that ever was, exalting himself above all that is called God, or is worshiped, showing himself that he is God, having a mouth speaking great things. Haman, like Antichrist, loved to have everybody else bow to him, and could not

---

1. The biblical text states that Ahasuerus, not God, promoted Haman.

2. At the bottom of MS p. 6, JE wrote: "See the page next after No. 167." The point of the reference is unclear.

bear it that Mordecai did not bow, nor do him reverence, as the true ministers of God will not submit or do obeisance to the Pope and his haughty clergy, which has always filled them with the greatest rage. Haman, like Antichrist, was of a most malicious, persecuting spirit, and persecuted and sought the destruction of all the people of God. Esther 3:6, "And he thought scorn to lay hands on Mordecai alone, for they had showed him the people of Mordecai; wherefore Haman sought to destroy all the Jews that were throughout the whole kingdom of Ahasuerus, even the people of Mordecai." The king gave him power to do as he would with this people. Esther 3:11, "And the king said unto Haman, The silver is given unto thee, the people also, to do with them as seemeth good to thee." So God gave Antichrist power over his people. Rev. 13:7, "And it was given unto him to make war with the saints, and to overcome them; and power was given him over all kindreds, and tongues, and nations." And Rev. 17:17, "For God hath put it into their hearts to fulfill his will, and to agree, and give their kingdom unto the beast." Deliverance is obtained for the Jews by Esther's humble prayer. So it will be by the earnest prayer of the church that God's people shall be delivered from Antichrist, and God will extend the golden scepter of his grace, as the king to Esther [5:2]. At that time the good works of God's people and ministers shall come into remembrance, to be recorded as Mordecai's; and God will not rest till he has delivered them, as Mordecai's good deeds were found by the king in the records [6:1–2]. Haman exceedingly affected pomp and sovereignty; he desired to wear the same apparel that the king wore, and to ride on the king's horse, and to wear the king's crown, and to be honored as the king himself [6:7–9]. So Antichrist would be honored and obeyed as God himself, assumes the power that belongs to God alone, assumes the power and is for wearing the crown of Christ himself, and usurps his throne, showing himself that he is God. But Haman, to his great mortification, sees Mordecai exalted to this same honor, and, which is more mortifying, he is forced to do it himself, and he is put in subjection to him, and made to run before him like a servant. He brought himself to this by the very means by which he intended to advance himself. Thus God is wont to order it with respect to the enemies of his people; those same means by which they proudly seek to advance themselves, God turns to their depression and the advancement [of his people]. And thus God has done and will do by Antichrist. God will exalt his people, and make them to reign with Christ, and to sit down with him in his throne, and to be partakers of his glory; and [they] shall be arrayed with holiness, which is the Christ's own royal robe. And Christ's delight in them and to honor them shall be publicly manifested, and his saints shall reign on earth. And Antichrist and all their enemies shall be put under their feet, and they shall gnaw their tongues for pain. Haman at last was hanged on the same gallows that he prepared for Mordecai. So God is wont to bring upon his people's enemies the very evil they intend for them,[3] and they fall into the pit which they have digged. So it will be with Antichrist. Rev. 13:10, "He that leadeth into captivity shall go into captivity; he that killeth with the sword must be killed with the sword." And Rev. 18:6, "Reward her even as she rewarded you, and double unto her double according to her works; in the cup which she hath filled, fill to her double." Haman intended[4] to hang Mordecai—a cursed death; so the Pope dispenses God's curses, but at length falls into it. So we find, Esther 8:1–2, that the house of Haman was given to Queen Esther, and Mordecai is put in his place. So shall it be with the saints. Europe, which has been the house of Antichrist, shall be in the possession of Protestants, and all his power and dominion shall be given to the saints. The Jews' glorious victory over all their enemies after these things, the growing greatness and honor of Mordecai, the gladness and feasting of the Jews, and their peace and prosperity afterwards, are figures of the glory, peace, and prosperity of the church after the final overthrow of Antichrist. Haman also is a type of the devil. See "Miscellanies," no. 710.[5]

47. JOHN 2:21. "But he spake of the temple of his body." And it seems to me likely that he should speak of his body in two senses: in one sense of the church, which is called his body, and is also called the temple of God, of which the temple of Jerusalem was a type. The temple of Jerusalem may signify the Jewish church, which Christ put an end to by his coming,[6] and in three ages after erected his spiritual temple, the Christian church.

3. I.e. God's people.
4. MS: "intend."
5. This reference and the preceding sentence are a later addition. "Miscellanies," no. 710, entitled "HEAVEN. SEPARATE STATE. RESURRECTION. DISPENSATIONS," includes a discussion of Haman as a "remarkable type of both the devil and Antichrist." Both Haman and the devil are destroyed by means intended for others.
6. JE deleted "so far as it was according to the rudiments of this world, and was made with hands."

48. I KINGS 6:7. "And the house, when it was in building, was built of stone made ready before it was brought thither; so that there was neither hammer, nor ax, nor any tool of iron heard in the house, while it was building." This temple represents the church of God, who are called God's temple, a spiritual house, Jesus Christ being chief cornerstone, and all the saints as so many stones. Particularly by Solomon's temple is meant the church triumphant, as by the tabernacle the church militant; by the exact fitting, squaring, and smoothing of those stones before they were brought thither, represents the perfection of the saints in glory. Heaven is not a place to prepare them; they are all prepared before they come there. They come perfectly sinless and holy into heaven. The world is the place where God hews them, and squares them by his prophets and ministers (I Kgs. 5:6), by the reproofs and warnings of his word, which God compares to a hammer, by persecutions and afflictions. There shall be no noise of these tools heard in heaven, but all these lively stones of this spiritual and glorious building are exactly fitted, framed, and polished before they come there.

49. I CORINTHIANS 11:14. "Doth not even nature itself teach you, that if a man have long hair, it is a shame unto him?" Having the head covered, by long custom, had been used to denote subjection; and as a note of subjection in man, it was plainly against nature itself. The plain light of nature had taught all nations the superiority of man to woman, and his right of rule over her. The Apostle had been pleading against man's long hair, or his covering the head, only on this score, that it was a debasing of man below the place that God had put him in, that it was unnatural and a shame, or debasing of man, and confusing of the order of nature, and in this sense against nature. In this, nature teaches the contrary. It is a disgrace to him, ἀτιμία, to appear below the woman, a debasing of him below his nature, and therefore nature teaches the contrary; not but that, if having the head uncovered were a note of subjection, it would have been as much against nature for the man to have his head uncovered. And that which is against nature in this sense, is against nature in a proper sense. It is against nature in a proper sense to bow down before an idol, because 'tis against nature to adore an idol; and bowing down, by universal custom, is used to denote adoration. But if bowing down by universal custom were used to denote contempt, it would not be against nature.

50. EPHESIANS 4:13. "Till we all come in the unity of the faith, and of the knowledge of God, to the measure of the stature of the fullness of Christ." That is, till we all come to agree in the same faith, which is fully conformed to Christ, and therein are come to his rule and measure; and in faith, and perhaps in other graces, the body of Christ becomes complete, being completely conformed to Christ. The church [is] the completeness of Christ, "the fullness of him that filleth all in all" [Eph. 1:23]. But this body is not complete, and but an imperfect embryo, till it is perfectly conformed to his mind in faith and to his image in other graces. Christ and his church, as here, so elsewhere, being as body and soul, are called one man. 'Tis as if he had said, "Till Christ's body is complete in stature." The church, the body of Christ, is called a man (Eph. 2:15).

51. GENESIS 4:14. It seems to me no way improbable that Cain's curse was intended and by him understood, not only of him personally, but of his posterity. Such he might learn from his father Adam, seeing the covenant that was made with him was made not only for himself, but for his posterity. If Cain understood it only of him personally, it seems something strange that he should express himself after such a manner. The inhabited earth was not broad enough for such expressions. The expression, "from thy face," may be in the same sense as David was shut out from the face of God when he dwelt in Ziklag [I Sam. 27:6–7], from his altar where his people sacrificed and worshiped him, and [where] he especially manifested himself. Doubtless there were then such things as well as afterwards.

52. JAMES 2:19. "The devils also believe, and tremble." They believe that Jesus is the Christ, etc., and tremble at the thoughts of the overthrow he will give them.

53. JOHN 11:51. "And this spake he not of himself; but being high priest that year, he prophesied that Jesus should die for that nation." By this it appears that things are ordered by God to be acted and spoken after such a particular manner, with a design to indigitate and represent heavenly things, without the least thought of the actors or speakers. See note on Gen. 22:8.[7]

7. This reference is a later addition and points to an entry in the "Blank Bible," not to No. 7 above. In the former JE writes, "Again we may observe here that which may confirm us,

54. PSALMS 65:8. "Thou makest the outgoings of the morning and the evening to rejoice." By "the outgoings of the morning and evening" may be meant the east and the west, and so signify the same as the "ends of the earth" in the former part of the verse.

55. MATTHEW 24:22. "But for the elect's sake those days shall be *shortened.*" *Inquiry.* What is meant here by being shortened? We in the Scriptures read of God's hastening the deliverance of his people, avenging them speedily, helping his church right early, and the like, though God suffers them for many ages to be persecuted. By it is intended that he will manifest his wisdom in swiftly turning the wheel of his providence, and with wondrous expedition, bringing things about that were necessary to be done before they could be delivered.

56. PSALMS 148:4. "Praise ye him, ye heavens of heavens, and ye waters that be above the heavens." That is, ye people and multitudes; not but that the Psalmist might think there were really waters there, but the Holy Ghost intended it not so. See "Theological Reflections," no. 229.[8]

57. II CORINTHIANS 5:1–2. The "house from heaven" means the body of the resurrection, as appears by the last clause[9] of the 4th verse.

58. MATTHEW 20:16. See "Exposition on the Apocalypse," Rev. 16:12.[1]

59. EXODUS 16:19–20. "Let no man leave of it till the morning," etc. Hereby perhaps we are designed to be taught our absolute dependence every day upon God for the supplies of his grace and spiritual food. We not only depend on him for the first conversion of the soul,

---

that the prophecies of the prophets often, according to the mind of the Holy Ghost, had respect to those things which the prophets themselves had no thought of; for Abraham, when he said, 'God will provide himself a lamb,' had no thought of any other than that Isaac was to be the lamb that was to be offered, and that God had provided for himself."

8. "God had a design and meaning which the penmen never thought of, which he makes appear these ways: by his own interpretation, and by his directing the penmen to such a phrase and manner of speaking, that has a much more exact agreement and consonancy with the thing remotely pointed to, than with the thing meant by the penmen" ("Miscellanies," no. 229, SCRIPTURE, *Works, 13,* 347–48).

9. Broken at margin.

1. "The 16th verse of the 20th [chapter].of Matthew seems to imply, that the Jews shall be some of the last that shall be converted to Christianity" ("Apocalypse," no. 40, *Works, 5,* 140).

but daily depend on him for his grace afterwards. This manna must be given us every day, or we shall be without food. We are taught not to rest in and live upon past attainments, but to be continually looking to God, and by faith fetching from him fresh supplies. We must not lay up in store the grace of this day for tomorrow, to save us the trouble of seeking and gathering more; we never have any to spare. Hereby we shall make a righteousness of what we receive and do; and when we make that use of it, it is like manna that breeds worms and stinks.

60. II CORINTHIANS 5:1.[2] 'Tis a confirmation that the Apostle meant the body of the resurrection by "an house not made with hands, eternal in the heavens," that Christ said, "Destroy this temple made with hands, and in three days I'll raise another made without hands" [Mark 14:58]; as the false witnesses testified, probably so far truly.

61. MATTHEW 9:24. When Christ said, "She is not dead but sleepeth," thereby is meant that her soul was not finally separated from her body, so as to enter into the spiritual and eternal world; nor had there that transformation passed upon her soul from a middle state to perfect holiness or misery. And her soul was kept in a state of insensibility, as in a sound sleep, that her resurrection might not be inconvenient. Therefore Christ also said, "Our friend Lazarus sleepeth" [John 11:11]. His state was not changed, his soul not purified from sin, nor any way altered so as to prepare it for glory; but his state was only intermitted.

62. PSALMS 40:6. "Mine ear hast thou opened," or bored. We read in the beginning of the 21st [chapter] of Exodus, that the servant that loved his wife and his children in his master's house so well, that he did not care to leave them at the six years' end, was then to have his ear bored through with an awl to the door, and to serve his master forever [vv. 5–6]. So Christ has his ear bored for the sake of his people, who are as his wife and his children. He, by the assumption of a body, appears in the form of a servant for them (Heb. 10:5). Christ's ear is as it were bored thereby to the door of God's house (his church) forever. The ear is that whereby the servant hears his master's commands; hearing is the same with obeying in Scripture phrase. And the door is that by which he goes in and out in execution of them, and where he waits to know them.

2. See above, No. 57.

63. EXODUS 23:20. "Behold, I send an angel before thee," etc. This does not seem to be the same angel spoken of in the 33rd chapter, [v. 2], which was a created angel, but the Son of God; for what was spoken here before was in the name of the Father.[3]

64. I SAMUEL 6:14–15. "And the cart came into the field of Joshua, a Bethshemite, and stood there, where there was a great stone. . . . And the Levites took down the ark, and set it on the great stone." The cart seems purposely to be stopped in this field, because of the name of the owner being the same with Christ's, who was signified by the ark, and because of the "great stone," which also represented Christ.

65. PROVERBS 4:23. "Keep thy heart with all diligence, for out of it are the issues of life." 'Tis probable here is an allusion to the blood's issuing from the heart. The heart is the fountain of the blood, which is called the "life" (Gen. 9:4, and other places). Solomon was so great a philosopher,[4] that doubtless he understood that the heart was the fountain of the blood.

66. JOHN 16:16. "A little while, and ye shall not see me; and again, a little while, and ye shall see me, because I go to the Father." "A little while, and ye shall not see me," when I ascend into heaven; "and a little while, and ye shall see me," that is, spiritually, when I shall send the Holy Ghost, who would not come if I did not go to the Father. "Seeing of Christ" is so understood (John 14:19).

67. II CORINTHIANS 1:24. "Not for that we have dominion over your faith," etc. This verse is to be joined to the 14th verse.

68. MALACHI 4:6. "Turn the heart of the fathers to the children, and the heart of children," etc. By "fathers" are meant all sorts of fathers: parents, rulers, and teachers. The hearts of these shall be turned to the children; that is, they shall faithfully rule and guide and teach them, take care of them, and consult their true good. "And the hearts of children shall be turned to their fathers"; that is, they shall be obedient, shall hearken to their teachers, etc. So 'tis explained, Luke 1:17, "the disobedient to the wisdom of the just."

3. JE began and then deleted the following unnumbered entry: "I JOHN 2:8. The Apostle says 'tis no new commandment."
4. I.e. natural philosopher, or scientist.

69. COLOSSIANS 2:11. "In putting off the body of the sins of the flesh by the circumcision of Christ." If this means the outward circumcision with which Christ was circumcised, our sins are put off by Christ's circumcision, after the same manner as by our own baptism; that is, Christ's circumcision signified the putting off our sins as much as our own baptism, for our body of sin was imputed to him. He bore it, and put it off in outward sign by his circumcision. Christ represented us: he came into the world without any original sin of his own, but with our original sin; and he was circumcised to signify the putting off our corruption of nature.

70. ACTS 1:15. "The number of the names together were about 120." Great respect seems to be shown to the number twelve in things pertaining to the church, as may be seen in the account of the New Jerusalem in Revelation; and the number of the sealed of every tribe were 12,000 [Rev. 7:5–8]. And here the number of the church, when the Holy Ghost was poured out upon it, is 120. There were twenty-four elders round about the throne [Rev. 4:4].

71. GENESIS 25:22. "And the children struggled together in the womb." I believe this had reference to the spiritual war there is in the[5] soul of the believer, Christ's spouse, between the flesh and spirit. "The flesh lusteth against the spirit, and the spirit against the flesh; and these two are contrary one to another" [Gal. 5:17].

72. I SAMUEL 25:41. "And she arose, and bowed herself on her face to the earth, and said, Behold, let thine handmaid be a servant to wash the feet of the servants of my lord." She was a type of the church, and herein spake that which represents the disposition of a true Christian, according to Christ's command and example (John 13:1–17).

73. NUMBERS 23:23. "According to this time shall it be said of Jacob and of Israel, What hath God wrought?" That is, God shall do a very strange and wonderful thing for Jacob and Israel. Such interrogations denote the wonderfulness of the thing about which the interrogation is, as Is. 63:1, "Who is this that cometh from Edom?" etc.; and Ps. 24:8, "Who is this King of glory?" See notes on that psalm.[6] "According to

5. JE deleted "heart of every."
6. This reference and the preceding sentence are later interlineations. Commenting on

this time," that is, what he hath done at this [time] is a shadow and representation of it. He hath now redeemed [them] out of Egypt with "the strength of an unicorn" [Num. 23:22]; and there is no enchantment against him, as in the words immediately foregoing. And hereafter he shall send Jesus Christ to redeem them out of spiritual Egypt; with a greater strength shall [he] redeem them from the power of the devil.

74. HEBREWS 6:4–6. "For it is impossible for those that were once enlightened, and have tasted of the heavenly gift," etc. (Let be added to this, No. 299.)[7] What is meant by these things here mentioned may be gathered from the foregoing verses. The Apostle exhorts us, when we have begun in Christianity, to go on and make progress to higher attainments, and not to have all to begin again, that when once we had laid the foundation, we should go on and build the superstructure, and not to keep always laying the foundation, or have occasion to lay it the second time, which foundation, or beginning, or first setting out in Christianity, consists in these things: "In repentance from dead works, and of faith towards God" [Heb. 6:1], which foundation was laid when they first turned from their erroneous and wicked ways, and embraced Christianity, and believed the gospel. And nextly, "in the doctrine of baptisms, and of laying on of hands" [Heb. 6:2], because when they first entered upon a profession of the gospel, they were baptized, and had hands laid on them, that they might receive the Holy Ghost. By the "doctrine of baptisms and laying on of hands," the Apostle means those plain instructions that were given them to prepare them for baptism and laying on hands. And lastly, "in the resurrection of the dead, and eternal judgment" [Heb. 6:2]. The doctrines of resurrection and the future state, or world to come, were the first principles of religion that they first began with.

Now by "those who were once enlightened," the Apostle means those that were once indoctrinated in Christianity, and brought so far to understand and believe it, as to make them forsake their former errors and vicious courses in their unbelief, as is evidently understood (Heb. 10:32). "Tasting of the heavenly gift, and being made partakers

---

Ps. 24:7–10, JE writes, "This has respect to God's or Christ's triumphant ascension into heaven after a battle and victory over his enemies here on earth, agreeable to the representation, Ps. 47:5" ("Blank Bible").

7. This cross-reference is a later interlineation.

of the Holy Ghost" are the same, and means their receiving the Holy Ghost, as they did by the laying on of hands. And lastly, "in tasting of the good word of God and the powers of the world to come" [Heb. 6:5]. Though 'tis probable there were many were made partakers of the gift of the Holy Ghost by laying on of hands than were true saints, yet I believe that when it was not accompanied with gracious exercises, yet it was always accompanied with great common illuminations and affections. 'Tis not probable that they should have the Holy Ghost dwelling in them with respect to his miraculous influences, and not feel anything of the power of it in their souls.[8] When the Holy Ghost was given them, they felt his presence, not only outwardly but inwardly, not only in their understanding, but affections. I believe never any had the Holy Ghost with respect to his extraordinary operations (see Num. 23:16 and 24:5–6, and I Sam 10:6)[9]—Balaam, Saul, nor unconverted men—but that he felt his influence this way. Thus they "tasted of the good word of God, and the powers of the world to come." They "tasted of the good word of God" as the stony-ground hearers who, anon with joy, received the word, and as the Galatians did, who thought it such a blessedness to hear the word of God, and would have plucked out their eyes and given them to the Apostle. They experienced in themselves "the powers of the world to come," that is, of the invisible world (see Eph. 1:21, and Heb. 2:5),[1] felt the powers of the invisible agents of that world upon their minds. 'Tis certain none exercised miraculous gifts without extraordinary influence of the Spirit of God to convince the judgment. I Cor. 13:2, "Though I have all faith, so that I could remove mountains, and have no charity, I am nothing." And doubtless, there was commonly an answerable or proportionable effect on the affections, as there was on the judgment. As that faith there mentioned is there distinguished from true grace or charity, and therefore differed in kind from saving faith, so do these things here mentioned from saving grace.

75. MATTHEW 17:21. "Howbeit this kind goeth not out but by prayer and fasting." This kind[2] as to the manner of possession and influence. There were dumb devils, and unclean devils, and a spirit of infirmity.

---

8. JE deleted "They felt his presence in their minds."
9. These references are a later interlineation.
1. Ibid.
2. JE deleted "of devil."

Some only took the advantage of bodily distemper and disorder of the brain; others possessed them in a more extraordinary manner, so as to have their bodies more absolutely under their influence, using[3] of them as they pleased, sometimes casting of them into the fire, and sometimes into the water, as that spoken of in this place [Matt. 17:15], and sometimes using their tongues as if they were their own, as in the man possessed with the legion [Mark 5:2–9].

76. MARK 1:24. "Saying, Let us alone; what have we to do with thee, thou Jesus of Nazareth? Art thou come to destroy us? I know thee who thou art, the Holy One of God." The devils were exceeding jealous of Christ; they understood of old that the Son of God was to come into the world to destroy them, and they dreaded that destruction. 'Tis probable that Christ came in a manner very unexpected to 'em, as well as to the Jews, but yet they were sensible who he was. They seemed to think that Christ appeared in so low and an obscure manner out of some secret design against them, that he came in disguise that they might not know of it, that he might some way or other be under better advantage to overthrow them. They therefore are willing to let him know that they knew who he was.

77. GENESIS 2:17. "In the day that thou eatest thereof, dying thou shalt die." This expression denotes not only the certainty of death, but the extremity: q.d. "Thou shalt,"[4] in the superlative and to the utmost degree; and so it properly extends to the second death, the death of the soul, for damnation is nothing but extreme death. And I am ready to think that God, by mentioning dying twice over, that he had respect to two deaths, the first and the second. And that 'tis to these words the apostle John refers, in the 20th [chapter] of Revelation and 14th [verse], when he says, "This is the second death." 'Tis much such a reference as he[5] makes in the 2nd verse of the chapter. There he explains who the serpent was that beguiled Eve: "the dragon, that old serpent, who is the devil and Satan." So here he explains what the second of these deaths that was threatened to Adam was. See notes on Rev. 20:14.[6] See further concerning this No. 325.

---

3. JE deleted "the bodies of the possessed as if they were their bodies."
4. MS: "Shall."
5. Conjecture for word at broken margin.
6. This reference and the following cross-reference are later additions. JE wrote, "In calling this the 'second death,' there seems to be respect had to the repetition there is made of

78. ISAIAH 53:1–2. "To whom hath the arm of the Lord been revealed? For HE shall grow up[7] before him as a tender plant," etc. That HE that the Prophet speaks of, as it's most natural to understand, [is] "the arm of the Lord," spoken of in the first verse, and in the two foregoing chapters, as in the 5th [and] 9th verses of the 51st chapter, and in the 10th verse of the 52nd [chapter], who is the same as his "servant" spoken of in[8] the three last verses of that chapter. Hereby two things are evident. 1. That he that is the subject of this chapter is no mere man, as the Jews suppose. This is evident by the 9th and 10th[9] verses of the 51st chapter. And 2. By the same verses it is evident that it was Christ, the second person of the Trinity, that went before Israel when they came[1] out of Egypt. God calls his Son his "arm," as Jacob calls his son "his right hand" (Gen. 35:18).

79. ISAIAH 42:3. "A bruised reed shall he not break, and the smoking flax shall he not quench; he shall bring forth judgment unto truth." The thing most directly intended in this verse seems to be the perseverance of the Christian church and of particular saints. The church shall not[2] be extinct, though it shall be greatly oppressed and persecuted, and shall be as a bruised reed, but it shall not be wholly broken. When once the fire is kindled, it shall never be quenched; but though it do but just smoke at first, afterwards it shall flame out. It shall be as a grain of mustard seed that by degrees shall become a great tree [Luke 13:19], or as the little leaven that was hidden in three measures of meal till the whole was leavened [Luke 13:21], or as the stone out of the mountain [Dan. 2:45]. Though the church sometimes be so suppressed that it's hardly visible—we can hardly see whether there be any fire or no, but only the smoke—yet it shall never be wholly destroyed. The same may be applied to particular saints, for he that has begun a good work in them shall carry it on to the day of Christ [Phil. 1:6].

80. JUDGES 16:25. When the Philistines had prevailed over Sampson and were making sport with [him], he overthrew them. The devils

---

the threatening to our first parents, 'dying thou shalt die,' as signifying two deaths" ("Blank Bible"). See also *Works*, 5, 145.

7. Broken at margin.
8. Conjecture for word at broken margin.
9. Broken at margin.
1. Ibid.
2. Ibid.

thought to have had fine sport with[3] God's people when he had[4] got him their captive; but their captivity to him was the occasion of one of them, who represented the rest of his brethren, even Christ, giving of them a most dreadful overthrow. And when they had Christ their captive, and thought to have triumphed and made themselves merry over him, for he was for a time in a sort their captive, being the captive of his ministers, and being more especially delivered to his power to tempt and afflict, as the Philistines did Sampson (Luke 22:53, "This is your hour, and the power of darkness."), I say, while they thought to have had good sport with him, yea, when they had actually brought him forth, and were making themselves sport with him as his instruments did, and doubtless the devil joined with[5] them, he gave them a most dreadful overthrow at his death, as Sampson did. He destroyed Satan's kingdom, overthrew Dagon's temple.

81. DANIEL 9:7. "O Lord, righteousness belongeth unto thee, but unto us confusion of faces, as at this day." By "confusion of faces," he don't mean so much shame and repentance as punishment. 'Tis an acknowledgment that they were justly punished, and brought to such sorrow and ruin as they were then the subjects [of], that is often represented by being ashamed and confounded. Therefore he says, "as it is this day"; he did not mean that they then were[6] ashamed with a shame of repentance, but that they then were in a ruined condition.

82. GENESIS 4:1. "And Adam knew his wife; and she conceived and bare Cain, and said, I have gotten a man from the Lord." In Eve's expressing herself so, it is probable she had an eye to what God said, that her seed should break the serpent's head [Gen. 3:15]; for now, seeing she had a son, her faith and hope was strengthened that the promise should be fulfilled.

83. ROMANS 5:18. "Therefore as by the offense of one, [judgment came][7] upon all men to condemnation, even so by the righteousness of one [the free gift came][8] upon all men to justification of life." Seeing the words "judgment" and "the free gift" are not in the original, I don't

3. JE deleted "man."
4. Broken at margin.
5. Conjecture for word at broken margin.
6. MS: "~~were~~."
7. JE's square brackets.
8. Ibid.

see why it would not have been better construing to have translated it thus: "Therefore as by the offense of one, the offense came upon all men to condemnation, so by the righteousness of one, righteousness came upon all men to justification of life." And so the word that is understood would have been the same with that that is expressed, though the placing of the same words in[9] the 16th verse gives considerable color for this translation.

84. ROMANS 8:15. "For ye have not received the spirit of bondage again unto fear, but ye have received the Spirit of adoption, whereby we cry, Abba, Father." That is, ye have not the spirit of slaves and bondservants[1] that works by slavish fear, but the spirit of children so that you ben't afraid, but dare cry, "Abba, Father," dare as children approach God with a holy boldness. The spirits are different: one is the spirit of God; the other is not.

85. CANTICLES 6:13. "What will ye see in the Shulamite? As it were the company of two armies," or "the company of Mahanaim."[2] The two armies that are the company of Mahanaim are the church of God in earth and in heaven, the company of Jacob and the company of the angels (see Gen. 32:2), the church militant and the church triumphant; for both these armies make one spouse of Jesus Christ.

86. CANTICLES 1:5. "As the tents of Kedar, as the curtains of Solomon." Kedar was a place where shepherds used to seat their tents and feed their flock, a noted place for shepherds, as you may see. Is. 60:7, "All the flocks of Kedar shall be gathered unto thee." And Jer. 49:28–29, "Concerning Kedar . . . . Their tents and their flocks; they shall take to themselves their curtains." The people of Kedar, it seems, used to dwell in tents, in movable habitations, and lived by feeding of sheep. And therefore the church is very fitly represented by these. It's agreeable to many other representations in Scripture where God's people are called his sheep, his flock, and Christ and his ministers shepherds. And the church is also compared to a tabernacle or tents; it's fitly compared to movable tents, for here we are pilgrims and strangers, and have no abiding place. These are the shepherds' tents referred to in the 8th verse.

9. Conjecture for word at broken margin.
1. MS: "bound Servants."
2. מַחֲנַיִם, literally "two camps."

87. ISAIAH 25:11. "And he shall spread forth his hands in the midst of them, as he that swimmeth spreadeth forth his hands to swim." Which was the posture that Christ was crucified in.[3]

88. LEVITICUS 12:6. "She shall bring a young pigeon or a turtle dove"; which typifies repentance as well as love. Ezek. 7:16, "They shall be as doves in the valleys, each one mourning for his iniquity." This is a proper sacrifice for original sin that the child brought into the world with it by the parents' means, a sacrifice both for the parents' and children's sin.

89. II CORINTHIANS 3:17–18. "Where the Spirit of the Lord is, there is liberty," that is, freedom of looking. And, behold, our sight is not hindered, as the children of Israel were, but we have liberty to see. "But we all, with open face beholding as in a glass[4] the glory of the Lord," with open face, not covered with a veil, as Moses' face was, as in the 7th and[5] 13th verses. "Are changed into the same image," as Moses was by beholding God's brightness; his own face shone. "From glory to glory," that is, changed from the glory of God, from a sight of his glory, "to glory," to a glory in ourselves like it.

90. ECCLESIASTES 1:6. "The wind goeth toward the south, and turneth about unto the north; it whirleth about continually, and the wind returneth again according to his circuits." Whenever the wind blows from one quarter for a long time, there must needs be a circulation in the atmosphere. When the wind blows from the north, there must at the same time be another wind from the south in some other place, otherwise long and strong winds would leave some region empty of air, and would mightily heap it[6] up in others. This I take to be what is meant in this place.

91. ECCLESIASTES 2:16. "There is no remembrance of the wise man more than of the fool." Man's reason[7] naturally[8] expects a future reward, that all the good that good and wise men have of their labor should not be confined to this short life.

3. JE wrote "vid.," but no reference follows.
4. Broken at margin.
5. Conjecture for word at broken margin.
6. Ibid.
7. Ibid.
8. MS: "natural."

92. I SAMUEL 1–2. By Hannah's song after the birth of Samuel, I am ready to think that Peninnah and Hannah were designed for types of the church of the Jews and the church of the Gentiles. The expressions are much like those that are used in the prophets when speaking of the calling of the[9] Gentiles. The whole song, and especially the 10th verse, seems evidently to refer to gospel times, [particularly] those expressions, "The Lord shall judge the ends of the earth; and he shall give strength unto his king, and[1] exalt the horn of his anointed" [I Sam. 2:10]. By God's "king" and "anointed," she did not mean any king that then ruled over Israel, for there was none; nor was it known that there ever would be one. There was no such design then on foot.

93. I SAMUEL 17:25. David won the king's daughter by victory over Goliath; so Christ wins the church by victory over Satan.

94. I SAMUEL 22:2. "And everyone that was in distress, and everyone that was in debt, and everyone[2] that was bitter of soul, gathered themselves to him; and he became captain over them." Herein he was a type of Christ.

95a. PSALMS 8:2. "Out of the mouth of babes and sucklings hast thou ordained strength because of thine enemies, that thou mightest still the enemy and the avenger." It seems to me that mankind are principally intended here by "babes and sucklings." 'Tis of God's lovingkindness to men that the Psalmist is speaking, to the end of the psalm. By "the enemy and the avenger" is meant the devil. Men are as babes and sucklings in comparison of the angelic. By so advancing of the human nature, the devils are disappointed and triumphed over.

95b. EXODUS 2. Moses in the ark upon the waters is a type of the church.[3] The church of God is like a babe, in infirmity and weakness, in helplessness of itself and dependence upon a superior help, and in that the members of it are all in a spiritual sense become as little children. And 'tis like a babe upon the waters, floating through all manner of changes, dangers, and troubles, and yet upheld and preserved in Christ the ark. He was especially a type of the church of the

9. Broken at margin.
1. Conjecture for word at broken margin.
2. Broken at margin.
3. JE wrote "and" followed by another clause that has broken off at the bottom of the page. This second clause, ending with "the church of the Jews," appears to be deleted by JE.

Jews in their oppressed condition in Egypt. 'Twas a wonder they were
not swallowed up by their enemies, and drowned, and lost in their
afflictions and the multitude of their adversaries. Moses, in the water
and not drowned, is much such another type as the bush, all in a flame
and not burnt [Ex. 3:2]. He was also herein a type of every elect soul
who is naturally all overwhelmed in sin, in misery and danger, and is
redeemed and delivered, as Moses was taken out of the water.

96. II CORINTHIANS 3:17. "Where the Spirit of the Lord is, there is
liberty." It seems to refer to that place, 51st Psalm, 12th verse, where
the Spirit of God is called the "free spirit."

97. JONAH 1–2. As the ship and company were saved by Jonah's
being cast into the waters, and his intended and supposed death, so
was the church, that is[4] several times typified by a ship, saved by Christ,
being cast into and overwhelmed by sorrows and troubles, which are
represented by water and by his death. His being swallowed of a whale,
or leviathan, represents Christ being as it were swallowed by him who
hath the power of death, the devil, the spiritual leviathan; but however,
it[5] was but a means of Christ's being under better advantages to come
at his heart, and to give him the more mortal wound. The whale
thought to have made a sweet feast of Jonah; he swallowed him at a
mouthful. But he found him a dreadful medicine; he was sick of him at
the heart, and vomited him up again. (See Jer. 51:44.)[6] So the devil
thought Christ was his food, but he proved not his meat, but his poison. The devil has been dreadful sick of putting Christ to death since
he has seen what the effect of it is. As Jonah was three days and three
nights[7] buried in the sea, so was Christ in his grave three days and
three nights.

It is said when Jonah was cast into the sea, the sea ceased from her
raging [Jonah 1:15]. When once Christ was swallowed up in God's
wrath, his wrath ceased from raging towards the church. The words of
Jonah's song (ch. 2) make the thing more apparent. He calls the belly of
the fish, "the belly of hell" [v. 2], or as in the margin,[8] "the belly of the
grave." Vv. 2 and 4, "I cried by reason of mine affliction. Then said I, I
am cast out of thy sight." So Christ said, "My God, my God, why hast

4. Conjecture for word at broken margin.
5. Ibid.
6. This reference is a later interlineation.
7. JE deleted "in the whale's belly, so was Christ t."
8. I.e. the margin of the KJV.

thou forsaken me?" [Matt. 27:46]. V. 3, "The floods compassed me about; all thy waves and thy billows passed over me"; the words of the Psalmist (Ps. 42:7; also Lam. 3:54), to signify the great sorrows and distress that God brought upon him. V. 5, "The waters compassed me about, even to the soul"; the words of the Psalmist for great trouble and anguish (Ps. 69:1). V. 6, "Yet hast thou brought up my life from corruption," agreeable to what is said of Christ, "Thou wilt not leave my soul in hell, nor suffer thine Holy [One] to see corruption" [Ps. 16:10].

98. MATTHEW 27:60. "And laid it in his own new tomb." Christ was laid in a disciple's grave. He suffered that death which belonged to us, and he was laid in our grave. He entered into the state of death in our stead; he went down into that deep pit where we were to have gone. He had no sin of his own, so he had no death of his own; it 'twas our sin and our grave, and our[9] tomb hewed out in a rock. Our state of death and misery was such that it would have been impossible for us to escape; for our prison that we're going to was strong. [. . .][1]

99. ROMANS 6:8–9. "Now if we be dead with Christ," etc. These two verses, with the context, seem irrefragably to prove perseverance.

100. DANIEL 3:25. "And the form of the fourth is like the Son of God." Christ redeems from the furnace by coming into it himself; so he redeems from wrath by enduring it himself.

101. JOB 26:7. "He stretcheth out the north over the empty place, and hangeth the earth upon nothing." By stretching out "the north over the empty place," in the former part of the verse, seems to be meant the extending [of] the northern parts of the wide plain of the earth, as they took it to be, over an empty abyss of space, much the same as hanging the earth "upon nothing," in the latter part of the verse.

102. ZECHARIAH 14:6–7. "And it shall come to pass in that day, that the light shall not be clear and[2] dark. But it shall be one day which shall be known to the Lord, not day, nor night; but it shall come to pass, that

9. Conjecture for two words at broken margin.
1. The bottom of the MS is broken away and what remains is illegible. Sereno Dwight completes the sentence with "as a solid rock" (Dwight ed., 9, 465).
2. KJV reads "nor."

at evening time it shall be light." That is, there shall no more be the successions of light and darkness, day and night, but it shall be one continued day; and it shall be light in the time of the night or evening.

103. GENESIS 44:32–33. "For thy servant became surety for the lad unto my father. . . . Now therefore, I pray, let thy servant abide in the stead of the lad a bondman to my lord, and let the lad go up with his brethren." Judah is herein a type of his offspring, Jesus Christ.

104. JUDE 9. "He[3] disputed about the body of Moses." The thing referred [to] is that mentioned, Zech. 3:2.[4] The church of the Jews is called the body of Moses, as the Christian church is called the body of Christ. Moses was herein a type of Christ.

105. MATTHEW 27:14. "And he answered him to never a word." The reason why he did [not] speak as accusing his accusers and those that sought his life, of falsehood, malice, unreasonableness, cruelty, was his wonderful meekness. In the midst of all the affronts and injuries, afflictions and vexations, that he was surrounded with, he chose that there should not be the least appearance of a disquieted, ruffled temper. And he did not speak as vindicating himself, because he knew it would signify nothing, and that there might be no appearance as if he flinched and gave back, and was not willing to suffer, or endeavored to avoid that which was his errand into the world, or repented when it came to that he had undertaken, so great a task for his people.

106. MALACHI 2:15. "And did he not make one? Yet had he the residue of the spirit." He makes them one flesh; their bodies are each other's, but the rest (or residue), which is the spirit, God reserves for himself. A man is one body with his wife, but one spirit with Christ (I Cor. 6:16–17). (The phrase in this sense is not different from what is common, as Deut. 21:8, "Thy people of Israel," the city of London, city of Jerusalem. And besides, it don't appear by the original but that the words are in opposition, and not in regimen. It might have been translated, "the residue, the spirit.")[5] Or if we interpret it as in the margin,[6] "the excellency of the spirit," then the meaning is that though God made them, and therefore they ought to be most nearly united in

---

3. I.e. Michael the archangel.
4. JE links Michael with "the angel of the Lord" who disputes with Satan in Zechariah.
5. וּשְׁאָר רוּחַ לוֹ This parenthesis is a later addition.
6. I.e. the margin of the KJV.

affection, yet he reserved to himself the soul's best love, the best of the heart.

107. HEBREWS 11:1. "Faith is the evidence of things not seen"; that is, it is their being evident. This verse is as much as if he had said, "Faith is the being present of things that are to come, and the being clearly seen of things that are not seen." "The substance of things hoped for" might have been translated, "the subsistence,"[7] that is, "their now subsisting."

108. ISAIAH 52:7. "How beautiful upon the mountains are the feet of him that bringeth good tidings!" etc. Jerusalem was compassed round with mountains, and therefore he that brought tidings to Zion must come over the mountains, and as he was coming over, might therefore be seen in the city. The like expression is in Nahum 1:15.

109. REVELATION 3:4. "They shall walk with me in white, for they are worthy." That is, they are fit, as we often use the word.

110. GENESIS 2:21. Adam received his Eve as he awaked out of a deep sleep; so Christ receives his church as he rises from the dead. Dr. Goodwin speaks of this deep sleep of Adam as a type of Christ's death (1st volume of his *Works*, Pt. 3, p. 58).[8]

111. JOB 8:8. "For inquire, I pray thee, of the former age, and prepare thyself to the search of the fathers." The people of God that lived before there was any written revelation depended very much upon the teaching and tradition of their fathers. Those that lived near the flood were but a few removes from Adam; they might have Adam's own instructions, without having of it through many hands. And those that lived in Job's time, they had doubtless abundance of traditions from the antediluvians that might be instructed from Adam himself, [who] through their vast age had vast opportunity to get abundance of knowledge and experience. 'Tis very probable that abundance of the

7. ἡ ὑπόστασις.

8. This reference to *The Works of Thomas Goodwin* (London, 1681), Vol. I, Pt. III, p. 58, is a later addition and refers to Goodwin's sermon on Eph. 5:30–31 where he compares the creation of Eve from Adam's rib with the establishment of the church through Christ's death. Goodwin writes, "And what hath Jesus Christ lost by his death? Nothing; he hath got a *Church* by the means. . . . He endured pain upon the Cross, he endured to have his side pierced, and his Soul wounded to have his *Church* taken out, all is closed up again, and the Man *Christ Jesus* is in Heaven for ever, and his Church shall be for ever with him."

learning that was in the heathen world was the corrupted remains of what was delivered to mankind by them that came out of the ark. Job lived in early days after the flood, and here is abundance of philosophy in this book, which in all probability they had from tradition from their fathers, as well as those high flights of divine knowledge. Therefore we often find the fathers quoted in this book, as here in this place, and ch. 15, vv. 10 and 18–19; there is a plain referring to tradition from the beginning of the world, or from the second beginning after the flood. 'Tis evident by the 18th verse, they quoted the fathers then as we do the Scriptures now.⁹

112. EXODUS 24:18. "And Moses was in the mount forty days and forty nights." Moses' being so long in the mount with God, when he received his mind and will to reveal to Israel, represents Christ's being in heaven with the Father to receive his mind and will [to] reveal to his church, his being from all eternity in the bosom of the Father. And it may be particularly "forty days," because when Christ came down from heaven, signified by this mount, it was¹ four thousand years from the beginning of time, and from the creation and fall of man, and since the covenant of grace first took place and Christ actually became the Mediator between God and man, which, putting ten for a thousand, and every age or century for a day, answers to forty days. That mount, when Moses was in it with God, typified heaven, as the Apostle teaches (Heb. 8:5).²

113. DEUTERONOMY 32:50. "And die in the mount whither thou goest up, and be gathered unto thy people, as Aaron thy brother died in Mount Hor, and was gathered unto his people." God ordered that Aaron and Moses should go up to the top of mountains to die, to signify that the death of godly men is but an entrance into a heavenly state.³ 'Tis evident that heaven is sometimes typified by the top of the mount, by Heb. 8:5 compared with 9:23. So Christ was transfigured in the mount [Luke 9:28–36], and appeared in glory with both Old Tes-

9. Following this, JE began a new unnumbered entry in large letters: "Faith may be defined: a hearty sense of the truth and reality, sufficiency and excellency, of Christ as a Savior, and an answerable inclination and application of the soul to him." He crossed out this definition, which appears appropriate for his notebook on "Faith," with a large "X."
    1. JE deleted "about."
    2. This sentence is a later addition.
    3. The remainder of this entry is a later addition.

tament and New Testament saints and the glory of God in a cloud, to be a type of the heavenly state. See note on Ex. 24:18, No. 112.

115.[4] JOB 33:14–16. "For God speaketh once, yea twice. . . . In a dream, in a vision of the night." Also Job 4:12–17. It was a common thing, before there was any written revelation, for God to reveal himself to holy men in visions and dreams. See Num. 12:6; Gen. 15:1, 12–21; Gen. 46:2.[5] "Man perceiveth it not." V. 16, "Then he openeth the ears of men, and sealeth their instruction." BY AFFLICTION: that is, when men won't hearken to God's instructions and warnings in his word (that in those days was wont to be given after this manner, and delivered from father to son), then he chastens them in his providence to make them hear.

116. JOSHUA 20:6. "And he shall dwell in that city, until he stand before the congregation." The seventy elders are here called the congregation or church, which are words of the same signification. So the elders of the church, they are called the church in the New Testament.

117. JOSHUA 10:13. "The sun stood still, and the moon stayed." "The moon stayed"; not that the moon's staying helped them, but 'twas because the earth was stopped, and so all the heavenly bodies were stopped, that is, kept their position with respect to the horizon,[6] except an inconsiderable alteration through the periodical revolution.

118. NUMBERS 12:6–8. "If there be a prophet among you, I the Lord will make known myself to him in a vision, and will speak to him in a dream. My servant Moses is not so; with him will I speak apparently, not in dark speeches." 'Tis evident by this that it was God's common manner to speak to the prophets in words that they did not understand themselves. Therefore in reading the prophets, we need not seek an interpretation which it would be natural for the prophets themselves to understand by it, for the Holy Ghost spake in what words he pleased to, and meant what he pleased, without revealing his meaning to the prophets. The prophecy of Scripture is not of a private interpretation, but they "spake as they were moved by the Holy Ghost" [II Pet. 1:21].

4. When renumbering the entries, JE failed to include a No. 114.
5. These references are later interlineations.
6. JE deleted "very nearly."

119. GENESIS 28:18, 22. "And he took the stone that he had put for his pillows, and set it up for a pillar, and poured oil upon the top of it. . . . And this stone, which I have set up for a pillar, shall be God's house." This anointed pillar is a type of the Messiah, or anointed, who is often called a stone or a rock, and is the house of God wherein the Godhead dwells and tabernacles. He was signified by the tabernacle and temple, as Christ tells us when he says, "Destroy this temple," etc. [John 2:19]. And he, we are told, is the temple of the New Jerusalem [Rev. 21:22]. This is the stone that was Jacob's pillow, to signify the dependence the saints have upon Christ, and that 'tis in him they find rest and repose, as Christ invites those that are weary to come to him, and they shall have rest [Matt. 11:28]. The Psalmist says he will lay him down, and sleep, and awake, the Lord sustaining of him [Ps. 3:5]. And as the stones of the temple rested on the foundation, the saints, the living stones, do upon Christ, building and resting upon that rock. This stone signified the same with the altar that he[7] built there when he returned (Gen. 35:7), and the pillar that he set up and poured a drink offering and oil upon it (v. 14).

120. I CORINTHIANS 16:21–24. "The salutation of me, Paul," etc. "If any man love not the [Lord] Jesus Christ, let him be Anathema Maranatha. The grace of our Lord Jesus Christ be with you." The Apostle concludes his epistle with a curse and a blessing. He curses all that don't love the Lord Jesus, but yet he blesses all that are of the church of Corinth; by which 'tis evident that those that are regularly of the communion of the Christian church are visible lovers of the Lord Jesus Christ, that is, they are so looked upon in public charity, and treated as if they were really such.

121. DEUTERONOMY 21:23. "For he that is hanged is accursed by God." The instances we have of those that were hanged are agreeable to this. Thus the heads of the people that joined themselves to Baal-peor were hung up before the sun, that the fierce anger of God might cease (Num. 25:3–4). So the seven sons of Saul were hanged to remove God's wrath[8] from the land [II Sam. 21:1–10]. Ahithophel, who was cursed by David in God's name, hanged himself [II Sam. 17:23]. Absalom was hanged in an oak for his rebellion against his father [II Sam.

7. I.e. Jacob.
8. JE deleted "against the nation."

18:9–10]; for it is written, "Cursed is everyone that setteth light by father or by mother" [Deut. 27:16]. The kings of the cursed cities of Canaan were hanged [Josh. 10:26]. Haman was hanged, for he was a type of Antichrist [Esther 7:10]. Judas hanged himself, having been declared accursed by Christ before [Matt. 27:5].

122. JOHN 1:16. "And of his fullness have all we received, and grace for grace." That is, he has a fullness of grace, and we receive grace from him, answerable to his grace—"grace for grace," that is, grace answerable to grace. The word ἀντί, translated "for," signifies so. Christ has many gifts from the Father, and we have gift for gift.

123. LUKE 22:31. "Satan hath desired to have thee, that he may sift thee as wheat." The wheat goes through, and nothing but the chaff [is] left. This Satan aimed at concerning Peter.[9]

124. MATTHEW 1:16. "And Jacob begat Joseph, the husband of Mary, of whom is born Jesus, who is called Christ." This genealogy proves that the kingdom of Israel was Christ's by right of inheritance. Christ, though [he] was not the real son of Joseph, yet he was the legal son, with greater reason than when a man took a wife, and died, and left no seed. His brother's seed by her were to be looked upon [as] his, and had a right of inheritance.

125. RUTH 1. The story of Ruth's forsaking her own people for the God and people of Israel. 1. It typifies the calling of the Gentile church. Naomi is a type of the Jewish church, that is the mother of the Gentile church; not the Jewish nation that was rejected, but the true church of God in Israel, to whom Ruth says in the 16th verse, "Whither thou goest, I will go, and where thou lodgest, I will lodge. Thy people shall be my people, and thy God my God." Naomi sets before her daughters the cost of going with her, and the advantages of staying in their own land. So did Christ set before men the cost of being his disciples, and so do his ministers in the church. And 2. It typifies the universal church, and the conversion of every believer. We are all born in sin, as Ruth was born in Moab, and was born a Moabitess. A state of sin is as it were our father's house, and sinners are our own people. When we are converted, we forsake our own people and father's house, as the church in the 45th Psalm.

9. JE marked this entry with a large "X."

126. GENESIS 37:28. "And they lift up Joseph out of the pit." Joseph was here a type of Christ; he was designed for death by his own brethren, as Christ was. He was cast into a pit, whereby his death and burial was signified. He was lift out again, and his resurrection was an occasion of their salvation from famine and death.

127. GENESIS 38:28–30. Zarah put his hand out first, but Pharez, from whom came Christ, broke forth before him. This imports much the same thing as Isaac's[1] casting out Ishmael [Gen. 21:10–14], or as Jacob's taking hold of Esau's heel when they were born, and afterwards getting the birthright of him [Gen. 25:26, 31–34], and David's getting the kingdom from Saul [II Sam. 5].

128. GENESIS 41:14. "And they brought Joseph out of the dungeon." By Joseph's being cast into the dungeon is signified the death of Christ; by his being delivered, his resurrection; and the ensuing great advancement of Joseph, to be next to the king, signifies the exaltation of Christ at the right hand of the Father. Joseph rose from the dungeon, and was thus exalted, to give salvation to the land of Egypt and to his brethren, as Christ to save his people.

129. GENESIS 15:17. "Behold a smoking furnace, and a burning lamp passed between those pieces." The "smoking furnace," I am ready to think, signified the same as fire from heaven to consume the sacrifices, that is, the wrath of God in the midst of[2] Jesus Christ. The furnace "passed between the pieces," that is, as it were through the midst of them. The "burning lamp" which followed was a fire of another nature; it was a clear bright light, whereas the other, though exceeding hot like a furnace, was all smoky. This signified the Holy Ghost, which is often compared to fire. It signified that light, glory, and blessedness, which followed Christ enduring wrath, and was purchased by it, both for himself and for his people. And doubtless this also has respect to the church in Egypt of Abraham's seed, and signified those things that God was now telling of Abraham in his deep sleep. The "smoking furnace" signified their suffering grievous persecution and affliction in Egypt, that is called the "iron furnace" [Jer. 11:4]; and the shining lamp signified their glorious deliverance in the

---

1. Abraham, not Isaac, cast out Ishmael and Hagar.
2. MS: "~~in the Soul of~~ (in the midst of)."

fourth generation, and being brought into the land of Canaan. Is. 62:1, "And the salvation thereof shall be as a lamp that burneth." The birds coming down, that Abraham frayed away [Gen. 15:11], were to typify the devils, and their endeavors to devour Jesus Christ and the church. This thing may also signify the terrors and consolations that attend the work of conversion, our deliverance out of spiritual Egypt.[3] See No. 353.

130. EXODUS 15:25–26. "And the Lord showed him a tree, which when he had cast into the waters, the waters were made sweet," etc. "I am the Lord that healeth thee." This tree is the tree of life, and signified Jesus Christ; it signifies God himself. And the waters are God's people, as it is here explained in the 26th verse. The tree's being cut down represented the death of Christ, and being cast into the waters, his uniting himself to his people by coming down from heaven, by taking our nature, and by his Spirit.

131. LUKE 8:28, 30–31. The legion of devils[4] beseech Christ that he would not torment them, and "that he would [not] command them to go out into the deep." This shows that the devils had a very trembling expectation of having their punishment completed, and being dreadfully destroyed some time or other by the Messiah.

132. NEHEMIAH 9:14. "And madest known unto them the holy sabbath." It seems that before they had lost the sabbath; that is, they had lost the beginning and ending of the week, reckoning from the creation, till God made it known to them upon occasion of their being brought out of Egypt on the same day of the week. And there was thereby a new occasion given for their sanctifying that day.

133. MALACHI 4:2. "But unto you that fear my name shall the Sun of Righteousness arise with healing in his wings," that is, in his beams. 'Tis very much like other metaphors that were common amongst those eastern people. The sun rises to fly through the heavens, and the bright beams by which it is encompassed are the wings.

134. JOHN 16:8–11. "And when the Comforter is come, he will convince the world of sin, of righteousness, and of judgment." "He

3. This sentence and the following cross-reference are later additions.
4. MS: "devil."

shall convince the world of sin," as men must be convinced of their guilt in order to their receiving of Christ. That is, the reason that sin and guilt lies upon them is because they believe not on Christ, as in the 9th verse, "Of sin, because they believe not on me"; and their rejecting Christ above all things enhances their guilt.[5] "Of righteousness," that is, he will convince them of the sufficiency of Christ's righteousness, of the way of removing guilt by him. Christ finished his work as priest, or what he did for the removing of guilt, by his ascending into heaven, his entering into the holiest of all with his own blood to make intercession for us, and thereby gave evidence to the world that what he had done was enough. Verse 10, "Of righteousness, because I go to my Father, and ye see me no more." "Of judgment," that is, he shall convince the world of Christ's sufficiency and excellency as a king and head of influence and government, as the sanctifier and deliverer of his people from their enemies, and he that brings them eternal life. He delivers from the influence and power of the devil, redeems his captives, and in spite of him, sanctifies and glorifies. In thus redeeming men by power, Satan is judged (John 12:31–32).[6] Verse 11, "Of judgment, because the prince of this world is judged." The conviction here spoken of righteousness and judgment is to the same purpose with that, Is. 45:24, "Surely, shall one say, in the Lord Jehovah have I righteousness and strength." And in the next verse, "In the Lord shall all the seed of Israel be justified, and shall glory."

135. HEBREWS 12:21. "And so terrible was the sight, that Moses said, I exceedingly fear and quake." The place referred to seems to me to be that, Deut. 9:18–19.[7] "I fell down, for I was afraid of the anger and hot displeasure," etc. God at that time manifested his displeasure by the extraordinary burning of the mount (v. 15).

136. LUKE 14:13–15.[8] "But when thou makest a feast, call the poor, the maimed," etc. "And thou shalt be blessed, for they cannot recompense thee. Thou shalt be recompensed at the resurrection of the just.

5. This last clause and the following deletion, "See note on John 3:18," are a later addition. In a note on John 3:18–19, JE asserted that the "foundation" of the condemnation of those who do not believe is not the coming of Christ, but rather that which is "antecedent to his coming, viz. the law of God and their evil deeds and wicked hearts, whereby they hate that which is good" ("Blank Bible").

6. This sentence is a later interlineation.

7. The remainder of this entry is a later addition.

8. JE mistakenly located this passage in the gospel of Matthew instead of Luke. Sereno Dwight repeated the error (Dwight ed., *9*, 438).

And when one of them [that] sat at meat heard these things, he said unto him, Blessed is he that shall eat bread in the kingdom of God." Christ had told his host that he should not invite his rich friends and neighbors, expecting to be invited to a feast again by them, but should invite those that could not invite him again; and he tells him he shall be blessed, and should "be recompensed at the resurrection of the just," intimating that he should be rewarded by feasting then. Now the Jews thought that the resurrection would be when the Messiah came. By the "kingdom of God" they understood the kingdom of the Messiah; and that is the reason that when Christ told the Pharisee he should be blessed, for he should feast at the resurrection, that he makes this reply, consenting to it: They shall be blessed indeed "that shall eat bread in the kingdom of God."

137. II TIMOTHY 2:18. "Who concerning the truth have erred, saying that the resurrection is past already; and overthrow the faith of some." The Jews, before Christ, had a general belief that there would be a resurrection, and they thought it would be when the Messiah came. When he came, [they] thought the saints that were of old, Abraham, and Isaac, and Jacob, and David, etc., would rise again. And there was a number of them did rise when Christ rose, as Matthew informs us [Matt. 27:52–53]; and therefore there were some, that the Apostle here speaks [of], that thought we were to expect no other resurrection.

138a. GENESIS 21:8. "And Abraham made a great feast the same day that Isaac was weaned." This typifies the weaning of the church from its milk of carnal ordinances, and ceremonies, and shadows, and beggarly elements, upon the coming of Christ. The church under the Old Testament is represented as being in its minority, and the Apostle tells [that] babes must be fed with milk, and not strong meat. Christ therefore dealt with his disciples just as a tender mother does with her child, when she would wean it from the breast. There was a great feast provided, which represents the glorious gospel feast provided for souls when the legal dispensation ceased by the coming of Christ. It may also signify the weaning of souls from the enjoyments of the world at conversion, and the spiritual feast which they find instead of them.

138b. JUDGES 13:2. Sampson's mother, before she bare him, was barren. So was Sarah before she bare Isaac [Gen. 16:1], and Hannah before she bare Samuel [I Sam. 1:2]. These women's being [barren], these persons evidently typified the church's bringing forth Jesus Christ spiritually; and their barrenness signifies the barrenness of our souls, their being utterly destitute of any good fruit, till Christ is born in our hearts.

139. JUDGES 13:20. "For it came to pass, when the flame went up toward heaven from off the altar, that the angel of the Lord ascended in the flame of the altar." Christ, by thus going into the flame in which the kid was sacrificed, and ascending in it, signified that he was the great sacrifice that was to be offered up to God, and was to ascend as a sweet savor to God from off the altar in the flame of his holy wrath. That was the substance represented by these shadows, the sacrifices of kids and lambs, etc.

140. II PETER 1:10. "Wherefore the rather, brethren, give diligence to make your calling and election sure, for he that doth these things shall never fall." The Apostle had exhorted to give diligence to add to our faith virtue, etc. [v. 5], and tells us that if we do these things, we shall not be barren and "unfruitful in the knowledge [of Christ]," etc. [v. 8]. Now he offers another argument; he tells us that to neglect these things is the way to doubtfulness about our condition. "He that lacketh these things has forgotten that he was purged from his old sins" [v. 9]. Therefore the meaning of this verse is, "the rather give diligence in these things, that you may make your calling and election sure"; as is evident by the following clause, "for he that doth these things shall never fall." "Wherefore the rather," is as much as to say, "the rather for this," viz. "that you may make your [calling and election sure]."

141. ROMANS 4:3–4. "What saith the scripture? Abraham believed God, and it was counted to him for righteousness." The Apostle lays stress upon the word "counted," or "imputed." If he had had a righteousness of his own, upon the account of which the reward was of proper debt, it would not have been expressed in this manner, as he evidently argues in the following verses.[9] Abraham's believing God was not righteousness, but was only counted for it. It was of God's grace looked upon as supplying the room of righteousness.

---

9. JE deleted "Its being counted for righteousness," a phrase written at the same time as the following two sentences which are a later addition.

142. HEBREWS 5:9. "And being made perfect, he became the author of eternal salvation to all them that obey him." By "obeying" here is not meant believing, but obedience to the law and commands of God, as it is understood in the foregoing verse.

143. EXODUS 28:30. "And thou shalt put in the breastplate of judgment the Urim," etc. Called "the breastplate of judgment," because in matters of judgment that were too hard for the judge, they[1] were to come to the priest, who was to inquire of God by Urim and Thummim in the breastplate for a determination, according to Deut. 17:8–9.

144. DEUTERONOMY 12:20. "When the Lord thy God shall enlarge thy border, . . . and thou shalt say, I will eat flesh, because thy soul longeth to eat flesh; thou mayst eat flesh, whatsoever thy soul lusteth after." That is, thou mayst eat it at home, without carrying of it to be sacrificed, as appears by the context.

145. BOOK OF JOB. It seems to have been the custom of those that were counted their wise men in those times, when they discoursed upon any head of wisdom, or delivered their minds in moral, spiritual, or philosophical matters, to take up this parable, and go on in long speeches in a lofty, and poetical, and dark, and mysterious style, that was their manner of teaching and discoursing. Now Job was one of those wise men that exercised himself very much in contemplation and instruction, and it seems that those that answered him were other wise men that were his companions, that he used to converse with upon matters of wisdom before. And therefore we have so many of these kind of discourses with Job upon this notable occasion. These discourses were called parables. So Balaam took up his parable [Num. 23:7]; so we read that "Job continued his parable" (Job 27:1 and 29:1). We read of these kind of speeches oftentimes in the Old Testament under the name of parables, as Prov. 26:7, 9. "As the legs of the lame are not equal, so is a parable in the mouth of fools; and as a thorn goeth into the hand of a drunkard, so is a parable in the mouth of fools." It was only them that were, or would be, accounted wise men, that used to utter their minds in such parables. Ps. 49:3–4, "My mouth shall speak of wisdom, and the meditation of my heart shall be of understanding. I will incline mine ear to a parable; I will open my dark saying upon the harp." And Ps. 78:2, "I will open my mouth in a parable; I will utter dark sayings of old."

1. I.e. the children of Israel. Word broken at margin.

146. PHILIPPIANS 2:11. "And every tongue should confess." In the place of the Old Testament that is here quoted, it is "every tongue shall swear" [Is. 45:23], which confirms that [by] swearing by God's name, so often spoken of in the Old Testament as a great duty of God's people, is meant publicly professing the true God, and entering into covenant with him.

147. SOLOMON'S SONG.[2] The[3] name by which Solomon calls this song confirms me in it that it is more than an ordinary love song, and that it was designed for a divine song, and of divine authority; for we read, I Kgs. 4:32, that Solomon's "songs were a thousand and five." This he calls the "song of songs" [Cant. 1:1], that is, the most excellent of all his songs, which it seems very probable to me to be upon that account, because it was a song of the most excellent subject, treating of the love, union, and communion between Christ and his spouse, of which marriage and conjugal love was but a shadow. These are the most excellent lovers, and their love the most excellent love.

Mr. Henry, in the introduction to his *Exposition* of this book, says, It appears that this book was "taken in a spiritual sense by the Jewish church, for whose use it was first composed, as appears by the Chaldee Paraphrase, and the most ancient Jewish expositors." In the same place he says, "In our belief, both of the divine extraction and spiritual exposition of this book, we are confirmed by the ancient, constant, and concurring testimony, both of the church of the Jews, to whom were committed the oracles of God, and who never made any doubt of the authority of this book, and of the Christian church, which happily succeeds them in that trust and honor."[4]

148. MARK 10:29–30. "There is no man hath left house, or brethren," etc., "but he shall receive an hundredfold now in this time, houses, and brethren, and sisters, and mothers, and children, with persecutions, and in the world to come eternal life." We may be helped to understand this place by Matthew's account of the same thing (Matt. 19:27–29), where we have an account that Christ told his disciples,

2. I.e. Canticles.
3. JE deleted "title of this song, viz."
4. This paragraph is a later addition. Matthew Henry, *An Exposition of All the Books of the Old and New Testament; Wherein the Chapters are summ'd up in Contents; the Sacred Text inserted at large, in Paragraphs, or Verses; and each Paragraph, or Verse, reduc'd to its proper Heads; the Sense given, and largely illustrated, with Practical Remarks and Observations* (6 vols. 3rd ed., London, 1725), *3*, 613.

upon Peter's asking this question at the same time, that they should "sit upon twelve thrones, judging the twelve tribes of Israel," i.e. they should be the means of the conversion of the world. The world should be given into their hands, should be brought to embrace their doctrine, and their word should be the standard of their faith and rule of their worship and practice. And thus they had "houses, and brethren, and sisters, and mothers, and children" an hundredfold. They had the houses of all the Christians to receive them. And at their service they had brethren and sisters, for all Christians were such in Christ. They had mothers, for so were the churches of Christ. We may observe in the foregoing verse, their forsaking fathers is mentioned; but fathers are not put in here as being restored an hundredfold, but only mothers. They had many mothers, but only one father, even their heavenly Father. They were to have children, for so were those they converted, and lands, for most regions of the earth were to be given to 'em.[5] The meek shall then "inherit the earth" [Matt. 5:5]. This is especially fulfilled in the glorious times of the church, after the fall of Antichrist.

149. JOB 36:30. "Behold, he spreadeth his light upon it, and covereth the bottom of the sea." In the original, "the roots of the sea,"[6] by which he means the extreme parts of the sea, where the clouds and the sea meet in the horizon, and those parts of the sea that are below the horizon, which they conceived to be deeper down; which is agreeable to the metaphor used in the foregoing, wherein the clouds that overspread the skies are represented by the curtains of a tabernacle [v. 29]. "He spreadeth his light upon it," that is, upon his tabernacle, upon those curtains, the cloud, which is like a bright covering on the inside of it.

150. I PETER 4:6. "For this cause was the gospel preached also to them that are dead, that they might be judged according to men in the flesh, and live according to God in the spirit." That is, that they might be judged according to what they did when they were alive here amongst men in the flesh, as other mortal men do. "Live according to God in the spirit," that is, that their spirits might live, might continue to exist before God, and as God doth, separate from fleshly bodies, and according as God pleases, to fix their state.

5. The remainder of this entry is a later addition.
6. שָׁרְשֵׁי הַיָּם.

151. I CORINTHIANS 11:22.[7] "What? Have ye not houses to eat and to drink in? Or despise ye the church of God, and SHAME THEM THAT HAVE NOT?"[8] That is, by sending them away empty. This supper was not to nourish the bodies of men and satisfy their hunger, but yet it seems as though they did make use of it also as a feast of charity, for the refreshment of the poor that had nothing to eat at home.

152. I CORINTHIANS 9:16. "For though I preach the gospel, I have nothing to glory of." That is, in case I had a dependence upon preaching the gospel for a livelihood, then might it be said that "necessity is laid upon me; yea, woe is unto me, if I preach not the gospel." That this is what the Apostle means, I think is evident by the context.

153. I CORINTHIANS 7:36. "But if any man think that he behaveth himself uncomely towards his virgin, if she pass the flower of her age." That is, if he should keep her till she pass the flower of her age, or in keeping her till she be past, and be past having children, because it was formerly reckoned[9] a great disgrace for women to be childless.

154. I KINGS 17:6. "And the ravens brought him bread and flesh in the morning," etc., which[1] typified the same thing as Sampson getting honey out of the lion [Judg. 14:8–9]. "Out of the eater came forth meat" [Judg. 14:14]. It was also more evidently miraculous that such a ravenous bird should bring him meat, and not eat it himself.

155. I CORINTHIANS 1:24. "But into[2] them which are called, both Jews and Greeks, Christ the power of God, and wisdom [of God]." The "power of God" answers to a sign or miracle, which the Jews sought after; and the "wisdom of God," to the wisdom which the Greeks sought after, mentioned in the last verse but one preceding [v. 22].

156. I CORINTHIANS 2:15–16. "For he that is spiritual judgeth all things, but he himself is judged of no man." He that has the Spirit of God to teach him truth, he is not in those things subject to the judgment or correction of any of the wise men of this world. The instruction, and judgment, and correction of a human master, of what he

7. JE marked this entry with a vertical line near the left margin.
8. JE deleted "or disappoint them."
9. Broken at margin.
1. JE deleted "signified."
2. KJV: "unto."

understands or believes by the Spirit of God, is what he needs not. In this case it don't take place; it will not alter him. "For," says the Apostle, "who hath known the mind of the Lord, that he may instruct him? For we have the mind of Christ." A man that has the mind of Christ is taught by his Spirit. If he should be subject to judgment and correction of men, that would argue that the mind of the Lord itself was subject to human correction.

157. I Corinthians 4:6. "And these things, brethren, I have in a figure transferred to myself and to Apollos for your sakes, that ye might learn not to think of men above that which is written, that no one of you be puffed up for one against another." It seems it was not Paul and Apollos particularly that the Corinthians were divided about; but what the Apostle means when he says, some say they are "of Paul," and others "of Apollos" [I Cor. 3:4], is that some were for one teacher, others for another. They overvalued their teachers, and built their faith upon them. He mentions his own name and Apollos', personating any human teachers whatsoever. He transferred it in a figure to himself and Apollos, that they might not be apt to suspect that he reproved them for being for this and that man, out of respect to himself; he would not have them set too much by men, though it were himself.

158. I Corinthians 15:28. "And when all things shall be subdued unto him, then shall the Son also himself be subject unto him that put all things under him, that God may be all in all." Christ as Mediator has now the kingdom and government of the world so committed [to] him, that he is to all intents and purposes in the room of his Father. He is to be respected as God himself is, as supreme, and absolute, and sovereign Ruler. God has left the government in his hands wholly, now since his exaltation, that he may himself have the accomplishment and finishing of those great things for which he died. He is made "head over all things to the church" [Eph. 1:22] till the consummation, as he is now king of the church and the world. In his present state of exaltation, he is not properly a subordinate ruler, because God hath entirely left the government with him, to his wisdom, and to his power. But after Christ has obtained all the ends of his labors and death, there will be no further occasion for the government's being, after that manner, in his hands. He will have obtained by his government[3] all the ends he

3. MS: "Governments."

desired; and so then God the Father will resume the government, and Christ and his church will spend eternity in mutual enjoyment, and in the joint enjoyment of God. Not but that Christ will still be the king and head of his church; he will be as much their head of influence and source of good and happiness as ever. But with respect[4] to government, God will be respected as Supreme Orderer, and Christ[5] with his church united to him and dependent on him, shall together be received[6] of the benefit of his government. See notes on v. 24.[7]

159. EXODUS 2:5. Pharaoh's daughter became the mother of Moses, which typified the calling of the Gentile church, that is naturally the daughter of Satan, the spiritual Pharaoh, which becomes the church of Christ, and so his mother; and also is to represent that all the saints, of which the whole church consists, are naturally the children of the devil, that by conversion become the spiritual mothers of Christ, as Christ says,[8] that "whosoever shall do the will of his Father which is in heaven, the same is his mother," etc. [Matt. 12:50]. The whole church, which is often represented as the mother of Christ, is in her constituent parts naturally an Egyptian, and the daughter of Pharaoh. She found Moses when she came down to wash herself in the river. The river here represents the Holy Ghost, and the washing is the washing of regeneration, by which souls are brought to Christ, which is signified by baptism, by which their admission into the Christian church is declared and sealed. Pharaoh's daughter is more than once made use of in Scripture to typify the church, especially the Gentile. So was Pharaoh's daughter that became Solomon's wife [I Kgs. 7:8], for the church is both the wife and mother of Christ. Add to this No. 384.[9]

160. EXODUS 2:16–17. "Now the priest of Midian had seven daughters; and they came and drew water, and filled the troughs to water their father's flock. And the shepherds came and drove them away, but Moses stood up and helped them, and watered their flock." Moses

4. Broken at margin.
5. JE deleted "as subordinate unto him together."
6. Broken at margin.
7. This reference is a later addition. JE's entry on I Cor. 15:24 in the "Blank Bible" refers to sources he was reading as well as to several entries in the "Miscellanies," including nos. 86, 609, and 736. For no. 86, entitled "KINGDOM OF CHRIST," see *Works, 13*, 250–51. Nos. 609 and 736, both entitled "CONSUMMATION of all things," discuss the manner in which Christ will continue to reign after that time to all eternity.
8. JE deleted "he that hears my word."
9. This cross-reference and the two preceding sentences are a later addition.

represents Christ; the seven daughters the church, or at least the daughter that he afterward married. The flock is the people or flock of the church; the water is the water of life. At the time when Christ [came], he found the people of God under the care of shepherds that caused them to err, that denied them, and drove them away from the water of life, instead of leading them to it; they would not suffer them that were entering into the kingdom of heaven to go in. But he helped the church, and watered the flock. He gave them the water which springs up to everlasting life [John 4:14], and married the church, as Moses did Zipporah [Ex. 2:21], and became the shepherd of the flock, as Moses did of the flock of Jethro, his father-in-law [Ex. 3:1].

161. GENESIS 24:15. Rebecca, and Rachel, and Zipporah, Moses' wife—these types of the church—all found their husbands, who were types of Christ, when coming out to fountains to draw water; which typifies this, that Christ is found by believers in a way of the use of the means of grace. The woman of Samaria found Christ coming to draw water [John 4:7].

162. II CORINTHIANS 8:10. "Who have begun before, not only to do, but also to be forward a year ago." It may seem strange that the Apostle says, "not only to do, but also to be willing." Doing is more than merely being willing. But 'tis as if he had said, "Ye have not only begun to do before now, but you have been ready to do for a long time, even a year ago." To be forward so long ago was something that might well be mentioned, in addition to their having now begun to do.

163. PSALMS 45:7. "Thou lovest righteousness, and hatest wickedness; therefore God, thy God, hath anointed thee," etc. The manifestation of Christ's loving righteousness and hating wickedness here spoken of, that was thus rewarded, was his humiliation and death, whereby he exceedingly manifested his regard to God's holiness and law, that when he had a mind that sinners should be saved, he was freely willing to suffer so much rather than it should be done with any injury unto that holiness and law.

164. II CORINTHIANS 11:4–5. It ought to have been translated, "ye have well borne,"[1] or "ye might well have borne with me." In the beginning of the chapter he desires them to bear with him, because he was jealous[2] over them, having betrothed them to Christ, that he[3]

1. καλῶς ἀνέχεσθε.
2. Broken at margin.
3. MS: "they."

might present them "a chaste virgin to Christ" [vv. 1–2]. He was jealous lest to other Christs they should yield themselves, to other lovers, and be defiled, and tells them in this verse that, seeing they were solicited to forsake Christ and to accept of other lovers, seeing that "he that cometh preacheth another Jesus," etc., he might well be jealous; and they might well bear with him in his boasting to set himself off, or rather to set off Christ, appearing, speaking, and working in him, to their affections, that so they might not like his rivals better.

Verse 5. "For I suppose I was not a whit behind the very chief," etc.; and so accordingly, now he begins to boast.

165. II CORINTHIANS 12:3. "Whether in the body, or out of the body, I cannot tell." When the Apostle said, "absent from the body, and present with the Lord" [II Cor. 5:8], he doubtless meant by "absent from the body," the same that he here means by "out of the body," which is a proper separation of the soul from the body.

166. GENESIS 8:21. "And the Lord smelt a sweet savor; and the Lord said in his heart, I will not," etc. It was not for the acceptableness of that sacrifice that made God promise that he would no more curse the ground, but the acceptableness of the sacrifice of Christ represented by it.

167. JOSHUA 10:13. "And the sun stood still, and the moon stayed." God thereby showed that all things were for his church; all was theirs. The whole earth, and the sun, moon, and stars, were made for them. See "Miscellanies," no. 702.[4]

168. PSALMS 91:11–12. "He will give his angels charge concerning thee, and they shall bear thee up in their hands, lest at any time thou dash thy foot against a stone."[5] As a father gives the elder children charge concerning the younger, to lead them, and bear them up, and keep them from falling.

4. This reference is a later addition. In no. 702, entitled "WORK OF CREATION. PROVIDENCE. REDEMPTION," JE asserts that "God's providence . . . is an operation and work of his superior to the work of creation." He also states in pt. 4 of the entry that "the works of creation" are "subordinate to the work of redemption." This was confirmed, he notes, when "the laws and course of nature" were set aside to "give place to the designs of redemption," including "God's causing the sun and moon to stand still in Joshua's time," demonstrating "that the whole frame of the universe was by him put in subjection to Christ's redeemed church."

5. JE conflated this passage with the New Testament versions of this text in Matt. 4:6 and Luke 4:10–11.

169. EPHESIANS 3:10. "That now unto the principalities and powers might be known by the church the manifold wisdom of God." That is, by the things done in the church, by what they see concerning the church.

170. II KINGS 6:6. "And he cut down a stick, and cast [it] in thither; and the iron did swim." The iron that sank in the water [v. 5] represents the soul of man that is like iron, exceeding heavy with sin and guilt, and prone to sink down into destruction, and be overwhelmed with misery, which is often compared to deep waters. The stick of wood that was cast in represents Christ, that was of a contrary nature, light, tended not to sink, but to ascend in the water and swim; as Christ, being of a divine and perfectly holy nature, though he might be plunged into affliction, and misery, and death, yet he naturally tended to ascend out of it. It was impossible he should be holden of it. Christ was plunged into our woe, and misery, and the death that we had deserved for ourselves, to bring us out of it. The stick, when that rose, brought up the iron with it; so Christ, when he rose, he brings up believers with him. They are risen with Christ, that they may walk in newness of life [Rom. 6:4]. "Christ is the first fruits; afterwards those that are Christ's" [I Cor. 15:23]. He rose again for our justification, and hath thereby begotten us again to a living hope [I Pet. 1:3].

171. PSALMS 40:6–8. "Sacrifice and offering thou didst not desire; mine ears hast thou opened, or bored. Burnt offering and sin offering thou hast not required. Then said I, Lo, I come. In the volume of the book it is written of me, I delight to do thy will, O my God: and thy law is within my heart." God often declared that willing obedience was better than sacrifice. The Psalmist is here declaring his giving of it the preference in his practice, according to God's mind. He did not rest in sacrifices, or look upon his duty as consisting mainly in them, but was willingly obedient. He delighted to do God's will; he loved his service. God had bored his ear, alluding to the law (Ex. 21:5–6) by which it was appointed that if the servant loved his master's service, and freely chose it, his master should bore his ear with an awl. "Burnt offering and sin offering hast thou not required. Then said I, Lo, I come," as a willing [servant] says to his master when he is called. "In the volume of the book it is written of me"; that is, it is written in the public records, that I voluntarily chose my master's service, and that my ears were bored, alluding still to that law and custom. If the servant loved his

master and chose his service, he was to be brought unto the judges, and was to declare his choice, and his ear was to be bored before them. And because the end of bringing of him to them was that they might take notice of it, and be witnesses of it, that the servant might afterwards be obliged by his act, we may conclude that there was a record written of it. It was not only trusted to their memories, for then if the judges should forget it or should die, the servant might go free; or if it was not the custom at first to record it, yet very probably it was in David's time. It seems they used to convey lands at first without writings (Ruth 4:7), but not afterwards. Jer. 32:10, "I subscribed the evidence," or as it is in the Hebrew, "I wrote in the book."[6] But the Psalmist also speaks here prophetically, and[7] as representing Christ. Christ freely and willingly became God's servant by becoming incarnate; therefore instead of the words, "mine ear hast thou bored," has these, "a body hast thou prepared me" [Heb. 10:5]. And as the servant that had his ear bored learned[8] obedience by what he suffered, it was a testimony of his real desire to serve him,[9] that he was willing to suffer this in order to it. So did Christ learn obedience by the things that he suffered by the sacrifice of his body; so that when it is said, "Sacrifice and offering thou dost not desire; mine ear hast thou bored," it is as much as if he had said, "These sacrifices of beasts, etc., are insignificant in themselves, but my crucifixion is the true sacrifice that God delights in."

172. EXODUS 15:27. "And they came to Elim, where were twelve wells of water, and threescore and ten palm trees; and they encamped there by the waters." These "twelve wells of water, and threescore and ten palm trees" are a representation of the church. The twelve wells of water answer to the twelve tribes, twelve patriarchs, twelve heads of the tribes, and twelve apostles. They signify the church itself, and then they answer to the twelve tribes. The church is compared to a fountain or spring of water (Cant. 4:12). The hearts of believers are like wells of living water, the water being the grace of the Spirit. Or they signify the ministry of the church, and so they answer to the twelve patriarchs and twelve apostles. The twelve patriarchs were the fathers and fountains of Israel, according to the flesh; the twelve apostles and gospel ministers are the fathers of Israel spiritually. Through the twelve apostles, Christ delivered his pure doctrine to the world, as through so many

6. וָאֶכְתֹּב בַּסֵּפֶר.
7. JE deleted "in the person of Christ."
8. Broken at margin.
9. Conjecture for word at broken margin.

fountains of pure water; and through gospel ministers in general, Christ communicates the living water of his Spirit to the church, as through so many springs, or pipes, or conveyancers (Zech. 4:12). Or the twelve fountains signify Christ himself; he is represented by twelve fountains, as the Holy Ghost is represented by "seven lamps" (Rev. 4:5), and he is called "twelve wells," according to the number of the instruments by which he communicates himself. However, in which sense soever we take it, the water represents the Holy Spirit. Christ communicates himself to his church only by his Spirit; he dwells in their hearts by his Spirit. The ministers of the gospel are instruments of the conveyance of the Spirit; the hearts of particular believers are fountains of living water, that is, of the Spirit.

The seventy palm trees signify the church, which is compared to a palm tree (Cant. 7:7–8). Deborah, the type of the church, dwelt under the palm tree [Judg. 4:5]. Believers are compared to palm trees. I Kgs. 6:29, "And he carved all the walls of the house round about with carved figures of cherubims, and palm trees," which represented saints and angels. The number seventy answers to the seventy elders, which were representatives of the whole congregation of Israel, and are called the congregation (Num. 31:12; Josh. 20:6), or church, which is a word of the same signification.

'Tis probable the palm trees grew so about these twelve fountains, that their roots were watered and received nourishment from them.

173. JOSHUA 6:26; I KINGS 16:34. "And Joshua adjured them at that time, saying, Cursed be the man before the Lord, that riseth up and buildeth this city Jericho: he shall lay the foundation thereof in his firstborn, and in his youngest son shall he set up the gates of it." Jericho herein was a remarkable type of the church of the elect. Jericho was a devoted[1] cursed city. It was devoted to perfect and to eternal destruction: to perfect destruction, in that every man, woman, and child, ox, sheep, and ass, were destroyed by God's command, and it was forbidden ever to be built again. So the elect are naturally under the curse of the law, which devotes those that have broke it to perfect and eternal destruction. However, this city was one very capable of being redeemed from that curse, but that was only by the curse being transferred upon him that built it. So the church of the elect could have the curse removed no other way, but by its being laid upon Christ that undertook to restore it. So Hiel the Bethelite represented Christ, who

1. I.e. doomed.

is from the true Bethel, or "house of God," even heaven. He was to lay the foundation of it in his firstborn, and in his youngest son to set up the gates of it. So his eldest son represented Christ, who is the firstborn of every creature, and is our elder brother. The foundation of the redeemed and restored church is laid in the blood of the first and only begotten Son of God. The gates of it were to be set up in his youngest son; so after the church is redeemed by Christ, the gates of it are to be set up in the blood of the martyrs. 'Tis in that way the church is to be erected, and finished, and brought to its determined glory and prosperity in the world, even through the sufferings and persecutions of believers. Jericho, though once an accursed city of the Canaanites, yet after it was thus redeemed from the curse, became a school of prophets (II Kgs. 2, 4:38, 6:1–2).[2]

174. JEREMIAH 7:33. "And the carcasses of this people shall be meat for the fowls of heaven, and for the beasts of the earth; and none shall fray them away." As this Tophet here spoken of represents hell, so those fowls and wild beasts, that feed upon the carcasses of those men, represent the devils who shall feed upon the souls of the wicked. The devils, we know, are compared to fowls of the air in the parable of the sower and the seed, as Christ himself explains it [Matt. 13:3–23]. Those fowls of the air that devoured those carcasses were ravens, and eagles, and other unclean and ravenous birds, that do fitly represent the impure spirits of the air; and those ravenous beasts do well represent him who is "as a roaring lion, going about seeking whom he may devour" [I Pet. 5:8].

175. ISAIAH 13:20–22. "It shall never be inhabited. . . . But wild beasts of the desert shall lie there, and their houses shall be full of doleful creatures, and owls shall dwell there, and satyrs shall dance there. And the wild beasts of the islands shall cry in their desolate houses, and dragons in their pleasant palaces." See Is. 34:11–15. Babylon represents the whole church of the wicked; by her being to be destroyed, never to be built or inhabited again, is represented the eternal destruction of the congregation of the wicked. By those "doleful creatures" here mentioned, their possessing of Babylon, are represented devils, which the church of the wicked shall be left to the possession of forever. Babylon, after its destruction, full of these creatures, represents the church of the wicked in its state of punishment. There-

2. This sentence is a later addition.

fore the apostle John, when speaking of the destruction of mystical Babylon, and alluding to this that is said of old Babylon, says expressly, she "is become the habitation of devils, the hold of every foul spirit, and a cage of every unclean and hateful bird" (Rev. 18:2).

176. JEREMIAH 10:16. "Israel is the rod of his inheritance." Deut. 32:9, called "the cord of inheritance,"[3] which in our translation is rendered, "the lot of his inheritance"; that is, he is the inheritance as it were measured by a cord, or by a rod. Sometimes they were wont to lay out and measure land by a cord, sometimes by a rod or pole.

177. JEREMIAH 12:3. THE PROPHETS PRAY FOR EVIL TO THEIR ENE-MIES. When we find passages of this kind in the Psalms or the Prophets, we are to look upon them as prophetical curses. They curse them in the name of the Lord, as Elisha did the children that mocked him [II Kgs. 2:24], as Noah cursed Canaan [Gen. 9:25]. We have instances of this kind, even in the apostles and the disciples of the Lamb of God, as Paul curses Alexander the coppersmith (II Tim. 4:14), and Peter says to Simon Magus, "Thy money perish with thee" [Acts 8:20]; or else they wish them ill, not as personal but as public enemies to the church. Sometimes what they say is in the name of the church (Jer. 51:34–35). See "Miscellanies," no. 600.[4]

178. JEREMIAH 13:12. "Therefore shalt thou speak unto them this word, Thus saith the Lord God of Israel, Every bottle shall be filled with wine. And they shall say unto thee, Do we not certainly know that every bottle shall be filled with wine?" *Quasi dicat,*[5] bottles were made, prepared to be filled with wine; they are fitted for it. You tell us no news in saying so. But so are wicked men vessels fitted to be filled with the wine of God's wrath, as bottles are fitted to be filled with wine; they are vessels of wrath fitted to destruction.

3. חֶבֶל נַחֲלָתוֹ.

4. This reference and the preceding sentence are a later addition. In no. 600, entitled "CHRISTIAN RELIGION. LOVE OF ENEMIES. PRAYING AGAINST THEM," JE writes, "It was not a thing allowed of under the Old Testament, nor approved by the Old Testament saints, to hate personal enemies, to wish ill to them, to wish for revenge, or to pray for their hurt, except it was as prophets, and as speaking in the name of the Lord; so that there is no inconsistence between the religion of the Old Testament and New in this respect." He then cites examples from both testaments, and closes the entry by suggesting that "some of the most terrible imprecations that we find in all the Old Testament are in the New spoken of as prophetical."

5. I.e. "as if he should say."

179. JEREMIAH 31:33. "But this shall be the covenant that I will make with the house of Israel; after those days, saith the Lord, I will put my law in their inward parts, and write it in their hearts, and will be their God, and they shall be my people." I think the difference here pointed forth between these two covenants lies plainly here, that in the old covenant God promised to be their God upon condition of hearty obedience; obedience was stipulated as a condition, but not promised. But in the new covenant, this hearty obedience is promised if a man be but of the house of Israel, as by faith he becomes so. God promises expressly in this new dispensation that he shall perform a hearty obedience, and so have God for his God. That old covenant they broke, as it is said in the foregoing [verse]. The house of Israel, those [that] were called so under the old testament,[6] could break that; but the new covenant is such as cannot be broke by the spiritual house of Israel, because obedience is one thing that God engages and promises. And therefore this is called an everlasting covenant upon this account, as is plain by Jer. 32:40.'Tis true the true saints in the Old Testament could not fall away any more than they can now, but they were not the Old Testament Israel; and though God had engaged in his covenant with Christ that they should not fall away, yet he had not expressly revealed that to them. God had not in those days so plainly revealed the primary and fundamental condition of the covenant of grace, viz. faith, but insisted more upon the secondary condition, universal and persevering obedience, the genuine and certain fruit of faith. See "Miscellanies," no. 439.[7]

188. JUDE 14–15.[8] "Enoch also, the seventh from Adam, prophesied of these, saying, Behold, the Lord cometh with ten thousands of his saints, to execute judgment," etc. 'Tis probable[9] that this prophecy of Enoch had the more direct respect to the destruction of the ungodly of the old world by the flood. Those sinners Jude speaks of were like them, and their destruction should be like theirs (II Pet. 2:5). It looks very probable that God would reveal his design to Enoch, of overthrowing the world, seeing that he was so intimately conversant with

6. I.e. old covenant.

7. In no. 439, "COVENANTS. TESTAMENTS," JE examines differences between the covenant made with the children of Israel and that established "with his people in these gospel times." No. 439, "probably written about the same time" as No. 179, includes explicit reference to this "explication of Jer. 31:33" (*Works, 13*, 487–89).

8. When renumbering the entries, JE dropped the numbers from 180–187.

9. MS: "Prophecy."

him, and the world was so much corrupted in his days, which was probably one reason why God took him out of the world. He would not suffer one so dear to him to live in the midst of such a wicked abominable crew, to have his soul continually vexed by them (Enoch's son Methuselah lived till the very year that the flood came [Gen. 5:27].);[1] and if so, 'tis exceeding probable that God would reveal something to him of his intended destruction of them. This prophecy is applied to those heretics and their destruction, very much after the same manner as many prophecies of the Old Testament are applied in the New, to other things than what they most directly signified. Many of the prophecies of Scripture are applicable to many things, as Christ's prophecy of the destruction of Jerusalem [Luke 21] is applicable to the destruction of heathenism in the Roman Empire, and to the end of the world. The all-knowing Spirit has an eye to many things in what he saith. When the Apostle says, Enoch "prophesied of these," he may be understood to mean those that were of this sort, i.e. of this lascivious kind of persons.[2] See No. 200.

189. II Samuel 23:1–5. See sermon on v. 5.[3]

190. I Peter 1:3. See sermon.[4]

191. II Samuel 23:4–5. "As the tender grass springing out of the earth by clear shining after rain, . . . although he make it not to grow."[5]

1. This parenthesis is a later interlineation.
2. This sentence and the following cross-reference are a later addition.
3. The text for this sermon, preached in November or December 1729, is "Yet he hath made with me an everlasting covenant, ordered in all things and sure." These are presented as among David's "last words which he probably spoke but a little before his death, and he spoke them not of himself, but by the inspiration of the Spirit of God." JE suggests that the text "shows where his [i.e. David's] chief dependence was, and what his heart was most upon by his dying breath." The Doctrine asserts "That the covenant of grace is every way so ordered as is needful in order to its being made firm and sure." The sermon includes a series of arguments supporting the claim that the promise of "justification and eternal life to all that believe in Jesus Christ" will be fulfilled. In the Application JE states, "If you trust in Christ, the covenant is so ordered in all things and sure, that you need not be afraid to fetch a leap into eternity. You shall be held up; you shall be kept safe."
4. This sermon, which is not extant, has been dated April–May 1729 because "Miscellanies," no. 409, reads, "Resurrection of Christ. See sermon on I Pet. 1:3" (*Works, 13,* 470). The biblical passage is "Blessed be the God and Father of our Lord Jesus Christ, which according to his abundant mercy hath begotten us again unto a lively hope by the resurrection of Jesus Christ from the dead" (KJV). See No. 264 for JE's later exposition of this text and its context.
5. JE deleted "I believe."

It is probable that it is from this that David speaks of the Messiah, that Christ is[6] called the branch, or the sprout. He is compared in Isaiah to "a tender plant" [53:2].

192. I CORINTHIANS 10:16. See sermon on the verse.[7]

193. I CORINTHIANS 8–10. See sermon on I Cor. 10:16.[8]

194. II SAMUEL 22:26–27. See sermon on the words.[9]

195. EXODUS 4:20. MOSES' ROD. "And Moses took the rod of God in his hand." This rod typified the Word, both the personal Word and the word of revelation. The word of God is called the rod of God's strength (Ps. 110:2); 'tis called the rod of Christ's mouth (Is. 11:4). 'Tis expressly represented by "the rod of an almond tree" (Jer. 1:11); Moses' rod was the rod of an almond tree [Num. 17:8].[1] Jesus Christ is also called a rod. "There shall come forth a rod out of the stem of Jesse, and a branch shall grow out of his roots" [Is. 11:1]. He is frequently called a branch, or sprout, a tender plant, etc.[2]

If we consider this rod as representing the revealed word of God, then Moses or Aaron, who kept and used the rod, represent Christ. A

6. JE deleted "so often."

7. The Doctrine of this sacrament sermon, preached sometime between January and April 1730, states, "The thing designed in the sacrament of the Lord's Supper is the communion of Christians in the body and blood of Christ." JE explains the immediate context of I Cor. 10:16 as the apostle Paul's argument against eating of the sacrifices offered to heathen idols because "those that eat things that are known to be offered to idols do visibly join, or have communion in, the worship of devils, in the same manner as all that partake of the elements of bread and wine in the Lord's Supper have visible communion in the worship of Christ."

8. See the preceding note. JE's textual exposition features the Apostle's efforts (chs. 8–10) to "dissuade Corinthian Christians from eating things offered to idols." The heathen population in Corinth celebrated festivals honoring their gods with "times of feasting and mirth." Christians who were invited to those feasts "had a notable temptation laid before them." Some pleaded that their "Christian liberty" allowed them to take part, JE notes, but the apostle Paul rejected that argument because eating meat offered to idols constitutes "a visible worshiping of idols," dishonors the Christian name, and offends the consciences of weaker brethren.

9. In this sermon preached in July 1730, JE describes the "song of praise that David sang towards the latter end of his reign and life" at a point when he was no longer engaged in warfare with his enemies. In that song David reflected on "God's different dealings with him and with his enemies," which leads JE to state in the Doctrine "That God will deal with all men according to their own temper and practice."

1. Aaron's rod is identified with the almond tree.

2. See above, No. 191.

rod is the instrument of a shepherd, by which he governs, directs, defends, and orders his flock. And this rod was that that Moses kept sheep with, which he was found with when he was feeding his father-in-law's sheep, when God appeared to him in the bush [Ex. 3:2–6]. The same that a rod or staff is to a shepherd and his flock, the same is the Word of God to Christ and his spiritual flock. As Moses used it in leading Jethro's flock of sheep, so he used it in leading God's people Israel. As the Word of God is the instrument Christ uses to save his people, and to destroy their enemies, and work those wonders that are wrought in bringing them to salvation, and which belong to the application of redemption, so Moses used this rod in the temporal deliverance of his people. 'Tis the Word of God that is used to remove all obstacles, and overcome all opposition in the way of a sinner's conversion and progress in holiness, as Moses' rod was made use of to divide the Red Sea [Ex. 14:21].

If the rod be considered as representing Christ, then Moses or Aaron represent God. Moses cast his rod "on the ground, and it became a serpent"; and he took it up, and it became a rod again [Ex. 4:3–4], signifying how that Christ, when he was sent down by God to the earth, was made sin for us, became guilty for our sakes, was accursed, and appeared in the form of sinful flesh. He appeared in our stead, having our guilt imputed to him, who are a generation of vipers. Thus when the children of Israel were bitten with fiery serpents, Christ was represented by the brazen serpent [Num. 21:9]. The rod, being become a serpent, swallowed the magicians' rods or serpents [Ex. 7:12]; so Christ, by his being made sin for us, destroyed sin and Satan. When Moses took up his rod from the ground, it was no longer a serpent, but became a rod again; so when God took up Christ from his state of humiliation, he was acquitted, justified. He had no longer the guilt of sin imputed to him; he no longer appeared in the form of sinful flesh. Rulers and princes are compared to rods (Ezek. 19:11–12, 14), and branches (Ps. 80:15, 17); so Christ himself is often called a rod and branch.[3]

'Tis by the Word of God, or by Christ, that God works all his wonders in and for the church; and Moses wrought wonders by his rod. 'Tis by Christ that all obstacles and difficulties are removed in order to our salvation, as the Red Sea was divided by Moses' rod. 'Tis by Christ, and in his name only, that God's people prevail over their enemies, as the

---

3. This sentence is a later addition.

children of Israel prevailed while Moses held up his rod,[4] and when he let it down, Amalek prevailed. Moses held up the rod in that battle, as the banner or ensign of the armies of Israel, as is evident by, as appears by, Ex. 17:11;[5] so Christ is lifted up as an ensign (Is. 11:10).[6]

When this rod budded, and blossomed, and bare fruit, that [which] it brought forth was almonds, intimating this,[7] the speediness of the Word of God in producing its effects in the world. It seems the almond tree is a tree of a very sudden growth, and speedily brings its fruit to perfection. See Jer 1:11–12. So the Word of God is quick and powerful. This is one way wherein the powerfulness of it is shown, in the suddenness of its producing its[8] great effects. Is. 66:7–8, "Before she travailed, she brought forth; before her pain came, she was delivered of a man child. Who hath heard such a thing? Who hath seen such things? Shall the earth be made to bring forth in one day, or shall a nation be born at once? For as soon as Zion travailed, she brought forth her children."

As Moses and Aaron represent God, then the rod represents Christ; as Moses and Aaron represent Christ, the rod represents the Word. As they represent ministers, the rod represents two things, viz. the Word of God which they preach, and their faith; for this rod was Moses' staff, and this staff represents the same as Jacob's and Elisha's staves. See note on Num. 21:18.[9] See further, No. 442.[1]

196. GALATIANS 5:18.[2] "But if ye be led by the Spirit, ye are not under the law." Here [is] inquired 1. In what sense they are not under the law; and 2. Why it is said, "Ye are not under the law, if ye are led by the Spirit," or wherein is the connection between being led by the Spirit, and not being under the law?

4. KJV: "hand."

5. The passage in Exodus refers to Moses' holding up his "hand."

6. This sentence is a later addition.

7. MS: "this that the ~~almond Tree word of God~~."

8. JE deleted "surprising effects."

9. In the "Blank Bible" JE suggests that the staves used by the princes to dig the well in the desert at Beer typify the faith of believers. "Faith is to believers as their staff in their journey through the wilderness of this world. They walk by faith; 'tis faith that supports them as a staff doth a man that goes in rough way and through a wearisome wilderness." For that reason Jacob is represented as leaning on his staff (Heb. 11:21), and Elisha as using a staff to perform a miracle (II Kgs. 4:29).

1. This paragraph is a later addition.

2. JE deleted "This I say then, Walk in the Spirit." He reworked this entry extensively. It contains changes too numerous to note individually, including deletions, interlineations, and later additions.

Inquiry 1. In what sense Christians are not under the law?

Answer. In one word, they are not under the law as servants, for this is what the Apostle had[3] insisted on, in the 4th chapter and latter end of the 3rd, that Christians are not under a schoolmaster, but a father (Gal. 3:25–26, and 4:2); that they ben't servants, but children (Gal. 4:1–7, especially the 7th verse); that they ben't the children of the bondwoman but of the free, and so are not in a state of bondage, but in a state of liberty, as Gal. 4:9–31. And 'tis the argument the Apostle is still upon in this chapter, as vv. 1 ff.

And 'tis evident that by being "under the law" in this verse [Gal. 5:18], the Apostle means being under the law as a servant, or as a being under the law is opposite to a state of liberty by the immediate context, [and] by the manner in which this and the intermediate verses are introduced by v. 13, "Brethren, ye have been called unto liberty; only use not liberty for an occasion to the flesh," etc., which may be seen. So the Apostle opposes being under the law to liberty, in the beginning of this chapter, and so in the latter part of the foregoing chapter, by the 21st verse compared with that allegory that follows, and by the Apostle's explanation of that allegory (v. 25). He tells us that Agar, the bondwoman, represents Mt. Sinai, the mount where the law was given. So a being under the law is called being under a schoolmaster, and under tutors and governors, which is opposed to being children (Gal. 3:24–26, and 4:2 with context). Yea, a being under the law is expressly opposed to being children (Gal. 4:5), and is called a being servants (v. 7).

By these things it is most evident that the Apostle here, when he says Christians are not under the law, means only that they were not under the law as servants or bondmen, or in any sense wherein a being under the law is opposite to liberty, or the state of children.

1st. They were not under the ceremonial law at all, which was a yoke of bondage, a law adapted to a servile state of the church, or the state of the church's minority, wherein it differs nothing from a servant; as Gal. 4:1–3, where 'tis evident the ceremonial law is especially intended by the expression of "the elements of the world" there used. 'Tis evident that by being under the law, the Apostle has a special respect to the ceremonial law, by Gal. 4:9–11 and 5:2–3, 6, 11, and by the occasion and drift of the whole epistle.

---

3. JE deleted "much."

2nd. They are not under the moral law as servants. Not only the ceremonial, but the moral law is intended in the words, as is evident by the context, as particularly the 14th verse and 23rd verse. Children in a family, where things are in their regular order, i.e. where the father has the proper qualifications and spirit of a father, and the children of children, ben't so properly under law as the servants. The commands of a father in such a family to his children, especially if the children be not in their minority, ben't called law in the same sense as the edicts of an absolute monarch to his subjects. Laws ben't made for children, and for intimate and dear friends, but for servants. A being under law, in the more ordinary use of the expression among the apostles, was inconsistent with liberty; a being under law and enjoying liberty were opposites, and therefore the phrase of "a law of liberty" [Jas. 2:12] is used by the apostle James as paradoxical. To be under law is to be under the declaration of the will of another, not only as an instruction or doctrine for our direction in acting, but to be under it as a rule of judgment, or a being under the justifying or condemning power of it. A being under the law in this sense is the Apostle's meaning, as is evident by the 4th verse of this chapter, and by chapter 3 *per totum.* See Rom. 8:1. For what is said in that 3rd chapter, introduces what follows in these two succeeding chapters. They can't be said to be under the law where the breaches of the law are not imputed to 'em. Sin is not imputed where there is no law, and vice versa (in a sense). There is no law, or persons are not under the law, where sin is not imputed.

The doctrine of the holy will of God, as revealed and directed to those that are in Christ, is improperly called "giving law." Where we find it so called, the word is used out of its strictly proper sense. The giving law to another is the exacting conformity to the declared will of the lawgiver. There may be a command without a law; a declaration of another's will without an exaction is not a giving law. A being under law is being under such an exaction, and they that receive a declaration of another's will, but at the same time han't it exacted of 'em, they have it not as a law, but only as an instruction or doctrine. God may be said to exact obedience of men to the commands of the law, when he signifies or makes known to them, that they are by [his] power held bound either to obedience or the penalty of the law. A declaration of a superior's will, without it being signified or supposed that it will be exacted by power, may be called a doctrine, a rule, a precept, or command, but not a law, unless improperly, as God's declaration of his will to his saints is called "the law of liberty." The expression shows that the word is not designed to be used in its strictly proper sense.

Objection. But is not sincere obedience exacted of believers, though perfect obedience be not? The Scripture often gives us to understand that no man can be saved, and that everyone shall perish, without sincere obedience.

Ans. 1. If sincere obedience be exacted of them, yet 'tis not the law by which it is exacted of them.[4] The thing that the law exacts is perfect, and not sincere, obedience. 'Tis a contradiction to suppose that any law requires and exacts any other than perfect conformity to itself, or which is the same thing, perfectly as much, or full as much, as it requires or exacts. Sincere obedience, or sincerely aiming at obedience, is not required or exacted by the law, any other way than as we consider it as a part of perfect obedience, or a part of that conformity to the law; and so it is no more exacted by the law than perfect obedience is. If the whole is not exacted, a part is no more exacted than the whole; part of conformity to the law can't be exacted by the law any more than conformity, because 'tis not exacted at all, only because 'tis a part of conformity and included in it. And therefore if conformity ben't exacted of believers by the law, or which is the same thing, perfect obedience no more is a part of conformity, so that no obedience at all is exacted of believers of the law, they are not under the law in whole, nor in part; for conformity is by the law exacted of all that are under it. Christ has freed them from the whole law by fulfilling the law for them.

So that if any obedience at all be exacted of believers, it is not by the law, but it must be by some other constitution, or superadded law. But,

Ans. 2. It is not properly exacted by any other constitution made since the law. There is indeed nothing properly exacted of any man whatsoever by any other constitution than the law. Indeed faith, and so sincere obedience, which is virtually implied in it, are by a new constitution made the conditions of salvation. Salvation is promised to them, and they are declared to be the only conditions of salvation; so that without them, we still lie under condemnation and must perish. Yet it

---

4. Here JE crossed out the following text with a large "X." "~~Tis obedience and Tis Conformity to the Law and not Sincerely aiming at Conformity~~ that is the thing that is ~~aimed at by~~ Exacted by the Law. Tis a Contradiction to Suppose that the thing that any Law Requires ~~is any thing~~ & Exacts is any thing Else than Conformity to it Self Now Conformity & Sincerely aiming at Conformity ~~are diverse things~~ may well be Considered as different things, as the thing aimed at and the aim are different one is the act & the other the object.

"But if we consider Sincere obed ~~as what~~ or Sincerely aiming at ~~Gon~~ Conformity to Gods Commands as."

won't hence follow that any new constitution or law does exact faith and sincere obedience, or require them upon pain of perishing or suffering any punishment at all of any man whatsoever, because 'tis not by virtue of the new constitution, which was only an offer or promise, that he perishes or suffers in unbelief, but by virtue of the[5] law only that he was under before. If a criminal is to be put to death for his breach of the law, and his prince offers him a pardon if he will accept of it at his hands, acknowledging his grace in it, if he refuses the king's offer, he is not pardoned but suffers; the law is executed upon him. But the prince can't be properly said by a new law or edict to exact it of him, that he should thankfully accept of pardon; for his execution is by virtue of a law made before that he had broke, and not by any new law, or that new act of his prince, his offering him pardon. 'Tis not by virtue of any threatening contained in that new act, but the threatening of the law that he had before broke, that he suffers. Yea, though besides his suffering for that breach of law, the pardon of which he refused, he may also suffer for his refusal. He may receive an additional punishment for his affronting the king in his contemptuous rejecting his gracious offer. Yet it won't follow that acceptance of pardon was properly exacted of him as by law, for that additional suffering for his affront may also be by virtue of the law that he was under before, and the threatening of that, and not any threatening implied in the king's offer that may be contained in the law, that whoever by his behavior affronts or casts contempt upon the king, shall be punished according to degree of the affront. And he may be punished for his rejection of the king's offer, by virtue of this, and not by virtue of any threatening contained in that new act of the king in offering pardon. Accepting the offer, indeed, is exacted of him, but 'tis exacted by the law, and not by the offer.

So faith,[6] and repentance, and sincere obedience are indeed exacted of sinners upon pain of eternal damnation, but not by the gospel. Eternal life is offered upon these terms by the gospel, and eternal damnation is threatened for the want of them by the law.

Unbelief in the present state of things is a great immorality, and as such forbidden by the law; and faith is strictly commanded, and as a duty of the law is exacted of all that are under the law. See No. 206.[7]

---

5. JE deleted "old constitution."

6. JE deleted "in Jesus."

7. This cross-reference is a later addition. Here JE crossed out the following text with a large "X": "To Exact obedience of any one is ~~by Power to hold one Bound by~~ to m Signify or

Inq. 2. Why it is said, "If ye are led by the Spirit, ye are not under the law," or what is the connection between being led by the Spirit, and not being under the law?

Ans. The connection consists in two things. 1. As this evidences their not being under the law. 2. It renders them not the proper subjects of law.[8]

1. Their being led by the Spirit is an evidence of their being in Christ, who has fulfilled the law, and delivered them from it. The Spirit is given in Scripture as the proper evidence of being in Christ (I Cor. 2:12, and 5:5; Eph. 1:13–14, and 4:30; Rom. 8:9; I John 3:24, 4:13). It is the proper evidence of their being children, for 'tis the "Spirit of the Son" (Gal. 4:6). "As many as are led by the Spirit of God are the sons of God," because 'tis the "Spirit of adoption" (Rom. 8:14–15). But children ben't under the law as servants.

2. A being led by the Spirit is a thing that causes that alteration with respect to them, that renders 'em unapt to be the subjects of law.

(1) By their having the Spirit given them, they are advanced to that state that don't agree with a state of subjection to the law. II Cor. 3:17, "Where the Spirit of the Lord is, there is liberty." See notes on that verse.[9] For hereby they are regenerated, are born of God, and do become the sons of God; they are hereby assimilated to the Son of God in nature and state. Being sons, it's suitable that they should be dealt with after another manner; to hold 'em under the law is to treat 'em as servants, as in the 6th and 7th verses of the preceding chapter. "And because ye are sons, God hath sent forth the Spirit of his Son into your hearts, crying, Abba, Father. Wherefore thou art no more a servant, but a son."

(2) The Spirit of Christ in Christians, or Spirit of adoption, actuating and leading, is a principle that supercedes the law and sets them above law, upon two accounts.

1. By their having this principle, so far as it prevails, they are above the need of the exaction of the law, and therefore are such as the law

---

make Known to him that he ⟨is⟩ ~~will be~~ by Power held bound ~~Either~~ to ~~Conform to his~~ obedience ⟨upon pain of⟩ ~~or to~~ a Suffering that is more opposite ⟨to him⟩ than obedience in any Case can be."

8. This paragraph is a later interlineation.

9. This reference and the preceding sentence are a later interlineation. JE has multiple notes on II Cor. 3:17. See above, Nos. 89 and 96. See also the "Blank Bible" where he writes, "So those that have the Spirit of the Lord, have a filial spirit and therefore a free spirit, a spirit of adoption, which is opposite to a spirit of bondage. If the Son gives us his own Spirit, we shall have a free spirit indeed."

was not given for, and are not aimed at in the law, and therefore are not under the law (I Tim. 1:9). They have a spirit of love and trust, that fulfills the thing that is aimed at by the law, as in the 14th and 16th verses of the context. They don't need the exaction of the law to drive 'em to their duty, for so far as they are led by the Spirit, they are of themselves naturally inclined to the same things that the law requires, and derive strength from God according to his promises to fulfill them. The fruits of the Spirit are such as they, by the Spirit without the law, are inclined and enabled to, such as love, joy, peace, etc., are such as the law is not against; as in the 22nd and 23rd verses of the context, "against such there is no law."

The filial spirit, or spirit of love and trust, fulfills the law; that is, the law obliges to no other things but what the Spirit inclines to, and is sufficient for. The law was not made for those that are already sufficiently disposed to all things contained in it. I Tim. 1:9, "The law is not made for a righteous man, but for the lawless and disobedient," etc. A filial spirit is law enough; 'tis a superior sort of law. The law of the Spirit of life is the best law, and makes free from any other law. The Spirit is better than the letter. They that have the Spirit of Christ in them have the law written in their hearts, according to God's promise by his prophets.

The Spirit of Christ is superior to the law, and sets a person above a subjection to the law, because 'tis a principle that is superior to a legal principle, or that principle which is the proper subject of the force and influence of the exaction of a law, viz. fear.[1]

So far as the Spirit of the Son, or the Spirit of adoption, prevails, so far he is above the need of that principle, and consequently above the need of being under the law.

2. The filial spirit, or Spirit of the Son, or Spirit of adoption, is a principle that, so far as it prevails, excludes and renders the saints incapable of fear, or a legal principle, or spirit of bondage. I John 4:18, "Perfect love casteth out fear." It casts it out as Sarah and Isaac cast out the bondwoman and her son, that we read of in the chapter preceding the text that we are upon [Gal. 4:30]. It is in Christians a principle of love, of childlike[2] confidence and hope, as in the 6th verse of the foregoing chapter, it cries, "Abba, Father." It evidences to 'em their

1. JE crossed out with a large "X" the balance of this paragraph which reads: "if a Person has not that Principle he is ~~he is not~~ a Proper Subject of Law because ~~he is ha~~ being destitute of that Principle the Law takes no hold of him."
2. JE deleted "trust."

being the children of God and begets that trust and assurance that renders 'em incapable of a legal principle. Rom. 8:15–16, "For ye have not received the spirit of bondage again unto fear, but ye have received the Spirit of adoption, whereby we cry, Abba, Father. The Spirit itself beareth witness with our spirits, that we are the children of God."

If a person has not that legal principle, or principle of fear, he has not that principle that the law, or that constitution which exacts obedience, was made to influence and work upon, and therefore is not a proper subject of law because, being destitute of that principle, the law takes no hold of him, for it finds no principle in him to take hold by.

A being led by the Spirit of the Son of God, as a Spirit of adoption, is inconsistent with a state of bondage, as sonship is inconsistent with servitude. II Cor. 3:17, "Where the Spirit of the Lord is, there is liberty."

197. MATTHEW 16:28. "Verily I say unto you, There be some standing here, which shall not taste of death, till they see the Son of man coming in his kingdom." The disciples saw sufficient to answer this promise. Some of them immediately after, as we have account in the beginning of the following chapter, saw Christ in his glory in his transfiguration, in the like glory with that in which he will come to judgment, as far as it could well be seen by them in their frail state, and by their feeble eyes. Again, they saw him coming in a glorious manner in the descent of the Holy Ghost on the day of Pentecost, for that was a coming of Christ wherein they saw him, agreeable to John 14:18–19. "I will not leave you comfortless; I will come unto you. Yet a little while, and the world seeth me no more; but ye see me." And this was a coming in his kingdom, for he came then to set him the[3] Christian church, to introduce the gospel dispensation, which seems to be called the "kingdom of heaven." And respect is doubtless had to this by John the Baptist, and by Christ after him, when they preached that "the kingdom of heaven is at hand" [Matt. 3:2, 4:17]. And again, some of them saw him coming in his kingdom at the destruction of Jerusalem; and an eye seems chiefly to be had to this event, for then was there a total end put to the Jewish church and the Jewish dispensation, which is compared to the end of the world. The world that then was,[4] the old state of things in the world with respect to religion, that had subsisted so long a time, was then utterly and finally done away, and the king-

3. JE deleted "gospel church."
4. JE deleted "then came to an end."

dom of heaven succeeded. The gospel dispensation or kingdom was then fully established; the state of things thenceforward in the church was boldly evangelical. Christ did then in a very awful manner, and with a signal manifestation of his hand, destroy the enemies of his kingdom, and remarkably delivered his people. He then came to judgment; he judged his adversaries, and delivered his chosen people. There was a remarkable rewarding [of] men according to their works then. 'Tis most apparent that Christ did call his appearing in that great event of the destruction of Jerusalem, and other events that attended it, his "coming" (Matt. 24:2–3). There Christ tells his disciples, when showing him the buildings of the temple, that not one stone shall be left on another; whereupon the disciples ask him, "when those things shall be, and what should be the sign of his coming, and of the end of the world?" And in his answer, he has respect still to the destruction of Jerusalem, as is evident by the 15th–20th verses. 'Tis expressly said to be the desolation of Jerusalem. Compare these texts in Matthew with Luke 21:20, "And when ye shall see Jerusalem compassed with armies, then know that the desolation thereof is nigh." And v. 23, "There shall be great distress in that land, and wrath upon that people." And in the 27th and 28th verses [of Matthew 24], he particularly gives his disciples a sign, whereby they might know the time and place of his coming, for Christ is there expressly speaking of his coming. Says he, "So shall the coming of the Son of man be. For wheresoever the carcass is, there will the eagles be gathered together," denoting it to be at Jerusalem, and at the time of its destruction by the Romans. See my notes on those verses.[5] There is no need of supposing that Christ here meant his coming in any other than a spiritual sense, for so Christ was wont to speak of things to come, when it is plain that he intended a spiritual fulfillment. So he speaks of the resurrection: "The hour is coming, and now is, when the dead shall hear the voice of the Son of God; and they that hear shall live" [John 5:25]. Here he speaks of the resurrection of bodies at the end of the world and the spiritual resurrection of souls together, including both in one and the same words, viz. "the dead shall hear the voice," etc. He speaks as if it were but one event that he had respect to; but yet when he says, it "is coming," he means one thing, even the resurrection of bodies, especially at the end of the

5. Commenting on Matt. 24:24–28, JE contrasts the public quality of Christ's second coming with the secret comings of impostors or false messiahs. In v. 28 he identifies the Romans as "the people of the prince that should come," the Jews having been forsaken ("Blank Bible").

world. When he says, it "now is," he means another thing, viz. the resurrection of souls by the preaching of the gospel; and the manner of speaking there is very parallel to that in this and the foregoing verse. In the foregoing verse Christ says, "For the Son of man shall come in the glory of his Father with his angels, and then shall he reward every man according to his works" [Matt. 16:27]. There he has a respect principally to his coming at the end of the world. But then in this verse, says he, "Verily I say unto you, there be some standing here, that shall not taste of death, till they see the Son of man coming in his kingdom." And now he has chiefly a respect to another event, viz. his appearing in the work that he will do at the destruction of Jerusalem. And therefore it can be no just objection against this explication, that Christ evidently meant the same coming in this as he did in the foregoing verse, for we ought not to dispute against plain fact. I can't see that, if we explain the words as I have done, the case is any more than exactly parallel to that in those other words, John 5:25. And 'tis plain and evident that 'tis a common thing in Scripture,[6] that things are said to be fulfilled that have been spoken of in the same context when they are only fulfilled in their type, and not in that which is ultimately intended. So Christ, speaking of his coming and the end of the world, says, "This generation shall not pass, till all these things shall be fulfilled" [Matt. 24:34]. So the apostle John, speaking of the predictions there had been of the coming of Antichrist, he speaks of those prophecies as being fulfilled in the false teachers there were then: "Even now," says he, "there are many antichrists" (I John 2:18).

But perhaps we are not sufficiently accurate, when we distinguish several events as so many distinct accomplishments of the prediction so often given of Christ's coming in his kingdom, to be understood in different senses; and so to look upon Christ's coming at the effusion of the Holy Ghost at Pentecost as one coming of Christ in his kingdom, and his remarkable appearing in the events that were at the destruction of Jerusalem as another coming of Christ in his kingdom, and his appearing in Constantine's time as another, and in the destruction of Antichrist as another, and at the end of the world as another. They seem rather to be spoken of in Scripture as several parts, or rather as several degrees, of one event, that great event spoken [of] in Dan. 7:13–14. "And I saw in the night visions, and, behold, one like the Son of man came with the clouds of heaven, and came to the Ancient of

6. JE deleted "when speaking to future events."

days, and they brought him near before him. And there was given to him dominion, and glory, and a kingdom, that all people, nations, and languages should serve him. His dominion is an everlasting dominion, which shall not pass away, and his kingdom that which shall not be destroyed." Which was what the Jews expected and called the kingdom of heaven, and which John the Baptist and Christ had reference to when they said, "The kingdom of heaven is at hand," and which Christ has respect to in this place, and also in the 24th [chapter] of Matthew. I say, this great event is gradually accomplished. It is accomplished by several steps and degrees; and the great events that were at the descent of the Holy Ghost at Pentecost, and at the destruction of Jerusalem, and in Constantine's time, and the destruction of Antichrist, and the end of the world, are all so many steps of the fulfillment of the same great event. When the Holy Ghost descended at Pentecost, it was fulfilled in a degree; then the Son of man came, and then was his kingdom set up in the world in a glorious manner. When Jerusalem was destroyed, it was fulfilled in another greater step; then did he remarkably exercise his kingly authority in judging his enemies, and putting an end to the old state of things in the church, and beginning a new world, establishing the Gentile church. When Constantine was destroyed, it was fulfilled in a yet higher degree, and still far more glorious [manner] at the destruction of Antichrist, but is fulfilled in its most complete and perfect degree at the end of the world.

So that Christ indeed has respect to the same great event here as he spake of in the foregoing verse, and promises that some there should see the accomplishment of that event before they tasted of death; i.e. they should see that, which indeed should be an accomplishment of it in the beginning of it, in a glorious degree, though not in its most glorious degree.

And hence also it can't be said that Christ meant the destruction of Jerusalem, when he speaks of his coming in his kingdom, or only that and what went before it, at the pouring out of the Holy Ghost at Pentecost; but it was this great event in general which was to be accomplished in several degrees, though when he said they should see it before they tasted of death, he did not mean that they should see [it] in all its degrees.

The forementioned prophecy of Daniel, without doubt, had a respect not only to Christ's coming at the end of the world, but also much of a respect to his coming, as he did, in those events that were before some of them tasted of death. See No. 279.[7] This prophecy of Daniel, Christ doubtless had in his eye when he spake this, and doubtless the disciples understood him as meaning that; for the event foretold in this was what they and the Jews were big with expectation of, and had their eye upon, and always understood one another of, when they spake of the coming of Christ in his kingdom. And therefore all that they would understand Christ of, was that they—some of them— should see that prophecy accomplished before they died.

It need be no difficulty that Christ's manner of expressing himself would lead 'em to expect that it should be accomplished in another manner, for the disciples knew that Christ was wont to speak to them in mystical language. And besides, Christ in expressing himself thus, does it but as referring to that prophecy or vision of Daniel. The expressions are taken out of that prophecy, and no wonder that events in visions and prophecies are represented mystically. And the disciples were not cheated in it, for there was as much accomplished as answered their expectation, while some of them lived, though not in the same manner, for they had poor mistaken notions what the kingdom of Christ was; yet they saw it accomplished in a more glorious sense than they expected. Add to this Nos. 414 and 464.[8]

198. II SAMUEL 12. It may be worth the while to observe the analogy there was between David's sin in the matter of Uriah, and the judgments after. He was guilty of shedding of blood, and he was punished with this in his own family, one of his own children shedding the blood of another, Absalom's shedding Amnon's blood [II Sam. 13:28–29], and afterwards he, though his[9] own son, seeking to shed his blood. And with Absalom, the greatest part of his subjects that used to be loyal and have a good affection for him, had their hearts turned against him [II Sam. 15:6], and became his enemies, and sought to shed his blood; and afterwards Absalom's blood was shed, greatly to the grief of David his father [II Sam. 18:14, 33].

He was guilty of most aggravated uncleanness in his adultery with Bathsheba, and he was punished with uncleanness in his own family in a most aggravated manner, by the horrid incest and rape of his own son upon his own daughter [II Sam. 13:14], and afterwards Absalom, his own son that was very dear to him, going in to his own concubines,

7. This cross-reference is a later interlineation.
8. These cross-references are later additions.
9. I.e. David's.

many of them, and that on the top of the house in the sight of the sun, and in the sight of all Israel [II Sam. 16:22], on purpose to render his father as odious and contemptible as possibly could be.

199. GENESIS 6:14. "Make thee an ark of gopher wood." "The word in the Hebrew language[1] seems to imply that the wood was of a bituminous or pitchy nature, and consequently more capable of resisting wet or moisture; and St. Chrysostom particularly calls it ξύλα τετράγωνα ἄσηπτα, 'square wood not liable to rot.' The learned Fuller rightly concludes it to be the cypress, from the affinity of the word; for cypress in Greek is κυπάρισσος, from whence, if the termination is taken away, *cuphar* or gopher consists of such letters as are often changed into each other. Neither is there any wood less subject to rottenness and worms than this is, as all writers do allow. Pliny saith that the cypress wood is not sensible of rottenness or age, that it will never split nor cleave asunder, except by force, and that no worm will touch it, because it hath a peculiar bitter taste. And therefore Plato advised that all records, that are to be preserved for the benefit of future generations, should be written upon tables of cypress. Martial saith that it will last for an hundred ages and never decay. Thucydides saith that the chests were made of cypress, in which the Athenians carried away the bones of those who died in war for their country; and the Scholiast gives this reason for it, because it would never decay. And the Pythagoreans abstained from making coffins of cypress, because they certainly concluded that the scepter of Jupiter was made of this tree. And no reason can be assigned for such a fiction among the poets, but because it was the fittest resemblance of that eternal power and authority which they attributed to him. Theophrastus, speaking of those trees which are least subject to decay, adds this as a conclusion, that the cypress tree seems to be most durable of all, and that the folding doors of the temple of Ephesus being made thereof, had lasted without damage for four generations. In this Pliny is more particular, and saith that those doors were made of cypress, and they had lasted till his time which, he saith, was near four hundred years, and still looked as if they were new. And Vitruvius speaks both of the cypress and of the pine tree, that they kept for a long time without the least defect, because the sap, which is [in] every part of the wood, hath a peculiar bitter taste, and is so very offensive that no worm or other consuming animal will touch it. He also tells us that such works, as are made of such wood, will last

1. I.e. עֲצֵי־גֹפֶר.

forever. And therefore he advises, that the beams of all chambers should especially be made of cypress wood, because such as were made of fir were soon consumed by the worm and rottenness.

"And as it was such a lasting wood, so it was also very fit for the building of ships. Peter Martyr of Angloria, as he is cited by the learned Fuller, saith that the inhabitants of Crete had their cypress trees so common, that they made the beams of their houses, their rafters, their rooms and floors, and also their ships of this wood. Plutarch saith that the ship carpenter in the first place useth the pine from Isthmus, and the cypress from Crete. And Vegetius adds that the galleys are built chiefly of the cypress, and of the pine tree, or of the larch and fir. And in the Epistle of Theodoricus to Abundantius the Prefect, in which he gives him a commission to build a thousand barks for the fetching provisions or bread corn, he commands him to inquire throughout all Italy of proper artists for wood for such work, and wherever he should find the cypress or pine trees near the shore, that he should buy them at a reasonable price. Neither was it thus only in Crete and Italy, but Diodorus proves that in Phoenicia there was timber sufficient to build ships, because Libanus near Tripoli, and Byblus, and Sidon were full of cedar trees, and larch trees, and cypress trees, which were very admirable for show and greatness. And Plato, among the trees that were fit for ship carpenters to use, places the cypress next to the pine and the larch tree. And even in later years, we are told that the Saracens did hasten from Alexandria to Phoenicia to cut down the cypress wood, and fit it for the use of the ships.

"And as the cypress tree was so very fit for this use, so it grew in great plenty in Assyria and Babylonia. And therefore Arianus and Strabo speak particularly of it, and that the numerous fleet, which Alexander the Great built in those parts, was made of the cypress, which he cut down, and which grew in Babylonia. For there was, as they say, a great plenty of these trees in Assyria, and that they had no other wood in that country, which was fit for such a purpose." Bedford's *Scripture Chronology*, pp. 111–12.[2] See No. 201.[3]

200. JUDE 14–15. (Let this be annexed to No. 188.) That Enoch prophesied of the flood, is yet more probable from the name that he

2. Arthur Bedford, *The Scripture Chronology Demonstrated by Astronomical Calculations, and also by the Year of Jubilee, and the Sabbatical Year among the Jews: or, An Account of Time, from the Creation of the World, to the Destruction of Jerusalem; as it may be proved from the Writings of the Old and New Testament* (London, 1730), pp. 111–12.

3. This cross-reference is a later addition.

gave his son, "Methuselah," for the first part of it, *methu*, signifies "he is dead," and *selah* signifies "sending"; so that what is implied in the name seems to be, "when he is dead, God shall send." And probably there is a prophecy couched in it, that when Methuselah was dead, God should send that great catastrophe that Enoch had foretold, which came to pass accordingly; for the flood came that very year that Methuselah died.

201. GENESIS 6:14. (Let this be annexed to No. 199.) Note that the reason why they needed a sort of wood not subject to decay or rottenness, was chiefly because the ark was so long in building. Had it not a kind of wood of extraordinary durableness, it would have decayed and spoiled in much less than an 120 years, being exposed to the weather.

202. THE BOOK OF JOB.[4] Extract out of Bedford's *Scripture Chronology*, pp. 365–66. "The place where *Job* lived is generally supposed to be Idumaea, because we meet with a person called Uz among the sons of Esau (Gen. 36:28), from whom a part of Idumaea was anciently called 'the land of Uz' (Lam 4:21). We meet also with Eliphaz, the son of Esau, and Teman his son (Gen. 36:15); and therefore it is probable that Eliphaz the Temanite, the friend of Job, might be [the] son of this Teman, and grandson of the other Eliphaz. And therefore many think that Job might be Jobab, one of the kings that reigned in the land of Edom (Gen. 36:33).

"But in answer to all this, it may be considered that there is another Uz, the son of Nahor, Abraham's brother (Gen. 22:20–21), who married Milcah of the same family, from which family Isaac and Jacob took wives by the direction of their parents, and consequently most likely to be a family in which religion might be kept up in that purity, as we find it to be in Job.

"As to the land of Uz, the Septuagint calls it Ausitis, but never calls that Uz in the land of Edom by this name. Nahor lived at Haran on the south of Euphrates, and no doubt his son might live with him, and his family give a name to this country. And we find in Ptolemy a people called Aisitae, which the learned Bochart supposes should be written Ausitae, who extended themselves from the river Euphrates south-

4. JE deleted "Gen. 22:13" before writing the title of this entry. The closing section of Gen. 22 relates directly to the excerpts cited from Bedford.

ward into Arabia Deserta; and here both he and Bishop Patrick, our excellent commentator, supposes Job to have been born. Besides, Job is said to be one of the greatest of all the men of the East. Now the land of Uz in Idumaea can in no respect be called the East. It lay almost north from Egypt, and south from Canaan, and southwest from the country of Midian, where Jethro, the father-in-law of Moses, lived. But the south part of the country of Ausitis or Uz lay not only east from Canaan, but eastward from all the countries in which the Israelites traveled whilst they were in the wilderness. As for the name of Eliphaz, it is not impossible but two men in different countries might have the same name; and then Eliphaz, the friend of Job, might not be the son of Esau from Teman, but the son of Ishmael from Tema (Gen. 25:13, 15), whom Abraham in his lifetime sent eastward to inhabit the east country (Gen. 25:6), and where we find them in the neighborhood of Uz. In those parts, it is probable that Bildad the Shuhite, or son of Abraham from Shuah by Keturah (Gen. 25:1–2), might live, who was also sent thither with the rest of his brethren (as in the forementioned Gen. 25:6). And as Buz was the brother of Uz (Gen. 22:20–21), so Elihu the Buzite, being of that family, might well live in those parts, especially since he seems to be of a religious family, the son of Barachel, that is, 'he blesseth God,' or 'God blesseth.' Besides, this Elihu was of the kindred of Ram or Aram, that is, a Syrian, as Laban was also called (Gen. 28:5), who dwelt with his ancestors in Padan Aram, or the country of Aram. [But 'tis more probable that the Ram here mentioned is the Aram mentioned, Gen. 22:21.][5] To this may be added, that the Sabeans, who took away Job's oxen, and the Chaldeans, who took away his cattle, were near neighbors to this part of the country of Uz, the son of Nahor, but lay so remote from Uz in Idumaea, that they could not make an excursion thither. It is allowed also that Job spoke the Arabic language in perfection, whence he is called 'the Divine of the Arabians,' and the book which goes under his name is full of Arabic words and phrases; and we may more rationally expect this language to be spoke in Arabia itself than in Idumaea. And therefore there is little reason to think that Moses would call him Job in one place, and Jobab in another, where the difference of words is not only evident in every translation, but in the Hebrew language they do not begin with the same letter, the one אִיּוֹב and the other יוֹבָב."[6]

---

5. JE's brackets. This editorial comment is a later interlineation.
6. Bedford, *Scripture Chronology*, pp. 365–66.

Thus far Bedford.[7] It seems likely that the land of Uz where Job lived was the former Uz,[8] upon this account: it is much more probable that we should find so much of religion and piety, and of the presence of God in the country of the posterity of Nahor, who is spoken of as an holy worshiper of the true God, whose covenant God God was (Gen. 31:53, "The God of Abraham, and the God of Nahor."), than in Idumaea among the posterity of so wicked a man as Esau, who is branded in Scripture for folly and impiety, of whom and his posterity 'tis recorded that God hated them [Mal. 1:3], who was[9] undutiful to his parents, and a persecutor, who began to struggle with Jacob in the womb, to signify that he and his posterity should be the enemies of the church, and whose posterity are always spoken of as the church's enemies, so that oftentimes the children of Edom are put for all the church's enemies in general. 'Tis much more likely to find piety among the posterity of Ishmael than of Esau, for there is no such promise concerning Esau, that he should live before God, as there is concerning Ishmael; and accordingly we find Eliphaz, in this book, an holy man of Ishmael's posterity. Esau's posterity, as they descended from a wicked father, so they chiefly descended from mothers of the accursed nations of Canaan that were Esau's wives, and were the more likely on that account to have wickedness descend to them, and God's curse entailed upon them.

Concerning the penman of the book of Job. Bedford thinks that the poetical part of it was[1] written originally by some person that belonged to Arabia, the country where the things were transacted and spoken, because "the style is not like the rest of the books of Moses, or indeed to any other parts of the Old Testament, but more concise and obscure, and that there are such a vast number of Arabic words and phrases to be found in it." It has been observed by several that the book of Job abounded with Arabisms, so that Job has been called "the Arabian divine." And he[2] thinks that the substance of this book was written originally "by Elihu, one of the speakers in it. First, because when Job's friends, who came to lament with him and to comfort him, [are numbered by name,] Elihu is not named among the number, because he

---

7. JE deleted "It seems much more probable that."
8. I.e. Uz, the son of Nahor.
9. JE deleted "a persecutor of Jacob while he lived."
1. MS: "was ~~Penn'd by Elihu one of the Speakers in it~~ & that ~~the whole~~ it was not written." Because JE's deletions are confusing, this reconstruction rests on Bedford's text.
2. I.e. Bedford.

himself was the historian and penman, who gave this account; and therefore he named not himself, when he named the rest. And secondly, because he[3] thinks that he seems to speak of himself as the historian. Job 32:15–17, 'They were amazed; they answered no more: they left off speaking. When I had waited (for they spake not, but stood still, and answered no more), I said, I will answer also; I also will show mine opinion.'"[4]

It looks to me probable chiefly on the former of these reasons, and if it was written originally by an inhabitant of that country, as the forementioned reason of the Arabic style argues strongly that it was, no person seems to be so likely as Elihu, for it was doubtless at first written by an inspired person, and probably therefore by some person in that country of eminent piety and wisdom, for such were the persons that were wont to be inspired, and to be improved as the penmen of holy inspired writings. And it probably also was some person that lived near the time when the things were transacted, for true religion vanished away out of Arabia not long after, and such men therefore were not there to be found. And 'tis not probable that there were any other persons of such eminent piety and wisdom as those mentioned in that book; but of them, be sure, none were so likely to be the penman as Elihu, who stood most indifferent in the affair, and was most approved of by God in what he said and acted in it, of any of them.

Bedford also thinks it probable that Moses, "when he kept the flock of Jethro, the priest of Midian, might meet with this book," which seems the more probable because priests, even in all nations, and in the most ancient times, used to be the keepers of books and records, especially those that were looked upon [as] sacred. And 'tis very likely that a priest of Midian should have this book, for the Midianites were related to the people that dwelt in Job's country, and particularly to one of the speakers in the affair, viz. Bildad the Shuhite, for Shuah and Midian were brothers, being both the children of Abraham by Keturah (Gen. 25:1–2). And it was so early then that the relation was more fresh in their memory, and 'tis more likely still that Jethro should have such a book, he being a priest of the true God, like Melchizedek. And Moses might probably take the more notice of the book, for its being so adapted for his improvement in the banished, afflicted circumstances he was then in, and also the circumstances of his brethren, the children

---

3. Ibid. JE inserted this and the following word.
4. Bedford, *Scripture Chronology*, pp. 296–97.

of Israel, in their great affliction in Egypt, for whose sake Bedford supposes he translated it into Hebrew, to teach them patience under their afflictions, and added the historical part; or he might alter the phrasing of the historical part, and add such expressions as would make it more intelligible to his own people, which were needless for readers in the country where the things were transacted.[5] See Bedford, *Scripture Chronology*, pp. 296–97, and 367–68.

203. PSALMS 90:10. Bedford, *Scripture Chronology*, p. 395. "When God had positively declared that the Israelites should wander forty years in the wilderness, and that all of them, except Joshua and Caleb, should die there, and when he did thus cut short the age of man to what it is at this time, then Moses penned a melancholy psalm, in which he tells us how they were consumed by God's anger for their impieties. And now man's age is come to seventy or eighty years, after which there is only labor and sorrow, instead of those hundreds which they lived before.

"Here we may observe, that as sin at first brought death into the world, so sin did afterwards shorten the age of man. Before the flood the patriarchs lived almost to a thousand years. But the sin which brought the flood took away one half of man's age, so that they who were born afterward never attained to the age of five hundred. At the confusion of Babylon, it was shortened again in the same manner, so that none born after that time lived up to two hundred and fifty, as it is easy to observe by computing those ages. After the death of the patriarchs, when the true worship of God was very much declined in their families, and the rest of mankind were overrun with superstition and idolatry, the life of man was shortened again, so that we read of none born since who exceeded an hundred and five and twenty. Neither did the ages of men stand at that measure, but at the frequent murmurings and provokings of God in the wilderness, a third part more, or thereabout, was cut off from the age of man; and the common stint of man's life was brought to seventy or eighty years, or thereabout, or more particularly to 83 or 84 years, which very few exceeded, and which Moses speaks of in the before-mentioned psalm composed upon that occasion. And though the sins of mankind have been very great and universal since that time, yet the age of man's life has not been shortened any more, because a shorter space would hardly have

5. Ibid., pp. 367–68.

been sufficient for the finding out and improvement of arts and sciences, as well as for other reasons."[6]

204. LEVITICUS 23:34–36; MATTHEW 1; LUKE 2. THE FEAST OF TABERNACLES. THE BIRTH OF CHRIST. LORD'S DAY. Bedford, in *Scripture Chronology*, makes it appear exceeding probable "that Christ was born on the feast of tabernacles";[7] as also Mather on the types. And besides what Mr. Mather on the types observes of this feast, and of the time of Christ's birth,[8] there are the following things observed by Mr. Bedford.

1. He shows that in this month, about the same time of the year that Christ was born, the world was created.[9] Thus the beginning of the new creation and the old, the creation of the first Adam and the second, are at the same time of year.

2. That Moses, the type of Christ, came down from Mt. Sinai, which was a type of heaven,

> on the first day of this month, and declared that God was appeased, and the people pardoned; and his face shone, as if the divinity had inhabited the manhood, so that the Israelites could not look upon him. And he then gave directions, that they should immediately set about building the tabernacle (which was hitherto hindered by and because of the golden calf), seeing that God would now dwell among them, and forsake them no more. Upon this the people bring their offerings, which were viewed and found to be sufficient. And then immediately they pitch their tents, knowing that they were not to depart from that place before the divine tabernacle was finished; and thus they set about this great work with all their might at this time of the year. Hence the fifteenth day of this month, and seven days after, were appointed for the feast of taber-

6. Ibid., p. 395.
7. Ibid., p. 400.
8. Samuel Mather, *The Figures or Types of the Old Testament, by which Christ and the Heavenly things of the Gospel were preached and shadowed to the People of God of old; Explained and improved in sundry Sermons* ([Dublin], 1683), pp. 532–45, contains a discussion of "The Gospel of the Feast of Tabernacles" which underscores one of the principal reasons for the festival, namely, that it pointed the children of Israel "to the time when God himself would come to tabernacle and pitch his Tent amongst men" (p. 534). Mather declared that "the Birth of Christ was at the Feast of Tabernacles," on the fifteenth day of the seventh month of the Jewish calendar (p. 535). He marshaled logical, chronological, and scriptural arguments in support of that date and in opposition to the more traditional dating of Christ's nativity.
9. Bedford, *Scripture Chronology*, p. 400.

nacles, in commemoration of their dwelling in tents in the wilderness when God dwelt in the midst of them.[1]

3. That Christ was not only born at the feast of tabernacles, and so circumcised on the last day or eighth day of that feast, which was a "great day," and probably appointed out of respect to the circumcision of Christ that was to be on that day, but also that the feast of tabernacles, on which Christ was born, fell out on the first day of the week, and so the eighth day of the feast on which he was circumcised also fell on the same day of the week.[2]

4. That the feast of the dedication of the temple of Solomon (which was a type of the body of Christ, as well as the tabernacle), was not only held on the feast of tabernacles, the feast on which Christ was born, but also that that feast "happened to be on a Sunday," as the day of Christ's birth was, and so "the last and great day of the feast" was also held on a Sunday. See *Scripture Chronology*, Bk. IV, ch. IV.[3]

5. I would further observe that in that day the Godhead did, in a sensible manner, descend in a pillar of cloud to inhabit the temple, as in the incarnation of Christ, the Godhead descended to dwell in flesh. See No. 396, note on Zech. 14:16–19.[4]

205. EXODUS 17:15. "And Moses built an altar, and called the name of it Jehovah Nissi,"[5] i.e. "the Lord my banner." Altars were types of Christ, and therefore were sometimes called by the name of God, as Jacob called the altar he built in Bethel, *El Bethel*,[6] or "the God of Bethel" [Gen. 31:13]. The special reason of Moses' calling this altar, that he built on occasion of their victory over Amalek, "the Lord my banner," was that Christ in that battle was in a special type represented as the banner of his people, under which they fought against their enemies, to which they should look, and by which they should be conducted as an army were by their banner or ensign, viz. in Moses' holding up the rod of God in his hand on the top of the hill, as verses 9–12. That rod was a type of Christ, as has been showed, No. 195. Moses, while the people were fighting with Amalek, held up this rod as the banner under which the people should fight. While Moses held up this rod, Israel prevailed; and when he let it down, Amalek prevailed.

1. Ibid., p. 401.
2. Ibid.
3. Ibid., p. 403.
4. This cross-reference is a later addition.
5. יְהוָה נִסִּי.
6. הָאֵל בֵּית־אֵל.

This is agreeable to what God commanded when the children of Israel were bitten with fiery serpents. Num. 21:8, "Make thee a fiery serpent, and set it upon a pole." In the original it is, "set it for a banner," or "ensign," or "upon an ensign."[7] In all likelihood, the brazen serpent was set up on one of the poles of the standards or ensigns of the camp, and probably on the standard of the tribe of Judah, which was a lion, and was a type of Christ, who is "the Lion of the tribe of Judah" [Rev. 5:5]. So it is prophesied that Christ should stand for an ensign. Is. 11:10, 12, "And in that day there shall be a root of Jesse, which shall stand for an ensign of the people; to it shall the Gentiles seek. . . . And he shall set up an ensign for the nations, and shall assemble the outcasts of Israel." See No. 473.[8]

206. GALATIANS 5:18. See No. 196, p. 108. 'Tis not by the gospel, but by the law, that unbelief is a sin that exposes to eternal damnation, as is evident, because we have the pardon of the sin of unbelief by the death of Christ, which shows that Christ died to satisfy for the sin of unbelief as well as other sins. But Christ was to answer the law, and satisfy that; he in his death endured the curse of the law (Gal. 3:10–13, and Rom. 8:3–4). 'Tis absurd to say that Christ died to satisfy the gospel, or to bear the punishment of that. See "Miscellanies," no. 399.[9]

207. JOSHUA 10:12–14. Concerning the sun and moon's standing still. This great event was doubtless typical; and as the sun was made to be a type of Christ, and is the most eminent type of him in all the inanimate creation, and is used as a type of Christ in Scripture—for he is the Sun of Righteousness and the Light of the world, etc.—so doubtless the sun here, when it stands still to give the children of Israel light to help them against their enemies, is a type of Christ. The sun did as it were fight for [the] Israelites by his light; so Christ fights for his people, and the way that he does is chiefly by giving them light. Hereby he helps them against the powers of darkness, and overthrows the kingdom of darkness. Christ was at that time actually fighting for Israel as the captain of the host; he had a little before appeared in a visible

7. וְשִׂים אֹתוֹ עַל־נֵס.

8. This cross-reference is a later addition.

9. In no. 399, "RIGHTEOUSNESS OF CHRIST," JE argues that the law "Christ was subject to and obeyed was the same that Adam was subject to and was to have obeyed," even though the "positive precepts" and "particular duties" differed because of their circumstances. Every act of Christ's obedience "was part of his righteousness"; but "all sins, even breaches of positive precepts as well as others, have atonement by the death of Christ" (*Works, 13*, 464–65).

shape "with a sword drawn in his hand," and told Joshua that "as the
captain of the host of the Lord," he was come (Josh. 5:13–14). And
there was now a double type of Christ's fighting for his people against
their spiritual enemies. Joshua was then fighting as the captain of the
host of Israel, who bore the name of Christ, for "Joshua" was the same
with "Jesus," and he was an eminent type of [him]; and at the same
time the sun stood over Joshua, fighting for Israel against their enemies. While Joshua, or Jesus, thus fought, the sun appeared also fighting in the same battle, being a type of the true Joshua, or Jesus. It was a
great thing for the sun to stand still, to fight for Israel, and to help
them to obtain the possession of Canaan, but not so great a thing as for
Christ, who is "the brightness of God's glory, and the express image of
his person" [Heb. 1:3], the creator and upholder of the sun, to appear
as he did, to deliver his people from their spiritual enemies, and to
make way for their obtaining the heavenly Canaan. The sun, though
so great and glorious an heavenly body, and though so high above the
earth, yet did forego its natural course, was greatly put out of the way,
and deprived of that which naturally belonged to it, for the sake of
Israel, laid aside its glory as the king of heaven, was as it were divested
of the glory of its dominion over heaven and earth, which it has by its
course through all heaven and round the earth. For 'tis by its course
that nothing is hid from its light and heat, by which it has influence
over all, and as it were rules over all (Ps. 19:6). The influence of the
heavenly bodies is called in Scripture their "dominion" (Job 38:32–
33), but this glory as king of heaven and earth was now laid aside to
serve and minister unto Israel. But this was not so great a thing as for
the eternal Son of God, the infinite fountain of all light, who is infinitely above all creatures, the Sun of Righteousness, in comparison of
whose brightness the sun is but darkness, and therefore will be turned
into darkness when he appears: I say, it was not so great a thing as for
him to lay aside his glory as king of heaven and earth, and appear in
the form of a servant, to serve men, and "come not to be ministered
unto, but to minister" [Matt. 20:28], and should even give his life to
destroy and confound our enemies, and obtain for us the possession of
the heavenly Canaan. The sun, who by his course was wont to fill
heaven and earth, now confined itself to the land of Canaan for the
sake of Israel; so Christ, who being in heaven filled all things (Eph.
4:10), by his incarnation confined himself to the land of Canaan and to
a tabernacle of flesh. Hence it is not any way incredible, not at all to be
wondered at, that God should cause such a miracle for the sake of the

Israelites, or that nature in so great an instance should be made to yield and give place to Israel's interest, when the God of nature did as it were deprive himself of the glory that he had from the beginning of the world, yea, "before the world was," even from all eternity (John 17:5), the glory that naturally belonged to him, and as it were give up all for man, that he should become incarnate, and deliver up himself to death for the spiritual Israel.

The moon also stood still at that time, to fight against the Amorites, who[1] is a type of the church; for the church fights with Christ against the spiritual [Amorites]. The church militant is Christ's army; they go forth with Christ, and under Christ, to fight the good fight of faith, and are soldiers of Jesus Christ. Christ and the church are represented going forth together in battle (Rev. 19:11–21). Both the sun and moon stood still at that time, that there might then be a representation of the same thing in heaven that there was on the earth. There was Joshua and Israel fighting God's enemies on earth, and there were the sun and moon fighting against them in heaven; and both represented Jesus and his church fighting against their spiritual enemies.

208. HABAKKUK 3:11. "The sun and moon stood still in their habitation; at the light of thine arrows they went, [and] at the shining of thy glittering spear." By this it is evident that there was not only a dreadful storm of hail, but thunder and lightning with it, on the day that the sun and moon stood still, as we commonly have thunder and lightning in storms of hail in the summertime. That by "the light of God's arrows" is meant the light of his lightning is evident by Ps. 144:6, "Cast forth lightning, and scatter them; shoot out thine arrows, and destroy them"; and especially Ps. 18:13–14, "The Lord also thundered in the heavens, and the Highest gave his voice, hailstones and coals of fire. Yea, he sent forth his arrows, and scattered them; and he shot out lightnings, and discomfited them." There lightnings are called God's arrows, and the instance that David has reference to was parallel with this, for it was an instance wherein God fought against David's enemies in a storm of hail, as he did against the enemies of Israel when the sun and moon stood still. And it was probably when God broke forth upon David's enemies before him, like the breach of waters at Baal-perazim, that we read of, II Sam. 5:20; and that which God did for David there is particularly mentioned as parallel with what God did for Israel at Gibeon, when the sun and moon stood still, in Is. 28:21. If this needed

---

1. I.e. the moon.

any further confirmation, it might be further confirmed by the last expression in this verse, "at the shining of thy glittering spear." The radix of the word that is translated "glittering," which is בָּרָק, signifies "to lighten": and the word itself, which is בָּרָק, properly signifies lightning; so that[2] the literal translation of the words are, "at the shining of the lightning of thy spear." And besides, we read, Josh. 10:10, that "the Lord discomfited them before Israel," and Mr. Bedford observes that the word used in the original "signifies to strike a terror by the noise of thunder" (*Scripture Chronology*, p. 510, margin). Wherever the same word in the original is used, and it is said that God discomfited these or those, this seems to have been the case, that God fought against them with thunder and lightning; so when Sisera and his host were discomfited, Judg. 4:15 (see notes on Judg. 5:20),[3] and so I Sam. 7:10, II Sam. 22:15, Ps. 18:14.[4]

It is here said that "the sun and moon stood still, but went or walked at the light of God's [arrows], and at the shining of the lightning of his spear," by which it seems that when the lightning began, the sun and moon began to move again, after they had stood still. The case seems to have been thus. As long as the sun and moon stood still, there was a serene air, that the children of Israel and their enemies might behold that great and wondrous miracle which God then manifested his power, and glory, and wonderful mercy to his people by. But then the storm began to arise, and appeared first at a distance with thunder and lightning, but approaching; and when the lightnings appeared, the sun and moon began to move, and then came the dreadful storm, and destroyed the Amorites. The lightning's appearing, and playing at a distance before the storm came, seems here to be compared to a man of war's brandishing his weapons when coming to battle. The sun and moon, God's creatures, had stood still to help Israel against their enemies; but when God himself appeared with brandished weapons coming to the battle, they withdrew, as conscious that now there was no further need of their help, seeing that God himself was coming, who needed not the help of his creatures, and did not need to have the sun and moon to stand still to give him time. He could do his work in a short time. And though God's fighting against the Amorites by hail is

---

2. MS: "that if the ~~wor~~."

3. JE's brief entry on this text in the "Blank Bible" asserts, "When God is doing some great thing for his church on earth, the hosts of heaven are engaged with the church on earth." A longer entry, more directly related to No. 208, follows in No. 211.

4. JE took these biblical references from Bedford, *Scripture Chronology*, p. 510, margin.

mentioned before the sun's and moon's standing still, yet doubtless it was after. When the sun stood still, it was to give them opportunity to fight for themselves, but there would have been no need of that if God was fighting for them. God did not appear thus to take burden of the battle immediately on himself, till they were weary. 'Tis not God's manner to appear, till after others have done their do; and then it must be either before or afterwards that God fought by the storm of hail, and not in the time of the sun's and moon's standing still, for if so, the storm would have hid the miracle. And 'tis unreasonable to suppose that it was afterwards, or that there was any need of the sun's standing still twelve hours together, to give opportunity for the children of Israel after God had taken the work into his own hands, and had so terribly destroyed them with hailstones. God don't need men to finish the work after he has taken it in hand; when he begins, he will also make an end.

In all probability, when God began with thunder, lightning, and hail, the children of Israel stood still and rested, while God fought for them. See Ex. 14:13–14, and also II Chron. 20:17. It could be no otherwise than that by that time the children of Israel needed rest, having been in battle and pursuit for about eighteen hours, and had traveled all the night before (Josh. 10:9), and the latter part of the time in the scorching heat of the sun (see No. 209),[5] it having stood still over their heads for twelve hours together. And besides, this destruction by hail was doubtless after the children of Israel had done, and not when they were mixed with their enemies, fighting with them; for if so, they themselves would be exposed to the hail, and thunder, and lightning, as well as their enemies. See notes on Ps. 68:8–9.[6]

'Tis signified in the margin of our Bibles,[7] that the words may be translated, "thine arrows walked in the light, and thy glittering spear in the shining," i.e. in the shining of the sun while it stood. But this is not so natural a translation; for by this way of rendering, the words are thus: "in the light thine arrows walked, and in the shining the glittering of thy spear." But this is not so natural a translation, for 1. There seems to be an evident antithesis in the words between "standing still" and "walking," and therefore they are to be attributed to the same subject, viz. the sun and moon. 2. 'Tis not a natural metaphor to [say] "a spear walked in the light"; for a spear is not a weapon that is to do its

5. This cross-reference is a later addition.
6. I.e. No. 210. This cross-reference is a later addition.
7. I.e. the KJV.

execution flying through the air, though arrows are. And 'tis less natural speaking to say, that "the glittering of the spear walks." 3. The shining spoken of seems evidently to relate to the word that next follows, viz. the glittering or lightning of the spear. 4. The prefix that is translated "at" is *lamed* and not *beth*, and therefore is more properly rendered "at" than "in." And besides, this translation confutes itself, because without doubt the thing that respect is had to here, when mention is made of God's appearing in battle himself with his own weapons, on that day when the sun and moon stood still, is God's fighting as he did against the Amorites, and destroying them by the storm of hail. But then God's arrows could not be said to walk in the light and shining of the sun, because the storm hid the shining of the sun. And besides that, 'tis not probable that [God] did do this execution while the sun continued to stand still, because the storm would have hid the miracle.

209. JOSHUA 10:12–14. Concerning the sun's standing still. This is supposed to give occasion to the story of Phaethon, the son of Sol and Clymene, who, desiring his father to let him guide the chariot of the sun for one day, set the world on fire. So we read that it was about the space of one day that the sun stood still, and this in all probability caused an extraordinary scorching and distressing heat in many parts of the world. And Mr. Bedford, in his *Scripture Chronology*, observes that mention is made of it in the Chinese history, "that in the reign of their seventh emperor Yao, that the sun did not set for ten days together, and that the inhabitants of the earth were afraid that the earth would be burnt, for there were great fires at that time. This happened in the sixty-seventh year of that emperor's reign, and so the time of it," Mr. Bedford observes, according to their account, "exactly agrees with Scripture history" (*Scripture Chronology*, p. 489). And he observes that "it's natural for men in things of great antiquity to enlarge beyond the truth." And what the Chinese history mentions about great fires in many places agrees, with the story of Phaethon's setting the world on fire.[8] And indeed, to have the day more than twenty-four hours (for besides the twelve hours that the sun stood, the time of the sun's course above the horizon was probably more than twelve hours, for it was probably later in the year than the vernal equinox), I say, to have the sun so long above the horizon, and twelve hours of it together extraor-

8. Bedford, *Scripture Chronology*, p. 489.

dinary near the meridian, shining down with a perpendicular ray all that time, must needs cause exceeding heat in many places.

210. PSALMS 68:8–9. "The earth shook, the heavens also dropped at the presence of God; even Sinai itself was moved at the presence of God, the God of Israel. Thou, O Lord, didst send a plentiful rain, whereby thou didst confirm thine inheritance, when it was weary." By this place, together with Judg. 5:4, it is manifest that there was a great shower of rain upon the camp of Israel at Mt. Sinai at the time of the giving the law there. The case seems to have been thus: On the day when the law was given, which was the day of Pentecost, there appeared a thick cloud upon Mt. Sinai, which was the same cloud that had gone before them and conducted them, now settled upon the mount, but only increased and gathered to a greater thickness. And there were great thunders and lightnings seen and heard out of that cloud, and "the voice of the trumpet exceeding loud, so that all the people that were in the camp trembled" [Ex. 19:16]. When God descended on the mount, the mount quaked greatly; and this earthquake was of great extent, so as to reach to distant countries (Hag. 2:6–7), and was so great as to move mountains, and throw down rocks and great parts of the mountains. Hence we have those expressions of "the mountains skipping like rams, and the little hills like lambs" [Ps. 114:4, 6], etc. And then Mt. Sinai appeared altogether on fire, which burnt to the midst of heaven; and then "the trumpet sounded long, and waxed louder and louder" [Ex. 19:19]. And then the Ten Commandments were given with a voice of awful majesty out of the midst of the fire. And when this was finished, it was followed with the most amazing thunders and lightnings from the thick cloud, the cloud of glory which was on the mount, which cloud spread wider and wider, till it covered the whole heavens. And there was a great shower of rain with thunder and lightning out of it, and the storm spread abroad so as to reach far countries which, with exceeding thunder and lightning, terrified distant nations. Hence the Apostle speaks of a tempest that was at this time from this place, in Heb. 12:18.[9] Thus when "the Lord gave the word, great was the company of them that published it" (Ps. 68:11). When God gave forth his voice at Mount Sinai and thundered there, by the ministration of angels the report was as it were carried into all nations round about; and there were thunders that uttered their voices in all parts of the world (or at least the adjacent countries) to

9. This sentence is a later interlineation.

answer it. Thus the prophet Habakkuk, speaking of this, Hab. 3:3, says, "His glory covered the heavens," i.e. the cloud that was called the "cloud of glory"; and the "glory of the Lord" appeared in the cloud, and covered the heavens in the blaze of lightnings that there then almost continually was, as in the next verse. V. 4, "And his brightness was as the light." And thus it was, as is expressed in the 6th and 7th verses, "He stood, and measured the earth. He beheld, and drove asunder the nations; the everlasting mountains were scattered, the perpetual hills did bow. . . . I saw the tents of Cushan in affliction, and the curtains of the land of Midian did tremble." And thus in Heb. 12:18, there is said to be at this time not only fire, and blackness, and darkness, but also tempest.

Corollary 1. Hereby we may the more fully see how lively a representation what was done on this day was of what was done afterwards on the same day of Pentecost in the days of the gospel. Now God descended from heaven on Mt. Sinai; then God descended from heaven on Mt. Sion, or on his church met together in Jerusalem. Now God revealed the law; then God did, in an extraordinary manner by his Spirit, make known the mysteries of the gospel. Now God's voice was uttered from Mt. Sinai in thunder, and great was the company of them that published. And the voice of his thunder went forth into all the world, and the world was enlightened with lightnings. Then was God's voice in his Word and in his glorious gospel uttered on the spiritual Mt. Sion. And the light of the glorious gospel then began to shine forth in Jerusalem, of which voice and light, thunder and lightning, is a type; "For the word of God is quick and powerful, sharper than any two-edged sword, piercing to the dividing asunder [of] soul and spirit, joints and marrow" [Heb. 4:12], and is as a fire and "hammer that breaks the rock in pieces" [Jer. 23:29]. This thunder and lightning was out of the cloud of glory, the symbol of God's presence; so the voice of the gospel is the voice of Christ, a divine person, and the light is the light of Christ's glory.[1] And then, or after that time, was first fulfilled what was typified by God's voice and light going forth from Mt. Sinai, and spreading abroad into all nations round about; for then first did the powerful voice of God's Word, and the powerful and glorious light of truth, go forth and spread abroad into Gentile nations. Then was the coming of Christ in the gospel, as "the lightning that cometh out of the east, and shineth even to the west" [Matt. 24:27]. The trumpet of

1. Ibid.

Mount Sinai was a type of the trumpet of the gospel.[2] As in the day of Sinai, there was a great earthquake; so consequent on the pouring out of the Spirit on the day of Pentecost, was there the greatest change and overturning of things on the face of the earth that ever had been. Earthquakes often denote great revolutions, in Revelations and elsewhere in Scripture. God's voice in the day of Sinai shook the heavens and earth, and shook all nations, as Heb. 12:26–27, compared with foregoing verses, and Hag. 2:6–7. As the earthquake then shook down towers, and palaces, and other buildings of the heathen, yea, and threw down rocks and mountains, so God's voice in the gospel, after the gospel Pentecost, overturned the heathenish kingdom of Satan, and shook down all its magnificence, the mighty fabric that Satan had been building up for many ages; and those things were overthrown that had been established in the heathen world time out of mind, and had remained till now immovable, like the everlasting hills and mountains. God's enemies abroad in the heathen world on the day of Sinai were greatly terrified, and scattered, and many of them destroyed, which is a type of the amazement that Satan and the powers of darkness were put into by the sudden and wonderful spreading of the gospel, and how the enemies of God were scattered and destroyed thereby. And God's pouring down a great and plentiful rain on the camp of Israel, on the day when the law was given (The refreshing shower that fell on Israel did well represent those divine instructions God was then giving them. Deut. 32:2, "My doctrine shall drop as the rain; my speech shall distill as the dew, as the small rain upon the tender herb, as the showers upon the grass."),[3] was a lively type of the great and abundant pouring out of the Spirit on the Christian church on the day of Pentecost, and on the world in consequence of that. The pouring out of the Spirit is often compared to showers of rain. This rain was the more lively type of the effusion of the Holy Spirit, because it was a very refreshing rain to the congregation of Israel, as 'tis said in the 9th verse of this psalm, "Thou didst send a plentiful rain, whereby thou didst confirm[4] thine inheritance, when it was weary." That was a weary land wherein they then were, being an exceeding dry and parched wilderness, where there is scarcely ever any rain. Horeb,[5] one name of Mt. Sinai, signifies "dryness," and it is called "a land of

2. Ibid.
3. This parenthesis is a later interlineation.
4. MS: "confirm ⟨or Strengthen⟩."
5. חֹרֶב.

drought" [Jer. 2:6]. And it lay far south, and it was now an hot time of the year, wherein the sun was just at the summer solstice, being about the end of May, so that the shower, by its cooling and sweetening the air, was very refreshing to them, and therefore was the more lively type of the sweet influences of the Spirit of God on the soul. And this shower was the more lively type of the pouring out of the Spirit still, because it was a shower out of the cloud of glory, or that cloud that was the symbol of God's presence, so that it was refreshment from God. As the fire from heaven on the altar proceeded out of [the] pillar of cloud and fire (Lev. 9:24), the manna, their early bread, came down on the camp out of the pillar of cloud and fire [Ex. 16], and so did more livelily represent the true bread from heaven, even Jesus Christ, who is a divine person, and dwells in the bosom of the Father.[6] And as their meat, so their water, the refreshing rain which signified also a divine person, viz. the Holy Ghost, was out of the cloud of glory.

Note that when mention is here made of God's sending a plentiful rain, whereby he did confirm or strengthen his inheritance when it was weary, respect is also probably had to the children of Israel's being refreshed by a shower of rain that descended on them, at the same time that a destructive hail fell on their enemies, on the day that the sun and moon stood still. For as has been observed in notes on Hab. 3:11, No. 208, that storm of hail did not arise till the end of the twelve hours of the sun's standing still; and the sun probably stood still near the meridian. And Joshua began the battle very early in the morning, after their traveling all the night before, so that after that night's watching and traveling, they had continued in battle and pursuit about eighteen hours, and great part of the time under a very great and extreme heat of the sun, which must necessarily arise from its standing still so long at a meridian height, and shining down on their heads with a perpendicular ray, so that by that time, without doubt the army of Israel were exceeding weary and faint. And the clouds that covered the heavens sent forth no hail on them, but probably it was rain where they were, and a very great shower, which cooled and sweetened the air, and was a great refreshment to them after such toil and extreme heat. If the rain was frozen in some places, doubtless it was a very cool rain where they were, which was needed to cool the air after such extreme heat. See No. 209. So that it was now with this cloud that arose, as it was

6. On the left margin JE lined out a box in which he wrote, "Manna out of the pillar of cloud and fire."

with [the] pillar of cloud and fire at the Red Sea. As that was a cloud and darkness to their enemies, and sent forth thunder and lightning to confound them (Ps. 77:16–19), but gave light to the Israelites, so now the cloud that arose sent forth destructive hail and thunder on the Amorites, but sent a most refreshing rain on Israel, whereby they were strengthened after they had been made faint with the heat of the sun and the toil of battle.

Corol. 2. Hence we may learn what the apostle Paul means by I Cor. 10:2, where he says that "their fathers were all baptized unto Moses in the cloud and in the sea."[7] They were baptized in the cloud by the cloud's showering down waters abundantly upon them, as it seems to have done at two times especially. One was while they were passing through the Red Sea, for there seems to have been a remarkable storm of rain, and thunder, and lightning, out of the cloud of glory, while the children of Israel were passing through the Red Sea, by Ps. 77:16–19. And thus God looked through the pillar of cloud and fire about the morning watch, and troubled all their host [Ex. 14:24]. He confounded them with perpetual flashes of thunder and lightning, which greatly affrighted the horses, and made them run wild, and jostle one against another, so as to overturn and break the chariots that they drew, and many of them lost their wheels [Ex. 14:25]. But it was only a plentiful shower on the Israelites; and so they were baptized by the water that came out of the pillar of cloud, representing the blood that came out of Christ, and the Spirit that comes forth from him. And so God now, at the time when they were coming out of Egypt (for the Red Sea was the bounds of Egypt), baptized them, to wash and cleanse them from the pollutions of Egypt, and to consecrate them to himself.

Another time was at Mt. Sinai, when God had brought them to himself there, when he first entered into covenant with them there, whereby they became his people and he their God; he consecrated them to him, and sealed that covenant by baptizing them by water out of the cloud.

Hence[8] an argument for baptism by sprinkling or affusion, for the Apostle calls[9] affusion or sprinkling, "baptism," comparing it to Christian baptism [I Cor. 10:2]. And when God himself immediately baptized his people, by a baptism by which he intended to signify the same

7. Jonathan Edwards, Jr., inserted "means that."
8. Jonathan Edwards, Jr., inserted "we have."
9. Jonathan Edwards, Jr., inserted "this."

thing that Christian baptism signifies, he baptized by affusion or sprinkling.

211. JUDGES 5:20. "They fought from heaven; the stars in their courses fought against Sisera." The learned Bedford, in his *Scripture Chronology*, p. 510, supposes that Sisera with his army had passed the river Kishon, and that when Barak came to engage him, God appeared against Sisera in a dreadful storm of thunder [and] lightning; and the battle continuing all day, and Sisera and his host being at last put to flight, the Israelites pursued in the night, and that the way that the stars fought for them was by shining with an extraordinary brightness to help the Israelites in their pursuing the enemy who, when they came to the river Kishon, went in, but the storm having swelled the river, the swift stream carried them away. And that there was thunder and lightning then, he argues from the 15th verse of the foregoing chapter, where it is said that "the Lord discomfited Sisera, and all his chariots, and all his host." He says, the word in the original[1] "signifies to strike a terror by the noise of thunder and lightning";[2] and the truth is, it is nowhere said that God discomfited the enemies of God's people where this word was used, but that it appears that God fought against them with thunder and lightning. So I Sam. 7:10 and Josh. 10:10 (see notes, No. 208, on Hab. 3:11), and II Sam. 22:15; Ps. 18:14.

There are several things that make this opinion of Mr. Bedford probable. This was an instance wherein God had extraordinarily appeared against the enemies of Israel, as appears by this song. And this verse of this song seems to intimate something miraculous of God's appearing in it, and it was the more probable that there was something miraculous for a prophetess being at the head of the army of Israel, and then God had in this manner appeared from time to time fighting against the enemies of his people. So he fought against the Egyptians at the Red Sea (Ps. 77:15–20); so he terrified his and his people's enemies in all neighbor countries with amazing thunder and lightning, when he entered into covenant with his people at Sinai. See No. 210. So God fought against the Amorites before Joshua; so God fought against the Philistines in Samuel's time (I Sam. 7:10). So God fought for David. See notes on Ps. 18:7–15.[3] So God seems to have

1. הָמַם.
2. Bedford, *Scripture Chronology*, p. 510.
3. In the "Blank Bible" JE suggests that God "probably had at sometime" fought against David's enemies, "literally" using hailstones, thunder, and lightning, as perhaps at one or both of his battles at Baal-perazim.

fought against Sennacherib's army in Hezekiah's time (Is. 30:30). See No. 218.[4] And so Hannah prophesied that God would appear against the enemies of his people (I Sam. 2:10). And the reason why Deborah begins this song with taking notice that God appeared with thunder and rain for his people in the wilderness (vv. 4–5), as he had done at the Red Sea and at Mt. Sinai, probably is because God now had so appeared for them in the deliverance that she celebrates by this song. God appeared so for his people when he took them first into covenant and made them his people. And now he had appeared in like manner again, and so appears to be still the same God; and she therefore mentions it as celebrating his covenant faithfulness. And then it is in no wise to be supposed that the river Kishon, that is elsewhere called a brook (Ps. 83:9), was by any means sufficient to sweep away and drown an army unless extraordinarily swelled by rain. Again 'tis probable because the great battle in which the enemies of the church shall be destroyed, and that shall usher in the glorious times of the church, that we read of in the 16th chapter of Revelation, is represented as being accompanied with thunder, lightning, and hail, but 'tis compared to this battle at Megiddo; and therefore the place where 'tis fought is said to be in the Hebrew tongue, *Ar Mageddon*, i.e. the mount of Megiddo. And 'tis probable that the way Mr. Bedford mentions was the way in which the stars fought against Sisera; 'tis most likely that the stars fought against Sisera the same way that the sun fought against the Amorites, viz. by giving light to Israel, that they might be avenged of their enemies (Josh. 10:13). As this that God wrought now was parallel with that in Joshua's time, in that God fought against the enemies of Israel in a storm of thunder and lightning, so if we suppose the stars shone at night with a miraculous brightness to help Israel against their enemies, it will in a great degree be parallel in another instance. For then the day was lengthened for them by the sun's standing still, and now the day is as it were lengthened by causing the stars in miraculous [manner] to supply in a great measure the want of daylight. The sun fought then, and the stars now, and both by giving light, but only there is this difference; the sun fought standing still, but the stars fought in their courses or paths, as 'tis in the original.[5] This instance is also very parallel with that at the Red Sea: for there God fought against their enemies with thunder and lightning, and drowned them in the Red Sea; and here God fought against them with thunder and lightning,

---

4. This cross-reference and the preceding sentence are a later interlineation.
5. מִמְּסִלּוֹתָם.

and drowned them with their horses and chariots in the river Kishon. Hence we may possibly see a reason why the great destruction of God's enemies before the glorious times of the church is compared to this instance, rather than to either of those two great instances of God's wonderfully destroying his enemies, viz. because this is parallel to both. And what is peculiar to both is here comprised, viz. the drowning of the Egyptians in the Red Sea, which is peculiar to the first, has here an equivalent in the drowning of the host of Sisera in Kishon, and the sun's standing still and fighting is here answered by the stars' fighting in their courses. And the Holy Ghost might rather choose to compare it to this, because the sun's standing still was a representation of Christ's humiliation. See note on Josh. 10:12–14, No. 207. But Christ will be far from fighting as in a state of humiliation, at that time when introducing the glorious times of the church, and Christ will not then presently appear fighting, as he did in his state of humiliation; but he will fight by his Spirit in his saints, which are called the stars of heaven (Dan. 12:3). Christ will fight by increasing their light, and so their enemies shall be destroyed; and they shall fight in their courses, and in running the race that God has appointed them. And 'tis compared to this rather than the instance at the Red Sea, for the children of Israel, and Moses, and the pillar of cloud being in the Red Sea was a type of Christ's humiliation. See "Miscellanies," no. 691, sec. 16 ff.[6]

That there should be such things at the battle with Sisera, and not mentioned particularly in the history, is not strange; for so there was thunder and lightning at the Red Sea, and on the day when the sun and moon stood still, and at Baal-perazim, and yet it is not mentioned in the history.

212. GENESIS 6:15. Concerning the DIMENSIONS of the ARK. [Bedford] says, "When our countryman, the ingenious and learned Mr. Greaves, traveled into Rome, Greece, Palestina, and Egypt, that he might be capable of discovering the ancient weights, money, and mea-

---

6. In no. 691, entitled "SABBATH. LORD'S DAY," JE argues that God instituted the Jewish sabbath on the day that the children of Israel passed through the Red Sea to commemorate their deliverance from bondage in Egypt. The Christian sabbath, in turn, commemorates the even greater redemption of Jesus Christ, of which the former deliverance was a type. "The children of Israel's being in the Red Sea was typical of Christ in his suffering state, and also the miserable and dreadful state and condition that Christ's people are in before they are delivered by his redemption. Misery, and wrath, and sore affliction are often in Scripture compared to great waters." Coming out of the Red Sea was a "lively representation" of Christ's resurrection in which the church, "the mystical body of Christ," also rises.

sures, both of length, solids, and liquids, he measured the pyramids in Egypt; and accordingly, comparing the account which Herodotus gives of them, he found the length of a cubit to be 21.888 inches, which is accordingly agreed to by other eminent writers (Arburthnet on Weights and Measures, Table 4; and Bishop Cumberland, Of Scripture Weights and Measures, pp. 34, 40, and 43). And therefore, though formerly a cubit was reckoned but 18 inches, and consequently the cube thereof to be but 5832 cubical inches, yet now the cube of a cubit, as it is now plainly known, is 10,267 inches; and therefore the capacity and weight of Noah's ark appears to be almost double of what it was once thought to be" (*Scripture Chronology*, p. 39).[7]

And that the cubit used in the antediluvian world was the same with that used in Egypt, by which the pyramids were measured, and also that used by the Israelites, Bedford argues thus (*Scripture Chronology*, p. 771).

> There is no doubt but that Ham, when he came into Egypt with Mizraim his son, brought with him the ancient measures, having a necessity to make use of some, that everyone might be restored to his own lands after the overflowings of the Nile, and neither having time nor the least necessity of making any alterations. Civil government cannot be supposed to be without determinate measures and weights; nor is there any reason to believe that Ham or Mizraim, in the lifetime of Noah, could be unacquainted with those which he used, or could see any cause to alter them in his lifetime, because the measures would in such a case be disproportionable to his own stature. Egypt is supposed to have been inhabited 190 years before the death of Noah, and the inhabitants had, no doubt, frequent commerce with him and his descendants dwelling in other lands, and such commerce would be facilitated by keeping up the same measures. But it must be made more troublesome, if not totally be broken off, by the change of them. Had the cubit been different, it would have been in vain for Moses to have described his measures by a word, the sense whereof was unknown; or if he had spoken of the measures in the country different from those, they would not upon reduction have fallen into such round even numbers, as he hath described them.[8]

7. Bedford, *Scripture Chronology*, p. 39.
8. Ibid., p. 771.

The same is confirmed by comparing the height of Goliath with the weight of his armor (see notes concerning Goliath's stature, I Sam. 17:4–7),[9] and by the stature of the Egyptian mentioned, I Chron. 11:23, compared with the staff of his spear, which is said to be "like a weaver's beam," which denotes him to have been a man exceeding ordinary men in bulk and strength much more than his being nine foot and nine inches high comes to, which would be his height if a cubit were but a foot and an half, as it used to be reckoned.

213. ISAIAH 32:2. "As rivers of water in a dry place, and as the shadow of a great rock in a weary land." There is an allusion here to the deserts of Arabia, which was an exceeding hot and dry place. One might travel many days' going, and see no sign of a river, brook, or spring, nothing but a dry and parched wilderness, so that travelers there were ready to be consumed with thirst, as the children of Israel were when they were in this wilderness, when they were faint because there was no water. Now when a man finds Jesus Christ, he is like a man that has been traveling in these deserts till he is ready to perish with thirst, and at last finds a river of cool and clear water; 'tis exceeding refreshing. Christ was once actually typified by a river of water that was miraculously caused to flow in the dry deserts of Arabia for the refreshing and satisfying [of] God's people when they were almost consumed with thirst, even by that stream of water out of the rock; for as the Apostle says, "that rock was Christ" [I Cor. 10:4]. This stream of water issued out of the rock that was in Horeb [Ex. 17:6], which word signifies "a dry place." This was a river in a dry place. Ps. 105:41, "He opened the rock, and the waters gushed out; they ran in the dry places like a river." This is called a "land of great drought" (Hos. 13:5). See also Deut. 8:15.[1] Christ is as a river of water, because there is such a fullness in him for the satisfaction of the needy thirsty soul, and enough not only for one, but for all the multitude of God's people, as the stream out of the rock was sufficient for the whole congregation, which was doubtless more than two million souls and their cattle.

And when Christ is said to be "as the shadow of a great rock in a weary land," the allusion is still to the deserts of Arabia. 'Tis not said, "as the shadow of a tree," because in those vast deserts there are no

---

9. This reference is interlined. In the "Blank Bible" JE cites Bedford's calculations, based on the revised measures, that Goliath stood 11 feet 9 inches in height and that his armor collectively weighed 243 pounds (Scripture Chronology, p. 535).

1. This reference and the preceding sentence are a later interlineation.

trees, nothing for shade to protect travelers, but here and there a great rock. Christ is to the weary soul as the cool shadow of a great rock, or a steep rocky mountain, in the scorched deserts of Arabia. See No. 261.[2]

214. ISAIAH 33:17. "Thine eyes shall see the king in his beauty; they shall behold the land that is very far off." This verse speaks of two different sorts of people that dwelt in Zion, viz. 1. The true citizens of Zion, described here in the two preceding verses, much as the true citizens of Zion are described in the 15th psalm and Ps. 24:3–5; and 2. Sinners in Zion, spoken of in the 14th verse. Of the former it is said, "Thine eyes shall see the king in his beauty," i.e. thou that art spoken of in the immediately foregoing words. "They shall see the land that is very far off," i.e. they that were spoken of before. There is an evident antithesis in the words, as they are opposite kinds of persons that are spoken of; so they are opposite things that are predicated of them. The one should see "the land that is very far off," i.e. should be led away captive thither, as it was threatened to the children of Israel if they were not obedient, that they should be driven out of their own land, and carried captive into a very far country. Deut. 28:49, "The Lord shall bring a nation against thee from far, from the end of the earth." And v. 64, "And the Lord shall scatter thee among all people, from one end of the earth even unto the other." And this is a judgment often threatened by the prophets to the wicked Israelites, and is threatened by this prophet in particular (Is. 5:26). Is. 13:5, "They come from a far country, from the end of heaven, even the Lord, and the weapons of his indignation, to destroy the whole land." But the other should "see the king in his beauty." This is here spoken of as the opposite to a being carried away into a far country. The literal and next meaning seems to be this, that while the sinners in Zion are cast out of Zion, and out of their own land to the ends of the earth, and made slaves to a foreign prince, thou shalt dwell peaceably and quietly in the land of Israel and in Zion (The true citizens of Zion shall abide in Zion, Ps. 15:1.), under the peaceable and happy government of thine own prince, the king of Zion, the king that sits in the throne of David, who had his palace in Zion. Thou shalt see the king that reigns in Zion in his beauty, reigning and governing his people in great glory and prosperity; and thou shalt enjoy the blessings of his prosperous and glorious reign. Beauty is often put for glory and prosperity, as Is. 28:1, and Ezek. 27:3–4, 11, and 28:12, 17, as v. 20 of this context. Thou shalt

2. This cross-reference is a later addition.

"see Jerusalem a quiet habitation," i.e. thou shalt enjoy the blessings of its safe and quiet state; as Ps. 128:5–6, "Thou shalt see the good of Jerusalem, . . . and thou shalt see peace upon Israel." The blessing here promised to the righteous in Israel seems to be the same with that which the queen of Sheba observed in Solomon's servants. II Chron. 9:7, "Happy are thy men, and happy are these thy servants, which stand continually before thee."

But although what the prophet here alludes to in the punishment threatened to the sinners in Zion be the captivity into Babylon, and what he alludes to in the reward promised to the righteous be the dwelling under the safe, and quiet, and prosperous government of their own king that sat on the throne of David, which was in Zion, yet the things chiefly meant are spiritual things that are typified by those temporal things; for there never was literally any such distinction made between the wicked and righteous Israelites, as is here spoken of, for when the Jews were carried away into Babylon, there was no king left reigning in Zion in peace and prosperity, but it was a time of universal calamity throughout the whole land. Therefore by being carried captive into a land very far off seems to be intended chiefly the eternal rejection and banishment of hypocrites, who though they for the present dwell in Zion in God's church amongst his people, yet the time will come when they shall be removed at the utmost distance from it, and shall be sent into eternal banishment. And by the king that is here spoken of, that the true citizens of Zion shall see in his beauty, is meant Jesus Christ, even David their king, as he is called (Jer. 30:9; and Hos. 3:5), the king spoken of in the beginning of the foregoing chapter, and everywhere throughout this book. They shall behold him in his beauty, and shall enjoy the blessings of his kingdom of grace here, and hereafter shall forever dwell in his presence, and see his face, and rejoice in his kingdom of glory.

215. II SAMUEL 24:9; I CHRONICLES 21:5. Concerning the seeming difference in the amount of the number of Israel when David numbered them in Samuel and in Chronicles, see Bedford, p. 559, *Scripture Chronology*. "The number of all Israel in the book of Chronicles were eleven hundred thousand men (I Chron. 21:5), and the book of Samuel saith that they were only eight hundred thousand (II Sam. 24:9), so that here are three hundred thousand difference. On the other hand, the book of Samuel saith that the men of Judah were five hundred thousand (II Sam. 24:9), and the book of Chronicles saith that they

were only four hundred and seventy thousand [I Chron. 21:5], so that
here also is thirty thousand difference. For the reconciling this great
and double diversity, it is to be observed that there were four and
twenty thousand soldiers and officers that attended David monthly, so
many every month (I Chron. 27:1–16); and these make in all two
hundred and eighty-eight thousand. These were like a standing guard
about the king every month, and ready for any sudden expedition.
There were besides these the rulers of the tribes, and the officers
under them, and therefore allowing a thousand officers to every
twenty-four thousand (as we cannot well allow less), there will be the
twelve thousand wanting, which added to the two hundred and eighty-
eight thousand, make just three hundred thousand; and these were
not put into the account in Samuel. Thus in the tribe of Judah, if
twenty-four thousand legionary soldiers and a thousand officers over
them be added to the four hundred and seventy thousand, there will
be but five thousand wanting in the number; and as this was David's
own tribe, which was faithful to him in all difficulties and troubles, it is
no wonder if so many of them were employed in some other extraordinary offices. These Joab put not into the account, because their number and list had been long known, and because the king would not put
a tax upon his own servants."[3]

216. II SAMUEL 23:1–5. These last words of David seem to be wholly
a prophecy of the Messiah. He begins as the prophets were wont to
begin their mystical speeches about things to come. "The spirit of the
Lord spake by me, and his word was in my tongue. The God of Israel
said, the Rock of Israel spake to me." He begins much after the manner
that Balaam began his two last prophecies (Num. 24), wherein he
prophesied of Israel's future happiness, and spake particularly of
Christ. What is here rendered, "He that ruleth over men must be just,"
might better be translated, "He that shall rule over men shall be just."
The words in the original are מוֹשֵׁל בָּאָדָם צַדִּיק. The two first words are
literally translated, "the ruler over men," or "the person ruling over
men," and may be referred to time present, past, or to come, indifferently. "Must be" is supplied in our translation; the word "just" only
is expressed in the original. And we may as well and better supply
"shall be just" than "must be," for the verb "is," or "be," is more frequently understood in either of the tenses than "must be" or "ought to
be." That he should rule "in the fear of the Lord" is agreeable to the

---

3. Bedford, *Scripture Chronology,* p. 559.

character of the Messiah given in Is. 11:1–3, where he is prophesied of, as he is here, as the branch of the stock or house of David; and that prophecy is very parallel to this. "And there shall come forth a rod out of the stem of Jesse, and a branch shall grow out of his roots. And the spirit of the Lord shall rest upon him, the spirit of wisdom and understanding, the spirit of counsel and might, the spirit of knowledge and of the fear of the Lord, and shall make him of quick understanding in the fear of the Lord." He is called "He that is to rule over men," rather than "He that is to rule over Israel," because when he comes, his kingdom should not be confined to that one people, but he should reign over all nations, and to the utmost ends of the earth; to him the gathering of the people should be [Gen. 49:10], and men should be blessed in him, and all nations should call him blessed [Ps. 72:17].

'Tis the Messiah that is intended, that "shall be as the light of the morning, when the sun riseth, even a morning without clouds, and as the tender grass springing out of the earth by clear shining after rain." Christ is both as the rain and the sun that causes the grass to grow, and also as the grass itself that flourishes under the benign influence of those. The person of Christ as head of the church is as the morning sun arising after a night of darkness, or as the clear sun breaking out of a thick cloud shining on the tender grass. Christ mystical, or Christ in his members, is "as the tender grass itself, springing out of the earth by clear shining after rain." This signifies both the glory and blessedness of his reign.

1. It signifies his prosperity and glory as a king. The springing and flourishing of grass is a simile elsewhere used to express the glory and prosperity. Ps. 92:7, "Though the wicked do grow[4] as the grass, and all the workers of iniquity do flourish," etc. So Job. 5:25, "Thou shalt know that thy seed shall be great, and thine offspring as the grass of the earth." So here the same is promised of the seed or offspring of David. Christ in his state of humiliation was a tender plant, and a root out of a dry ground, having no form nor comeliness; but when he rose from the earth, God made him to spring as the grass out of the earth. And after his resurrection, he was a glorious, and flourishing, and most fruitful branch, as is prophesied of the branch of the stock of David. Is. 4:2, "In that day shall the branch of the Lord be beautiful and glorious, and the fruit of the earth shall be excellent and comely." Jer. 23:5, "Behold, the days come, saith the Lord, that I will raise unto

---

4. Conjecture for unclear word. The KJV reads "spring."

David a righteous branch, and a king shall reign and prosper." And so in many other places, wherever Christ is prophesied of under the appellation of the branch, he seems to be spoken of as a flourishing branch. David here in his last words comforts himself in the respect of the glorious prosperity of his offspring.

2. Hereby is signified the happiness of his kingdom, not only the glory of the king, but the happiness of those that enjoy the blessings of his reign, which is still the prosperity of Christ mystical. Ps. 72:6–7, "He shall come down like rain on the mown grass, as showers that water the earth. In his days shall the righteous flourish."

Verse 5. "Although my house be not so with God; yet he hath made with me an everlasting covenant, ordered in all things, and sure, for this is all my salvation, and all my desire, although he made it not to grow." "My house," that is, my offspring, my posterity, those of my family that are to succeed me in the throne. We often find the posterity of David called the "house of David," though my successors and offspring be not just, and don't rule in the fear of God (as David by the Spirit foresaw that they would not), though they ben't "as the light of the morning," and "as the tender grass springing out of the earth." "Though he make it not to grow," i.e. "my house," for that he was speaking of. 'Tis the same, in other words, that was expressed in the first clause of the verse, "though my house be not so with God." And there is special reference had to the last clause of the preceding verse, where it was foretold that the Messiah should be "as the tender grass springing out of the earth." "Though my house or offspring be not so," be not made to grow as the grass; the house or lineage of David seems here to be spoken of under the figure of the root or stock of a plant, as a family or race is often so called in Scripture. Judg. 5:14, "Out of Ephraim was there a root of them against Amalek." Is. 14:29, "Out of the serpent's root shall come forth a cockatrice," i.e. the serpent's race or offspring; and so v. 30, "I will kill thy root with famine, and he shall slay thy remnant." Dan. 11:7, "Out of a branch of her root shall one stand up," i.e. one of her posterity. And so Hos. 9:16, "Ephraim is smitten, their root is dried up, they shall bear no fruit; yea, though they bring forth, yet will I slay the beloved fruit of the womb." The family or lineage of Jesse or David is particularly in the prophecies of the Messiah compared to the root or stem of a plant, as in the forementioned Is. 11:1–2. "And there shall come forth a rod out of the stem of Jesse, and a branch shall grow out of his roots."

And to these last words of David, all the prophets seem to refer to when they prophesy of Christ under the name of the Branch, for he is here prophesied of[5] "as the tender grass springing out of the earth"; and the lineage of David seems to be spoken of under the figure of a root or stock. And when it is said, "though he make it not to grow,"[6] the word signifies "to grow as a branch." It might have been translated, "though he make it not to branch forth." The word here used is of the same radix as the word used when Christ is prophesied of as the Branch. The word that is translated "branch" is צֶמַח, and the verb that signifies "to grow" is צָמַח, which is the verb here used. David here foresaw that God would not make his root or stock to grow in his successors that should reign in the kingdom of Judah. And therefore, with reference to this, the prophet Jeremiah foretelling of Christ, says, Jer. 33:15, "In those days, and at that time, I will cause the Branch of righteousness to grow up unto David; and he shall execute judgment and righteousness in the land." His being called a "righteous Branch," and his executing judgment and justice in the land, seems to be with reference to David's last words, where it is said, "He shall be just, ruling in the fear of the Lord" [II Sam. 23:3]. So Jer. 23:5, "Behold, the days come, saith the Lord, that I will raise up unto David a righteous Branch, and a king shall reign and prosper, and shall execute judgment and justice in the earth."

217. II SAMUEL 24:18–25; AND I CHRONICLES 21:18–22:1. The temple and altar, where those sacrifices were to be offered that were typical of the sacrifice of Christ, were by God's order erected on a threshing floor, a place where wheat was wont to be threshed that it might become bread to support men's life. The wheat that was here threshed, or the bread that was made of it, seems to be typical of Christ, that bread which came down from heaven, who is often typically represented by bread, by flour, and wheat. See note on II Kgs. 4:41.[7] And the threshing of this wheat to prepare it for our food seems to represent the sufferings of Christ, by which he was prepared to be our spiritual food.[8] And therefore this very wheat that was threshed on this floor was the first meat offering that was offered to God on the

---

5. MS: "out."

6. כִּי־לֹא יַצְמִיחַ.

7. In the "Blank Bible" JE writes, "Wheat and other corn is often made use as a type of Christ. It was so in the sheaf of the first fruits, and in the first fruits of wheat harvest, in the wave loaves offered at Pentecost, and in all their meat offerings. Christ compares himself to a corn of wheat which, except it die, abideth alone; and how often is Christ compared to bread. This meal was corn ground to powder; so Christ, before we can be healed by him, must suffer to the greatest extremity."

8. JE deleted "So that this place, before the temple was built on it, was a place where the sufferings of Christ were typified."

altar that was built in this place. And the threshing instruments, that were typical of the instruments of Christ's sufferings, in being the instruments wherewith the corn was threshed, is made use of as the fuel for the fire, in which David offers sacrifice in this place; and the fire in which that very wheat that they had threshed was burnt, and the same oxen that in that place were wont to labor in treading out the corn, were the first sacrifice that was there offered, so that before they were sacrificed on the altar, they in their labors in that place were typical of Christ, who underwent such great labors to procure bread for our souls. And they were sacrificed for men there, in that very place where they were wont to labor for the good of men, as Christ was crucified in that very land where he had laboriously spent his life for the good of men, and where his goodness had been so distinguishingly manifested for so many ages, and in that very city, Jerusalem, where he had especially labored, and which city had been for many ages distinguished by his goodness above all others in the world. Those oxen were sacrificed in a fire that was made of their own instruments, their own yokes, and other instruments that they had borne (II Sam. 24:22), as Christ carried his own cross.

218. ISAIAH 30:27–31:9. Mr. Bedford supposes (*Scripture Chronology*, p. 671) that what is here said respects the time when Rabshakeh came against Jerusalem, and God did so wonderfully appear for the defense of the city, and miraculously slew such a multitude of their enemies in one night. Is. 30:28, 'Tis said that "his breath, as an overflowing stream, should reach to the midst of the neck," i.e. should reduce them to the utmost extremity. This is very agreeable to the manner in which Dr. Prideaux very probably supposes that Rabshakeh's army was destroyed, viz. by God's bringing on them "an hot pestilential wind." See *Connection*, pp. 34–35.[9] And when it is said here that "there shall be a bridle in the jaws of the people, causing them to err," this is agreeable to what is said concerning Rabshakeh and his army (Is. 37:29). 'Tis here said, v. 29, that they should "have a song, as in the night when an holy assembly is kept, and gladness of heart, as when one goeth with a pipe to come into the mountain of the Lord, to the Mighty One of Israel." And God wrought this great deliverance by slaying Sennacherib's army in the night, as before he had done in Egypt by slaying the firstborn in the night, and thereby gave occasion

---

9. Humphrey Prideaux, *The Old and New Testament Connected in the History of the Jews and Neighbouring Nations, from the Declension of the Kingdoms of Israel and Judah to the Time of Christ*, Pt. I, Vol. 1 (10th ed., London, 1729), pp. 34–35.

to keep the night of the passover in a joyful manner, and with songs of praise, which probably was the "holy solemnity" that the prophet had a special respect to, as Bedford supposes.[1] What is said in the 30th verse, together with the 32nd, of "battles of shaking," renders it probable that there was an earthquake accompanying that judgment, and also thunder, and lightning, and hail, as was common when God miraculously fought against the enemies of his people, as it was when [he] fought against Pharaoh and the Egyptians at the Red Sea (Ps. 77:15–20). So God fought against the Amorites in Joshua's time, not only with hail, but thunder and lightning (Hab. 3:11). So God seems to have fought against Sisera and his host. (See note on Judg. 5:20.)[2] So God fought against the Philistines in Samuel's time. So God seems to have fought sometimes for David against his enemies, and particularly at Baal-perazim. (See notes on Ps. 18:7–15.)[3] So Hannah prophesied that God would appear against the enemies of his people (I Sam. 2:10). Thunder, lightning, hail, and rain is God's artillery, that he was wont to make use of when he appeared in battle. Job 38:22–23, "Hast thou entered into the treasures of the snow, or hast thou seen the treasures of the hail, which I have reserved against the time of trouble, against the day of battle and war?" 'Tis probable that the greater part of them might be slain by such a sudden and extraordinary pestilence while asleep, and that God might pursue the rest that awoke and escaped the pestilence with a tempest of thunder, lightning, and hail, till the greater part of them were destroyed. And what is said,[4] v. 32, seems to be much better translated in the margin,[5] viz. "In every passing of the rod founded,[6] which the Lord shall cause to rest upon him, it shall be with tabrets and harps." This translation is word for word, as it is in the original,[7] meaning the rod of God's anger on the Assyrian. In the foregoing verse with this, 'tis foretold that the Assyrian, that beat down others with his rod, should be beaten down in his turn with God's rod.

1. Bedford, *Scripture Chronology*, p. 671.
2. I.e. No. 211.
3. In the "Blank Bible" JE began his entry: "The things here spoken of God probably had [been] at sometime or times literally accomplished for David and against his enemies. He had at sometime wondrously appeared on David's side in the time of battle, and fought against his enemies when they were too strong for him, and he cried unto him, with mighty thunder [and] lightning."
4. JE deleted "V. 33 seems well to agree with the place where this great destruction was, viz. Tophet, or the valley of the son of Hinnom."
5. I.e. of the KJV.
6. KJV: "grounded staff."
7. כֹּל מַעֲבַר מַטֵּה מוּסָדָה.

And thus to speak of the "rod of God's anger" is agreeable to the phraseology of Scripture, particularly to call a judgment that God had appointed, a "rod that God had founded or established," and to express his subjecting them to the judgment, by God's "causing the rod to rest upon them," and to call the smiting with the rod at each stripe to be "the passings of the rod." We read of these passings of the rod (Is. 28:18–19).[8] And when it is said, "it shall be with tabrets and harps," the meaning is that when God's people shall behold the punishment which he shall bring upon [the Assyrians], it shall cause joy and songs in them, agreeable to v. 29. They shall as it were lift up the voice of music and joy at every time, as they hear the voice or sound of God's avenging rod on their enemies, which is agreeable to what is said with respect to this very judgment on Rabshakeh's army (Is. 37:22).

And what is said, v. 33, seems well to agree with the place where this great destruction was, viz. "Tophet, or the valley of the son of Hinnom, which was near Jerusalem on the south side, whither Rabshakeh came from Lachish, Libnah, and Cush, and where he encamped before he could form the siege of the place," as Bedford observes.[9]

The time when they were thus threatened by Sennacherib and Rabshakeh was a time when they relied on Egypt for help, as appears by the words of Rabshakeh (Is. 36:6–9), which agrees with the beginning of the 31st chapter. And what is said in the 4th, 5th, and 8th verses of that chapter exceedingly agrees with the way in which God did by himself, immediately, without making use of the sword of men, defend and fight for Jerusalem. And what is said in the 9th verse, of the Assyrian's passing "over to his stronghold for fear," agrees with what is said, Is. 37:7, 29, 34, and 37.

219. MATTHEW 23:34–35. "Wherefore, behold, I send unto you prophets, and wise men, and scribes; and some of them ye shall kill and crucify, and some of them ye shall scourge in your synagogues, and persecute them from city to city, that upon you may come all the righteous blood shed upon the earth, from the blood of righteous Abel unto the blood of Zacharias son of Barachias, whom ye slew between the temple and the altar." The learned Bedford in his *Scripture Chronology*, speaking of Zechariah, the son of Jehoiada, whose murder in the court of the temple we have account of (II Chron. 24:20–22), says, "There are some of good authority, who look upon this Zechariah to be

8. This sentence is a later interlineation.
9. Bedford, *Scripture Chronology*, p. 671.

the person of whom our Savior spake in this place. But," says [Bedford],

> as our Savior begins with Abel the first instance, so we may suppose that he concluded with the last. And as he here speaks of future things, so this may be one instance among the rest; and the naming the name of both father and son is such an instance of his knowledge, the like whereof was never given by any other. We may therefore conclude, that the Zecharias, which our Savior speaks of, was one whom Josephus mentions in the time of the Jewish wars, and of whom he gives us this account, that he was the son of Baruch, a man of the first rank, a friend to all good men, and an enemy to the wicked, a man who had very great authority, virtue, and wealth. This Zecharias the Zealots looked upon as a man so very popular, that they themselves could not be safe, without taking away his life. For this purpose they bring him before a court of their own setting up, and falsely accuse him of a conspiracy to betray Jerusalem to the Romans, and treating with Vespasian about it. When the court, contrary to their own expectation, had declared him innocent, two of the greatest ruffians of the company fall outrageously upon Zecharias, and murder him in the middle of the temple, with this insolent raillery in their mouths, "Now we have given you your discharge too, and you are much surer of this, than you were of the other." And so they cast his body down the precipice of the mountain.[1]

220. The accounts of the four evangelists concerning the resurrection of Christ reconciled.[2] In the first place, "there was a great earthquake. An angel of the Lord descended from heaven, and came and rolled back the stone from the door, and sat upon it. His appearance was like lightning, and his raiment white as snow; and for fear of him the keepers did shake, and became as dead men" (Matt. 28:2–4). And presently, as soon as their extraordinary surprise would allow 'em, they ran away into the city. And then, soon after they were gone, Mary Magdalene, from her extraordinary affection, came to see the sepulcher before the other women, "while it was yet dark, and sees the stone taken away from the sepulcher," and finds not the body there, and "then runneth, and cometh to Simon Peter and the other disciple

1. Ibid., p. 641.
2. JE deleted "Calvary the place where the sepul According to Mr. Prince, Calvary, the place where the sepulcer was, was about a mile from Jerusalem. In the first place."

whom Jesus loved, and saith unto them, They have taken away the Lord out of the sepulcher, and we know not where they have laid him." Then Peter and John came running to the sepulcher, and Mary returns with them, or comes after them as fast as she could. Peter and John went into the sepulcher, and see the linen clothes lying, but found not the body of Christ, and not knowing what to make of things, went away again [John 20:1–10]. Mr. Prince supposes that Luke speaks of this coming of Peter to the sepulcher in [the] 24th chapter of his gospel, 12th verse, and supposes the word should have been rendered thus, "Now Peter also had risen, and ran to the sepulcher, and stooping down, saw the linen clothes lying by themselves, and departed, wondering in himself at what was done."[3] But when they was gone, Mary stayed behind, and would not go away; she probably stayed, waiting for the company of women that she expected would presently come with spices to anoint the body. But as she stood there weeping, "she stooped down, and looked into the sepulcher, and sees two angels in white sitting, one at the head, and the other at the feet, where the body of Jesus had lain." They speak to her, and ask her why she wept? She answers, "Because they have taken away my Lord, and I know not where they have laid him. And when she had thus said, she turned herself back, and saw Jesus standing, and knew not that it was Jesus (probably because the twilight was yet dim). Jesus asked her why she wept. "She, supposing him to be the gardener, says to him, Sir, if thou have borne him hence, tell me where thou hast laid him, and I will take him away. Jesus saith to her, Mary." And she then knew him, and worships him. Christ bids her go, and inform his disciples, etc., on which Mary went away in haste to tell his disciples, and did not wait till the women came with the spices, as she intended (Mark 16:9–11; John 20:1–19).

The other women that were concerned in the design of anointing the body of Jesus, they meet together in order to go to the sepulcher

3.[Nathan Prince], *An Essay to Solve the Difficulties that attend the Several Accounts given by the Evangelists of Our Saviour's Resurrection and His Appearances to his Followers on the day He rose. Wherein the Opinion of the most celebrated Harmonists and Commentators whether Protestants or Papists, of our own Nation or Foreigners are impartially represented and examined* (Boston, 1734), p. 3. Prince (1698–1748), identified on the title page as "a Fellow of Harvard College," served as a tutor at Harvard from 1723–42. In the *Essay* he acknowledges the assistance of Judah Monis, a rabbinically-trained Jew who taught Hebrew at Harvard beginning in 1722 and who converted to Christianity in that same year (Thomas J. Siegel, "Professor Stephen Sewall and the Transformation of Hebrew at Harvard," in Shalom Goldman, ed., *Hebrew and the Bible in America: The First Two Centuries* [Hanover, Univ. Press of New England, 1993], pp. 230–31).

about break of day, and come to the sepulcher about sunrise, after Mary Magdalene was gone, whom they had not seen, nor she them. "And they said among themselves, Who shall roll us away the stone from the door of the sepulcher?" And when they came, they found "that the stone was rolled away" (Mark 16:2–4). And Luke 24:1–2, "And they entered in" (the angel now not appearing on the stone), "and found not the body of Jesus there, and while they were much perplexed thereabout, behold, two men stood by them in shining garments." And one of them, of a distinguished brightness and glorious appearance, being the same, the glory and majesty of whose appearance had so terrified the keepers, he sat "on the right side, clothed in a long white garment" (Matt. 28:4–5; Luke 24:3–4; Mark 16:5). This angel on the right side is he that speaks to them, saying, Fear ye not; I know that ye seek Jesus of Nazareth, who was crucified. Why seek ye the living among the dead? He is not here, for he is risen, as he said. Come, see the place where the Lord lay; and remember how he spake unto you while he was yet in Galilee, saying, The Son of man must be delivered into the hands of sinful men, and be crucified, and the third day rise again. But go your way quickly, tell his disciples and Peter that he goeth before you into Galilee; there shall ye see him, as he said unto you. Lo, I have told you" (Matt. 28:5–7; Mark 16:6–7; Luke 24:5–7).[4] "And they remembered his words, and they came out quickly, and fled from the sepulcher; for they trembled and were amazed, nor said they anything to anyone, for they were affrighted. They came out with fear and great joy, and they ran to bring his disciples word" (Matt. 28:8; Mark 16:8; Luke 24:8). "And as they went to bring his disciples word, lo, Jesus met them, saying, All hail. And they came to him, and held him by the feet, and worshiped him. Then said Jesus unto them, Be not afraid. Go tell my brethren that they go into Galilee, and there shall they see me" (Matt. 28:9–10). "And they returned from the sepulcher, and told all these things unto the eleven, and to all the rest" [Luke 24:9].

221. Amos 1:6–13. The injuriousness and cruelty of the Philistines, Tyrians, and Edomites towards the children of Israel, that is here spoken of, and for which God's judgments are by the prophet denounced against them, seem to have been acted at the time that those things were done, that we read of in II Chron. 21:8–10, 16–17, and 22:1. The judgments spoken of concerning the Philistines seem

4. This account is a composite from the three synoptic gospels.

in part to have been fulfilled before the prophecy of Amos, in what we have an account of, II Chron. 26:6–7, when Uzziah, king of Judah, "went forth and warred against the Philistines, and brake down the wall of Gath, and the wall of Jabneh, and the wall of Ashdod, and built cities about Ashdod, and among the Philistines," and his God helped, so that he was successful. Accordingly the words of the prophecy may be interpreted, "And I have sent a fire upon the wall of Gaza, and have cut off the inhabitants from Ashdod." And as the prophets frequently speak of things to come in the same manner as if they were past or present, so it was further fulfilled in the time of Hezekiah, who "smote the Philistines, even unto Gaza, and the borders thereof, from the tower of the watchmen to the fenced cities" (II Kgs. 18:8), or both in town and country, where they built little cottages, where they watched their flocks by night. And therefore the prophet Isaiah bids the Philistines not to rejoice, because the rod that smote them was broken, or Uzziah was dead, who had sorely afflicted them (Is. 14:29–32); for Hezekiah should come out of his root, or be descended from him, who should more grievously gall them. And it was more fully completed, when Sennacherib, king of Assyria, marched against Egypt; and the better to open his way into that country, he sent Tartan, one of his generals, before him, who fought against Ashdod, and took it. Secondly, the prophet Amos prophesieth also against Tyre for this reason, that God would "send a fire upon the wall of Tyrus, which should devour the palaces thereof." This was also fulfilled when Shalmaneser, king of Assyria, made war upon Tyre in the reign of Elulaeus their king, and having sent an army, invaded the whole country of Phoenicia; and taking it very heinously to see the Tyrians to be the only people who disputed his authority, he sent a large fleet against them, which being beaten, the king of Assyria returns, and sets guards along the river, and upon all springs and aqueducts to keep the Tyrians from water, which distress continued for five years, when they were forced to relieve themselves by pits of their own digging. After this Nebuchadnezzar, continuing a long and terrible siege of thirteen years, made himself master of it; who finding but little spoil therein to reward his soldiers for their great pains, was so inflamed with anger, that he razed the whole town to the ground, and slew all that he found therein, from which time it nevermore recovered in glory. But the city on the island became the Tyre, which was afterwards so famous, and this was ever after a village called by the name of Old Tyre. And lastly, the prophet for the same reasons foretells the destruction of Edom, that God would "send a fire upon Teman," their capital city, which should "devour the palaces of Bozrah," a city in the confines of Moab. This seems first to have been fulfilled when Shalmaneser, king of Assyria, came against Samaria, and having conquered the country of Moab, ravaged and destroyed the country of Edom, the neighboring kingdom, the better to secure himself from any disturbance on that side. And also when Sennacherib, king of Assyria, went with his forces into Egypt; for the same reason that induced him to send Tartan into Ashdod, would induce him to overrun all Idumaea, which lay directly in his way, and would open a freer communication with his own country. And after this the army of Nebuchadnezzar ransacked the country, when Tyre was taken, and when he marched into Egypt, and his soldiers were hungry for want of plunder, as it had been foretold by the prophets Obadiah (throughout his prophecy) and Jeremiah (49:7–23), when the accomplishment thereof was nearer at hand.

Bedford, *Scripture Chronology*, pp. 633–34.

222. II CHRONICLES 22:1–2. "So Ahaziah, the son of Jehoram, king of Judah reigned. Forty and two years old was Ahaziah when he began to reign." Here a great difficulty ariseth. "For whereas Joram[5] was thirty and two years old when he began to reign, and he reigned eight years in Jerusalem, and so he died when he was forty years old, and immediately the inhabitants of Jerusalem set Ahaziah upon his throne, who was his youngest son; yet this Ahaziah was forty-two years old when he began to reign, and so he will prove to be two years older than his father.

"*Answer.* The book of Chronicles doth not mean in this place, that Ahaziah was so old, when he began to reign, for the book of Kings tells us plainly, that he was twenty-two at that time. So that those forty-two years have reference to another thing, particularly to the house of Omri, and not the age of Ahaziah. For if we count from the beginning of the reign of Omri, we shall find that Ahaziah entered into his reign in the two and fortieth year from thence. The original words therefore

5. Joram and Jehoram were the same person.

are not to be translated, as we render them, 'Ahaziah was two and forty years old,' but 'Ahaziah was the son of the two and forty years.' And this was anciently observed in that history among the Jews called 'Seder Olam,' or 'The Order of the World.' Now the reason why his reign is dated differently from all the rest of the kings of Judah is because he did according to all the wickedness of the house of Omri; for Athaliah, his mother, was Ahab's daughter, and she both perverted her husband Joram, and brought up this her son Ahaziah in all the idolatry of that wicked house. And therefore Ahaziah is not thought fit to be reckoned by the line of the kings of Judah [and of the house of David, and the ancestors of Christ],[6] but by the house of Omri and Ahab. Thus a particular mark is set upon Joram by the evangelist Matthew, who leaves out the three succeeding generations, viz. Ahaziah, Joash, and Amaziah, and mentions Uzziah as the next. Here the three descents are omitted, according to what the Psalmist saith, Ps. 37:28, 'The seed of the wicked shall be cut off.' See the letter ע, which is the last letter of זֶרַע, 'the seed,' and of רָשָׁע,[7] 'the wicked,' cut out of that acrostical and alphabetical psalm in that very place. Dr. Lightfoot, Vol. 1, p. 417, saith, 'That this omission is most divinely done from the threatening of the Second Commandment, "Thou shalt not commit idolatry, for I visit the sins of the fathers on the children unto the third and fourth generation" [Ex. 20:4–5].[8] It is the manner of Scripture very often to leave out men's names from certain stories and records, to show a distaste at some evil in them. Thus all Cain's posterity is blotted out of the book of Chronicles, as it was out of the world by the flood. So Simeon is omitted in Moses' blessing (Deut. 33:6–25), for his cruelty at Shechem and to Joseph. So Dan [and Ephraim][9] at the sealing of the Lord's people (Rev. 7:4–8), because of idolatry, which began in the tribe of Dan (Judg. 18:30–31) [and afterwards had its principal seat in the tribe of Ephraim].[1] So Joab from among David's worthies (II Sam. 23), because of his bloodiness to Abner and Amasa. And such another close intimation of God's displeasure at the wickedness of Joram is to be seen, II Chron. 22:1–2, where the reign of his son Ahaziah is not dated according to the custom and manner of the other kings of Judah, but by the style of the continuance of the house of Omri.'

6. JE's brackets and insertion.
7. JE incorrectly wrote צָרַע, the Hebrew for "leper" or "leprosy."
8. JE is citing Lightfoot from Bedford.
9. JE's brackets and insertion.
1. Ibid.

"And Ahaziah, alone among all the kings of Israel, might be reckoned in this manner, because in his time the whole house of Ahab was cut off by Jehu, after the battle at the field of Naboth the Jezreelite, where Joram, the last king of Israel of the house of Ahab or Omri, was slain; and Ahaziah was slain with him, and two and forty of his brethren perished with the house of Ahab."[2] (This, I suppose, is from Bedford.) 'Tis not unusual in Scripture to mention a number of years or a certain date without expressing the epocha; so in Ezek. 1:1, 8:1, 20:1, 24:1, 26:1, 29:1, 31:1, 32:1, 29:17, 30:20. That Hebrew phrase, "the son of (so many) years," don't always signify the person's being so old. As, for instance, I Sam. 13:1, "Saul reigned one year"; in the original it is, "Saul was the son of one year."

It may be noted further, that the Scripture, in dating kings' reigns, don't always make the person's birth the epoch from whence the date is taken, as concerning Absalom, II Sam. 15:7. See also *Synopsis Criticorum* on II Kgs. 24:8.[3]

223. JUDGES 11:30–40. Concerning JEPHTHAH's Vow and his offering up his daughter.[4] That Jephthah did not put his daughter to death and[5] burn her in sacrifice, the following things evince.

I. The tenor of his vow, if we suppose it to be a lawful vow, did not oblige him to it. He promised that whatsoever come forth of the doors of his house to meet him, should surely be the Lord's, and he would offer it up for a burnt offering. He was obliged to no more by this vow than only to deal with whatsoever come forth of the doors of his house to meet him, as those things that were holy to the Lord, and by right burnt offerings to God were to be dealt with, by God's own law and the rules that he had given. Supposing it had been an ass, or some unclean beast had come forth to meet him, as Jephthah did not know but it would, his vow would not have obliged him to have offered it in sacrifice, or actually to have made a burnt offering of it. But he must have

---

2. Bedford, *Scripture Chronology*, p. 599.

3. This paragraph and the previous passage beginning with the parenthetical reference to Bedford are a later addition. Matthew Poole's exposition of II Kgs. 24:8 lists several ways of dealing with conflicting chronological data in II Chron. 36:9, such as attributing it to a scribal error or making the point of reference the reign of Jehoiachin's father, or perhaps even the reign of Nebuchadnezzar. Poole finds similar expressions elsewhere in the Bible. See *Synopsis Criticorum aliorumque Sacrae Scripturae Interpretum*, (4 pts. in 5 vols., London, 1669–76), *I*, Pt. II, cols. 708–09.

4. JE wrote "No. 223. Jephthah's Vow" as a running head on the pages of this entry.

5. JE deleted "actually."

dealt with it, as the law of God directed to deal with an unclean beast that was holy to the Lord, and that otherwise must have been actually a burnt offering to the Lord, had it not been for that legal incapacity of the impurity of its nature. All living things that were consecrated were to be as it were burnt offerings to God, i.e. they were actually to be offered up a burnt sacrifice, if not of a nature that rendered it incapable of this, and then in that case something else was to be done that God would accept instead of offering it up a burnt sacrifice. The direction we have in Lev. 27:11–13, "And if it be any unclean beast, of which they do not offer a sacrifice unto the Lord, then he shall present the beast before the priest; and the priest shall value it, whether it be good or bad. As thou valuest it, who art the priest, so shall it be. But if he will at all redeem it, then he shall add a fifth part thereunto of thy estimation"; i.e. it should be valued by the priest, and the man should, after it was valued, determine whether he would redeem it, or no. And if not, he was to break his neck if an ass (Ex. 13:12–13); or if other unclean beast, it must be sold according to the priest's estimation, Lev. 27:27 (as is elsewhere directed to be done to unclean beasts that were holy to the Lord, Ex. 34:20). But if he would redeem it, if it were an ass, he was to redeem it with a lamb (Ex. 13:12–13); if other unclean beast, he was to add the fifth part to the priest's estimation, that is, he was to give the value of the beast, and a fifth part more.[6] And if Jephthah had done this in case an unclean beast had met him, he would have done according to his vow. If he had, in such a case, gone about to have offered an unclean beast as a burnt sacrifice, he would dreadfully have provoked God. His vow could be supposed to oblige him to no other than only to deal with the unclean beast that was consecrated, as the law of God directed to deal with it, instead of offering it a burnt offering. And so when it was his daughter that met him, he might do to her according to his vow, without making her a burnt sacrifice, if he did that to her which the law of God directed to be done to a dedicated person, instead of actually making them a burnt sacrifice, by reason of the incapacity which, by the mercy of God, attends a human person to be a burnt sacrifice. For to offer either a man or an unclean beast in sacrifice to God are both mentioned as a great abomination to God, and as what were universally known so to be. Is. 66:3, "He that killeth an ox is as if he slew a man; he that sacrificeth a lamb, as if he cut off a dog's neck; he that offereth an oblation, as if he offered swine's blood." But the more

---

6. JE deleted "the prefix ו, which is rendered by the particle 'but' in the 13th verse, this would have obscured the sense less if it had been ~~tra~~ rendered 'and.'"

fully to clear up the difficulties that attend this matter, I will particu-lar[ly] observe some things concerning the laws, that related to persons that were consecrated so as to become holy to the Lord.[7]

First. Every living thing that was holy to the Lord, whether of man or beast, was by right a burnt offering to God, and must be either actually made a burnt sacrifice, or something else must be done to it, that God appointed to be in lieu of burning it in sacrifice. Thus the firstborn of man and beast, they were all holy to the Lord,. and must either be offered up a burnt sacrifice, or to be redeemed. The firstborn of men and of unclean beasts were to be redeemed.

Second. Persons that were devoted to God by a singular vow (unless they were those that were devoted to be accursed, of which, Lev. 27:28–29), were to be brought and presented before the Lord, that the priest might estimate them; and they were to [be] redeemed according to the priest's estimation. But beasts that might be sacrificed were to be sanctified (Lev. 27:7–9). See *Synopsis Criticorum* on v. 2.[8]

Third. Persons that were thus devoted to God by the vow of their parents were yet to remain persons separate, and set apart for God, after they were redeemed; and this may appear by several things.

1. The redemption was only to redeem them from being slain in sacrifice; it was not to redeem them from being holy to the Lord, or persons set apart and sanctified to him.

2. The firstborn were appointed to [be] given or consecrated to God (Ex. 13:2 and 23:19); and they were by God's law holy to the Lord, in the very same manner as persons devoted to him by a singular vow, as is evident because they were to be redeemed in the same manner and at the same price, as is evident by comparing the beginning of the 27th chapter of Leviticus with Num. 18:15–16. God, in giving the rule for the redemption of the firstborn in the latter place, evidently refers to what he had before appointed in the former place, concerning per-sons devoted by a singular vow.[9] And so likewise, the firstlings of unclean beasts were to be redeemed, in the same manner as unclean

7. Here JE crossed out the following with a large "X": "1. Though there were several ways in which persons might come to [be] holy to the Lord, or consecrated to him, yet there was one law or rule for them when they were so, except they were things devoted to be accursed, which are spoken of, Lev. 27:28."

8. This reference and the preceding sentence (excepting the biblical location) are a later addition. Poole, discussing ancient temple procedures, notes that not all redemption rates were equal (*Synopsis Criticorum*, *1* [London, 1669], Pt. 1, cols. 617–18).

9. JE deleted "and therefore does as it were but briefly hint at something, and is not particular in the directing."

beasts that were devoted, as appears by comparing Lev. 27:11–13 with v. 27; but yet the firstborn still remained separated to God, as his special possession, after they were redeemed. Hence the Levites were accepted for the firstborn, to a tribe separated to God, after the firstborn were thus redeemed.

3. Persons that were devoted to God by the vow of their parents were Nazarites, as well as those that were separated by their own vows. The word "Nazarite"[1] signifies "one that is separated"; they might be separated by their parents' vows, or their own. This is very evident in instances that we have in Scripture. Thus Samuel was a Nazarite by the vow of his mother. I Sam. 1:11, "And she vowed a vow, and said, O Lord of hosts, if thou wilt indeed look on the affliction of thine handmaid, and remember me, and not forget thine handmaid, but will give unto thine handmaid a manchild, then I will give [him] unto the Lord all the days of his life, and there shall no razor come upon his head." And so it was with respect to Sampson (Judg. 13:5). But the Nazarite was to continue separated to God, as long as he remained under the vow by which he was devoted.

4. Those that were thus devoted to God to be Nazarites were, to the utmost of their power, to abstain from all legal pollutions (Lam. 4:7). With respect to defilements by dead bodies, they were required to keep themselves pure, with greater strictness than the very priests, except the high priest alone, and were obliged to as [great] strictness as the high priest himself (Num. 6:6–7, compared with Lev. 21:10–11). And though only some legal impurities are expressly mentioned, as what the Nazarite was to avoid, yet it is to be understood, that he is to his utmost to separate himself from all legal defilements, agreeable to his name, a Nazarite, or a "separate person." The Nazarite was to abstain from all legal impurities, in like manner as the priests, and even as the high priest; there are like directions given to one as to the other. The high priest was on no account to defile himself with the dead, and were forbidden to drink wine, or strong drink, when they went into the tabernacle of the congregation (Lev. 10:9). The priests were to abstain from all manner of legal defilement, as far as in them lay (Lev. 22:1–9).

If it be objected against this, that the Levites, who were accepted to be the Lord's instead of the firstborn that were holy to the Lord, were not obliged to such strictness, I answer, that this may be one reason

1. נָזִיר.

why God did not look on the firstborn as being fully redeemed by the Levites' being substituted in their stead, but there were still extraordinary[2] charges required of them for the maintenance of the Levites,[3] much more than in proportion to the bigness of the tribe; and God might accept this as an equivalent for their not being so strictly separated, as he accepted extraordinary redemption money for the odd number of the firstborn that were more than the Levites (Num. 3:46–47, and 18:15–16).

5. Those that were devoted to God to be Nazarites by a singular vow were to devote themselves wholly to religious exercises, and to spend their lives in the more[4] immediate service of God. For though this ben't particularly expressed, but only some things are expressed that they should abstain from, yet this is implied in their being God's, his being separated to the Lord (Num. 6:5), his being holy to the Lord. Num. 6:6, "All the days that he separateth himself unto the Lord," he shall be holy; and v. 8, "All the days of his separation, he shall be holy unto the Lord." In like manner, as in the Second Commandment, there are only some things particularly mentioned that we should abstain from on the sabbath, but 'tis not expressly said that the[5] day should be spent in religious exercises, yet 'tis implied in that, that the seventh day is the sabbath of the Lord our God, and that we are commanded to keep it holy. This was evidently Hannah's intention in her vow, whereby she devoted Samuel to be a Nazarite, as was explained by her own words and practice. I Sam. 1:28, "Therefore also I have lent him to the Lord; as long as he liveth he shall be lent to the Lord." And accordingly she brought him, and left him in the sanctuary to dwell continually there, and there to spend his time in sacred business. I Sam. 2:11, "And Elkanah went to Ramah to his house. And the child did minister unto the Lord before Eli the priest." V. 18, "But Samuel ministered before the Lord, being a child, girded with a linen ephod."

6. It was necessary that a woman that was devoted to be a Nazarite (for a women might be a Nazarite, Num. 6:2), that she should thenceforward avoid marrying, and refrain from all carnal intercourse with men. If she was a virgin when she was devoted, it was necessary that she should continue a virgin till her vow was ended;

2. MS: "~~Great~~ ⟨Extraordinary⟩."
3. The remainder of this paragraph is a later interlineation.
4. MS: "~~Special~~ ⟨more Immediate⟩."
5. JE deleted "whole."

and if she was devoted for her whole life, she must continue a virgin forever. And if she was a widow, she must continue in her widowhood, and that on two accounts.

(1) Marrying would be contrary to the obligation, that has been taken notice of, that the Nazarite was under, with the utmost strictness to avoid all legal defilements, for marrying unavoidably exposed to great legal impurities, and of long continuance. See Lev. 12. There were scarcely any legal impurities to which the children of Israel were exposed, excepting the leprosy, that were so great[6] as those that marriage brought women into. Being therefore devoted to God, to be holy to the Lord in the utmost possible legal purity, she must avoid marrying. And then those legal impurities rendered her incapable of those sacred offices and services that she was devoted to. It incapacitated her from conversing in holy things, or drawing near to God in ordinances, as much as being defiled by the dead body of a man incapacitated a priest from his work and office. Lev. 12:4, "And she shall then continue in the blood of her purifying three and thirty days; she shall touch no hallowed thing, nor come into the sanctuary till the days of her purifying be fulfilled," which, in all, for a son made up forty days, and for a daughter fourscore days, which must needs be very inconsistent with the circumstances of the Nazarite, that was devoted wholly to attend on God and holy exercises in the[7] way of the Jewish ordinances. If the Nazarite were a male, his marrying did not expose him to such legal impurities. The Nazarite was to observe as strict a legal purity as the high priest himself, as has been observed; but he, for the greater purity, was allowed to marry none but a virgin. Therefore doubtless the woman herself, that was a Nazarite, was obliged to continue a virgin. See how some things were required in the law of Moses by consequence, though not expressly, in my papers of "Infant Baptism."[8]

(2) Marrying would utterly destroy the main design of her being dedicated in the vow of a Nazarite, which was, that she might be wholly devoted to the more immediate service of God in sacred things. If she was married, her time must unavoidably be exceedingly taken up in

6. JE deleted "and long."
7. JE deleted "observance of."
8. This sentence is a later addition. No separate papers on infant baptism are extant. See "Table to the 'Miscellanies'" for references to JE's discussions of infant baptism in that series and in the "Blank Bible" (*Works, 13*, 126). See also David D. Hall's discussion of the issue in the Introduction to *Works, 12*.

secular business and cares, in tending and bringing up children, and in providing for and taking care of a family, which exceedingly fills married women's hands and hearts, and is as inconsistent as possible with the design of the vow of the Nazarite. Hence the women that were devoted to the special service of God's house in the primitive church (though not devoted to God so solemnly, nor in so great a degree, as the Nazarite), must be one that was not married, and never like to marry; and it was looked upon and spoken of by the apostles as sinful in such to marry. I Tim. 5:11, "But the younger widows refuse; for when they have begun to wax wanton against Christ, they will marry." And the reason that is given why they should be widows, that were like ever to continue so, and free from all worldly care, was that they might be the more entirely at liberty for religious duties. Vv. 3–5, "Honor widows that are widows indeed. But if any widow have children or nephews, let them learn first to show piety at home, and to requite their parents, for that is good and acceptable before God. Now she that is a widow indeed, and desolate, trusteth in God, and continueth in supplications and prayers night and day." Those widows in the primitive church seem to be, in some degree, in imitation of the Nazarites in the Jewish church. Anna the prophetess was in all probability a Nazarite, or one that, after her husband's death, had devoted herself to the service of God by such a vow as that we have been speaking of, and therefore continued in widowhood to so great an age, because her vow obliged her to it. And therefore she, throwing by all worldly care, devoted herself wholly to the immediate service of God. Luke 2:36–37, "And there was one Anna, a prophetess, the daughter of Phanuel, of the tribe of Aser. She was of a great age, and had lived with an husband seven years from her virginity; and she was a widow of about fourscore and four years, which departed not from the temple, but served God with fastings and prayers, night and day," the like expression with that that the Apostle uses concerning widows (I Tim. 5:5).

And therefore,[9] when we have an account that after Jephthah's daughter had been let alone two months, to go up and down the mountains with her companions to bewail her virginity, that she returned to her father, who did to her according to his vow. That which Jephthah did was this: he took her up to the sanctuary before the Lord, and presented her before the priest, that he might estimate her, and then paid according to his estimation (Thus the Jews that came

---

9. JE deleted "'tis probable."

out of the captivity vowed that they would offer the firstborn of their sons, Neh. 10:36.),[1] whereby she was redeemed from being made a burnt sacrifice, according to the law. And by thus presenting her in the sanctuary, and offering up that which [was] accepted instead of her blood, she was actually separated according to the vow. Her separation began from that time, and thenceforward she was to begin her strict abstinence from all legal impurities, and to spend her time in sacred offices. And 'tis probable that Jephthah thenceforward left her in the sanctuary, to dwell there as long as she lived, as Hannah did to her son Samuel, whom she had devoted to be a Nazarite. I Sam. 1:22, "I will not go up till the child be weaned, and then I will bring him, that he may appear before the Lord, and there abide forever"; and as the other Hannah, or Anna, did with herself after she had devoted herself to perpetual widowhood as a Nazarite, of whom we read, Luke 2:37, that she was widow of fourscore years old, and "departed not from the temple." And there probably Jephthah's daughter continued in supplications and prayers night and day, for she was eminently disposed and prepared for such duties by that remarkable spirit of piety that appeared in her, by her resignation with respect to the vow her father had made concerning her. And what time she did not spend in duties of immediate devotion, she might spend in making of priests' garments (Ex. 35:25–26), or[2] in other business subservient to the work of the sanctuary, as there might be enough found that a woman might do.

II. The nature of the case will not allow us to suppose that that was done, that was so horrid and so contrary to the mind and will of God, as putting of her to death, and offering her up as a burnt sacrifice. God took great care that never any human sacrifice should be offered to him. Though he commanded Abraham to offer up his son, yet he would by no means suffer it to be actually done, but appointed something else with which he should be redeemed [Gen. 22]. And though God challenged the firstborn of all living things to be his, yet he appointed that the firstborn of men should be redeemed, and so in all cases wherein persons were holy to the Lord, the law makes provision that they should not be slain, but redeemed. See No. 290 *.[3] And God, by the prophet Isaiah, declares such sacrifices to be abominable to him

---

1. This parenthesis is a later interlineation.
2. JE deleted "ministring," as in the sense of "serving."
3. MS: "* See after No. 289, last page." This cross-reference is a later interlineation. The "last page" refers to the last page of Book 1 where JE wrote a few lines about Jephthah.

in the forementioned Is. 66:3. See also Jer. 7:31, with my note on that text.[4] It would have been symbolizing with the abominable customs of the heathen nations that were round, especially that [of] offering human sacrifices to the idol Moloch, which God ever manifested a peculiar detestation of [Lev. 20:2]. Here particularly observe Deut. 12:29–32.[5] And the nature of the case won't allow us to think that Jephthah, in this instance, committed such abomination. 'Tis not likely but that he, being a pious person, as he is spoken of by the Apostle [Heb. 11:32], would have been restrained from it by God. And then what was done was doubtless agreeable to the mind and will of God, for God otherwise would not, in so extraordinary a manner, have assisted her so quickly and readily to resign herself to it. There seems most evidently an extraordinary divine influence on her mind in the affair, for her resignation did [not] arise from senselessness or indifference of spirit, as is evident, because she desired time so to bewail what was to be done to her. And upon the supposition that she was to be slain, it would be impossible, without an extraordinary influence on her mind, for her to be so resigned. Her resignation was from pious considerations, and holy and excellent principles, as is evident by what she says to her father, when she sees him passionately lamenting the issue of his vow, of which we have an account in the 36th verse. "And she said unto him, My father, if thou hast opened thy mouth unto the Lord, do to me according to that which hath proceeded out of thy mouth; forasmuch as the Lord hath taken vengeance for thee of thine enemies, even of the children of Ammon."

If what he had vowed to do was so abominable a thing, as to kill her in sacrifice, it would not have been her duty to say, as she does, "do to me according to that which hath proceeded out of thy mouth." But she seemed to be influenced to express herself as she did by the Spirit of God, and her resignation is recorded of her as a very excellent thing in her.

III. Her being to be slain in sacrifice seems inconsistent with her request to go up and down the mountains to bewail her virginity; it would have been rather to bewail her untimely end.

---

4. This reference is a later interlineation. In the "Blank Bible" JE observes that God "never commanded" the sacrifice of children, nor did it ever once come into his heart "to require parents to put such a face on their natural affection" in serving him. JE's entry on Jer. 7:31 cites Matthew Henry.

5. This sentence is a later addition.

IV. It seems evident that she was not slain, by the 39th verse. 'Tis said, that "it came to pass that at the end of two months, she returned unto her father, who did with her according to his vow which he had vowed"; and the consequence of it is immediately added, "and she knew no man." This clause seems evidently to be exegetical of the foregoing, viz. that he did to her "according to his vow"; or to explain what that was that he did, viz. devote her to God in a perpetual virginity. If she had been slain, 'tis not at all likely that it would have been mentioned, that "she knew no man," for that she had known no man before this had been already expressed, in her going up and down the mountains to bewail her virginity; and nobody would suppose that she would marry and have children after she was devoted to death, and it had been determined, both by herself and her father, that it should be put in execution. And besides, there would have been no occasion to mention not knowing man, because as soon as the two months was out, wherein she bewailed her virginity, and she had returned from going up and down the mountains, the vow was immediately executed.

V. It is no argument that Jephthah thought himself obliged to put her to death, that he so lamented when his daughter met him, as v. 35. "And it came to pass, when he saw her, that he rent his clothes, and said, Alas, my daughter, thou hast brought me very low, and thou art one of them that trouble me; for I have opened my mouth unto the Lord, and I cannot go back." For she, being his only child, by her being devoted to be a Nazarite, his family was entirely extinct. He had no issue to inherit his estate, or keep his name in remembrance, which in those days was looked upon an exceeding great calamity. "Thou hast brought me very low," i.e. thou hast quenched my coal, and brought perpetual barrenness on thyself. See Poole's *Synopsis*, at the end of Judg. 11.[6]

224. JOSHUA 11:8. "And the Lord delivered them into the hand of Israel, who smote them, and chased them even unto great Zidon." Bedford, in his *Scripture Chronology*, pp. 195 and 493, supposes that great numbers of them made their escape from thence, and from neighboring seaports, by shipping to all the shores which lay round the Mediterranean and Aegean seas, and even to other parts of Europe,

6. This reference is a later addition. Poole contains an extensive discussion of the interpretive dilemma posed by Jephthah's vow and the division among earlier commentators over alternative ways of understanding his grief at his daughter's "perpetual barrenness" (*Synopsis Criticorum, 1* [London, 1669], Pt. 1, cols. 1148–55).

Asia, and Africa; of which, says he, the learned Bochart hath given us a large account in his incomparable *Canaan*,[7] and particularly shown that the names of most places are of Phoenician or Hebrew extraction. About this time they set up their two pillars at Tangier with this inscription in the Phoenician language: "We are they who fled from the face of Joshua the Robber, the son of Nun."[8] About this time they built the city of Carthage, which at first they called Carthada, which in the Chaldee and Syriac languages signifies "The New City." "This building of Carthage," says he, p. 195, "not only appears from the common consent of all historians, but also from the remains of the Carthaginian language, which we have in Plautus, where he brings in a youth from thence, speaking in such a manner, that many learned men have proved it to be the Hebrew or language of Canaan. And the Carthaginians are frequently called Phoenicians and Tyrians, because they came from this country. Being thus used to sailing and merchandise, they soon carried on a larger trade, and settled other colonies near Gibraltar, both in Asia and Africa. The learned Bochartus tells us, that these expeditions were computed to be in the times of the heroes."[9] And Bedford says, p. 493, that hence "the story of Dido and Aeneas, as mentioned in Virgil, must be false and groundless. Neither is it probable," says he,

> that the widow of a priest flying the country, unknown to the king, could carry with her so great a number of men to a new colony, as should undertake to build so great a city; so that she brought not inhabitants there, but found them there, and did not so properly build as only repair and enlarge the town to which she came. She built the tower, which was called *Bozrah*, or a "fort" in Hebrew, and from thence called *Byrsa*, or a "hide" in Greek, and so occasioned the fabulous story, that Dido bought the place to build the city on with little bits of leather marked, which was anciently used instead of money. But others tell us, that when she arrived on the coasts of Africa, she was forbidden to tarry there by Hiarbas, king of the country, lest she with her company might seize on great part of his

7. In his "Catalogue" JE refers to Samuel Bochart's *Canaan* as "a book often quoted by Bedford in his *Scripture Chronology*, and spoken of by him with high commendable [sic], and once spoken of as an incomparable thing" (p. 6). *Canaan* appeared as Part II in *Geographica sacrae: Phaleg, seu De dispersione gentium et terrarum divisione facta in aedificatione turris Babel; Chanaan, seu De coloniis et sermone Phoenicum* (Cadomi, 1646).

8. Bedford, *Scripture Chronology*, pp. 195–96.

9. Ibid., p. 195.

dominion, and therefore she craftily desired of him only to buy so much ground as might be compassed with an ox hide; which, when she had obtained, she cut it into small thongs, and therewith compassed two and twenty furlongs, on which she built the city afterward named Carthage, and called the castle *Byrsa*, or "Hide." All this we owe to the fertile invention of the Greeks, to make everything derived from them. Whereas Dido, coming from Tyre, knew nothing of that language; and besides, the old Carthaginian language was the Phoenician or Hebrew, as appears by the old remains thereof, which we have in Plautus's *Paenulus*.[1]

It looks exceeding probable that when Joshua had smitten the vast army of Hazor, and the kings that were with him, and chased them unto Zidon, that all that could, would flee by ship, for that was a great seaport; and therefore they had opportunity to escape this way, and they had had enough to terrify them to it. For they had heard how God, with a strong hand, had brought off the people from Egypt, and had divided the Red Sea, and drowned the Egyptians there; and fear and dread had fallen upon them, and their hearts had melted at the news (Ex. 15:14–16). And they had heard how that God was among the people in the wilderness, and how he was seen face to face, and how that his cloud stood over them, and how he went before them in a pillar of cloud by day and a pillar of fire by night (Num. 14:14). And their dread and astonishment was renewed by hearing how they had destroyed Sihon, king of the Amorites, and Og, the king of Bashan; and they had trembled, and anguish had taken hold on them at the news (Deut. 2:25). As Rahab told the spies, their terror was fallen upon them, and all the inhabitants of the land did faint, and even melt; neither was there any more courage left in any man because of them (Josh. 2:9–11). God did as he promised. Ex. 23:27, "I will send my fear before thee, and I will destroy all the people to whom thou shalt come, and I will make all thine enemies turn their backs unto thee."[2] Their terror was greatly increased by God's drying up Jordan (Josh. 5:1), and then causing the walls of Jericho to fall down flat [Josh. 6:20], and after that his causing the sun to stand still [Josh. 10:13], and so miraculously destroying the five kings of the Amorites in a storm of thunder, lightning, and hail, and their utterly destroying their cities in all the southern parts of Canaan. And they had heard how that Joshua was pos-

---

1. Ibid., p. 493.
2. JE deleted "and after this."

itively commanded to smite them, and utterly destroy them, and make no covenant with them, nor show mercy unto them, and how that Joshua had given no quarter to their neighbors. And now when the kings and people in all the northern parts of Canaan had gathered together such a vast strength, peoples as the sand upon the seashore, with innumerable horses and chariots, as Josh. 11:4, and yet they were suddenly vanquished, and Joshua was still pursuing with a design utterly to destroy them according to his order, and had pursued them even to great Zidon, when they therefore came there, they must needs be in the utmost consternation. And if there were any ships there, it could be no otherwise but that all that could, fled in them, and that they would [not] trust to the walls of Zidon, for they did not know but they would fall down flat, as the walls of Jericho had done, and that not only multitudes should be slain, but many of [them] driven away to the ends of the earth, agrees best with the expression so often used of God's driving them out before the children of Israel.

And besides, there could be no room for such multitudes in Zidon and a few neighboring cities, for they, with those that Joshua had slain of them, had before filled all the land of Canaan north of the tribe of Ephraim, even to Mt. Hermon and to Zidon; and they were under a necessity to seek new seats abroad where they could find them.

225. LUKE 22:44. "And being in an agony he prayed more earnestly." This was in his second prayer; he prayed more earnestly than in his first. But we can't justly suppose that 'tis meant that he prayed more earnestly than before that this cup might pass from him, for this was after the "angel appeared to him from heaven, strengthening him,"[3] as in the foregoing verse. This angel came from heaven on that errand, to strengthen him with the more cheerfulness to take the cup and drink, and to go through with the sufferings that were before him, that were so dreadful to him; and therefore we must suppose that in consequence of it, Christ was more strengthened in it. And though Christ seems to have had a greater sight of his sufferings given him after this strengthening than before, that caused such an agony, yet he was strengthened in order to fit him for a greater sight of them, and he had greater strength and courage to conflict and grapple with those awful apprehensions than before. His strength to bear suffering is increased with his suffering. And then, seeing this angel came to

3. MS: "of him."

strengthen [him] with courage to go through his sufferings, and Christ knew it, we must suppose that Christ, now in answer to what he said to God in his former prayer, herein had it signified that it was the will of God that he should drink that cup. And so 'tis not to be supposed that, immediately upon it, he prayed more earnestly than before that the cup might pass from him; that he should so do is utterly inconsistent with Matthew's account of this second prayer. The account we have of this second prayer of Christ in the other Evangelists, together with John 12:27–28 and Heb. 5:7, serve well to lead us into an understanding of the matter of this prayer. Indeed, when the evangelist Mark gives us an account of this second prayer, he says that he "spake the same words" that he did before (Mark 14:39); but by what the evangelist Matthew says of it, we are not to understand this as though he spake all the same words, but the same words with the last part of his former [prayer], viz. "not what I will, but what thou wilt." The account Matthew gives of it is this. Matt. 26:42, "He went away again the second time, and prayed, saying, O my Father, if this cup may not pass away from me, except I drink it, thy will be done." By Matthew's account, he prays the second time as if he had received a signification from God, since he prayed before, that it was his will that the cup should not pass from him. And the evangelist Luke tells us how, viz. by the angel that came from God to strengthen [him]. And therefore, though he prays now more earnestly than before, yet he only prays that God's will may be done, i.e. not only in his sufferings, but in the effects and fruits of them, that God would so order it, that his end and will may be obtained by them in that glory to his name,[4] particularly the glory of his grace and mercy in the salvation and happiness of his chosen ones, which he intended by them. Christ's second request here, after it was signified and determined that it was the will of God that he should drink the cup, corresponds with his second request that was made on the same account that we have in John 12:27–28. The first request was the same as here, and in like trouble. "Now is my soul troubled; and what shall I say? Father, save me from this hour." And then after this he was determined within himself as now, that the will of God must be otherwise, that he should not be saved from that hour. "But for this cause came I to this hour." And then his second request after this is, "Father, glorify thy name." So this was the purport of this second request, as Matthew gives us an account of it, saying the same also the third time (v. 44),

4. JE deleted "and blessedness to his chosen people which purposed by them."

wherein the evangelist Luke says, "He, being in an agony, prayed more earnestly"; which seems to be the "strong crying and tears" that the Apostle has respect to, Heb. 5:6–8, as he saith also in another place, "Thou art a priest forever after the order of Melchizedek, who in the days of his flesh, when he had offered up prayers and supplications with strong crying and tears unto him who was able to save from death, and was heard in that he feared; though he were a Son, yet learned he obedience by the things that he suffered."

The thing that he feared, and the thing that he prayed to be delivered from in those prayers and supplications, that he offered up with such earnestness and agonies to him that was able to save him from death, that so the Father's will might be done, and his glory attained in his sufferings, was that he might be "saved from death"; that though he must drink the cup, and pass through death, that he might not be swallowed up, that he might not fail and sink in so great a trial, but might overcome, as Christ is represented praying, Ps. 69:14–15. He prayed that his heart might not utterly fail in his last passion, and that it might be effectual for the obtaining of God's will and glorious ends proposed. If he had failed, all would have failed, and the whole affair entirely frustrated. The man Christ, in such an extraordinary and terrible sight of the cup he had to drink, did not trust in his own feeble human nature to support him, but looked to God to support [him]. If he had not overcome in that sore trial and dreadful conflict, he would never have been "saved from death" (for his resurrection was a release from the grave, was in token that he had vanquished, and fulfilled, and satisfied God's will); and then all would have failed, and we should never have been redeemed. Our faith would have been vain, and we should have remained yet in our sins [I Cor. 15:17]. The things which Christ prayed for, and the things in which he was heard, were those two things mentioned in Is. 49:8. When Christ prayed to be delivered from death, it was not as a private person, but as a common head; his deliverance from death is virtually the deliverance of all the elect. Thus this High Priest (for he is spoken of as such in that place in Hebrews; see verse foregoing [Heb. 5:6]) offered up prayers and supplications with his sacrifice, as the Jews were wont to do. He mixed strong crying and tears with his blood that was shed out and fell down to the ground in his agony, praying that the effect and end of that blood might be obtained. Such earnest agonizing prayers were offered with his blood, and his infinitely precious and meritorious blood was offered with his prayers. How effectual must such prayers be! And how sure may those be of salvation that have an interest in those supplications! See further, No. 311.[5]

226. MARK 11:13. "And seeing a fig tree afar off having leaves, he came, if haply he might find anything thereon. And when he came to it, he found nothing but leaves, *for the time of figs was not yet.*" By "the time of figs" here seems to be meant the fig harvest, or the time of the ingathering of figs, as the author of the reply to Woolston with great probability supposes, agreeable to the manner of expression in Matt. 21:34, "when the time of the fruit drew nigh," καιρὸς τῶν καρπῶν; and Ps. 1:3, "yield its fruit in its season."[6] This is given as a reason why Christ came seeking and expecting figs on the tree. The time of ingathering of 'em was not yet come, and therefore he might well expect to find them hanging. The particle ("for") has reference not separately to the last words, viz. "and when he came to it, he found nothing but leaves"; but it has reference to the whole sentence taken together, signifying that he came seeking and expecting fruit, and was disappointed. These words, "for the time of figs was not yet," contain a reason both why he came, and why it was a disappointment to him to find none, both which are understood and necessarily implied in the words preceding. See No. 229 *.[7] And though the fig harvest was not yet come, or the time of general ingathering of figs, yet it was a time of year, as the forementioned author observes, wherein Christ might expect to find some ripe figs fit for eating on the tree; for, as he observes, the more common sort of fig tree in those parts brings two crops in a year (see Hos. 9:10), and that the first ripe fruits of the first crop might be expected then, and that Josephus says that at the time of the passover some Jewish robbers made an excursion from the castle of Masada, and carried off the ripe fruits belonging to the town of Engaddi, and that he, describing the fruitfulness of the country of Gennesaret, says it affords figs and grapes for ten months without intermission, and that Pliny says those two crops of figs kept pace with the harvest and vintage, and that if so, the first crop will be ripe at about the time of the passover, and that the end of the winter and beginning of spring in Judea was, at latest, about the middle of Febru-

5. This cross-reference is a later addition.
6. JE was reading the reply to Thomas Woolston's *Discourses on the Miracles of our Saviour* (In 6 pts. London, 1727–29) by Zachary Pearce, *The Miracles of Jesus Vindicated. In Four Parts* (3rd ed., London, 1730). Woolston elicited more than sixty responses by his attack on Jesus' miracles.
7. This cross-reference is a later addition.

ary, and then the fig tree began to put forth green figs, agreeable to Cant. 2:13. And therefore, unless the text is to be interpreted in this sense, but only the contrary, that in the words "the time of fruit is not yet" is signified that not the barrenness of the tree, but only that the proper time wherein figs used to be ripe was not yet come, was the reason why Christ did not find eatable figs on the tree. It never would have been expressed, as 'tis here, that he found "nothing but leaves," but rather that he found "nothing but green figs"; for undoubtedly by what has been observed, there must be green figs on all fig trees that were not barren long before this time.[8]

227. HEBREWS 6:4–6. "For it is impossible," etc. Those that the Apostle here has respect to must be such as were guilty of the unpardonable sin. The falling away that he speaks of is an apostasy from Christianity. It could not be otherwise but that those, who in those days had been Christians, and then openly renounced Christianity, must openly reproach that[9] Spirit that Christians were then so generally endued with in his miraculous gifts, which was so notorous, and was so great a thing, and the principal thing in them that drew the eyes of the world upon them, and was the greatest seal that God gave them, to evidence in the sight of the world that they were his people, and which was the argument that was principally effectual for the gaining others to them. When they openly renounced Christianity that they once had appeared to embrace, their renunciation contained a great and open reproach, for it was an avowed casting away and rejecting a thing that has been received, as having found it naught and vile.[1] He that admits and receives another in the capacity of a wife,[2] or husband, or lord, or other relation, and then afterwards on trial rejects them, and turns them out of doors, casts a vastly greater reproach on them than those that never received them; much more those that received anyone for their God. So those apostates here spoken [of], in renouncing Christianity, did openly cast the greatest reproach on Christianity; and therefore the Apostle says, v. 6, they "put him to an open shame." And indeed, an open declared renunciation of Christianity, after it had been embraced, is itself an open reproaching and blaspheming of it in words. And they that apostatized and openly renounced Christianity

8. Pearce, *Miracles*, pp. 45–50.
9. JE deleted "Holy Ghost."
1. JE deleted "and an open renunciation can scarcely be without declaring this in words."
2. MS: "wife ⟨or Husband or Lord⟩ ~~or Servant~~ or ~~any~~ other."

in those days, and the church being in those circumstances that have already been mentioned, must openly renounce and reproach that Spirit that the Christians were endued with and confirmed by, for that Spirit was the principal and most notorous thing in that Christianity that they renounced and reproached. And especially must it be so, when those openly renounced Christianity that had themselves been endued with the Holy Ghost, as those here spoken of had been. In renouncing Christianity, they must renounce that Spirit, that great seal of Christianity that they had had. And those that had such experience of the evidences of the truth of Christianity that those had, as has been explained, No. 74, must do it against light and the conviction of their own consciences; and so what they did amounts to the sin against the Holy Ghost, as explained, "Miscellanies," nos. 475 and 703.[3] And those that apostatized from Christianity under these circumstances would naturally be abundant in their reproaches of the religion they had renounced, and the Spirit that confirmed, that they might justify themselves, and that they might not appear inconsistent with themselves in the eye of the world. The same apostates are evidently spoken of in Heb. 10:25–29, where he speaks of their forsaking the assemblies of Christians, and sinning willfully, after they had received the knowledge of the truth, and treading underfoot the Son of God, and renouncing the blood of the covenant wherewith they had been sanctified, and doing despite to the Spirit of grace. See further of this last place,[4] No. 230.[5]

228. SOLOMON'S SONG 4:8. "Come with me from Lebanon, my spouse, with me from Lebanon; look from the top of Amana, from the top of Shenir and Hermon, from the lions' dens, from the mountains of the leopards."[6] This call and invitation of Jesus Christ may be looked upon as directed either to her that is already actually the

---

3. In no. 475 entitled "SIN AGAINST THE HOLY GHOST," JE develops at length "three things essential to this sin, viz. conviction, malice and presumption (presumption in expressing that malice)." See the same entry for a discussion of JE's reading of Richard Baxter's sermon, *For Prevention of the Unpardonable Sin against the Holy Ghost* (*Works*, *13*, 517–22, n. 2). In no. 703, similarly titled, JE discusses the fact that this sin involves "avowed malicious opposition and contumacy against the Holy Ghost in his work and office, and as communicated to men and acting in them either in his ordinary or extraordinary influences and operations." He also asserts that the "ground of the unpardonableness of this sin" is the "arbitrary constitution" of God.

4. I.e. Heb. 10:25–29.

5. This cross-reference is a later addition.

6. JE deleted "She that is here called may be looked upon to either as alread[y]."

spouse of Christ, or her that is[7] called and invited to be his spouse, that is already his spouse no otherwise than in his gracious election. So the Gentiles are called a "sister" in the last chapter of this song, even before they were in a church estate, before she had any breasts [Cant. 8:8]. So in the 43rd of Isaiah, where respect is had to the calling of the Gentiles, God calls those his sons and daughters that were so as yet only in his decree of election. V. 6, "I will say to the north, Give up; and to the south, Keep not back: bring my sons from far, and my daughters from the ends of the earth."

Lebanon, Amana, Shenir, and Hermon were certain noted mountains in the wilderness, in the confines of the land of Canaan, that were[8] wild and uninhabited. Hence the wonderful work of God in turning barbarous and heathenish countries to Christianity is compared to the turning such a wild forest as Lebanon into a fruitful field. Is. 29:17, "Is it not yet a very little while, and Lebanon shall be turned into a fruitful field, and the fruitful field shall be esteemed as a forest?" They were mountains that were haunts of wild beasts, and probably some of them at least very much frequented by lions and leopards, those most fierce and terrible of wild beasts. They were places where lions had their dens, and either these or some other noted mountains in the wilderness were so frequented by leopards, that they were called "the mountains of the leopards." 'Tis from such places as these that the spouse, or she that is invited to be the spouse, is invited to look to Jesus Christ, where she was[9] without the limits of the pleasant land of Canaan, wandering and lost in a howling wilderness, where she was in continual danger of being devoured,[1] and falling a prey to these terrible creatures. Christ graciously calls and invites her to look to him from the tops of these desolate mountains towards the land of Canaan, and towards the holy city Jerusalem where he dwelt, though far off. Yea, to come with him, for Christ is come into this wilderness to seek and save her that is lost, to come and leave those horrid places, and come and dwell with him in the pleasant land, yea, in the city Jerusalem, that is the perfection of beauty, the joy of the whole earth. Yea, though the lions had actually seized her and carried her into their dens, there to be a feast for them, yet Christ calls and encourages her to look to him from the lions' dens.

7. JE deleted "not now his spouse but is."
8. JE deleted "desolate."
9. JE deleted "far off."
1. JE deleted "by wild beasts."

David represents his praying to God in a state of exile and in distressing circumstances by his remembering God from the land of the Hermonites (Ps. 42:6). Christ saves souls out of the dens of lions, as he did Daniel [Dan. 6], and out of the mouths of wild beasts, as David did the lamb from the mouth of the lion and the bear [I Sam. 17:34–36]. He[2] invites sinners that are naturally under the dominion of Satan, that roaring lion that goes about, "seeking whom he may devour" [I Pet. 5:8], and invites saints under the greatest darkness, and distresses, and temptations, and buffetings of Satan to look to him.

229. MARK 11:13. Join this to No. 226, at this mark *. If we suppose the particle ("for") here has no reference at all to the last words, viz. "when he came to it, he found nothing but leaves," but look on the words as a parenthesis, this is no difficulty, for we have an instance fully parallel in Luke 19:24–26. "And he said unto them that stood by, Take from him the pound, and give it to him that hath ten pounds. (And they said unto him, Lord, he hath ten pounds.) *For* I say unto you, That unto everyone that hath shall be given; and from him that hath not, even that he hath shall be taken away from him," where 'tis most evident that the causative particle "for" has no reference to the words immediately preceding, viz. "And they said unto him, Lord, he hath ten pounds," but to those before. See also a parallel instance, Mark 16:3–4.[3]

230. HEBREWS 10:25–29. Let this be added to No. 227. That the sin against the Holy Ghost is here intended, is confirmed from the place in the Old Testament that seems to be referred to in the 28th and 29th verses, for the place that seems especially to be referred to is that in Num. 15:30–36, where God, having been speaking of the sins of ignorance that should be atoned with sacrifice, tells what sin should not be atoned with sacrifice, in these words: "But the soul that doth ought presumptuously, whether he be born in the land, or a stranger, the same reproacheth the Lord; and that soul shall be cut off from among his people. Because he hath despised the word of the Lord, and hath broken his commandment, that soul shall be utterly cut off" [vv. 30–31]. And then in the words next following, there is an instance given of such a man so sinning presumptuously, viz. the sabbath-breaker that gathered sticks on the sabbath, and how no sacrifice was accepted for

2. I.e. Christ. JE deleted "saves."
3. This sentence is a later addition.

him, but he perished without mercy by all the congregation's stoning him with stones. See margin of the Hebrew Bible.[4] That the Apostle here refers [to Num. 15:30–36] seems evident by these things: the Apostle is here speaking of a sin for which there remains no more sacrifice, and in that in Numbers shows what sins were not to be atoned by legal sacrifice. He speaks here of him that "despised Moses' law," which agrees with those words in that place in Numbers, "Because he hath despised the word of the Lord, and hath broken his commandment," the reason given in that place why no sacrifice was to be accepted for him; so here the reason given why no more sacrifice remains, is that he sins willfully. In that place another reason why [he] should perish without accepting a sacrifice was that he "reproached the Lord." So here the reason given why there remained no sacrifice for this was that he had insolently and maliciously reproached the Spirit of grace, for so the words in the original signify, which are translated "hath done despite to the Spirit of grace."[5] See Mastricht, p. 363, col. 1.[6] Another reason there given is that "he had despised the word of the Lord"; a reason here given is that he had trampled on the Son of God, who is the *Word* of God. The man gathering sticks perished by the hand of all the congregation; all, the whole congregation, were commanded to stone him with [stones], to be a testimony that none had mercy on him, agreeable to God's direction in such a case. Deut. 13:8–10, "Neither shall thine eye pity him, neither shalt thou spare. But thou shalt surely kill him; thine hand shall be first upon him to put him to death, and afterwards the hand of all the people. And thou shalt stone him with stones, that he die." Thus the sabbathbreaker perished without mercy, and he died under the hand of two or three witnesses, as the Apostle concluded from the law in such a case.

Hence we may gather the meaning of the word "willfully" in this place, that the Apostle means by it in the same sense as the man in Numbers is said to sin "presumptuously." The phrase in the original is "with an high hand," or rather, "a lifted-up hand,"[7] as of one that is

---

4. This sentence is a later interlineation. Here JE may have reference to the import of the Hebrew verb in v. 35, מוֹת יוּמַת, which implies "being put to a violent death."

5. τὸ πνεῦμα τῆς χάριτος ενυβρίσας.

6. Petrus van Mastricht, *Theoretico-practica theologia, qua, per singula capita Theologica, pars exegetica, dogmatica, elenchtica, & practica, perpetua successione conjugantur*, ed. nova (Trajecti ad Rhenum & Amstelodami, 1715), p. 363, col. 1, contains a discussion of reasons why the sin against the Holy Ghost is unforgivable.

7. בְּיָד רָמָה.

going to strike another. The same word is used of Jeroboam. I Kgs. 11:26, "He lift up his hand against the king."

231. THE BOOK OF SOLOMON'S SONG. The divinity of this song is confirmed from the allusions there seem to be in the New Testament to things herein contained; and particularly Christ, in John 4:10–14, speaking of a well of "living water," seems to allude to the 15th verse of the 4th chapter of this song, "a fount of gardens, a well of living waters." So in Eph. 5:18,[8] there seems to be an eye to 5:1 of this song. See notes on that in Ephesians.[9]

232. EPHESIANS 5:30–32. "For we are members of his body, of his flesh, and of his bones. For this cause shall a man leave his father and mother, and shall be joined unto his wife, and they two shall be one flesh. This is a great mystery, but I speak concerning Christ and the church." Christ did as it were leave his Father in order to obtain and be joined to the church; he came down from heaven, and did as it were leave the bosom of his Father. He left the sweet and joyful manifestations of his Father's love, and became subject to the hidings of his Father's face, and even to the expressions of his wrath, and gave himself to his church, that he might be joined to his church, and "that he might present it to himself a glorious church," etc., as vv. 25–27. So he also left his mother, which was the church of the Jews,[1] to cleave to the New Testament church as his wife. The Old Testament church was as it were the mother of Christ. Christ was born of the Jews, and the Jewish [church] of old as it were held Christ in its womb. All those ordinances and legal observances, Christ was hid in them, as the infant is hid in the womb. All God's dispensations towards that church, his calling of them by Moses, his giving them such ordinances, his so ordering their state from age to age, was in order to bring forth Christ into the world. This Old Testament church is represented by Sarah, Isaac's mother, and the New Testament church by Rebecca, that Isaac loved, and took into his

8. JE deleted "probably."

9. JE contrasts being drunk with wine and being filled with the Spirit. He writes, "There is excess in being full of wine, but no excess in being filled with the Spirit; there is no excess in spiritual enjoyments. We may be drunken with the Spirit, and there is no excess in that, as 'tis said, Cant. 5:1, 'Drink, and be drunken, O beloved.'" From this JE draws the following corollary: "Hence we may learn the authority of that book of Canticles" ("Blank Bible").

1. JE deleted "or the Old Testament."

mother's tent, and in whom he was comforted after his mother's death. See Gen. 24:67 notes.[2] The Old Testament church was as Christ's mother, but the New Testament church is his wife, whom he is joined to, and whom he treats with far greater endearment and intimacy. He forsook his mother also in this respect, viz. as he made a sacrifice of that flesh and blood, and laid down that mortal life which he had from his mother, the Virgin Mary. "That which [is] born of the flesh is flesh," though he did not derive[3] flesh from his mother in the sense in which it is spoken of, John 3:6, viz. corrupt sinful nature, and therefore did not forsake his mother for the church in the same sense wherein the church is advised to forsake her father's[4] house for Christ's sake, viz. to forsake sin and[5] lusts derived from parents, by crucifying the flesh with the affections and lusts. Yet Christ derived flesh from his mother, viz. the animal nature and human nature, with that corruption that is the fruit of sin, viz. with frailty and mortality. This Christ forsook, and yielded to be crucified for the sake of the church.

233. LUKE 18:35. "And it came to pass, that as he was come nigh unto Jericho, a certain blind man sat by the wayside begging." Here this is said to be as he "came nigh unto" the city; in the original 'tis said, ἐν τῷ ἐγγίζειν, "in his approaching" to the city. And we have an account afterwards, in the first verse of the next chapter, of Jesus' entering and passing through Jericho. And yet it is said in Matthew 20:29, that it was "as they departed from Jericho," or as 'tis in the original, ἐκπορευομένων αὐτῶν, "they going out" of Jericho. And in Mark the same is said, and there we have an account before of his coming to Jericho. Mark 10:46, "And they came to Jericho; and as he went out of Jericho with his disciples and a great number of people, blind Bartimaeus," etc. It seems to me the difficulty and seeming inconsistence is thus to be solved, viz. that Jesus passed over Jordan the day before, from the other side where he had been (John 10:40–42, Matt. 19:1–2, Mark 10:1), and came to the suburbs of Jericho that night, and that this is what is meant by Mark, when it is said, "they came to Jericho," in the first words of Mark 10:46, now mentioned, and that Christ did not go

2. JE suggests that Rebecca represents 1) "the soul of a believer whom Christ espouses to himself, and brings into his church" to enjoy its privileges in this world and in heaven, and 2) "the Gentile or New Testament church," which is called into the tent following the apostasy of the Jews. "Thus Christ is as it were comforted concerning the loss of the Jewish church by the calling of the Gentiles" ("Blank Bible").

3. JE deleted "corruption."

4. MS: "Father ~~and her mother~~ ⟨House⟩."

5. JE deleted "corruption and."

into the main city that night, but lodged in the suburbs for the comfort of lodging, and to avoid the crowd and throng of people. For 'tis evident that the people there were now in a great disposition to flock after him and throng him, by the whole context of these places. If [he] had gone into the midst of so populous a city as Jericho that evening, the multitude would necessarily have greatly distressed him that night. And that Christ did lodge somewhere, after he came over Jordan into Judea, before he entered the main city of Jericho, seems evident by this, that otherwise we shall not find room for the four days that Lazarus had been dead before he came to Bethany, if we suppose the day that he was raised to be the fourth day. For we are told that when Christ heard he was sick, that "he abode two days still in the same place where he was, even beyond Jordan" (John 11:6, compared with the next verse, and the 40th verse of the foregoing chapter).[6] Lazarus died after Christ heard this news, as is evident by what Christ said, by v. 11. It was when Christ was going out of that place into Judea that he said to his disciples, "Our friend Lazarus sleepeth, but I go that I may awake him out of sleep." By this we can't rationally suppose that he died sooner than the day before he went over Jordan, which may be reckoned one day of his being dead. And when he came over Jordan, and lodged in the suburbs of it, there was two days. And the next day he passed through Jericho and lodged at Zacchaeus's (Luke 19:5–10), and the next day he came to Bethany, which is four days. There is a necessity of supposing that [Christ] lodged somewhere on this side Jordan before he came to Zacchaeus's, but it seems evident that he did not lodge at all in the old city of Jericho, but passed directly through it, and came to Zacchaeus's house the same day that he entered and passed through the city, by Luke 19:1–2. "And Jesus entered and passed through Jericho. And, behold, there was a man named Zacchaeus," etc.

Another thing further strengthens the probability that Christ had lodged a night on this side Jordan before that day that he passed through the city and came to Zacchaeus's, viz. that if he went through the city to Zacchaeus's the same day that he came over Jordan, it is not at all likely there would have been gathered such a multitude to him; there would not have been time for it.[7] The multitude was exceeding

---

6. JE deleted "Lazarus died after Christ heard this news, as is evident by supposing he went out of that place the second day after."

7. JE deleted "Christ seems to have been alone with his disciples when he passed into Judea from beyond Jordan, by Luke 31, etc."

great, as appears by the blind man's taking so much notice of the noise they made as they passed (Luke 18:36), and by Zacchaeus's being forced to climb a sycamore tree to see him.

And therefore thus the seeming inconsistence between the Evangelists is solved. Jesus' coming from beyond Jordan to the suburbs of Jericho and lodging there, Mark calls his coming to Jericho (10:46). And when Christ set out on his journey the next morning, to go from Jericho further towards Jerusalem, Mark calls [that] his setting out from Jericho, or his going forth from that city, though the main city was in his way, and he passed through it in his journey, which is not disagreeable to our vulgar ways of speaking. If a man that belongs to a certain town—suppose the town of Northampton—living on the outskirts of it on the north side, sets out to go a journey to another town south of Northampton, supposing Hartford, and anyone at his journey's end should ask him at what time it was that he set out from Northampton, such a question would be understood to mean at what time he began his journey from his own home at Northampton, though he after that passed through the main body of the town. Or if he was on a journey before, and lodged at Northampton for a night at an house in the utmost northern skirts of it, and so went forward on his journey to Hartford the next morning, this don't alter the case. The case seems to have been thus: that Jesus, lodging in the eastern suburbs of Jericho, the people flocked to him in the morning before he set out on his journey. And when he set forth on his journey, in order to leave that town in the bounds of which he then was, Mark and Matthew speak of him as then going out of Jericho. But between the place where he lodged and the walls of the main city, which he must pass through in his way, the blind man cried for mercy; and therefore Luke says it was as he was entering into the city.

Note that the supposition of his coming over Jordan is not agreeable to Doddridge's *Harmony*. See how he reconciles the Evangelists, in note in the "Blank Bible" on Luke 18:35.[8]

234. JOHN 10:34–36. "Jesus answered them, It is written in your law, I said, Ye are gods. If he called them gods, unto whom the word of God

8. This paragraph is a later addition. In the "Blank Bible" JE cites Philip Doddridge's judgment that ἐν τῷ ἐγγίζειν only signify "'when' or 'while he was near it,'" a view found in *The Family Expositor: or, a Paraphrase and Version of the New Testament: with Critical Notes; and a Practical Improvement of each Section. Containing the Latter Part of the History of our Lord Jesus Christ, as recorded by the Four Evangelists, Disposed in the Order of an Harmony* (6 vols. London, 1739–56) 2, 271. Vol. 2 was published in 1740.

came, and the Scripture cannot be broken, say ye of him," etc. The rulers of God's people were called gods, because unto them the word of God came, i.e. his law was come to them, was committed to them, and betrusted with them for them to enforce and execute. They were herein instead of God to the people, because they held forth the law, or word of God. The law of God was in a sense their law. They were judges or executors of the law for God, for the judgment was God's (Deut. 1:17, and II Chron. 19:6). Herein they were types of Christ, to whom the Father hath committed all judgment. Thus it was a ceremony in Israel, in inaugurating a king, to bring the law and commit [it] to him, as II Kgs. 11:12. "And he brought forth the king's son, and put the crown upon him, *and gave him the testimony*; and they made him king, and anointed him; and they clapped their hands, and said, God save the king." Thus the word of God came to him.[9] This interpretation of this expression of Christ is confirmed by what God says to Moses, Ex. 4:16. "And he shall be thy spokesman unto the people: and he shall be, even he shall be unto thee instead of a mouth, and thou shalt be to him *instead of God*"; i.e. by speaking the word of God to him, he was instead of God, because *the word of God came to him*, or was committed to him to speak in God's name. And so in the 7th chapter, 1st verse, "And the Lord said unto Moses, See, I have made thee a god to Pharaoh; and Aaron thy brother shall be thy prophet." He represented God before Pharaoh, by the word of God in his mouth as he spake in his name, and by his word wrought miracles before[1] [him].

These earthly rulers were called gods, because the external word of God came thus to them, whereby they were rendered types and images of the Son of God, the internal word of God. Hence they have not only [been] called gods, but the sons of God. Ps. 82:6, "I have said, Ye are gods, and all of you children of the Most High." And if they were called gods only for thus resembling God's Son, how much[2] is Christ to be justified, who was himself that Son of God, when he called himself God. See No. 482.[3]

235. EPHESIANS 1:22–23. "And gave him to be head over all things to the church, which is his body, the fullness of him that filleth all in all." By "fullness," according to the Apostle's use of the phrase, is signified

9. JE deleted "and therefore they were only rulers of Israel that were called gods. ~~other~~ ~~the~~ We never find the rulers of the heathen called gods."
1. JE deleted "and what is more full to the purpose still is that in."
2. JE deleted "more."
3. This cross-reference is a later addition.

the good of any being, all that by which any being is excellent and happy, including its perfection, beauty, riches,[4] and joy, and pleasure. Rom. 11:12, "Now if the fall of them be the riches of the world, and the diminishing of them be the riches of the Gentiles, how much more their fullness?" The word "fullness," in the former part of this verse, is doubtless to be understood in like manner as the word "filleth," in the latter part. By Christ's filling "all in all" seems evidently to be intended that he supplies all the creatures in heaven and in earth, angels, and blessed spirits, and men, with all good, as in Eph. 4:10. "He that descended is the same also that ascended far above all heavens, that he might fill all things," viz. that he might supply all intelligent creatures in heaven and earth with good. So when it is said, Eph. 3:19, "that ye might be filled with all the fullness of God," the meaning seems to be, that ye might have your souls satisfied with a participation of God's own good, his beauty and joy. "For our communion is with the Father, and with his Son Jesus Christ" (I John 1:3). So when the Apostle says, Christ emptied himself, as Phil. 2:7, he means he appeared in the world without his former glory and joy. See John 17:5.[5] So that here the Apostle teaches that Christ, who fills all things, all elect creatures in heaven and earth, himself is filled by the church. He, who supplies angels and men with all[6] that good in which they are perfect and happy, receives the church as that in which he himself is happy. He, from whom and in whom all angels and saints are adorned and made perfect in beauty, himself receives the church as his glorious and beautiful ornament, as the virtuous wife is a crown to her husband. The church is the garment of Christ, and was typified by that coat of his that was without seam [John 19:23], [which] signified the union of the various members of the church, and was typified by those garments of the high priest that were made "for glory and for beauty" (Ex. 28:2), as seems evident by the 2nd verse of the 133rd psalm, and by the precious stones of his breastplate in a particular manner, on which were engraven the names of the children of Israel. Is. 62:3, "Thou shalt also be a crown of glory in the hand of the Lord, and a royal diadem in the hand of thy God," i.e. in the possession of God. So Zech. 9:16–17, "And the Lord their God shall save them in that day as the flock of his people, for they shall be as the stones of a crown, lifted up as an ensign

4. MS: "riches ⟨Honour⟩ ɉ & Joy & blessedness Pleasure."
5. This reference, the preceding sentence, and the word "elect" in the following sentence are a later interlineation.
6. JE deleted "their excellency and beauty and divine ornaments himself receives the."

upon his land." As 'tis from and in Christ that all are supplied with joy and happiness, so Christ receives the church as that in which he has exceeding and satisfying delight and joy. Is. 62:5, "As the bridegroom rejoiceth over the bride, so shall thy God rejoice over thee." This seems to be the good that Christ sought in the creation of the world, who is the beginning of the creation of God, when all things were created by him and for him, viz. that he might obtain a spouse that he might give himself to and give himself for, on whom he might pour forth his love, and in whom his soul might eternally be delighted. Till he had attained this, he was pleased not to look on himself as complete, but as wanting something, as Adam was not complete till he had obtained his Eve (Gen. 2:20). Here add No. 481.[7]

236. JEREMIAH 30:21. "Their nobles shall be of themselves, and their governor shall proceed from the midst of them; and I will cause him to draw near, and he shall approach unto me. For who is this that engaged his heart to approach unto me?" This, as Dr. Ridgley in his *Body of Divinity*, vol. I, pp. 366–67, observes, seems to be a prophecy of Christ. The chapter is evidently a prophecy of the gospel times of the church, the times when the spiritual David was to be their noble and governor, as appears by v. 9. "They shall serve the Lord their God, and David their king, whom I will raise up unto them." And what is in this verse translated "nobles,"[8] is in the Hebrew in the singular number, their "noble."[9] 'Tis the more probable that this is to be understood of Christ, and not of Zerubbabel, or any other governors after the Babylonish captivity, because the supreme governor of Israel was very rarely of themselves after the captivity, even till their destruction by the Romans. They scarcely ever had this privilege in this sense, to so great a degree, as before their captivity. But [as] we look on this chapter, we can't think it is a prophecy of less prosperity to God's people than what they now enjoyed. And then what is said here of this governor or noble agrees peculiarly to Christ, and particularly that clause, "For who is this that hath engaged his heart to approach unto me?" The word translated "engaged" is עָרַב, "to become or act the surety for anyone, to mingle himself with another, or unite himself to another, as a surety"; and so the word is commonly used in Scripture, as Gen. 43:9, and 44:32, and Prov. 11:15, Job 17:3, II Kgs. 18:23, and elsewhere. See

7. This cross-reference is a later addition.
8. JE deleted "ought to b."
9. אַדִּירוֹ.

Buxtorf.[1] So that the words might well have been translated, "Who is this that hath mingled or united his heart as a surety to approach unto me?" It is here inquired with a note of admiration, "Who is this that hath engaged his heart in suretyship to approach unto me?" probably for two reasons, viz. because of the wonderfulness of his person, and because of the greatness of the undertaking. And whether we understand by the Israel whose prosperity is here prophesied of, the Israelitish nation or God's spiritual Israel, yet Christ, their governor, is of themselves. He has taken on him the human nature; he is of the human race, and is our brother, and he is a child of the church. He has sucked the breasts of our mother [Cant. 8:1]. He is one [of] the holy nation, the spiritual seed of Abraham; and he is also of the Israelitish nation. He took on him the seed of Abraham in a literal sense. In the following verse is mentioned the consequence of Christ's approaching to God as his people's surety, viz. their covenant[2] interest in God: "And ye shall be my people, and I will be your God."[3]

237. GENESIS 7. Concerning the flood. *Revelation Examined with Candor*, Vol. 1, p. 189. "Examine the highest eminences of the earth, and they all, with one accord, produce the spoils of the ocean deposited upon them on that occasion; the shells and skeletons of sea fish, and sea monsters of all kinds. The Alps, the Apennines, the Pyrenees, Libanus, and Atlas, and Ararat, every mountain of every region under heaven where search hath been made, from Japan to Mexico, all conspire in one uniform, universal proof, that they all had the sea spread over their highest summits. Search the earth; you shall find the mouse deer, natives of America, buried in Ireland; elephants, natives of Asia

1. Buxtorf translates עָרַב with *Miscuit* and *Commiscuit*, as well as figuratively with *Spondere*, which is used of the solemn promises made in covenants and treaties. It is this last use he identifies with Jer. 30:21, "*Qui spondeat cum animo suo.*" See Johann Buxtorf, *Lexicon Hebraicum et Chaldaicum* (6th ed., London, 1646), p. 544.

2. JE deleted "relation to God and."

3. JE drew the substance of this entry from Thomas Ridgley's discussion of Question 31 in the Westminster Assembly's Larger Catechism which reads, "With whom was the covenant of grace made?" For example, the judgment concerning the singular number of the Hebrew for "nobles" in Jer. 30:21, the association of the prophecy with Christ instead of Zerubbabel, and the list of parallel passages containing the Hebrew word for "engage" are derived directly, as is the notion of "suretyship." Ridgley writes, "Now this proves an eternal transaction between the Father and the Son, in that the Father wills, or determines, that he shall draw near, or approach to him, as a surety, and the Son consents, in that he has engaged his heart to do it; and all this with a design that his covenant should be established, and that he should be a God to his people." See *A Body of Divinity wherein the Doctrines of the Christian Religion are Explained and Defended being the Substance of several Lectures on the Assembly's Larger Catechism* (2 vols. London, 1731), *1*, 366–67.

and Africa, buried in the midst of England; crocodiles, the natives of the Nile, in the heart of Germany; shellfish, never known in any but the American seas, together with entire skeletons of whales, in the most inland regions of England; trees of vast dimensions, with the roots and tops, and some also with leaves and fruit, at the bottoms of mines and marls; and that too in regions where no tree of that kind was ever known to grow, nay, where it is demonstrably impossible they should grow. Nay more, trees and plants of various kinds, which are not now known to grow in any region under heaven."[4]

238. GENESIS 9:12–15. Concerning the rainbow that God gave for a token of the covenant to Noah. The author of *Revelation Examined with Candor* supposes that the rainbow was never seen before Noah saw it, on occasion of his revealing his covenant to him, and says, "The tradition of antiquity concerning the rainbow seems strongly to confirm this opinion, for *Iris*, which is the name of the rainbow with the Greeks, is said to be the daughter of *Thaumas*, i.e. 'wonder,' and the messenger of Jupiter, to carry his great oath to the other gods when they had offended. Now this seems to be a fable, plainly founded upon the solemn covenant now mentioned, which God made with man after the deluge. The covenant of God on this occasion plainly implies the oath of God, as you may learn from Is. 54:9, where God, declaring his resolution of mercy to the Gentiles, useth these words, 'For this is as the waters of Noah unto me; for as I have sworn that the waters of Noah should no more go over the earth, so have I sworn that I would not be wroth with thee, nor rebuke thee.'"[5]

239. GENESIS 19:26. CONCERNING LOT'S WIFE. *Revelation Examined with Candor.* "The unseasonable delay of Lot's wife was, without question, occasioned by her solicitude for her children which she left behind her. The story of *Niobe* weeping for her children, and being stiffened into stone with grief, is doubtless founded upon this history. Possibly too, the fable of Orpheus being permitted to redeem his wife from hell, and losing her afterwards by looking unseasonably back, contrary to the express command given him, and then through grief,

4. JE draws this citation from Patrick Delany's assertion that the evidence of natural philosophy, or science, supports the Mosaic description of the height of the waters of the deluge. See *Revelation Examined with Candour. Or, a Fair Enquiry into the Sense and Use of the Several Revelations Expressly Declared, or sufficiently Implied, to be given to Mankind from the Creation, as they are found in the Bible* (2 vols. London, 1733), *1*, 189.

5. Ibid., pp. 212–13.

deserting the society of mankind, and dwelling in deserts, might be derived from some obscure tradition of this history. Sodom was now the liveliest emblem of hell that can be imagined. It was granted to Lot, by a peculiar privilege, to deliver his wife thence. He was expressly commanded, Gen. 19:17, 'Look not behind thee.'" By her looking back, contrary to this command, "his wife was lost; after which he quits the city, and dwells alone in the mountains. Here are all the main circumstances of the fable, and the poets had nothing to do, but to vary and embellish as they liked best."[6]

240. GENESIS 11:7. Concerning the confusion of languages. The[7] state of the world of mankind, with respect to variety of language, now and in all past ages that we can learn anything of by history, does exceedingly confirm this account of the confusion of languages. Without this, 'tis very unaccountable how there should be so great a variety of language in so little a time, or indeed ever at all. Concerning this, the author of *Revelation Examined with Candor*, [writes] as follows.

'Tis true, the English and all living languages are in a perpetual flux; new words are added, and others die and grow obsolete. But whence does this arise? Not at all from the necessary mutability of human things, but most evidently from the mixture of other tongues. Scholars add new words or terminations from the learned languages, either through affectation of learning, or desire of adorning their native tongue, with some words of more elegance or significance; and others, from a commerce with other countries of different languages, naturally adopt some of their phrases and expressions into their own, and so our language varies. And what then? How does this affect the question concerning the continuance of the same language, where no other was ever taught or heard?—The Jews spake the same language from Moses to the Babylonish captivity. If their polity had continued, would they not speak the same language to this day?

(And here I would insert what Bedford in his *Scripture Chronology* observes, viz. that the Arabic continued the same from the time of Job till later ages. "The Arabic spoken by Christians in Asia at this day is the same with that spoken by Mahomet the Imposter," which was much the same with that used in Job's time; and "the Chaldee re-

6. Ibid., 2 (1732), 230–31.
7. JE deleted "present and past."

mained the same from the time of Jacob till the date of the Babylonish Talmud"; and the Greek continued "the same from the days of Homer to St. Chrysostom." See Bedford, pp. 297 and 512.)[8] The author of *Revelation Examined with Candor* goes on.

Some of the inland inhabitants of Africa are found to speak the same language now which they spake two thousand years ago (and, in all probability, the same observation is true of our neighbors the Welsh). Could they keep to one language for 2000 [years], and could not the descendants of Noah keep to one language 200? Could they keep their language amidst a variety of so many others about them, and when 'tis scarcely possible that they should be clear of all commerce with people of different tongues, and could not these keep their language, when it was impossible they should have any commerce but with one another? These Africans, to say nothing of the Welsh, now keep their own tongue, though there are so many others in the world to taint, and by degrees to abolish it; if there were no other language in the world but theirs, does any man believe they would not continue to speak it for 2000, or 10,000 years more, if the world lasted so long? 'Tis true, as arts increased and customs changed, new terms and phrases might be added. What then? New words would increase and adorn the tongue; but sure no man would say it would destroy it, unless it be believed that new branches, or fruit, or flowers, do daily destroy the tree they shoot out from.

The learned author of the *Letter to Dr. Waterland*[9] seems to think, that all other languages sprang as naturally from the Hebrew, as many shoots from the same root, or many branches from the same stock. But I am confident whoever carefully considers the genius of each of the ancient languages now extant, will find as little reason to believe that they all had their original from the Hebrew, as that all the variety of forest and fruit trees in the world were originally but so many shoots and branches from the palm tree of Judea.

Besides all this, if we consider that the language of Adam (if we could suppose it imperfect in him, when it was demonstrably inspired by God, yet) had time enough to arrive at full perfection in 1656 years, and that Noah and his sons had time enough to learn it

---

8. Bedford, *Scripture Chronology*, pp. 297, 512.

9. Conyers Middleton, *A Letter to Dr. Waterland; containing Some Remarks on his Vindication of Scripture: in answer to a book, intituled Christianity as Old as the Creation* (London, 1731).

in perfection, before the flood, the youngest of his sons being about 100 years old at that time, and himself 600, we cannot with any color of reason imagine that there could be any necessity of adding so much as one word to it before the building of Babel.[1]

Thus far the author of *Revelation*[2] *Examined with Candor*. And besides all this, the greater excellency and regularity of some of the ancient languages so early, when arts were in their first beginning, as the Latin and Greek, the latter of which was in great perfection in the days of Homer, seems to argue something divine in it. If the art and learning of the nation had so early brought their language to such a pitch of perfection, they had made infinitely greater progress in this than in other things that pertain to human life.

The manner in which God seems to have confounded the language of the posterity of Noah seems to be by confounding their memory with respect to their former language, but not utterly destroying of it, so but that they still retained some notion of many of the words and phrases of their former language. Hence 'tis found that other languages have in many words affinity with the Hebrew.

241. GENESIS 16:10–12. "I will multiply thy seed exceedingly, and it shall not be numbered for multitude. . . . And shalt call his name Ishmael, because the Lord hath heard thy affliction. And he will be a wild man; his hand will be against every man, and every man's hand against him; and he shall dwell in the presence of all his brethren." The following observations [are] taken principally out of a book entitled *Revelation Examined with Candor*.[3] This prophecy is remarkably verified in the Arabs. The Arabs are the undoubted descendants of Hagar and Ishmael. "Ishmael was circumcised at thirteen years of age; so have all these his sons, from him, till the establishment of Mahometanism; and many of them to this day, though some of them circumcise indifferently in any year, from the eighth to the thirteenth, but all professing to derive the practice from their father Ishmael. He was an archer in the wilderness; his sons, the Arabs, have been the most remarkable archers in the world, and are so to this day, and in the

1. Delany, *Revelation Examined*, 2 (1732), 107–10.
2. MS: "Religion."
3. Patrick Delany's "Dissertation IV" in vol. 2, entitled "Concerning the predictions relating to Ishmael," comprises pp. 114–51. JE draws heavily on Delany in this entry, at times citing his text verbatim, at other times summarizing or paraphrasing *Revelation Examined*. Only the locations of direct quotations are cited in the notes.

wilderness too, where culture is not known." Hagar "was a concubine, and an hireling"; and while she dwelt with Abraham, "Abraham dwelt in tents," and was continually moving from place to place. "Ammianus Marcellinus observes of the Arabs, that they had mercenary wives, hired for a time."[4] The learned Dr. Jackson[5] makes it exceeding evident, that the Arabs and the Saracens were descended from Ishmael, and also the writers of the Life of Mahomet, and the writers of travels "and voyages without number. In short, it is a point universally agreed upon, all over the East and South."[6] As the Ishmaelites lived under twelve princes by Moses' account, so these principalities remained till later times bearing the names of the twelve sons of Ishmael, as *Le Clerc*[7] makes very evident.[8]

The first part of this prophecy, viz. "I will multiply thy seed exceedingly, that it shall not be numbered for multitude," is fulfilled in them. The Hagarenes, spoken of in Scripture, and "the Arabs, especially the Scaenitae,[9] were very numerous; and the Saracens were more numerous than either." But this prophecy is most eminently fulfilled in that vast empire that the Saracens have set up in the world.[1]

The next part of the prophecy is that he should be "a wild man." "The word which is translated 'wild' in this place, signifies 'a wild ass.' The literal construction of the phrase in Latin is *erit onager homo*, 'he shall be a wild ass man.'" The Arabs are, above all nations, a wild people, and have been so through all ages.[2] "Throughout so many hundred generations, they vary no more from their progenitors' agrest and fierce qualities, than the wild plants of the forest, never accustomed to human culture, do from the trees whence they are propagated."[3] The dwelling of those Arabs and the wild ass is alike, and indeed the same. See Job 39:6.[4]

The next part of the prophecy, "His hand shall be against every man, and every man's hand against him; he shall dwell in the presence of all his brethren." The meaning of which words seems to be that they

---

4. Here JE deleted "marrying in one place."
5. Thomas Jackson (1579–1640), sometime president of Corpus Christi College, Oxford.
6. *Revelation Examined*, 2 (1732), 121–24.
7. Jean Le Clerc (1657–1736), Swiss Protestant theologian.
8. *Revelation Examined*, 2 (1732), 148–49.
9. I.e. those dwelling in tents.
1. *Revelation Examined*, 2 (1732), 124–25.
2. Ibid., pp. 118–19.
3. Ibid., p. 127.
4. This reference and the preceding sentence are a later interlineation.

should be "in perpetual enmity with all mankind," and yet should subsist in the face of the world. [And such a sense of this prophecy seems to be agreeable to the idiom of Scripture phrase. Thus when the Scripture speaks of "brethren" with respect to nations, sometimes nothing is intended but only other nations that are round about. So when it is said concerning Canaan, Gen. 9:25, "A servant of servants shall he be unto his brethren," it is not intended only, nor chiefly, and it may be not at all, that he should be a servant of servants to his brethren, as Cush, Mizraim, and Phut, the other sons of Ham, but that he should be a servant to other nations; and it was fulfilled especially in his posterity's being subdued by the posterity of Shem and Japheth.[5]

When it is said, "they shall dwell," the meaning is that they shall remain a nation, and still retain their habitation and possession, without being cut off or carried captive from their own land. In such a sense the word is used, Ps. 37:27, "Depart from evil, and do good; and dwell forevermore." This expression is explained by other passages in the psalm, as v. 3. "Trust in the Lord, and do good; so shalt thou dwell in the land." V. 9, "Evildoers shall be cut off, but those that wait on the Lord shall *inherit* the earth." Vv. 10–11, "Yet a little while, and the wicked shall *not be*; yea, thou shalt diligently consider *his place*, and it shall not be. But the meek shall *inherit* the earth." V. 18, "The Lord knoweth the days of the upright, and their *inheritance shall be forever*." And v. 22, "For such as be blessed of him shall inherit the earth, and they that be cursed of him shall be cut off." V. 29, "The righteous shall inherit the land, and dwell therein forever." V. 34, "And he shall exalt thee to inherit the land; when the wicked are cut off, thou shalt see it."

It is also agreeable to a Scripture way of speaking when it is said, "He shall dwell in the presence of all his brethren," to understand it that they, after all their opposition to it, shall see him still subsisting, and retaining his own habitation in spite of them. So the expression, "in the presence," seems evidently to signify. Ps. 23:5, "Thou preparest a table before me in the presence of mine enemies."][6] This is also remarkably fulfilled in the Arabs, for they have ever lived in professed enmity with all mankind, and all mankind in enmity with them. They have continued in a state of perpetual hostility with the rest of their brethren, and yet have subsisted perpetually under it, before their faces, and in spite

---

5. JE deleted "So when Isaac says, All his brethren have I given him for servants, to Esau concerning Jacob" [Gen. 27:37].

6. JE's brackets. The section enclosed by brackets, including portions of this and the preceding two paragraphs, represents JE's own reflections.

of them all.[7] They have neither been destroyed, nor lost, by mingling with other nations; "they marry only in their own nation, disdaining alliances with all others."[8] [Their language, continuing so much the same through all ages (as Bedford, in his *Scripture Chronology*, observes, it continued much the same from the days of Job till latter ages), shows that their nation has never been much mixed with other nations.][9] "They, and the Jews only, have subsisted from the remotest accounts of antiquity, as a distinct people from all the rest of the mankind, and the undoubted descendants of one man."[1] [And the Arabs never were subdued and carried captive, as the Jews have been.][2] "Alexander the Great intended an expedition against them, but was prevented by death. What Alexander intended, Antigonus, the greatest of his successors, attempted, but without success, being repulsed with disgrace, and the loss of above 8000 men." He made a second and greater attempt, but without success.[3]

They had wars afterwards with the Romans and Parthians, "but were never either subdued or tamed, resembling in this (the only comparison in nature that suits them) the wild ass in the desert, and sent out, by the same hand, free as he, whose house is also the wilderness, and the barren land his dwelling; alike disdainful of bondage, scorning alike the multitude of the city, and the cry of the driver." Pompey made war with them, and some part of them seemingly submitted, but never remained at all in subjection to him. After this they "misled and deluded Crassus to his destruction. Anthony, after this, sent his horse to ravage" Palmyra, but the city was defended from them by archers, who were probably Arabs. Afterwards their chief city was besieged by Trajan, one of the most warlike and powerful of all the Roman emperors. He went in person with his army against them with great resolution to subdue them; but his soldiers were strangely "annoyed with lightnings, thunders, whirlwinds, and hails, and affrighted and dazzled with the apparition of rainbows, and so was forced to give over the siege."[4] After this Severus, a great conqueror, after he had subdued all his enemies, marched in person against them with great resolution to subdue them, with his greatest force and warlike prepa-

7. *Revelation Examined*, 2 (1732), 127–29.
8. Ibid., p. 124.
9. JE's brackets. *Scripture Chronology*, pp. 367–68.
1. *Revelation Examined*, 2 (1732), 120–21.
2. JE's brackets.
3. *Revelation Examined*, 2 (1732), 131–32.
4. Ibid., pp. 132–36.

rations, besieges the city twice, but is twice repulsed with great loss. And when they had actually made a breach in the wall of the chief city, they were strangely prevented from entering by unaccountable discontents arising among the soldiers; and so they went away baffled and confounded. These Ishmaelites, when their wall was broke down, being invited to a treaty with the emperor, disdained to enter into any treaty with him. After this the Saracens set up a vast empire, and so the prophecy of their becoming a great nation that could not be numbered was most eminently fulfilled.[5]

[They also have dwelt in the presence of all their brethren in another sense, viz. that all their brethren, the posterity of all the other sons of Abraham, and even the posterity of Isaac themselves, have seen them remaining unsubdued and holding their own dwelling, while they, all of them, and even the posterity of Isaac and Jacob themselves, were conquered and carried away out of their own dwellings.][6]

242. ISAIAH 7:17. "The Lord shall bring upon thee, and upon thy people, and upon thy father's house, days that have not come, from the day that Ephraim departed from Judah, even the king of Assyria." This seems not to be spoken of the king of Israel[7] mentioned in the foregoing verse, but of Ahaz, the king of Judah, to whom the Prophet was then speaking. It could not be meant of Pekah, the king of Israel, because it speaks of bringing the king of Assyria on his father's house; but the family of Pekah was not cut off by the king of Assyria, but by Hoshea, the son of Elah, who conspired against him, "and slew him, and reigned in his stead" (II Kgs. 15:30). God, by the Prophet, had offered great encouragement to Ahaz under his present distress and fear of Pekah and Rezin, and gave him a glorious sign, which he would not give heed to, as appears by v. 12. His confidence was not in God for help, but in the king of Assyria, whom he had hired by the treasures of both church and state, and by basely promising to be his servant (II Kgs. 16:7–8). Seeing he would not believe God's promises, nor take encouragement from his signs, therefore he should not be established; and though God would do great things for his people by the Immanuel that should be born in his family, yet he should have no benefit of it. And though it was true, as the Prophet had told him, that he should not be hurt by the kingdom [of Syria][8] and kingdom of

5. Ibid., pp. 140–43, 148.
6. JE's brackets.
7. JE deleted "as I once thought."
8. See Is. 7:1–9.

Ephraim that was now plotting his ruin, yet seeing he would not believe, he should not be the better for it. For there should come a greater calamity upon him than ever the kingdom of Judah suffered from the kingdom of Israel, and indeed greater than ever they suffered since the kingdoms were divided from 'em, and became unfriendly to them, and that from the king [of] Assyria himself, whom he trusted so much in for help against the kingdom of Israel. This calamity came upon him in his lifetime in a measure, as 'tis said in this verse ("upon thee"), for when the king of Assyria came up, he "distressed him, and strengthened him not" (II Chron. 28:20–21); and afterwards, it came upon his father's house and on his people.

243. ISAIAH 9:9–10 ff. "And all the people shall know, even Ephraim and the inhabitant of Samaria, that say in the pride and stoutness of their heart, The bricks are fallen[9] down, but we will build with hewn stones. The sycamores are cut down, but we will change them into cedars." They disregarded those awful and repeated judgments God had lately executed upon 'em, whereby he had already greatly diminished their numbers, and their wealth, and the extent of their dominions, when Pul, the king of Assyria, came up against the land, and took "a thousand talents of silver" out of the land, as II Kgs. 15:19, and when afterwards Tiglath Pileser, in the days of Pekah, he that was now king, came and destroyed so great a part of the land beyond Jordan, and in the northern parts, as II Kgs. 15:19 and I Chron. 5:26. They were insensible and unhumbled under these awful rebukes of heaven, as v. 13; "For the people turneth not to him that smiteth them." But when the hand of heaven was so evident against them to diminish them, yet they were full of contrivances, and big with expectations of conquests and enlarging their dominions, as appears in Pekah's conspiring with Rezin, king of Syria, to go and conquer the kingdom of Judah, of which in the two foregoing chapters. Thus even in the midst of God's awful judgments, they were full of haughty ambitious designs, and big with expectations of aggrandizing them, and making themselves bigger than they were before. Though they had lost their western and northern countries, yet they hoped to obtain the kingdom of Judah, that should more than make up their loss, and so said, Though "the bricks are fallen down, we will build with hewn stone," etc.

9. MS: "hewn"; KJV: "fallen."

244. Romans 6:14. "For sin shall not have dominion over you, for ye are not under the law, but under grace." The law, or covenant of works, is not a proper means to bring the fallen creature to the service of God. It was a very proper means to be used with man in a state of innocency, but it has no tendency to answer this end in our present weak and sinful state; but on the contrary, to have been kept under the law would have had a tendency to hinder it, and would have been a bar in the way of it, and that upon two accounts. 1. It would have tended to discourage persons from any attempts to serve God, because under such a constitution it must necessarily have been looked upon as impossible to please him or serve him to his acceptance; and one in despair of this would have been in no capacity to yield a cheerful service to God, but would rather have been far from any manner of endeavors to serve him at all, but to have abandoned himself to wickedness. By such a despair the dominion of sin would have been dreadfully established, and all yielded up to it, as in the damned in hell. 2. God must necessarily have been looked on as an enemy, which would have tended to drive from him and stir up enmity against him. A fallen creature held under the covenant of works can't look on God as a father and friend, but must necessarily look on him as an enemy, for the least failure of obedience by that constitution, whether past or future, renders him so. But this would greatly establish the dominion of sin or enmity against God in the heart. And indeed, it is the law only that makes wicked men hate God. They hate him no otherwise than as they look upon [him] as acting, either as the giver or judge of the law, and so by the law opposing their sins, and the law tending to establish the hatred of God. Hence 'tis necessary to be brought from under the dominion of it, in order to a willing serving of God.

Corollary. Hence men, when they are convinced of the law under awakenings, and have God represented to 'em as a strict lawgiver and judge, before they are convinced of the gospel, sometimes such sensible exercises of enmity of heart are stirred up against God.

But those that are redeemed from the bondage of the law, they have, 1. Great encouragement to serve God, in that their poor and imperfect obedience may be accepted; and 2. They have a great deal to win them to an ingenuous obedience, for God now represents himself as a merciful God, a God ready to pardon past transgressions and future infirmities. And he promises that if we will yield ourselves willingly to serve him as we are able, he will be our friend, and will treat us as a merciful and gracious father.

If a man does perform an external service while under the bondage of the law, 'tis no real service; 'tis merely forced by threats and terrors. 'Tis not performed freely and heartily, but is a dead, lifeless obedience. But a being delivered from the law and brought under grace tends to win men to serve God from love, and with the whole heart. Rom. 7:6, "But now we are delivered from the law, that being dead wherein we were held, that we should serve in newness of the spirit, and not in the oldness of the letter."

246. ISAIAH 10:26.[1] "And the Lord of hosts shall stir up a scourge for him according to the slaughter of Midian at the rock Oreb." The Prophet is speaking here of the destruction of Sennacherib's army,[2] and of himself afterwards. There was a remarkable agreement between the destruction of his army and that of the vast army of the Midianites, which was without the children of Israel's striking a blow (Judg. 7:20 ff.). And as Oreb, one of their princes, was taken afterwards, and slain after the battle was over and he was returning to his own land, so Sennacherib, after he had fled, was slain in the temple of his god Nisroch (Is. 37:38). So was that prayer against the enemies of the church, Ps. 83:11, "Make their nobles like Oreb, and like Zeeb," now fulfilled in Sennacherib.

247. HOSEA 1:4. "For yet a little while, and I will avenge the blood of Jezreel upon the house of Jehu." This prophecy was given in the days of Jeroboam, a king of the house of Jehu, not long before the destruction of that house; for Zachariah, Jeroboam's son and successor, was the last that reigned of that family, and he reigned but six months. Jehu's killing all that were of the house of Ahab was both rewarded and punished. It was rewarded, because as to the matter of it, it was agreeable to God's command (see II Kgs. 10:30), but was done in a wicked manner. He did not do it so much from a spirit of obedience as from an aim at his own advancement, for he little regarded God's honor in it, as afterwards plainly appeared by his idolatry, the very sin for which he was bid to kill Ahab and destroy his family. God saw that he did it with a murderous heart, and so punishes it by the overthrow of his family. As Jehu, with a murderous heart, slew Ahab and all his family, so shall the posterity of Jehu be slain, and his family overthrown in their turn. So the house of Baasha was rooted out, because he did the like to Jer-

1. JE skipped No. 245 in his numbering sequence.
2. JE deleted "before Jerusalem."

oboam (I Kgs. 16:7). Because Jehu performed the matter of God's command, he was rewarded by continuing the crown of Israel in his family unto the fourth generation; but because he did it in a wicked manner, as his after-behavior manifested, therefore it was continued no longer, but then taken away. His doing the matter of his duty was rewarded, but his doing it in a murderous manner was punished, which two things are not at all inconsistent.

248. HOSEA 2:2–5. God in these verses threatens that he will deal with the church of Israel, "as the just and jealous husband at length doth with an adulterous wife, that hath filled his house with a spurious brood, and will not be reclaimed. He turns her and her children out of doors, and sends them a-begging." And that seeing she ascribed her food and drink, and her clothing and ornaments, to her lovers, that therefore she and her children should be deprived of that food and drink, ornaments and raiment, and should be both naked and famished; and that she should be set naked and in the wilderness, "as in the day that she was born." The time when the church of Israel was born was the time of their slavery in Egypt, and wandering in the wilderness; then was she naked. She was in a state of poverty and abject slavery in Egypt, and afterwards in wearisome travail in a desolate wilderness; and so God threatens that she should be again. Henry.[3]

249. I KINGS 11:3. "And he had seven hundred wives, princesses, and three hundred concubines." Solomon could not but know the law of Moses, in which is prescribed concerning the king, Deut. 17:16–17, "But he shall not multiply horses to himself, nor cause the people to return to Egypt, to the end that he should multiply horses; forasmuch as the Lord hath said unto you, Ye shall henceforth return no more that way. Neither shall he multiply wives to himself, that his heart turn not away; neither shall he greatly multiply to himself silver and gold." But without doubt Solomon either put some wrong interpretation upon this law, or on some account or other thought himself exempt from the obligation of it. Possibly because when God had appeared to him, and asked him what he should give him, and he requested a wise and understanding heart, and did not ask that earthly glory that other kings set their hearts upon, God told him that he would give him riches and honor, so that there should not be any among the kings like unto [him] all his days [I Kgs. 3:13], i.e. that God would give him[4] outward

3. Henry, *Exposition*, *4* (1725), 612–13.
4. JE deleted "a greater degree of."

state and glory above all that other kings valued themselves upon. But in those days it was looked upon among the kings of the earth as great part of the state and grandeur of a king to have a great number of wives, and concubines, and horses, as well as to have a great deal of silver and gold. Solomon might look on this promise of God to him as a dispensation from the obligation of that whole law of Moses, which was given to restrain the ambition, and set bounds to the earthly grandeur of the king of Israel.

250a. GENESIS 3:7.[5] "And the eyes of them both were opened, and they knew that they were naked; and they sewed fig leaves together, and made themselves aprons." That our first parents, while they remained in innocency, had a luster or brightness on their bodies in which they shone, which left them when they fell, seems on many accounts probable, and among others, the signification of their name, by which God called them in the day that God created them. Gen. 5:2, "Male and female created he them, and blessed them, and called their name Adam, in the day when they were created." The signification of the Hebrew word "Adam"[6] is not only *rubuit*,[7] "he was red or ruddy," but means likewise as much as *splenduit*,[8] "he was bright and beautiful." That it bears this sense may be gathered from the word *Adamdameth*[9] (Lev. 13:19).

250b. HOSEA 7:14. "And they have not cried unto me with their heart, when they howled upon their beds." They are represented as, in their being in the calamities they suffered, compared to sick and wounded men, as Hos. 5:13. And many of them were doubtless literally sick, wounded men in grievous pain on their beds, by reason of the continual wars that they had of late been embroiled in. They howled in pain and distress on their beds, and cried that God would help them. When he slew them, then they sought him, but it was all in hypocrisy. And probably they cried in their prayers under distress with a loud voice, as they used to cry to Baal and other idols, as if they must be awakened, or could be prevailed upon by the loudness of the noise they made; but God, to show his abhorrence of it, calls it "howling."

5. JE deleted "250" and crossed out the entire entry with a large "X." He numbered the following entry No. 250.
6. אָדָם.
7. From the Latin *rubeo*.
8. From the Latin *splendeo*.
9. אֲדַמְדֶּמֶת.

"They assembled themselves for corn and wine, and they rebel against me." They assemble themselves to fast and pray for these blessings, when they were by divine judgments cut short in them; but they sought in such a manner that God looked upon it as rebellion, as the prophet Isaiah says, Is. 1:13, "The calling of assemblies, I cannot away with; it is iniquity, even the solemn meeting."

251. GENESIS 3:1. "Now the serpent was more subtile," etc. "What is an argument *ex posteriori*, of the devil's having assumed the form of a serpent in his temptation of our first parents, is the pride he has ever since taken, of being worshiped under that form, to insult as it were, and trample upon fallen man. To this purpose we may observe, that the serpent has all along been the common symbol and representation of the heathen deities (*Jul. Firmic. de errore Profan. Relig.*, p. 15). That the Babylonians worshiped a dragon, we may learn from the Apocrypha; and that they had images of serpents in the temple of Belus, Diodorus Siculus, Lib. 2, ch. 4, informs us. Grotius, out of several ancient authors, has made it appear that in the old Greek mysteries, they used to carry about a serpent, and cry Εὔα, the devil thereby expressing his triumph in the unhappy deception of our first mother. The story of Ophioneus, among the heathens, was taken from the devil's assuming the body of a serpent in his tempting of Eve (*Orig. contra Celsus*, Lib. 6). And, to name no more, what Philip Melanchthon tells us of some priests in Asia is very wonderful, viz. that they carry about a serpent in a brazen vessel, which they attend with a great deal of music and many charms in verse, while the serpent, every now and then, lifts up himself, opens his mouth, and thrusts out the head of a beautiful virgin [as having swallowed her],[1] to show the devil's triumph in this miscarriage among these poor deluded idolaters (Nichol's *Conference with a Theist*, vol. 1)." *Complete Body of Divinity*, p. 285, margin.[2]

252. HOSEA 10:9–10. "O Israel, thou hast sinned from the days of Gibeah. There they stood; the battle in Gibeah against the children of iniquity did not overtake them. It is in my desire that I should chastise them," etc. When the Benjamites committed such wickedness in Gi-

1. JE's brackets and editorial insertion.
2. Thomas Stackhouse, *A Complete Body of Divinity. Consisting in Five Parts: The Whole Extracted from the best Ancient and Modern Writers, but chiefly from the Works of such, as have been reputed the most able Divines, and celebrated Preachers amongst us* (London, 1729), p. 285.

beah, they stood and defended them,[3] and were victors in the first and second battle that was fought against them; and at last the battle did not overtake them all, but six hundred made their escape [Judg. 20:47]. And they have stood and remained in their successors in their wickedness to this very day, till the generation of such wicked men in Israel has now at length so increased, till they have overspread not only one tribe but all the tribes of Israel. That wicked tribe of Benjamin was not overtaken or rooted out[4] by the battle in Gibeah. "But I have a design now that the battle shall overtake them; my desire is that I should chastise 'em," as it follows in the next verse. When the Benjamites committed such wickedness in Gibeah, the other tribes had a desire to chastise them by wholly rooting out that tribe. They seemed to be greatly engaged about it, but failed of it; there they stood or remained notwithstanding. "Now I have a desire to chastise them. I myself will take it in hand, and I will make more thorough work. I will root out all of them; none shall be able to stand against me."

"And the people shall be gathered against them, when they shall bind themselves in their two furrows" [v. 10]. That is, when they shall fortify themselves in their two furrows, where they "have plowed wickedness" and sowed iniquity (v. 13), i.e. Dan and Bethel, the places of their two calves, or in the service of their two gods. In this field they bind themselves; they are resolute not to depart from those two furrows that they have plowed. They remain there as if they were bound there. They are obstinate in their wicked works, in their two furrows. Their two ways of wickedness, or two wicked works, viz. their worshiping the two calves, are here compared to two furrows that they have plowed, in analogy to the rest of the allegory in the following verses. In those wicked works they persist, and think to stand it out as the Benjamites did; but they shall not be able to defend themselves as they did. But "the people shall be gathered against them," as the tribes of Israel were gathered against the wicked Benjamites, and to more effect.

253. HOSEA 10:11. "I will make Ephraim to ride, Judah shall plow, and Jacob shall break his clods." In the preceding words God had threatened that he would put a yoke on Ephraim's fair neck, that she might be made to do harder work than treading out the corn, to wit, plow the field. Here the comparison is in part continued, and in part

---

3. I.e. themselves.
4. MS: "~~extirpated~~ ⟨rooted out⟩."

altered, from the labors of the cattle in plowing to that of the men that plow, wherein one was wont to ride to guide the beast that drew the plow, another to hold the plow, and another to break the clods. God here says that he would cause Ephraim to ride, i.e. he should go foremost in this labor God had to call 'em to; and Judah should plow, i.e. Judah should follow in it, as he that held [the] plow did him that rid; and then Jacob, i.e. the whole nation of Israel in all the tribes, should be in the same calamity, and reduced to the same slavery, as he that broke the clods in plowing came last. See Hos. 12:1–2.

254. PSALMS 78:43. "How he had wrought his signs in Egypt, and his wonders in the field of Zoan." Wells, in his *Sacred Geography*, from hence very probably supposes that Zoan, in the time when Moses wrought those miracles in Egypt, was the royal city, or the city where the Pharaohs had their seat. For we know that Moses wrought those miracles in the presence of Pharaoh, and therefore doubtless near the city where he dwelt, or in the field about that city. Zoan was probably from the beginning the seat of their kings, and that 'tis because it was so noted a city, and especially so known to the children of Israel, who had been bondslaves in Egypt under Pharaoh who dwelt in Zoan, that such particular notice is taken of it in Num. 13:22. "Now Hebron was built seven years before Zoan in Egypt." And Dr. Wells observes that this seems to have been the royal seat long after, even till Isaiah's time, though "Noph and Hanes were two other cities where the kings of Egypt did then sometimes reside." Is. 19:11, "Surely the princes of Zoan are fools; the counsel of the wise counselors of Pharaoh is become brutish. How say ye unto Pharaoh, I am the son of the wise, the son of ancient kings?" V. 13, "The princes of Zoan are become fools, the princes of Noph are deceived; they have seduced Egypt, even they that are the stay of the tribes thereof." Is. 30:4, "For his princes were at Zoan, and his ambassadors came to Hanes." Zoan is the same with Tanis. By the Seventy interpreters,[5] Noph is the same with Memphis; Hanes is the same with Tahapanes (Jer. 2:16) and Tahpanhes, where we read "that Pharaoh had an house" (Jer. 43:9), called in Ezek. 30:18, Tehaphnehes, the same that was called Daphne by the Greeks. Soon after Isaiah's time, Noph, or Memphis, became the capital city (Ezek. 30:13). Wells, *Sacred Geography*, pp. 8–9, and pp. 49–50.[6]

5. I.e. in the Septuagint.
6. Edward Wells, *An Historical Geography of the Old Testament* (3 vols. London, 1711), 2, 8–9, 49–50.

255. ISAIAH 51:9. "Art thou not it that hath cut Rahab, and wounded the dragon?" The word "Rahab" here is not the same with Rahab the harlot in Joshua [Josh. 2:1]. That is "Rachab" with ח; this is with ה. The word signifies "pride," probably so called from the exceeding pride that the Egyptians manifest in the time of that here spoken, viz. when God cut or broke that land, "and wounded the dragon." The taskmasters of the Israelites and Pharaoh, the dragon here spoken [of], manifested an exceeding haughtiness of spirit in so flouting of it out with God, who appeared in such awful judgments against them. On this account Egypt is the more fit type of the antichristian church, that is spiritually called Sodom and Egypt, and Pharaoh, the dragon here spoken of, the fitter type of the great red dragon with seven heads and ten horns [Rev. 12:3], and the Pope his image.

256. EZEKIEL 26:5, 14. "It shall be a place for the spreading of nets in the midst of the sea." And v. 14, "And I will make thee like the top of a rock, and thou shalt be a place to spread nets upon." Mr. Maundrel, a minister of the Church of England, who went there A.D. 1697, gives this account of new Tyre, that which was built on the island, as Dr. Wells in his *Sacred Geography*, vol. 4, pp. 96–97, relates. "On the north side it has an old Turkish ungarrisoned castle, besides which you see nothing here but a mere Babel of broken walls, pillars, vaults, etc., there being not so much as one entire house left. Its present inhabitants are only a few poor wretches, harboring themselves in vaults, and subsisting chiefly upon fishing, who seem to be preserved in this place by divine providence, as a visible argument how God has fulfilled his word concerning Tyre, viz. that it shall be as 'the top of a rock, a place for fishers to dry their nets on' (Ezek. 26:14)."[7]

257. GENESIS 6:4. Add this to No. 5. And their great bulk, and strength, and renown, besides the pride of such persons and churches as join the religion, doctrines, and worship, and profession of his church with the deluding glories and bewitching pleasures of this world, and of the heathenish and other humane and carnal churches and societies of it (here typified by the beauty of "the daughters of men"), I say, besides the pride of such churches, these things seem to denote the earthly pomp and splendor, and worldly renown and glory,

---

7. Edwards Wells, *An Historical Geography of the New Testament: In Two Parts. Part I. The Journeyings of our Lord and Saviour Jesus Christ. Part II. The Travels and Voyages of St. Paul, &c* (4th ed., London, 1734), pp. 96–97. This publication, which appeared originally in 1708, was published as vol. 4 in the 1734 ed. of the *Historical Geography of the Old Testament*.

and great temporal power that such churches affect, and are commonly in providence suffered to arrive to, as the Church of Rome and others.

258. HOSEA 12:1. "He daily increaseth lies and desolation." "Those that make creatures their confidence make fools of themselves, and take a great deal of pains to put a cheat upon their own souls, and to prepare vexation for themselves. 'He daily increaseth lies,' i.e. multiplies his correspondences and leagues with his neighbors, which will all prove deceitful to him; nay, they will prove desolation to him. Those very nations that he makes his refuge will prove his ruin. 'They that observe lying vanities forsake their own mercies' [Jonah 2:8]." Henry.[8]

259. GENESIS 8:4.[9] The country where Noah built the ark was probably in Babylonia, or the region thereabout, which abounds with cypress or gopher trees. "The Gordyaean mountains in Armenia seem to be at a proportionable distance; and since they are allowed to be the highest in the world, there is no reason for receding from the commonly received opinion, viz. that these were the hills whereon the ark stopped. Here it is, that the generality of geographers place the ark; here it is, that almost all travelers have found the report of it; and lastly, here it is, that the inhabitants of the country show some relics of it, and call places after its name, to this very day." *Complete Body of Divinity*, p. 324.

"'In Armenia, est altior mons, quam sit in toto orbe terrarum, qui Arath vulgariter nuncupatur; et in Cacumine illius montis arca Noe post diluvium primo sedit. Et licet, propter abundantium nivium, quae semper in illo monte reperiuntur, nemo valet illum ascendere; semper tamen apparet in ejus Cacumine quoddam nigrum, quod ab hominibus dicitur esse arca.' Haitho Hist. Orient, ch. 9.

"The mount Gordion, called by the Turks, Ardagh, is the highest in the world. The Jews, the Armenians, and the Mussulmans affirm, that the ark of Noah stopped at this mountain after the deluge (La Boulaye's *Voyages*). They tell us likewise, that the city Naksivan, which is about three leagues from the mountain Ararat, is the oldest in the world; that Noah dwelt therein when he came out of the ark; that the word *Naksivan* is derived from *Nak*, which signifies a 'ship,' and *Sivan*, which signifies 'to stop or stay'; and that this name was given to it,

8. Henry, *Exposition*, *4* (1725), 645.
9. JE supplied no biblical reference for this entry.

because the ark stopped at this same mountain. Tavernier's *Travels,* Tom. IV." Ibid., margin.[1] See further No. 455.[2]

260. HOSEA 12:12–13. "And Jacob fled into the country of Syria, and Israel served for a wife, and for a wife he kept sheep. And by a prophet the Lord brought Israel out of Egypt, and by a prophet was he preserved." 1. Israel are here put in mind of their former meanness in the same two instances that they were commanded every year to remember and confess anew, when they offered the basket of first fruits. Deut. 26:5, "And thou shalt speak and say, A Syrian ready to perish was my father, and he went down into Egypt, and sojourned there with a few." God puts 'em in mind from what small beginnings he raised them. Their father served and kept sheep for their mothers. He came to Syria a poor fugitive, and lived there a servant. He came to Syria with nothing; he had nothing to endow a wife with, and therefore was forced to serve for a wife. And again they were poor slaves in a strange land in Egypt. 2. They are put in mind of God's great mercies of old to their forefathers, in twice bringing them out of banishment and out of servitude. See v. 9. And he brought them out of Egypt, and led and preserved them in the wilderness; it was by a prophet, which shows their ingratitude in their despising and rejecting the prophets,[3] the successors of Moses (v. 10).

261. ISAIAH 32:2. "And a man shall be an hiding place," etc. Here Christ is compared to three things, that correspond with several things in the congregation in the wilderness, that were typical of Christ. *First,* Christ is called "an hiding place from the wind, and a covert from the tempest," which corresponds with the tabernacles. Tabernacles are made to shelter travelers in a strange land, where they have no abiding place, from the injuries of the weather. And a tabernacle is also an hiding place; the secret of God's tabernacle is especially spoken of as such. Ps. 27:5, "In the time of trouble he shall hide me in his pavilion, in the secret of his tabernacle." And so in other places there cited in the margin,[4] and in the 4th chapter of Isaiah ultimo [v. 6], Christ is expressly compared to a tabernacle in both these respects, viz. as a shelter, and as an hiding place or refuge.

1. Stackhouse, *Complete Body of Divinity*, p. 324.
2. This cross-reference is a later addition.
3. JE deleted "that God so often sent v. 10."
4. I.e. margin of the KJV.

Secondly, Christ is compared to "rivers of water in a dry place," which answers to those rivers of water out of a rock in that land of great drought. See No. 213. And *thirdly*, Christ [is] compared to "the shadow of a great rock in a weary land," which answers to the pillar of cloud which shaded the children of Israel in that[5] parched wilderness, to which Christ is compared (Is. 4:5, Ps. 121:5, Is. 25:4–5); and that it was not the shade of a rock, yet it was a rock that refreshed 'em otherwise, viz. with its cooling refreshing waters.

262. REVELATION 2:17. "To him that overcometh will I give to eat of the hidden manna." By this hidden manna is doubtless meant that spiritual heavenly food with which God feeds the saints, that spiritual heavenly good that the souls of the saints are refreshed, and comforted, and satisfied with, that is reserved and laid up for them, and appropriated to them as to his dear children and peculiar favorites. This excellent bread is no other than the Holy Spirit in his sweet, soul-strengthening, and satisfying communications, as we may learn from three things. First, Christ compares the Holy Spirit to the children's bread. "If a child ask bread of any of you that is a father, will he give him a stone? . . . How much more shall my heavenly Father give the Holy Spirit to them that ask him?" [Luke 11:11, 13]. And again in the 6th chapter of John, when Christ informs the Jews that he is the true manna or bread from heaven, and that they must eat him or they have no life in them, on the Jews' being stumbled at it, he informs them that he don't speak of his flesh properly, but that it must be his Spirit that they must receive in order to their living forever. V. 63, "It is the spirit that quickeneth; the flesh profiteth nothing." It is the Spirit that is truly the bread that quickeneth, or giveth life. Persons must feed on Christ by receiving of his Spirit. And thirdly, those first fruits of the Spirit, that were given on the day of Pentecost, were of old typified every year by the bread of the first fruits of their harvest, that was offered on the same day of Pentecost (Lev. 23:17).

In this expression of the HIDDEN MANNA, there is an allusion to the pot of manna that was laid up in the ark (Heb. 9:4), whereby was typified that excellent divine good and happiness that God [gives]. I Pet. 1:4, "An inheritance incorruptible, and undefiled, and that fadeth not away, reserved in heaven for you." That manna was hid as a most precious treasure in the secret of God's tabernacle. Hidden treasures and hidden riches is put for the most excellent treasure. It was hidden

5. JE deleted "scorching."

in the secret of God's presence, laid up most safely in God's chest, in his cabinet, as the ark was. Things that are laid up in an ark are hidden; hence "hidden or secret things" in Latin is *arcana*.[6] This food and treasure of the saints is so excellent, and such is God's great favor for them, that he reposits it in his own tabernacle, and not only so, but in the holy of holies, and not only so, but in the very ark itself, the immediate symbol of his presence. This ark, overlaid with gold, was a type of Christ, God's dear Son in whom is his infinite delight, as in his cabinet of precious jewels. In him are hid all the treasures of wisdom and knowledge, and all God's treasures. So infinite is God's favor to his saints that he lays up their life and happiness safely in this cabinet; their "life is hid with Christ in God" (Col. 3:3). Our life, our treasures, our stores of food, are safe in him; we can't be spoiled of them unless Christ, him the cabinet of God, can be stolen or robbed.

Our food and life is hid in Christ; he is the life (John 1:4). He is "the true God, and eternal life" (I John 5:20). Our souls are fed out of that ark, by partaking of the fullness of that cabinet, or of that good that that cabinet is full of; he is "full of grace and truth, and of his fullness all we receive, and grace for grace" (John 1:14, 16). We are happy and blessed no other way than by communion with Christ. Our food, our life, our joy and blessedness, is first in him, and then in us: first in the head and then in the members, first in this chest and then given into our mouths. The Holy Spirit, that is this manna and is the sum of all good, is given to us no other way than by our partaking of Christ's fullness. God has given the Spirit not by measure unto him; he has reposited an inexhaustible stock of this manna in this ark, and thence we are fed. The Holy Spirit descends to us, as the oil that was poured on Aaron's head ran "down to the skirts of his garments" [Ps. 133:2].

263. JOHN 7:38–39. "Out of his belly shall flow rivers of living water. But this spake he of the Spirit." The Spirit of God in the saints is called "living water" upon three accounts. Firstly and chiefly, 'tis meant that the water had life in it. Common water is mere passive, dead matter, but this water is alive. 'Tis a living divine person; so Christ is called "a living stone" (I Pet. 2:4). This water is not only something living, but 'tis life itself. 'Tis that Spirit that is the very life of God, and so is divine and infinitely perfect life, and act, and energy; for which cause partly the Spirit of God is called "water of life" (Rev. 22:1), because divine life is the very matter of this water. 2. He is living water as he is life-giving

---

6. This sentence is a later interlineation.

water, as Christ is called "the living bread" (John 6:51), and as the Spirit of God is called living bread there in that chapter, v. 63. See No. 262. He is living bread as he is life-giving bread, for so Christ explains himself in that chapter. 3. 'Tis living water in those in whom it is, as it is like a spring that never fails; as it gives life, so it will infallibly maintain life forever. So it seems to be explained by Christ, John 4:10–11, 13, and especially 14. So Christ is called "bread of life," because they that eat of him shall never die, but live forever (John 6). So the Christians' hope that they are begotten to "by the resurrection of Christ from the dead," is said, I Pet. 1:3, to be "a living hope," i.e. a never-dying, never-failing hope. See notes *in loc.*[7] But yet probably it don't appear that this water would on the account of its perpetuity be called "living water," if there was no life in the water, and life was not the thing that was perpetual; for it don't appear that springs of water that were never dry were, on that account, called "living springs" then, as now, but it seems to be a metaphor invented since.

264. I PETER 1:3, with the context. The Apostle, directing his epistle to the Christians in Pontus, etc., takes notice in the foregoing verse of the hand that each of the persons of the Trinity had in their being so distinguished from the rest of the world, as to be Christians or saints: "Elect according to the foreknowledge of *God the Father*, through sanctification of *the Spirit*, unto obedience and sprinkling of the blood of *Jesus Christ*." And having mentioned the blood of Christ and referred to his death, which is in itself, considered without what followed, a melancholy subject, as Christ says, Matt. 9:15, "The days come when the bridegroom shall be taken from them, and then shall they fast," he therefore in this verse leads their thoughts to the resurrection, a more joyful subject. The death of Christ, without a resurrection following, might justly have damped and killed the hope of all his disciples; but his resurrection revives their hearts, and renews and everlastingly establishes their hopes, no more to be thus damped. 'Tis probable that the Apostle, when he wrote this, remembered how it was with him and the rest of the apostles when Christ was dead. Before, they were full of hope of being advanced with Christ in his kingdom; but when he was dead, their hopes seem to be quashed and dead as it were with him. But when Christ was raised to life again, so were their hopes renewed and abundantly established, and their hearts were filled with joy.

7. This cross-reference is a later interlineation pointing to JE's discussion of the hope of resurrection in the next entry, No. 264.

Christ by his resurrection is said to be begotten. Acts 13:33, "God hath raised up Jesus again: as it is written, Thou art my Son; this day have I begotten thee." When the Father raised Christ from the dead, he was as it were begotten again of the Father. And so his disciples were with him begotten again to a "lively hope," or as it probably might have been better translated, a "living hope." The expression of a "living hope" seems to denote three things.

1. That as Christ, since his death, is alive again, so their hope was alive, and not dead, as the hope of the disciples was while Christ was dead, though Christians suffered persecution (vv. 6–7).

2. That their hope by Christ's resurrection is exceedingly established, and made strong and lively, so that they greatly rejoiced, as v. 8, yea, rejoiced "with joy unspeakable and full of glory."

3. Which seems more especially to be intended, their hope that is begotten and established by Christ's resurrection is an immortal and never-dying hope, as the Spirit of grace in the saints is called "living water," because it springs up into everlasting life (John 4:14), and Christ is called "the bread of life," because he that eateth thereof shall not die but live forever (John 6:51). The hope that the disciples had before Christ's death was in a great measure dead when he was dead, but now Christ is risen and is "alive forevermore" (Rev. 1:18). So the hope that is begotten and established by the resurrection of Christ is a living, never-dying hope; 'tis now too much established by that glorious resurrection of Christ ever to die again to that degree that the hope of the disciples died when Christ died. God the Father raised Christ,[8] incorruptible, never to die more, and thereby begot them "to an inheritance incorruptible" [I Pet. 1:4]. A rich father begets a child to an inheritance; so God, the Father of their Lord Jesus Christ, and their Father here spoken of, [has] begotten them to an inheritance, and this inheritance is incorruptible, "and that fadeth not away." And as their inheritance, that they are begotten to, is immortal and unfading, so is their hope a living and unfading hope (v. 4). The same power of God that raised Christ immortal will keep their faith alive, that it shall never die, as v. 5, "Who are kept by the power of God through faith unto salvation." So that their faith and hope lives still, though they be subject to great trials, even as refined pure gold will bear the fire (vv. 6–7). And therefore the Apostle exhorts them to "hope to the end" (v. 13), or to hope with a living and never-dying hope.

---

8. MS: "~~Christ rose~~ ⟨God ~~raise~~ the Father raised X⟩."

265. II Peter 1:11–21. V. 11, "So an entrance shall be ministered to you abundantly into the kingdom of our Lord and Savior Jesus Christ." By the kingdom seems to have been intended by the Apostle, and to be understood by the Christians in those days, the kingdom that Christ would set up and establish at his second coming, spoken of in the 16th verse. That was the principal accomplishment of that prophecy of the kingdom of the Son of God, in the 2nd and 7th chapters of Daniel, and was the greatest thing intended by Christ when he spake of his coming in his kingdom.

V. 12, "Wherefore I will not be negligent to put you always in remembrance of these things, though ye know them, and be established in the present truth." By "the present truth" seems to be intended the doctrine of Christ's second coming, because there were some apostates and false teachers among them lately risen up, spoken of, chs. 2 and 3, that denied it and opposed it; they denied "the Lord that bought them" (II Pet. 2:1), and of consequence, denied the second coming of Christ,[9] as appears by ch. 3. They were "scoffers, walking after their own lusts, saying, Where is the promise of his coming?" [vv. 3–4], for the Apostle in that chapter don't only speak of such a sort of men as future, but as what was now present, as having been foretold by the apostles of the Lord Jesus (v. 2). The apostles had foretold of scoffers that should come before the coming of Christ, as they knew, and the Apostle[1] speaks of that sort of men he had described in the second chapter as being in part a fulfillment of their prediction, as the apostle John says, I John 2:18. "Little children, it is the *last time*: and as ye have heard that Antichrist shall come, even now are there many antichrists; whereby we know that it is the *last time*." So here, II Pet. 3:2–3, the apostle Peter puts 'em in mind how the apostles of the Lord Jesus had told 'em, and they knew by their word, that "*in the last days* scoffers should come." Therefore the Apostle would not have them shocked by them, now they were come. 'Tis evident that the Apostle speaks of them as present, and not only future, by the following part of that chapter, particularly vv. 5, and 8–10, and 15–17. So that 'tis the doctrine of the second coming of Christ that was the doctrine that was especially opposed by apostates among them at that day, and therefore that doctrine is what the Apostle calls "the present truth." The Apostle in this verse signifies that he writes this epistle to establish them in, and

9. JE deleted "One principal end of the Apostle's writing this epistle is to establish those that he wrote to in this tra."
1. JE deleted "plainly."

put them in remembrance [of] what he calls "the present truth." But 'tis the truth of Christ's second coming that he writes this epistle to establish them in, as appears by the beginning of the 3rd chapter, where he uses the same expression of putting them in remembrance. "This second epistle I now write unto you; in both which I stir up your pure minds by way of remembrance, that ye may be mindful of the words spoken before by the holy prophets, and the commandment of us the apostles of the Lord and Savior." And that word and commandment was what they told 'em of Christ's second coming, as appears by what there follows.

Verse 16, "For we have not followed cunningly devised fables, when we made known unto you the power and coming of our Lord Jesus Christ." "*We*, i.e. the apostles, have not followed cunningly devised fables, when we taught you the *present truth* of the second coming of our Lord Jesus Christ," for he speaks of this as a doctrine that the apostles had taught them before (II Pet. 3:2). These apostates gave out that what Jesus had said about his second coming was only a fable cunningly devised by him, perhaps to maintain[2] the credit of his former pretences of being the Messiah prophesied of, that was to set up the kingdom of heaven, when otherwise he would have lost it all by his sufferings and disgrace that he met with while he lived, and to keep up the zeal of his followers, and so his name and honor after his death.

Verses 16–18, "But were eyewitnesses of his majesty," etc. They, the apostles, had not only "heard" him say that he would come in his kingdom in power and great glory, but they were in a sort eyewitnesses of it, in that they were eyewitness of something in Christ that was a remarkable and wonderful earnest and prelibation of it, viz. the glory of his transfiguration. The glory of the transfiguration was manifested to Peter, that wrote this epistle, and two other disciples, to that very end, that it might be an earnest[3] of what he had been telling them of his coming in his kingdom, and a specimen of the glory of his second coming; for in each of the three evangelists, the account of Christ's transfiguration follows next after Christ's foretelling them of his coming in his kingdom. What they saw of the glory of Christ's transfiguration was an evidence of two things that were dependent one on another, both which these apostates denied.

2. JE deleted "the hopes of his followers and keep up."
3. MS: "~~a specimen~~ ⟨an earnest⟩."

First, it was an evidence that he was the Son of God, the same that was declared by the voice which said, "This is my beloved Son."[4] This these apostates denied, II Pet. 2:1, "denying the Lord that bought them." This was evident by that glory that they saw, as,

1. The glory that Christ then appeared in was so divine and admirably excellent, and had such a bright and evident appearance of divinity, such an admirable and ineffable semblance of the infinitely glorious perfection of God, his awful majesty, his purity, and infinitely sweet grace and love, that evidently denoted him to be a divine person. The Apostle says, "He received from the Father honor and glory." The term is doubled and varied, thus to signify the exceeding excellency of the glory.

There was doubtless an inward sight, or lively sense of heart, of Christ's spiritual glory that accompanied Peter's sight of the visible glory of Christ. There was an ineffable beauty, majesty, and brightness in his countenance that held forth and naturally represented the excellencies of his mind,[5] his holiness, his heavenly meekness, and grace, and love, and that majesty that spake his union with the deity, and by the influence of the Spirit of God accompanying, excited in Peter and the other two that were with him a great sense of those perfections, and their immense excellency, adorableness, and sweetness. And the Spirit of God doubtless accompanied the word of God that Peter and the others then heard, so that that word was spiritually understood and believed, so that Christ's glory then was manifested to the disciples three ways. By the rays of light, it was exhibited to their eyes; by the voice, it was declared to their ears, and by the Spirit, to their souls. The last was the most convincing and certain evidence to them of Christ's divinity.

This glory of Christ that the apostles then saw, both the outward glory and that spiritual glory that the outward glory had a semblance of, did most remarkably appear to be such as exceedingly became the only begotten, dearly beloved, and infinitely lovely Son of God. Therefore the apostle John, who was another eyewitness of it, speaking probably with special reference to this, John 1:14, [says], "We beheld his glory, the glory as of the only begotten of the Father, full of grace and truth." It exhibited not only the divine greatness in the majesty, of which the apostle Peter in this place especially speaks, but the divine grace and love in the sweetness of it.

4. E.g. Matt. 3:17, Mark 9:7, Luke 9:35.
5. JE deleted "and of his divinity."

2. This glory that appeared in the[6] person of Christ did exactly resemble that excellent glory that the Apostle speaks of, out of which the voice came (v. 17). For there was there in the mount an external glory as a visible symbol of the presence of God the Father, and by which he was represented, as well as an external glory in God the Son, viz. that bright cloud that overshadowed them. There was a glory in that cloud that the Apostle calls an "excellent glory." When it is said in the evangelists that "a bright cloud overshadowed them" [Matt. 17:5], 'tis not meant a light or white cloud, as by a cast of light upon it by something shining, such as are some clouds by the bright reflections of the sun's light, but a cloud bright by an internal light shining out of [it], which light the Apostle calls an "excellent glory." It [was] probably an ineffably sweet, excellent sort of light, perfectly differing from and far exceeding the light of the sun. All light is sweet, but this seems to have been immensely more sweet than any other that ever they had, impressing some idea that we can't conceive of, having never seen it, as we can conceive of nothing of light more than we have seen. We could have conceived of no such light as the light of the sun, had not we seen it, nor of any color—blue, red, green, purple, nor any other. God doubtless can excite other ideas of light in our minds besides any of those that we have had, and far exceeding them, a light affording sweetness and pleasure to the sight far exceeding all pleasure of the grosser and inferior senses. Therefore Peter, the Apostle that writes this epistle, was exceedingly delighted with it in the time of it, which made him say, "It is good for us to be here" [Matt. 17:4], and made him talk of building tabernacles, and think of spending the rest of his days there. And he still (though now old and near his end, by vv. 13–14) retains a lively sense of the exquisite gloriousness and pleasantness of that light when he expresses himself, as he does here, calling [it] the "excellent glory." (See "Miscellanies," no. 721.)[7] And there probably was an exact resemblance between the glory that the disciples saw in Christ's face and that which they saw in this cloud, which declared him to be the Son of God; for they saw him to be his express image.

6. JE deleted "body and."

7. This reference is a later addition. In no. 721, entitled "HAPPINESS OF HEAVEN," JE asserts that after the resurrection the saints will have "external perception or sense" and that "every perceptive faculty shall be an inlet of delight," including the "noblest of all external senses," that of sight. Additionally, he notes, "the light of heaven, which will be the light of the brightness of Christ's glorified body, shall be a perfectly different sort of light from that of this world," as is "evident from the circumstances of Christ's transfiguration" and from Moses' vision of God on Mt. Sinai.

The apostle John who saw this, he probably afterwards in his visions saw the very same sort of light and glory as an emanation of the glory of God filling the New Jerusalem, which he now saw filling the mount of transfiguration, the type of it which he gives an account of in Rev. 21:11. "Having the glory of God, and her light was like unto a stone most precious, even like a jasper stone, clear as crystal." The light he then saw seems to be perfectly differing in nature from any that is to be seen in this [world], and immensely more sweet and excellent. He evidently wants[8] words and similitudes to set it forth; he wants something excellent, and sweet, and precious enough to set it forth. He says it was like "a stone most precious"; he knew none precious, or bright, or excellent enough to the sight. But he says it was "like a jasper stone," more resembling that than any other; but that is not sufficient, and therefore he adds, "clear as crystal." And from the whole we may gather it was something he could not express, and that there was nothing like. (See note on the verse.)[9] So it was the same kind of light that this beloved disciple had the glory of God represented by. Rev. 4:3, "He that sat was like a jasper and a sardine stone." A jasper and a sardine stone were of different colors, one green and the other red. How then could the light appear like both? By this it is plain that, indeed, it was like neither, and that the Apostle could find nothing to represent it by. There was all that was excellent in both. This is something like his seeing that the street of the New Jerusalem was like "pure gold," and yet like transparent "glass" (Rev. 21:18).

3. This glory that they saw in Christ appeared to them as communicated from that glory in the cloud, for the Apostle says, "He received from the Father honor and glory" [II Pet. 1:17]. The light in Christ's person appeared to them to be as it were lighted[1] up, or begotten as it were, by that in the cloud; or[2] the glory in the cloud appeared shining on Christ, and so communicating the same excellent brightness. This again declared him to be the Son of God, for it showed him to be the express image of the Father, and to be from the Father as begotten of

---

8. I.e. lacks.

9. JE's exposition of Rev. 21:11 focuses on the green of the jasper stone, the color easiest to the eyes, from which he infers that "the visible brightness and glory that will be seen in heaven, especially in the human nature of Christ, the person who is the brightness of God's glory, . . . will be exceeding great and doubtless immensely exceeding the coruscation of the sun." Yet it will not be painful, but rather "perfectly easy" and "infinitely sweet and pleasant" to the saints. Similarly, the spiritual glory of God will not be "overbearing" ("Blank Bible").

1. MS: "light."

2. JE deleted "rather."

him. Thus the glory of Christ's transfiguration was an evidence that he was the Son of God.

Secondly, it was also a special and direct evidence that what he had said a little before of his second coming was true, as it was given as a specimen of that glory that he should then appear in, and showed that this was the person that the prophet Daniel foretold would come in so glorious a kingdom, that the Jews called the kingdom of heaven, by the agreement there was between this glory they saw in Christ, and that which Daniel describes to be in that person that should set up that kingdom, whose garment is said to be "white as snow" (Dan. 7:9), as Christ's garments were said to be "white as the light" [Matt. 17:1], and "so as no fuller on earth can white them" [Mark 9:3].

And nextly, besides this visible glory, the Apostle mentions the voice that there was from the excellent glory in the cloud, "This is my beloved Son, in whom I am well pleased; hear him" (though the last clause, "hear him," is not here mentioned). It is observable that it is the very same that the glory that was "in the cloud" declared to the eyes of the apostles, that the voice "in the cloud" declared to their ears. The communication visible from this[3] glory to Christ, one glory as it were begetting another, and the exact resemblance of the glory begotten, declared him to be God's Son. And the sweet and exact agreement between one and the other, and the union that appeared by communication, denoted the love between the Father and Son, or that he was well-pleased in him. And this glory being given, as a specimen of the glory of his second coming, declared the truth of what he had so lately told 'em of his second coming, the same that the voice implicitly declared when it bid them "hear him," or believe what he said, which the disciples that heard it must especially apply to the things he had most lately told them and instructed them in.

Verse 19, "We have also a more sure word of prophecy; whereunto ye do well that ye take heed, as unto a light that shines in a dark place, until the day dawn, and the daystar arise in your hearts." By the "word of prophecy" is here meant the standing written revelation that God had given to his church, as appears by the two next verses. This is spoken of as surer than a voice from heaven. But the Apostle has a special respect to the prophetical part of this written revelation, and most of all those parts that speak of the glory of Christ's kingdom, which is the principal subject of scripture prophecy, particularly that

3. JE deleted "light."

prophecy in the 7th chapter of Daniel that speaks of the kingdom of heaven. This word of prophecy is "as a light that shines in a dark place." The time[4] of Christ's coming is here spoken of as the morning, when Christ, who is the sun, shall arise and appear; and his happy kingdom, that he shall then set up, is represented as the daytime. But the time that goes before that is here represented as nighttime, or a time of darkness, and we that live in that time as being in "a dark place." The "word of prophecy" is as a light shining in a dark place, or as the light of a bright star in this night, a light preceding the day of Christ's coming, like the morning star that is a forerunner of the day. The prophecies of that day foretell it, as the daystar foretells the approaching day. The prophets were harbingers of that blessed season, as the morning star is the harbinger of the day. By the prophecies of that day that go before it, something of the light of that day is manifested beforehand and is reflected to it, so that some of the light of the sun is anticipated, as by the daystar while it is yet night. If we give heed to these prophecies, we shall enjoy this foregoing light in our hearts, and so this daystar will arise there. Our faith in these prophecies will be the evidence of that glorious sun that is now not seen, and will render his light that is hoped for in some measure present in this dark world, and in our dark hearts. We shall in a measure have the joy of the morning of Christ's coming beforehand. We shall have a light in our hearts that will be an earnest and forerunner of the glorious light of that day, as the dawning of the day before sunrise.

This world is a dark place without Christ, and therefore is dark till he comes, and till his kingdom of glory is set up. It appeared to be so now, especially in the circumstances of the Christians that the Apostle now writes to, a world of heresies, grand delusions, and dreadful wickedness. They were in a dark place; they were not only surrounded with heathens and subject to persecution, as appears by Peter's first epistle that was written to the same Christians, as is evident by II Pet. 3:1, but were in the midst of vile heretics and apostates, as has been said already. And Christ delayed his coming, and they had many temptations to deny the present truth, and lose their hopes of the sun's rising. When a man is in a dark place, and is in danger of stumbling, and falling, and being lost, and has a light held forth to him to guide him in it, it behooves him to take heed to it, and keep his eye upon it, lest he get out of the way and fall into mischief.

4. MS: "~~day~~ ⟨time⟩."

266. EXODUS 33:18–23. Moses, when he beseeches God to show him his glory, seems to have respect to a visible glory, something to be seen with his bodily eyes, not exclusive of an inward sweet sense of those glorious perfections, of which the external glory that God manifests himself by is a semblance, which was wont to accompany the external discoveries of divine glory that God made to the prophets, the external glory being by the Spirit of God accompanying, being made a means of a sense of the spiritual glory, as the music of a song of praise is the means of a sense of the excellency of divine things. But by the context it is manifest that it was a visible glory that Moses had a most immediate respect to. Moses seems to have apprehended, from what he had seen of the visible manifestations that God had made of himself to him, and it may be from the apprehensions other holy men before him had entertained concerning God, from what God had revealed to them, that there was some transcendent external majesty and beauty, some immensely sweet and ravishing brightness, that the sight of would exceedingly fill the soul with delight that was immensely above all that he had seen yet. And God, in his answer to Moses and in what he did in compliance with his request, seems to allow Moses' apprehension, which probably was because it was God's design to all eternity to appear to the bodily eyes of his saints in such an external glory in the person of Christ, God-man. And Moses argued right from the visible manifestations of an external glory that God had often made. These were indeed an intimation that there was such a transcendent external glory in some sort belonging to God, even to the second person of the Trinity, in that it was established in God's gracious decree and eternal agreement of the persons of the Trinity, on the foot of which establishment were all God's proceedings with the church of Israel, that Christ should everlastingly be united to an external nature, and in that be manifested to his church in an external glory. The external manifestations that he had made of himself to Moses and other holy men were presages and prelibations of this. Moses longed to see and enjoy that [of] which they were specimens and prelibations. Christ is the glory of God and his image; and no man hath seen God at any time, but 'tis he that always manifested himself by visible appearances. God granted to Moses to see something of this glorious brightness, as he passed by, so much as was to be seen in his back parts. Probably God's back parts, as he passed by in a visible [manner], shone with an ineffably sweet and glorious brightness, far exceeding all the brightness that is ever seen in this world for glory and delightfulness. (See No. 265, even the preced-

ing note, pp. 213–16, of that note.) But God tells him that he cannot see his face, for no man should see him and live [v. 20], i.e. not only could they not see that spiritual glory that he manifests himself in in heaven, but there is evidently a respect to an external glory. No man should see that external glory of God's face, that God intended to manifest himself in to his saints in heaven to all eternity, in the face of Jesus Christ.

Corol. Hence the glory of Christ at his transfiguration was not that glory in which the human nature of Christ appears in in heaven, and especially that which it will appear in after the day of judgment, but only a shadow and faint resemblance of it. For that glory, God says, is such as no man can see and live; and so, of the appearances of Christ's visible glory that Isaiah, and Ezekiel, and Daniel, and the apostle Paul, and the apostle John had.

267. Exodus 33:18–19. "And he said, I beseech thee, show me thy glory. And he said, I will make all my goodness pass before thee, and I will proclaim the name of the Lord before thee, and will be gracious to whom I will be gracious, and will show mercy on whom I will show mercy." Moses, by his finding his great acceptance and favor with God in the power that his prayers and intercessions had with him, so as it were to appease God's wrath against the congregation of Israel, which was so great for their making the golden calf, and his obtaining by prayer the promise of so great a favor as that God's presence should go with them, which promise was made with this gracious declaration made of God's favor to him—"For thou hast found grace in my sight, and I know thee by name" [v. 17]—and God having in all this spoken to Moses as a man speaks to his friend, this great mercy of God to him has two effects on Moses. 1. It gives him a sense of God's excellency and glory, especially the excellency of his mercy and free goodness, by this manifestation of it to him and his people after their great sin, and makes him long for a full sight of the glory of [so] excellent and good a being. 2. It encourages him to ask for this exceeding great mercy of seeing God's glory. God's mercy and favor, being so very great in past instances, encourages him to ask yet further and more exceeding favor. And we don't find that God rebukes Moses as being too forward and presumptuous in such a request, and not being content with so great mercy as he had received already, but on the contrary seems to manifest an approbation of his making such an improvement of mercy already received, for he grants his request so far as is consistent with his present state.

Several things are observable concerning the manner of God's show-ing Moses his glory, wherein, though it was extraordinary, is agreeable to the manner of God's discovering himself to the souls of his people in this world.

1. It was not face to face, which is reserved for the heavenly state (I Cor. 13:12), but it was God's back parts.

2. It was as passing by. Herein is a great difference in the manner in which the saints have the discoveries of God's glory, and that wherein they shall see him hereafter. Hereafter they shall dwell in his presence. They shall be fixed in an everlasting view of the glory of God; their eye shall be perpetually feasted with a full vision of his face. But here, when the saints have extraordinary discoveries of the glory of God, they are transient and short; sometimes 'tis only a glance. Christ stands behind the wall for the most part; and when he shows himself, it is through the lattice, as passing by a window. But hereafter they shall be in his presence-chamber with him. Here the saints see God as passing by before them, and then he is gone.

3. Hereby is livelily represented how[5] [imperfect] the spiritual dis-coveries the saints have of God here. They see God as it were when he is gone by. They have something of a sight of him, but yet very imperfect, as of the back parts of one that is just gone by, giving of them a sense that he is indeed an infinitely glorious one, if they could but have a full sight of him. They can see so much as to give a sense what is to be seen, if they could but come at it. They seem to be as it were on the borders of seeing it; and their appetite is excited to see it, but while they are admiring, and longing, and reaching after it, it is gone and passed away.

4. The discovery of God's spiritual glory is not by immediate intu-ition, but by the Word of God is the medium by which it is discovered. 'Tis by God's proclaiming his name; so God reveals himself to the saints in this world by proclaiming his name in the joyful sound of the gospel.

5. 'Tis by causing his goodness to pass before him, which is agreeable to the way in which God discovers himself to his saints by the gospel, which in a peculiar manner [is] a manifestation of the glory of divine grace or good. Divine grace is the leading attribute in that discovery God makes of his glory by the gospel, wherein God's goodness is re-vealed more than any; wherein, and wherein especially it is revealed as

5. MS: "how ithe."

free and sovereign, and which is another thing that is a peculiar glory of the gospel. It is a revelation of free and infinite grace, as consistent with strict justice in punishing sin; and therefore both are mentioned together in that proclamation God makes of his name to Moses, as in the 5th, 6th, [and] 7th verses of the following chapter. (* See further, No. 358.)[6]

Another reason why God makes all his goodness to pass before Moses seems to be that this was the attribute that God had wonderfully been exercising towards Moses and the congregation of Israel, whereby Moses was now especially affected with that attribute, and especially longed to see the glory of it, as was before observed. And at the same time God tells Moses that he will be gracious to whom he will be gracious, and will show mercy on whom he will show mercy, because he had wonderfully manifested the sovereignty of his mercy in forgiving, as he had done, a people that had so exceedingly transgressed, as the congregation of Israel had done in making the golden calf, and also that Moses might not be lifted up by God's bestowing such unspeakable favors on him, as he had done and now promised to do, in answer to his request, but might be sensible that it was not for his worthiness, but his sovereign pleasure. And another reason is that the glory of God's goodness is that part of God's glory that such a poor, feeble, corrupt creature as man is can best bear the sight of while he lives and remains such, for 'tis the most mild and gentle attribute; and the manifestation of it affords a cordial and support to enable to bear it.[7]

268. I Corinthians 1:1. "Paul, called to be an apostle of Jesus Christ *through the will of God.*" St. Paul, when he calls himself an apostle, does commonly add some such clause, as here, "through the will of God." So II Cor. 1:1, "Paul, an apostle of Jesus Christ by the will of God"; and the very same words, Eph. 1:1, and Col. 1:1, and II Tim. 1:1. And I Tim. 1:1, "Paul, an apostle of Jesus Christ by the commandment of God our Savior, and Lord Jesus Christ"; and Rom. 1:1, "Paul, a servant of Jesus Christ, called to be an apostle, separated unto the gospel of God." V. 5, "By whom we have received grace and apostleship," which was because he continually carried a deep sense of his unworthiness to be an apostle, who before was so great a sinner; and how it was not

---

6. This cross-reference is a later addition.
7. This sentence is a later addition.

owing to anything in him that he was promoted to such dignity, but only to the sovereign will, and pleasure, and free grace of God, that, of a persecutor of the church, made him an apostle in the church. Therefore when he takes the honor of the name of an apostle, he[8] ascribes [it] to God's sovereign pleasure and grace. The cause of it is a sense of what he expresses in I Cor. 15:9–10. "For I am the least of the apostles, and am not meet to be called an apostle, because I persecuted the church of God. But by the grace of God I am what I am." Eph. 3:8, "Unto me, who am less than the least of all saints, is this grace given, that I should preach among the Gentiles the unsearchable riches of Christ."

269. ZECHARIAH 1:8. "I saw by night, and behold a man riding upon a red horse, and he stood among the myrtle trees that were in the bottom; and behind him were there red horses, speckled, and white." The grove of myrtle trees signifies the church. It was a grove of myrtle trees down in a bottom, hid by the adjacent hills, so that you were not aware of [it] till you were just upon it. This represents the low, dark, solitary, melancholy condition of the Jewish church at this time. They were overtopped by all their neighbors, buried in obscurity, as the woman in the wilderness (Rev. 12:6). Being in a valley is evidently used to signify being in mean, depressed, afflicted circumstances. Is. 32:19, "And the city shall be low in a low place." And being set on high on a mountain denotes a state of great honor and prosperity. Is. 2:2, "The mountain of the Lord's house shall be established on the top," etc. Hence Babylon, though built on a plain, is called a mountain (Jer. 51:25).[9] The man upon the red horse in the midst of this myrtle grove is no other than Jesus Christ, the same that appeared to Joshua "with his sword drawn in his hand, . . . as captain of the host of the Lord" (Josh. 5:13–14), and to St. John, as captain of the armies of heaven, sitting on a white horse, "clothed with a vesture dipped in blood," and out of his mouth going "a sharp sword, that with it he should smite the nations," who should "rule them with a rod of iron," and that "treadeth the winepress of the fierceness and wrath of Almighty God," having the armies of heaven following on white horses (Rev. 19).

Though the church was in a low condition, yet Christ was present in the midst of it. He was riding as a man of war, as a man in haste, riding on the heavens for the help of his people (Deut. 33:26). He rode on a

8. JE deleted "does so commonly."
9. The preceding three sentences are a later interlineation.

red horse, either naturally so or dyed red with the blood of war, as this same victorious prince appears red in his apparel, by treading on his enemies and besmearing his raiment with their blood, as in the forementioned place of Revelation and Is. 63:3. Red is a fiery color, noting what is said, vv. 14–15, that he was "jealous for Jerusalem and for Zion with great jealousy," and that he was "very sore displeased" with their enemies. Christ, under the law, appeared on a red horse, noting the terror of that dispensation, and that he had yet his conflict before him when he was to resist unto blood. But under the gospel, he appears on a white horse (Rev. 19:11), noting that he has now gained the victory, and rides in triumph, and hangs out the white, not the bloody flag. Here also follows him an army on horseback, as in the 19th chapter of Revelation. Behind him were some on red horses, some speckled, some white—angels attending on the Lord Jesus Christ, ready to be employed by him, some in acts of judgment, others of mercy, others in mixed events. And probably they appeared in the order in which they are mentioned, the red first, and the speckled next, and the white last: the red that appeared first, noting God's indignation[1] and just judgments against the church of Israel in their captivity, mentioned, v. 12, "Jerusalem and the cities of Judah, against which thou hast had indignation these threescore and ten years"; the speckled, that were partly red, partly white, noting God's present dealings with them, since their captivity, that were mixed. God had exercised great mercy towards them in restoring them out of captivity to their own land, and it was far otherwise with them than it had been. But yet it was a time of great adversity with them, which is signified by the myrtle trees being in a low place, and which was the occasion of the earnest intercession of him that stood among the myrtle trees for them (v. 12). The white horses that were last note that glorious prosperity which God now promises to his church, that shall be the conclusion and issue of all those troubles (vv. 13, 16–17). The color white sometimes is made use of to signify holiness or purity, and sometimes mercy and prosperity, sometimes freedom or purity from the evil of sin, and sometimes freedom from the evil of affliction. So it is evidently used, Rev. 7:14, "These are they which came out of great tribulation, and have washed their robes, and made them white in the blood of the Lamb."

270. REVELATION 4:3. "And there was a rainbow round about the throne, in sight like unto an emerald." The rainbow, we know, was

1. MS: "~~Anger~~ ⟨Indignation⟩."

appointed of God as a token of his gracious covenant with mankind. God is encompassed with a rainbow, which signifies that as he sits, and reigns, and manifests himself in his church, he appears as encompassed with mercy, as of old the throne of God in the holy of holies, where God manifested himself in the church of Israel, was called the mercy seat. So here there is a rainbow, the sign of God's gracious covenant, round about the throne that he sits on. This rainbow was "in sight like unto an emerald," which is a precious stone of an exceeding lovely green color, so green that this color appears in nothing else so lively and lovely. This color is a most fit emblem of divine grace; it is a very lively color, not so dull as blue or purple, and yet most easy to the sight, more easy than the more fiery colors of yellow and red. It is the color of all the grass, herbs, and trees, and growth of the earth, and therefore fitly denotes life, flourishing, prosperity, and happiness, which are often in Scripture compared to the green and flourishing growth of the earth. As the benign influence of the sun on the face of the earth is shown by this color above all others, so is the grace, and benign influence, and communication of God fitly represented by this color. This color is the color of joy and gladness. The fields are said to shout for joy, and also to sing, by their appearing in a cheerful green. As the color red is made use of to signify God's revenging justice, in Zech. 1:8 and elsewhere, so is green the emblem of divine grace. As Dr. Doddridge observes, this don't imply that the rainbow had no other color, "but that the proportion of green was greater than ordinary."[2]

271. REVELATION 12:1. The moon is a type of the revelation God made and the ordinances he instituted under the Old Testament, or of the Old Testament constitution and administration, and is so used (Rev. 12:1). See notes *in loc.*[3] And it is made use of in Scripture also as a type of the church; it is so in the festival of the new moon. See notes on Num. 10:10.[4] The church under the Old Testament, in the institution

2. This sentence, a later interlineation, dates from at least 1756. JE is citing Doddridge, *Family Expositor, 6*, 466.

3. In the "Blank Bible" JE asserts that "the moon under her feet" [Rev. 12:1] refers to "all sublunary or earthly things under her feet, the whole of this lower world, the earth with all the region that appertains to it, near to the orb of the moon. The moon is an attendant or satellite to this earth, and may be looked upon as the highest thing that appertains to the earthly system. All is under the feet of the church, that is clothed with the sun." In that location JE also references "Images," no. 139 (*Works, 11*, 99).

4. JE identifies the new moon as "a type of the beginning the new and glorious dispensation introduced by Jesus Christ, wherein the gospel was to be clearly and plainly preached

of that festival, must be supposed to be represented under the type of the moon before its conjunction with the sun, i.e. Christ the Sun, from whom the church borrows her light. The gospel light granted to the Old Testament church in its different successive ages was very much like the light of the moon in the several parts of the revolution it performs, which ends in its conjunction with the sun. The first[5] calling of Abraham, the father of the nation and founder of their church, as separated from the rest of the world by God's revealing, and establishing, and sealing his covenant to him and his seed, and bestowing the privileges of it upon them, and also the first institution of the administration of the church of Israel by Moses, may each of them be looked upon as the beginning of the moon's course in this revolution, wherein it sets out in the beginning of its month for a conjunction with Christ, its sun, at the conclusion of it. Christ's coming, and so mercifully and remarkably appearing to Abraham from time to time as his friend, and sometimes in the form of a man, as if incarnate, eating and drinking with him, and doing such great things for him and by him, and particularly his entering into covenant with him as the father and founder of this church, may be looked upon as this moon's first conjunction with the sun, or with Christ, from whence in her revolution she set out for the other conjunction at Christ's coming by his incarnation and resurrection. Abraham was not only the natural, but in some sense the spiritual, father of the church (as he is called in the New Testament, the father of believers), and therein is a type of Christ, and was in some respect a father instead of Christ, till Christ came.[6] After this, that[7] nation and church at first was very small and weak, but they gradually grew greater and more and more flourishing till Solomon's time, which was about the middle of the space between Abraham and Christ, or the middle of the revolution from one conjunction to an-

---

and proclaimed unto all nations. The moon is a lively image of the church, as she borrows all her light from the sun; so doth the church receive light from Christ, the Son of Righteousness." He contrasted the old moon, the church under the Old Testament, with the new moon, the church under the New Testament. The former received light from "Christ yet to come," and the latter "from Christ already come." JE associates "the conjunction of the sun and moon in the time of the change" with the incarnation of Christ, and he cites Arthur Bedford's judgment that Christ's conception probably occurred in the Virgin Mary at the "time of the change of the moon" ("Blank Bible").

5. JE deleted "revelation that was made of Christ or of gospel truth by Moses' institution of the Mosaic administration by Moses was like the first beginning of the moon's course in this revolution."

6. This sentence is a later interlineation.

7. JE deleted "posterity."

other. And then it was full moon; then both the nation and church were in their greatest glory. But from that time they were gradually diminished and dwindled, first by the nation's dividing into two kingdoms, and then by the captivity of the ten tribes, and then the captivity of the kingdom of Judah, and then after that by various calamities they suffered after the captivity, under the Persian, Grecian, and Roman monarchies, until at last the scepter departed from Judah, and they were put under a Roman governor; and their light was as it were put out, as the moon when she is just come to her conjunction with the sun.

But as the calling of Abraham, the father of the church and nation, may be looked upon as the beginning of the revolution with respect to the being and prosperity of the nation or church itself, so Christ's revealing himself to that people by Moses, the teacher of the church and the father of the prophets, by whom the administration they were under was first instituted, and who gave the first written revelation to it, may be looked upon as the beginning of the revolution with respect to the light that church had by prophecy and revelation by God's word, as written in the Old Testament, which Old Testament revelation is, as has been already observed, compared in Scripture to the reflected light of the moon in the night, to serve in the absence of the sun. Christ's coming, as he did to the children of Israel in Moses' time, his appearing first to him in the burning bush, and in such a wonderful way redeeming them out of Egypt—which was, if I may so say, the Old Testament redemption—redeeming them and revealing himself to them by Moses, and entering covenant with them by Moses (their great prophet, and king, and intercessor, like to Christ, and that was instead of God to Pharaoh, and instead of Christ to the people, and was as it were the Old Testament Christ; and therefore that church is called his "body," by Jude, v. 9 of his epistle), his coming down out of heaven to dwell amongst the people, whereby he as it were bowed the heavens and came down [Ps. 18:9], and the mountains flowed down at his presence [Is. 64:3], his speaking to the people with an audible voice, his speaking to Moses face to face, as a man speaks with his friend, his appearing in the form of a man to the seventy elders [Num. 11:24–25] (when they saw the God of Israel, and did eat and drink, which is spoken of as a new thing), and afterwards leading them into Canaan, and working such wonders for them by Joshua, who bears the name of Jesus, and was called the shepherd and stone of Israel in Jacob's blessing of Ephraim [Gen. 49:24], and was to the people in Christ's stead, as their leader and captain of salvation—I say, these things were as it were the first conjunction of the moon with the sun, whence she set out in her revolution, when the gospel light, or the revelation of Christ and the great truths respecting him, was but very small and dim, being almost wholly hid under types and shadows. After this it gradually increased; the prophets that were afterwards in Israel were more clear than Moses was in what they taught of gospel truth. The succession of prophets began in Samuel, and David had much of the spirit of prophecy. Gospel light was much more full and clear in the revelations made by him than it had been in any revelation the church enjoyed before. But in the revelations that were given by the prophet Isaiah, gospel light is fullest and clearest of all, beyond what we have in any other Old Testament revelation. This was at about the middle of the space between Moses and Christ. In Isaiah, the Old Testament church enjoyed gospel light as it were reflected from a full moon. There was no prophet afterwards that spake so fully of Christ, and afterwards the spirit of prophecy diminished. It continued in a smaller degree till some time after the captivity, and then wholly ceased in Malachi, or a little after his time; and the minds of the people became more [and] more darkened as to their notions of Christ and his kingdom, till Christ's time when they were exceeding corrupt and carnal, [and] expected a temporal messiah. They were under blind guides that led 'em into the ditch, and had in a great measure made void the commandment of God by their tradition, as the light of the moon ceases as she approaches to her conjunction with the sun.

272. GALATIANS 1:17.[8] "Neither went I up to Jerusalem to them which were apostles before me; but I went into Arabia, and returned again to Damascus." 'Tis probable that this was Arabia Deserta, which was that part of Arabia that lay next to Damascus, lying east of the land of Canaan, and reached up to the very neighborhood of Damascus. By the Apostle's going from Damascus into Arabia, and returning from thence into Damascus again, it looks as if the Arabia that he went into was that which was[9] neighboring to this city. "As Christ after his baptism withdrew into the wilderness,[1] before he actually began to preach, so 'tis no improbable conjecture, that St. Paul, after his conversion and baptism, withdrew into the deserts of Arabia, there to receive

8. JE marked this entire entry with a vertical line on the left side of the text one inch from the margin. He subsequently crossed out that line with circular countermarks.

9. JE deleted "bordering to."

1. JE deleted "of Judea."

the knowledge of the gospel by immediate revelation from Christ; and that this being done, he returned to Damascus, and after this his return, straightway preached Christ in their synagogues," as Acts 9:20. (See Wells' *Sacred Geography*, Pt. 2, pp. 22–23.)[2] This very well agrees with this context in which the scope òf the Apostle is to show that he had his gospel not from man, "but by revelation of Jesus Christ," as v. 12. "For I neither received it of man, neither was I taught it, but by revelation of Jesus Christ." And vv. 15–16, "But when it pleased God, who separated me from my mother's womb, and called me by his grace, to reveal his Son in me, that I might preach him among the heathen, immediately I conferred not with flesh and blood." Then come in the words of this verse that we are upon, to show how he did not confer with flesh and blood, but was taught immediately of Christ. "Neither went I up to Jerusalem to them which were apostles before me; but I went into Arabia, and returned again unto Damascus." This is a desert, uninhabited country; and therefore 'tis the more probable that the Apostle went thither for this end, and not to preach the gospel to any that dwelt there. And the inhabitants that were in Arabia Felix, under whose king, Aretas, Damascus then was, they were chiefly[3] heathens; but preaching to the heathens was not yet begun, though there were then some Jews that were then inhabitants of Arabia, of which we read in the 2nd chapter of Acts, "Cretes and Arabians" [v. 11].

273. I KINGS 7:15–22. Concerning the brazen pillars, Jachin and Boaz. These pillars were set in the porch of the temple, or at the entry into the temple, which was a type of heaven, to show how strongly the entrance of God's elect and covenant people into heaven is secured by God's immutable establishment and almighty power, and also how certain [they] there shall be when once they are entered, and that their happiness, which is supported by these pillars, shall be as perpetual and immovable as the pillars, as Rev. 3:12. "Him that overcometh will I make a pillar in the temple of my God, and he shall go no more out."[4] Jachin, "he shall establish,"[5] signifies both God's decree and promise; for they, by the covenant of redemption, become the same. God's decree of election is in Christ an eternal promise and oath, and the

---

2. Wells, *Historical Geography of the New Testament*, Pt. 2 (3rd ed., London, 1718), pp. 22–23.
3. MS: "~~probably~~ ⟨Chiefly⟩."
4. JE deleted "and I will write upon him the name of my God."
5. יָכִין.

promise made in time is but an expression of that for the dependence and comfort of the saints. 'Tis as it were a temporal decree. A promise is but an expression of a purpose; 'tis that in words that a purpose is in heart. The chapiters were made of lilies and pomegranates, the lilies especially denoting the honor, glory, and beauty of the saints. Lilies and flowers are used for a representation of honor, glory, and beauty in Scripture. Is. 28:1, "Woe to the crown of pride, to the drunkards of Ephraim, whose glorious beauty is a fading flower, which are on the head of the fat valleys," etc. Cant. 2:1–2, "I am the rose of Sharon, and lily of the valleys. As the lily among thorns, so is my love among the daughters." The pomegranate signifies the sweet fruit they shall bring forth and enjoy, the fruit of holiness that they shall bring forth, and the fruits of happiness, or that pleasure and satisfaction they shall enjoy. These spiritual fruits are often compared to pomegranates in Solomon's Song, and more frequently than to any other sort of fruit, as Cant. 4:3, 13, and 6:7, 11, and 7:12, and 8:2.

There was a very great number of these pomegranates on those chapiters, to signify the abundant happiness that is laid up for the saints. These fruits were hung on network and chainwork, to show how the graces of God's Spirit and the spiritual fruits of holiness and happiness are interwoven one with another, and are connected together, and depend one on another as it were by a concatenation.

274. JONAH 2:6. "The earth with her bars were about me forever." It alludes to the bars of a prison. He speaks of himself as having as it were been in hell. V. 2, "Out of the belly of hell cried I," which in Scripture is often spoken of as being in the bowels of the earth, and under the bottoms or foundations of the mountains. Deut. 32:22, "A fire is kindled in mine anger, and shall burn to the lowest *hell*, and shall consume the earth with her increase, and set on fire the *foundations of the mountains*." So here, "I went down to the bottoms of the mountains." So hell is spoken of as being under the bottom of the sea, in Job 26:5–6. "Dead things are formed from under the waters, and the inhabitants thereof. Hell is naked before him, and destruction hath no covering." (See notes on the place.)[6] Hell and destruction here seem to be synonymous

6. JE associates the "dead things," the *Rephaim*, with the dead inhabitants of the "infernal world," an abode called both "destruction" and "hell" in the Old Testament. These inhabitants include devils, giants and other sinners destroyed by the flood, uncircumcised heathen, and the wicked. When the apparitions of these evil ones appear, they are "very frightful and terrifying." The same term may also refer to "whales, and crocodiles, and other water

terms. Hell is by a metonymy called destruction. So Ps. 88:11, "Shall thy lovingkindness be declared in the grave, or thy faithfulness in destruction?" So Prov. 15:11, "Hell and destruction are before the Lord"; and Prov. 27:20, "Hell and destruction are never full"; and in other places.[7] This prayer of Jonah was indited by the Spirit of God, and so is mystical; and the Holy Ghost in it has an eye to Christ, who as it were went into hell in our stead. Hell is here represented as a prison in the heart of the earth, that hath the earth with its rocks and other strong and immovable parts for its walls and bars; and therefore 'tis such a prison as cannot be broken through, but effectually forever confines those that are prisoners there. And therefore it is said, "The earth with her bars were about me forever," i.e. it would have been so were it not for the wonderful power of God delivering me, which was stronger than the walls and bars of this prison.

275. GENESIS 13:10. "And Lot lifted up his eyes, and beheld all the plain of Jordan, that it was well watered everywhere, before the Lord destroyed Sodom and Gomorrah, even as the garden of the Lord, like the land of Egypt, as thou comest unto Zoar." Zoar here probably is the same city which was elsewhere called Zoan, which was of old the chief city of Egypt. (See No. 254.) The Hebrew letter *nun* seems easily convertible into *resh*, as in Achan, Achor, Nebuchadnezzar, Nebuchadrezzar. Zoan was probably at this time the most famous and the royal city in Egypt. It stood in the delta of Egypt, or that part of it that was near the sea, through which the river Nilus ran in many branches, so that it was well watered everywhere, as the land about Sodom is here said to be, for "it had not only the river Jordan running through it, but the river Arnon from the east, the brook Zared (Num. 21:12), and the famous fountain Callirrhoe (Pliny, Lib. 5, ch. 16), from the south, falling into it." [Stackhouse,] *Complete Body of Divinity*, p. 350. (Probably this fountain is the same with the well which the princes of Israel digged with their staves, Num. 21:16–18.) And probably, being a low flat country, which is sometimes called a plain, sometimes a valley (Gen. 14:10), [it] was in the time of the swelling of Jordan overflowed, as Egypt was with the Nilus.

---

monsters which God forms from under the waters . . . terrible huge monsters" ("Blank Bible").

7. JE deleted "So here in this verse in the next words it follows, Thou hast brought back my life from destruction." He then failed to delete "i.e from *hell*."

276. GENESIS 19:24–28. Concerning the destruction of Sodom and parts adjacent.[8] The very ground of that region, great part of it, seems to have been burnt up, for it was in great measure made up of bitumen, or what the Scripture calls slime. Gen. 14:10, "And the vale of Siddim was full of slime pits; and the kings of Sodom and Gomorrah fled, and fell there." And because of the abundance of bitumen in the lake of Sodom, it was called of old, and is still, *Lacus Asphaltites.* "It is full of bitumen, which, at certain seasons, boils up from the bottom in bubbles like hot water."[9] "This bitumen, [which] is a very combustible matter, is in some places liquid, and in others firm, and not only lies near the surface of the earth, but lies sometimes very deep, and is dug out of the bowels of it."[1] So that the streams of fire that came from heaven set the very ground on fire; and therefore 'tis here, in the 28th verse, that Lot "looked toward Sodom and Gomorrah, and toward all the land of the plain, and beheld, and, lo, the smoke of the country went up as the smoke of a furnace." So that the country burning was a very lively representation of the general conflagration; and by the melting of the bituminous ground in many places was probably a burning lake, and so was a lively image of hell, which is often called the lake of fire, and the lake that burns with fire and brimstone [Rev. 19:20] (Note that bitumen is a sulfurous substance. Bailey's *Dictionary*),[2] and therefore is fitly compared to hellfire in Scripture (Jude 7). There seems to be an evident allusion to the manner of the destruction of this country in Isaiah 34:9–10. "And the streams thereof shall be turned into pitch, and the dust thereof into brimstone, and the land thereof shall become burning pitch [or bitumen].[3] It shall not be quenched night nor day; the smoke thereof shall go up forever; from generation to generation it shall lie waste; none shall pass through it forever and ever." Deut. 29:23, "And the whole land thereof is brimstone, and salt, and burning, that is not sown, nor beareth, nor any grass groweth therein, like the overthrow of Sodom and Gomorrah,

8. JE deleted "It is the very soil of that."
9. Stackhouse, *Complete Body of Divinity*, p. 352.
1. Ibid., p. 351.
2. The parenthesis is a later interlineation. "BITUMEN, an inflammable Matter fat and unctuous, which Naturalists distinguish into three Sorts, hard, soft and liquid or oily; some Bitumens are fossils, others are found floating on lakes, and others spring out of the Earth like fountains, one kind of it is a sort of Slime, clammy like Pitch, and smelling something like Brimstone. The Ancients used it instead of mortar for building, and also instead of oil for lamps. It is an imperfect fatty Sulphur, consisting of an Oil and a vague acid combined" (Nathan Bailey, *An Universal Etymological English Dictionary* [London, 1736], n.p.).
3. JE's brackets.

Admah, and Zeboim, which the Lord overthrew in his anger and in his wrath," where we are expressly taught that the very ground of this country was burnt. The ground burning up sunk the land, and made this valley deeper, so that after that the waters of Jordan perpetually overflowed it; and besides, there was probably an earthquake at the same time by which the ground subsided, as the tradition of the heathen was. 'Tis probable that the same time as the meteors of their air were enflamed, the bitumen and other combustible matter that was in the bowels of their earth was also enkindled; or the fire, that was first kindled on the top of the ground, might run down in the bituminous and sulfurous veins deep into the earth, and being there pent up, might cause earthquakes after those cities and inhabitants were all consumed, which might make the country to sink, and turn it into a bituminous and exceeding salt lake. The ground there was doubtless very likely to sink by an earthquake, being hollow, as 'tis evident it is still, in that since the surface of the earth hath been broken to let down the water of the river Jordan and other streams, there is no outlet out of the lake above ground, but they have a secret passage under the earth. The bitumen there is mixed with an abundance of niter and salt which, by their repugnant quality, might cause a more violent struggle in the fire that burnt down into the caverns of the earth to cause an earthquake. See many of these things in *Complete Body of Divinity*, pp. 351–52.[4]

277. EXODUS 7:9–12. Moses' rod,[5] when cast unto the earth, became a serpent. So Christ, when sent down to the earth, appeared in the form of sinful flesh; he was made sin for us. So Christ was represented by the brazen serpent [Num. 21:9], that was made in the form of the fiery serpents that bit the people. Moses' rod, when on the ground in the form of a serpent, swallowed up the serpents of the magicians. So Christ, by being made sin, he swallowed up the devils, the parents of sin. When he appeared in the form of sinful flesh and for sin, he condemned sin in the flesh. By being made a curse, he destroyed the curse; by suffering the punishment of sin, he abolished the punishment of sin. And at the same time that being made sin, he destroyed sin and the devil, and so swallowed up the serpents in that sense, so he received and embraced sinners (that are in themselves serpents) by his

4. Stackhouse, *Complete Body of Divinity*.
5. The biblical text states that Aaron, not Moses, cast his rod on the ground.

love and grace, so that they became as it were his pleasant food; and so he swallowed down serpents. In this sense God's people are represented as his pleasant food; so they are represented as the wheat in opposition to tares, and as his good grain in opposition to chaff. See also Is. 6:13. "But yet in it shall be a tenth, and it shall return, and shall be eaten: as a teil tree, and as an oak, whose substance is in them, when they cast their leaves; so the holy seed shall be the substance thereof." See further, No. 385.[6]

278. II CHRONICLES 25:9. "And Amaziah said to the man of God, But what shall we do for the hundred talents which I have given to the army of Israel? And the man of God answered, The Lord is able to give thee much more than this." Amaziah seemed to look upon it an hard thing to part with so great a sum, but the words that the Prophet spake to him were not vain words. God plentifully rewarded Amaziah for obeying God's command in this particular, for God gave him success against his enemies that he was going to war with; and he obtained victory over the children of Edom, as in vv. 11–12, so that he obtained the same end without the help of the army of Israel, that he aimed at by paying the hundred talents to hire their help, and therefore lost nothing by not taking them with him. And probably Amaziah was much more than paid for his hundred talents by the spoils of his enemies. But yet this was not all that God did in reward for his obeying his command by the Prophet, for though he carried himself very wickedly after this, so as to bring God's judgments on himself during his life, yet God seems to have remembered what he had done in his son Uzziah's days; and Amaziah's success in this very expedition against the Edomites was the occasion of vastly enriching his son Uzziah. For that which seems in times past to have been the principal source of the wealth of the kings of Judah was the trade that they had by the Red Sea to Ophir, for gold, which was carried on from two seaport towns upon the Red Sea, viz. Eloth and Ezion-geber, which places were in the land of Edom, as appears by I Kgs. 9:26–27. "And king Solomon made a navy of ships in Ezion-geber, which is beside Eloth, on the shore of the Red Sea, in the land of Edom." And by means of this trade very much, it was in all probability that Solomon so enriched the country in his time, so as to make silver as plenty as stones there. The principal seaport that was made use of till Jehoshaphat's time was Ezion-geber;

6. This cross-reference is a later addition.

but Jehoshaphat, having there lost his fleet that he had prepared to send from thence to Ophir, his ships being broken to pieces on the rocks there, as I Kgs. 22:48, they seem after that to have made use of Eloth instead of Ezion-geber, as being a safer harbor. The kings of Judah continued in the possession of this trade to Ophir as long as they continued in the possession of the land of Edom, where those seaports were, which was till the days of Jehoram, the son of Jehoshaphat. But "in his days Edom revolted from under the hand of Judah, and made a king over themselves," as II Kgs. 8:20. And so the kings of Judah, from that time, lost Eloth and their trade to Ophir, until the days of Amaziah, who conquered them, and brought 'em into subjection again in that expedition spoken of in the context, to assist in which he had given the hundred talents to the army of Israel. But God gave him such success without this hired army that he brought the country under, and so recovered Eloth; and his son Uzziah rebuilt it, and so renewed the trade to Ophir from thence, as in the next chapter, verses 1–2. "Then all the people of Judah took Uzziah, who was sixteen years, and made him king in the room of his father Amaziah. He built Eloth, and restored it to Judah"; and by this means he became an exceeding wealthy prince, and filled the land with riches. And therefore Isaiah, who in the beginning of his prophecy prophesied in the days of Uzziah, says, Is. 2:7, "The land also is full of silver, and there is no end of their treasures."

"This king lost one hundred talents by his obedience; and we find just that sum given to his grandson, Jotham, as a present (II Chron. 27:5). Then the principal was repaid, and for interest, ten thousand measures of wheat, and as many of barley." Henry.[7]

279. DANIEL 7:13. "I saw in the night visions, and, behold, one like the Son of man came with the clouds of heaven, and came to the Ancient of days, and they brought him near before him." Here both Christ's humanity and divinity is signified: his humanity, in that it is said, "one like the Son of man," and his divinity, in that he "came with the clouds of heaven." Appearing with bright clouds, or with the Shekinah, is a token of divinity, for this is often in Scripture called "the glory of the Lord" [Ex. 16:10], and sometimes "the cloud of glory" [I Kgs. 8:10–11].

7. This paragraph is a later addition. Henry, *Exposition*, 2 (1725), 564.

Another thing that may be observed of these words is that it is not said, that he descended with the clouds of heaven, or that he ascended, but he "came with the clouds of heaven, and came to the Ancient of days," which is equally applicable to both his ascension into heaven, when he went to receive his kingdom and to be invested with his royal dominion and glory, and his last coming at the day of judgment, which is called his "coming in his kingdom," and doubtless includes both, for one was like the other, and might very well both be spoken of under one. For as the angel told the disciples of Christ's ascension, "This same Jesus shall come in like manner as he was seen to go into heaven" [Acts 1:11]; he shall descend in the same manner as he ascended. In both he comes with clouds of heaven (Acts 1:9). In both he comes attended with hosts of angels, and probably in both with the whole multitude of the heavenly hosts; in both he is attended with risen saints, for 'tis probable that those saints that came out of their graves with him also ascended with him. In both he comes to the Ancient of days, and is brought near before him: he is so in his ascension, for he ascended to his Father to appear before him, there to receive a kingdom of him; and when he comes at the last day, he will come to the Ancient of days in a more mystical sense, for all the glory that he will be invested with on that day will be by his Father, and all that he will do in the day of judgment will be as acting from his Father, and in his name. He shall then, in the most glorious manner of all, receive a kingdom from his Father; he shall then be brought near to the Father, and set down in the Father's throne in the most eminent manner of all. He shall then most fully receive his church, the kingdom of his grace, that is made up of all peoples, nations, and languages, as in the next verse [Dan. 7:14]. Both these are remarkable periods, or epochs, of the commencement of the kingdom of heaven, of which the Messiah is the king, and are so spoken of in the New Testament.

This prophecy doubtless has respect to Christ's ascent into heaven, for to that 'tis much the most obviously and directly applicable; that is most plainly spoken of in the New Testament, as the time when he went to God, the Ancient of days, to receive his kingdom. It also doubtless has respect to his coming to judgment, for that coming to judgment seems often in the New Testament spoken of with reference to this very prophecy; with reference to this, 'tis called his "coming in his kingdom." The Jews seem to have taken that phrase of the Messiah's "coming in his kingdom" [Matt. 16:28] from this prophecy; and with reference to this, it seems often to [be] spoken of in the New

Testament as "the Son of man's coming in the clouds of heaven" [Matt. 24:30].

280. EXODUS 12:15. Concerning LEAVEN. It was a most fit type of the corruption of the heart by reason of its sourness, and because of its infecting, spreading nature, so that "a little leaven leavens the whole lump" [I Cor. 5:6] (in which respect also it is a fit type of false doctrine, as Matt. 16:6, 11–12), and because of its swelling nature, for the nature of corruption is to swell self. It radically consists in inordinate self-love, and primarily is manifest in pride and self-exaltation. The swelling nature of leaven represents the nature of corruption with respect to its principle, viz. inordinate self-love; and the sourness of it represents its nature with respect to its tendency, which is enmity.

But especially is leaven a fit type of original sin by reason of the manner of its propagation; for as original sin is propagated from father to son, and so from generation to generation, so it is with leaven. One lump leavens the next, and that the next, and so leaven is propagated from lump to lump to lump forever. The old lump leavens the new, and therefore is called the old leaven. See Papers on Original Sin, p. 86.[8]

281. I KINGS 3:1. Solomon's marrying Pharaoh's daughter seems to be a type of two things. 1. Of the calling of the Gentile church. The Egyptians were aliens from the nation of Israel, but now she that was an Egyptian is not only made an Israelite, but she is made the queen in Israel. So the Gentile church, when she was called, was not only received to like privileges that the Jewish church were wont to enjoy, but to vastly greater privileges. 2. The union of Christ with his whole church in all ages is typified, for the church is made up altogether of those that were sinners by nature, aliens from God and Christ, and the children of the devil. Pharaoh is often used in Scripture as a type of the devil. She that is made the church and spouse of Christ is naturally the daughter of the spiritual Pharaoh.

8. JE's reference points to his "Book on Controversies" (MS, Yale coll.) where he asserted, "That LEAVEN is so much made use of in the law of Moses as a type of sin is an argument that sin is an evil nature derived from our parents." He compares the communication of "sourness and fermentation" from the old lump of leaven to the new with the "corruption of nature" passed "from father to son through successive generations." Page 86 contains a reference to No. 280. JE used the "Controversies" notebook to record his thoughts on a variety of theological topics, including "Original Sin."

But especially does this seem to typify what shall come to pass in the last and most glorious times of the church, for the reign of Solomon is especially a type of those times. At that time especially will there be a great gathering of the Gentiles unto Christ; multitudes of nations, that till then were gross heathens, will be espoused unto Christ. And then will the grace and love of Christ be in a most remarkable manner exercised towards sinners, and great sinners, and those that were distinguished as the children of the devil. Then will many nations be brought to the church that before were the church's greatest enemies, as Pharaoh was a grand enemy of God's church and people, but yet now his daughter is married to the prince of Israel. And particularly the nations that have been subject to Antichrist, who is spiritually called Pharaoh, shall then be espoused by Christ. This type is fulfilled at the same time with those prophecies. Is. 19:24–25, "In that day shall Israel be the third with Egypt and with Assyria, even a blessing in the midst of the land, whom the Lord of hosts shall bless, saying, Blessed be Egypt my people, and Assyria the work of my hands, and Israel mine inheritance." Egypt and Assyria were remarkable enemies of Israel, and both in their turns held them in bondage and slavery. See also other prophecies of the calling of Egypt.[9]

282. JEREMIAH 2:2–3. "I remember thee, the kindness of thy youth, the love of thine espousals, when thou wentest after me in the wilderness, in a land that was not sown. Israel was holiness to the Lord, and the first fruits of his increase." See also v. 21, "Yet I had planted thee a noble vine, wholly a right seed." See Ps. 68:14.[1] This has not respect to that generation that went out of Egypt, whose carcasses fell in the wilderness, that were a very corrupt generation, but the generation of their children, spoken of Num. 14:31. "But your little ones, which ye said should be a prey, them will I bring in, and they shall know the land that ye have despised." So Deut. 1:39. It has respect to those spoken of Jer. 31:2, "The people which were left of the sword that found grace in the wilderness."[2] The same generation that entered into the land of Canaan with Joshua, and took possession of the good land,[3] it was the

9. See, for example, Ps. 68:31, Is. 11:11, and Zech. 10:10.
1. This reference and preceding sentence are a later interlineation. JE explains the phrase "white as snow in Salmon" [Ps. 68:14] as a reference to "the holiness of that generation that first entered into Canaan under Joshua" from which God had fully cleansed "the pollutions of Egypt" ("Blank Bible").
2. This sentence is a later interlineation.
3. The remainder of this sentence is a later interlineation.

generation that God planted in Canaan, as is evident by v. 21. And the going after God in the wilderness, that is here spoken of, is not the going of the children of Israel out of Egypt into the wilderness of Sinai, but their following God through that dreadful[4] wilderness that the congregation long wandered in after they went back from Kadesh-barnea, which is spoken of, Deut. 8:15. "Who led thee through that great and terrible wilderness, wherein were fiery serpents, and scorpions, and drought, where there was no water." Although this generation had a much greater trial than the generation of their fathers had before they came to Kadesh-barnea, yet [they] never murmured against God in anywise as their fathers had done; but their trials had a contrary effect upon them, viz. to humble them and fit them for great mercy. Deut. 8:2–3, "And thou shalt remember the way which the Lord thy God led thee these forty years in the wilderness, to humble thee, and to prove thee, and to know what was in thine heart, whether thou wouldst keep his commandments, or no. And he humbled thee," etc. And vv. 15–16, "Who led thee through that great and terrible wilderness," etc., "that he might humble thee, and that he might prove thee, to do thee good in thy latter end." And therefore it is said, Hosea 13:5, "I did know thee in the wilderness, in the land of great drought."

This generation were eminent for piety, as appears by many things said of them in the book of Numbers, and especially Joshua. See Josh. 23:8, and 22:2. See Deut. 4:3–4. See also note on Hos. 11:1.[5] [See] Jer. 31:2–3; Hos. 9:10; Jer. 2:21; Ps. 68:14; Josh. 1:16–18; Judg. 2:7, 17, 22.[6] Though there were some wicked men amongst them, they were not like their fathers, an unbelieving generation, but believed God, and followed him, and by faith overcame Sihon and Og, and the giants and mighty nations of Canaan. They showed a laudable and fervent zeal for God on several occasions, on occasion of Achan's sin, but especially when they suspected the two tribes and half had set up an altar in opposition to the altar of burnt offering before the tabernacle.

4. MS: "~~Great & terrible~~ ⟨dreadfull⟩."

5. JE notes that Israel, when called out of Egypt by God, was a "child" not only "because he was young at that time as a nation, but that generation that God loved and brought into Canaan were literally children when God called 'em out of Egypt" ("Blank Bible").

6. All of these references are later interlineations. It is unclear whether JE intended these biblical citations as simple scriptural references or as references to notes elsewhere in his writings. For example, he spoke of "a remnant that were redeemed, that found favor, [and] were brought into Canaan" in his exposition of Jer. 31:2 ("Blank Bible"). He identified the "grapes in the wilderness," spoken of in Hos. 9:10, with Israel's forefathers who were accounted a "delight and pleasure" (ibid.). On Ps. 68:14, see above, note 1; on Judg. 2:7, see below, note 7.

Israel feared and served the Lord all the days that the men of that generation lived. Add to this No. 296. See notes on Judg. 2:7.[7]

283. II Kɪɴɢs 2:11–13. Concerning Elijah's translation. Elijah's ascension into heaven seems to be a type of the ascension of Christ. Before he ascended, he asked his disciple Elisha what he should give him; so Christ, when he ascended, gave gifts unto men. When Elijah ascended, his mantle fell from him, which is a type of the righteousness of Christ, as righteousness is often in Scripture[8] represented by a garment. Christ, though he himself went away, yet left his righteousness for his church and people here below. The efficacy of what he did and suffered still remained for the justification of sinners here below, though he himself was gone; and the saving fruits and benefits of it were communicated more abundantly after his ascension than before. "God exalted him with his own right hand to be a prince and a Savior, to give repentance unto Israel, and remission of sins" [Acts 5:31]. Elisha received a double portion of his spirit when he ascended; so when Christ ascended, he sent down abundant measures of his Holy Spirit on his disciples and followers. The condition of Elisha's receiving a double portion of Elijah's spirit was his seeing him when he ascended; so it is by faith in the ascended Savior that we receive the Holy Spirit from [him]. We can receive no spiritual benefits from him any otherwise than as we see him in his glorious exaltation by an eye of faith.

284. Hᴇʙʀᴇᴡs 6:19. "Which hope we have as an anchor of the soul, both sure and steadfast, and which entereth into that within the veil." That which is here called "hope" is the same with the grace of "faith," but only with respect to one kind of its exercises, viz. those that respect God's promises, or our own future promised good. 'Tis no other than trust in God (or rather faith in God) through Christ for salvation. This agrees with the context, beginning with the 12th verse, and with the description given of hope in the words themselves, for 'tis faith in Christ that is the stability of the soul. Faith is that by which we are built on that strong rock, so that we can't be overthrown; and the same is the anchor by which we are held fast, and can't be driven to and fro of wind and storms, and shipwrecked, and lost. That which is here called

7. This reference and the preceding cross-reference are later additions. In the "Blank Bible," JE cites briefly "traditions preserved . . . among the heathen" concerning the righteousness of the first generation of Jews in Canaan.
8. JE deleted "compared."

"hope" is the very same that is elsewhere called "faith"; and saving and justifying faith is often in the New Testament called by the name of hope, as in Rom. 8:24–25. "For we are saved by hope, but hope that is seen is not hope: for what a man seeth, why doth he yet hope for? But if we hope for that we see not, then do [we] with patience wait for it." How are we saved by hope, but as we are saved or justified by faith? It further appears that by "hope" here is meant "faith," by the following words, "But hope that is seen is not hope," etc., compared with the words of the same Apostle, Heb. 11:1, "Faith is the evidence of things not seen"; and by the next verse, "But if we hope for that we see not, then do we with patience wait for it," compared with the 12th verse of the context in this 6th [chapter] of Hebrews, "That ye be followers of them who through faith and patience inherit the promises." And it may be further confirmed by comparing this last place with the foregoing verse, "And we desire everyone of you to show the same diligence to the full assurance of hope to the end," and also comparing both with the 19th verse, the text we are upon. That "faith" with the Apostle sometimes signifies the same with "hope" is manifest from his description of it, in the first verse of Hebrews 11, "FAITH is the substance of things HOPED for." And Gal. 5:5, "We through the Spirit wait for the HOPE of righteousness through faith." And Col. 1:23, "If ye continue in faith grounded and settled, and be not moved away from the hope of the gospel." "Continuing grounded and settled in faith," and "unmoved in the hope of the gospel," are expressions evidently used as exegetical one of another. And Heb. 3:6, "If we hold fast our confidence and rejoicing of hope firm unto the end"; our confidence and our hope seem to be synonymous. So Rom. 4:18, "Who against *hope believed in hope*"; I Tim. 1:1, "Jesus Christ, which is our hope." So the apostle Peter seems to use the term hope. I Pet. 1:21, "Who by him do believe in God, that raised him up from the dead, and gave him glory, that your faith in hope might be in God." So I Pet. 3:15, "Be ready to give a reason of the hope that is in you with meekness and fear," that is, to give a reason, or declare the grounds, of your faith. So hope seems to be used for faith by the apostle John. I John 3:3, "Every man that hath this hope in him purifieth himself, even as he is pure."

Hope, in the New Testament, is often spoken of as a great Christian grace and virtue, and one of the main things that distinguishes a true Christian, which would be difficult to understand or account for, if by hope is meant no more than what we commonly understand by the word, viz. his thinking well of his own state, or hoping well of his future state. That is not hard to do; 'tis what nature is prone to. But by hope they doubtless meant something more, viz. an embracing the promises of God, and fiducial relying on them, through Christ for salvation. This is that great Christian grace that the Apostle speaks of in the 13th chapter of I Corinthians, where he speaks of faith, hope, charity. And by faith, there and elsewhere, where it is distinguished from hope, is meant faith in a larger sense, viz. acquiescing in the truth in whatever he testifies or reveals, without any special regard to our own concern and future interest in what he reveals. Hope is our acquiescing and relying on God's truth and sufficiency as to what concerns our own future happiness.

285. EXODUS 25:10–22. "And they shall make an ARK of shittim wood," etc. The ark was upon many accounts a lively type of Jesus Christ. The ark was united to the Godhead; it had the cloud of glory over it and upon it, which was the symbol of God's immediate presence. The ark was the throne of God (Jer. 3:17); i.e.[9] it was that that was his immediate seat, and where he was present in an higher manner than he was in any other place, or to which his presence was united in a more immediate manner than anything else. God was present in the land of Canaan, or the Holy Land, more than in any other part of the face of the earth.[1] God was present in Jerusalem, the holy city or city of God, above all other places of the land of Canaan; and he was present in his temple above all other places in that city, as a king is more immediately present in his own house than in any other part of the royal city. But God was present with the ark, which was his throne, more than in any other part of his house. So the human nature of Christ is as it were the throne of God, where God is present more than in any other part of the whole universe. It is, of all created things, the highest and most immediate seat of the divine presence, that in which God resides in a higher and more eminent manner than in any other part of the highest heaven itself, that is, his temple. The ark in itself was, in some respects, a mean thing for the throne of God, and for the symbol of God's most immediate presence; it was only a wooden chest. It appeared without that form and pomp that the heathen images did, on which account the heathen despised it, and the children of Israel were often ashamed of it, and had a mind to have images in the stead of

9. JE deleted "the place."
1. JE deleted "therefore this land is called the place of his seat, Jerusalem."

it, as the heathen had. So the human nature of Christ is in itself a mean thing; man is but a worm. The human nature has no glory in itself; it is but a vessel that must receive its fullness from something else. As this chest in itself was empty, its fullness was what was put into it. Christ, when he was on the earth, appeared without form or comeliness [Is. 53:2], without external pomp and glory. The Jews, when they saw him, saw no beauty wherefore they should desire him; and he was despised by the Gentiles. He was "to the Jews a stumbling block, and to the Greeks foolishness" [I Cor. 1:23]. Though the ark was in some respect mean, yet it was exceeding precious; though it was made of wood, yet it was overlaid with gold. So the man Christ Jesus was exceeding excellent, though he was a man, one of the mean race of mankind; yet he was an holy man, perfectly holy, endowed with excellent graces and virtues. Christ, God-man, Mediator, is wonderful; his name is secret. His person and offices are full of unfathomable mysteries. Hence Christ's name is called "Wonderful," as the prophet Isaiah says [Is. 9:6]; and the angel that wrestled with Jacob says, "Why askest thou after my name?" [Gen. 32:29], seeing it is secret or wonderful. And Isaiah, ch. 53, says, "Who shall declare his generation?" [v. 8]; and Agur, in Prov. 30:4, says, "What is his son's name, if thou canst tell?" As an ark is a thing shut up, what is in it is secret; hence secret things are called arcana. The mercy seat was upon the ark, and never was separated from it, which shows that God's mercy is only in and through Jesus Christ. The ark was God's chest or cabinet. Men's cabinets contain their most precious treasure, which denotes the infinite dignity and preciousness of Christ in the sight of God the Father, and the infinite love the Father hath to him, and delight he hath in him. The beloved Son of God is his most precious treasure, in which God's infinite riches, and infinite happiness, and joy from eternity to eternity does consist. Cabinets are made to contain a treasure. So the ark contained the precious treasure of the law of God and the pot of manna, the one signifying divine holiness, of which the law of God is an emanation and expression, and the other signifying divine happiness, for manna was spiritual and heavenly bread or food. But food is the common figure in Scripture to represent happiness, delight, and satisfaction; or in one word, those two things that were contained in this cabinet signified the Holy Spirit, which is the same with the divine good or fullness of God, his infinite holiness and joy. Christ is the person in whom is the Spirit of God, and therefore is called the Anointed. "In him dwells the fullness of the Godhead" [Col. 2:9]; he is the cabinet of God the Father, in which is contained all his treasure. In him the Father beholds infinite beauty (or holiness, which is the beauty of the divine nature); and in him the Father has his food, or infinite delight and satisfaction.

The ark in the temple was not only God's cabinet, containing his treasure, but it was also Israel's cabinet; it contained the greatest treasure of the children of Israel. See note on Is. 4:5.[2] So Christ is the greatest treasure of his church: he is their pearl of great price; he is the church's portion and chief good. In him is contained all the church's fullness; "Of his fullness she receives, and grace for grace" [John 1:16]. All her happiness, all the covenant blessings that she hath, are bound up in Christ. The church hath the Holy Spirit, which is the sum of all her good, no otherwise than through Christ and in Christ. God hath given the Spirit, not by measure unto him and from him [John 3:34]; it flows to his members, as the oil on Aaron's head "went down to the skirts of his garments" [Ps. 133:2]. Particularly, 'tis only in and through Christ that the church hath holiness, expressed in the law of God, and happiness, expressed by the pot of manna.

The ark itself, considered separately from the things it contained, was only a repository and vehicle to contain other things more precious than itself. So the human nature of Christ is only a repository or vehicle to contain and convey that which is infinitely excellent and precious. In this human nature of Christ dwelt God himself; the divine Logos dwelt in it by his Spirit, signified by the law and manna. The Spirit of God never dwelt in any other creature in anywise as it dwells in the man Christ Jesus; for in him it dwells without measure, on which account also he is called Christ, or Anointed. By the Spirit of God's dwelling in so high and transcendent a manner, the human nature is united to the divine in the same person. And as the human nature of Christ is as it were the container of the deity, a vessel full of the divine nature, so it is as it were the vehicle of it by which it is conveyed to us, in and through which it might be as it were ours in possession. For 'tis by the Godhead's being united to the nature of man, that it becomes the portion of men, as the ark of old was as it were the vehicle of the deity to the children of Israel. It was that by which they had the deity, whose

2. JE speaks of the pillar of cloud and fire as a defense for the children of Israel and the covering of the tabernacle as a shelter for its beautiful contents. From these examples he generalizes about the sanctuary provided by God. "The glory of God's people, their most precious treasure, shall be hid safe in God's pavilion." In like manner, "the life of every Christian is hid with Christ in God, and his treasure is laid up in heaven" ("Blank Bible").

dwelling place is in heaven, dwelling amongst them as their God, and by which God maintained a gracious communication with them.

The human nature of Christ had the Logos, or the Word of God, dwelling in it, as the divine eternal person of the Son is often called. This was typified by the ark's containing the word of God in it, written in tables of stone and in the book of the law. Christ is the Light of the world, as that law contained in the ark is represented as the light of the congregation of Israel. Deut. 33:2, "From his right hand went a fire of law for them." Christ is the Bread of life that came down from heaven; he is that that was signified by the manna in the wilderness, as Christ teaches in the 6th chapter of John. And he is so by the Spirit that dwells in him, and that he communicates, which was typified by the ark's containing manna, the bread from heaven.

The law that was put into the ark signified the righteousness of Christ, containing both his propitiation and obedience. Christ's preparedness for both is signified in the 40th psalm by that, "Thy law is within mine heart" [v. 8]. God's law was put within Christ's heart, as the law was put within the ark. Hence he satisfied the law by his sufferings, for it was out of regard to the honor of God's law that, when he would save them that had broken it, he had rather himself suffer the penalty of the law than that their salvation should be inconsistent with the honor of it; and it was also because God's law was within his heart that he perfectly obeyed it.

God was wont to manifest his glory from above the ark in the holy of holies; so it is only by Christ that God manifests his glory to his church. They see the glory of God in the face of Jesus Christ; he is the effulgence, or shining forth, of his Father's glory. So God was wont to meet with the children of Israel over the ark, and there speak with them, and give forth his oracles and answers; so it is by Christ only that God reveals himself to his church. "No man hath seen God at any time; the only begotten Son, that is in the bosom of the Father, he hath declared him" [John 1:18].

The ark is called the ark of the covenant; the covenant that [God] made with the people was contained in it. The covenant that God hath made with mankind is made in[3] Christ. The covenant was made with him from eternity; the covenant was then committed to him for us. The promises were given us in Christ, and 'tis he that reveals the covenant, and he is the mediator and surety of the cove-

---

3. JE deleted "and by."

nant. The book of the covenant was shut up in the ark, which denotes the mysteriousness of the things contained in this covenant.
As was said before, things shut up in an ark are secret, or arcana;
and especially hereby seems to be signified that the great things of
the covenant were in a great measure hidden under the Old Testament. They were covered as with a veil. As Moses put a veil over his
face [Ex. 34:33], so he hid the covenant in an ark. The ark itself was
hidden by the veil of the temple, and the book of the covenant was
hid by the cover of the ark; i.e. they were as it were hidden under
Christ's flesh. The carnal typical ordinances of the Old Testament
are in Scripture represented as Christ's flesh (Rom. 2:1–4;[4] Col.
2:14). The veil signified the flesh of Christ (Heb. 10:20), and so doth
the cover of the ark, or the ark considered as distinct from what was
contained in it. The covenant of grace was, and the glorious things
of the gospel were, contained in that book that was laid up in the
ark; but it was as it were shut up in a cabinet, hid under types and
dark dispensations. Christ rent the veil from the top to the bottom;
so he opened the cabinet of the ark. The faces of the cherubims
were towards this ark, and the mercy seat upon it, to pry into the
mysteries of the person of Christ, and of this covenant of grace; for
these things, as the apostle Peter says, "the angels desire to look
into" [I Pet. 1:12].

The ark was carried on staves on the Levites'[5] shoulders; so Christ is
brought to his church and people in the labors[6] of the ministers of the
gospel.

It seems, by Jer. 3:16–17, as though the ark were a type of the
church as well as of Christ; but no wonder, for the church hath such an
union and communion with Christ that almost all the same things that
are predicated of Christ are also, in some sense, predicated of the
church. Christ is the temple of God, and so is the church. Believers are
said to be his temple, and they together are said to be "built up a
spiritual house," etc. [I Pet. 2:5]. The law is in Christ's heart (Ps. 40), as
the law was in the ark; so God promises to put his law into the hearts of
his people. Christ is the pearl of great price; he is the Father's treasure,
his chief delight. So the church is his cabinet, and believers are his
jewels. The ark represents the human nature of Christ especially, or
body of Christ; the church is called the "body of Christ" [Eph. 4:12].

4. This biblical reference seems unrelated to JE's discussion.
5. MS: "P̶r̶i̶e̶s̶t̶s̶ ⟨Levites⟩."
6. MS: "h̶a̶r̶d̶ Labours."

286. HAGGAI 2:8. "The silver is mine, and the gold is mine, saith the Lord of hosts." This is to remove a great objection that was a principal ground of their discouragement in building the temple, viz. their poverty. They had not silver and gold wherewith to do the work, as Solomon had. The first temple was exceedingly adorned with silver and gold, but they had not wherewith thus to adorn this house. Cyrus commanded his subjects to help them with silver and gold (Ezra 1:4); but Artaxerxes, he that was now king of Persia, instead of that, forbid their proceeding in the building (Ezra 4:23–24). But in this verse God signifies to them that God don't need their being rich in order to his fulfilling his promise of making this latter temple glorious. Though the silver and gold was not theirs, yet it was God's, and in his hand; and if he needed it to accomplish his promise, he could find ways that enough of it should be produced. And it was needless for 'em to be much concerned about adorning the house with silver and gold, and so dedicating silver and gold to him, for all the silver and gold in the world was his already, as Is. 66:1–2. "Where is the house that ye build to me, and where is the place of my rest? For all those things have my hands made, and all those things have been, saith the Lord; but to this man will I look," etc. And there were other ornaments of greater importance than these, of a spiritual nature, as God elsewhere shows of how little importance the offering of their beasts to God was, in comparison of other things that were spiritual, by that, that all the beasts of the field were his already, "and the cattle on a thousand hills" [Ps. 50:10–11].

287. I JOHN 3:9. "Whosoever is born of God doth not commit sin." I.e. he don't relapse, or fall away from righteousness into sin again. "For his seed remaineth in him," i.e. the seed of which he is born of God. The same seed, by which he is begotten of God, remaineth in him; and therefore he don't fall away to a state and trade of sin again, out of which he was begotten and born by that seed.

288. HEBREWS 10:1. "The law having a shadow of good things to come, and not the very image of the things." Here a shadow is distinguished from images or pictures, as being a more imperfect representation of the things represented by it. The types of the Old Testament are[7] compared to this kind of representations of things, not only here, but Heb. 8:5 and Col. 2:17, which fitly resemble them on several ac-

---

7. JE deleted "often."

counts. The shadow of a thing is an exceeding imperfect representation of it, and yet has such a resemblance that it has a most evident relation to the thing, of which it is the shadow. Again, shadows are dark resemblances; though there be a resemblance, yet the image is accompanied with darkness, or hiding of the light. The light is beyond the substance, so that it is hid. So was it with the types of the Old Testament; they were obscure and dark. The light was beyond the substance; the light that was plainly to reveal gospel things came after Christ, the substance of all ancient types. The shadow was accompanied with darkness and obscurity; gospel things were then hid under a veil.

289. HEBREWS 13:12–14. "Wherefore Jesus also, that he might sanctify the people with his own blood, suffered without the gate. Let us go forth therefore unto him without the camp, bearing his reproach. For here we have no continuing city, but we seek one to come." Christ suffered as one that was not fit to live amongst men, nor to die in a place where men dwelt, and therefore was carried forth as execrable, without the gate, to suffer there. Such *reproach* did Christ suffer, and such were the circumstances of the Christian church in those days, that those that would be the faithful followers of Christ must suffer like reproach. They that were cast off by the generality of men, they were looked upon as not fit for human society, worthy to be shut out from dwelling with men. Matt. 10:22, "And ye shall be hated of all men for my name's sake." If they would cleave to Christ, they must e'en go forth with him without the camp, reputed as unclean as he was; they must be shut without the gates of the city as execrable too, and must bear his reproach, or the same reproach that he bore. So the Apostle advises 'em to be willing "to go forth u⸳ ⸳o him without the camp, bearing his reproach,"[8] and for his sake to be willing to leave the city, and as it were to dwell without the gate where he suffered. And to encourage 'em to this, the Apostle tells them that here they have no continuing city, but they seek one which is to come. It need not so much grieve to go forth to Christ without the gates of the earthly city, or to do that which shall expose 'em to be shut out from the society of the bulk of mankind as not fit for human society, or to dwell with them in their cities, for here in this world is no continuing city. The cities that we are born in and where we have dwelt are not continuing cities. The privileges and benefits that men, that were well received in them, enjoyed were no

8. JE later marked off the remainder of this paragraph with horizontal lines across the page and a vertical line down the middle of the entry.

abiding things; and this might be a great encouragement to them, that if they, for Christ's sake, left these earthly cities and possessions that are,[9] at longest, of short continuance, they should for them receive a continuing city and incorruptible inheritance hereafter.

But by going forth to Christ "without the camp," or the gate of the city, the Apostle here seems especially to mean exposing themselves to be shut out as unclean from the congregation of the Jews, and from the temple and city of Jerusalem, and from the religious society of the Jews in their synagogues, by their forsaking the ancient legal sacrifices and other legal observances for Christ (v. 9). The city of Jerusalem, at that time especially, was not a continuing city, for it was dreadfully destroyed by the Romans in about four years after this epistle is supposed to have been written.[1]

290.[2] JUDGES 11:30–40. Add this to No. 223, concerning Jephthah's vow, at the place marked *. 'Tis particularly forbidden in the law of Moses, in the strictest manner, that the children of Israel should not worship God by offering up their children in sacrifice to him (Deut. 12:30–31). There God charges them not to worship him in the manner that the inhabitants of Canaan had worshiped their gods, and then mentions, as the most abominable thing in their worship, that they had offered up their children for burnt offerings.

291. THE BOOK OF REVELATION. Concerning the authority of the book of Revelation, see "Preface" of Lowman's *Paraphrase*, pp. i–iii. "The book of Revelation is, for very good reasons, received as one of the sacred books of the New Testament; the reasons for which are to be seen in many authors, and are represented, with great evidence and strength, by Sir Isaac Newton, who observes he does not find any other book of the New Testament so strongly attested, or commented upon so early as this.

"Mr. Lardner has collected, with great care and faithfulness, the testimonies of the most early Christian writers, to the books of the New Testament, in a late excellent treatise of *The Credibility of the Gospel History*.[3] I shall just mention the testimony of the most eminent, to the authority of this book as a part of the Holy Scripture.

9. JE deleted "not of an abiding nature."
1. JE marked off this sentence with horizontal lines at the top and bottom and a vertical line about one third of the way from the left margin.
2. This number, which was not JE's, was added later by another hand.
3. Concerning Nathaniel Lardner, see *Works*, 5, 66–67.

"Tertullian wrote about the year of Christ 200, and so somewhat above one hundred years after the time in which St. John writ the Revelations. He observes, 'John, in the Apocalypse, is commanded to correct those who eat things sacrificed to idols and commit fornication.' And again, 'We have churches, disciples of John; for though Marcion rejects his Revelation, the succession of bishops, traced to the original, will assure us that John is the author of it.' It is no wonder Marcion should reject the Revelation, who rejected all the Old Testament, and of the New received only the Gospel of St. Luke, and ten epistles of St. Paul, which also he had corrupted and altered.

"Somewhat before this, Clement of Alexandria quotes these Revelations as St. John's: 'As John says in the Revelation.' And he refers to them as the words of an apostle, or having the authority of apostolical writings.

"Yet earlier, Theophilus of Antioch, in a book of his against the heresy of Hermogenes, makes use of testimonies from John's Apocalypse.

"We have another witness of great character still nearer the times of St. John: Irenaeus writ about A.D. 178, within seventy or eighty years of him. He expressly ascribes the Revelation to John, the disciple of the Lord. His testimony to this book, as Mr. Lardner observes, 'is so strong and full, that considering the age of Irenaeus, it seems to put it beyond all question, that it is the work of St. John, the apostle and evangelist.'

"Still nearer the times of St. John, Melito, bishop of Sardis, one of the seven churches, writ a book on the Revelations of John. Some think it was an entire commentary; however that be, it will show he esteemed it a book of canonical authority.

"Justin Martyr, a person of eminent name, about the year of Christ 140, and so about fifty or sixty years after the writing this book, expressly calls it a prophecy, and ascribes it to John the apostle. 'A man from among us,' says he, 'by name John, one of the apostles of Christ, in the Revelation made to him, has prophesied.' In fine,

"The church, nearest the times of writing this book, received it with so full consent, that in a very few years, as Dr. Mills observes, it was acknowledged and placed in the number of apostolical writings, not only by the churches of Asia, but by the neighboring churches of Syria and Samaria, by the more distant churches of Africa and Egypt, by Rome, and the other churches of Europe. Such reasons there are to receive this as one of the books of the Holy Scriptures of the New

Testament, that hardly any one book has more early, full, or authentic attestations given to it."[4]

292. MATTHEW 24:21–24 ff. "For then shall be great tribulation, such as was not since the beginning of the world to this time, no, nor ever shall be. And except those days should be shortened, there should no flesh be saved; but for the elect's sake those days shall be shortened. Then if any man shall say unto you, Lo, here is Christ, or there; believe it not. For there shall arise false Christs, and false prophets, and shall show great signs and wonders; insomuch that, if it were possible, they shall deceive the very elect," etc.

1. By those days of great tribulation that Christ here speaks of, is not to be understood only the tribulation that accompanied the taking and destroying the city of Jerusalem by Titus, but 'tis a day of tribulation to the spiritual Jerusalem as well as the literal. 'Tis a day of tribulation wherein the elect, or true Christians, should be concerned, as seems to appear from v. 22, and also by the 23rd verse. For it seems to be partly for this reason, that Christ warns his church to beware that, under such a day of extraordinary temptation, they should not be overforward to believe any that appeared in his name, pretending to be Christ appearing in his second coming to deliver 'em from their sufferings. For that was all the primitive Christians expected, that when Christ came the second time, he would deliver his church from its sufferings and tribulations. And Christ speaks of his second coming at this time, as the day of their redemption out of their tribulation. Luke 21:28, "Then lift up your heads, for your redemption draweth nigh."[5] And therefore, knowing that through their great tribulation they would be earnestly waiting for his coming, and so under temptation to listen to any that pretend in his name to set up for their deliverers, and appear to lead[6] them to war against their enemies, therefore Christ warns them not to listen or follow such impostors. The Christian church was especially under this temptation under the persecutions of Rome heathen, for in those days especially there prevailed an opinion in the church that Christ would soon appear for their deliverance.[7]

4. Moses Lowman, *A Paraphrase and Notes on the Revelation of St. John* (London, 1737), pp. i–iii.

5. The last two sentences are later interlineations.
6. MS: "head."
7. This sentence is a later interlineation.

2.[8] When Christ says, "Except those days should be shortened, no flesh should be saved; but for the elect's sake those days shall be shortened," Christ seems to have respect to those days of tribulation, that he had been speaking of in the former part of the chapter, not only in the 21st verse, but in the 7th-10th verses, that those earthquakes, famines, etc. (Mark 13:8), are said to be the beginning of, which were not only sorrows to the Jews, but Christians, as is evident by what immediately follows. "Then shall they deliver you up to be afflicted, and shall kill you; and ye shall be hated of all nations for my name's sake. And then shall many be offended, and shall betray one another, and shall hate one another."

3. Therefore the time of tribulation here spoken [of] is, as the prophet Jeremy expresses it, the time of Jacob's tribulation. Jer. 30:7, "Alas, for that day is great, so that none is like it: it is even the time of Jacob's trouble, but he shall be saved out of it." It is the time of the trouble, both of the literal and spiritual Jacob. The literal Jacob shall be saved out of it, when the time come that the Apostle speaks of in the 11th of Romans, when "all Israel shall be saved" [v. 26]. And the spiritual Jacob shall be saved out of it, as appears by the words of Dan. 12:1, where there seems to be reference to those words of Jeremiah. "And at that time shall Michael stand up, the great prince which standeth for the children of thy people. And there shall be a time of trouble, such as never was since there was a nation, even to that same time. And at that time thy people shall be delivered, everyone that are found written in the book." And that the spiritual Jacob, or the elect, shall be delivered out of it, appears by the words of Christ in this place, where Christ seems to have reference to what had been before said by both these other prophets.

The prophecies of the Old Testament that speak of Israel, Jacob, Jerusalem, Zion, commonly have respect, both to the Christian church, and also the nation of the Jews, in things that are to be fulfilled to both in the latter days; and so it is here in the 24th of Matthew. See note on Num. 24:23–24.[9]

8. MS: "2. ~~It further~~ It further appears by the 8. 9. & following verses where X Speaks of the beginning of ~~Sor~~ those Sorrows or tribulations ~~where X he there Speaks of the tribulation both of the Jews by Gods Judgment & also of his own People by Persecution~~." JE crossed out these words with a large "X."

9. This reference is a later addition. JE states that Num. 24:23–24 points prophetically to "the great and unparalleled calamities and troubles" that shall occur to both "the natural and spiritual posterity of Abraham." The Jews were to suffer "amazing destruction" at the hands of the Romans, and the Christian church was to suffer "both from Rome heathen and

4. More particularly, by the time of tribulation here spoken of is meant the whole time of the tribulation and suffering, both of the literal and spiritual Israel, from the Roman Empire, or the whole time wherein both the literal and spiritual Jerusalem shall be trodden underfoot by Rome, or the spiritual Babylon, beginning with the troubles that both Jews and Christians suffered under Nero, about which time was that "beginning [of] sorrows," spoken of in the 7th, 8th, and 9th verses, and ending with the "time, and times, and half a time" [Rev. 12:14] of the reign of Antichrist.[1] That this tribulation should be suffered from Rome, or in the spiritual Babylon, is signified by Christ, in v. 28. "Wheresoever the carcass is, there will the eagles be gathered together." The tribulation is by the eagles, i.e. the Roman powers preying on the carcasses of Israel.[2]

5. The tribulation of the literal and spiritual Jews from Rome both began about the same [time], and therefore both the sufferings of the Jews and the persecution of Christians from the Romans are mentioned together in the preceding part of this chapter, and called "the beginning of sorrows" [v. 8]. About the same time that the troubles of the Jews from the Romans began, the persecution of Christians began under Nero, who persecuted both Jews and Christians together. And both will end together, viz. when the power of Rome, the city that has brought this tribulation upon them, ends. Much as of old, the captivity of the Jews ceased when Babylon, that carried them captive, was destroyed; so when the spiritual Babylon falls, the Christian church shall be delivered, and the Jews shall be called.

6. The tribulation of the literal Jerusalem and the Jewish nation, spoken of by Christ, at the time that we have an account of in this chapter, was not any short tribulation, or something that should soon be over, but is expressly spoken of by Christ as that which [shall] be continued for many ages, and even till the commencement of the glorious times of the Christian church in the latter ages of the world. Luke 21:23–24, "There shall be great distress in the land, and wrath upon this people. And they shall fall by the edge of the sword, and shall be led away captive into all nations; and Jerusalem shall be trodden down of the Gentiles, until the times of the Gentiles be fulfilled."

---

antichristian." This was the "great tribulation" spoken of by Christ in Matt. 24 ("Blank Bible").

1. JE deleted "which Christ in this place calls the 'times of the Gentiles' (Luke 21:24)."
2. The last two sentences are a later interlineation.

The calamity or judgment upon the Jews, here spoken of, is manifestly the same with the tribulation spoken of in Matthew, so far as that nation were the subjects of it. But this calamity or judgment, here spoken of, is the great and sore judgment of God on the Jewish nation, that has now continued for many ages, begun in the destruction of Jerusalem by the Romans, their state of captivity and dispersion into all nations, and being trodden down of all nations. But this calamity yet continues, and is spoken of in the words as what shall be continued, "till the times of the Gentiles be fulfilled." This tribulation was but begun when Jerusalem was destroyed. The calamity was not ended when the destruction was finished; it is not ended till they are delivered from that destruction, or till the state of destruction they were then brought into ceases. The calamity of being killed, or brought into a state of death, is not ended as soon as a man is killed; it is then but brought to perfection. It is not ended till the resurrection comes. The tribulation on the Jews can't be said to be ended as long as the ruin of the city and dispersion of the nation brought by it remain. These are the great judgments spoken of as included in this tribulation, and as long as the judgments remain, the tribulation is not ended.[3]

7. And as the calamity brought on the Jewish nation by Rome continues all this time, so is the Christian church throughout this time kept in a state of tribulation and oppression. There was indeed a short intermission of their trouble after Constantine came to the throne, but this was no proper end to their day of tribulation, but only a short breathing spell. It is represented by St. John as silence for "half an hour" [Rev. 8:1]. But soon after this, the church of Christ began again to be persecuted by the power of the Roman Empire, first by Arian emperors, and afterwards by the[4] power of Rome antichristian, and is to be persecuted to the end of Antichrist's reign, or that "time, times, and an half" that the holy city is to be trodden underfoot, and that forty-two months, or 1260 days, wherein the woman is to remain in the wilderness [Rev. 12:14], and the witnesses are to prophesy in sackcloth [Rev. 11:3]. This whole space of time may be called "the time of Jacob's trouble" [Jer. 30:7], or the time of the tribulation of the church of God, a time of far greater outward affliction than ever the church of God saw, from the beginning of the world till that time, and greater than ever it should see again. This long period of suffering of his

3. The preceding three sentences are a later interlineation.
4. JE deleted "An Pope of Rome and the Roman hierarch."

church Christ had respect to when he said, he did not come to send peace on the earth, but a sword [Matt. 10:34]. This whole time is what is called the time of "the mystery of God," as 'tis called, Rev. 10:7; and the time of "these wonders," as 'tis called, Dan. 12:6, i.e. the time of God's mysterious and wonderful dealings with his own people in their great sufferings. See note on Rev. 10:7.[5] This is properly the time of the church's travail; for from Nero's time till now, the church has been in travail, to bring forth the glory of the approaching millennium, or the establishment of Christ's kingdom through the earth. When the millennium begins, then will the church, that God has redeemed from being an accursed Jericho by the blood of his firstborn, have gates set up; but from the time of the laying the foundation in the blood of that firstborn till this time, even all the while this Jericho is in building, it has been by the shedding the blood of God's younger children [I Kgs. 16:34]. This long space of time is the time of the slaying those children, being the time of the building of the city, till it is finished in setting up the gates of it. And all this tribulation has been from one enemy, viz. the spiritual Babylon, or the idolatrous empire of Rome.

The church in all ages in this world may be said to be, in a degree, in a militant state, and the triumphant state to be reserved for heaven. But of the different states of the church in this world, compared one with another, one may be called the militant, and another the triumphant state of the church. And the state of the church from Christ's time till the downfall of the spiritual Babylon, may be called its militant state, and after that, during the millennium, it is in its triumphant state. This is properly "the time of Jacob's trouble," beyond all that went before it or shall follow it. The church's sufferings properly follow Christ's sufferings, as the church's glory follows his. The church bears the cross after Christ, and so follows him to the crown; 'tis made "conformable to his death" [Phil. 3:10], that it may be conformable to his resurrection. The troubles of the church come after Christ's, to fill up, as the Apostle expresses it, what is behind of the sufferings of Christ [Col. 1:24]. The sufferings of the head is, in some respects, a forerunner of the sufferings of the members, as the glory of the head is of the glory of the members. This whole time is the time of the captivity of God's people in the spiritual Babylon.

---

5. This reference and the preceding sentence are a later interlineation. In "Apocalypse," JE states that the "mystery of God," the suffering of the church, shall be finished at the time of the "fall of the Roman antichristian church" (*Works*, 5, 172–73).

8. Christ in these words probably has an eye to what is said by the prophet Jeremy, in the place forementioned, ch. 30 of his prophecy, 6th and 7th verses, where he speaks of the church's travail, and says, "Ask ye now, and see whether a man doth travail with child? Wherefore do I see every man with his hands on his loins, as a woman in travail, and all faces are turned into paleness. Alas, for that day is great, so that none is like it. It is even the time of Jacob's trouble, but he shall be delivered out of it." Here the prophet seems indeed to have some respect to Jacob's trouble from the literal Babylon, and the deliverance of the Jews out of their captivity unto that Babylon. But 'tis manifest that 'tis something else he has a main respect to under that time, viz. the time of Jacob's trouble under Rome, the spiritual Babylon. And that deliverance out of this trouble that he speaks [of], is not what the Jews had on their return from the Babylonish captivity, nor at any time before the calling of that nation at the beginning of the glorious times of the church. For 'tis said, v. 8, that at that day "strangers shall no more serve themselves" of them, and that "Jacob shall return, and shall be in rest, and in quiet, and none shall make him afraid. . . . And their nobles shall be of themselves, and their governor shall proceed from the midst of them," as vv. 8, 10, 21; but these things have never yet been accomplished to that nation. And then 'tis mentioned as the peculiar glory that shall attend this deliverance, that they should serve David, their king, whom the Lord would raise up unto them, which was not accomplished on the Jews' return out [of] Babylon, for this king did not appear till many hundred years after; and when he did appear, they did not serve him, but crucified him. And his rising again was followed with the destruction of that land and Jerusalem, instead of building it on her own heap, as v. 18, so that this has never yet been accomplished.

9. But that this great tribulation, that Christ speaks of, is no short tribulation, finished when Jerusalem was destroyed by the Romans, but that which is not ended till the reign of Antichrist is ended, and respects not only the sufferings of the outward but also the spiritual Jerusalem, is more fully manifest from what the prophet Daniel says of it. Dan. 12:1, "And at that time shall Michael stand up, the great prince that standeth for the children of thy people. And there shall be a time of trouble, such as never was since there was a nation, even to that same time. And at that time thy people shall be delivered, everyone that is

found written in the book."[6] Concerning these words in Daniel, several things are manifest.

(1) 'Tis manifest that this is a time of trouble and great trial to the church and people of God, and that 'tis the same people that is first in this trouble, that through Michael's standing up and appearing for them in their distress, shall deliver them out of trouble, as 'tis often spoken of in Scripture, as God's manner of dealing with his people, first to bring 'em into great distress, and then to appear or stand up for them in their extremity, and deliver [them]. Probably here is an eye to the forementioned prophecy of Jeremy, where this time of trouble is said to be "the time of Jacob's trouble" [Jer. 30:7], and that the same Jacob should be delivered out of it. Daniel made use of those prophecies of Jeremy, at the time that he had these revelations, as appears by Dan. 9:2. And 'tis further manifest by the 7th verse, where, speaking of the time when this time of trouble should be ended, 'tis said to be "when he should have accomplished to scatter the power of the holy people" [Dan. 12:7].

(2) 'Tis manifest this is a time of trouble, that was to be in the Christian church after the Messiah had appeared in the world; for after the Prophet, in the foregoing chapter, had been giving an account of many successive events that be between the time that then was and the coming of the Messiah, he now in the beginning of this chapter proceeds to give an account of the Messiah's coming, and what should befall God's church after that. "And at that time shall Michael stand up, the great prince that standeth for the children of thy people," etc.

(3) 'Tis manifest that this time of trouble, here spoken of, is not to be ended till "the time, and times, and half a time" of Antichrist is ended; for when the angels, being tenderly and greatly concerned for the church under such great trouble, say to Jesus Christ, "How long shall it be to the end of these wonders?," Christ, for the comfort of them and his church, lest his people should faint under such tribulation, holds up his right hand and his left to heaven, and swears by him that lives forever and ever, that it shall continue no longer than "for a time, and times, and an half" (vv. 6–7).

(4) 'Tis manifest that the time of great tribulation, spoken of by Christ in the 24th of Matthew, is the same with that spoken of by Daniel

6. JE crossed out with two large "X's" the following: "It can scarcely be doubted whether Christ has reference to these words of Daniel in this 24th of Matthew, which prophecy he had just cited in foregoing words, v. 15, and refers to time after time in the chapter."

in this place. It can scarcely be doubted whether Christ has reference to these words of Daniel in what he says here, his words being so much like them, and he having just before expressly cited Daniel's prophecy (v. 15), and refers to it from time to time in the chapters, and particularly has reference to Daniel's words in this chapter, in what he says of the continuance of those days of tribulation. But this may be more particularly considered under the next head,[7] viz. that,

10. All this will be more abundantly manifest, and will be put beyond dispute, by comparing three scriptures together, viz. what Christ says of the continuance of those days of tribulation in that forementioned place, Luke 21:24, "And Jerusalem shall be trodden down of the Gentiles, until the times of the Gentiles be fulfilled"; with what Daniel says in this 12th chapter of his prophecy, of the continuance of this time of great trouble, till "a time, times, and an half"; and what is said in Rev. 11:2, "But the court which is without the temple leave out, and measure it not, for it is given unto the Gentiles. And the holy city shall they tread underfoot forty and two months." Concerning these three scriptures I would observe,

(1) That nobody doubts whether these forty-two months that St. John speaks of, in which the holy city should be trodden underfoot of the Gentiles, be the same with the "time, times, and an half" that Daniel speaks of, till the end of which the time of great tribulation was to last.

(2) Both Christ in the 21st of Luke, and John in the Revelation, speak of treading down Jerusalem, for by the "holy city" is meant Jerusalem, that was commonly called the holy city; and both speak of treading down Jerusalem by the Gentiles. And probably in that place of Revelation, reference is had to those words of Christ.

(3) Hence we may infer that when Christ says, "Jerusalem shall be trodden down of the Gentiles, till the times of the Gentiles be fulfilled," by the "times of the Gentiles" he means the same with that forty-two months of the prevailing of the Gentiles against Jerusalem, or the Jews, that St. John speaks of, and the same with the "time, times, and half," that Daniel speaks of; and probably in the phrase he uses, "*times* of the Gentiles," [he] has reference to these "time, and times," etc., of Daniel, whose prophecy he had [been] referring to. The "times of the Gentiles" Christ here speaks of are the same with that time that

---

7. JE deleted "of argument which I now proceed to."

the angel swears shall be no longer (Rev. 10:6 compared [with] Dan. 12:7).

(4) That the Jerusalem that Christ speaks of is especially the literal Jerusalem, and that by the Jerusalem or holy city that John speaks of is the spiritual Jerusalem, from all which it is greatly confirmed, that the time of tribulation that Christ speaks of is the same that Daniel speaks of, and that it respects the continuance of the tribulation, or treading down both of the literal and spiritual Jerusalem, and that it shall last till the fall of Antichrist.

11. It seems to be intimated that the time in itself was very long, by the 22nd verse. "And except those days should be shortened, there should no flesh be saved; but for the elect's sake those days shall be shortened." The days are shortened[8] by taking out many days out of this long period of time for times of respite and rest. Then the proper time appointed for Jacob's trouble is from Nero's time till the fall of Antichrist, which is a great many ages; but "for the elect's [sake]," the tribulation is not constantly continued through this whole time, for if it should be so, it would wear out the saints, and would wholly root out and destroy the church. Therefore, "for the elect's sake," God will take out many of those days for respite, so that the days of actual tribulation shall be much fewer than this whole period. Thus there was respite between the ten heathen persecutions, and there was a remarkable time of rest after the tenth and hottest of them, upon Constantine's coming to the throne. And towards the end of the antichristian persecutions, many of the days should be taken out, and many parts of the church should have rest after the Reformation, being out of the reach of the persecuting power of Rome, which is possibly what is signified by the witnesses rising and standing on their feet, and being caught up to heaven out of the reach of their enemies [Rev. 11:11–12].

It is further evident, that the tribulation Christ speaks [of] is not merely a calamity that was brought on Judea and Jerusalem, or limited to that people or land, by those things that Christ says are the beginning of this tribulation (vv. 7–8). "For nation shall rise against nation, and kingdom against kingdom; and there shall be famines, and pestilences, and earthquakes, in diverse places. All these are the beginning of sorrows." Now it can't be supposed that wars between other nations, and earthquakes, and pestilences in other countries can be

---

8. JE deleted "not so much by cutting off some of the days at the end but."

signs and forerunners only of a calamity upon the nation of the Jews, and troubles in their land.

12. What has been said is further confirmed by the 29th [verse] of this 24th [chapter] of Matthew. "Immediately after the tribulation of those days shall the sun be darkened, and the moon shall not give her light, and the stars shall fall from heaven, and the powers of the heavens shall be shaken." I.e. "immediately after the tribulation of those days" shall those great events be accomplished, which are signified by those places in the Prophets that speak of the sun's being darkened, etc., which you have often read and heard discourse of. It is observable that almost throughout this whole discourse of Christ with his disciples he refers to things that had been said by the ancient prophets; and what Christ says don't imply that what the prophets have said in those things is to be understood literally, but he seems to intimate the contrary, viz. that their meaning is mysterious, in that expression, v. 15, "Whoso readeth, let him understand." The places in the Prophets that speak of these things have reference to the great events, and the wonderful changes in the face of things, that shall be brought to pass at the beginning of the glorious times of the church, and particularly the utter overthrow of the kingdom of Satan, and casting down all powers and authorities by which false religion has been maintained, and the putting out all their glory, as in Joel 3:15. "The sun and moon shall be darkened, and the stars shall withdraw their shining." And then the Prophet goes on to speak of the glorious times of the church in the following verses. Jerusalem shall be holy [v. 17], and "the mountains shall drop down new wine," etc. [v. 18]. And Joel 2:31, speaking of the time when God shall pour out his Spirit on all flesh, it is said, "The sun shall be turned into darkness, and the moon into blood, before the great and terrible day of the Lord come." And Is. 13:10–11, "For the stars of heaven and the constellations thereof shall not give their light: the sun shall be darkened in his going forth, and the moon shall not cause her light to shine. And I will punish the world for their evil, and the wicked for their iniquity; and I will cause the arrogancy of the proud to cease, and will lay low the haughtiness of the terrible." And v. 13, "Therefore I will shake the heavens, and the earth shall remove out of her place," agreeable to what Christ says, "The powers of the heavens shall be shaken" [Matt. 24:29]. This had its first fulfillment in the destruction of Babylon, but has a further and more full accomplishment in the destruction of the spiritual Babylon, of which that was a type. Again, in Ezekiel 32:7–8, it

is said of Pharaoh and Egypt, "And when I shall put thee out, I will cover the heaven, and make the stars thereof dark; I will cover the sun with a cloud, and the moon shall not give her light. All the bright lights of heaven will I make dark over thee, and set darkness upon thy land, saith the Lord." This will have a further accomplishment in the destruction of that city, of which it is said in Revelation, that it is spiritually called Egypt [Rev. 11:8]. And again, Is. 24:23, "Then the moon shall be confounded, and the sun ashamed, when the Lord of hosts shall reign in Mt. Zion, and in Jerusalem, before his ancients gloriously." Possibly there may also [appear] some strange phenomena in the heavens just before that time, by which there may be something of a literal accomplishment, as in the events signified by the pouring out of the fourth vial on the sun [Rev. 16:8], there was both a figurative and literal accomplishment of it. See Lowman, *On the Revelation*.[9]

13. Now if we understand these days of tribulation in the sense in which I have explained them, these great events do immediately follow them. If we understand them in a more limited and restrained sense, for the days of the church's suffering under Rome heathen, which was much the greatest under the last of the ten persecutions, then immediately after the tribulation of those days, there was a remarkable accomplishment of this. Then was the sun and moon darkened, and the stars fell from heaven, and the powers of heaven were shaken [Matt. 24:29], in the sense of Scripture prophecy, as appears by Rev. 6:12–14, which speaks of those times. "And I beheld when he had opened the sixth seal, and, lo, there was a great earthquake; and the sun became black as sackcloth of hair, and the moon became as blood; and the stars of heaven fell unto the earth, even as a fig tree casteth her untimely figs, when she is shaken of a mighty wind. And the heavens departed as a scroll when it is rolled together; and every mountain and island were moved out of their places." But if we understand, as in its greatest and full extent, it is to be understood for the whole time of Jerusalem's lying waste, and the church's suffering under the idolatrous, persecuting Roman power, then also those great events shall

---

9. Moses Lowman's discussion of the pouring of the fourth vial, which he dates from the late fourteenth century through the first third of the sixteenth century, includes both literal and figurative interpretations of the "Power given unto the Sun, to scorch Men." He points to the impact of intemperate heat in France between 1528–1534 and to the distemper in sixteenth-century Germany and England as evidence of the former, and to evils, including warfare and schism, brought on the earth by the ambition, envy, and covetousness of the popes as proof of the later (*Paraphrase and Notes*, pp. 188–95).

immediately follow, which are a yet[1] much greater accomplishment of these things, these events seem plainly to be spoken of.[2]

14. Then the sun is darkened, and the moon turned into blood, and the stars fall, and the heavens are shaken, immediately after the captivity of God's people in the spiritual Babylon, just as[3] those things came to pass with respect to the Babylonish empire, that the prophet Isaiah signifies by the very same expressions (Is. 13:10–13), as soon as ever the seventy years of the Jewish captivity were ended.

15. But if we understand Christ, by this time of tribulation, to mean only the time of the besieging and taking the city of Jerusalem by the Romans, those things did not come to pass in any sense, as we have any account, immediately after those days. The overthrow of the heathen empire, the nearest event after this signified by those expressions, was about 250 years after this.

16. When Christ had said that "immediately after the tribulation of those days the sun shall be darkened," etc., he then adds in the next verse, v. 30, "And then shall appear the sign of the Son of man in heaven. And then shall all the tribes of the earth mourn, and they shall see the Son of man coming in the clouds of heaven with power and great glory." "Then shall appear," i.e. after those things are accomplished, not signifying that it should be immediately after, but that it should not be till all those things are first accomplished, as the Apostle says, II Thess. 2:3, "Let no man deceive you by any means; for that day shall not come, except there come a falling away first," etc. So Christ is here telling his disciples what great events are to be accomplished before his last coming, how that there should be a time of great tribulation; and then after that, there should be great signs in the heavens, in the sun, and in the moon and stars, and on the earth distress of nations [Luke 21:25]. That is, there should be very great, extraordinary, and wonderful things brought to pass, such as never were before, causing great and universal changes in the state of things in the world, such as never were seen before. And then the next sign or wonder that shall be seen [added] to this, shall be the sign of the Son of man; i.e. this shall be the last great revolution, or change of the state of things in the world, before the last judgment. This darkening of the sun and moon, etc., shall be the last great step of providence towards finishing the state of things in this world, and setting up Christ's heavenly kingdom, except-

---

1. JE deleted "more full."
2. This last clause is a later interlineation.
3. JE deleted "Babylon was destroyed and."

ing the personal appearing of the Son of God to judgment. The manner of expression, "then shall such, or such an event, be," don't, in the manner in which the prophets use it, signify that it shall be immediately upon it. The prophets often express themselves after that manner, when the event is to be many ages after. So when the prophets are foretelling the return of the Jews from the Babylonish captivity, they often speak of the coming of Christ as what shall be, as they express themselves, "at that time," or "in that day." So here, when Christ is speaking of the return of his people from their captivity in the spiritual Babylon, he speaks of the second coming of the Messiah as what shall be at that time. For it shall be at the conclusion of the state of things that he introduced by that dispensation of providence, though much degenerated by an apostasy at the latter end of the period, as the first coming of Christ was at the conclusion of that state of the Jewish church that it was brought into after the return from the literal Babylon.[4]

Corol. 1. Hence when Christ, v. 24, speaks of false prophets and false Christs that shall arise in this time of tribulation, "that should show great signs and wonders, insomuch that if it were possible, they should deceive the very elect," 'tis probable that Christ has not only respect to those false Christs and false prophets that arose at or near the time of the destruction of Jerusalem, but that he has especial respect to the great Antichrist, to the Pope and his clergy, that are from time to time stigmatized in the Revelations by the name of the false prophet, and by the character of the false prophet that works miracles. Rev. 16:13–14, "And I saw three unclean spirits like frogs come out of the mouth of the dragon, and out of the mouth of the beast, and out of the mouth of the *false prophet.* For they are the spirits of devils, *working miracles.*" And the false prophet that works miracles, by which he deceives the world: Rev. 19:20, "And the beast was taken, and with him the *false prophet that wrought miracles before him, with which he deceived them,* which had received the mark of the beast," etc. Rev. 13:13–14, "And he doth great *wonders,* so that he maketh fire come down from heaven on the earth in the sight of men, and *deceiveth them that dwell on the earth by the means of those miracles,* which he had power to do in the sight of the beast." And so II Thess. 2:9–11, "Even him, whose coming is after the working of Satan with all power and signs and lying wonders, and with all de-

4. JE crossed out the following sentence with three large "X's": "That Christ, when he says, Then shall appear the sign of the Son of man" [Matt. 24:30], don't mean *at the same time,* ~~more~~ but *after that,* more fully appears ~~from Luke~~."

ceivableness of unrighteousness. . . . For this cause God shall send them strong delusions." And again, this great false prophet is a false Christ, for the false Christs here spoken of are those that personate Jesus, the true[5] Christ that was crucified. Concerning which, see notes in "Blank Bible."[6] This false prophet pretends to be Christ's vicar, and therein is Antichrist. He shows that he is vested with all the power and authority of Christ, as if he were Christ, or God on earth, and challenges the glory and worship due to Christ alone. Thus he has "horns like a lamb" (Rev. 13:11), and he "sitteth in the temple of God, showing himself that he is God," in that he showeth himself that he is Christ, and therein exalteth himself above Christ (II Thess. 2:4).

Christ nowhere foretells the coming of Antichrist, if not here. It is not probable that Christ would omit so great an event as the coming of Antichrist, which is the principal subject of New Testament prophecy, next to those events signified by the coming of Christ himself. I say, 'tis not probable that Christ would omit so great an event in those predictions, that he is giving his disciples, of the great events that should come to pass in his church till his second coming, when he was about to leave the world after his first coming. Indeed, all that Christ has respect to, in this prediction of false prophets and false Christs, is either the great Antichrist and false prophet, or those lesser false prophets and antichrists that were his types and forerunners. Compare I John 4:1, "Many false prophets are gone out into the world," with I John 2:18, "As ye have heard that Antichrist should come, even so now are there many antichrists."

Corol. 2. This leads us to interpret those things in the Old Testament that speak of the glory of the Christian church, of the state of the church in the millennium, for that is the time of her glory on earth. The time foregoing, excepting some intermissions by which God has graciously shortened those days, is the time not of her prosperity, but her great tribulation.[7]

5. JE deleted "Messiah."

6. In a note on Matt. 24:24–28, JE identifies the "false Christs" with impostors who "pretend to be the same Jesus that was crucified, returned a second time, according to his promise" rather than with those "persons that set [themselves] up for messiahs in opposition to Jesus." The former come "in a private manner" in secret places by contrast with Christ's authentic second coming which will be "in a very public manner" and with "conspicuous glory" ("Blank Bible").

7. This entry draws heavily on a variety of topics discussed in Lowman, *Paraphrase and Notes*.

293. ISAIAH 8:7–8. "Now therefore, behold, the Lord bringeth up upon them the waters of the river, strong and many, even the king of Assyria, and all his glory; and he shall come up over all his channels, and go over all his banks. And he shall pass through Judah; he shall overflow and go over." The river Euphrates was the ancient boundary that God had set to the possession of the children of Israel, and to the dominion of their princes. This is, from time to time, mentioned as their eastern limits in the books of Moses; and over all on this side the river, the kings of Judah and Israel had formerly reigned. And their territories were overrun by the people that dwelt about that river. 'Tis well represented as though the river Euphrates, their ancient boundary, broke its banks, and not only encroached upon them to the straitening their limits, but even overflowed all their possessions. They have no more their own, by God's grant, than is left them on this side the river Euphrates; and therefore, when those waters come to overflow all, they have none left. See note on Is. 28:17.[8]

294. JEREMIAH 5:22. "Fear ye not me? saith the Lord. Will ye not tremble at my presence, which have placed the sand for the bound of the sea by a perpetual decree, that it cannot pass it: and though the waves thereof toss themselves, yet can they not prevail; though they roar, yet can they not pass over it?" The unreasonableness and folly of their not fearing God appears from the consideration of the greatness and majesty of God appearing in his works. And this work of his ruling and curbing the raging waves of the sea is mentioned in particular, because that wickedness of theirs, described in the foregoing part of the chapter, might fitly be compared to the raging waves of the sea in a storm. We are told, Is. 57:20, that "the wicked are like the troubled sea, when it cannot rest, whose waters cast up mire and dirt." God puts a stop to the waves of the tempestuous sea, let them toss themselves never so proudly, and rage never so violently, as though they would carry all before them, and scorned any restraint. So the mighty God was able to put a stop to that rage and violence of theirs in wickedness, spoken of in vv. 3, 5, 7–8, 12. However headstrong, obstinate, and violent they were in it, God could curb and tame them by his almighty hand. He that looks on everyone that is proud and abases him, could

8. This reference is a later addition. JE links the "hail" mentioned with "the northern armies of Assyria" and the overflowing of the river Euphrates with "the armies of Chaldea" ("Blank Bible").

bring down their pride [Job 40:11–12], whereby they as it were tossed themselves up against the heavens like the waves of the sea. He could break their power, and subdue their spirits; he would bring 'em down with a strong hand, however set they were in their way. He could do it very easily by weak and despicable means. He could crush them before a moth [Job 4:19]. He could show them that his weakness was stronger than they, and would say concerning their wickedness, "Hitherto shalt thou come, and no further: and here shall thy proud waves be stayed" [Job 38:11], as the highest and most raging waves of the sea were brought down, and broken, and brought to nothing, by such[9] contemptible means as the sand. Thus God often pours contempt on wicked men, and even the greatest princes. Such was the obstinacy and violence of the men of Judah and Jerusalem, that men and means could do nothing with them; no human power could stop them. The prophets had tried, and used their utmost endeavors to counsel them; [it] was like preaching to the raging waves of the sea, as vv. 3–5, 12–13. Therefore God would take the work in hand himself.

God's subduing the rage of the sea, and the rage of men's spirits, and the wickedness of his enemies, are spoken of as parallel works of God. Ps. 65:7, "Who stilleth the noise of the seas, the noise of their waves, and the tumult of the people." And Ps. 89:9–10, "Thou rulest the raging of the sea: when the waves thereof arise, thou stillest them. Thou hast broken Rahab in pieces, as one that is slain; thou hast scattered thine enemies with thy strong arm." However for a while, and sometimes, wicked men may seem to carry all afore 'em, and their wickedness rages without control. Yet there are certain limits set to it that are unalterable, as the sands on the seashore, which here are said to be placed "for the bound of the sea by a perpetual decree."

295. LUKE 10:38–42. Concerning Mary's and Martha's different ways of showing their respect to Christ. Martha and Mary seem to be types of different churches, or rather different parts of the Christian church, the one showing their respect to Christ by much external service and ceremony, as "Martha was cumbered about much serving" [v. 40], the other that part of the church that is more pure and spiritual in their worship, as Mary "sat at his feet, and heard his word" [v. 39]. Particularly, Martha represents the Jewish Christian church in the

---

9. JE deleted "weak and."

come, and hearkening to the call, and flying for refuge to the ark, and getting into the ark. So the way by which we are saved by Christ is by flying from the deluge of God's wrath, and taking refuge in Christ, and being in him.

The ark was a refuge from storm and from wind. The rain that poured down out of heaven in a very dreadful manner, it did not hurt those that were in the ark. So Christ is "an hiding place from the wind, a covert from the tempest" (Is. 32:2). He is "a place of refuge, and a covert from storm and from wind" (Is. 4:6). He is to his church "a refuge from the storm, when the blast of the terrible ones is as a storm against the wall" (Is. 25:4). He that is built on Christ, when the wind blows, the rain descends, and floods come and beat upon his house, it will not fall [Matt. 7:25].

The company in the ark was safe in the greatest catastrophe, when the world was as it were dissolved. So they that have Christ for their refuge and strength need not fear, "though the earth be removed, and though the mountains be carried into the midst of the sea (as they in a sense were in the flood: they were in the midst of the sea; the sea surrounded 'em and overwhelmed them), though the waters thereof roar and are troubled, though the mountains shake with the swelling thereof" (Ps. 46:1–3). Though the waters were so exceeding great and overwhelming, yet those that were in the ark did not sink in them. Though the waters overtopped the highest mountains, yet they could not overwhelm them. Though the ark, when it stood on the ground, was a low thing in comparison of other things that the waters over-whelmed, yet the waters could not get above them; but let the waters rise never so high, yet the ark kept above them, which livelily repre-sents the safety of the church in Christ in the greatest dangers, so that "when she passes through the waters, he will be with her;[2] and through the rivers, and they shall not overflow her" (Is. 43:2). Con-cerning those that belong to the church of Christ, it is promised, as Ps. 32:6, "Surely in the floods of great waters they shall not come nigh thee." And though the church often appears as a low thing, as though the mighty waters that come against it could immediately overflow it, yet the church is kept above water, let 'em come in never so fiercely and rise never so high. If it was not the Lord that is on their side, oftentimes her enemies would swallow her up quick [Ps. 124:1–3]. This also rep-

---

2. MS: "~~them~~ ⟨her⟩."

resents to us how Christ was kept from sinking under his sufferings. It was impossible that Christ should fail in the great work that he undertook; and though his sufferings were so great, though the deluge that came upon [him] was so very great, the billows of wrath so mighty, enough to overwhelm a whole world, and to overwhelm the highest mountains, to overtop the stoutest and mightiest, yet Christ did not sink and fail, but was kept above water. He kept above all, and in the issue triumphed over all, as his church also in him shall obtain the victory over all her enemies, and shall appear finally above them, let 'em rise never so high and deal never so proudly. As the ark kept still above water, when the waters were mounted up even to heaven, the ship wherein Christ was could not sink (Matt. 8:24–26).

They that were in the ark were saved, when thousands and millions of others were destroyed. So he that dwells in the secret place of the Most High, that make Christ their refuge and the Most High their habitation, thousands shall fall at their side, and ten thousand at their right hand. Only with their eyes shall they behold, and see the reward of the wicked. But no evil shall befall them, nor any plague come nigh their dwelling (Ps. 91).[3]

There was but one ark that any could resort to for refuge in the whole world; so there is no other name, but the name of Christ, "given under heaven amongst men, whereby we must be saved" [Acts 4:12]. There was no other refuge but the ark. If they got up to the tops of their houses, or to the tops of the highest mountains, it was in vain; the waters overtopped them. So if men trust in their carnal confidences, in their own strength, their own works, and mount high in a towering conceit of their own righteousness, it is in vain. In vain is salvation looked for from the hills and the multitude of the mountains, for there is no safety but in the Lord. Other refuges did then probably look far more likely to save them then than the ark, for they could scarce conceive of such a way of safety, by the floating of such a building on the waters, the art of making ships having not been discovered[4] before that time. So men's own righteousness looks more likely to men to save them than Christ. They are ready to say of the Lord's anointed, "How shall this man save us?" [I Sam. 10:27].

There was but a few saved, when all the rest of the world was destroyed; so the church of Christ is but a little flock.

3. This paragraph is an example of the freedom JE exercises when citing biblical texts and of the editorial difficulty in determining when to use quotation marks.

4. JE deleted "till then."

The door of the ark was open to receive all sorts of creatures—tigers, wolves, bears, lions, leopards, serpents, vipers, dragons—such as men would not by any means admit into the doors of their houses, but if they came there, would soon have beat 'em out again.[5] So Christ stands ready to receive all, even the vilest and worst; he came to save the chief of sinners. There were all kinds of creatures[6] in the ark; so in the Christian church are gathered together persons of all nations, kindreds, tongues, and peoples, persons of all degrees, all kinds of tempers and manners.

In the ark the wolf dwelt with the lamb; the leopard lay down with the kid. All were peaceable together in the ark, even those that were the greatest enemies, and were wont to devour one another before, as 'tis prophesied that it should be in the Christian church (Is. 11:6 ff., and 65:25).

All in the ark was subject to Noah, as the church is subject to Christ. All was saved by his righteousness (Gen. 7:1), as the church is saved by Christ's righteousness. There is no rest anywhere for God's people but in Christ, as the dove that Noah sent forth found no rest for the sole of her foot but in the ark. When she wandered from the ark, she found no rest till she returned again. The dove therein was a type of a true saint, as the raven was a type of a false professor, who departs from Christ, and returns to him no more.

The ark was taken up from the earth, and after being long tossed to and fro in the waters, was not steered by the wisdom of Noah, was only under the care of providence, rested on the top of an exceeding high mountain, as it were in heaven, and was brought into a new world. So the church of Christ in this world is tossed to and fro, like a bark on the water, passes through great tribulation, and appears ready to be overwhelmed (Is. 54:11), but at last, through God's care of it and mercy to it, rests in heaven. The ark, in the midst of the flood, rested on a mountain, a strong and high rock; so the church, when ready to be overwhelmed, rests on a rock higher than she.[7] See "Miscellanies," no. 1069, pp. 221–25.[8]

5. JE deleted "This represents."
6. JE deleted "under heaven."
7. This paragraph has multiple later interlineations, including this entire sentence.
8. This reference is an even later interlineation. No. 1069, entitled "Types of the Messiah," concerns "THE THINGS OF THE OLD TESTAMENT [THAT] ARE TYPES OF THINGS APPERTAINING TO THE MESSIAH AND HIS KINGDOM AND SALVATION." The pages in question focus on the resemblance between the Old Testament account of the Flood and occurrences in the time of the Messiah's kingdom, including the destruction of the wicked and the gathering

298. PSALMS 17:4. "Concerning the works of men, by the word of thy lips I have kept myself from the paths of the *destroyer*." By the "destroyer" here is doubtless meant the devil, the same with him that is called Abaddon and Apollyon in the Revelation.[9] God's people under the old testament[1] were sensible that there was an evil and malignant spirit, or invisible agent, that sought the ruin of men, as even the heathen nations had a notion of evil demons. This evil spirit the Hebrews were wont to call by several names; one was Satan, or the adversary. So it is said, "Satan stood up against Israel, and moved David to number the people" [I Chron. 21:1]; so in several other places in the Old Testament. Another name was the "destroyer"; so devils are called destroyers in Job. 33:22. "Yea, his soul draweth nigh unto the grave, and his life to the destroyers."

299. HEBREWS 6:4–6. Let this be added to No. 74. If any think that the Apostle here used expressions too high to denote any gifts of the Spirit common to good and bad men, though miraculous gifts, I answer that the drift of the Apostle, and his argument in these words, led him to set forth the greatness of the privilege that such persons had received, that he might the better show the exceeding aggravations of their apostasy, whence what the Apostle says might be the more easily believed, viz. that it was impossible "to renew them again to repentance." For 'tis certain that he intends the aggravatedness of their crime as a reason of it, because he himself gives it as a reason of it (v. 6), in these words, "seeing they crucify to themselves the Son of God afresh, and put him to an open shame."

300. EPHESIANS 2:7. "That in the ages to come he might show the exceeding riches of his grace in his kindness towards us through Christ Jesus." Intimating that this was not made known in ages past, but in a great measure kept hid, as 'tis said in the next chapter at the 5th verse, "Which in other ages was not made known to the sons of men, as 'tis now revealed unto his holy apostles and prophets by the Spirit." The "riches of God's grace in his kindness through Christ Jesus," here spoken of, is the same with those "unsearchable riches of Christ,"

---

and preservation of the church. JE seems to have consulted No. 297 when writing no. 1069. The text of no. 1069 is printed in *Works*, *11*, 191–324.

9. See Rev. 9:11. Here JE deleted "The devil is called by several names in the."

1. JE deleted "had the knowledge."

spoken [of] in the next chapter, 8th and 9th verses, which the Apostle there says, was a "mystery which, from the beginning of the world, had been hid in God." So Rom. 16:25, "According to the revelation of the mystery, which was kept secret since the world began." And Col. 1:26–27, "Even the mystery which hath been hid from ages and generations, but is now made manifest to his saints; to whom God would make known what is the riches of the glory of this mystery among the Gentiles, which is Christ in you, the hope of glory." The Apostle, in this text we are upon, speaks of it as being now made known for the present and all future ages, brought to light for the last ages of the world, which were now begun.

Upon second thoughts, I am inclined to think that by τοῖς αἰῶσιν τοῖς ἐπερχομένοις is meant the "world." Αἰών is almost everywhere put for "world," and αἰὼν ἐρχόμενος, or μέλλων, is always put for the "world to come," though here it be in the plural number. See Eph. 1:21, and this chapter, v. 2, in the original. See No. 504.[2]

301. GENESIS 17:10. CIRCUMCISION signified or represented that mortification, or the denying of our lusts, that is the condition of obtaining the blessings of the covenant. Totally denying any lust is represented in Scripture by "cutting off"; so cutting off of a right hand, or right foot, is put for the denying of some very dear lust. So cutting off the privy member, so prone to violent lust, signifies a total denying of our lusts. A main reason why lust, or our natural corruption, is represented by this instrument of generation is because we have all our natural corruption or lust by generation, i.e. by being the natural offspring of the corrupt parents of mankind. Therefore when God would signify that our original or natural corruption should be mortified, he appoints that the instrument of propagation of corruption should be cut off.

Another reason why the seal of the covenant that God made with Abraham was appointed to be affixed to this member of the body, seems to be that God made this covenant not only with Abraham and for him, but him and his seed. It mainly respected his seed, as abundantly appears by the tenor of the words in which the covenant was revealed from time to time; and therefore the seal was to [be] affixed to that part of the body whence came his seed. The covenant was made, not with a man, but with a race of men, ordinarily to be continued by natural

2. This paragraph is a later addition, and the cross-reference is an even later addition.

generation; and therefore the sign of the covenant was a sign affixed to the instrument of generation. The sign was a purgation of the member of the body by which offspring was, to be a sign of the purification of the offspring. God seeks a godly seed and children that are holy.

Corol. Hence we learn that, seeing the Gentiles, now in the days of the gospel, are admitted to be the seed of Abraham as the Jews were, and are admitted to an interest in Abraham's covenant, and to the blessing of Abraham, so that Abraham is become the father now, not of one nation, but many nations, in the way of that covenant, as the apostle Paul abundantly teaches, then the posterity of Christians by natural generation are now God's people, and are a holy seed by Abraham's covenant, as the Israelites were of old. There is but two ways of persons'[3] being of Abraham's covenant, race, or generation. One is[4] by generation by the natural instruments of generation, to which the seal of that covenant was affixed, and so continued from root to branches; or [the other], by ingrafting a new branch into that stock, that shall, after ingrafting, grow, and bring forth branches, and bear fruit upon that stock, as the other branches did that were cut off to make room for them. In this way now many nations or generations are of Abraham's race, instead of one nation or family.

302. GENESIS 14:15–16 ff. Abraham, in thus conquering the great kings and princes of the earth, and their united hosts, is a type of Christ and of the church. God seems to have granted this great victory to Abraham as some earnest of those great blessings he had promised to him, the belief of which promises was attended with so much difficulty. Here was given some specimen of what Abraham's promised seed should do, which includes Christ and his church. Abraham might well represent Christ, for Christ is Abraham's seed; and he might well represent the church, for he was the father of the church, the father of all that believe, as the Apostle testifies [Rom. 4:11]. And besides, Abraham and his household was then as it were God's visible church; God had separated Abraham from the rest of the world to that end, that his church might be continued in his family. And though there were as yet some other true worshipers of God that were not of his family, yet soon after, the church was confined to his posterity. This victory of Abraham was doubtless intended as a sign and earnest of the

3. JE deleted "having a title to Abraham's covenant."
4. JE deleted "generation by those parts of the body."

victory that Christ and his church should obtain over their enemies, and over the nations of the world, because God himself makes use of it to this purpose, in [the] 41st chapter of Isaiah. "Keep silence before me, O islands; and let the people renew their strength; let them come near; then let them speak; let us come near together in judgment. Who raised up the righteous man from the east, called him to his foot, gave the nations before him, and made him to rule over kings? He gave them as the dust to his sword, and as the driven stubble to his bow. He pursued them, and passed safely, even by the way that he had not gone with his feet" [vv. 1–3].[5] 'Tis not probable that this victory of Abraham would be spoken of in such lofty language, and in expressions so much like those that are elsewhere made use of to represent Christ's glorious victories over the powers of earth and hell, if the one were not a type of the other. This victory of Abraham is in this place mentioned to that end, that the church, the seed of Abraham, might take it as a sign and evidence that they should not be subdued, but should subdue and conquer the world, as appears by what follows. V. 8, "But thou, Israel, [art] my servant, Jacob whom I have chosen, the seed of Abraham my friend." Vv. 10–11, "Fear thou not, for I am with thee; be not dismayed, for I am thy God. I will strengthen thee; yea, I will help thee; yea, I will uphold thee with the right hand of my righteousness. Behold, all they that were incensed against thee shall be ashamed and confounded: they shall be as nothing; and they that strive with thee shall perish." V. 15, "Behold, I will make thee a new, sharp threshing instrument having teeth; thou shalt thresh the mountains, and beat them small, and shalt make the hills as chaff."

Abraham conquered the chief nations and princes of the world, which was a seal of what God promised him, "that he should be the heir of the world" (Rom. 4:13). He conquered them, not with an hired army, but only with the armed soldiers of his own household; so the armies that go forth with Christ unto battle to subdue the world (Rev. 19:14), they are his church, which is his household. Abraham conquers the kings of the earth and their armies, united and joining all their force together; and therein his victory was a type of Christ's victory, as in the 41st of Isaiah, 6th [and] 7th verses, speaking of this victory. "They helped everyone his neighbor; and everyone said to his brother, Be of good courage. So the carpenter encouraged the goldsmith," etc.

5. JE deleted "This is here mentioned ~~to~~ by God to encourage his church that they shall not be conquered."

Abraham, by this conquest, rescued Lot his kinsman; so Christ, our near kinsman, by his victory over our enemies that had taken us captive, delivers us. And he[6] redeemed him and the other captives freely, and would take nothing of them for his pains; so Christ freely redeems us. Abraham redeemed the people of Sodom and Gomorrah, that wicked people, which is a type of Christ's redeeming sinners.[7]

303. ISAIAH 1:18.[8] "Come now, let us reason together, saith the Lord. Though your sins be as scarlet, they shall [be] as white as snow; though they be red like crimson, they shall be as wool." The reasoning together, here spoken of, is not to be understood merely of a reasoning with the people about the fairness and righteousness of that method of dealing with them, that God declares in the context. 'Tis not so properly a *demand* or *challenge* of them, to bring forth an objection against God's dispensations towards [them]; but the words are rather in the form of[9] an invitation, by faith to come to him, and reason or plead with him for mercy, being convinced and humbled by his reasoning or pleading with them, concerning their great transgressions against him, and the unreasonableness and inexcusableness of it. 'Tis a reasoning together, in order that should precede their pardon or justification, as being in order to it,[1] as in that parallel place, Is. 43:25–26. "I, even I, am he that blotteth out thy transgressions for mine own sake, and will not remember thy sins. Put me in remembrance. Let us plead together; declare thou, that thou mayst be justified." God, in this context as in that, is pleading with them concerning their wickedness, and the justice of his judgments for their sins. He invites them, that they being convinced thereby, [he] would have them also to come to [him].[2]

304. I CORINTHIANS 13:13. "And now abideth faith, hope, charity, these three; but the greatest of these is charity." The Apostle in this place is not comparing these together as three distinct graces, but gifts of the Spirit of God. They can't be properly three distributively dis-

---

6. I.e. Abraham.
7. This sentence is a later interlineation.
8. This entry, which is unfinished, has one large "X" through it in the center of the page.
9. JE deleted "a call."
1. JE deleted "and not follow it."
2. JE failed to complete the sentence and left space at the bottom of the page as though he intended to write more.

tinct graces, or saving virtues, because charity is the sum of all saving virtue, as abundantly appears from the foregoing part of the chapter, and from innumerable other places of Scripture. Charity is an ingredient in saving faith, and is the most essential thing in it, is its life and soul; and so it is in hope. The Apostle is here comparing gifts of the Spirit, and not graces, as is manifest from the last verse of the foregoing chapter, and the former verses of this, and the beginning of the next. What is in faith and hope, which is distinct from love, which are principles or exercises of mind that are called also by those names of faith and hope, though they are not Christian and saving faith and hope yet, they are principles that are gifts of God. And in these three gifts of the mind—faith, hope, and love[3]—are the three gifts into which all Christianity, as a principle in the mind, is to be resolved.

The first, viz. faith, as distinct from love, hath its seat purely in the understanding, and consists in an understanding of divine things and an apprehension of their reality. Hope, if we mean that hope that is distinct from love, has its seat both in the understanding and natural will, or inclination, and apprehends not only the reality of divine things, but our interest in them. Love has its seat in the spiritual will, and apprehends divine things as amiable. And in these three consists the whole of that respect that the mind of man has to divine things, wherein the Christianity of the mind consists. And these three, when joined together and united in one, constituteth saving faith, or the soul's savingly embracing Christ and Christianity. But of these three constituents of justifying faith, love is the greatest. The other two are the body; this is the soul.[4]

305. I CORINTHIANS 13:8–12. "Charity never faileth; but whether there be prophecies, they shall fail. . . . For we know in part, and we prophesy in part. But when that which is perfect is come, that which is in part shall be done away. When I was a child. . . . Now we see through a glass darkly," etc. There is a twofold failing, or ceasing, of those miraculous and other common gifts of the Spirit, both of which the Apostle has doubtless respect to. One is their failing at the end of the

3. JE deleted "does consist."

4. This entry relates directly to the series of sermons on I Cor. 13 JE preached between April and October 1738, published posthumously first in 1852 under the title *Charity and Its Fruits; Or, Christian Love as Manifested in Heart and Life* (*Works, 8*, 123–397). JE wrote the closing lines of this entry in an uncharacteristically large script as though to emphasize his assertions.

present state of probation, or the present imperfect state of God's people in time, with respect to particular persons that have common gifts at death, and with respect to the church of God, collectively considered, at the end of the world. And the other is the failing of miraculous gifts in the church of Christ, even while yet remaining in its temporary and militant state, as they failed at or about the end of the apostolic age, that first and more imperfect, and less settled and established state of the Christian church, before it was wholly brought out from under the Mosaic dispensation, wherein it was under tutors and governors, and before the canon of the Scripture was fully completed, and all parts of it thoroughly collected and established. Miraculous and other common gifts of the Spirit cease at the end of the imperfect state of the church, wherein the church knows in part, and is in a state of childhood, in comparison of the more perfect state that follows. So there is a twofold perfect state of the church to answer them, wherein the church may be said to be in a state of manhood with respect to those more imperfect states that they succeed. The first state of the church[5] in its first age on earth, before the canon of the Scripture was completed, etc., is its imperfect state, wherein the church knows in part, and is as a child, and speaks, and understands, and thinks as a child, and sees "through a glass darkly," in comparison of the state of the church in its latter ages, wherein it will be in a state of manhood, in a perfect state, and will see "face to face," in comparison of what it did in its first infant state. And so the gift of prophecy and tongues, etc., ceased at the end of the church's age of childhood, but charity remains when the elder age of the church comes, and when it shall "put away childish things." That age shall be an age of love; but there shall be no miraculous gifts of the Spirit, as being needless and more proper helps for the church in a state of infancy than in that state of manhood. Again the church, all the while it remains in a militant state, is in an imperfect state, a state of childhood, sees "through a glass darkly," thinks, speaks, and understands as a child, in comparison of what it will be in its heavenly and eternal state, when it shall come to "the measure of the stature of the fullness of Christ" [Eph. 4:13], when it shall see face to face, and know as it is known [v. 12]. Then it shall put away such childish things, such leading strings and gocarts, as the miraculous gifts of the Spirit, but love shall gloriously prevail. That world shall be a world of love. If we thus understand the Apostle, it

5. MS: "Chh. ~~in the Apostolical age~~ ⟨in its first age on earth⟩."

fully proves that the gifts of tongues and miracles, etc., are not to be upheld in the church in the millennium. See sermon on v. 8, 1st Inference.[6]

306. REVELATION 21:21. "And the street of the city was pure gold, like unto transparent glass." This does most livelily represent the perfect purity of that city and its inhabitants. In the most stately and magnificent cities in this world, however beautiful the buildings are, yet the streets are dirty and defiled, being made to be trodden underfoot; but the very streets of this heavenly city are so pure, that their being like pure gold don't sufficiently represent the purity of them, but they appear also like clear glass or crystal. If there be the least dirt or defilement, it discovers itself in that which is transparent; but those golden streets appeared perfectly clear, without the least speck to lessen the transparency. Christ represents as though the saints that he has washed, though they are clean, yet while in this world have defiled feet; they need to be often washing their feet. But in that world, their feet shall be perfectly pure so as not at all to defile the streets. This is an evidence that what is treated of in these two last chapters of Revelation is the heavenly[7] state of the church.

307. NUMBERS 19. The ashes of the red heifer, of which was made the water of separation, for the purification of those that were legally unclean. This heifer, being a female, doubtless does more directly signify the church of Christ than Christ himself. She was to be an heifer "without spot," having "no blemish" [v. 2], because it was the church of saints that are pure and upright ones, those that are not defiled with any pollution, showing hypocrisy or want of evangelical perfection (They are Israelites, indeed, "in whom is no guile" [John 1:47].), and those in whom God does not behold iniquity or see perverseness. The slaying and burning [of] this heifer signifies the sufferings and persecutions of the church of Christ, the fiery trial which she was [to] undergo. The persecutions of the church of Christ have mainly been carried on by burning. The purifying with the ashes of this heifer signifies that the church and people of God should be

6. JE's sermon on I Cor. 13:8, preached in October 1738, is the 14th in the series entitled *Charity and Its Fruits*. The first inference in the Application addresses the question whether there is "any reason to think as some have thought, that the extraordinary gifts of the Spirit of God are to be restored in the future glorious times of the church." JE's answer in that sermon parallels his discussion in this entry. See *Works, 8*, 361–63.

7. MS: "Heavenly & most perfect & Eternal State."

purified by her sufferings, and as it were by the ashes of the martyrs. The purifying of God's people, and taking away their sins, and refining them as silver, and making them white, is often declared to be the end of the suffering and persecutions of God's people; and 'tis the way in which it has pleased God to lay the foundation of the purity of his church, viz. by continuing it for many ages under extreme persecutions, first under the tyranny of Rome heathen, and nextly under Antichrist, and so to fill up, as the Apostle expresses himself, what is lacking in the sufferings of Christ [Col. 1:24]. For Christ does as it were suffer in his members; in all their affliction, he is afflicted. The church is his body, and in this sense the slaying and burning [of] this heifer represents the suffering of Christ, as they represent the sufferings of his people, whereby they are made conformable to Christ's death, and partakers of his sufferings. It pleases God to lay the foundation of the spiritual purity and prosperity of his church, in the first place, in his eldest Son, even Jesus Christ, and secondarily, in the blood of the martyrs, Christ's younger brethren, that are as it were God's youngest son. See notes on Joshua's prophecy concerning the rebuilding of Jericho.[8]

This was not to be a cow, but an heifer, and also without spot or blemish [v. 2], which is very agreeable to the description that is given of the church of Christ in Revelation, in the time of her persecution. Rev. 14:4–5, "These are they which were not defiled with women, for they are virgins. . . . And in their mouth was found no guile, for they are without fault before the throne of God."

And it must be a red heifer [v. 2], which signifies the militant state the church is in under those sufferings, conflicting with her enemies. The color red is often so used in Scripture. So Christ, while he is warring with his enemies, is represented as being red in his apparel (Is. 63:2), and as being "clothed with a vesture dipped in blood" (Rev. 19:13). So God's saints are clothed in red, till they have got through their sufferings and are in a triumphant state; then they are represented as having "washed their robes, and made them white in the blood of the Lamb" (Rev. 7:14).

It was to be an heifer on which never had come yoke [v. 2], which most fitly represents the spirit and practice of God's true church in the time of persecution from her enemies, which refuses to submit to the yoke, that they would oppose whatever cruelties they exercise them

8. See above, No. 173.

with. She will not call any man on earth master or lord, won't be subject to their impositions, won't forsake the commands of God nor be subject to the commandments of men, will "follow the Lamb whithersoever he goeth" [Rev. 14:4], will not worship the beast, nor his image, nor receive his mark in their foreheads nor in their hand [Rev. 20:4], stand fast in the liberty wherewith Christ hath made them free, not submitting to the yoke of bondage (Gal. 5:1).

This heifer was sacrificed to God; so are the martyrs represented as sacrificed. They offer up themselves a sacrifice to God through the Holy Spirit, and the souls of the martyrs are represented as souls under the altar [Rev. 6:9]. She was to be burnt "without the camp" [v. 3], as the martyrs, especially suffering under Antichrist, are rejected and cast out of the communion of their persecutors as not being of the church of Christ.

"Her skin, and her flesh, and her blood, with her dung" [v. 5], were to be burnt; the sufferings of the martyrs burns up their carnality and corruption, and cleanses all their filthiness.

The peculiar use of the ashes of the red heifer [vv. 17–19] was to purge from pollutions by dead bodies. So the use for which God designs the suffering and persecutions of his church is to rouse his people from coldness and deadness in religion, and from carnality, and worldly- or fleshly-mindedness, whereby men become as dead[9] carcasses, for he or she that liveth in pleasure is dead while he liveth. Carnal things are well compared to dead carcasses, for they are fleshly, and they are filthy and loathsome like stinking flesh.

308. PSALMS 24:7–10. "Lift up your heads, O ye gates; and be ye lift up, ye everlasting doors, that the King of glory may come in." The gates and doors here spoken of are the gates and doors of God's holy place, or sanctuary, on his holy hill, spoken of, v. 3, so that here the Psalmist is speaking of Christ's ascension to heaven. He before had inquired who should ascend there, and he answered, "He that has clean hands, and a pure heart," etc. [vv. 4–5]. In one sense, all Christ's sincere disciples and followers are such; they are pure in heart and hands, with a purity of sincerity and universal obedience. But in another sense, Christ alone is so, who was perfectly free from any defilement of heart or hands. This psalm treats of the ascension, both of the head and members of the church of Christ, into heaven.

9. MS: "a dead."

When Christ ascends into heaven after his sore conflict with his enemies and his glorious victory over them, wherein he appeared to be "the Lord strong and mighty, the Lord mighty in battle" [v. 8], and the word was proclaimed to the gates and doors of that everlasting temple of God, that they should be lift up, that the King of glory may come in, the heavenly hosts are represented as inquiring with wonder and great admiration, "Who is this King of glory?", as being in their eyes a very wonderful person, and one that had done very wonderful things, as though some very new thing appeared, a remarkable person coming, appearing in such wise as never had been before, a person that appeared with very wonderful glory, and such an one as that it was wonderful that one, with those things that had appeared in him of late and now appeared, should have the title of "the King of glory," as though it was admirable that such glory should be united with those other things that appeared in this person, which yet it most plainly appeared there had, that appeared in him, by which he appears sufficiently to merit the character of the King of glory, viz. his appearing so strong and mighty in battle, as he had done, and gaining such a glorious victory, as he had done. And therefore it is answered, "The Lord strong and mighty," etc. [v. 8].

So David, the type of Christ, after he had come from his conflict with Goliath, and had slain him with his own [hand], drew the eyes and admiration of others upon him. Saul inquired, "Whose son is this youth, whose son is the stripling?" [I Sam. 17:55–56]. He appeared a wonderful person, one that had done a wonderful thing, and now appeared in a remarkable manner. A new thing appeared, a youth, a stripling, in such honor and glory, with the head of such a giant in his hand. It appeared wonderful that such glory should be united with such things as appeared in him, viz. such youth, such tenderness. And when it is said here, "the Lord strong and mighty, the Lord mighty in battle," this is like the song of the daughters of Israel that came out to meet King David, when he came from the slaughter of the Philistine, saying, David has slain his ten thousands [I Sam. 18:7].[1] So it is inquired of Christ in Isaiah 63:1, "Who is this that cometh from Edom, with dyed garments from Bozrah, this that is glorious in his apparel, traveling in the greatness of his strength?" So we find, once and again, that Christ's name is called "Wonderful." See Ps. 118:22–23. See obser-

1. This sentence is a later interlineation.

vations on this psalm in my "Treatise of the Prophecies of the Messiah."[2]

309. HEBREWS 3:6–4:11. "Whose house are we, if we hold fast the confidence and the rejoicing of the hope firm unto the end. Wherefore, as the Holy Ghost saith, Today, if ye will hear his voice, harden not your hearts, as in the provocation," etc. The Apostle here supposes that when the Psalmist here says, "*Today*, if ye will hear his voice, harden not your hearts," it is as much as if he had said, "Although that was a long time ago, and though their day was long since past, yet hear his voice, and don't harden your hearts now in this your day, and see that you never harden your hearts while your day lasts. For if you don't harden your hearts, there is a rest of God that you may enter into, as well as they; but if you continue to harden your heart, your day in a little time will be past as well as theirs." The former part of this sense, viz. that by the expression "today," the Psalmist means, "in this day that you now have so long after their day is past," is evident by Heb. 4:7; and the latter part, viz. that he means, "Take heed that your heart be at no time hardened during your day," is evident, because in the 8th verse the words are brought in as a motive to perseverance. It is still more evident by the manner of the Apostle's bringing [in] the words in the 11th and 12th [verses], and also in the 14th and 15th verses, and by the Apostle's paraphrase of the words, or gloss he puts upon them there, "while it is called today" (v. 13), and "while it is said, today" (v. 15), which is the same thing as "during the continuance of this day."

From the Psalmist's exhorting us to hear God's voice today, so long a time since the carcasses of the children of Israel fell in the wilderness, and so they failed of entering into God's rest, and so long a time after others that believed entered into that temporal rest that Joshua

2. This cross-reference and the preceding biblical reference are later interlineations. There is some ambiguity in the reference to "this psalm." JE has entries on both Ps. 24 and Ps. 118 in "Prophecies of the Messiah," a treatise comprised of three entries in the "Miscellanies." Section 23 contains a brief comment on Ps. 118:22–26 which concludes with "See how the Jews interpret this psalm of the Messiah. Poole's *Synopsis* on the argument of the psalm and on verse 22" ("Miscellanies," no. 922). Section 85 is a longer discussion of Ps. 24 which JE declares "to have respect to the times of the Messiah." He suggests the psalm was occasioned by the removal of the ark from the sanctuary in ancient Israel; and he points to parallels between David's triumph over Goliath and Christ's ascension following his triumph over his enemies. Yet the "King of glory" spoken of seems properly to refer to one who "was in a peculiar manner free of sin, of clean hands and a pure heart, and therefore above all others had a right to ascend God's holy hill, and to stand in his holy place" ("Miscellanies," no. 1067).

brought them into, the Apostle would argue that there remains still another rest to the people of God to be entered into. As God spake concerning the children of Israel in the wilderness, as if there was a rest of God still to be entered into, though there had been a rest of God many ages before that, viz. that rest, or sabbatism of God, which God enjoyed on the seventh day of the creation, resting from the works of creation, which had been distinguished as God's rest, or his sabbatism, but yet there then remained another rest of God to those that believed, viz. Christ's rest in Canaan after the Egyptian bondage and his redemption of his people out of Egypt, as is implied in his swearing in his wrath that those that did not believe should not enter into rest, so there still remains another rest also, besides God's rest from that redemption, as is implied in the Psalmist. When speaking so long after of the unbelievers in the wilderness failing of entering into that rest, he still exhorts and says, "Today, if you will hear his voice, harden not your hearts, as they did," implying that it won't be in vain for us, even now, to hearken, but we shall enter in God's rest still if we hearken, even that rest that Christ entered into in heaven, after his great bondage here on earth and his finishing the work of redemption, by which may be understood the force of the Apostle's reasoning in vv. 3–11 of the next chapter.

310. HEBREWS 8:1. "We have such an high priest, who is set on the right hand of the throne of the Majesty in the heavens." This is often taken notice of in this epistle, as Heb. 1:3, and 10:12, and 12:2. This High Priest, when he enters into the holy of holies with his own blood, don't only appear there standing before the throne, or mercy seat, as the high priests of old were wont to do when they entered into the holy of holies once a year with the blood of others, but sits down on the throne in the holy of holies on the right hand of God, which shows the exceeding dignity of the priest, his nearness and dearness to God, and the absolute sufficiency of the sacrifice that he had offered, the blood of which he entered in there with, and the dignity and honorableness of the manner of interceding there, which was not merely by supplicating, as one in humble posture before the throne, but by[3] representing his will to the Father, as one sitting in glory with him on the throne, as John 17:24, "Father, I will that they that thou hast given me, be with me," etc. His thus being admitted and invited of God to sit with him on

3. JE deleted "manifesting."

the throne denotes [that] God's full, and perfect, and great satisfaction, and well-pleasedness rest on this High Priest. When he had offered his sacrifice, and entered into the holy of holies with the blood of it, to obtain of God what he shed that blood for, God immediately receives him, and accepts him and his plea, and says to him, "Sit thou on my right hand, till I make thine enemies thy footstool" [Heb. 1:13]. And it is a note of Christ's perfect assurance of the Father's acceptance of him as priest, and his rest, as having virtually obtained what he intercedes for, having all things put into his hands, being made "head over all things to the church" [Eph. 1:22]. He don't merely stand before the throne, supplicating, hoping, and waiting, as the legal high priests did, but sits down in perfect rest, as being satisfied in his full acceptance and virtual possession of all he seeks. He sits on the throne as a royal priest, as "a priest on the throne," agreeable to the prophecy in Zech. 6:13, being made to reign, to accomplish the ends of his priesthood, according to his own will; for God has given all power in heaven and on earth, that Christ may give eternal life to as many as God hath given him.

311. LUKE 22:44. This to be added to No. 225. Christ, in those strong cries and tears, wherein he wrestled with God in a bloody sweat for the success of his sufferings in the salvation of the elect, hath given us example how we should seek our own salvation, and the salvation of others whose souls are committed to our care, viz. as striving, wrestling, and agonizing with God. See Prov. 2, at beginning.[4] When Christ says, Luke 13:24, "Strive to enter in at the strait gate," the word in the original for "strive" is ἀγωνίζεσθε, "agonize."

312. HEBREWS 9:28. "So Christ was once offered to bear the sins of many; and unto those that look for him shall he appear the second time without sin unto salvation." The first time that Christ appeared, he did not appear without sin, for he bare the sins of many; he appeared in that form, in those circumstances, and with those labors and sufferings, that were tokens of imputed sin or guilt that lay upon him. But then he perfectly freed himself from this imputed sin; he perfectly abolished this guilt by those sufferings he underwent, as the Apostle is here arguing in the preceding parts of the chapter. And

4. In a note on Prov. 2:1–5, JE describes "true seekers" as "those that seek from love and [a] sense of the value of [the] thing sought, and with longing desire after the thing for its own sake" by contrast with "natural men" who "seek only from fear and self-love" ("Blank Bible").

therefore, when he appears the second time, it shall be without sin, without any of those tokens of imputed guilt which he had in his state of humiliation; he shall be exceeding far from them. The state in which he will then appear will be immensely different from the state of one under the tokens and fruits of guilt and wrath, for he shall appear in the glory of his Father, with all the holy angels, as the supreme head and judge of the universe, with ineffable and inconceivable glory and magnificence. Had not Christ perfectly satisfied for the sins of men, and so done away all his imputed guilt, he could not have appeared a second time without sin, but must always have remained under the tokens of God's curse for sin. But at the day of judgment he will appear infinitely far from that. The glory he will appear in at the day of judgment will be the greatest and brightest evidence of all, of his having fully satisfied for sin. His resurrection is a glorious evidence of, and therefore is called, his "justification" [Rom. 4:25]. His ascending into heaven, and sitting on the right hand of God there, is a still brighter evidence, as 'tis a higher degree of his exaltation. But the glory that he will appear in at the day of judgment will be the brightest evidence of all, as herein appears the glory of his exaltation in its highest degree of all, and is the highest reward which the Father bestows on him for it, and so is the highest token of his acceptance of it as sufficient and perfect. Besides the glory of the special affair of that day which Christ shall bear, then will be the beginning of the consummate glory and reward of both Christ and his church, to last throughout eternity. And not only the glory that Christ will then appear in, but the nature of the business that he will come upon, will show him perfectly to have done away all the sins of his elect, which will be judged,[5] and save those that have believed in him. God would not have committed this affair to one that had undertaken for them, unless he had satisfied for them.

He will appear "without sin to salvation." The first time he appeared, it was with sin to procure salvation. The second time he will appear to bestow salvation, which will in the event show that salvation is fully procured.

313. JOHN 21:25. "And there are also many other things which Jesus did, the which, if they should be written every one, I suppose that even the world itself could not contain the books that should be written." If here, by the "things that Jesus did," be not only meant the actions of

5. MS: "judge."

Christ, but the things done or accomplished by those actions, we may suppose it to be literally true, that if they were written every one, the world itself is not large enough to "contain the books that should be written." There are other things that belong to what Christ did, besides merely the external action that was immediately[6] visible to the eye, or the words that might be heard by the ear, which we must suppose are included in what the Evangelist means by the "things that he did." There was the internal manner of doing, the design with which it was done, what moved and influenced Christ in doing, the ends and events brought to pass by doing. The evangelists do mention some of Christ's ends and motives, etc., in acting. The apostle John in this history mentions some of them, but to mention all would be to write a declaration of all the glorious wise purposes and designs of God's wisdom and grace, and the love of Christ, and all that belongs to that manifold wisdom of God, and those unsearchable riches of wisdom and knowledge in the work of redemption that we read of in the Scripture, which, if they should be all written, 'tis probable the universe would not contain the books. For here are the multitude of God's mercies that we read of, in Ps. 5:7; 51:1; 69:13, 16; 106:7; and 119:156. These works, that the Evangelist speaks of that Christ wrought, are the same with those spoken of, Ps. 40:5–10. "Many, O Lord my God, are thy wonderful works which thou hast done, and thy thoughts which are to usward. They cannot be reckoned up in order unto thee; if I would declare and speak of them, they are more than can be numbered. Sacrifice and offering thou didst not desire. . . . Then said I, Lo, I come; in the volume of the book it is written of me, I delight to do thy will, O my God, and thy law is within my heart. I have preached righteousness in the great congregation," etc. And Ps. 71:15, "My mouth shall show forth thy righteousness and thy salvation all the day; for I know not the numbers thereof." And Ps. 139:17–18, "How precious are thy thoughts unto me, O God! How great is the sum of them! If I should count them, they are more in number than the sand." The wonderful things designed and virtually accomplished in what Christ did when on the earth are so manifold as to be sufficient to employ the contemplation of saints and angels to all eternity, who will discover more and more of the manifold wisdom of God therein, and yet never will discover all.[7]

---

6. This word is a later interlineation.
7. After this JE later interlined "Job 5:9" and then deleted it.

314. LUKE 1:35. "And the angel answered and said unto her, The Holy Ghost shall come upon thee, and the power of the Highest shall overshadow thee. Therefore also that holy thing that shall be born of thee shall be called the Son of God." The Virgin Mary, the mother of Christ, was a type of two things. She was a type of the church, that is often in Scripture represented as Christ's mother, that travails in pain with him and brings him forth. She brings him forth in the hearts of believers, and especially those that are ministers in the church, who (as the Apostle said he did) do "travail in birth" with souls [Gal. 4:19]; and he, being brought forth, appears and lives in their lives. The church is also represented as a chaste pure virgin [II Cor. 11:2]; she is often called his "undefiled" in Canticles.[8] As she brings Christ forth, so she nourishes Christ, or grace, in the hearts of the saints at the breasts of ordinances, and those means of grace that are[9] maintained in the church. She affords the sincere milk of the word, which believers, as newborn babes, are nourished and do grow by. And the blessed Virgin, in conceiving and bringing forth Christ, is an eminent type of every believing soul, who is Christ's brother, and sister, and mother. As Christ was formed in her, so is he in every true convert. He was formed in her by the Holy Ghost coming upon [her], and the power of the Highest overshadowing her, which is a lively representation of the manner in which the new creature is formed in the saints. The mother of Christ was a pure virgin; so are believers represented in Scripture. They are presented as [a] chaste virgin to Christ; they are those that are "not defiled with women, for they are virgins," as 'tis said in Rev. 14:4. The blessed Virgin brought forth Christ with travail, pains, and throes; so is Christ commonly brought forth in the hearts of believers, with those convictions, and that repentance and sorrow for sin, that self-denial and mortification, that may fitly be compared to the pains of a woman in travail. As the blessed Virgin nourished her babe with milk from her paps, with nourishment from her breast, and as it were flowing from her heart, so Christ is as it were refreshed with the exercises of grace that flow from the hearts of the saints, and their good works, which are often represented in Scripture as the fruit and food that Christ expects, feeds on, and is delighted in. 'Tis that which is food to Christ in the heart, or the principle of grace there, which is as a newborn child, and causes it to grow. And the exercises and fruits of

---

8. See Cant. 5:2 and 6:9.
9. JE deleted "enjoyed."

grace, that come from the hearts of the saints, do as it were nourish Christ's interest in the world, and cause Christ's mystical body, which is small as in infancy, to be strengthened and increased. The mother of Christ was very careful of Christ when he was an infant, tended him with great care, was careful in watching over him lest he should be hurt, and was careful to feed and nourish him, when he was wounded to heal him, to please and gratify him, and by all means to promote his health and growth, as tender mothers are wont to do to their little children; so should the saint do with respect to Christ in the heart.[1] The care that a tender mother has of her infant is a very lively image of the care that a Christian ought to have of grace in the heart. 'Tis a very constant care; the child must be continually looked after. It must be taken care of both day and night. When the mother wakes up in the night, she has her child to look after, and nourish at her breast; and it sleeps in her bosom, and it must be continually in the mother's bosom or arms, there to be upheld and cherished. It needs its food and nourishment much oftener than adult persons; it must be fed both day and night. It must be very frequently cleansed, for 'tis very often defiled. It must in everything be gratified and pleased. The mother must bear the burden of it as she goes to and fro. This is also a lively image of the care that the church, especially the ministers of the gospel, should have of the interest of Christ committed to their care. I Thess. 2:6–9, "We might have been burdensome, as the apostles of Christ. But we were gentle among you, even as the nurse cherisheth her children. So being affectionately desirous of you, we were willing to have imparted unto you, not the gospel of God only, but also our own souls, because ye were dear unto us. For ye remember, brethren, our labor and travail: for laboring night and day, because we would not be chargeable unto any of you, we preached unto you the gospel of God." That the church, when spoken of under the character of a mother, the ministers are especially meant, see notes on Cant. 3:11, at the latter end.[2]

1. JE deleted "and so should the church do with respect to the interest of Christ in the world."

2. JE's exposition includes the judgment that "by 'his mother' seems especially to be meant the church, as holding forth the word of Christ and administering the ordinances of Christ, whereby souls are converted and brought forth and brought to an union and spiritual marriage with Christ. And therefore the ministers of the gospel seem especially to be intended by 'his mother,' for they travail in birth with souls till Christ be formed in them." The "character of a mother" has special reference also to "the instructing part of the church" ("Blank Bible").

315. NUMBERS 10:10. This in addition to[3] note on Num. 10:10.[4] Concerning the festival of the new moon. The change of the moon at her conjunction with the sun seems to be a type of three things.

1. Of the resurrection of the church from the dead by virtue of her union with Christ, and at the coming of Christ, for the moon at her change, that lost all her light, and was extinct, and seemed to die, revives again after her conjunction with the sun.

2. Of the conversion of every believing soul, which is its spiritual resurrection. The soul in its conversion comes to Christ and closes with Christ, as the moon[5] comes to the sun into a conjunction with him. The soul in conversion dies to sin and to the world, crucifies "the flesh with the affections and lusts" [Gal. 5:24], dies as to its own worthiness or righteousness, whereby it is said in Scripture to be "dead to the law" that it may receive new life [Gal. 2:19], as the former light of the moon is extinct at its conjunction with the sun, that it may receive new light. In order to coming to Christ aright, we must [not] come with our own brightness and glory, with any of our own fullness, strength, light, or righteousness, or happiness, but as stripped of all our glory, empty of all good, wholly dark, sinful, destitute, and miserable, as the moon is wholly divested of all her light at her conjunction with the sun. We must come to Christ as wholly sinful and miserable, as the moon comes to the sun in total darkness. The moon, as it comes nearer the sun, grows darker and darker; so souls, the more they are fitted for Christ, are more and more emptied of themselves, that they may be filled with Christ. The moon grows darker and darker in her approach to the sun; so the soul sees more and more of its own sinfulness, and vileness, and misery, that it may be swallowed up in the rays of the Sun of Righteousness.

3. The change of the moon at her conjunction with the sun signifies the change of the[6] state and administration of the church at the coming of Christ.

The sun is sometimes eclipsed in his conjunction with the moon, which signifies two things, viz. (1) The veiling of his glory by his incar-

3. JE deleted "Numb. No. 271."
4. JE associated the festivities at the new moon described in Num. 10:10 with the proclamation of the "glad tidings of the gospel." "The moon is a lively image of [the] church," the old moon being linked to "the church under the Old Testament ," and the new moon to the New Testament church. The time of the change of the moon "seems to represent the coming of Christ" into the flesh and his uniting with the church ("Blank Bible").
5. JE deleted "closes with the sun."
6. JE deleted "dispensation."

nation. For as the sun has his light veiled by his conjunction with the moon in its darkness, so Christ had his glory veiled by his conjunction, or union, with our nature in its low and broken state. As the moon proves a veil to hide the glory of the sun, so the flesh[7] of Christ was a veil that hid his divine glory. (2) It signifies his death. The sun is sometimes totally eclipsed by the moon at her change; so Christ died at the time of the change of the church from the old dispensation to the new. The sun is eclipsed at his conjunction with the moon in her darkness; so Christ, taking our nature upon him in his low and broken state, died in it. Christ assumed his church and people in their[8] guilt and misery, and in their condemned, cursed, dying state, into a very close union with him, so as to become one with him; and hereby he takes their guilt on himself, and becomes subject to their sin, their curse, their death, yea, is made a curse for them, as the sun as it were assumes the moon in her total darkness into a close union with himself, so as to become one with her. They become concentrical, and become as it were one body, circumscribed by the same circumference; and thereby he takes her darkness on himself, and becomes himself dark with her darkness, and is extinct in his union with her. The moon, that receives all her light from the sun, eclipses the sun, and takes away his light; so Christ was put to death by those that he came to save. He is put to death by the iniquities of those that he came to give life to, and he was immediately crucified by the hands of some of them. And all of them have pierced him in the disposition and tendency of that sin that they have been guilty of, for all have manifested and expressed a mortal enmity against him. 'Tis an argument that the eclipse of the sun is a type of Christ's death, because the sun suffered a total eclipse miraculously at that time that Christ died.

The sun can be in a total eclipse but a very little while, much less than the moon, though neither of them can always be in an eclipse; so Christ could not, by reason of his divine glory and worthiness, be long held of death, in no measure so long as the saints may be, though it ben't possible that either of them should always be held of it.

The sun's coming out of his eclipse is a figure of his resurrection from the dead. As the sun is restored to light, so the moon that eclipsed him begins to receive light from him, and so to partake of his restored light. So the church, for whose sins Christ died, and who has pierced

7. JE deleted "in Scripture is represented as a veil."
8. JE deleted "sinfulness."

Christ, rises with Christ, is begotten again to a living hope by the resurrection of Christ from the dead [I Pet. 1:3], and is made partaker of the life and power of his resurrection, and is partaker of the glory of his exaltation, is raised up together, and made to sit together in heavenly places [Eph. 2:6]. In him they live, yet not they, but Christ lives in them [Gal. 2:20]; and they are married to him that is risen from the dead. God, having raised Christ, quickens them who were totally dark and dead in trespasses and sins; and they are revived by God's power, according to the exceeding greatness of his power that wrought in Christ Jesus when he raised him from the dead.

The moon is eclipsed when at the full, in its greatest glory, which may signify several things. (1) That God is wont to bring some great calamity on his visible church when [in] its greatest glory and prosperity, as he did on the Old Testament church when in the height of its glory in David's and Solomon's time, by David's adultery and murder, and those sore calamities that followed in his family, and to all Israel in the affairs of Amnon and especially Absalom, and in the idolatry of Solomon, and sore calamities that followed, and particularly the dividing the kingdom of Israel. So he did also in the church of the New Testament, after Constantine, by the Arian heresy, etc. God doth thus "to stain the pride of all glory" [Is. 23:9], and that his people may not lift up themselves against him, that he alone may be exalted. (2). That 'tis often God's manner to bring some grievous calamity on his saints, at times when they have received the greatest light and joys, and have been most exalted with smiles of heaven upon them, as Jacob was made lame at the same time that he was admitted to so extraordinary a privilege as wrestling with God, and overcoming him, and so obtaining the blessing [Gen. 32:24–28]. And so Paul, when he was received up to "the third heaven," received "a thorn in the flesh"; lest he should be exalted above measure, he had "a messenger of Satan" to buffet him. So grievous calamity it was that he labored under, that he besought the Lord thrice that it might be taken from him [II Cor. 12:2–8]. Sometimes extraordinary light and comfort is given to fit for great calamities, and sometimes for death, which God brings soon after such things. So when God gives his own people great temporal prosperity, he is wont to bring with it some calamity to clipse it, to keep them [from] being exalted in their prosperity and trusting in it.

316. ECCLESIASTES 6:3. "So that the days of his years be many, and his soul be not filled with good, and also that he HAVE NO BURIAL; I say,

that an untimely birth is better than he." "Have no burial," i.e. be one that God takes no care of in his death, does him no honor, takes no care of either soul or body, as having any value or care of either, or any respect for their memory. For 'tis the wicked that the wise man is here speaking of, the same that is spoken of, Eccles. 8:12–13, which is a place very parallel with this; and it will be further evident by comparing this and the following verse with Eccles. 5:13–17. Burial is the respect which friends show to the memory and remains of those that are dead. God will show no regard to anything that remains of wicked men after death. God treats their souls when they die, and will treat their bodies at the resurrection, with contempt, as men treat the dead bodies of those creatures they have [no] honor or regard for, and are abominable to them, as are the carcasses of unclean beasts. Jer. 22:19, "He shall be buried with the burial of an ass, drawn and cast forth beyond the gates of Jerusalem." And Is. 14:19–20, "But thou art cast out of thy grave like an abominable branch, and as the raiment of those that are slain, thrust through with the sword, that go down to the stones of the pit, and as a carcass trodden under feet. Thou shalt not be joined unto them in burial, because thou hast destroyed thy land." God takes care of the righteous when they die; he finds a repository of rest for their souls, and their dust is precious to him. As God buried Moses in the mount, they are gathered to their fathers, and received into Abraham's bosom. But God treats the souls of the wicked when they die as men treat the dead, rotting, stinking carcass of an ass or a dog; they are cast forth out of the city of God's Jerusalem, and shall be forever shut out thence.

317. ISAIAH 40:1–2. "Comfort ye, comfort ye my people, saith your God. Speak ye comfortably to Jerusalem, and cry unto her, that her warfare is accomplished, that her iniquity is pardoned; for she hath received of the Lord's hand DOUBLE for all her sins." God often executes very severe judgments on his visible church for their sins; and though their punishment be never double to her deserts, or more than her deserts, yet she oftentimes suffers double in two respects. 1. Double to the[9] sufferings which their sins, their violations of duties of the second table of the law, have brought cn others, in which sense the false church is commanded to be punished. Rev. 18:6, "Reward her even as she rewarded you, and double unto her double; in the cup

9. JE deleted "injuries that."

which she hath filled, fill to her double." 2. Double to all the pleasure or benefit, the wealth or worldly advancement, which she hath obtained or aimed at by her sins, as in that place in Revelation. It follows in the next verse, "How much she hath glorified herself, and lived deliciously, so much torment and sorrow give her." By "double" is not meant precisely twice so much, but vastly more. Thus God don't only punish Babylon, or the false church, but his own visible church, when they corrupt themselves, and make themselves in a great measure a false church, as Jerusalem and Israel of old did. God punished them with great severity; he punished them doubly. Jer. 16:18, "I will recompense their iniquity and their sin double, because they have defiled my land."[1] God caused all the idolatrous nations to drink the wine-cup of God's fury, and especially Sheshach, or Babylon; but he, in the first place, gave it to Jerusalem (Jer. 25). God takes notice of the great severity with which he had punished Jerusalem, for this is manifestly the language of compassion. A father, while in wrath he is correcting his child, makes light of its sufferings; but when his heart begins to relent, and bowels of compassion to yearn, his sufferings begin to look great in his eyes. God is often represented as thus exercising the bowels of a merciful father towards his people after severe correction. See Judg. 10:16, Jer. 31:20, and Is. 63:15–16. See Neh. 9:32.[2]

318. ROMANS 1:16–18. JUSTIFICATION. CHRIST'S RIGHTEOUSNESS. "For I am not ashamed of the gospel of Christ," etc., "For therein is the righteousness of God revealed from faith to faith; as it is written, The just shall live by faith. For the wrath of God is revealed from heaven against all ungodliness and unrighteousness of men." In these verses I would note two things.

First, that here, in the beginning of this discourse of his of the wickedness of the whole world, both Jews and Gentiles, that is continued from this place to the 19th, 20th, and 21st verses of ch. 3, as well as in the conclusion in that part of the 3rd chapter, he manifests his design in it all to be to show that all are guilty, and in a state of condemnation, and therefore can't be saved by their own righteousness, that it must be by the righteousness of God through Christ received by faith alone. He here in the 17th verse asserts that 'tis thus only that men have justification, and then in the 18th verse enters on the reason why, "For

1. This sentence and the last four words of the preceding sentence are a later interlineation.
2. This reference is a later addition.

the wrath of God is revealed from heaven against all ungodliness and unrighteousness of men, who hold the truth in unrighteousness"; and so goes on, setting forth the ungodliness and unrighteousness of men through most of those three first chapters, and then at the end, concludes his argument as he began it, that, seeing all are under sin, "Therefore by the deeds of the law shall no flesh living be justified in his sight" [v. 20], but that 'tis by "the righteousness of God which is by the faith of Christ" [v. 22].

Secondly, I observe that by "the righteousness of God" in this place can't be meant only God's way of justifying a sinner, but hereby is meant the moral, legal righteousness which God had provided for sinners. 'Tis evident by two things. 1. 'Tis the righteousness or justice which those that are justified have, by which they are righteous or just, as is evident by the Apostle's selecting that passage of the Old Testament to cite on this occasion, "The *just* shall live by faith" [Hab. 2:4]. 2. 'Tis evident by the antithesis, for here 'tis most manifest that the "righteousness of God," by which God's people are just, in one verse, is opposed to the "unrighteousness of men," by which they in themselves are unjust, as is evident by the argument of the Apostle in these verses. 'Tis a righteousness that believers are vested with, as is evident by Rom. 3:22–23. The same is also manifest by the antithesis in that place; the same is manifest both those ways, by Phil. 3:9.

The same is very manifest by Rom. 10:3–4. "For they being ignorant of God's righteousness, and going about to establish their own righteousness, have not submitted themselves to the righteousness of God. For Christ is the end of the law for righteousness to everyone that believeth." The antithesis here makes it evident that by "God's righteousness" is meant a righteousness, in having which we are righteous. And the 4th verse shows that this righteousness was procured for every believer by Christ, as he was subject to the law. "Christ is the end of the law for righteousness," the natural meaning of which is that,[3] as to what concerns the elect, or them that believe, the Lawgiver, in making the law and establishing of it as a rule for them, had respect to Christ only for its being answered. The law that requires righteousness looks to Christ only to produce that righteousness that it requires, who of God is made to be righteousness, and who is "the Lord our righteousness" [Jer. 23:6]. I can find no instance in the New Testament where the τέλος, here translated "end," is anywhere used in Scripture

---

3. JE deleted "God in making the law had a main respect."

for final cause, but it seems properly to signify the final term, finishing, or accomplishing; so that the words might be rendered, "Christ is the finishing and completing of the law, as to the righteousness it requires, as it respects all them that believe."

There is one place where the same word in the original is used as here, and also speaking of the end of the law or commandment, that exceedingly confirms this interpretation, viz. I Tim. 1:5. "Now the end of the commandment is charity," i.e. the accomplishment or fulfillment of the law, as the same Apostle says, "Charity is the fulfilling of the law," in this epistle of Romans, 13:8, 10. So that 'tis manifest from this place that that righteousness, which this Apostle calls the "righteousness of God," consists in Christ's fulfilling or answering the law; and therefore that 'tis the same thing with what we call the "righteousness of Christ."

This righteousness of God, which the Apostle so often speaks of in the matter of our justification, is in Christ. II Cor. 5:21, "He was made sin for us, that we might be the righteousness of God in him." "He was made sin," i.e. sin was imputed to him. And what sin was it? Why, that sin that was *in us.* So we are made "the righteousness of God." But what righteousness of God is it that we are made? Why, that which was in Christ our Mediator. See "Miscellanies," no. 1271.[4]

It is not called by the Apostle "Christ's righteousness," because the righteousness, by which a believer stands just before God, does but in part consist in that which can properly be called Christ's righteousness, for 'tis only the obedience of Christ that is properly his righteousness. But this is not all that by which we stand just before God, for, besides this, his sufferings as our[5] atonement were necessary. Without this we are not righteous, but must appear sinful before God, because our old sins would remain. These sufferings, abating the obedience that was in them, were not in themselves Christ's righteousness; and therefore the Scripture don't ordinarily call them so, but calls the whole of the provision made of God in Christ, for our appearing just, consisting both in his obedience and atonement, "God's righteousness" and "the righteousness of God which is by the faith of Christ" (Rom. 3:22). See notes on Rom. 10:3; "Miscellanies," no. 637, Argument 2.[6]

---

4. This reference is a later addition. In no. 1271, JE asserts that "THE RIGHTEOUSNESS by which believers are justified is called GOD'S RIGHTEOUSNESS" because that righteousness is "inherent in God" as a "divine person."

5. JE deleted "substitute."

6. Both references are later additions. In a lengthy discussion of Rom. 10:3, JE states,

319. Psalms 68.[7] The bringing up the ark of God out of the house of Obed-edom the Gittite, into the city of David on the top of Mt. Zion, on which occasion this psalm was penned, was the most remarkable type of the ascension of Christ that we have in the Old Testament. Then Christ rode "on the heavens by his name Jah" [v. 4]. Before, his divinity was veiled; he appeared as a mere man, and as "a worm, and no man" [Ps. 22:6]. He had as it were laid aside his glory as a divine person, emptied himself of the name and form of God; but now he appears[8] in his ascension as God, in the glory of his divinity, in the name and glory of the great Jah and Jehovah (v. 4).[9] Then he rode "upon the heavens of heavens, which were of old" (v. 33); as the Apostle says, he "ascended up far above all heavens" [Eph. 4:10]. As the inhabitants of the land of Canaan were gathered together to attend the ark in this its ascension into Mt. Zion (II Sam. 6:15, 19; I Chron. 15:3, 25, and 28; 16:2), so without doubt the inhabitants of the heavenly Canaan were gathered together on occasion of Christ's ascension to attend him into heaven. For he ascended into heaven "in like manner" as he shall descend at the last day (Acts 1:11), with like glory and magnificence, and with a like attendance. He shall come at the last day in the glory of his Father; so he, without doubt, ascended in that glory after his human nature was transformed, as it was as it passed out of our atmosphere. That Christ entered heaven with divine glory is manifest by Ps. 24:7–10. "Lift up your head, O ye gates, that the King of glory may come in," etc. Christ will descend at the last day with the clouds of heaven, and so he ascended into heaven (Acts 1:9, and Dan. 7:13 with

---

"The reason why the righteousness of Christ from time to time is called by the name of God's righteousness may probably be this, that the grand difference between the righteousness of the two covenants is this, that one is a mere human righteousness; the other is a divine righteousness, or the righteousness of a divine person." This difference has the practical effect of bringing "mankind to a greater dependence on God" and recognition of God as "the sum of their objective good," for human righteousness, or that of the first covenant, is insufficient for justification. God's righteousness, by contrast, comes "immediately of God by his gift and imputation" ("Blank Bible"). In "Miscellanies" no. 637, JE asserts, from Rom. 10:3 and other texts, that "it is evident that trusting in our own righteousness is fatal to the soul." Those who are "ignorant of God's righteousness" do not understand or believe the "doctrine of imputed righteousness," but rather seek "to establish their own righteousness" in the matter of justification.

7. JE wrote "The Removal of the Ark and Christ's Ascension, No. 319" at the top of two pages of this entry.

8. JE deleted "as the great God."

9. JE deleted "Then Christ ascended on high, and led captivity captive, and received gifts for men, even for the rebellious (v. 18)."

notes).[1] Christ will descend to judgment, and so he ascended to judge and confirm the angels, to give repentance unto Israel and remission of sin, and by his knowledge to justify many, and to judge the prince of this world, and to execute judgments on the wicked. And as he will descend with all the heavenly hosts of both saints and angels, so he ascended. They came forth out of heaven to meet the King of glory as he ascended. As the Roman generals, after a signal battle and victory over their enemies abroad, far distant from Rome, when they returned in triumph (which is a great type of Christ's ascension), had multitudes to attend them, so had Christ in his ascension into heaven. See in how many respects the Roman triumphs were like Christ's ascension (Mastricht, p. 597, col. 2).[2] See also the description of a Roman triumph in Chambers, *Dictionary*.[3] As Christ's descent will be attended with the general resurrection, so was his ascension with the risen bodies of many of his saints, and was followed with a great spiritual resurrection of the world.

As the ark in its ascension into Mt. Zion was attended with "the princes of the people" (Ps. 68:27; 47:9), and with the captains of their hosts (I Chron. 15:25), and with the ministers of the sanctuary (I Chron. 15:4 ff.), so Christ in his ascension was attended with the angels, who are called the principalities and powers of heaven [Col. 1:16], and are the mighty champions in God's armies, and the ministers of the heavenly sanctuary, as they are represented in Revelation. Shall a departing soul of a saint ascend to heaven with a convoy of angels, being carried by angels into Abraham's bosom, and shall not the King of saints and angels in his ascension into heaven be attended with myriads of angels? That Christ was attended with multitudes of angels in his ascension into heaven is manifest by the 17th and 18th verses of this 68th psalm. "The chariots of God are twenty thousand, even thousands of angels; the Lord is among them, as in Sinai, in the holy place.

1. For JE's "notes" on Dan. 7:13, see No. 279.

2. This sentence is a later addition. See "Images," no. 81, on the Roman triumph. Mastricht, *Theoretica-practica theologia*, pp. 597–98, points to a number of similarities including the fact that both processions were accompanied with songs and celebrations, that the cloud bearing Christ was like unto the Roman chariot, that in both the conquerors gave gifts, and that Christ's ascent to heaven was like that of the victor's ascent to the Capitol in Rome.

3. This sentence is a later addition. Ephraim Chambers described the honors given to a "victorious general" on his entry into Rome, including an account of the chariot procession and of the fate accorded to the captured enemies. "The *triumph* was the most pompous spectacle known among the ancients," he wrote (*Cyclopaedia: or, an Universal Dictionary of Arts and Sciences* [2 vols. 2nd ed., London, 1738], 2, entry on "Triumph, Triumphs," n.p.).

Thou hast ascended on high," etc. These are the chariots in which
Christ ascended, as Elijah in his ascension into heaven did not ascend
without chariots and horses of fire to convey him [II Kgs. 2:11]. These
were a symbol of the convoy of angels by which he was conducted into
heaven, as those chariots and horses of fire were that defended the city
where Elisha was from the Syrians, as appears by II Kgs. 6:16–17.
These in Christ's triumphal entrance into heaven answer to the triumphal chariot in which the victors entered the city of Rome. Christ also
was attended with the princes, and elders, and captains of his people,
and ministers of his sanctuary, as he was attended with the patriarchs,
and prophets, and holy princes, and martyrs, and more eminent saints
of the Old Testament, or that church which was in being before
Christ's ascension, and with many of them with their risen bodies.

Though many of the angels attended Christ from the top of Mt.
Olivet, yet it appears to me probable that the place where he was met by
the whole multitude of the heavenly hosts, saints, and angels, was in
the upper parts of the earth's atmosphere, beyond the region of the
clouds, at the place where, 'tis said, a cloud received Christ out of the
sight of the disciples, as they stood beholding him as he went up [Acts
1:9], and that that cloud that received him was a symbol of that glorious host of saints and angels. An heavenly multitude is called a
"cloud." See Heb. 12:1, with notes.[4] An host of angels seems to have
been represented by that cloud of glory in which God appeared on Mt.
Sinai, spoken of in this 68th psalm in the 17th verse, where the Psalmist
speaks of the thousands of angels that conveyed Christ to heaven. 'Tis
added, "The Lord is among them, as in Sinai, his holy place." (See the
places there cited in the margin.)[5] When Christ passed out of the sight
of earthly inhabitants, then he joined the heavenly inhabitants. The
atmosphere belongs to this earthly world; so far Satan's power extends, who is god of this earthly world and prince of the power of the
air. When Christ had gotten out of this world, then heaven met him,
and received him. And 'tis probable that Christ's human nature there
had its transformation into its glorious state. It was not transformed at
his first resurrection, for he appeared as he used to, and conversed,
and eat and drank with his disciples. Nor was it transformed at its first
ascent from the surface of the earth, for the disciples beheld him, and

4. JE writes, "An heavenly multitude is especially fitly represented by a cloud, for clouds
have their place in heaven; they are dark in themselves, but receive brightness and glory
from the sun. So is it with the saints in heaven" ("Blank Bible").
5. I.e. margin of the KJV. For example, see Deut. 33:2.

knew him as he went up, because he appeared as he used to do. The disciples beheld him so long, till he was transformed, for so long they might behold him; but when he was transformed into his heavenly glory, it was not meet that they should behold him any longer while in this mortal state, for this state is not the state appointed for us to behold Christ in his glory, nor indeed could they see him so and live. And therefore when he was transformed, a cloud hid him from them. As long as Christ was within the limits of this earthly world, it was meet that he should remain in his earthly state; but when he passed out of this world and met heaven, it was meet that he should be transformed into his heavenly state. An earthly body might subsist as far as the region of the clouds, but it could not subsist further. Christ ascended from thence to heaven in his glorified state,[6] with all his holy angels; and at the last day he will descend from heaven in the same glorified state, with all the holy angels, and no further. For there the saints on earth shall meet him, being caught up in the clouds, or to the region of the clouds, to meet the Lord in the air; and from thence shall Christ be seen in his glory by all that shall remain on this earth. When Christ came to meet the heavenly hosts in their glory, and to be in the midst of them, it was not meet that he should remain any longer in his earthly state, for "flesh and blood shall not inherit the kingdom of God" [I Cor. 15:50]. So far Christ ascended slowly and gradually, as earthly bodies are wont to move, so that the disciples could see him as he went up; but from thence, without doubt, he mounted with inconceivable swiftness, answerable to the agility of an heavenly glorious body.

As they attended the ark in its ascension with great joy, with shouting, and the sound of the trumpet, and all kinds of music, singing God's praises (II Sam. 6:15; I Chron. 15:28, with the context in that and the following chapter), this represents the glorious joy and praise with which the heavenly hosts attended Christ in his ascension. Ps. 47:5, "God is gone up with a shout, the Lord with the sound of a trumpet," the very same as is said concerning the ascension of the ark in II Sam. 6:15. That was [an] exceeding joyful day in Israel; 'tis said they brought up the ark with joy (I Chron. 15:25). II Sam. 6:14, "David danced before the Lord with all his might"; so Christ's ascension is represented as an exceeding joyful occasion. Ps. 47:6 ff., on that occasion, "Sing praises to God, sing praises: sing praises to our King, sing praises," etc. And in this 68th Psalm, [v.] 3, "Let the righteous be glad;

6. The preceding six words are a later interlineation.

let them rejoice before the Lord: yea, let them exceedingly rejoice."
And v. 25, "The singers went before, and the players on instruments
followed after; amongst them were the damsels playing with timbrels."

When the ark was ascended and placed on the throne of God, or
mercy seat, David "dealt among all the people, even among the whole
multitude of Israel, as well to the women as men, to everyone a cake of
bread, and a good piece of flesh, and a flagon of wine" (II Sam. 6:19,
and I Chron. 16:3). So, speaking of Christ in this psalm, v. 18, the
Psalmist says, "Thou hast ascended on high; thou hast led captivity
captive, and received gifts for men, yea, for the rebellious also."

David brought the ark into the tabernacle in Zion with sacrifices
offered to God; and when he had offered the sacrifices, "blessed the
people in the name of the Lord," and gave 'em gifts[7] (I Chron. 16:1–3,
and II Sam. 6:17–19). So Christ, when he ascended, entered into
heaven[8] with his own blood, the blood of that sacrifice that he had
offered, and so obtained the blessing for men, which he then gave to
them by sending down the Holy Spirit upon them.

David, when the ark was ascended, returned to bless his household.
So Christ, when he was ascended, returned by his Spirit to bless his
church, which is the household of God and is Christ's house, as the
Apostle calls it in the 3rd chapter of Hebrews.

When David thus returned to bless his household, Michal, that had
been his wife before, despised him because he humbled himself so
much, and made himself so vile. And therefore was Michal rejected,
and had no child; but of the maidservants, whom Michal condemned,
was he had in honor [II Sam. 6:20–23]. So the Jewish church, that had
been Christ's church before his ascension, yet because Christ humbled
himself so much and made himself so vile, they despised and rejected
and called him "King of the Jews" in contempt, as Michal calls David
"King of Israel" in contempt. Therefore when Christ returned by his
Spirit to bless his household after his ascension, the church of the Jews
was rejected and became barren, but the Gentile nations that the
Jewish church used to contemn as poor slaves, while they called themselves the children of God and free, of them was Christ had in honor.
Michal was Saul's daughter, David's persecutor, that was at the head of
affairs in Israel before David; but David tells Michal that God chose
him before her father. So the priests, and elders, and scribes were the
father of the Jewish church, were at the head of affairs in God's church

7. The preceding four words are a later interlineation.
8. JE deleted "the holy of holies."

before Christ, and were Christ's persecutors; but God chose him before them.

The glorious attendants and consequents of Christ's ascension are livelily represented in this psalm, and other divine songs that seem to be penned on occasion of the recovering the ark, as particularly Christ's glorious victory over his enemies (vv. 1–2, 18), the destruction of Satan's kingdom and his church's enemies that followed (vv. 12, 14, 16, 23, 30), a terrible manifestation of wrath against obstinate sinners (vv. 6, 21), the publishing [of] the gospel in the world (vv. 11, 33), a remarkable pouring out of the Spirit (v. 9), a great increase of the privileges of the church and a more abundant measure of spiritual blessings (vv. 3, 10, 13, 18, 19, 24, 29, 34–35), the calling of the Gentiles (vv. 6, 29, 31–32), a glorious salvation from slavery and misery for sinners and enslaved (vv. 6, 13, 20, 22). The like might be observed of other songs penned on this occasion, as Ps. 47, and that which is given us in the I Chronicles, 16th chapter.

320. GENESIS 2:17. "In the day that thou eatest thereof, thou shalt surely die." This in addition to notes in "Blank Bible."[9] And besides, Adam died that day, for he was ruined and undone that day; his nature was ruined, the nature of his soul, which ruin is called "death" in Scripture (Eph. 2:1, 5; Col. 2:13; Matt. 8:22; John 5:25). The nature of his body was ruined that day, and became mortal, began to die; his whole man became subject to condemnation, to death. He was guilty of death. And yet that all was not executed that day was a token of his deliverance. And his not dying that day a natural death is no more difficult to reconcile with truth than his never suffering at all that death that was principally intended, viz. eternal damnation. And probably there were beasts slain the same day by God's appointment in their stead, of which God made them "coats of skins" [Gen. 3:21]; for 'tis probable God's thus clothing them was not long delayed after that they saw that they were naked [Gen. 3:7].

321. MALACHI 4:1–2. "For, behold, the day cometh that shall burn as an oven; and all the proud, yea, all that do wickedly, shall be stubble:

9. Concerning Gen. 2:17, JE asserts, "It don't seem to me necessary that we should understand this, that death should be executed upon him in that day when he eats." Rather it indicates that death was "made sure" to Adam that very day. Additionally, the words "signify that perfect obedience was the condition of God's covenant that was made with Adam, as they signify that for one act of disobedience he should die" ("Blank Bible").

and the day that cometh shall burn them up, saith the Lord of hosts, that it shall leave them neither root nor branch. But unto you that fear my name shall the Sun of Righteousness arise with healing in his wings; and ye shall go forth, and grow up as calves of the stall." The day here spoken of is the day of the coming of Christ, the day spoken of in the first, second, and third verses of the foregoing chapter. "Behold, I will send my messenger, and he shall prepare the way before me. And the Lord, whom ye seek, shall suddenly come to his temple, even the messenger of the covenant, whom ye delight in: behold, he shall come, saith the Lord of hosts. But who may abide the DAY of his coming, and who shall stand when he appeareth? For he is like a refiner's fire," etc. This day shall burn as an oven with respect to the wicked. Christ, who will then come, the Sun of Righteousness, whose coming or rising will usher in that day, and who then will be as a refiner's fire, will scorch and burn up the wicked as stubble and dry and dead plants, so that it shall leave them neither root nor branch. But with respect to them that fear God's name, his beams shall not be scorching, but healing, of a benign healthful nature, as the warm pleasant sunbeams are to living plants and animals, which makes 'em to grow and flourish, so that they shall "grow up as calves of the stall." He that then [will] be as a refiner's fire will then only refine the sons of Levi and others that fear God's name, that are as gold and silver that are not consumed but refined in the fire; but he will consume the wicked that are as dross. Christ shall then prune and purge the fruitful branches; but as for those that are dead, barren, dry branches, they shall be cut off, and cast into the fire, and burnt. The Sun of Righteousness that shall come on that day when he is risen, shall be as the pillar of cloud and fire was of old, which gave light to the Israelites, and was a defense unto them, was their sun and shield; but it confounded and destroyed the Egyptians.

Thus it will be at Christ's last coming. The light and glory of his appearance will be intolerable to the wicked; it shall be like the fire of a furnace to their souls, and shall make the day like an oven to them. And his coming shall actually be attended with a dreadful conflagration of the fiercest glowing heat in which they shall be burnt. But the appearance of his glory shall be exceeding pleasant, and joyful, and healthful to the saints. The sight of this glory shall perfectly heal them, shall drive away all remains of sin and make 'em perfectly holy, shall drive away all corruptibility and ill qualities of their bodies; and they shall be changed, in the twinkling of an eye, into a state of glorious health, strength,[1] perfection, activity, and incorruptibility. It shall perfectly heal of all trouble and sorrow, and shall forever banish all such things. However, the church of God shall then be found in a very distressed state; so it was at Christ's first coming. That coming was infinitely for the benefit of the elect, but to the unspeakable misery of the wicked many ways, as might be shown; [it] brought on a glorious state of the church, but a most fearful destruction of unbelievers, as in the destruction of Jerusalem and the whole land. So it was at Christ's coming in Constantine's time, and so it will be at his coming at the destruction of Antichrist.

322. GENESIS 3:20. "And Adam called his wife's name Eve, because she was the mother of all living." What Adam in this has respect to, doubtless is that which God had signified in the 15th verse, viz. that Eve was to be the mother of that seed that was to bruise the head of the serpent, the grand enemy of mankind, that had brought death on them, and had the power of death, and so was to be the author of life to all that should live, i.e. all that should escape that death. So Eve was the mother of all living, as all that have spiritual and eternal life are Christ's, and so the woman's seed, because Christ was of the woman. Adam, when he had eaten the forbidden fruit and his conscience smote him, had a terrible remembrance of the awful threatening, "Dying thou shalt die" [Gen. 2:17], and therefore took great notice of those words that God spake concerning Eve's seed bruising the serpent's head, which seem to afford some relief from his terror, and therefore thought it worthy to give Eve her name from it, as the most remarkable thing that he had observed concerning Eve, and the thing that he thought most worthy to be remembered, and could think of with greater delight and pleasure than anything else concerning her, and therefore thought it above all things worthy that her name should be [a] continual memorial of it.

That it was not her being the universal mother of mankind, or the *universality* of her maternity, but the *quality* of those that she was to be the mother of, viz. *living* ones, that was the thing that Adam took special notice of in giving his wife [this name], is evident from the name itself, which expresses the latter and not the former. The word *Chavah*,[2] which we render "Eve," expresses life, the quality of those that she was to be the mother of, and not the universality of her

1. JE deleted "spirituality."
2. חַוָּה.

maternity. And 'tis not likely this would have been, if there was nothing in this quality of her posterity that did at all distinguish her from any other mother, which would have been if all that was intended by her being the mother of those that were living was that she was to be the mother of such as were to live in the world, for so all other mothers might be called *Chavah* as well as she, or by some name that expressed that quality of life. A name is given for distinction, and therefore doubtless Adam gave her a name that expressed something that was distinguishing. But if what was meant was only that she was the mother of all mankind, then the only thing that was distinguishing of her was the universality of her maternity, and not at all the quality of her posterity. And why then was not the universality the distinguishing thing expressed in the name, rather than the quality that was not at all distinguishing?

Again, it is not likely that Adam would give her a name from that which did not [at] all distinguish her from him. If persons have not names that shall distinguish them from all others, yet doubtless they ought to have names to distinguish 'em from those that they always live with, from whom there is most occasion to distinguish them. But if it was not the quality of her posterity, but only the universality of her progeniture of mankind that he had respect to, that was what was common to her with himself.

If it had been only her being the mother of all mankind that Adam had respect to, it would have been more likely that he would have given her this name on her first creation and being brought to him, which was after that benediction, "Be fruitful, and multiply" [Gen. 1:28]. But we find that this name was not given on that occasion, but then Adam gave her another name (Gen. 2:23). He called [her] *Ishah*,[3] from her being "taken out of man." But the name of *Chavah*, as the mother of all living, is given on another occasion, viz. just after God had promised that the seed of the woman should bruise the serpent's head, and immediately after God had pronounced the threatening of death on Adam, as in the verse immediately foregoing, "till thou return to the ground, for dust thou art, and unto dust thou shalt return" [Gen. 3:19]. While Adam is under the terror of this sentence of death, he comforts himself with the promise of life couched in what God had said to the serpent. Adam gave Eve a new name on this occasion, from that new thing that appeared concerning [her] after the Fall. As she

3. אִשָּׁה.

had her first name from the manner of her creation, so she has her new name given her from Christ's redemption. And Adam [gave] her her name from that which comforted him, with respect to the curse that God had pronounced on him and the earth, as Lamech named Noah. Gen. 5:29, "And he called his name Noah, saying, This same shall comfort us concerning our work and toil of our hands, because of the ground which the Lord hath cursed."

It was a common thing for the progenitors of Christ to have names given them from something that [had] respect to him, or his redemption, or some of his benefits; so was[4] Seth, and Noah, and Abraham, and Sarah, and Israel, and Judah, and others named.

And besides, we have no parallel place in the Bible to justify our understanding this expression, "all living," to be understood of all mankind that shall hereafter live upon the earth, or including them with those that are now living. See further, No. 399.[5]

323. GENESIS 5:29. "And he called his name Noah, saying, This same shall comfort us concerning our work and toil of our hands, because of the ground which the Lord hath cursed." Noah comforted God's people concerning that labor and fatigue that was the fruit of God's curse on the ground. 1. And chiefly, as the Redeemer was to be of him, who should deliver his people from all their labors and sorrows, and should procure them everlasting life in the heavenly Canaan, a better paradise than that which was lost, where the ground is not cursed, and shall spontaneously yield her rich fruit every mouth, where there remains a rest to the people of God, who shall rest from their labors, and their works shall follow them [Rev. 14:13]. 2. He first invented wine, which is to comfort him that is faint and weary with the fatigue and the toil of his hands, and makes glad man's heart, a remarkable type of the blood of Christ and his spiritual benefits. 3. To him was given leave to eat flesh, as a relief from the fruit of the curse on the ground, which render the fruits of it less pleasant and wholesome. God gave Noah leave to feed on the flesh of other animals, to comfort him under his toil of his hands in tilling the ground. And this is another type of our feeding on Christ, and having spiritual life and refreshment in him, for in feeding on the flesh of animals, our food and the nourishment of our lives is obtained at the expense of their

4. JE deleted "Sarai Sarah named as a princess."
5. This cross-reference is a later addition.

lives and shedding their blood, as we come to feed on Christ by his laying down his life. And those things that should be in Noah matter of comfort under God's curse, are the rather taken notice of in him, because in his time the curse on the ground was to be more fully executed than ever it had been before. The good constitution[6] of the earth was to be overthrown by a flood, and its wholesomeness and fertility greatly diminished; and so the toil of his hands would be greatly increased, were it not for this relief given that has been mentioned.

4. Before Noah, God's people did not know how far this curse would proceed; they probably foresaw that God intended to execute the curse on the ground in a much further degree than ever yet he had done. God had not comforted his people by any limits set in any promise made to them, but to Noah God made a gracious promise, setting limits to the curse, promising in some respects a certain measure of success to the labor of their hands, promising that "seedtime and harvest," etc. [Gen. 8:22], should not cease.

324. MATTHEW 21:1–11. Christ's solemn entry into Jerusalem, that we have an account of [in] this place, seems to represent[7] his ascension into heaven; that which had before been very remarkably represented by the carrying the ark into Jerusalem, and its ascending into Mt. Zion into the sanctuary there, is here again represented by the entering of Christ himself, the antitype of the ark, into the same city Jerusalem, and his ascending up into the mountain of the temple into the sanctuary there, as in the Roman triumph, the triumphing general entered Rome and went straight to the Capitol, the chief temple in all the city. See "Shadows of Divine Things."[8] So that there was a literal ascension of Christ at this time in the mountain of the temple, the greatest type of heaven upon earth; and Jerusalem itself, the city he then entered into, was the next greatest type of heaven to the temple, for heaven is called the "Jerusalem which is above" [Gal. 4:26].

In this his solemn entry into Jerusalem, he passed from the Mount of Olives, the same mount from which he ascended into the heavenly

6. MS: "~~frame~~ ⟨Constitution⟩."
7. MS: "~~Shadow~~ represent."
8. "Shadows of Divine Things," no. 81, dated by Wallace E. Anderson as written in early 1739, is an extended comparison between the Roman triumph and Christ's ascension into heaven. JE's description of the triumph draws heavily on the entry in Ephraim Chambers' *Cyclopaedia* cited above in No. 319, n. 3. See *Works, 11*, 82–84.

Jerusalem. He ascended from the Mount of Olives, the mount of peace. Olive branches were used as a symbol of peace among the Gentiles, and so was the olive branch brought by Noah's dove [Gen. 8:11]. Christ ascended after he had made peace, or finished the work of reconciliation; without his reconciliation he could not have ascended. He entered into the holiest of all by his own blood; God was as it were reconciled to him by his blood, who was before as it were the object and mark of God's wrath, for our sins he had taken upon him. It was the mountain where he had his agony and sweat that blood, by which he obtained peace, and where he was betrayed to endure the cross. The ascension and glory of Christ, and the glory of the saints, is consequent on and procured by Christ's sufferings, by which he wrought out reconciliation. The place on Mt. Olivet that he ascended from was Bethany (Luke 24:50), the "house of affliction,"[9] signifying that his exaltation was consequent on his sufferings. So he ascended into Jerusalem from Bethany and Bethphage (Mark 11:1, Matt. 21:1, Luke 19:29–30), which latter signifies the "house of first ripe figs,"[1] signifying that Christ entered into heaven as the first fruits, Christ the fruits, and afterwards they that are Christ's at his coming.

He entered Jerusalem as a king, sitting on an ass, for kings formerly were wont to ride on asses; so he ascended into heaven as the King of glory.[2] His riding an ass betokened two things, viz. kingly glory, and great humility and meekness, agreeable to the passage in Zech. 9:9, cited on this occasion. As Christ ascended in great glory, so he also ascended in unparalleled humility and meekness, a most admirable conjunction of diverse qualifications appearing in him, which may probably be signified by the colt's being found at a place where two ways met, denoting that two things that seem very diverse, and seem to have a very diverse relation and tendency, meet here, as two men that go diverse ways meet together at the meeting of two paths. The path of humility seems to lead him that walks in it a diverse way from the path of honor; one seems to tend downward, and the other upwards. Yet indeed they both meet, and become the same; both carry a man to the same place, as the ass was a token both of kingly honor and great humility. The ass, the symbol of humility, carries a king on his back;

---

9. JE'S etymology here is unclear. The Mount of Olives is also called "the mount of corruption" in II Kgs. 23:13.

1. βηθφαγὴ.

2. JE deleted "Ps. 24."

and on an ass does the King of glory ascend into the city and temple of the great King, as by humiliation Christ ascended into heaven.

The ass on which Christ rode was a colt, a new ass, on which never man sat. So Christ's humiliation was new, such as there never had been a parallel of, or anything like it; and it carried him into glory as unparalleled.

Zion is called upon to rejoice on this occasion; so heaven rejoiced on occasion of Christ's ascension. They cut down branches of palm trees, the symbol of victory, and spread them in the way [v. 8]; so Christ's ascension to heaven was a triumphant ascension, having obtained the victory in his sore conflict with his enemies. (See of the Roman triumphs, in "Images of Divine Things.")[3] A great multitude attended Christ; so a vast multitude attended him in his ascension into heaven, a multitude of saints and angels. They spread their garments under his feet, which is like the angels and elders casting down their crowns at his feet. They consecrate all their honor to Christ's honor, and put it under his feet. He sat on their garments, and went on them. He is attended with great and joyful acclamations and praises, all the way as he went avant up into the mountain of the temple, the children crying, "Hosanna," there in the temple. As the multitudes attended the ark in all its ascent into Jerusalem and Mt. Zion, that was then the mount of the house of the Lord, all the way with most joyful acclamations and songs, so the saints and angels attended Christ all the way, as he went from the uppermost regions of our air, with most joyful praises and acclamations, to heaven.

As he came into Jerusalem, "all the city was moved, saying, Who is this?" So on occasion of Christ's ascension, the inhabitants of heaven say once and again, "Who is this King of glory?" (Ps. 24). See notes on the place.[4]

'Tis very remarkable that one thing that the multitude cry in their acclamations is "Peace in heaven, and glory in the highest" (Luke 19:38), being wonderfully directed thus to express the joy and glory there would be in heaven, the highest heaven, at the ascension of Christ.

---

3. See above, p. 307, n. 8.

4. JE explains Ps. 24:7 as a representation of "Christ's triumphant ascension into heaven after a battle and victory over his enemies here on earth." He makes his "entrance into heaven from the earth through that vault which is conceived as the pavement of heaven." The doors open to the King of glory, the "most proper inhabitant" and the "rightful owner of the house," and he is readily received ("Blank Bible").

God was pleased thus to give Christ such a representation and earnest of the ascension and glory that should be the reward of his sufferings, a little before those sufferings, to encourage him to go through them, as he had before done another way in his transfiguration.

325. GENESIS 2:17. "Dying, thou shalt die." This in addition to No. 47. If we sometimes find such kind of doubled expressions, and also this very expression, "Dying, thou shalt die," as in Solomon's threatening to Shimei [I Kgs. 2:42], when no more is intended than only the certainty of the event, yet this is no argument that this don't signify more than the certainty, even the extremity as well as certainty of it, because such a repetition or doubling of a word, according to the idiom of the Hebrew tongue, is as much as our speaking a word once with a very extraordinary emphasis. But such a great emphasis, as we use it, signifies variously: it sometimes signifies certainty, at other times extremity, and sometimes both.

326. MATTHEW 17:27. "Notwithstanding, lest we should offend them, go thou to the sea, and cast an hook, and take up the fish that first cometh up; and when thou hast opened his mouth, thou shalt find a piece of money. That take, and give unto them for me and thee." Which signifies that ministers of the gospel should receive of the temporal things of those that they preach the gospel to, whose souls they catch for Christ, for they are the fish, of which gospel ministers are the fishers. Peter was a fisherman by trade; and Christ had commanded him to leave his net, and to follow him, and he would make him a fisher of men [Matt. 4:19].

327. SOLOMON'S SONG 7:2.[5] "Thy belly is like a heap of wheat set about with lilies." I.e. thy womb is very fruitful. The good fruit brought forth by thee may, for abundance, be compared to the multitude of grains of corn in an heap of wheat; and the fruits of thy womb are as food to thy husband, as wheat, and are pleasant and delightful like beautiful lilies. Rom. 7:4, "Wherefore, my brethren, ye are become dead to the law by the body of Christ; that ye should be married unto another, even to him who is raised from the dead, that ye should bring forth fruit unto God." Here the Apostle evidently compares the good fruits Christians bring forth by their spiritual marriage to Christ, to the fruit of the womb that is brought forth by a woman's marriage to an husband.

5. I.e. Canticles.

The fruits of the saints are both profitable as wheat, and also beautiful as lilies. The womb of the spouse of Christ is like an heap of wheat, as having already brought forth much fruit, and also is set about with fair blossoms, as being likely to continue still to bear fruit. Jer. 17:8, "Neither shall cease from yielding fruit." John 15:2, "Every branch in me that beareth fruit, he purgeth it, that it may bring forth more fruit." And v. 16, "I have ordained you, that you should go and bring forth fruit, and that your fruit should remain."

328. PSALMS 19:4–6. "In them hath he set a tabernacle for the sun, which is [as] a bridegroom coming out of his chamber, and rejoiceth as a strong man to run a race. His going forth is from the end of heaven, and his circuit unto the ends of it; and nothing is hid from the heat of it." It appears to me[6] very likely that the Holy Ghost, in these expressions which he most immediately uses about the rising of the sun, has an eye[7] to the rising of the Sun of Righteousness from the grave, and that the expressions that the Holy Ghost here uses are conformed to such a view. The times of the Old Testament are times of night in comparison of the gospel day, and are so represented in Scripture. And therefore the approach of the day of the New Testament dispensation in the birth of Christ is called "the dayspring from on high," visiting the earth. Luke 1:78, "Through the tender mercy of our God, whereby the dayspring from on high hath visited us." And the commencing of the gospel dispensation, as it was introduced by Christ, is called the Sun of Righteousness rising (Mal. 4:2). But this gospel dispensation commences with the resurrection of Christ. Therein the Sun of Righteousness rises from under the earth, as the sun appears to do in the morning, and comes forth as a bridegroom. He rose as the joyful glorious bridegroom of his church; for Christ, especially as risen again, is the proper bridegroom or husband of his church, as the Apostle teaches. Rom. 7:4, "Wherefore, my brethren, ye also are become dead to the law by the body of Christ, that ye should be married to another, even to him who is raised from the dead, that we should bring forth fruit to God."

He that before was covered with contempt, and overwhelmed in a deluge of sorrow, hath purchased and won his spouse (for he loved the church, and gave himself for it, that he might present it to himself [Eph. 5:25–27]), now comes forth as a bridegroom to bring home his

6. JE deleted "exceeding."
7. JE deleted "in the manner of expression."

purchased spouse to him in spiritual marriage, as he soon after did in the conversion of such multitudes, making his people willing in the day of his power, and hath also done many times since, and will do in a yet more glorious degree. And as the sun, when it rises, comes forth like a bridegroom gloriously adorned, so Christ in his resurrection entered on his state of glory after his state of sufferings. He rose to shine forth in ineffable glory as the King of heaven and earth, that he might be a glorious bridegroom in whom his church might be unspeakably happy.

Here the Psalmist says that God has placed a tabernacle for the sun in the heavens; so God the Father had prepared an abode in heaven for Jesus Christ. He had set a throne for him there, to which he ascended after he rose. The sun, after it is risen, ascends up to the midst of heaven, and then at the end of its race descends again to the earth; so Christ, when he rose from the grave, ascended up to the height of heaven and far above all heavens, but at the end of the gospel day will descend again to the earth.

'Tis here said that the risen sun "rejoiceth as a strong man to run his race." So Christ, when he rose, he arose as a man of war, as "the Lord strong and mighty, the Lord mighty in battle" [Ps. 24:8]. He rose to conquer his enemies, and to show forth his glorious power in subduing all things to himself, during that race which [he] had to run, which is from his resurrection to the end of the world, when he will return to the earth again.

Here the going forth of the sun "is from the end of heaven, and his circuit to the end of it, and that nothing is hid from the heat thereof." So Christ rose from the grave to send forth his light and truth to the utmost ends of the earth, that had hitherto been confined to one nation, and to rule over all nations in the kingdom of his grace. Thus his line goes out through all the earth, and his words to the end of the world, so that "there is no speech or language, where his voice is not heard" [v. 3], as is here said of the line and voice of the sun and heavenly bodies, in the two foregoing verses, which are by the Apostle interpreted of the gospel of Jesus Christ. Rom. 10:16–18, "But they have not all obeyed the gospel. For Esaias saith, Lord, who hath believed our report? So then faith cometh by hearing, and hearing by the word of God. But I say, Have they not heard? Yes, verily, their sound went into all the earth, and their words unto the end of the world."

That the Holy Ghost here has a mystical meaning, and has respect to the light of the Sun of Righteousness, and not only the light of the natural [sun], is confirmed by the verses that follow, in which the Psalmist himself seems to apply them to the word of God, which is the light of that Sun, even of Jesus Christ, who himself is called the Word of God. See the very next words, "The law of the Lord is perfect, converting the soul," etc. [v. 7].

329. II THESSALONIANS 2:7. "For the mystery of iniquity doth already work." As *Christianity*, or the scheme for setting up the kingdom of God, and advancing his glory, and the salvation of men by *Christ*, is called "the mystery of godliness" [I Tim. 3:16], so *antichristianism*, or the scheme for setting up the kingdom of the devil, and accomplishing the destruction of men by *Antichrist*, is called "the mystery of iniquity." The Christian scheme is called "the mystery of godliness" very much on that account, that all the ancient mysteries, types, shadows, and prophecies relating to the kingdom and interest of godliness, have their fulfillment in it. So antichristianism is "the mystery of iniquity," because in this the types and prophecies that relate to the kingdom and interest of iniquity have their principal fulfillment. Here is fulfilled what was shadowed forth of old by the murder of Cain and his city in the land of Nod [Gen. 4:8, 17], and by the building of the tower of Babel [Gen. 11:1–9], and by the city of Babylon, and by the mighty Nimrod [Gen. 10:9], and Belus, or Bel [Jer. 50:2], and by the city of Sodom, by Egypt and Pharaoh; and the great things that were done in Egypt, in the time of Moses and Aaron, are types of what is done by and to the Church of Rome. Here is the antitype of Jabin and Sisera, Oreb and Zeeb, Zebah and Zalmunna [Ps. 83:9, 11], the Moabites, and the Ammonites, the Philistines, and especially the Edomites. Here is the antitype of proud Nebuchadnezzar, and Belshazzar, and Haman. Here is the antitype of the city and king of Tyrus, and of Antiochus Epiphanes. And here is the chief fulfillment of the ancient prophecies of Daniel and other prophets that relate to the kingdom of iniquity, and also of most of such prophecies in the New Testament. On the same account the antichristian church is called "Mystery, Babylon the Great" [Rev. 17:5].

330. MATTHEW 21:12–16. Concerning making Christ's house a den of thieves, etc. The apostate Jewish church that was in Christ's times was in many things an image of the apostate Christian church, or rather the antichristian church. And among other things, the Jews making Christ's Father's house an house of merchandise and den of

thieves was typical of what the clergy of the Church of Rome do. And Christ's overthrowing them, and driving them out of the temple, is typical of what Christ hath done and will further do with respect to that church. It shows how displeasing and provoking to Christ their so doing is, how Christ abominates such practices. They sold doves in the temple [v. 12]; so the merchants of the Church of Rome pretend to sell those things that are the gifts of the Holy Spirit, the heavenly dove. These gifts are called "spirits" in Paul's epistles; and so in the Revelation the Spirit of God, with respect to his various gifts and operations, is called "seven spirits" [Rev. 1:4]. They do as Simon the Sorcerer, who desired to buy a power to confer the gifts of the Holy Ghost on whomsoever he would, to that end that he might make merchandise of them [Acts 8:18–19]. So the clergy of the Church of Rome sell baptism, regeneration, and salvation; they sell forgiveness of sins, and sanctification in confirmation, and the Eucharist, and ordination, consecration, and extreme unction, etc. The Holy Spirit is the great commodity that their merchandise consists in.

Christ casts these Jewish merchants out of his temple; so Christ casts such merchants out of his church. When Christ came into his temple at Jerusalem, this was the effect; so when Christ returns into his church after its great apostasy, this is the consequence. At the same time, the blind and the lame come to Christ, and he heals them [v. 14]; so when Christ comes to drive out the antichristian merchants out of his house, there will be a great flocking of poor miserable souls to Christ to be healed. At the same time also the children cry, "Hosanna," in the temple, and the priests and scribes are sore displeased [v. 15], which are all typical of what will be when Christ comes to revive religion and execute judgments on the Romish church. Then will the mouths of God's people be filled with praises to Christ, and there will be a remarkable fulfillment of that saying, "Out of the mouth of babes and sucklings, thou hast perfected praise" [v.16], which will greatly displease and provoke the chief priests and scribes of the Church of Rome.

Because this was typical of something very remarkable that should surely come to pass in the church, therefore it was repeated, as Pharaoh's dream was, concerning the years of famine and plenty [Gen. 41:1–7]; for Christ thus drove out the merchants out of his temple once before (John 2:13–16).

331. ISAIAH 41:25. "I have raised up one from the north, and he shall come: from the rising of the sun shall he call on my name, and he

shall come upon princes as upon mortar, and as the potter treadeth clay." Probably some respect may be here had to Cyrus, who came from the northeast, being sent by the king of Media to destroy Babylon; and so this place seems parallel with Is. 44:28, and 45:1 and 13. But yet the Holy Ghost seems principally to have an eye here to some other prince, an antitype of Cyrus, that shall come from the northeast to destroy the spiritual Babylon, or antichristian church, which shall be raised up at the time when that glory shall be accomplished for the church that is here prophesied of in this chapter, and the foregoing and following chapters. The chief of them that are called "the kings of [the] East," that are represented as coming to destroy the spiritual Babylon on the drying up [of] the river Euphrates, in Rev. 16:12, as Cyrus and other princes of the East had their way prepared to destroy literal Babylon on the drying up [of] the literal river Euphrates, is[8] probably the emperor of Muscovy. (See notes on that passage in Revelation, "Revelation," no. 78, at the latter end.)[9] This better agrees with the context, which evidently speaks of the glorious times of the church of God; it better agrees with the words themselves, that speak of the person that shall be "raised up," as one that shall call on God's name, which was not fully accomplished in Cyrus, though he showed great respect to the true God, yet never properly became a worshiper of the true God, but lived and died an idolator. And it better agrees with the following words, which speak of the glory of God in foretelling this thing so long aforehand [v. 26].

The princes that the emperor of Muscovy shall probably come[1] upon as mortar, are those two great princes that the devil has set up in opposition to Christ, viz. the emperor of the Turks and the Pope—the emperor of the Turks first, so drying up the river Euphrates, and then the Pope, when his way is thus prepared. And probably herein, at least in the former,[2] the princes[3] of these very countries, whose former

---

8. MS: "&."
9. No. 78 is an interpretation of the sixth vial in Rev. 16:12. JE equates the drying up of the Euphrates with the destruction of the "wealth, revenues and incomes" of the Church of Rome, a process carried out by Protestant European nations. He also linked the Turkish Empire with the Euphrates, and suggested that the destruction of the latter was a further blow to the Church of Rome. In a closing comment, JE adds, "And possibly the emperor of Muscovy, who lives in the northeast, is meant in Isaiah 41:25" (*Works*, 5, 191).
1. MS: "⟨probably⟩ come."
2. The last five words are a later interlineation.
3. MS: "~~People~~ ⟨Princes⟩."

princes overthrew the literal Babylon, will be joined with the princes of Muscovy, as they have of late been in war against the Turks.[4]

332. MATTHEW 3:2. "Repent ye, for the KINGDOM OF HEAVEN is at hand." The following are the places of the Old Testament from whence probably the Jews principally took their notion of the kingdom of heaven.

Dan. 2:44–45; 7:9–15, and 26–27.

Ps. 96, especially the four last verses; Ps. 50:1–7, compared with Dan. 7:9–15; Ps. 97 and 98, especially [the] last verse.

Is. 2:1–6, and 15–22; 9:6–7; 11–12; 24:23; and 25, especially vv. 9–11; and 26–27; 32:1–9; and 35; and 40:3–5, 10–11; and 41; and 42:1–22; and 49; and 60–62; and 63:1–7; and 64:1–2; and 65:17–25; and 66.

Jer. 23:5–9; and 30:9; and 31; and 33, especially vv. 15–16.

Ezek. 21:27; 34:20–31; and 37:20–28.

Hos. 2:16–23.

Joel 2:28–32; and 3:9–21.

Amos 9:11–15.

Micah 4:1–9; and 5; and 7:8–20.

Obad. 17–21, especially vv. 15–16.

Nah. 1:15.

Zeph. 3:8–20.

Hag. 2:1–10, and 21–23.

Zech. 2:10–13; 3:8–10; 6:9–15; 8:20–23; 9:9–17; 10; 12–14.

Mal. 3:1–7, and 16–18; and 4.

333. ACTS 4:32–37. The reasons why the primitive Christians of the church of Jerusalem had ALL THINGS COMMON seem to be these.

1. Great part of the members of this church were strangers, or Hellenists, or Grecians, as here called. The first Christian church was set up in Jerusalem, the center of the resort of the Jews from all nations, when they came up to their three great feasts. And therefore the Christian church of Jerusalem, as it was the only Christian church then in the world, was as it were the house for the reception and entertainment of the people of Christ that came from all parts of the world, as we read that this church was constituted of Jews from "every nation under heaven" [Acts 2:5]. But these strangers did not bring their estates with them; and yet it was very needful that they should

4. I.e. the Russo-Turkish War of 1735–39.

mostly keep together in their new and infant state, and not disperse by returning into their several countries. It was fit therefore that the Hebrew[5] Christians should entertain them, and give them of what they had. They all lived upon the estates of the Christians that properly belonged to Judea. And therefore it came to pass that there soon arose a complaint that the Grecians were neglected in the daily ministration [Acts 6:1]; for the estates, being originally the Hebrews', they, some of them, began to begrutch to bestow so freely of it on them as on themselves. The circumstances of this church being such, it was thought meet that the church of Jerusalem, which was the first church, and then the only Christian church, and a long time after as a mother to all other churches, should be as a common father's house, where all the children from the utmost ends of the earth might be freely entertained, without money and without price, representing the manner of their spiritual entertainment in their Father's house.

2. Many of them were to be continually employed as teachers, as the apostles, and[6] the whole number of that first 120, on every one of which the Holy Ghost was poured out in his extraordinary gifts, sitting on each of them in the appearance of cloven tongues of fire [Acts 2:3], to fit them and mark them out for teachers. And accordingly, they all began to exercise their gifts in teaching, as appears by the beginning of the 2nd chapter of Acts. And after this the same miraculous gifts were given to great numbers of others among them, to fit them also to be teachers; for it was agreeable to the circumstances the church was then in, a little flock in the midst of a dark blind world, and agreeable to the design of God, of a swift propagation and diffusion of the gospel over great part of the world, that great numbers of the first Christians should be teachers. But those being constantly employed in this work, it was necessary that they should be maintained by the substance of others, and there being so many of them was another thing that made it needful that they should have all things common.

3. The state that this church was in, in the midst of an enemy's country, liable to be sorely persecuted, and driven to and fro, made this requisite on several accounts.

First. It was needful that their possessions should be turned into that which was portable, so that when persecuted in one city, they might fly to another.

5. MS: "~~Jewish~~ ⟨Hebrew⟩."
6. JE deleted "probably."

Secondly. Their being subject to such great and continual persecution made it needful that they should not be entangled in the world, or cumbered with worldly cares about their estates. This made it needful that they should do as a man that is going a journey, about to remove to some other country: sell what he has, and carry the effects with him. A man in his journey has no care but only to use what he carries with, to lay out his money to support him from hand to mouth; or as a man that goes into the wars, he has no care about anything but fighting, receiving his food daily from a common stock.

Thirdly. This made them less liable to the rage of their persecutors. A people that are supported one by another, by what they have among them in common, are not so liable to be deprived of all support, as he that has nothing but a possession of his own to depend on; for when things are in common, if they took one, and took from him what he had about him, yet there remained others to help him. A portable estate, consisting in moneys, is also more easily concealed, and kept out of the way of persecutors, than a real estate.

334. JOB 15:14, 25:4, and 14:4. "What is man, that he should be clean, and he which is born of a woman, that he should be righteous?" "How can he be clean that is born of a woman?" "Who can bring a clean thing out of an unclean? Not one." These places imply that it is impossible to be anyway of the race of mankind, that is corrupt and guilty, without being some way a partaker of the sin of that race, and that a proceeding from this corrupt guilty race, either by man or woman, will necessarily be attended with this consequence. And so it is, for Christ, who was born of a woman, and was of the race of mankind only by the woman, and was in himself perfectly holy and innocent, yet he did in a sense derive guilt from his mother. By being born of a woman, he lay under imputed guilt; we, by being the seed of the man, have Adam's guilt imputed to us. And Christ, by being born of a woman, had the guilt of mankind, or at least the elect part of it, the guilt of every individual, imputed to him. For though Christ, in that he was not the seed of the man, was not naturally of the corrupt race, and so did not naturally and necessarily derive guilt, and had not a corrupt nature, yet his being born of a woman, one of the corrupt race, showed that he voluntarily took that corrupt race, at least a part of them, assumed them into union with himself, and so voluntarily took their guilt, for the unavoidable consequence of voluntarily assuming the guilty race to him was his assuming their guilt. So that a being, in one respect or other, partaker of the guilt

of mankind, is the unavoidable consequence of being of the race of mankind either of these ways. None can be of the race of mankind by the man, but as he is naturally of that race, and so is included in the covenant made with the first man and his seed, and so[7] naturally partakes of his guilt and corruption. And if anyone becomes of the race of mankind only by the woman, it shows that he voluntarily assumes this guilty race to himself, and so that he voluntarily takes their guilt on himself. He that is guilty naturally, as being of the guilty race by his own nature, and as originally included in man's covenant, is guilty in himself, and guilty with the rest of guilty mankind, and so dies in himself and with the rest. But he that takes their guilt only voluntarily, as not being in himself one of the guilty race, but only takes them voluntarily on himself and their guilt with them, is not guilty in himself as guilty with the rest, but is guilty by a voluntary mutuation, as being guilty for the rest, and so dies not in himself, but for them.

335. II Corinthians 3:18. "But we all, with open face beholding as in a glass the glory of the Lord." The word in the original, *katoptrizomenoi*,[8] signifies "beholding as in a reflecting glass, or looking glass." If "beholding through a transmitting glass," the word *dioptomenoi*[9] would rather have been used, which signifies "to see through," or "to look through."

We behold the glory of God as in a glass, in two respects, both which seem to be intended in these words.

1. We behold the glory of God as in the face of Jesus Christ, who is the brightness of God's light or glory, as it were reflected, and is the express image of the Father, the perfect image of God, as the image in a plain and clear looking glass is the express image of the person that looks in it. And that is the only way that the glory of God is seen by his church; he is seen no other way, but in this perfect and as it were reflected image. For "no man hath seen God at any time; the only begotten Son of God, that is in the bosom of the Father, he hath declared him" [John 1:18]; he is "the image of the invisible God" [Col. 1:15]. And he that hath seen the Son, hath seen the Father [John 14:9]; and the Father is seen no other way, but by the Son. And 'tis only by this image is Christ seen in heaven by the saints and angels there. Yea, 'tis by this image only that God sees himself, for he sees himself in his own

7. JE deleted "necessarily."
8. κατοπτριζόμενοι.
9. διοπτόμενοι.

perfect substantial idea. And that one thing here meant by the image in the glass, is the image of Christ that is to be seen in Christ's face, may be argued from two things. (1) The Apostle is here comparing the glory of God that we see in Christ to that reflected glory of God which the children of Israel beheld in Moses, where Moses' face was instead of a glass to them, in which they beheld the glory of God reflected to their view, though with this difference, that a veil was put over the glass then, or there was a veil between their eyes and Moses' face, that was the glass that reflected God's glory, because the children of Israel could not bear to look upon the glass immediately; but now we all "with open face" behold the image in the glass. (2) Another thing that [this] argues, is what follows here in the continuance of the Apostle's discourse on this subject, in the 4th verse of the next chapter, where the Apostle, speaking of the same glory, speaks of it as the light of God's glory that we see in Christ as "the image of God" (i.e. as the image in the glass is the image of the man it represents). And in the 6th [verse], he speaks of this same glory as that which is seen in the face of Christ, alluding to the children of Israel's seeing as it were the reflected light of God's glory in the face of Moses.

2. We behold the glory of God as in a looking glass in another respect, and that is as we behold it by the intermediation of the outward means of our illumination and knowledge of God, viz. Christ's ministers, and the gospel which they preach, and his ordinances which they administer, which serve instead of a looking glass to reflect the glory of the Lord. When men read the Holy Scripture, they there may see Christ's glory, as men see images of things by looking in a glass; so we see Christ's glory in ordinances. Ministers are burning and shining lights, but then they don't shine by their own light, but only reflect the light of Christ. They are called stars that are held in the right hand of Christ [Rev. 1:16], and shine by reflecting Christ's light, as the stars shine by reflecting the light of the sun; and so they are as mirrors that bring the light of Christ's glory to the view of the church. They are lights set up in golden candlesticks. By looking on those lights, they see light; they see the light of Christ reflected. 'Tis evident the Apostle is here speaking of the light of Christ's glory, as ministered and communicated by ministers of the gospel and ministers of the Spirit, which is that light and glory, as we shall show presently (so vv. 2–6). So in the words next following in the beginning of the next chapter, vv. 1–2, 5, and which is strongly to the purpose in the 6th verse, he expressly speaks of the light of this glory as communicated to men by ministers

this way, viz. by first shining upon them or into their hearts, and then being communicated or given from them to others, which is just as light is communicated from a reflecting glass. "For God, who commanded the light to shine out of darkness, hath shined in our hearts, to give the light of the knowledge of the glory of God in the face of Jesus Christ." And in the next, or 7th, verse, they are spoken [of] as the vessel that conveys the treasure; now a vessel is to the treasure that it conveys, as a glass is to the light that that conveys.

And it further argues that the Apostle has respect to ministers, and so the means of grace, as a glass in which we see the glory of the Lord, by that which he here alludes to, viz. the children of Israel's seeing the glory of the Lord in Moses' face. But Moses[1] is here by the Apostle spoken [of] as in this representing both Christ and gospel ministers. That he speaks of him as in this thing representing Christ, is most evident by the 6th verse of the next chapter; and that he also speaks of him as herein like gospel ministers, the apostles, and others, because the Apostle does expressly compare Moses' holding forth the glory of God on his face to ministers' holding forth the glory of Christ, as in the 12th and 13th verses.

And herein the sight that the saints have of the glory of Christ in this world, differs from that sight that the saints have in heaven; for there they see immediately, face to face, but here by a medium, by an intervening looking glass, in which the glory is but obscure in comparison of the immediate glory seen in heaven. I Cor. 13:12, "Now we see through a glass darkly, then face to face." But it is a very plain and clear sight in comparison of that which was under the law; 'tis beholding with open face in comparison of that, though the face that is seen be in a glass. The sight we have now is by a medium as well as then, though the[2] medium made use of now excels that made use of under the law, as much as a glass for discovery exceeds a veil.

"Are changed into the same image" [v. 18]. In this there is an agreement in our looking in this glass and a person's looking in a material glass, that there is an exact resemblance between the image in the glass and the person that beholds it, in both cases. But in this there is a difference, that whereas, when a person looks in a glass, the image in the glass is conformed to him, as being derived from him as his image, he impresses his image upon the glass; but when a person looks in this

1. JE deleted "in the context."
2. JE deleted "transcends it." The next thirteen words are a later interlineation.

spiritual glass, the image that he beholds there conforms him to it. It is not his image, but the image of God, and reflects and impresses its likeness on the beholder. See No. 341.[3]

336. CANTICLES. 'Tis one argument that the BOOK OF CANTICLES is no common love song, that the bridegroom or lover there spoken of so often calls his beloved, "my sister, my spouse."[4] This well agrees with Christ's relation to believers, who is become our brother and near kinsman by taking upon him our nature, and is our brother, and the son of our mother by his incarnation, as thereby he became a son of the church, and used the ordinances appointed in it, and so has sucked the breasts of our mother [Cant. 8:1]; and we are become his brethren also by the adoption of his Father. But this appellation would not well suit a common spouse among the Jews, who were so strictly forbidden to marry any that were near of kin to them, and particularly to marry a sister. Lev. 18:9, "The nakedness of thy sister, the daughter of thy father, or the daughter of thy mother, whether she be born at home, or born abroad, even their nakedness thou shalt not uncover." 'Tis neither likely that the Jews would marry such in Solomon's time, nor that it would be the custom to compare their spouses to such, especially that they would insist so much on such an appellation, as though it was an amiable thing, and a thing to be thought of and mentioned with delight and pleasure, to have a spouse that was a sister, when God's law taught them to dread and abhor the thoughts of it.

337. NUMBERS 11:10–15. "Then Moses heard the people weep throughout their families, every man in the door of his tent. And the anger of the Lord was kindled greatly; Moses also was displeased. And Moses said unto the Lord, Wherefore hast thou afflicted thy servant, and wherefore have I not found favor in thy sight, that thou layest the burden of this people upon me? Have I conceived all this people? Have I begotten them, that thou shouldst say unto me, Carry them in thy bosom, as a nursing father beareth the sucking child, unto the land which thou swarest unto their fathers? . . . If thou deal thus with me, kill me out of hand, . . . and let me not see my wretchedness." Moses, though God gives this testimony concerning him, that he "was very meek, above all men upon the face of the earth" [Num. 12:3], yet could not bear the perverseness of the congregation of God's people. How

3. This cross-reference is a later addition.
4. See Cant. 4:9–10, 12; 5:1.

much therefore does Christ's meekness go beyond Moses'? Moses was not willing to bear the burden of all that people upon him; but Christ, the angel of God's presence, is willing to bear them all with all their frowardness and perverseness. Moses said, "Have I conceived this people? Have I begotten them, that thou shouldst say, Carry them in thy bosom, as a nursing father beareth a sucking child, unto the land which thou swarest unto their fathers?" But Christ willingly thus carries his people in his bosom unto the promised land, for they are his children; he has begotten them, and he never casts them off for their frowardness. He willingly obeys his Father when he commands him, saying, "Carry this people," etc. Is. 63:8–9, "For he said, Surely they are my people, children that will not lie; so he was their Savior. In all their affliction he was afflicted, and the angel of his presence saved them. In his love and in his pity he redeemed them; and he bare them, and carried them all the days of old." Deut. 1:31, "And in the wilderness, where thou hast seen how that the Lord thy God bare thee, as a man doth bear his son, in all the way that ye went." Is. 40:11, "He shall feed his flock like a shepherd; he shall gather the lambs with his arm, and carry them in his bosom, and shall gently lead those that are with young." Moses said, "Wherefore hast thou afflicted thy servant?"; but Christ was willingly afflicted and tormented for the sake of a perverse people, his enemies. Moses desired to be killed, to be delivered from the burden of bearing the people to the land of promise, rather than bear it; but such was Christ's love to them, that he desired to be killed that he might bear them to the land of promise.

338. LUKE 22:31. "And the Lord said, Simon, Simon, behold, Satan hath desired to have you, that he may sift you as wheat." The true meaning of these words seems to be this: "'Tis ordered in providence that Satan should, at this time extraordinary, seek and hope to have you. And 'tis so ordered to that end, that by his temptations he might sift you as wheat; that is, that there might be a separation made between you and your corruptions, your pride, and self-confidence, as wheat is separated from chaff by sifting," which proved to be the effect of those trials that Peter and the rest of the disciples had at that time. They were sifted, and purified, and came forth abundantly brighter than before, as gold that is tried in the fire. 'Tis not Satan's end in desiring to have them, that is here spoken of, but God's end in so ordering it, that Satan should desire to have them. Satan's end in desiring to have the saints is not to sift them, and pu-

rify the wheat from chaff, but to destroy them. See "Images of Divine Things," no. 94.[5]

339. MATTHEW 27:45. "Now from the sixth hour there was darkness over all the land unto the ninth hour." This darkness seems to be a presage of the approaching destruction of that land for that sin of crucifying Christ. This darkness began at noon, whereby the sun as it were went down at noon. The prophet Amos, in the 8th chapter of his prophecy, foretelling the destruction of the land, when the end shall come upon the people Israel, and God will not pass by them any more, and the songs of the temple shall be turned into howlings, and "there shall be many dead bodies in every place" [vv.2–3], says in the 9th verse, "And it shall come to pass in that day, saith the Lord God, that I will cause the sun to go down at noon, and I will darken the earth in the clear day."

This also seems to be a fulfillment of Jer. 2:12–13. "Be ye astonished, O ye heavens, at this, and be ye horribly afraid; be ye very desolate, saith the Lord. For my people have committed two evils; they have forsaken me, the fountain of living waters," etc.[6]

340. MATTHEW 27:51. "And, behold, the veil of the temple was rent in twain from the top to the bottom." This was the veil that hindered our access to the throne of grace, or the mercy seat, in the holy of holies. That hiding of the mercy seat, and hindering of our access to the mercy seat, signified a twofold hindrance of access to God. 1. The hindrance by which all men are kept off while they remain under the first covenant of works. They are hindered by their guilt, God's law, and justice. And 2. That hindrance of free access that was under the first testament, while the church was in a legal state, and in its minority, and under carnal ordinances, so that access was rare and difficult, only allowed to the high priest, and that but once a year. So that the veil signifies two things, viz. the sin of man, both guilt and corruption of heart, which both in diverse respects are a veil to hide the mercy seat, and hinder our access.

Both these were typified by the flesh of Christ. The sin of God's people, or elect church, was typified by Christ's flesh, for sin is called

---

5. JE compares the "threshing and winnowing" and the "grinding and sifting" at harvest to the trials and persecution the godly suffer following times of "a remarkable harvest in the church." No. 94, dated in late 1739, cites Luke 22:31 (*Works*, *11*, 87).

6. This paragraph is a later addition.

"flesh" in Scripture. And the elect church is Christ mystical, so that Christ, in taking flesh upon him, took their sin upon him; he was sin for us. And when his flesh was crucified, when his human nature died, then this veil was removed, for that abolished the sin of the elect church. So likewise, Christ in the flesh, in his infirm weak state, signified the church, or Christ mystical, in its old testament minority, when it was in its weak, infirm, and carnal state under carnal ordinances, under the elements of the world; and those carnal ordinances and carnal dispensation that mystical Christ was under, was as it were the flesh of Christ. When Christ died, then there was an end to those types and shadows, because they were then all fulfilled.

Christ's human nature was a temple; it was the antitype of the temple. And his flesh, or the infirmity and imperfection of his human nature, was the veil that hid the glory of God, or the divinity that dwelt in him, and was in his person. So that the veil of the temple, in the third place, typified the literal flesh of Christ, that hid and veiled his glory, which it ceased to do when his state of humiliation was at an end.

Christ himself, our great High Priest, entered into the holy of holies through the veil of his own flesh. That day that Christ died was the great day of atonement, typified by the day of atonement of old, when the high priest entered into the holy of holies. Christ, as God-man, could enter into heaven no other way than by rending this veil. Christ offered his sacrifice in the outward court, in this world, and then in the conclusion of it, rent the veil, that his blood might be sprinkled within the veil.

341. II CORINTHIANS 3:18. "Behold as in a glass." What seems especially to be meant by the looking glass here spoken of, is the[7] figurative representation of gospel things in the Old Testament, especially the law of Moses, which to the Jews, who did not know the meaning of them, nor see the image of Christ or gospel things in them, was as a veil. But to us, to whom the image plainly appears as unveiled by the gospel, these types and other figurative representations are as a glass in which we see the image of Christ's face.

342. GENESIS 1:2. "The earth was without form, and void." The first state of the earth, or this lower world, shows what it was to be afterwards, viz. a world of confusion and emptiness, full of evil, vanity of

---

7. JE deleted "typical."

vanities. So in the first state of man, in his infancy, is an image of what man always is in himself, a poor, polluted, helpless worm.

343. GENESIS 2:8. "And there he put the man whom he had formed." "Man was made out of paradise, for after God had formed him, he put him into the garden. He was made of common clay, not of paradise dust. He lived out of Eden before he lived in it, that he might see all the comforts of his paradise-state owing to God's free grace. He could not plead a tenant-right to the garden, for he was not born upon the premises, nor had anything but what he received. All boasting was hereby forever excluded." Henry.[8]

344. GENESIS 4:7. "If thou dost well, shalt not thou be accepted? And if thou dost not well, sin lieth at the door." Cain was not accepted in his offering, because he did not well, because, 1. He "was a wicked man, led an ill life, under the reigning power of the world and the flesh, and therefore his sacrifice was 'an abomination to the Lord' (Prov. 15:8), 'a vain oblation' (Is. 1:13). God had no respect to Cain himself, and therefore no respect to his offering, as the manner of the expression (v. 5) intimates. But Abel was a righteous man; he is called 'righteous Abel' (Matt. 23:35). His heart was upright, and his life was pious; he was one of those whom God's countenance beholds (Ps. 11:7), and whose prayer is therefore his delight (Prov. 15:8). God had respect to him as a holy man, and therefore to his offering as a holy offering. The tree must be good, else the fruit cannot be pleasing to the heart-searching God. 2. There was a difference in the offerings they brought. 'Tis expressly said, Heb. 11:4, Abel's was 'a more excellent sacrifice' than Cain's: either, (1) In the nature of it. Cain's was only a sacrifice of acknowledgment offered to the Creator; the meat offerings of the fruit of the ground were no more, and for ought I know, might have been offered in innocency. But Abel brought a sacrifice of atonement, the blood whereof was shed in order to remission, thereby owning himself a sinner, deprecating[9] God's wrath, and imploring his favor in a Mediator. Or, (2) In the qualities of the offering. Cain brought of the fruit of the ground, anything that came next to hand, what he had not occasion for himself, or was not merchantable.[1] But Abel was curious in the choice of his offering: not the lame, or the lean,

---

8. Henry, *Exposition*, *1* (1725), 10.
9. I.e. trying to avert by prayer.
1. MS: "mar̶k̶e̶t̶(chantable)." Henry reads "marketable."

or the refuse, but the firstlings of the flock, the best he had, and the fat thereof, the best of those best. 3. The great difference was this, that Abel offered in faith, and Cain did not. . . . Abel was a penitent believer, like the publican that went away justified. Cain was unhumbled, and his confidence was in himself, like the Pharisee who glorified himself, but he was not so much justified before God [Luke 18:13–14]." Henry, on verses 3–5.[2]

"If thou dost not well, sin lieth at the door." Not at Cain's door, but at God's door. His wicked doing lay as it were at the door of God's temple, to prevent his admittance and acceptance with God, stood as a partition wall between God and him. Wicked men's sins are as a cloud that their prayer can't pass through, and a veil to hinder their offerings being brought into the holy place; they are a thick veil before the door of the holiest of all, to hinder their access to God. I John 3:21–22, "Beloved, if our heart condemn us not, then have we confidence towards God. And whatsoever we ask, we receive of him, because we keep his commandments, and do those things that are pleasing in his sight."

345. GENESIS 4:7. "And unto thee shall be his desire, and thou shalt rule over him." God shows Cain "that he had no reason to be angry at his brother. 'Unto thee shall be his desire'; he shall continue his respect to thee as an elder brother, and thou, as the firstborn, shalt rule over him as much as ever. God's acceptance of Abel's offering did not transfer the birthright to him (which Cain was jealous of), nor put upon him that 'excellency of dignity, and excellency of power,' which is said to belong to it (Gen. 49:3). God did not so intend it; Abel did not so interpret it. There was no danger of its being improved to Cain's prejudice. Why then should he be so much exasperated? Observe here, 1. The difference which God's grace makes doth not alter the distinctions which God's providence makes, but preserves them, and obliges us to do the duty which results from them. Believing servants must be obedient to unbelieving masters. Dominion is not founded in grace, nor will religion warrant disloyalty or disrespect in any relation. 2. That the jealousies which civil governments have sometimes conceived of the true worshipers of God as dangerous to their government, enemies to Caesar, and hurtful to kings and provinces (on which suspicion persecutors have grounded their rage against them), are

2. Henry, *Exposition*, *1* (1725), 21.

very unjust and unreasonable. Whatever pretenders are, 'tis certain good Christians are the best subjects, and quiet in the land. Their desire is towards their governors, and they shall rule over them." Henry, *in loc.*[3]

346. GENESIS 8:7–11. Concerning the raven and the dove that Noah sent forth. The dove is an emblem of a gracious soul that, finding no rest for its foot, no solid peace or satisfaction in this world, this deluged defiling world, returns to Christ, as to its ark, as to its Noah. The carnal heart, like the raven, takes up with the world, and feeds on the carrions it finds there. But "return thou to thy rest, O my soul," to thy "Noah";[4] so the word is, Ps. 116:7. "O that I had wings like a dove," to flee to him (Ps. 55:6). The olive branch, which was an emblem of peace, was brought not by a raven, a bird of prey, nor by a gay and proud peacock, but by a mild, patient, humble dove. 'Tis a dove-like disposition that brings into the soul earnests of rest and joy.

347. GENESIS 9:5–6. "And surely your blood of your lives will I require. . . . Whoso sheddeth man's blood, by man shall his blood be shed." We have an account of murthers before the flood, but nothing that looks as though murther was wont then to be revenged with death by men in an established course of public justice. Lamech, when[5] he had been guilty of murther [Gen. 4:23], seems not to have been executed for it by men. And by the story of Cain, it should seem that God took the punishment of murder then into his own hands. In all probability, a little before the flood, when we read that the earth was filled with violence, the earth was filled with murders, and that those giants, that became such "mighty men" and "men of renown" [Gen. 6:4], were guilty of many murthers, and that it was in the earth, as it was in corrupt times in Israel, and the land was filled with oppression and violence in other respects. Their hands were "full of blood" (Is. 1:15; Jer. 2:34), and the land was "full of blood" (Ezek. 9:9). "By swearing, and lying, and killing, and stealing, and committing adultery, they brake out, and blood touched blood" [Hos. 4:2]. The like in many other places. And there being [no] human laws for[6] putting murtherers to death, therefore God did in a remarkable manner take that

3. Ibid., 22.
4. נֹחַ.
5. MS: "what."
6. JE deleted "the revenge of murther."

work into his own hands in the destruction of those murtherers by the waters of the deluge. But now God establishes it as a rule, henceforward to be observed, that murther shall be revenged in a course of public justice.

Another reason why God now does expressly establish and particularly insist on this rule is, that God had now just given 'em leave to shed the blood of beasts for food, which had not been granted till now, which liberty they would have been in danger of abusing, to make shedding blood appear a less terrible thing to them, and so taking encouragement the more lightly to shed man's blood, had not God set up this fence.

348. GENESIS 9:12–17. Concerning the RAINBOW,[7] the token of the covenant. This is on many accounts a token of God's covenant of grace, and this special promise of no more overthrowing the earth with a flood in particular.

It was a most fit token of the covenant of grace, of which this particular covenant was a part and also an image, as appears by Is. 54:8–10. Tokens of things that appertain to the covenant of God do as fitly confirm this promise, as they did that promise mentioned in the 7th chapter of Isaiah, v. 14.

'Tis light, which is the symbol of God's favor and blessed communications to those that are the objects of his favor, and a symbol of hope, comfort and joy, excellency and glory.

'Tis a very pleasant light, excellently representing that grace and love that is manifested in the covenant of grace, and that sweet comfort, peace, and that excellent grace and glory, that is the fruit of that love.

'Tis light manifested in all the variety of its beautiful colors, which represent, as has been elsewhere shown,[8] the beauties and sweetness of the divine Spirit of love, and those amiable sweet graces and happy influences that are from that Spirit.

'Tis a pleasant sweet light in a cloud, which is the symbol of the divine presence, and especially of God manifest in the flesh, or in the human nature of Christ, and therefore fitly represents the pleasant

---

7. See JE's "Of the Rainbow" (*Works*, *6*, 298–301). See also Stephen J. Stein, "Jonathan Edwards and the Rainbow: Biblical Exegesis and Poetic Imagination," *New England Quarterly* 47 (1974), 440–56.

8. See "Miscellanies," nos. 362 and 370 (*Works*, *13*, 434–35, 441–42); and "Images," no. 58 (ibid., *11*, 67–69).

grace and sweet love of God as appearing in Christ, God-man. The light of the sun is more beautiful and pleasant to our weak eyes appearing thus in a cloud, where the[9] dazzling brightness of it is removed, and its pleasantness retained and illustrated, than when we behold it in the sun directly. So the divine perfections, as appearing in Christ, God-man, are brought down to our manner of conception, and are represented to the greatest advantage to such weak creatures as we are, appear not glaring and terrifying, but easy, sweet, and inviting. The light of the rainbow[1] in a cloud teaches the like mystery with the light of fire in a pillar of cloud in the wilderness [Ex. 14:24], even the union of the divine and human nature, or God dwelling in flesh.

'Tis a pleasant light in the bosom of a dissolving cloud, that is wearied with watering, and is spending itself for the sake of men, and in order to shed down its fatness, its nourishing, benign, refreshing influences on the earth, and so fitly represents the beauty, and love, and excellent fullness of Christ, as it is manifested in his dying for men. The drops of rain fitly represent Christ's blood, and also his word, and the blessed communications of his Spirit, which come by his death, and are compared to the rain in the Scripture [Is. 55:10–11].

As the cloud fitly represents the human nature of Christ's person, so also it doth of Christ mystical, or the human nature of the church. In the rainbow the light of the sun is imparted to and sweetly reflected from a cloud, that is but a vapor, that continues for a little while and then vanishes away, is an empty, unsubstantial, vanishing thing, driven to and fro with the wind, that is far from having any light or beauty of its own, being in its own nature dark.

The multitude of drops, from which the light of the sun is so beautifully reflected, signify the same with the multitude of the drops of dew, that reflect the light of the sun in a morning, spoken of, Ps. 110:3. (See notes on the place.)[2] They are all God's jewels; and as they are all in heaven, each one by its reflection is a little star, and so do more fitly represent the saints than the drops of dew.[3] These drops are all from heaven, as the saints are born from above; they are all from the dissolv-

---

9. JE deleted "glaring brightness of."

1. MS: "~~Sun~~ ⟨Rainbow⟩."

2. JE explains Ps. 110:3 as "a prophecy of the great success of the gospel soon after Christ's ascension and in the primitive times of the Christian church." He finds multiple ways in which the dew of the morning represents aspects of the church's situation in those times. For example, Christ, the Sun of Righteousness, has his light reflected from the "souls on the earth" who are represented as "a multitude of dewy drops" ("Blank Bible").

3. This sentence is a later interlineation.

ing cloud. So the saints are the children of Christ; they receive their new nature from him, and by his death they are from the womb of the cloud, the church. So Jerusalem, which is above, is "the mother of us all" [Gal. 4:26]. The saints are born of the church that is in travail with them, enduring great labors, and sufferings,[4] and cruel persecutions; so these jewels of God are out of the dissolving cloud. These drops receive and reflect the light of the sun just breaking forth, and shining out of the cloud that had been till now darkened, and hid, and covered with thick clouds. So the saints receive grace and comfort from Christ rising from his state of humiliation, suffering, and death, wherein his glory was veiled; and he that is the brightness of God's glory was as it were extinguished, as was signified in the time of it by that eclipse of the sun. The light, which in the sun, its fountain, is one and unvaried, as it is reflected from the cloud, appears with great variety; so the glory of God, that is simple, is reflected from the saints in various graces. The whole rainbow, composed of innumerable, shining, beautiful drops, all united in one, ranged in such excellent order, some parts higher and others lower, the different colors, one above another in such exact order, beautifully represents the church of saints of different degrees, gifts, and offices, each with its proper place, and each with its peculiar beauty, each drop very beautiful in itself, but the whole as united together much more beautiful. Num. 24:5–6, "How goodly are thy tents, O Jacob, and thy tabernacles, O Israel! As the valleys are they spread forth, as the gardens by the riverside, as the trees of lign aloes which the Lord hath planted, and as the cedar trees beside the waters." Ps. 48:2, "Beautiful for situation, the joy of the whole earth, is Mount Zion." Ps. 50:2, "Out of Zion, the perfection of beauty, hath God shined." Ps. 122:3, "Jerusalem is builded as a city compact together."

Part of this bow is on earth and part in heaven, as 'tis with the church. The bow gradually rises higher and higher from the earth towards heaven; so the saints, from their first conversion, are traveling in the way towards heaven, and gradually climb the hill till they arrive at the top. So this bow in this respect is a like token of the covenant with Jacob's ladder [Gen. 28:12–15], which represented the way to heaven by the covenant of grace, in which the saints go from step to step, and from strength to strength, till they arrive at the heavenly Zion. So on this bow, the ascent is gradual towards the top in the way to heaven; the beginning of the ascent is steepest and most difficult. The higher you

---

4. JE deleted "and death."

ascend, the easier the ascent becomes. On earth this bow is divided; the parts of it that are here below are at a distance one from another, but in heaven it is united and perfectly joined together. So different parts of the church on earth may be divided, separated as to distance of place, have no acquaintance one part with another, and separated in manners of worship and many opinions, and separated in affection, but will be perfectly united in heaven. The parts of the rainbow, the higher you ascend, the nearer and nearer do they come together; so the more eminent saints are in knowledge and holiness, the nearer they are to an union in opinion and affection, but perfect union is not to be expected but in heaven.

The rainbow, if completed, would be a perfect circle, the most perfect figure, in every part united, fitly representing the most excellent order and perfect union that there shall be in the church of Christ. The rainbow is sometimes in Scripture represented as a circle. Rev. 10:1, "And a rainbow was upon his head." The reason why the circle is not now complete, is because a part of it is as it were under the earth; but if we, by standing on an high mountain or otherwise, could see it all raised above the earth, we should see it a complete circle. So the church of Christ is now incomplete, while a part of the elect church is buried under the earth, and a part has never yet received being; but after the general resurrection, when that part of the church which is now under the earth shall be raised above it, then the church of Christ would be in its complete state. If we could view the resurrection church from an high mountain, as the apostle John viewed it [Rev. 4:3], and saw it in the colors of the rainbow reflected from those precious stones, we should see the circle completed without any part wanting, all disposed in the most perfect union and beautiful order. The order of the drops of the rainbow, supposing them to represent saints, and the sun to represent Christ, is the most apt, commodious, and beautiful, both with respect to the sun and each other. They are in the most apt order with respect to the sun, all opposite to him, and so placed in a fit posture to view the sun, and to receive and reflect his rays, all at an equal distance from the sun, and all in a sense round about him, to testify their respect to him, and yet none behind him, but all before his face, and all in the most apt order to behold and reflect light on, and converse together, and assist and rejoice[5] one another. On the whole, here is an image of the most pleasant and perfect harmony, of a great,

5. The seven preceding words are a later interlineation.

and amiable, and blessed society, dependent on, blessed in, and showing respect to, the fountain of all light and love.

The sun is as it were in the center of this beautiful circle of little jewels or stars, as the sun is in the center of the orbits of the planets, and as the ark, and mercy seat, and the seven lamps were in the midst of the tabernacle of blue, and purple, and scarlet, those colors of the rainbow; and as[6] Christ is in the midst of the seven golden candlesticks, and as the throne of the Lamb is in the midst of the saints of heaven, who are round about that throne, and also "a rainbow round about the throne" (Rev. 4:3–4); and as the Lamb, who is the light of the New Jerusalem, has that city adorned with the colors of the rainbow round about him.

Each drop contains in itself a beautiful image of the sun reflected after its manner, according to that part of the sun's glory which is most conspicuous in it. One contains a red image of the sun, another a yellow one, another a green one, and another a blue one, etc. (as each saint reflects the image of Christ, though each one has his particular gift, and there be some particular grace or spiritual beauty that is most conspicuous in him). And the whole bow, when completed into the form of a circle, or all that multitude of shining jewels or stars together united into that excellent form and order, do together constitute one complete image of the sun, though the image differs from the sun itself in the following things. 1. That whereas the disk of the sun is full within its own circumference, the image is empty; 'tis a circle not filled, but left empty, to be filled with the sun. So Christ has all fullness in himself, but the church is in itself an empty vessel, and Christ is her fullness. 2. Whereas the light is simple in the sun, in the bow it is diversified, reflected in a great variety, the distinct glories of the sun as it were divided and separately reflected, each beauty by itself, as 'tis in Christ and his church. 3. Though there be so many that each one reflect a little image of the sun, and the whole bow or circle be of so great extent, and be so beautiful, yet the sun infinitely exceeds the whole in light; the whole reflects but a little of the brightness[7] of the fountain.

This beautiful pleasant light appears after darkness, after the heavens have been covered with blackness, and have poured out rain on the earth, seeming to threaten its destruction by a deluge. So it is a

6. JE deleted "the glorifie."
7. MS: "~~Light~~ ⟨brightness⟩."

fit symbol of his mercy after his anger, the turning away of his anger, his mercy appearing in the forgiveness of sins. So the glorious gospel follows the law, and Christ's glory follows his sufferings, and comfort in the hearts of the saints follows terrors of conscience. Yea, this light is light in darkness; 'tis a beautiful light reflected from the dark cloud, showing God's love in his anger, his love appearing in his frowns. God's love never so greatly appeared as in the sufferings of Christ, the greatest manifestation of his anger against sin; and his love, when the shower is over, appears in past threatenings, and convictions, and terrors of conscience, which the saints have been the subjects of.

A drop of rain fitly represents[8] man; it is a very small thing, of little value and significancy. A drop of the bucket and light dust of the balance are mentioned together as small and worthy of no consideration [Is. 40:15]. It is a very weak [thing], very mutable and unstable, exceeding liable to perish, soon falls and is dissipated, and can't be made up again. The continuance of a drop of rain is but short; 'tis a thing of a very passing nature. Its course is swift; and in a moment it sinks into the earth, and is no more, which fitly represents the frailty and mortality of man, whose "days are swifter than a weaver's shuttle" [Job 7:6], who is but a momentary thing, and hastens with a swift course to the grave. Man's dying and sinking into the grave is compared to this very thing, of waters being spilt on the ground, sinking into the earth, and so being irrecoverably gone (II Sam. 14:14).[9]

The drops of rain reflecting the light of the sun in the rainbow fitly represent the saints, for in them fire and water are mixed together, which fitly represents the contrary principles that are in the saints, flesh and spirit. In those drops is a bright spark of heavenly fire in the midst of water, and yet is not quenched, is kept alive by the influence of the sun, as the heavenly seed and divine spark is kept alive in the saints in the midst of corruption and temptation, that seem often as if they would overwhelm and extinguish it. So God suffers not the smoking flax to be quenched [Is.42:3]. The drop in itself is wholly water, as the nature of man in itself is wholly corrupt. In the saints, that is, in their flesh, dwells no good thing; they have no light or brightness in them, but only what is immediately from heaven, from the Sun of Righteousness. In the drops of the rainbow is represented both the saints' descending to the grave by the flesh, and also their ascending to heaven by the spirit of holiness; for the water descends swiftly to be buried in

8. JE deleted "the nature of."
9. This sentence is a later addition.

the earth, but by the fire, a beautiful light in them, is represented an ascent as it were up an hill from the earth to heaven.

These drops fitly represent the saints on another account, as Mary's alabaster box of precious ointment [Mark 14:3] represented the heart of a saint. This drop, though itself weak and frail, yet is clear and pure as alabaster, and contains as it were a spark or star of beautiful heavenly light in it, which represents the same divine grace that Mary's precious ointment did.

349. PSALMS 84:3. "Yea, the sparrow hath found an house, and the swallow a nest for herself, where she may lay her young, even thine altars." The expletive "even," which is not in the original, hurts the sense.[1] "Thine altars, O Lord of hosts, my King, and my God!" seems to be a distinct sentence from the foregoing, and comes in as an ardent exclamation, expressing the longing of David's soul after God's altars, as is rather to be added to the foregoing verse, where the Psalmist had said, "My soul longeth, yea, even fainteth for the courts of the Lord; my heart and my flesh crieth out for the living God." And then his thoughts of the birds' having a nest, and so being distinguished from him, a poor exile that was cast out of house and home, and had not where to lay his head, and was banished from God's house, which is the worst part of his banishment, this comes in as it were a parenthesis; and then follows the exclamation, "Thine altars, O Lord of hosts, my King, and my God!" Such an interpretation is exceeding agreeable with the context and the frame the Psalmist was in.

350. GENESIS 23. Concerning Abraham's buying in Canaan the possession of a burying place. Canaan is the land that God made over to Abraham by covenant, and yet "he gave him none inheritance in it" to live upon, as Stephen observes, "no, not so much as to set his foot on" (Acts 7:5). But the first possession he had in it was the possession of a burying place, or a possession for him to be in after he and his were dead; which signifies this, that the heavenly Canaan, the land of promise, the rest that remains for the people of God, is a land for them to possess, and abide and rest in, after they are dead. They don't enter upon the possession of it till after they are dead, and then they are gathered to their possession in Canaan. Therefore it was so ordered, that Jacob and Joseph so much insisted on it to be buried in that land.

1. MS: "Sun." Dwight's suggested reading is "hurts the sense" (Dwight ed., 9, 356).

351. EXODUS 12:35–36. "And they borrowed of the Egyptians jewels of silver, and jewels of gold, and raiment. And the Lord gave the people favor in the eyes of the Egyptians, so that they lent unto them such things as they required. And they spoiled the Egyptians." The treasures that the children of Israel by this means carried forth out of Egypt were very great, even so as in a great measure to leave Egypt empty of its wealth, and so as to enrich the Israelites. Ps. 105:37, "He brought them forth also with silver and with gold." And Gen. 15:14, "They shall come out with great substance." When a person is redeemed by Christ out of spiritual bondage, at the same time they are set at liberty, they are also enriched. They have great substance given, as it were gold tried in the fire; and those riches are the spoils of their enemies. All that spiritual wealth, glory, and blessedness, and even heaven itself, is in some sort the spoils of Satan, that which God has deprived him of to give to the saints. As the earthly Canaan was taken away from the Canaanites and giants of that land, the enemies of the Israelites, and given to them, so heaven was taken from the fallen angels; they were driven out thence by the spiritual Joshua, to make room for the saints. The devils lost heaven, in all probability, by their opposition and envy towards the saints, and rising up in open hostility against Christ as their head, revealed to be such in God's decree, and so their hostility against the spiritual Moses, and Joshua, and their seed, and seeking to keep them down. Those spiritual Egyptians and Canaanites lost their spiritual and heavenly possessions, riches, and honors, and inheritance; and God took it from them, and gave it to them that they opposed and sought to impoverish and destroy, and impoverished them to make those they hated rich with their riches. Yea, they themselves, though their enemies are made in some sense to give them their own riches, so enrich them and impoverish themselves, for they are made by divine providence the occasions of their being brought to their spiritual and eternal riches and glory. Satan has been the occasion of the saints' heavenly riches and glory in tempting men to fall, and so giving occasion for the work of redemption, and then in procuring the death of Christ, and oftentimes is made the occasion of particular advantages that the church obtains at one age and another. And his opposition to the welfare of particular elect souls is always turned to be an occasion of their riches and fullness, so that all the wealth and glory that the church has is in a sense, and indeed in many ways, from Satan, though he seeks nothing but her destruction.

Another thing signified by it is that the church of Christ, when redeemed from her enemies and oppressors, especially from Rome, heathen and antichristian, that is spiritually called Egypt [Rev. 11:8], should have their wealth and glory given into their hands, as is foretold by the prophets. Ps. 68:30, "Rebuke the company of spearmen, the multitude of the bulls, with the calves of the people, till everyone submit himself with pieces of silver." Zech. 14:14, "And Judah also shall fight at Jerusalem; and the wealth of the heathen round about shall be gathered together, gold, and silver, and apparel in great abundance." See Is. 60:5–6, 9–10, 13, 16–17; and 61:6, which was fulfilled in the days of Constantine the Great, and will be more gloriously fulfilled at the fall of Antichrist. Thus the wealth of the sinner is laid up for the just, and Christ shall have a portion divided to him with the great, and "shall divide the spoil with the strong" [Is. 53:12].

It is to be noted that the tabernacle in the wilderness was made of these spoils the children of Israel took from the Egyptians—it was made of those jewels of silver, and gold, and raiment—so all the utensils and holy vessels of the tabernacle, the ark, and the mercy seat, and the cherubims, and the candlestick, and table of shewbread, and altar of incense, and laver, and his foot, and also the priests' vestments, the twelve precious stones of the breastplate. As afterwards, the temple was built chiefly of those vast treasures that David took from his enemies. Whereby is signified several things.

1. That God's church, that in Scripture is represented as Christ's house or temple, and as his raiment and ornament, and as a golden candlestick, etc., is wholly constituted of those saints that are his jewels, that are the spoils of his enemies, that were once his enemies' possession, but that he has redeemed out of their hands. Those precious gems that are near his heart, and are as it were his breastplate,[2] are Satan's spoils.

2. That Christ himself, that is the antitype of the tabernacle and temple, and especially of the ark and the altar, is one that has been rescued out of Satan's hands, and comes to be our ark and altar, no other way than by his resurrection and ascension, whereby he was delivered from captivity to Satan.

3. Hereby is signified that the church of Christ, when it shall be fully redeemed from the tyranny of Rome, that is spiritually called Egypt, shall be adorned and beautified with the wealth[3] of her enemies. That

2. JE deleted "were redeemed."
3. JE deleted "and glory."

vast wealth, that has hitherto been improved to gratify the avarice and pride of the church's enemies, shall then be improved to holy purposes, to build up the church of Christ,[4] to beautify the place of God's sanctuary, and to make the place of his feet glorious. And the kings of the earth shall bring their glory and honor into the church. Thus Satan shall be spoiled of his wealth [and] glory; and that which used to be improved in his service shall be taken from him, and shall be improved in the service of Christ, so that what he hath swallowed down, he shall vomit up again [Job 20:15].

352. JUDGES 1:12–15. Concerning Othniel and Caleb's daughter. Othniel in this story is a type of Christ. As Othniel, Caleb's nephew, obtained Caleb's daughter, his first cousin, to wife by war, and the victory he obtained over Caleb's enemies, and taking a city from them to be a possession for Caleb and his heirs, so Christ, who is nearly related to both God and us, and so fit to be a mediator betwixt God and us, has obtained the church, God's daughter, by war with God's enemies, and the victory he has obtained over them, and by redeeming a city, the spiritual Jerusalem, or Zion, out of their hands, to be a possession for God and his heirs. Achsah, Othniel's wife, moves her husband to ask of her father a blessing and an inheritance; so it is by the intercession of Christ that the church obtains of God the blessings and the inheritance she needs. She complains to her father that she inherited a "south," i.e. a dry desert land. She asks of him "springs of water," and Caleb granted her request. He gave her freely and abundantly; he gave her the "upper springs and the nether springs." And if men, being evil, know how to give good gifts to their children, how much more shall our heavenly Father "give good things to [them] that ask him" [Matt. 7:11]. When Caleb's daughter inhabited a south land, and dwelt in the parched places of the wilderness, and asked "springs of water," both "the upper and the nether springs," so when the souls of God's people are in a droughty, pining, languishing condition, 'tis not a vain thing for them to go to their heavenly Father, through the mediation of Christ, for all such supplies as they need. He'll give 'em springs of water, both "the upper and the nether springs." Godliness hath the promise of the things of this life, and that which is to come [I Tim. 4:8]. God "will give grace and glory, and no good thing will he withhold from those that walk uprightly" [Ps. 84:11]. Achsah im-

4. JE deleted "agreeable to prophecies."

proved that time to move her husband to intercede for [her], when she came to him, which should teach us, when we are brought especially nigh to Christ, and have special seasons of communion with him, to be careful then to improve our interest in him, and to seek his intercession for us with the Father for such blessings as we need.

But this probably has a special respect to some particular seasons of God's blessings on the church, and the accomplishing a glorious alteration in the state of things for her sake, and particular [in] two seasons.

1. That glorious change [that] was made at and after Christ's first coming. The church before that did as it were inhabit "a south land," was held under "weak and beggarly elements" [Gal. 4:9], was under the ministration of death, the letter and not the spirit. But then Christ came nigh to the church; he took her nature upon him. He came and dwelt with us, and received his church into a much greater nearness to himself; and through his mediation was obtained of God a far more glorious dispensation, springs of water in abundance, a ministration of the Spirit. The Spirit was abundantly poured out upon her, and her inheritance was greatly enlarged. Instead of being confined only to the land of Canaan, she had the Roman Empire given, with all its wealth and glory, and so had the nether springs as well as the upper.

2. That glorious change that will be accomplished in favor of the church at the fall of Antichrist. Now the church of Christ does as it were inherit[5] a dry land, and has so done for a long time, dry both upon spiritual and temporal accounts, both as to the upper and nether springs, and is much straitened in her inheritance. But the days will soon come, wherein Christ will come in a spiritual sense, and the church shall forsake worldly vanities and her own righteousness, and shall come to Christ; and then God will gloriously enlarge her inheritance, and will bestow both spiritual and temporal blessings upon her in abundance.

353. GENESIS 15:17. "And it came to pass, when the sun went down, and it was dark, behold a smoking furnace, and a burning lamp that passed between those pieces." Here were four things that were significant of the death and last sufferings of Christ, all at the same time. 1. There were the sacrifices that were slain and lay there, dead and divided. Christ feared when his last passion approached, lest Satan should utterly devour him, and swallow him up in that trial, and cried

5. MS: "~~inhabit a dry~~ inherit a dry."

to God, and was heard in that he feared; and those fowls were frayed away that sought to devour that sacrifice, as Abraham frayed away the fowls that attempted to devour this sacrifice while it lay upon the altar [Gen. 15:11]. 2. The smoking furnace that passed through the midst of the sacrifices. 3. The "deep sleep that fell upon Abraham," and the "horror of great darkness" that fell upon him [Gen. 15:11]. 4. The sun, that greatest of all natural types of Christ, went down and descended under the earth, and it was dark.

"'Tis probable this furnace and lamp, which passed between the pieces, burned and consumed them, and so completed the sacrifice and testified God's acceptance of it (Judg. 6:21), [as] Manoah's (Judg. 13:19–20), and Solomon's (II Chron. 7:1)." This was of old God's manner of manifesting his acceptance of sacrifices, viz. kindling a fire from heaven upon them. "And by this we may know that he accepts our sacrifices, if he kindle in our souls a holy fire of devout affections in them." Henry.[6]

354. GENESIS 7:8–9, 14–16. Concerning the resorting of all kinds of birds, and beasts, and creeping things to the ark before the flood. The particular animals that were gathered together to the ark and saved there, when all the rest of their kind were destroyed, were those that God had pitched, and in his sovereign pleasure chosen out of the many thousands and millions that were of their kind; and yet they were of every kind, as it were of every nation of birds and beasts. So that here was a lively image of that gathering together the elect from the four winds, from one end of heaven to the other, that there was before the destruction of Jerusalem, and before the terrible judgments of God that came on the earth at and before Constantine's time, and that will be before the great destruction of God's enemies that will be about the time of the destruction of Antichrist, when the harvest of the earth shall be gathered in before the vintage; and the gathering together there will be to Christ before the great, and general, and last destruction of the wicked by the general conflagration, when the world shall be destroyed by a deluge of fire. There are elect of every nation that shall [be] gathered in before the final destruction of the wicked world, as is often said in Scripture, especially in the book of Revelation.

The doves and other birds then flocked to the window of the ark, representing that flocking of souls to Christ, which shall be as doves to

6. *Exposition, 1* (1725), 58.

their windows. They flocked together, the eagle, the vulture, and other[7] rapacious birds, together with doves and other such birds, without preying upon them, representing times of great ingathering of souls to Christ, wherein the wolf dwells with the lamb, and the leopard lies down with the kid, etc. [Is. 11:6].

355. GENESIS 18. Isaac, the interpretation of whose name is "laughter,"[8] was conceived about the same time that Sodom and the other cities of the plain were destroyed; and he was born soon after their destruction. So the accomplishment of the terrible destruction of God's enemies, and the glorious prosperity of his church, usually go together, as in Is. 66:13–14. First the enemies of the church are destroyed, and then Isaac is born, or that prosperous state of the church is brought about, wherein their mouths are filled with laughter, and their tongue with singing. So the Egyptians were first overthrown in the Red Sea, and then Moses and the children of Israel rejoiced in peace and liberty, and sung that glorious song of triumph. So first Babylon is destroyed, and then the captivity of Israel is returned, and Jerusalem rebuilt. So when the heathen Roman Empire was overthrown, then commenced that prosperous and joyful state of the church that was in the days of Constantine. So when Antichrist is destroyed, then will follow that joyful glorious state of the church we are looking for. Isaac was the promised seed of Abraham, the father of all the faithful, the blessing he had long waited for; and when Sarah brought him forth, it represented the same thing as the woman in the 12th chapter of Revelation. The accomplishment of the prosperous state of the church is in Scripture often compared to a woman's bringing forth a child, that she had been in travail with; it is so in particular by our Savior (John 16:19–22). Hereby is especially represented the accomplishment of the church's glory, joy, and laughter after the destruction of Antichrist, or the Church of Rome, that is spiritually called Sodom [Rev. 11:8].

356. MATTHEW 11:25–26. "At that time Jesus answered and said, I thank thee, O Father, Lord of heaven and earth, that thou hast hid these things from the wise and prudent, and hast revealed them unto babes. Even so, Father, for so it seemed good in thy sight." Christ don't

7. JE deleted "birds of prey with."
8. יִצְחָק.

only *praise* God, as God may be praised or glorified for his majesty and greatness, sovereignty or justice, or any perfection or glorious work of his, but he *thanks* him as one interested, as though it were a work of God, whereby he had received a benefit. And so it was; these persons to whom his Father had revealed these things were his before God had revealed them to them, for they were given him from eternity, and he had set his love upon them before the foundation of the world, and for their sakes he came into the world, and he knew them all by name. Their names were written on his heart, and he looked upon them as himself. And therefore he thanks the Father for revealing those things to these that were his, that he so loved and was so greatly concerned for, though they were but poor, weak, helpless, and despicable creatures, when he had passed by others more noble, more wise, and prudent; as a loving father, if he had a number of poor children in themselves very mean and contemptible, might well be the more affected with the goodness of God, and justly have his heart more enlarged with thankfulness, if God should look on his poor children, bestowing infinite blessings upon them, when he saw that the rich and noble, potent and learned, were generally passed by. Persons themselves, that see themselves very weak and distinguishingly contemptible, have the more cause to thank God for saving mercy to them, when they consider how they are distinguished from many far greater and more considerable than they. And so Christ looked upon it that he had like cause of thankfulness on this account, because they being from eternity given to him, he looked on them as himself, and on himself as they. Christ, the head of the elect church, here thanks the Father, with rejoicing in spirit, as Luke tells us [Luke 10:21], for that which will be the matter of the most exalted thanksgivings of the church itself to all eternity.

Christ thankfully acknowledges[9] God's kindness herein, because he did it of his own will. "Even so, Father, for so it seemed good in thy sight," that is, without regard to their meanness, or others' greatness. Compare this text with Rom. 6:17.[1]

357. JUDE 14. "And Enoch also, the seventh from Adam, prophesied of these, saying, Behold, the Lord cometh with ten thousand of his saints." 'Tis observable that Enoch, the first of all the prophets, prophesied of the last event that is the subject of prophecy, and that event

9. MS: "acknowledges ~~the Sovereignty~~ of Gods."
1. This sentence is a later addition.

which is the greatest subject of the prophecies of Scripture, and in which the rest of the prophecies of Scripture terminate. Though this ben't the most wonderful event that is the subject of prophecy, for that was the death of Christ, yet this is the greatest event that is the fruit of that event. In this is completed the end of Christ's death. And this last coming of Christ, and what is accomplished by it, is in many respects the greatest of all events; and 'tis so in this respect, that 'tis what all that God has made, and all that Christ has done and suffered, and all the events of providence from the beginning of the world, and all that he has foretold, ultimately terminates in. Therefore with this does Scripture prophecy both begin and end. It begins in Enoch's prophecy, which is the first prophecy we have an account of in Scripture; and it ends with this in the last words of the last of the prophets, even John, in the conclusion of the Revelations.

358. EXODUS 33:18–23. Add this to No. 267, sec. 5, at this mark *. 6. While God draws nigh to Moses, and he is in God's presence, Moses is commanded to hide himself in the clefts of the rock, that God may not be a consuming fire to him, and that he may be secured from destruction, while the burning blaze of God's glory passes by (as Watts expresses himself),[2] which typifies the same Redeemer that is as the munitions of rocks, and as a strong rock and hiding place of his people, that is as compared to a great rock to secure from the burning heat of the sun by its shadow, and was typified by the rock out of which water

2. JE appears to have in mind Isaac Watts' hymn entitled "Divine Wrath and Mercy." The first three verses read:

Adore and tremble, for our God
   Is a *Consuming Fire*
His jealous Eyes his Wrath enflame,
   And raise his Vengeance higher.

Almighty Vengeance, how it burns!
   How bright his Fury glows!
Vast Magazines of Plagues and Storms
   Lie treasur'd for his Foes.

Those heaps of Wrath by slow degrees
   Are forced into a Flame,
But kindled, oh' how fierce they blaze!
   And rend all Natures frame.

See Watts, *Hymns and Spiritual Songs. In Three Books. I. Collected from the Scriptures. II. Compos'd on Divine Subjects. III. Prepar'd for the Lord's Supper* (2nd ed., London, 1709), p. 31.

was fetched for the children of Israel [Ex. 17:6]. God's[3] people can be secured from destruction when they are in the presence of God, and in his approaches and converse, no other way than by being in Christ, and sheltered by him from being consumed by the flames of God's pure and spotless holiness.

7. God covered him with his hand while he passed by [v. 22], not only that he might not see more of the glory of God than he could bear, but also that his deformity and pollution might not be discovered, to bring on him destruction from the presence of that infinitely pure and holy God, and from the glory of that power that passed by. So in Jesus, God covers our deformity and pollution. He beholds not iniquity in Jacob, nor sees pollution in Israel; he turns away his eye from beholding our transgression. Therefore it is that we are not consumed in our intercourse with God.

8. Moses beholds God's glory through a crevice or hole of the rock, as through a window at which he looked out, which represents the manner of God's discovering himself to his people in this world, which [is] as standing behind a wall and showing himself through the lattice.

359. GENESIS 19:23–24. "The sun was risen upon the earth when Lot entered into Zoar. Then the Lord rained upon Sodom and upon Gomorrah brimstone and fire from the Lord out of heaven."[4] This signified that the terrible destruction of the wicked is at the beginning of the glorious day wherein the Sun of Righteousness rises on the earth, and at Christ, Lot's antitype, his coming and visiting his church, the little city, the antitype of the church. So it was in the days of the apostles, in the morning of the gospel day, when Judea and Jerusalem were so terribly destroyed. So it was in the days of Constantine, and so it will be at the fall of Antichrist, and so it will be at the end of the world. See Job 38:13 note.[5]

360. JOSHUA 7. Concerning Achan, the troubler of Israel. Achan was that to the congregation of Israel, that some lust or way of iniquity indulged and allowed is to particular professors. Sinful enjoyments are accursed things; wherever they are entertained, God's curse at-

---

3. MS: "God."
4. JE deleted "Hence I note that."
5. This reference is a later addition. JE suggests that in Job 38:13 God has an eye toward events that will accompany "the morning of that glorious day of the church when the Sun of Righteousness shall arise" ("Blank Bible").

tends them. The accursed things that Achan took were "a goodly Babylonish garment, and two hundred shekels of silver, and a wedge [of gold] of fifty shekels weight" [v. 21], that when he saw he coveted. So the objects of men's lusts, which they take and indulge themselves in the enjoyment of, are very tempting and alluring, appearing very beautiful, and seeming very precious. Achan took those and hid them in his tent underground, so that there was no sign or appearance of them above ground; they were concealed with the utmost secrecy. So very commonly the sins that chiefly trouble professors, and provoke God's displeasure, and bring both spiritual and temporal calamities upon them, are "secret faults" [Ps. 19:12], as David calls them, hidden by some lust, or Achan, as it were underground. Lust is exceeding deceitful, and will hide iniquity, and cover it over with such fair pretenses and excuses that it is exceeding difficult for persons to discover them, and to be brought fully to see and own their fault in them. The silver and gold was covered over with the goodly Babylonish garment (as it is said, the silver was under it [v. 21]); so persons are wont to cover their secret wickedness with a very fair, hypocritical profession. An hypocritical high profession is a Babylonish, or antichristian, garment; 'tis the robe of the false church. God charges Israel not only with stealing, but dissembling. When Israel had transgressed in the accursed thing, and God was not among them, [they] were carnally secure and self-confident; they thought a few of them enough to vanquish the inhabitants of Ai [v. 3], which represents to us the frame that. professors[6] are commonly in when they indulge some secret iniquity. But they could not stand before their enemies; they were smitten down before them [vv. 4–5]. So when [they] secretly indulge some one lust, it makes 'em universally weak; they lie dreadfully exposed to their spiritual enemies, and easily fall before them. The congregation seem to wonder what is the matter, that God hides himself from them; so Christians oftentimes, when they are going on in some evil way that the deceitfulness of sin hides from them, wonder what is the reason that God hides himself from them. They lay long upon their faces, crying to God without receiving any answer. So when persons harbor any iniquity, 'tis wont[7] to prevent any gracious answer to their prayer. Their prayers are hindered; their iniquity is a cloud that their prayer can't pass through. When they were troubled and distressed, they took

6. MS: "~~Persons~~ (Professours)."
7. JE deleted "effectually."

a wrong course. They betook themselves to prayer and crying to God, as though they had nothing else to do, whereas their first and principal work ought to have been diligently to have inquired whether there was not some iniquity to be found among them, as is implied, v. 10. So Christians, when God greatly afflicts them, and hides his face from them, and manifests his anger towards them, are commonly wont to do. They cry, and cry to God, as if they had nothing else to do, but still secretly entertain[8] the troubler; and it never comes into their hearts, "Am I not greatly guilty, with respect to such a practice or way that I allow myself in, in my covetousness, or in my proud, or contentious,[9] or sensual, or peevish, and froward behavior?" God mentions it as an aggravation of the sin of the congregation in Achan, that they had even put the accursed thing among their own stuff; so when professors allow themselves in any unlawful gain or enjoyment, they[1] commonly put it among those things that are theirs, that they may lawfully enjoy or make use of. If men continue in such evil ways, and don't depart from them, they are ruinous to the soul, however they may plead that they think there is no hurt in them. There is a way that seems right to a man, but the end thereof are the ways of death. So God says to Israel, v. 12, "Neither will I be with you anymore, except ye destroy the accursed thing from among you." God directed the congregation of Israel to make diligent search in order to find out the troubler; all were to be examined, tribe by tribe, and family by family, and man by man [v. 17]. So when God hides his face from us and frowns upon us, we ought diligently and thoroughly to examine all our ways, and to take effectual care that none escape thorough examination, to examine them first in their several kinds, as they may be ranked with respect to their objects, times, and otherwise, and then to proceed to a more special examination and inquiry, and never leave till we have thoroughly examined every particular way and practice, yea, to examine act by act, and to bring all before God to be tried by him, by his word and Spirit, as all Israel was brought before the Lord to be tried by him. By this means Achan was thoroughly discovered, and brought to confess his wickedness. So if we be thus thorough in trying our ways, and bring all to the test of God's word, seeking the direction of his Spirit also with his

---

8. MS: "~~indulge~~ entertain."

9. MS: "contention."

1. Here JE crossed out "~~are commonly~~ guilty of placing their happiness partly in it; they make that sinful enjoyment part of their portion, which is an high aggravation of their wickedness."

word, 'tis the way to discover the sin that troubles us, and thoroughly to convince the conscience, and make it plainly to confess the iniquity. The congregation, after they had found out the accursed thing, they brought it out of the earth, and out of the tent, and spread it before the Lord [v. 23]. So persons, when they have found out the sin that has troubled them, should confess those sins, and spread 'em before the Lord. And we must not content ourselves only with confessing the sin to God, but must deal with it, as the children of Israel did with Achan. We must treat it as a mortal, and most hateful, and pernicious enemy;[2] we must turn inveterate implacable enemies to it, must have no mercy on it. We must not spare it at all, or be afraid of being too cruel to it; we must aim at nothing short of the life of it, and must resolve utterly to destroy and extirpate it, must as it were stone it with stones, and burn it with fire (So "Samuel hewed Agag in pieces before the Lord"; see notes on I Sam. 15:32–33; see also II Cor. 7:12.),[3] and must not only destroy that sin, but all its offspring, its whole family, and its oxen and asses [v. 24], and all that belongs to it, everything that[4] spring from it, every evil that has attended or sprung from [it]. We must serve them all alike.

And as this was done to Achan, not only by a particular executioner, but by all Israel [v. 25], so we must do it with all our hearts and souls; we must be full in it. There must be nothing in our[5] hearts that is favorable to the troubler, or that has not a hand in its death. Israel, after they had thus slain the troubler, raised over him "a great heap of stones" [v. 26] as a monument of what had been. So when we have slain the troubler, we must keep a record of the mischief we received by that sin, to be a constant everlasting warning to us to avoid it and everything of that nature for the future. This is the way to have the Lord turn from the fierceness of his anger [Deut. 13:17].

361. GENESIS 21:10–11. "Wherefore she said unto Abraham, Cast out this bondwoman and her son, for the son of this bondwoman shall not be heir with my son, even with Isaac." The son of the bondwoman is men's own righteousness, which is the son of the first covenant, given

---

2. MS: "enemies."

3. This parenthesis is a later interlineation. JE compared Samuel's response to Agag with that of Christians to their "most beloved lusts." Both Agag and lusts "must be utterly destroyed without mercy." Similarly, JE explains that the godly sorrow that Paul provoked among the Corinthian Christians was "out of regard to the well-being of the church, the state of religion, and the welfare of the souls of the people in general" ("Blank Bible").

4. JE deleted "is akin to it."

5. MS: "his."

at Mt. Sinai, which is Hagar. And Isaac, the son of the free woman, is Christ, as applied to the soul by faith; he is the child of promise, and the son of the free woman. At least this is part of the signification. 'Tis Sarah, the mother of Isaac, that urges the casting out the son of the bondwoman; so 'tis the church in its ministry and ordinances, which is the mother of Christ in the souls of believers, that urges the casting out our own legal righteousness. 'Tis Christ that is the heir of the blessings of the covenant; 'tis his merits only that have a right or title to those blessings. We must cast out our own righteousness, and not have any manner of regard to that, as though that had a right, or as though a right came by that. "And the thing was very grievous in Abraham's sight because of his son" [v. 11], which signifies how very hard and grievous it seems to persons wholly to cast out their own righteousness, the son of the legal covenant from Mt. Sinai, because they are our own works, our own brats, that are dear to us, as Ishmael was to his father Abraham.

362. GENESIS 22. Concerning Abraham's offering up his son Isaac. God's command to Abraham to offer up his son Isaac, considered with all its circumstances, was an exceeding great trial. Abraham had left his own country, and his father's house, and all that [was] dear and pleasant to him, and followed God, not knowing whither he went. First he left Ur of the Chaldees with his father. That was a great trial, but that was not enough. After this he was required also to leave Haran, and his father's house there, after he had been there settled, in hopes of a blessing, which God encouraged him that he would give him in a posterity. When he came there, he found a famine in the land, and [was] forced to fly the country, and go down into Egypt for sustenance. And God appeared to him time after time, promising great things concerning his posterity. Abraham waited a long time, and saw no appearance of the fulfillment of the promise, for his wife continued barren; and he made his complaint of it to God. And God renewed and very solemnly confirmed his promise, but did not tell him that it should be a child by his wife; and therefore, after he had waited some time longer, he went in to his maid. But God rejected her son, and he waited thirteen years longer, till he was an hundred years old, before he obtained the son promised; and then God gave him but one, without any hopes of his having any other. And after this, at God's command, he cast out his son Ishmael, though it was exceeding grievous to him, on encouragement of great blessings in Isaac and his posterity.

And now at last God commands him to take him, and offer him up for a burnt offering. He don't only call to see him die, though that would have been a great trial under such circumstances; but he is to cut his throat with his own hands, and when he has done, to burn his flesh on the altar in offering to God, to that God that carnal reason would have said had dealt so ill with him, after he had lived long enough to get fast hold of his affections, and after he was weaned from Ishmael, and had set all his heart on Isaac, and after there began to be a most hopeful prospect of God's fulfilling his promises concerning him. And "God gave him no reason for it. When Ishmael was to be cast out," the reason assigned was that in Isaac, his seed should be called; but now, in seeming inconsistency with that reason, "Isaac must die, and Abraham must kill him, and neither one nor the other must know why, nor wherefore." And as Mr. Henry observes, "How would he ever look Sarah in the face again? With what face could he return to her and his family with the blood of Isaac sprinkled on his garments? 'Surely a bloody husband hast thou been to me,' would Sarah say, as Ex. 4:25–26."[6]

363. II CORINTHIANS 2:14–16. "And maketh manifest the savor of his knowledge by us in every place. For we are unto God a sweet savor of Christ, in them that are saved, and in them that perish. To the one we are the savor of death unto death, and to the other we are the savor of life unto life." This last verse might more literally and more properly have been translated thus: "To those, indeed, we are a savor of death unto death, but to these a savor of life unto life,"[7] which makes the sense much less perplexed. Ministers are as it were the vessels that carry the sweet ointment of the name of Christ, whose name is said to be as ointment poured forth. When they preach the gospel, this ointment is poured forth. Christ is the fragrant rose. That knowledge of Christ that is diffused by his ministers is the savor of this rose, and this is the savor that the Apostle speaks of, which in the 14th verse he calls "the savor of his knowledge." This is always a sweet savor to God. The name of Christ is ever delightful to God; and the preaching of Christ in the world, whether to elect or reprobates, is acceptable to God, as he delights in having the name of his Son glorified, for Christ's being made known to those that perish shall be greatly to the glory of Christ. God loves to have the name of his Son made known to all men for his

6. Henry, *Exposition*, *1* (1725), 76.
7. οἵς μὲν ὀσμὴ ἐκ θανάτου εἰς θάνατον, οἵς δὲ ὀσμὴ ἐκ ζωῆς εἰς ζωήν.

Son's glory, so that the knowledge that reprobates receive of Christ, by the preaching of the gospel, is a sweet savor to God; for wherever the name of Christ is found, it is acceptable to God. But yet it is not always a sweet savor to them to whom the gospel is preached, though it be to God. Indeed, to the elect, to those that are saved, 'tis a sweet savor, as well as to God; 'tis a savor of life. We are to them a savor of a living Redeemer. They believe him to be a risen and glorified Redeemer. He is a savor of life unto life, i.e. not only a sweet savor as of a living Redeemer, but a refreshing, renewing, life-giving savor.

But to them that perish, he is a savor of death unto death. The preaching of Christ crucified is not a sweet savor unto them, but a stinking savor, as of a slain dead carcass. They don't believe his resurrection; they look upon him dead still. The doctrine of Christ crucified is nauseous to them. 'Tis a savor of death unto death; 'tis a stench as of a dead carcass, that kills them, and brings them into a state of death.

364. JUDGES 6:37–40. Concerning Gideon's fleece. There being first dew on the fleece, when it was dry upon all the earth beside, and then dew on all the ground, but dry upon the fleece, was a type of the Jews' being, in the first place, the peculiar people of God, and favored with spiritual blessings alone, when all the world besides were destitute, and then the Jews' being rejected, and remaining destitute of spiritual blessing, when the Gentile nations all around 'em were favored with them. Gideon was a type of Christ; his overcoming that innumerable multitude of Gentile nations with trumpets, and lamps, and earthen vessels, typifies Christ's conquering the Gentile world by the[8] sound of the trumpet of the gospel, and by carrying the light of the gospel to them by ministers that are as earthen vessels. This event was accompanied with what was typified by the fleece. A sheep is a creature often used to typify Christ. The Jewish nation was as it were Christ's clothing; they are sometimes represented as such. First they only had the word, and ordinances, and the blessing of the Holy Spirit. It was remarkably poured out on them on the day of Pentecost; then was that plentiful dew that was a bowl full of water, when the Gentile nations were destitute. But afterwards, the Gentile nations received the gospel, and God's Spirit was poured out on them, and the Jews were rejected,[9] and have now remained dry for many ages.

8. JE deleted "preaching of the go."
9. MS: "reject."

365. ROMANS 2:29. "But he is a Jew, which is one inwardly; and circumcision is that of the heart, in the spirit, and not in the letter; *whose praise is not of men, but of God.*"[1] That by this last expression, "whose praise is not of men, but of God," the Apostle has respect to the insufficiency of men to judge concerning him, whether he be inwardly a Jew, or no, and would signify that it belongs to God alone to give a voice in that matter, is confirmed by the same Apostle's use of the like phrase in I Cor. 4:5. "Therefore judge nothing before the time, until the Lord come, who both will bring to light the hidden things of darkness, and will make manifest the counsels of the hearts: *and then shall every man have praise of God.*" The Apostle in the two foregoing verses says, "But with me it is a very small thing that I should be judged of you, or of man's judgment; yea, I judge not mine own self. For I know nothing of myself; yet am I not hereby justified, but he that judgeth me is the Lord" [I Cor. 4:3–4]. And again, it is further confirmed, because the Apostle in this 2nd chapter to the Romans, directs himself especially to those that had a high conceit of their own holiness, made their boast of God, and were confident of their own discerning, and that they knew God's will, and approved the things that were more excellent, "*or tried the things that differ,*" as it is in the margin[2] (v. 18), and were confident that they were guides of the blind, a light of them which are in darkness, instructors of the foolish, teachers of babes, and so took upon them to judge others. See vv. 1, and 17–20. These things show that for any to take upon [themselves], by only a little occasional conversation with others that are professors of godliness, [to judge them] as hypocrites, unexperienced and unconverted men, is a great error.

The same is confirmed by I Cor. 2:15. "But he that is spiritual judgeth all things, but he himself is judged of no man," or (as it is in the margin),[3] "is discerned of no man."

Everything in the saints that belongs to the spiritual and divine life is spoken of in Scripture as "being hidden," known only to God and to himself. His life is said to be "hid with Christ in God," but to appear and to be made manifest at the day of judgment, when Christ shall appear

1. JE wrote, "365. Judging and Discerning the State of Others' Souls," as a running head on the pages of this entry. He used materials in this entry when he delivered the commencement address at Yale College on Sept. 10, 1741, subsequently published as *The Distinguishing Marks of a Work of the Spirit of God* (*Works*, 4, 283–86).

2. I.e. margin of the KJV.

3. Ibid.

(Col. 3:3–4). Their joy is said to be what others intermeddle not with. Their spiritual food is said to be hidden. Rev. 2:17, "To him that overcometh will I give to eat of the hidden manna." So Christ told his disciples that he had meat to eat that they knew not of [John 4:32]. And their new name, which is the name they have as new creatures, as born again, is said to be what no man knows, but he that receives it (Rev. 2:17). The heart, which is the thing that God looks at, and in which are those spiritual ornaments and graces by which persons are sincere Christians, is called "the hidden man." I Pet. 3:4, "But let it be the hidden man of the heart, in that which is not corruptible, the ornament," etc.

Again, the same is confirmed from that in the parable of the good seed and the tares, in the 13th chapter of Matthew, [vv.] 28–30. "The servants said unto him, Wilt thou that we go and gather them up? But he said, Nay, lest while ye gather up the tares, ye root up also the wheat with them. Let both grow together until the harvest, and in the time of harvest I will say to the reapers, Gather ye together first the tares, and bind them in bundles to burn them, but gather the wheat into my barn." The servants of the householder can be interpreted of nothing better than ministers, who were represented by Abraham's servant [Gen. 24:2]; and by the servants of the householder, in the parable of "the king that made a marriage for his son, and sent forth his *servants* to call" guests [Matt. 22:2]; and by the servant of the man that made a great supper in the 14th [chapter] of Luke; and by the servants of the householder to whom he committed the care of his family when traveling into a far country [Luke 19:13]; and by the servants of the householder that waited for the coming of their lord in the 12th chapter of Luke; and by the servant or steward in the same chapter, that gives to everyone his "portion of meat in due season" [Luke 12:42]; and the servant that beat his fellow servant [Luke 20:10]; and the servants of the householder that dressed, and adorned, and fed the returning prodigal [Luke 19:22–23]; and the servants that were sent to receive the fruit of the vineyard (Luke 20). The same that were there to take care of the fruit of the vineyard are those that in this parable have the care of the fruit of the field. The servants of the householder are oftentimes very apt to conceit themselves sufficient to separate between the wheat and the tares, but the householder says, "No." He is aware of more dangers of their rooting up the wheat with the tares than they are, and therefore commands that they should let both grow together till the harvest, and signifies that that is the proper time of doing it. This parable shows plainly that the proper time of judgment in this respect, viz. of judging who[4] of professors are sincere and who not, is the day of judgment, and that therefore if any take it upon them to do this now, they do it out of its proper season. And therefore judging men in this sense comes under that prohibition forementioned, I Cor. 4:5, "Therefore judge nothing before the time."

When we are so often forbidden to judge that we be not judged [Luke 6:37], without doubt [is meant] a judging of men's state, or of their sincerity and hypocrisy, good and evil principles, of their hearts in general as well as of particular actions; for what is meant by that prohibition is doubtless that we should not take God's work out of his hands, and anticipate the proper business of the day of judgment. In the place just now mentioned, we are forbidden to judge; in I Corinthians we are forbidden to judge others upon that account, because it is before the time. And in the 14th [chapter] of Romans, at the 4th verse, we are forbidden to judge others upon the other account, because we therein go out of our place, and take God's work into our hands. Rom. 14:4, "Who art thou that judgest another man's servant? To his own master he standeth or falleth." And Jas. 4:12, "There is one Lawgiver, that is able to save and to destroy. Who art thou that judgest another?"

These two reasons are given as good reasons in Scripture against judging others, but they are as strong against judging the state of men's hearts in general as against judging the state of their hearts with regard to particular actions.

For, 1. It is as much the proper work of God and his prerogative, to judge the state of men's hearts in general, to determine what hearts are good, and what not, what hearts are sincere, and what not, as to judge the state of the heart with regard to particular actions. + + Here add No. 370.[5] 'Tis often challenged by God as[6] one of his most glorious prerogatives, to search the heart and try the reins of the children of men. And this is challenged as God's prerogative, especially as it relates to the trial of the general state of the hearts of professors,[7] in Rev. 2:22–23. There Christ threatens to destroy and damn certain professors, except they repent, and adds, "And all the churches shall know that I am he which searcheth the reins and the hearts; and I will give unto everyone of you according to your works." And again, I Chron. 28:9, this divine prerogative is asserted, with respect to judg-

4. JE deleted "are godly."
5. This cross-reference is a later addition.
6. JE deleted "his peculiar."
7. MS: "the ⟨general State⟩ ~~State~~ of ⟨the Heart of⟩ Professours."

ing of the state of the heart in general, and in order to that salvation, or destruction and casting off forever, that depends on it. "And thou, Solomon my son, know thou the God of thy father, and serve him with a perfect heart and with a willing mind; for the Lord searcheth all hearts, and understandeth all the imagination of the thoughts. If thou seek him, he will be found of thee; but if thou forsake him, he will cast thee off forever." So Ps. 7:9–11, "Oh let the wickedness of the wicked come to an end; but do thou establish the just: for the righteous God trieth the hearts and reins. My defense is of God, which saveth the upright in heart. God judgeth the righteous, and God is angry with the wicked every day." So trying the hearts is spoken of as God's prerogative, and the furnace tries what is gold, and what is dross or base metal. Prov. 17:3, "The fining pot is for silver, and the furnace for gold, but the Lord trieth the hearts." So the Psalmist prays in the 26th psalm, that God would judge him with respect to his integrity and trusting in God, and that he would examine him, and prove him, and try his reins and his heart, and not gather his soul with sinners, nor his life "with bloody men" (v. 9). So it was part of Christ's prerogative to know which of his followers and professed believers on him were to be depended on, and which not. John 2:23–25, "Many believed in his name, when they saw the miracles which he did. But Jesus did not commit himself unto them, because he knew all men, and needed not that any should testify of man; for he knew what was in man." 'Tis God's prerogative to weigh the spirits and ponder the hearts of men (Prov. 16:2, and 21:2). It belongs to him to weigh men in the balances, and say who is found wanting (Dan. 5:27). This certainly is as much, and much more, claimed in Scripture as God's prerogative, than taking vengeance is; and therefore for anyone to take upon him to decide what professors are sincere and what insincere, and to draw a dividing line between 'em, is as much, and much more, invading the divine prerogative than private revenge is.

2. If that reason why we should not judge men be a good one, that in so doing we shall judge men before the time, because the proper time for this is the day of judgment, then this [is] a good reason why we should not take upon us to judge professors with respect to their state; for this is one great and principal part of the work of the last judgment, and one special end of the day of judgment, to make an open distinction between the sincere and hypocrites, to separate between sheep and goats, between wheat and tares, between good grain and chaff, between gold and dross, as is manifest by Mal. 3:2. "But who may abide

the day of his coming, and who shall stand when he appeareth? For he is like a refiner's fire, and like fuller's soap." And Matt. 3:12, "Whose fan is in his hand, and he will thoroughly purge his floor, and gather his wheat into the garner; but he will burn up the chaff with unquenchable fire." Yea, in most of the descriptions we have in Scripture, this is all the work that is mentioned. This is all that is mentioned in that description we have of the day of judgment, in the explication of the parable of the good seed and tares, in the 13th chapter of Matthew. And this is all the business that is mentioned in that famous description that Christ gives of the day of judgment, in the 25th chapter of Matthew; and this is all the business mentioned in that description we have in the 20th chapter of Revelation, which is the most famous of any we have in the Bible, excepting that in the 25th of Matthew.

Yea, judging of persons' state, and sentencing or damning them, is chiefly intended by Christ when he forbids us to judge them, for this is most properly judging them, or judging and condemning their persons. We may blame a man for many things he does, yet not condemn or sentence the man. 'Tis the doing the part of the great Judge of men that is chiefly forbidden, which is either to justify them, or condemn them as wicked or righteous. See further No. 367, and also No. 392.[8] See sermon on Ps. 55:12–14.[9]

The eleven disciples, though they were all true converts, did not know but that Judas was also converted, and always supposed him to be so, though they had such abundant opportunity of conversation with him. And Christ all along treated him as if he had been a true disciple, and even sent him forth to preach the gospel, because he therein acted as a minister of the visible church. He did not take it upon him to act as an omniscient judge at that time, but as setting an example for his disciples and ministers how to behave themselves in the visible church. The Psalmist, though so wise a man, and a man so greatly acquainted with the word of God, and a man of such great experience, did not find out that Ahithophel was not a convert, though he had so long been so intimately acquainted with him, but always looked upon him as a saint, and an eminent saint, and delighted in him as such. Ps. 55:13–14, "But it was thou, a man mine equal, my guide,

---

8. These cross-references are later additions.

9. This reference is a later addition. The doctrine of this sermon, preached in September 1741, reads, "Men are not sufficient positively to determine the state of the souls of others that are of God's visible people" (MS, Yale coll.).

and mine acquaintance. We took sweet counsel together; we went to the house of God in company."

And besides, we are nowhere directed to judge of men chiefly by the account they give of their experiences, but chiefly by their works. And it is evident it was not the manner of the apostles to judge of Christians' sincerity chiefly by the account they gave of the manner of the work on their hearts, but by their behavior. See sermon on Jas. 2:18.[1] See No. 370 at this mark #.[2]

366. GENESIS 19:23–24. Add this to No. 359. So Dagon fell, once and again, before the ark early in the morning [I Sam. 5:4]. So after the disciples had toiled all night and caught nothing, yet in the morning Christ came to 'em, and they had a great draught of fishes [Luke 5:5–9]. So Christ rose from the dead early in the morning. 'Tis said concerning God's church, that weeping may continue for a night, but joy will come in the morning [Ps. 30:5]. The children of Israel were all night pursued by their enemies at the Red Sea; in the night they were in the sea, in a great and terrible east wind. But in the morning watch, the Lord looked through the pillar of cloud and fire, and troubled the host of the Egyptians. And in the morning the children of Israel came up out of the sea, and the host of the Egyptians was destroyed, and the children of Israel rejoiced and sang [Ex. 15:1]. Jacob, after wrestling with the angel in the night, obtained the blessing in the morning [Gen. 32:24–29]. He that rules over men "shall be as the light of the morning, when the sun riseth, even a morning without clouds, and as the tender grass springing out of the earth by clear shining after rain" (II Sam. 23:4). Ps. 49:14, "The upright shall have dominion over them in the morning." In the morning, when the Sun of Righteousness shall rise "with healing in his wings," the day comes "that shall burn as an oven" (as that day burnt on which, when Lot entered into Zoar [Gen. 19:23]), "and all the proud, yea, all that do wickedly, shall be stubble," and the righteous "shall tread down the wicked, and they shall be as ashes under the soles of their feet" (Mal. 4:1–3). The church, in the 59th psalm, after expressing her great troubles from her enemies, and declaring[3] how God should destroy them, says, v. 16, "But I will sing of thy power; yea, I will sing aloud of thy mercy in the morning, for thou

1. JE's sermon, preached earlier in May 1736, sounds a similar theme in its doctrine: "A manifestation of godliness in a man's life and walk is a better ground of others' charity concerning his godliness than any account that he gives about it in words" (MS, Yale coll.).

2. This cross-reference is a later addition.

3. MS: "declared."

hast been my defense and refuge in the day of my trouble." So likewise the church, in speaking of her troubles, in Ps. 143, where she says, v. 8, "Cause [me] to hear thy lovingkindness in the morning." 'Tis said of the church, Ps. 46:5, "God is in the midst of her; she shall not be moved. God shall help her, when the early morning appeareth," for so 'tis in the original.[4] And then in the 8th verse, 'tis said, "Come, behold the works of the Lord, what desolations he hath made in the earth." Hos. 6:1–3, "Come, and let us return unto the Lord; for he hath torn, and he will heal us. After two days he will revive us: in the third day he will raise us up, and we shall live in his sight. Then shall we know, if we follow on to know the Lord; his going forth is prepared as the morning."

367. ROMANS 2:29. Add this to No. 365. As to that text, Judges 12:6, "Then said they unto him, Say now Shibboleth; and he said *Sibboleth*, for he could not frame to pronounce it right. Then they took him, and slew him at the passages of Jordan." Though that be an undoubted truth, that want of experience has a tendency to cause men as it were to lisp, and greatly to fail, and blunder in talking of experimental religion, which may very fitly be compared to the failing of the Ephraimites in pronouncing "*Shibboleth*," yet we can't infer from it that we are warranted to go as far in judging men's state, by what we think of their rightly expressing themselves in spiritual and experimental language, any more than we can infer that 'tis committed to us to proceed upon it, as far as they did on the wrong pronunciation of "*Shibboleth*." We can't carry the inference so far, because the thing here principally typified is not the language of false professors, as it sounds in the ears of fellow professors in this world, but in the ears of their Judge and of the saints as assessors with him "at the passages of Jordan," i.e. in their passage out of this world into the next, or when they are attempting to pass out of this world into the heavenly Canaan. In Christ's ears, no man can learn the language of the Canaanites, but those that are indeed Canaanites, even as no man can learn the song of the 144,000, but only those that are redeemed from the earth. What is wanting is the heart and the practice, which are the essential part of the song; and 'tis the language of the heart and practice that are the essential part of the language of a Christian. And these are what we are often told professors of religion shall hereafter be judged by, by him that searches the hearts, and tries the reins, and renders to everyone

4. לִפְנוֹת בֹּקֶר.

according to his works [Rev. 2:23]. See further No. 370 *.[5] "Passing over Jordan" can't mean admitting into the visible church here on earth, and "slaying" an exclusion out of the church, as two[6] things make evident. 1. If by a "*Shibboleth*" the saints could decide who were true Christians and who not, with a certainty sufficient to fix the dreadful sentence upon them, there would be no such thing as false professors in the visible church, which is contrary to the whole stream of Scripture, which holds forth everywhere that a very great part of the visible church are false professors. 2. However excommunication, or excluding from the church after persons have been admitted in, implies a dreadful sentence, and is an awful punishment, and might in some respects be represented by death, yet a mere keeping out,[7] or refusing to receive those that never were received, can't properly be represented by such an execution.[8] Christ did not judge Judas, or withdraw from him as an hypocrite, because he would not then act towards him as a judge, but to set us an example, especially an example to pastors of churches.[9]

368. JOHN 2:1–10. Concerning the marriage at Cana of Galilee. The company [that] were here at this wedding represent the church of Christ, who are often represented as the guests called together to a marriage feast. Jesus, and his mother, and his disciples were there; thus it is in the church. The former circumstances of the marriage, wherein "they wanted wine" [v. 3], represents the state of the church before Christ came, or rather before the evangelical dispensation was established. The latter state of the wedding, wherein they had plenty of wine, represents the latter state of the church after the glorious pouring out of the Spirit at Pentecost, and especially after the fall of Antichrist. The wine represents the spiritual supplies of his church, the grace and comforts of the Holy Spirit, which are often represented by wine in Scripture. Their wine ran very low, and was just out. Formerly, the Old Testament church had a supply of wine, but when Christ came into the world, it was just out; they had in a manner "no

5. This cross-reference is a later addition.
6. MS: "~~three~~ ⟨two⟩."
7. MS: "~~Shutting out~~ ⟨Keeping out⟩."
8. Here JE crossed out the following with a large "X": "3. Jordan is used in Scripture as a type of death, or that change we pass under in going out of this world into an eternal state, but there is nothing passed through in an admission." At the same time he substituted "two" for "three" above.
9. This sentence is a later interlineation.

wine." But when Christ came and ascended up to heaven, he soon gave his church plenty of wine, and much better wine than ever the Jewish church had enjoyed, as 'tis said, "Thou has kept the best wine until now" [v. 10]. So again, before the glorious times of the church commence, the church's wine runs very low, and is almost out; what they alouted with is water—human learning, sapless speculations and dispensations, and dead morality. Formerly the Christian church had wine, as in the times of the primitive church, and in the times of the Reformation, but now their wine is just gone. But after the beginning of those glorious times, their water shall be turned into wine, and much better wine than ever they had before. The mother of Jesus represents the more eminent[1] ministers of the gospel, or the public ecclesiastical authority as exercised in synods, public schools, etc. They, in a dark and dead time of the church, complain to Christ of their unsuccessfulness, of the want of wine in the church, and look to him for a supply, but must not expect an answer till Christ's time is come [v. 4]. Their prayers are not answered till then, and then they shall be fully answered. Their prayers are not rejected; they are offered up with incense. The cries of the souls under the altar, that cry "How long, Lord, holy and true?" ben't rejected; but yet 'tis said to them that they should wait till God's time comes. The servants represent gospel ministers; they have a command from Jesus' mother, i.e. from the church in her public authority, to do whatever Jesus commands [v. 5], whence we may note that the way to have a plentiful effusion of the Spirit with his Word and ordinances is to be faithful in their work. They are to fill up the water pots of purification with water [v. 7]; that is all that they can do. They can, in the use of the ordinances of God's house and appointed means of grace and purification, "be instant in season and out of season" [II Tim. 4:2]. They can fill the water pots up to the brim. They can be abundant in preaching the word, which, as it comes only from them, is but water, a dead letter, a sapless, tasteless, spiritless thing; but this is what Christ will bless for the supply [of] his church with wine.

369. GENESIS 26:19–22. "The two first wells that Isaac's servants digged were Esek and Sitnah, 'contention' and 'hatred.' . . . At length Isaac removed to a quiet settlement, sticking to his peaceable principles, rather fly than fight, and unwilling to dwell with them that hated peace. Those that study to be quiet seldom fail of being so. The last well

1. MS: "~~faithfull~~ ⟨more Eminent⟩."

they called Rehoboth, 'enlargement,' 'room enough.' In the two former wells we may see what this earth is, straitness and strife. This well
shows us what heaven is, enlargement and peace, room enough there;
for there are many mansions." Henry.[2]

370. ROMANS 2:29. Add this to No. 367 at this mark *. And the
signification of the word "*Shibboleth*" seems to intimate the same thing,
which is "an ear of corn." This seems to intimate that 'tis the fruit or
ear, that is the grand characteristic by which the true friends of
Jephthah[3] may be known from hypocrites,[4] or the wheat known from
tares. 'Tis the fruit that we shall be judged by at last; our fruits shall be
weighed in the balances, and if they are found wanting, we shall be
slain on this [side of] Jordan, and never suffered to go over into Canaan. 'Tis probable that, according to the dialect of Ephraim, an ear of
corn was called "*Sibboleth*," and so that was the name of the fruit of
Jephthah's enemies; but "*Shibboleth*" was the name of the fruit of
Jephthah's friends, according to the dialect of Gilead. This therefore
signifies that, if at last our fruit be found to be not the fruit of the
friends of Christ, but [of] his enemies, we shall be slain.

Add[5] this to No. 365 at this mark ++. When knowing the hearts of
men is so often ascribed to God as his great prerogative, one thing
principally intended is his knowing the state of their hearts, whether
they are sincerely godly, or no, as is evident by what Peter says concerning the conversion of the Gentiles before the council of Jerusalem.
Acts 15:7–8, "God made choice among us, that the Gentiles by my
mouth should hear the word of the gospel, and believe. And God,
which knoweth the hearts, bare them witness, giving them the Holy
Ghost, even as he did unto us."

[See No. 365, this mark] #. It seems very probable that the devil,
though he sees and hears a great deal more what men do and say than
we, and has infinitely more experience, yet don't know who are converted and who not. Thus he did not know that Peter was converted,
and therefore hoped to overthrow him [Luke 23:54–62]. So he did not
know that Job was, as God told him, "a perfect and an upright man"
[Job 1:8]. He questioned it, though he was so eminent a saint; he
doubted whether he would not fail in the trial (unless we may suppose

2. *Exposition, 1* (1725), 89.
3. MS: "~~Gileadites~~ ⟨friends of Jephthah⟩."
4. MS: "~~Ephraimites~~ ⟨Hypocrites⟩."
5. JE repeated "370" at the beginning of this paragraph. This paragraph, the one preceding, and the one following all relate to Rom. 2:21.

that the devil seeks to overthrow particular Christians, only as he seeks to overthrow the church of God, which he does what he can to destroy, though God has promised that it shall never be destroyed).

377. JUDGES 14–16.[6] The history of Sampson. Sampson was charmed with the daughters of the uncircumcised Philistines, and as it were bewitched with them. These daughters represent those lusts, or objects of their lusts, with which men are charmed and infatuated. Sampson's uniting himself with these daughters of the Philistines proved his ruin. He had warning enough to beware of them before he was utterly destroyed by them. First he was deceived by one of them, and suffered great damage by her falseness, by the woman of Timnath. Though he loved her, she proved an enemy to him, and treacherously deprived him of thirty sheets and thirty change of garments; and then she was taken from him [Judg. 14:20]. She proved false to him, and left him; and he never enjoyed her [Judg. 15:1]. So she served him, as the objects of men's lusts often serve them; they promise them a great deal, but never afford 'em anything. They are like a pleasing shadow at a distance, that do us a great deal of damage in the pursuit; and when we come nigh them, and hope to embrace them, and to be paid for our damages, they afford us nothing but disappointment. Sampson's being thus served by a daughter of the Philistines might be a warning to him, not to be concerned with them any more. But after this Sampson was ensnared again, and went in to an harlot at Gaza, which suddenly brought him into eminent danger of his life, so that he very narrowly escaped, as in the beginning of ch. 16. But yet after this, he unites him[self] with Delilah, and had sufficient from her to make him sensible that she was his enemy time after time, had he not been utterly infatuated and bewitched; but yet he would not take warning, and at last she[7] deprived [him] of the seven locks of his head [Judg. 16:19], which signified the consideration and sense of the mind, and bringing a person to a stupid and senseless state. (See notes on Num. 6:5,[8] concerning the Nazarite's not shaving his head.) When

6. JE misnumbered the series at this point, omitting Nos. 371–376. However, in the "Blank Bible," he mistakenly referenced this entry as "No. 371."

7. JE deleted "betrayed him into the hands of the Philistines that."

8. JE suggests the prohibition against shaving the head signifies that the great purity of the Nazarites must not be profaned and that they are to devote their lives to "divine contemplations," because "the growing of the hair seemed to signify increasing in spiritual knowledge." JE also stated that Nazarites typify ministers who are to devote themselves to such contemplations ("Blank Bible").

persons' sense, consideration, and watchfulness is gone, their strength will soon be gone. And then God departed from Sampson, and [he] became the miserable, condemned captive and slave of the Philistines, who tormented him and insulted over him, made themselves sport in his misery [Judg. 16:21–25]; and at last it proved his death.

378. ISAIAH 31:9. "Saith the Lord, whose fire is in Zion, and his furnace in Jerusalem." I.e. there he has his throne of judgment, where he sits to judge the nations of the world, to try men as in a refiner's fire, to prove the righteous and justify them, and to consume the wicked. God, in judging, is represented in Scripture as doing the part of a refiner of metals. Mal. 3:2–3, "But who may abide the day of his coming, and who shall stand when he appeareth? For he is like a refiner's fire, and like fuller's soap; and he shall sit as a refiner and purifier of silver." The place where the refiner tries metals is where he has his furnace; and so the place whence God judges the nations of the world, and executes judgment and justice in the earth, is where he has established his throne, which is in Zion. There God is represented as having his throne, and from thence all his judgments that are executed on the earth are represented as proceeding. So in the 1st chapter of Amos, God's judgments upon Syria, and upon the Philistines, Tyrus, and Edom, and upon the Ammonites, are represented as proceeding from God in Zion and from Jerusalem, as v. 2, "The Lord will roar from Zion, and utter his voice from Jerusalem," together with what follows in that chapter. So God is represented as judging all nations from thence, in the last chapter of Joel, as vv. 16–17. "The Lord also shall roar out of Zion, and utter his voice from Jerusalem; and the heavens and the earth shall shake. . . . So shall ye know that I am the Lord your God dwelling in Zion, my holy mountain." And v. 21, "For the Lord dwelleth in Zion," together with the rest of the chapter. So it is said, Ps. 76:2–3, "In Salem also is his tabernacle, and his dwelling place in Zion. There brake he the arrows of the bow, the shield, and the sword, and the battle." So God is represented as judging the nations of the world out of Zion. Ps. 50:1–4, "The mighty God, even the Lord, hath spoken, and called the earth from the rising of the sun unto the going down thereof. Out of Zion, the perfection of beauty, hath God shined. Our God shall come, and shall not keep silence; a FIRE shall devour before him. . . . He shall call to the heavens from above, and to the earth, that he may judge his people." So Is. 2:3–4, "For out of Zion shall go forth the law, and the word of the Lord from Jerusalem. And

he shall judge among the nations, and shall rebuke many people." So here God is represented as judging the Assyrians from Mt. Zion. He that sits in Zion as a refiner is represented as bringing their young valiant men to the furnace there, and melting them in the fire; as in the foregoing verse, "his young men shall be for melting," as 'tis in the Hebrew.[9] So in the 33rd chapter, he is represented as destroying the enemies of Israel, as one that dwelleth on high, and fills Zion with judgment and righteousness[1] [vv. 3–5]. And as God's judgments on his enemies is represented as coming out of Zion, so is the salvation of his people, as Ps. 14:7, and 53:6, and 20:2, and 110:2, and 128:5, and 134:3. The Assyrians that besieged Jerusalem are represented as consumed by fire. Is. 9:5, "Every battle of the warrior is with confused noise, and garments rolled in blood; but this shall be with burning and fuel of fire."[2]

379. MATTHEW 22:31–32. "But as touching the resurrection of the dead, have ye not read that which was spoken unto you by God, saying, I am the God of Abraham, and the God of Isaac, and the God of Jacob? God is not the God of the dead, but of the living." The argument is very strong for the immortality of the soul, considering how often God manifested his great favor to those patriarchs in their lifetime, time after time entering into covenant with them, and professing himself to be their God, declaring to them that he was God all-sufficient, and that he was their shield and their exceeding great reward, promising that he would be with them and would bless them, and considering what great and manifold afflictions they met with while they lived, especially Abraham and Jacob, how little good they ever saw of those promises that God had made[3] in this life. God promised 'em the land of Canaan, but they were[4] pilgrims and strangers in it; they had no settled habitation in it, but dwelt in tents, removing to and fro. Other people had the possession of the land, and oftentimes molested them, as Abimelech in particular did [Gen. 20:2]. They were driven out of the land by famines; all three of them were so. Abraham came from a far country, left his own kindred and his father's house, and went out not knowing whither he went, for the sake of this land [Gen. 12:1]; but

9. וּבַחוּרָיו לָמַס יִהְיוּ.
1. MS: "Righteousness (~~See Isai 14.25~~)."
2. The last two sentences are a later addition.
3. JE deleted "and particularly those promises that was chiefly in."
4. MS: "will."

yet God gave him none inheritance in it, no, not so much as to set his foot on. Jacob had the promise of this land, but yet he was first driven out of the land by Esau, that had no promise of it [Gen. 27:41], and lived in exile from it twenty years for fear of him, in a state of servitude and in abundance of trouble. And in the latter part of his life he was forced to leave it, to go down into Egypt with all his family, and posterity, and flocks, and herds; and there he died. Though Canaan was the promised land, yet the principal quietness Jacob had in this world was in Egypt, that seventeen years he lived there with Joseph his son, and not in Canaan. Another thing that was chiefly insisted on in God's covenant with them was their being blessed in their posterity, that should be numerous and happy; but how little did they see of this while they lived. How long did Abraham wait before he had any child; and after he had one, he was[5] obliged to cast out his first child, greatly to his grief. And he was an hundred years old before he saw one child in whom his seed should be called, and then God gave him but one, so that he saw nothing like a numerous posterity while he lived. And Isaac never had but two sons, and concerning his eldest and best beloved, it was revealed that his seed was not to be called in him. And he was obliged to disinherit him, and he had a great deal of grief in him and his wives. And his other son, that was to be his heir, he was obliged to part with into a strange land, and saw him not for twenty years together. And Jacob, though he had a numerous family, yet he had abundance of sorrow and trouble in them. His eldest son committed incest with his own concubine [Gen. 35:22]; his two next sons were guilty of barbarous murder [Gen. 34:25–26]. Judah, in whose posterity chiefly it was that Jacob's posterity were to be blessed, behaved himself very sinfully [Gen. 38], and so, as doubtless, was greatly to his father's grief. Joseph, his best beloved son, he went long mourning for as lost and having come to an untimely and sorrowful end [Gen. 37:34]. The sons of the handmaids seem to have been none of the best beloved. Esau's posterity seem to have come to greater[6] prosperity than Jacob's, as Esau himself seems to have been vastly richer and more potent than his brother. Considering these things, how can it be imagined that God's so often speaking of it as so great, and inestimable, and distinguishing an happiness[7] that he had admitted them to, that he was their God, and insisting on these covenant promises that he made

5. JE deleted "forced to cast him."
6. MS: "Great."
7. MS: "~~Priviledge~~ ⟨Happiness⟩."

to them, as so exceeding great and precious, I say, how can it be imagined, but that God, in thus saying and promising, had respect to something that they should see and enjoy further than they ever enjoyed in this life? See No. 381.[8]

380. GENESIS 19:26. "But his wife looked back from behind her,[9] and she became a pillar of salt." What happened to Lot's wife, when she looked back as she was flying out of Sodom, is typical of what commonly happens to men that are guilty of backsliding, when they have begun to seek deliverance out of a state of sin and misery, and an escape from the wrath to come. She was there stiffened into a hard substance, which signifies the tendency that backsliding has to harden the heart. She became a senseless statue, which typifies the senselessness persons bring on them by backsliding. There she was fixed, and never got any further, which typifies the tendency that backsliding has to hinder persons ever escaping eternal wrath.

381. MATTHEW 22:31–32. Add this to No. 379. The same may be argued, and in some respects more strongly, from God's still revealing himself as "the God of Abraham, and the God of Isaac, and the God of Jacob," after they were dead. It was with respect to the promises that had been made to them while living, which it was known that they never saw the fulfillment of, never had received the promises, but had received a great deal of the contrary affliction. And therefore, if their being was now finally extinct, and they no more capable of seeing or enjoying the fulfillment of any promise, why should God mention and insist on his friendship, and love, and promises to them, as what still moved him to do great things for their sakes? And why should God still delight to characterize himself by his being their covenant God and friend, where there appeared so little foundation for it in any benefit that ever they had received by it, or were ever like to receive? It was because they were still capable of receiving the benefits of his favor and friendship, that he was "not ashamed to be called their God." Heb. 11:16, "But now they desire a better country, that is, an heavenly; wherefore God is not ashamed to be called their God, for he hath prepared for them a city." If it had not been for this, God's being their God, spoken of so much, and as so great a thing, would come to a very small matter, hardly worth the mentioning.

8. This cross-reference is a later addition.
9. KJV: "him."

From these things we may not only argue that the patriarchs continued to be, and did enjoy something after they were dead, but also that they lived to see and enjoy the fulfillment of those promises that were made to them, with respect to which it is that God calls himself their God, both before and after their death, and that their happiness in great part consisted in seeing the fulfillment of those promises in the course of his providence to their seed, i.e. in the dispensations of providence towards the church. And so I would argue that the happiness of departed souls in heaven, in great measure consists in beholding and contemplating God's glorious dispensations towards the church in this world, and seeing his wonderful wisdom, and infinite grace, and other perfections therein manifested, as the principal employment of great part of the heavenly hosts, viz. the holy angels, is about these things. That in which the angels do chiefly behold the manifold wisdom and other perfections of God is in these things, and the same is that wherein chiefly the souls of departed saints do chiefly behold God's glory. The fulfillment of the promises God made to him, concerning[1] what should be accomplished in and for his seed, and for the church of God after his death, he said was all his salvation and all his desire; and therefore doubtless great part of the happiness he enjoyed after his death consisted in fulfilling that desire of his. See "Miscellanies," no. 811, at the latter end of that number.[2]

382. GENESIS 48:21.[3] "And Israel said to Joseph, Behold, I die; but God shall be with you."[4] So Joseph, when he was near his death, said to his brethren after the like manner. Gen 50:24, "And Joseph said unto his brethren, I die; and God will surely visit you, and bring you out of this land unto the land which he sware to Abraham, to Isaac, and to Jacob." Thus the blessing of the presence of God with the children of Israel, and his favor and salvation, is consequent on the death of their father, and their brother, and savior, shadowing this forth, that the favor of God, and his presence, and salvation is by the death of Christ. He, when near death, said to his disciples, John 16:7, "It is expedient

1. JE deleted "the good they i he would do."
2. In no. 811, entitled "SEPARATE Souls of SAINTS in HEAVEN acquainted with what is done on earth," JE asserts that Christ's argument in Matt. 22 proves that the patriarchs were alive in heaven "to enjoy the fulfillment of those promises" made to them before their death.
3. JE began an entry on Ex. 1:6–7, but changed his mind. See below, No. 383.
4. JE deleted "So Christ, the antitype of Jacob, when he was going to die, said to his spiritual children."

for you that I go away: for if I go not away, the Comforter will not come unto you; but if I depart, I will send him unto you"; and elsewhere promises that the Father and the Son will come to 'em, and make their abode with them [John 14:23]. Isaac's and Jacob's blessing their children before their death, and as it were making over to them their future inheritance, may probably be typical of our receiving the blessings of the covenant of grace from Christ, as by his last will and testament, the final covenant of grace represented as his testament. Christ, in the 14th, 15th, 16th chapters of John, does as it were make his will, and conveys to his people their inheritance before his death, [in] particular the Comforter, or the Holy Spirit, which is the sum of the purchased inheritance.

383. EXODUS 1:6–7. "And Joseph died, and all his brethren, and all that generation. And the children of Israel were fruitful, and increased abundantly, and multiplied, and waxed exceeding mighty; and the land was filled with them." "After the death of Christ, our Joseph, his spiritual Israel began abundantly to increase; and his death had an influence upon it. It was like the sowing of a corn of wheat, which, 'if it die, bringeth forth much fruit' (John 12:24). From the call of Abraham, when God first told him he would make of him a great nation, to the deliverance of his seed out of Egypt, was 430 years, during the first 215 of which they were increased but to seventy; but in the latter half, those seventy multiplied to 600,000 fighting men. So sometimes God's providences may seem for a great while to thwart his promises, and go counter to them, that his people's faith may be tried, and his own power the more magnified. And though the performance of God's promises is sometimes slow, yet 'tis always sure; 'at the end it shall speak, and not lie' (Hab. 2:3)."[5]

384. EXODUS 2:5 ff. Add this to No. 159. Pharaoh's daughter came to wash herself in the same river into which Moses was cast. So if we would find Christ, and be the spiritual mothers of Christ, we must die with Christ, be "made conformable to his death" [Phil. 3:10], be "buried with him by baptism" [Rom. 6:4], must die to sin, must be crucified to the world [Gal. 6:14], and die to the law, and be willing to suffer affliction and persecution with him. By such mortification and humiliation is the soul washed in the river into which Christ was cast.

5. Henry, *Exposition, 1* (1725), 152.

385. EXODUS 7:9–10. Add this to No. 277.[6] Moses' rod, that had been a shepherd's staff to lead, protect, and comfort a flock of sheep, and by which Moses led and comforted Israel as a flock, when cast upon the land of Egypt, became a serpent, a terrible, hurtful, and destructive creature. So Christ, that is a shepherd to his people, is their protection and comfort, is destructive to unbelievers, "a stone of stumbling and a rock of offense" [I Pet. 2:8]; his salvation is poison to them through their rejection of it. They have a greater fall by the Second Adam than by the first, and Christ will at last be a lion to destroy them, as that pillar of cloud and fire, that gave light to the Israelites, was a cloud and darkness to the Egyptians [Ex. 14:20]. So the word of God (which is another thing signified by the rod), which is a means of the salvation of Israel, is a sword to destroy the Egyptians. Christ was represented by a serpent in the wilderness, because he was made sin *for* believers, but he will be made sin *to* unbelievers. He was made a curse for Israel, a serpent for them, but he will be the greatest curse to sinners, a terrible serpent to the Egyptians. So the savior of Israel proved the most dreadful destroyer of the Egyptians; and the word of God by Moses, which proved the salvation of his people, was their destruction. This seems to be one thing intended by this miracle, for there seems to be something threatening to the Egyptians. For the serpent had a very terrible appearance and motion, as appears by Moses' fleeing before it when he first tried the experiment at Mt. Sinai [Ex. 4:3]; it was something threatening of the plagues that were coming. God was pleased first to threaten the Egyptians, and give 'em warning of approaching judgments, before he began to execute 'em.

386. EXODUS 7:14–24. Concerning the plague of turning the waters of Egypt into blood. 1. It was "a dreadful plague," as upon other accounts, so upon this, that it was the death of the fish (v. 21). "And Ps. 105:29, he 'slew their fish.' Fish was much of their food (Num. 11:5). When another destruction of Egypt long after is threatened, the disappointment of those that made 'sluices and ponds for fish' is instanced in Isaiah 19:10. 2. It was a righteous plague, and justly inflicted upon the Egyptians. For, *First*, the river Nilus was an idol" that they worshiped. This is one instance wherein God executed judgment upon the gods of Egypt, as it is said. Moses is directed to meet Pharaoh by the riverside, as he went out to the river in the morning, probably to

---

6. JE deleted "Aaron's."

pay his morning devotions to this idol, that this judgment may be executed upon his god while he is worshiping it, and upon him for his idolatry while he is committing it. "*Secondly*, they had stained the river with the blood of the Hebrew children." They had sacrificed those children to that idol, and now God turned the river into blood. The bloodthirsty genius of that river, who was their god, had now blood enough. He had a river of nothing but blood; and the Egyptians, that shed innocent blood, had "blood to drink, for they were worthy (Rev. 16:6). 3. It was a significant plague; Egypt had a great dependence upon their river (Zech. 14:18), so that in smiting the river, they were warned of the destruction of all their products, till it came at last to their firstborn. And this red river proved a direful omen of the ruin of Pharaoh and all his forces in the Red Sea." Thus the first of the ten plagues was not only itself a great plague, but it was (as was fit) a fair and loud warning of those other greater plagues that would come if they continued obstinate. "This plague of Egypt is alluded [to] in the prediction of the ruin of the enemies of the New Testament church (Rev. 16:3–4). But there the sea, as well as the rivers and fountains of water, are turned into blood," for God's plagues upon the spiritual Egypt shall be much more dreadful than upon the temporal. "And it may be observed in general concerning this plague, that one of the first miracles Moses wrought was turning water into blood; but one of the first miracles our Lord Jesus wrought was turning water into wine [John 2:11]. For the law was given by Moses, and it was a dispensation of death and terror; but grace and truth, which like wine makes glad the heart, came by Jesus Christ." Henry.[7]

387. Acts 17:26–27. "And hath made of one blood all nations of men for to dwell on all the face of the earth, and hath determined the times before appointed, and the bounds of their habitation; that they should seek the Lord, if haply they might feel after him, and find him." I.e. God hath so ordered the state of the world of mankind, though scattered abroad upon the face of the earth, that provision should be made in providence at all times, that the nations of the world, if their heart had been well disposed to seek after the truth, might have had some means to have led 'em in their sincere and diligent inquiries to the knowledge of the true God and his ways, partly by making 'em all of one blood, and partly by an adjustment of the particular place and

7. *Exposition*, *1* (1725), 168.

limits of the habitation of the people that had the knowledge of the true religion, and might hold forth light to others, and the Gentiles that had it not, and the different times, changes, and circumstances of the world of mankind, that the bounds of their habitations and the state of the times might be so adapted one to another, that the Gentile world might always be under a capacity of receiving light from the Jews. The world had great advantage to obtain the knowledge of the true God by their being all "made of one blood"; by this means the knowledge of true religion was for some time kept up in the world by tradition. And there were soon great corruptions and apostasies crept in, and much darkness overwhelmed great part of the world. Yet there was so much light remained till Moses' time, that tradition and memory of things past would have afforded means sufficient to an honest, sincere, and faithful inquirer, to have come to the knowledge of the true religion, at least that, together with what there was here and there of revelation, here and there among those that still held the true religion (the bounds and limits of whose habitation was appointed and fixed to that end). And afterwards, even till Christ's time, there remained by tradition many scraps of truth among the heathen, that would greatly have served well-disposed inquirers as a clue in their search after truth.

About Moses' time, when truth, that had been upheld by tradition, was very much lost, and former things became much out of sight by being far off, and the professors of the true religion, excepting in the posterity of Jacob, very much ceased in the world, God took care that there might be something new, [which] should be very public, and of great fame, and much taken notice of abroad, in the world heard, that might be sufficient to lead sincere inquirers to the true God; and those were the great things God wrought in Egypt, and at the Red Sea, and in the wilderness, for the children of Israel. Those things were very publicly wrought. Egypt, where many of them were wrought, was one of the most noted heathen nations in the world. And we often read how that those great miracles that God wrought actually were taken notice of by the heathen nations round about; and probably most, if not all, the heathen nations heard of them[8] (See Ex. 9:16, "And in very deed for this cause have I raised thee up," etc.), for then the bounds of their habitations were so appointed, that they did not live near so much dispersed abroad as afterwards they did. See Gen. 41:56–57.

8. JE interlined and then deleted "See Deut. 2:25."

They were probably almost all within hearing of these great things which, it is likely, became yet more public, and were carried further abroad in the world, together with other great things that God did in Canaan, when the sun stood still [Josh. 10:13] (which was a miracle done in the presence of the whole world), and Joshua had conquered that land, and multitudes of the inhabitants were driven out and went, some to Africa, to Carthage and other parts, and to the isles of the sea, to many parts of Europe as well as Asia, to carry the tidings of those things, and to interpret the miracle of the sun's standing still; so that, in a manner, the whole world heard of these great things. See Deut. 2:25, "This day will I begin to put the dread of thee and the fear of thee upon the nations that are under the whole heaven, who shall hear report of thee, and shall tremble, and be in anguish because of thee." And the memory of these things was kept up a great while among the nations, as appears by the accounts we have of the occasional mention, which the neighbor nations from time to time make of them, till about David's time, when the memory of those things began to be lost among them. And then God did new things to make his people Israel, who had the true religion, [be] taken notice of in the heathen [nations], viz. his subduing all the nations from Euphrates to Egypt under David, and setting Israel at the head of the greatest empire in the world, in his days and the days of his son Solomon (This there is respect to in many such passages in the Psalms, as that, Ps. 98:2, though there be also a prophetic respect to what should be in gospel days.),[9] and the great wisdom and prosperity of Solomon, and the great things that were done by him, the fame of which filled the world to the utmost bounds of it, though by that time God had enlarged the bounds of their habitation. That one design of providence in these things was that the heathen nations might hear the fame of the God of Israel, and so have opportunity to come to the knowledge of him, is confirmed by I Kgs. 8:41–43. The memory of these things kept up the fame of that nation and of their God for several hundred years. They were remembered till the Jews were carried captive into Babylon, as appears by the mention that the enemies of the Jews make of them in their letter to Artaxerxes, and by Artaxerxes' answer in the 4th chapter of Ezra. But then, when the memory of those things was decaying, and the bounds of the habitation of the heathen nations was enlarged, God altered the place of the habitation of his people, and carried them to Babylon, the

9. This parenthesis is a later interlineation.

mistress of the world, where some of them, especially Daniel and his companions, raised the fame of the true God, and caused it to go from thence through the world, by the great things he wrought by and for them, and also by what he wrought for Daniel in Persia. After this, the appointed bounds of the Jews' habitation were not the limits of any one land, but they were dispersed all over the world, as they were very much in Esther's time, when they were a people very famous through the world by what was done respecting [them] in her time, and afterwards were much more dispersed abroad in the world, and so remained till Christ's time; so that the heathen world had opportunity by them to have come to the knowledge of the true God.

God appointed the particular place of the habitation of the Jews to be as it were in the midst of the earth, between Asia, Africa, and Europe; and in the great contests there were between the great empires of the world, they were always in the way. And before the days of the gospel, the bounds of the world of mankind seem not to have been near so extensive as since; and particularly, 'tis probable that America has been wholly peopled[1] since. See Is. 45:19; Ezek. 5:5.[2]

388. EXODUS 10:21–23. Concerning the plague of darkness.

"1. It was a total darkness. We have reason to think, not only that the lights of heaven were clouded, but that all their fires and candles were put out by the damps, or clammy vapors, which were the cause of this darkness, for 'tis said, v. 23, that 'they saw not one another.' 'Tis threatened to the wicked, Job. 18:5–6, that 'the spark of his fire shall not shine' (even the sparks of his own kindling, as they are called, Is. 50:11), and that 'the light shall be dark in his tabernacle.' Hell is utter darkness. 'The light of a candle shall no more at all shine in thee' (Rev. 18:23).

"2. That it was darkness which might be felt (v. 21), felt in its causes by their fingers' ends, so thick were the fogs felt in its effects (some think) by their eyes, which were pricked with pain, and made the more sore by their rubbing them. Great pain is spoken of as the effect of that darkness, Rev. 16:10, which alludes to this.

"3. No doubt it was very frightful and amazing. The tradition of the Jews is, that in this darkness they were terrified by the apparition of evil spirits, or rather, by dreadful sounds and murmers which they made. And this is the plague which some think is intended (for other-

1. MS: "people."
2. These references are later additions.

wise it is not mentioned at all there) in Ps. 78:49. He poured 'upon them the fierceness of his anger by sending evil angels among them.'

"4. It continued three days; six nights, saith Bishop Hall, in one; so long were they imprisoned by those chains of darkness, and the most lightsome palaces were perfect dungeons. No man rose from his place (v. 23). They were all confined to their houses, and such a terror seized them that few of them had the courage to go from the chair to the bed, or from the bed to the chair. Thus were they 'silent in darkness' (I Sam. 2:9). Now Pharaoh had time to consider, if he would have improved it. Spiritual darkness is spiritual bondage; while Satan blinds men's minds that they see not, he binds their hands and feet that they work not for God, nor move towards heaven. They sit in darkness.

"Let us dread the consequences of sin. If three days darkness was so dreadful, what will everlasting darkness be?" Henry.[3]

389. EZEKIEL 1. Concerning Ezekiel's wheels.[4] Divine providence is most aptly represented by the revolution or course of these wheels. Things in their series and course in providence, they do as it were go round like a wheel in its motion on the earth. That which goes round like a wheel goes from a certain point or direction, till it gradually returns to it again. So is the course of things in providence.

God's providence over the world consists partly in his governing the natural world according to the course and laws of nature. This consists wholly as it were in the revolution of wheels. So the annual changes that appear in the natural world are as it were by the revolution of a wheel, or the course of the sun through that great circle, the ecliption,[5] or the ring of that great wheel, the zodiac. And so the[6] monthly changes are by the revolution of another lesser wheel within that greater annual wheel, which, being a lesser wheel, must go round oftener to make the same progress. Ezekiel's vision was of wheels within wheels, of lesser wheels within greater, which all went round as though running upon several parallel planes, each touching the circumference of its respective wheel, and all making the same progress, keeping pace one with another; and therefore the lesser wheels must go round so much oftener, according as their circumference was less. So again, the diurnal changes in the natural world are by the revolu-

3. *Exposition, 1* (1725), 175–76.
4. JE wrote "Ezekiel's Wheels No. 389" as a running head on the pages of this entry.
5. I.e. the ecliptic.
6. JE deleted "diurnal changes in the face of nature are also by the."

tion of a wheel still within the monthly wheel, and going round about thirty times in one revolution of the other. ++ Here add No. 394.

So 'tis with the motion of the air in the winds; it goes and returns according to its circuits. And so it is with the motion of the water in the tides, and in their course out of the sea, and into the clouds, springs, and rivers, and into the sea again. So it is with the circulation of the blood in a man's body, and the bodies of other animals. So it is with the life of man; it is like the revolution of a wheel. He is from the earth, and gradually rises, and then gradually falls, and returns to the earth again. Dust we are, and unto dust we return [Gen. 3:19]. We come naked out of our mother's womb, and naked must we go and return as we came, as it were into our mother's womb. The dust returns to earth as it was, and the spirit returns to God who gave it. So 'tis with the world of mankind; it is, the whole of it, like a wheel. It as it were sinks, and goes down to the earth in one generation, and rises in another, as 'tis with a wheel; at the same time that one side is falling to the earth, another part of the wheel is rising from the earth. Solomon takes notice of these things, Eccles. 1:4–8. "One generation passeth away, and another cometh; but the earth abideth forever. The sun also ariseth, and the sun goeth down, and hasteth to the place where he arose. The wind goeth toward the south, and turneth about unto the north; it whirleth about continually, and the wind returneth again according to his circuits. All the rivers run into the sea, yet the sea is not full; unto the place from whence the rivers come, thither they return again. All things are full of labor; man cannot utter it."

So it is in the course of things in God's providence over the intelligent and moral world; all is the motion of wheels. They go round and come to the same again; and the whole series of divine providence, from the beginning to the end, is nothing else but the revolution of certain wheels, greater and lesser, the lesser being contained within the greater. What comes to pass in the natural world is, in this respect, typical of what comes to pass in the moral and intelligent world, and seems to be so spoken of by the wise man in that forementioned place in Ecclesiastes. The words that follow next, after those that were mentioned respecting the natural world, do respect the intelligent world. Vv. 9–10, "The thing that hath been, it is that which shall be; and that which is done, is that which shall be done. And there is no new thing under the sun," etc.

Things in their series and course in providence do as it were return to the same point or place whence they began, as in the turning of a wheel; but yet not so, but that a further end is obtained than was at first, or the same end is obtained in a much further degree. So that in the general there is a progress towards a certain final issue of things, and every revolution brings nearer to that issue, as 'tis in the motion of a wheel upon the earth, as in the motion of the wheels of a chariot, and not like the motion of a wheel by its axis, for if so, its motion would be in vain.

The entire series of [7] events in the course of things through the age of the visible universe may fitly be represented by one great wheel, exceeding high and terrible, performing one great revolution. In the beginning of this revolution, all things come from God, and are formed out of a chaos; and in the end, all things shall return into a chaos again, and shall return to God, so that he that is the Alpha will be the Omega. This great wheel contains a lesser wheel, that performs two revolutions while that performs one. The first begins at the beginning of the world, and ends at the coming of Christ, and at the ending of the Old Testament dispensation, which is often represented as the end of the world in Scripture. The first revolution began with the creation of the world; so the second revolution began with the creation of new heavens and a new earth.

The course of things, from the beginning of the world to the coming of [Christ], may be represented as one great wheel performing one revolution. All things in the beginning of this revolution were from Christ, the Creator of man; and the whole motion henceforward till Christ came was to bring things about to Christ again, and to prepare the way for his coming, and to introduce him as the Redeemer of man. This wheel contains a lesser wheel, that performs two revolutions while the great one does one: the first revolution ending at the calling of Abraham, at which time God did as it were plant the tree of his church anew, that he had planted at first in his revealing the covenant of grace to Adam; the second ending at the coming of Christ, the promised seed of Abraham and his antitype, in whom all the families of the earth are blessed, and in whom the church was planted anew and in a far more glorious manner.

The course of things from the beginning of the world to the flood may be looked upon as the revolution of a wheel. At the beginning of it, God created the world, and the face of the earth was covered with waters, and the world was all of one man and his posterity. At the end

---

7. JE deleted "divine."

of it, the world was destroyed and reduced to the same state again; the world was covered with waters, and the world of mankind was begun anew with one man and his posterity. The course of things from the flood to Abraham was as it were the revolution of another wheel, or another revolution of the same wheel. As at the beginning of it, the world was corrupt, and therefore one man and his family separated to be the father of the church; so it was again at the end of it. The space from Abraham to Moses was as it were another revolution of the same wheel; for as God established his covenant with Abraham, and then separated his church from the heathen in calling Abraham out of Chaldee and Syria, so in the end of it he again renewed his covenant, and again separated his church from the heathen world by bringing of them up out of Egypt. From Moses and Joshua to Samuel, David, and Solomon, was another revolution of the same wheel. As in the beginning of it, God gave the spirit of prophecy to Moses, so he renewed it in Samuel. As in the beginning of it, God gloriously conquered the enemies of Israel, and settled them in Canaan in peace by the hand of Moses and Joshua, so in the end of it, God gloriously subdued the enemies of Israel, and subdued the remains of the old inhabitants of Canaan and the nations round about, and gave 'em the full and peaceable possession of the land of promise, in the full extent of it, from the river Euphrates to the river of Egypt. The space from David and Solomon to the return out of the captivity is another revolution of the same wheel. In the beginning of it, the temple was built; in the end, it was[8] built again, and the temple of worship and the courses of the priests and Levites again restored, that David and Solomon had established. And the church state of the Jews, as it had been settled by David and Solomon, was again renewed. From the return out of the captivity till Christ came and established the Christian dispensation, is another revolution of the same wheel. At the beginning of it, God redeemed the church out of Babylon; at the end of it, he redeemed his church from sin and Satan, accomplished that great redemption, of which the redemption from the Babylonish captivity was a great type.

The course of things during the Jewish state was as it were the revolution of a great [wheel]. This course, as it respects the national state of that people, began with Abraham, Isaac, and Jacob, the fathers of that nation; the national state of that people was then in its infancy. The wheel then began to rise from the ground, and it rose

8. JE deleted "destroyed."

to the height in Solomon's time, when the temple was built, and Solomon's kingdom [was] in its greatest prosperity, which was at about the middle of the space between the birth and calling of Abraham and Christ, and the destruction of Jerusalem. Thenceforward they declined in numbers, and wealth, and strength, till they came to the ground again, when Christ came, and Jerusalem was destroyed by the Romans. That state, with respect to their ecclesiastical constitution, began in Moses, the first prophet, and came to the height in Isaiah's time, that most evangelical prophet, who lived about the middle of the space between Moses and Christ, and came to the ground again in Christ's time. It was with the Jewish state in this respect, as 'tis with the life of man, which I before showed was as the revolution of a wheel, that began at the ground, and gradually rose to the height, and then gradually came to the ground again. So it is with kingdoms and empires; their state and course is very much like the revolution of a wheel, beginning at the ground, and rising to the height, and coming to the ground again. So it was with the four great monarchies of the world, and so it is with the reign of Antichrist, and the continuance of the Mahometan empire, and other states and kingdoms. And when nation or kingdom comes to the ground, another comes to the greatest height, that before was at the ground, as 'tis with the different parts of a wheel in motion.

The space of time from Christ to the end of the world is as the revolution of a great wheel. In the beginning of it, Christ comes into the world, and the wicked Jews were judged at the destruction of Jerusalem, and after them the wicked heathen world in Constantine's time; and the old world comes to an end, and the church's glory follows. And then things in the Christian church gradually sink, till they come to the ground in the darkest times of Antichrist, and then gradually rise again, till Christ comes again, and judges the world, and destroys the church's enemies, and destroys the old heaven and earth; and then the church's glory follows.

The whole series of things through the age of the world may be represented as a wheel of various rings, one within another and less than another, each one going round but once, the lesser ones finishing their revolution soonest, and each beginning at the creation of the old heavens and earth, which in some respects had different beginnings, one when Adam was created, another in Noah's time, the settling of the world after the building of Babel, and another at the establishment of the Jewish state. And the revolution of each wheel ends in an end of the world, and a day of judgment, and a creation of new heavens and a new earth. The least wheel finishes its revolution at the coming of Christ, and the[9] destruction of Jerusalem, and overthrow of the heathen empire that followed, when the world in a sense came to an end, and there was a day of judgment,[1] which began at the creation of the Jewish state in the time of Abraham, Isaac, Jacob, and Moses, and Joshua, and the total apostasy of the Gentile world to heathenism. The next wheel, which is larger, began its revolution at Noah's coming out of the ark, and the building of Babel, and dispersing of nations, and settling the world from thence, which is as it were another beginning of the world, and ends at the destruction of Antichrist, or the spiritual Babylon, and Satan's visible kingdom on earth, which began in the building of Babel, and the commencing of the glorious times of the church. This is another end of the world, and day of judgment, and building of the new heavens and new earth. The third and greatest wheel begins its revolution at the creation, and finishes at Christ's second coming to judge the world and destroy heaven and earth, in a literal sense.

Every wheel in every revolution begins and proceeds from God, and returns to God; as in Ezekiel's vision, God is represented as appearing above the wheels, so that to him they continually returned. God remarkably appears both in the beginning and ending of each of these wheels that have been mentioned, especially in those that respect the state of the church of God. As to human [things], such as human kingdoms and empires, they rise from the earth, and return to the ground again; but spiritual things begin their revolution from God on high, and thither they return again.

The changes that are in the world with respect to the profession of the truth, and rise and fall of heresies, is very much like the motion of wheels; they rise and fall, and rise and fall again.

Those wheels in this vision are represented as God's chariot wheels. The world is the chariot of Jesus Christ, the Son of God, in which he makes his progress to that glory, that glorious marriage with his spouse, that eternal feast, that everlasting kingdom of rest, and love, and joy, which the Father hath designed him. * Add here No. 391.

This chariot is drawn on those wheels by the four animals, which denote God's power, wisdom, justice, and mercy; and all proceed on

9. JE deleted "pouring out of the Holy Ghost."
1. JE deleted "the next finished its revolution."

calves' feet, because the great work of providence, that is as it were the sum of all providences, is that work of mercy, the work of redemption.[2]

390. EXODUS 5–11 and 14.[3] Concerning Pharaoh's hardness of heart and obstinacy in refusing to let the children of Israel go, and the manner of God's dealing with him. In Pharaoh's behavior is very livelily represented the behavior of impenitent sinners when the subjects of reproofs [and] corrections for their sins, and under convictions of conscience, and warnings, and fears of future wrath, with respect to parting with their sins, or letting go the objects of their lusts. And indeed it is an instance of it, for Pharaoh, in refusing to let the people go, refused to let go the objects of his lusts; in keeping them in bondage, he kept his sins. His pride was gratified in his dominion over that people. He was loath to let them go, because he was loath to part with his pride. His covetousness was also gratified by the profits he had by their slavery; he would not let them go, because he would not part with the object of his covetousness.

God commanded him to let the people go; he sent his commands from time to time by the hand of Moses and Aaron, and warned him of the ill consequence if he refused. So God counsels and warns sinners in his word by his ministers. God first made known his will to Pharaoh in a mild and gentle manner[4] (ch. 5 at the beginning),[5] but that was so far from being effectual that he was only the worse for it. Instead of letting the people go, he only increased their burdens. So God is wont, in the first place, to use gentle means with sinners; but impenitent sinners are not the better, but the worse, for the gracious calls and counsels of the word of God. They sin with the greater contempt for it, as Pharaoh took God's command in disdain. He said, "Who is the Lord, that I should obey his voice?" [Ex. 5:2]. Then God proceeded to lay greater matter of conviction before Pharaoh, and to warn him of the mischief [that] would come upon him by his refusal, by turning the rod into a serpent. (See notes on that miracle, Ex. 7.)[6] And when he still hardened his heart, then God[7] began to chastise him by turning the waters into blood, which was not only a chastisement, but also a clear

2. See *Works*, 9, 517–18.
3. JE wrote "Pharaoh's Obstinacy and God's Dealings with him. 390" as a running head on the pages of this entry.
4. JE deleted "and when that did not succeed."
5. JE deleted "and what that did not do then."
6. See above, Nos. 277 and 385.
7. JE deleted "proceed to correct."

and loud warning of the future destruction he would bring upon himself by his obstinacy. (See notes on that plague.)[8] So God is wont to give sinners fair warning of the misery [and] the danger of their sins before he destroys them. After this, when God's hand pressed Pharaoh, and he was exercised with fears of God's future wrath, he entertained some thoughts of letting the people go, and promised he would do it; but from time to time he brake his promises when he saw there was respite. So sinners are often wont to do under convictions of conscience and fears of wrath. They have many thoughts of parting with their sins, but there is never a divorce actually made between them and their lusts. 'Tis common for sinners, when under afflictive and threatening dispensations of providence, to make promises of amendment, as in times of sore sickness, and when in danger of death and damnation, but soon to forget them when God's hand is removed and future damnation more out of sight. In such cases sinners are wont to beg the prayers of ministers, that God would remove his hand and restore them again, as Pharaoh begs the prayers of Moses and Aaron.[9] Ex. 8:8, "Then Pharaoh called for Moses and Aaron, and said, Entreat the Lord, that he may take away the frogs from me, and from my people; and I will let the people go, that they may do sacrifice unto the Lord." And so v. 28; so Ex. 9:27–28, and 10:16–17. Pharaoh was brought by God's judgments and terrors to confess his sin with seeming humility,[1] as Ex. 9:27. "And Pharaoh sent, and called for Moses and Aaron, and said unto them, I have sinned this time. The Lord is righteous, and I and my people are wicked." This was when there were mighty thunderings, as it follows in the next verse. "Entreat the Lord that there may be no more mighty thunderings." So Ex. 10:16–17, "And he said, I have sinned against the Lord your God, and against you. Now therefore forgive, I pray thee, my sin only this once." So sinners, oftentimes under affliction and danger of future wrath, and when God thunders upon their consciences, seem very penitent, and humble, and are much in confessing their sins, but yet have not their

8. See above, No. 386. JE also commented on Ex. 7:19–21 in the "Blank Bible," where, citing Thomas Stackhouse's *Complete Body of Divinity*, he compared the bloodthirstiness of the Egyptians in Moses' time to that of "spiritual Egypt" in later times. In both cases, those who shed the blood of innocents were forced to drink bloody water.

9. JE was drawing on his own ministerial experience in this comment. See Stephen J. Stein, "'For Their Spiritual Good': The Northampton, Massachusetts, Prayer Bids of the 1730s and 1740s," *William and Mary Quarterly*, 3rd ser., 37 (1980), 261–85.

1. JE deleted "so are sinners under are sinners oftentimes under afflictions and dangerous dispensations."

hearts divorced from them, have no thorough disposition to forsake them.

Pharaoh, in the struggle there was between his conscience and his lusts, was for contriving that God might be served, and he enjoy his lusts that were gratified by the slavery of the children of Israel. Moses kept insisting upon it, that God should be served and sacrificed to. Pharaoh was willing to consent to that, but he would have it done without his parting with the children of Israel. Ex. 8:25, "And Pharaoh called for Moses and Aaron, and said, Go ye, sacrifice to your God in the land." So 'tis oftentimes with sinners under fears of divine wrath; they are for contriving to serve God, and enjoy their lusts too. They are willing to be very devout in many duties of religion, but without parting with their beloved sins. How do some wicked men amongst the papists and elsewhere seem to abound in acts of devotion! How much pains do they take! How much trouble and cost are they at! They are like the Samaritans that worshiped the God of Israel, and served their own gods too. So did the Jews. Jer. 7:9–10, "Will ye steal, murder, and commit adultery, and swear falsely, and burn incense unto Baal, and come and stand before me in this house?" And Ezek. 23:39, "For when they had slain their children to their idols, then they came the same day into my sanctuary to profane it; and lo, thus have they done in the midst of mine house." Moses objected against[2] complying with Pharaoh's contrivance and proposal in this matter, that serving God and continuing in the land of Egypt among the Egyptians in slavery to them did not agree together, and were inconsistent one with another; that the Egyptians, their taskmasters, would abhor that service that God required, and would not tolerate it, but would kill God's worshipers. And therefore there was a necessity of a separation to be made between Israelites and Egyptians in order to God's being served. So the service of God and our still continuing in the service of our lusts are inconsistent one with another; as Christ says, "Ye cannot serve God and mammon" [Matt. 6:24]. There is a necessity of forsaking one in order to cleave to the other. If we retain our sins, if we don't part from them, [they] will kill those duties wherewith God is served.

When Pharaoh saw that it would not be consented to, that the people should only sacrifice to their God in the land, then he consented to let them go, provided they would not go far away; he was not willing to part with them finally, and therefore would not let them go clear, but

---

2. JE deleted "their sacrificing."

would have 'em within reach, that he might bring 'em back again. So it is often with sinners with respect to their sins; they will refrain a while from them, but won't wholly part with them, taking an everlasting leave of them, quitting all hopes or expectations of ever having anything more to do with them.

Afterwards, when God's plagues came still harder upon Pharaoh, he consented to let the men go, if they would leave the women and children (Ex. 10:8–10). And then after that, when God's hand pressed him still more sorely, he consented that they should go, men, women, and children, provided that they would leave their cattle behind them; but he was not willing to let them go, and all that they had (Ex. 10:24). So it oftentimes is with sinners, when pressed with God's judgments or fears of future wrath. They are brought to be willing to part with some of their sins, but not all; they are brought to part with the more gross acts, but not so to part with their lusts in lesser indulgences of 'em, whereas we must part with all our sins, little and great, and all that belong to 'em. Men, women, children, and cattle, they must all be let go, with their young and with their old, with their sons and with their daughters, with their flocks and with their herds. There must not be an hoof left behind. At last, when it came to extremity, Pharaoh consented to let the people all go, and all that they had; but he was not steadfastly of that mind. He soon repented, and pursued after them again. And then, when he was guilty of such backsliding, he was destroyed without remedy, which is often the case with sinners. Note, when there is only a forced parting with sin, though it be universal, yet 'tis not sincere, nor is it like to be persevering.[3]

God exercised abundance of patience with Pharaoh before he destroyed him, and the warnings that were given him were louder and louder, and God's judgments upon him greater and greater,[4] and God's hand and design in them became more and more manifest. First, God only sends a command from him, directing Moses to deliver it, and let it be accompanied with humble entreaties, paying him the honor due to a king (Ex. 3:18, and 5:3). After that, Moses spake with more authority: God made him "a god to Pharaoh," and he more beseeched him as a subject (Ex. 7.1), and his word was confirmed by miracles. But in the first place, the miracles were such as did not hurt them, but only warn them, as that turning the rod into a serpent. And

---

3. This sentence is a later interlineation.
4. JE deleted "and then God holding forth clearer and clearer instruction."

then God proceeded to miracles that were hurtful, which yet were imitated by the magicians. But then God proceeded further, to do things that the magicians could not imitate, but themselves confessed manifested the finger of God. And then, that the evidence might be still clearer, and God's meaning in these plagues plainer, God proceeded to[5] sever between the land of Goshen, where the children of Israel dwelt, and the rest of Egypt. And then in the next plague, God severed even between the cattle of Israel and the cattle of Egypt. And then the next plague, the plague of boils and blains, was not only beyond what the magicians could do, but the magicians themselves were the subjects of the plague, and were grievously tormented, so that they could not stand before Moses. And this plague were brought upon them by the ashes of the furnace, wherein they employed the children of Israel in their slavery in burning the brick they made, that Pharaoh might see wherefore God was thus angry and did so chastise him. After this, Pharaoh was more particularly and fully warned, in the warning of God by his word, than ever before, and was forewarned what those plagues would at last come to, if he continued still obstinate (Ex. 9:13–19). And then after this, God brought the plague of hail and thunder, that was more terrifying and threatening than any heretofore; and then to complete the destruction caused by the hail, the locusts were sent to eat up what the hail had left. Then came the plague of darkness with frightful apparitions of evil angels (see notes),[6] which was more terrifying still than any that had gone before; and the distinction made in it between the children of Israel and the Egyptians was more remarkable, for they had light in their dwellings, not only in Goshen, but in other dwellings where they dwelt mingled with the Egyptians. And then before that great destruction by the last plague, Pharaoh was again particularly warned of what was coming, and when, and in what manner it would come, much more fully and particularly than ever (Ex. 11:4–8). And then came the last and greatest plague that preceded Pharaoh's own destruction, attended with the greatest tokens of God's wrath, and[7] a remarkable distinction between the Israelites and the Egyptians. And last of all, Pharaoh himself, with all the prime of Egypt, was destroyed in the Red Sea.

5. JE deleted "make a distinction be."
6. See above, No. 388. JE also wrote a brief entry on Ex. 10:23, based on Matthew Henry's *Exposition*, comparing the distinction made between the Israelites and the Egyptians in this plague and that later during the death of the firstborn ("Blank Bible").
7. JE deleted "the most visible dist."

391. EZEKIEL 1. Add this to No. 389, "Concerning Ezekiel's wheels," towards the close, at this mark *. What Ezekiel here saw was designed to represent God's chariot, in which God rode, and those wheels are the wheels of his chariot. And God, who sat in his throne above the firmament, over those wheels and[8] cherubim, is represented as in the seat in which he rides, and makes progress with the wheels and cherubim. God came to Ezekiel to speak to him, and give him his mission on this chariot, and is so represented in the first chapter. In the second and third chapters, we have an account what he said to him from this seat. In the 12th and 13th verses of the third chapter, we have an account of his departure, when he had done speaking with him, which was with "a great rushing," and noise of the wings of the cherubim, and the noise of the wheels. God rode on these cherubim, as those that drew his chariot, as 'tis said, Ps. 18:10, "He rode on a cherub, and did fly." And Ps. 68:17, "The chariots of God are twenty thousand, even thousands of angels." And therefore God, in being on the chariot drawn by these cherubims, is said to be upon the cherub. Ezek. 9:3, "And the glory of the God of Israel was gone up from the cherub, whereupon he was, to the threshold of the house." And God appeared about to leave the temple; and his glory departed from off this threshold into this same chariot (Ezek. 10:18, with the foregoing verses). And then it is said, "the cherubims lift up their wings, and mounted up from the earth" in his sight, and the wheels also went beside them, "and the glory of the God of Israel was over them above" [v. 19]. And after this, Ezek. 11:22–23, God is represented as departing in this manner up out of the midst of the city, ascending up to the top of Mt. Olivet, being about from thence to ascend into heaven, from whence this same person afterwards ascended after his resurrection. (See notes on that verse.)[9] And when it was represented in vision to Ezekiel, how God would afterwards return to the city and temple in those happy days that were to come, he is represented as returning in the same manner (Ezek. 43:2–4).

This chariot represents the world, which is confirmed by this, that one part of it is called the "firmament," which was the upper part, but

8. JE deleted "che living."

9. Commenting on the departure of the "glory of the Lord" from Jerusalem before its destruction by the Babylonians in Ezek. 11:23, JE states that "it was now the same person that ascended, that afterwards ascended hence in his human nature." JE also asserts that "he ascended from the same mountain, from whence he afterwards ascended when he left them before their second destruction by the Romans" ("Blank Bible").

yet the pavement of it, above which was the seat of God, who sat and rode in this chariot, agreeable to that in Deut. 33:26, "Who rideth on the heaven in thine help, and in his excellency on the sky." And Ps. 68:4, "Extol him that rideth upon the heavens by his name Jah." And v. 33, "To him that rideth upon the heaven of heavens, which were of old." God appeared here on the same pavement as he appeared to the seventy elders on Mount Sinai. See notes on Ex. 24:10.[1] What is signified by the wheels, which were under the firmament but above or upon the earth, is God's providence in this visible world, especially respecting mankind that dwell on the earth.

Christ was the person that appeared riding in this chariot, as[2] is confirmed from that, that he appeared in the likeness of a man (v. 26), and also from the description that is given of his appearance. See notes on v. 27.[3]

Corol. Hence I would argue, that the affairs of heaven have doubtless great respect to the affairs of this lower world and God's providence here, and that the church in heaven, in the progress it makes in its state of glory and blessedness, keeps pace with the church on earth, that the glory of both is advanced together. Those great dispensations of providence, by which glorious things are brought to pass for the church on earth, are accompanied with like advances made at the same time in the church in heaven; and also that the affairs of the church in heaven have some way or other a dependence on God's providence towards his church on earth, and that their progress is dependent on the progress of things in God's providence towards his church here. For heaven and earth are both framed together. 'Tis the same chariot; one part has relation to another, and is connected with another, and is all moved together. The motion of one part depends on the motion of the other. The upper part moves on the wheels of the lower part, for heaven is the room and seat of the chariot that is above the firmament, that moves on the wheels that are under the firmament, and that go upon the earth. When those wheels are moved by the cherubim, then the

---

1. According to JE, Mount Sinai was a "type of heaven." The surface of the mountain was described as "a paved work of a sapphire stone," which JE links with "an azure, or sky, color" and "with the pavement that appeared under God's seat in Ezekiel's chariot" ("Blank Bible"). He equates the pavement of heaven with the sky or firmament.

2. JE deleted "pe may be argued."

3. JE stated that Jesus was the man in Ezekiel's vision. He explains the amber, or "flesh color," as representing the human nature of Christ, and the fire as his "divine nature." But amber also resembles gold, and therefore in Ezek. 1:27 it represents "both Christ's incarnation and his preciousness" ("Blank Bible").

upper part moves; when they stop, that stops; and wherever the wheels go, that goes. 'Tis on these wheels that Christ, the King of heaven, in his throne in heaven, makes progress to the final issue of all things. 'Tis on the wheels of his providence that move on earth that he, on his throne in heaven, makes progress towards the ultimate end of the creation of both heaven and earth, and the ultimate end of all the affairs of both. For this is the end of the journey of the whole chariot, both wheels and throne, for both are moving towards the same journey's end; and the motion of all is by the wheels on earth. And if so, doubtless 'tis on those wheels that all the inhabitants of heaven, both saints and angels, are carried towards their ultimate end, for all are Christ's family; they are either his servants and attendants in the affair of redemption, which is the grand movement of the wheels, and are the ministers that draw the wheels, or are his members[4] and parts of his body.

This therefore confirms that the saints and angels in heaven do make progress in knowledge and happiness, by what they see of God's works on earth. We know that all the happiness of the saints in heaven is entirely dependent on those great things that Christ did on earth in the work of redemption, as it was purchased by it. And there is reason to think that their knowledge and glory is, in other respects, by what they see of those great works of providence which God carries on [in] the world, in the prosecution of the grand design of redemption.

See "Miscellanies," nos. 804, and 805, and 811, and 776, 777, and 778.[5]

392. ROMANS 2:29. Add this to No. 365. When Christ and his apostles so much warned against judging others, they doubtless had especially respect to judging their hearts. And Christians in those days understood this to be the thing so strictly prohibited, and a practice marked out as so presumptuous, as is confirmed by the manner of the apostle James introducing what he says, in the 2nd chapter of his

---

4. MS: "member."

5. The "Miscellanies" entries referenced here focus on the knowledge the saints in heaven have of the state of the church on earth. No. 777 asserts, the "HAPPINESS of HEAVEN is PROGRESSIVE, and has various periods in which it has a new and glorious advancement, and consists very much in BEHOLDING the manifestations that God makes of himself in the WORK OF REDEMPTION." Likewise, the misery that is enacted on the devils and the souls in Satan's kingdom is progressive (no. 805). The saints in heaven are acquainted with all aspects of the dispensations of providence on earth, and the glory of the church in heaven is "advanced by like steps and degrees at the same time" (no. 804). No. 804 contains a cross-reference to this corollary in No. 391.

epistle, at the 4th verse. Speaking of their preferring of a man of gay appearance to the man in mean apparel, he says, "Are ye not then partial in yourselves, and are become *judges of evil thoughts?*"

393. EZEKIEL 1:4. "And I looked, and, behold, a whirlwind came out of the north, and a great cloud, and a fire enfolding itself, and a brightness was about it, and out of the midst thereof as the color of amber, out of the midst of the fire." This that was here seen by Ezekiel was the Shekinah, or the symbol and representation of the deity. Here is a cloud and fire, as God appeared in the wilderness in a pillar of cloud and fire. Ps. 18:11, "His pavilion round about him were dark waters and thick clouds of the skies." And Ps. 97:2, "Clouds and darkness are round about him." And there was a whirlwind, which was an usual symbol of the divine presence, as Job 38:1. "Then the Lord answered Job out of the whirlwind." So again Job 40:6. And Nah. 1:3, "The Lord hath his way in the whirlwind."

The fire that appeared, which did in a special manner represent the divine essence, is said to be "a fire enfolding itself," or "catching itself," as it is in the margin,[6] or receiving or taking itself into its own bosom, which represents the action of the deity towards itself, in the action of the persons of the TRINITY towards each other. The Godhead is perceived only by perceiving the Son and the Spirit, for "no man hath seen God at any time" [John 1:18]. He is seen by his image, the Son, and is felt by the Holy Spirit, as fire is perceived only by its[7] light and heat, seen by one and felt by the other. Fire, by its light, represents the Son of God, and by its heat, the Holy Spirit. God is light, and he is love. This light, in the manner of the subsisting of the Father and the Son, shines on itself; it receives its own brightness into its own bosom. The deity, in the generation of the Son, shines forth with infinite brightness towards itself; and in the manner of the proceeding of the Holy Ghost, it receives all its own heat into its own bosom, and burns with infinite heat towards itself. The flames of divine love are received and enfolded into the bosom of the deity.

'Tis the nature of all other fire to go out of itself, as it were to fly from itself, and hastily to dissipate; the flames are continually going forth from the midst of the fire towards the exterior air. But this fire received itself into its own bosom.

6. I.e. margin of the KJV.
7. JE deleted "brightness."

Ezekiel saw this cloud of glory and fire enfolding, or taking in, itself, before he saw the chariot of God, the cherubims, and wheels, and firmament, and throne, and the appearance of a man above upon it, which came out of that cloud and fire. And therefore this "fire enfolding itself" does especially represent the deity before the creation of the world, or before the beginning of the[8] being of this chariot with its wheels, when all God's acts were only towards himself, for then there was no other being but he.

This appeared coming "out of the north," from whence usually came whirlwinds in that country, and possibly because in the north is the empty place. The chariot of the world comes forth out of nothing.

394. EZEKIEL 1. Add this to No. 389, "Concerning Ezekiel's wheels," at this mark + +. The system of the universe very exactly answers what is here said of these wheels, and livelily represents God's providence in the government of the moral world. There is as it were a wheel within a wheel; the whole system is nothing else but wheels within wheels, lesser wheels within greater, revolving oftener. There is the sphere of the fixed stars, which is the greatest wheel, and includes all the other, [and] is many thousand years in performing its revolution. This includes the circle of Saturn's course, which is a lesser wheel within the other, finishing its revolution in about thirty years. That includes the circle of Jupiter, a lesser wheel, revolving in about twelve years; that includes the circle of Mars, that the circle of the earth, that of Venus, that of Mercury, that the sun, which revolves about its own axis. And some of the greater wheels include lesser ones of various kinds, as the grand wheel of Saturn, besides those of the inferior planets, has annexed to it those lesser wheels of his satellites, one within another, and then its ring, and then its own body about its axis. So of Jupiter, and so of the earth and moon. So some of the grand revolutions of providence, that are but parts of the grand system of providence, have a particular system as it were belonging to themselves, wherein the great revolution includes lesser revolutions, that are not parallel with any like 'em, continued from the beginning to the end of time, but begin their various revolutions with that particular great wheel that they are affixed to, and end with it. So 'tis with that great wheel, the continuance of the Jewish state; so 'tis with the continuance of the Christian church; so 'tis with the state of some particular kingdoms and empires.

8. JE deleted "course of the wheel."

395. CANTICLES 2:7. "I charge you, O ye daughters of Jerusalem, by the roes, and by the hinds of the field, that ye stir not up, nor awake my love, till he please." In the 2nd verse of this chapter is represented the church in her state of persecution. In the 3rd, 4th, 5th, and 6th verses is represented the comforts and supports Christ gives her in this state of hers. In this verse is represented her duty in patience, meekness, and love to her enemies, and humble and patient waiting for Christ's deliverance in Christ's time, while she is in this state of suffering. In the five following verses is represented Christ's coming to her deliverance, to put an end to the suffering state of the church, and introduce its prosperous and glorious day. In this 7th verse, it is strictly charged upon all professing Christians, that they should not stir up nor awake Christ till he please, i.e. that they should not take any indirect courses for their own deliverance, while the church is in her afflicted state, and Christ seems to neglect her, as though he were asleep; but that they should patiently wait on him till his time should come, when he would awake for the deliverance of his church. He that believeth shall not make haste; they that take indirect courses to hasten their own deliverance, by rising up against authority, and resisting their persecutors, are guilty of tempting Christ, and not waiting till his time comes, but going about to stir him up, and force deliverance before his own time. They are charged by the roes and hinds of the field, who are of a gentle and harmless nature, are not beasts of prey, don't devour one another, don't fight with their enemies but fly from them, and are of a pleasant loving nature (Prov. 5:19). So Christians should flee when persecuted, and should not be of a fierce nature to resist and fight, but should be of a gentle and loving nature, and wait for Christ's awaking.[9]

The same charge is repeated in the 3rd chapter, 5th verse. There, in that chapter in the 1st verse, is represented the fruitless seeking of the church in her slothful, slumbering, dark state that precedes the glorious day of the Christian church. And then is represented her seeking him more earnestly when[1] more awakened (v. 2), and then the introduction of her state of light and comfort by that extraordinary preaching of the word of God, which will be by the ministers of the gospel. And then in the 5th verse is the church to wait patiently for Christ's appearance, without using undue indirect means to obtain comfort

9. JE later interlined and then deleted the following: "the ~~spousing~~ spouse's charging the daughters of Jerusalem by the roes and hinds of the field is something like the Apostle's beseeching by the meekness and gentleness of Christ."
1. JE deleted "stirred up."

before his time comes. And then in the following verses is more fully represented the happy state of the church, after Christ has awaked, and come out of the wilderness where he had hid himself. The like charge we have again, Cant. 8:4, which in a like sense also agrees well with the context.

396. ZECHARIAH 14:16–19. "Shall even go up from year to year to keep the feast of TABERNACLES. And it shall be, that whoso will not come up of all the families of the earth," etc., "upon [them] shall be no rain. . . . This shall be the punishment of Egypt, and the punishment of all nations that come not up to keep the feast of tabernacles." The feast of tabernacles here spoken of is that glorious spiritual feast that God shall provide for all nations in the last ages of the world, and in the expected glorious state of the Christian church, which is spoken of, Is. 25:6. This feast was on the seventh month of the year, which was a kind of an holy sabbatical month, as the seventh day of the week was an holy day, and the seventh year an holy year, and also the year of jubilee at the end of seven times seven years. So this glorious state of the church is to be on the seventh age of the world, or seventh thousand years. The feast of tabernacles was the greatest feast on that month. It was to be kept on that month, after Israel were prepared for it by the feast of trumpets and the day of atonement, both on the same month. So way shall be made for the joy of the church of God in its glorious state on earth by the preaching of the gospel, and deep repentance, and humiliation for its great sins, and long continued deadness, and carnality.

The feast of tabernacles was the last feast they had in the whole year[2] before the face of the earth was destroyed by the winter. Presently, after the feast of tabernacles was over, a tempestuous season began. See Acts 27:9, "Sailing was now dangerous, because the feast[3] was now already past." So this feast of the church will [be] the last feast she shall have on earth, the last pouring out of the Spirit before this lower world is destroyed. The feast of tabernacles was kept when they had "gathered in the fruit of their land" (Lev. 23:39), and is called the feast of ingathering at the end of the year. So this great spiritual feast of the church shall [be] after God's ingathering of both his harvest and vintage, spoken of, Rev. 14. It will be the time of his gathering in all his good fruits before winter as it were, that is, before the destruction of

2. JE deleted "So that glorious state."
3. KJV: "fast."

the world, a time wherein the fruits of the earth will come to their full ripeness.

The feast of tabernacles was kept in commemoration of God's setting up his tabernacle among the children of Israel in the wilderness, but in that glorious time God will, above all other times, set up his tabernacle amongst men in the midst of his spiritual Israel, as is prophesied, Ezek. 37:27, and proclaimed in Rev. 21:3. The world was created about the time of the feast of tabernacles. See No. 204. So this is the creation of the new heavens and new earth. The temple of Solomon was dedicated at the time of the feast of tabernacles; then God descended in a pillar of cloud, and dwelt in the temple. So this is the time wherein the temple of God should be erected, and beautified, and dedicated; and God shall come down from heaven to dwell in his church. The church of God shall as it were go up to the mountain of the house of the Lord, as they did on that great occasion of Solomon's dedicating the temple [I Kgs. 8].

Christ was born, and came to tabernacle in flesh, on the feast of tabernacles; so then shall Christ be born. The woman in travail shall then bring forth her son, that is to rule all nations; and then mankind, above all other times, shall enjoy the benefit of the birth of Christ. Christ shall then be born in the souls of men.

There seems to be greater tokens of rejoicing on this feast than any other. The people dwelt in booths of green boughs, which represent the flourishing, beautiful, pleasant state the church shall be in, rejoicing in God's grace and love (represented by the color green). She shall yet dwell in tabernacles on this side [of] heaven, her land of rest. Their branches of palm trees represent the church's flourishing as the palm tree, and the glorious victory the church shall then have obtained. The willows of the brook they shall make use of, represent the flourishing state of the souls of God's people, as a tree planted by the rivers of waters (Lev. 23:40). The olive branches (Neh. 8:15) represent the church's fullness of the Spirit, the antitype of the oil of the olive. At the feast of tabernacles God's people left their houses to dwell in booths, which represented two things that should be in the glorious times, viz. their great weanedness from the world, and joy in God.

Thus the two great feasts of the Jews that followed the passover represent the two[4] great seasons, consequent on the death of Christ, which was at the passover, of the communication of the benefits of

---

4. JE deleted "grand periods."

Christ's redemption to his church on earth; one, that which was in primitive ages of the Christian church, which began on the day of Pentecost, in which the Holy Ghost was not only given in ordinary, sanctifying, saving influences, but also in extraordinary gifts of inspiration for the revealing the mind and will of God, and establishing the standing rule of the faith, worship, and manners of the Christian church, which answered to the giving of the law at Mt. Sinai, which was on the feast of Pentecost. The other is that which shall follow the destruction of Antichrist, which answers to the setting up the tabernacle in the wilderness, and the gifts, sacrificings, and rejoicing that were on that occasion, which was on the same day of the year that the feast of tabernacles was. These three great feasts do prefigure those three grand[5] events that are brought to pass for the church of God in the progress of the work of redemption, viz. the death of Christ to purchase salvation for the church, and those two great outpourings of the Spirit to apply it. See note on Ezek. 45:25.[6]

Those that would not come to keep this feast, that would not acknowledge God's glorious works, and praise his name, and rejoice with his people, upon them should be no rain [Zech. 14:17], i.e. [they] should not partake of that shower of divine blessing that then should descend on the earth, but God would give 'em over to hardness of heart and blindness of mind. For the rain is mystical rain, as is evident (18th and 19th verses); for 'tis said that Egypt, that had no rain, yet should be subject to the same plague that other nations had, if they kept not the feast of tabernacles.[7]

397. GENESIS 2:9 and 3:22–24. Concerning the TREE OF LIFE. This tree seems manifestly to have been designed for a seal of Adam's confirmation in life, in case he had stood, for two reasons: first, because its distinguishing name is the "tree of life"; and second, because by what is said in the latter end of the third chapter, there appears to have been a connection by divine [constitution] between eating of that tree and living forever, or enjoying a confirmed, certain, and everlasting life.

5. MS: "~~Greatest~~ (Grand)."

6. This reference is a later addition. JE contrasts the glory of the "first outpouring of the Spirit in the apostles' days" with that in the "joyful and glorious state of the church after the fall of Antichrist, when there should be a more full ingathering of God's elect, which was represented by the feast of tabernacles." The former, he writes, pales in comparison ("Blank Bible").

7. JE deleted "See concerning the feast of tabernacles, No. 204."

But yet here are those difficulties attending such a supposition. If it was so that this fruit was intended as a seal of Adam's confirmation in life, and was by divine constitution connected with confirmed life, then it should seem that it was something kept in store, reserved by God to be bestowed as a reward of his obedience and overcoming all temptations, when his time of probation[8] was ended. There seems to be an allusion to this in Rev. 22:14, "Blessed are they that do his commandments, that they may have right to the tree of life." And Rev. 2:7, "To him that overcometh will I give to eat of the tree of life." And so that it was not to be come at till the time of his trial was ended, for if he had eat of the tree before his probation was ended, confirmed life would doubtless have been as much connected with it as after he fell, and that would have defeated God's design, which was that he should [not] have confirmed life till his obedience was tried. And if so, why was not there need of cherubims and a flaming sword before, to keep Adam from the tree before he fell, as well as afterwards? Whereas there seems to be nothing to keep him from this tree; the tree was not forbidden him, for he had leave to eat of every tree, but only the tree of knowledge of good and evil. And as there was no moral hindrance, so there seems to be no natural fence to keep him off. It don't seem to be out of his reach; for, if so, what occasion was there for placing cherubims and a flaming sword after he fell? The tree don't seem to be hidden from Adam; for if it was sufficiently secured from him by this means before he fell, so it was afterwards, and so what need of the cherubims and flaming sword? And by the account which Moses gives of the place of this tree, that it was in the midst of the garden, it appears probable that it was in the most conspicuous place in the whole garden (as the tree of life is said to grow in the midst of the street of the heavenly paradise, Rev. 22:2; the street of a city is the most public place in it), that Adam might have it in view, to put him in mind of the glorious reward promised to his obedience, to engage him to the greater care and watchfulness, that he might not fail.

The most probable account that is to be given of this matter is this, that the fruit of the tree of life was not yet produced, but that it was revealed to Adam, that after a while, that tree should produce fruit, that whosoever eat of [it] should live forever, that he might eat if he persisted in his obedience, and did not so expose himself to death before that time, and so cut himself off from ever tasting of it. The tree

---

8. MS: "~~obedience~~ ⟨Probation⟩."

probably made a most lovely and excellent appearance, and sent forth a sweet fragrancy, and perhaps was gay in the blossom, promising most excellent fruit.

This tree, as it grew in the midst of the garden, so probably it grew by the river that run through the midst of this paradise. See Rev. 22:2, and Ezek. 47:12. See further No. 469.[9]

Corol. This is a confirmation, that the angels were not confirmed till Christ had ended his humiliation, and till he ascended into glory, for Christ is the tree of life in the heavenly paradise, in the native country of the angels, as this tree we have been speaking of was the tree of life on earth, the native country of men. And the Scripture gives us to understand that[1] this person, who is the tree of life in this heavenly paradise, is angels' food. And so we may infer, that the fruit of this tree was the food by which the angels have their eternal life, or confirmed life. But as man, who was made under a like covenant of works with the angels, would not have been confirmed, if he had persevered in his obedience, till this tree had brought forth its fruit, and till the fruit of the tree was ripe, so 'tis not probable that the angels were confirmed till the Christ, the tree of life in the heavenly paradise, had brought forth his fruit. But what is the fruit that grows on this heavenly tree, the second person of the Trinity, but the fruit of the Virgin Mary's womb, and that fruit of the earth spoken of, Is. 4:2, that son born, that child given, etc. (How often are the children that are born in a family in Scripture compared to the fruit that grows on a tree.) When this holy child had gone through all his labors and sufferings, and had fulfilled all righteousness, and was perfected (as 'tis expressed in Luke 13:32, Heb. 2:10, 5:9), then he was seen of angels, and received up into glory, and then the fruit was gathered. Christ, as full ripe fruit, was gathered into the garner of God, into heaven, the country of angels, and so became angels' food. Then the angels fed upon the full ripe fruit of the tree of life, and received of the Father the reward of everlasting life. Christ did not become the author of eternal salvation till he was made so; neither did he become the author of confirmed eternal life to the angels till he was made perfect. Thus the fruit of this tree of life did not become the food of life to either men or angels till it was ripe.

This tree of life did as it were blossom in the sight of the angels when[2] man was at first created in an innocent, holy, pleasant, and

---

9. This cross-reference is a later addition.
1. JE deleted "Christ."
2. JE deleted "Adam."

happy state, who was that creature from whence this future fruit of the tree of life was to spring, the blossom out of which the fruit was to come. It was a fair and pleasant blossom, though a weak and feeble (and proved a fading) thing, like a flower. When man fell, then the blossom faded and fell off. Man came forth like a flower, and was cut down; but the blossom fell in order to the succeeding fruit. The fall of man made way for the incarnation of Christ; it gave occasion to the production and ripening of that fruit, and to it blessed consequences.

Thus, though Christ, God-man, ben't the Savior of the angels, as he is of men, yet he is the tree of life to the angels, and bread of life as well as to men.

398. GENESIS 1:27–30. COVENANT WITH ADAM. "So God created man in his own image; in the image of God created he him. Male and female created he them. And God blessed them, and God said unto them," etc. Here is described the sum of the blessedness that man had in his first estate. Here is first his inherent spiritual good, which lay in his being created in God's image. Here is the happiness that he had in the favor of God; his blessing of him is a testimony of it. Here is the happiness he had in his intercourse with God, for his thus talking with him in this friendly manner is an instance of it. Here is all his external good, which consisted in two things: first, in human society, implied in that expression, "Male and female created he them," and in those words, "Be fruitful and multiply." Here is the sum of their outward good in the enjoyment of earthly good. Here is the possession of the earth, and the enjoyment of the produce of it, and dominion over the inferior creatures in it. These things were evidently given to Adam as the public head of mankind. God, in blessing them, evidently speaks to them as the head of mankind. The blessings he pronounced are given him in the name of the whole race, and therefore the favor manifested in blessing them is implicitly given to him as the head of the race. God's making them in his own image, and then blessing them, implies his bestowing these blessings pronounced on the subject blessed, as [if it] continued such an excellent subject as he had made it, as it now stood forth to receive his blessing, or continued in such an happy capacity to enjoy the blessings as he now was; otherwise the blessing would be in a great measure made void. For in order to man's being happy in the blessing, two things were needful: first, that the enjoyments granted should be good; and second, that the subject should be good, or in a good capacity to receive and enjoy them. Therefore both these are

doubtless implied in the blessing here pronounced, which is plainly pronounced on him in the name of the whole race. And therefore in like manner, when Adam[3] is threatened with a being deprived of all these on his disobedience, Adam must understand it in like manner as a calamity to come on the whole race; and consequently the implicit promise of life, or the confirmation and increase of the blessing, respects also the whole race. Hence the covenant must be made with Adam, not only for himself, but all his posterity.

399. GENESIS 3:20.[4] Add this to No. 322. There are also these further arguments to confirm that Adam don't give his wife the name of Eve, which signifies "life," because she was the mother of all mankind, but because she was the mother of Christ, and of his living seed, who are the seed of the woman God had just spoken of. 1. This name is exceeding proper and suitable to signify the latter, because "in Adam all die, but in Christ shall all be made alive" [I Cor. 15:22]. "By man came death; so by man also came the resurrection of the dead" [I Cor. 15:21]. The second Adam is made a quickening spirit [I Cor. 15:45]; in him was life, and he is *the Life*. All mankind, by the first Adam, are in a state of death, dead in trespasses and sin; but Christ is the Bread of Life [John 6:35], which he that eats shall live forever. And he is thus the fountain of life to the children of men, by bruising the head of the serpent, or destroying him that has the power of death, even the devil, which God had just before promised[5] should be by the seed of *Ishah*,[6] the name that Adam gave his wife at first.

2. 'Tis not likely that Adam would give this, viz. "Living Ones," as a distinguishing name for mankind, to distinguish them from other creatures, for the same name is, from time to time in the preceding chapters, given to other creatures, as Gen. 1:21, 24, 28,[7] and 2:19, where the word is radically the same. And so afterwards, the name is often given to other animals (Gen. 6:19, and 7:4, 23, and 8:1, and in many other places of Scripture). And especially is it unlikely that he would give this as a distinguishing name to mankind immediately upon man's fall, whereby he was ruined, and had brought that threat-

3. MS: "God."
4. "Eve Why So Called. No. 399" appears as a running head on the second page of this entry.
5. MS: "promise." This is but one example of many errors made by JE in this entry.
6. אִשָּׁה.
7. JE deleted "where the word is of the same radix."

ening on himself, "in the day that thou eatest thereof, thou shalt surely die" [Gen. 2:17], and immediately after he had been told by God that he was dead[8] (in effect so): "Dust thou art, and unto dust thou shalt return" [Gen. 3:19]. Adam could not mean by "all living," as we sometimes use such an expression, indeed to signify "mankind," but not all that have the human nature, as though life was a distinguishing property of that nature, but to mean those that are now alive, to distinguish them from those that are dead, or are not yet born. And 'tis exceeding unlikely that Adam would now first find out this name to distinguish mankind, even those that yet had no life or being, as though life was a distinguishing property and dignity of human nature, on occasion of so great, awful, and affecting an event as the first entrance of any such thing as death into the world, to waste, and destroy, and make fearful havoc of all mankind, all Eve's posterity, and that firstly by her means. If Adam had meant by "the living," all mankind that now have a being in this world, the name was very improper for her, for he that was living of mankind was the only person of all mankind that she was not the mother of. He was rather the father of her, for she was taken out of him, and not he out of her. But in the other sense, it is true that Eve was the mother of all living universally, "of every living one," as it is in the original.[9] [There is] not one, that has spiritual and eternal life, of all mankind, that in this sense is excepted, not Adam, nor Christ, no, nor herself; for in this sense, as she was the mother of Christ, she was her own mother.

3. 'Tis remarkable that Adam had before given his wife another name, viz. *Ishah*, when she was first created and brought to him, but now on the occasion of the Fall, and what God had said upon it, changes her name, and gives her a new name, viz. *Life*, because she was to be the mother of everyone that has life, which would be exceeding strange and unaccountable, if all that he meant was that she was to be the mother of mankind. If that was all that he intended, it would have been much more likely to be given to her at first, when God gave them that blessing, viz. "Be fruitful and multiply," by virtue of which she became the mother of mankind, and when mankind was hitherto in a state of life, and death had not yet entered into the world. But that Adam should not give her this name now, but call her *Ishah*, and then after that change her name, and call her name *Life*, immediately upon

8. JE deleted "virtually."
9. כָּל־חָי.

their losing their life and glory, and coming under a sentence of death with all their posterity, and the awful melancholy shadow and darkness of death being brought on the whole world, occasioned first by Eve's folly, is altogether unaccountable, if he had only meant that she was the mother of mankind.

4. That Adam should change her name, and call her name *Life*, after he had given her another name, doubtless was from something new that appeared that was very remarkable concerning Eve; and doubtless we have an account what that remarkable thing was. The Scripture history is not so imperfect as to give us an account of such an event as a person's name being changed, without mentioning the occasion of that change. We have several times elsewhere an account of the change of persons' names in Scripture, but always have an account of the[1] reason why; but we have no account of anything new concerning Eve, that could give Adam occasion thus to change her name, and call her *Life*, but only what God said concerning her and her seed after her fall. We have an account of the change of her name immediately upon it, and therefore must understand that as the occasion of it. This was an exceeding proper occasion for such a name, and it is natural to suppose that Adam's mind might now be so affected by the curse of death just pronounced by God, and the promise of life by Eve, as to induce him to change her name from *Ishah* to *Life*.

5. 'Tis most likely that Adam would give Eve her name from that which was her greatest honor, since 'tis evident that he had respect to her honor in giving her this name. The name itself, *Life*, is honorable; and that which he mentions, her being the "mother of every living one," is doubtless something he had respect to as honorable to her. Since he changed her name from regard to her honor, 'tis most likely he would signify in it that which was her peculiar honor; but that was the most honorable of anything new that had happened concerning [her], viz. that God said that she should be the mother of that seed that should bruise the serpent's head [Gen. 3:15], and was the greatest honor that God had put upon her. We find persons' names changed elsewhere, to signify something that is [the] person's peculiar honor, as Abraham's, Sarah's, and Israel's new names.

6. All new names, that we have an account of in Scripture, are given with respect to some great privilege persons have by some special relation to Christ, or interest in him and his redemption. So Abraham's and Sarah's new names were given 'em of God on occasion

---

1. JE deleted "cause."

of the promise made to them, that in their seed all the families of the earth should be blessed [Gen. 22:18]. And Jacob's new name of "Israel" is given, because as a principal he had prevailed with Christ in wrestling with him, and had obtained the confirmation of Abraham's and Isaac's blessing to him and his seed, when he and his posterity were in danger of being cut off by[2] Esau.[3] See "Prophecies of the Messiah" ("Miscellanies," no. 1067, sec. 96, pp. 108–109).[4] See No. 466. See note on Ezek. 26:20.[5]

400. GENESIS 10:6. How what the heathen said of Jupiter is evidently taken from Ham, the son of Noah. Noah is the Saturn of the heathen, as is evident by note on Gen. 1:27.[6] 'Tis fabled that Saturn had three sons, Jupiter, Neptune, and Pluto, who divided the world between them. "Sanchoniathon says, 'The son of Saturn was Zeus Belus,' or Baal, the chief god among the Phoenicians. It was a name assumed by Jehovah, the God of Israel, before abused to superstition, as appears by Hosea 2:16. It is elsewhere written Beel, as Βεελσάμιν, which answers to the Hebrew, *Baal Shamaiim*, the 'Lord of heaven.' Zeus is derived from ζέσιν, which signifies 'heat,' and answereth exactly to the Hebrew *Cham*, from the radix *Chamam*, to 'wax hot.' Herodotus tells us that the Egyptians called Jupiter, *Ammon*, from their progenitor Ham, whence Egypt is called the land of Ham (Ps. 105:23, 27). Also Plutarch testifies that Egypt, in the sacreds of Isis, was termed Χημία; whence this but from Cham? And Africa of old was called Hammonia. The Africans were more wont to worship Ham under the name of Hammon. [These things are more largely treated of by Cudworth, pp. 337–39. See "Miscellanies," no. 1359.][7] Again, Sanchoniathon terms Jupi-

2. JE deleted "Ishmael."
3. This word and the references that follow are later additions.
4. In sec. 96, focusing on Gen. 3:20, JE asserts, "That it is with respect to the salvation and benefits of the Messiah that Adam called his wife's name Eve because she is the mother of all living." He then cites biblical passages in support of that contention (MS, Andover coll.).
5. JE explained "the land of the living" (Ezek. 26:20) as a reference to Israel, "the land of the righteous," where God bestowed "the blessing of spiritual and eternal life," rather than as a reference to the "whole habitable earth" ("Blank Bible"). This is analogous to the distinction JE makes here between Eve being called Eve because she was the mother of all mankind, or because she was the mother of Christ and his seed.
6. Based on his reading of Theophilus Gale, in his note JE described in detail the ways in which the "heathen fables" concerning Saturn seem to be derived from the biblical stories involving Adam, Abraham, and Noah ("Blank Bible").
7. JE's brackets. The bracketed material is a later addition. In a discussion of the names of gods among the ancient nations based on the testimony of Herodotus, Ralph Cudworth stated that the Egyptians, among their many deities, acknowledged one supreme god whom they called *Hammon* or *Ammon*, which he linked to Ham, the son of Noah. Cudworth asserted

ter, Sydyk, or, as Damascius in Photius, Sadyk. Now this name is evidently taken from the Hebrew Saddik, the 'Just,' which is a name given to God, as also to the first patriarchs, whence Melchizedek. The name Jupiter (as Muis on the Psalms well observes) is evidently the same with *Ia Pater*, or Ἰεὺ πατήρ, that is, Father *Jah*, or *Jeu*. That God's name *Jah* was well known to the Phoenicians, who communicated the same to the Grecians, is evident by what Porphyry says of Sanchoniathon's deriving the materials of his history from Jerombalus, the priest of the god Ἰαώ. So Diodorus, Lib. [I], tells us, that Moses inscribed his laws to the God called *Jao*. So the oblique cases of Jupiter are from God's name Jehovah, as Jovi, Jove, etc. This same name *Jao*, in the Oracle of Clarius Apollo, is given to Bacchus. Again Jupiter was Sabasius, from that title of God, Jehovah Sabaoth. [This Cudworth also takes notice of, pp. 259–60.][8] The fable of Jupiter's cutting off his father's genitalia seems to arise from Ham's seeing his father's nakedness [Gen. 9:22]. Again, in the *Metamorphosis* of the gods of Egypt, 'tis said that Jupiter was turned into a ram, which fable Bochart supposeth to have had its rise from the cognation between the Hebrew words אֵל, *El*, and אַיִל, *ajil*, a 'ram,' the plural number of which are both the same, *Elim*. The tradition of Bacchus's being produced out of Jupiter's thigh" seems to come from the Hebrew expression, to signify the natural proceeding of posterity from a father, their coming out of his thigh, which in our translation is "to proceed out of his loins." Gale's *Court of the Gentiles*, Pt. 1, Bk. 2, ch. 1, pp. 10–13.[9]

401. GENESIS 10:8.[1] "And Cush begat Nimrod; he began to be a mighty one in the earth." Many of those things that the heathen said of Bacchus were taken from Nimrod. The name Bacchus is

that the names of gods were "a mixture of *Herology* or *History*, together with *Theology*" (*The True Intellectual System of the Universe: The First Part; Wherein All the Reason and Philosophy of Atheism is Confuted; and Its Impossibility Demonstrated* [London, 1678], pp. 337–39). No. 1359, is entitled "EXTRACTS FROM DR. CUDWORTH CONCERNING THE OPINIONS AND TRADITIONS OF HEATHEN PHILOSOPHERS agreeable to truth concerning matters of RELIGION."

8. JE's brackets. The bracketed material is a later interlineation. Cudworth notes "that *Zeus Sabazius* was a name for the Supreme God, sometime introduced amongst the Greeks, and derived in all probability, from the Hebrew *Sabaoth*, or *Adonai Tsebaoth, the Lord of Hosts*) or the Supreme Governour of the World" (*True Intellectual System*, pp. 259–60).

9. Theophilus Gale, *The Court of the Gentiles: Or A Discourse touching the Original of Human Literature, both Philologie and Philosophie, From the Scripture & Jewish Church* (2nd ed., Oxford, 1672), Pt. 1, Bk. 2, ch. 1, pp. 10–13.

1. "Fables applied to Bacchus of Sacred Extract. No. 401," appears as a running head on the pages of this entry.

derived from the Hebrew, or Phoenician (which is the same), *Bar-Cush*, the son of Cush, whence also those νέβριδες in Bacchus's garment, as also in his chariot, נִמְרִין, i.e. *Tigres*, which are allusions to the name Nimrod, or *Nebrodes*. As for the Greek —Ἴαχχος, it seems the same with the Hebrew *Jah-Chus*, i.e. Jah the son of Chus. Thence also in the Oracle of Clarius Apollo, the name *Iao* is attributed to Bacchus, whence some derive the name *Io-Bacchus*, i.e. the God Bacchus. Bacchus was also called Ἄττης, according to that of the Rhodian Oracle. "*Magnum Atten placate Deum,*" etc. What the proper import of this name was, the Grecians know not. So Eustathius *Odyss.* "It is not for us to find out the origin of *Atta*; neither has it any interpretation." But what they knew not, the Hebrews well understood; for *Atta*, as all know, is the same with the Hebrew אַתָּה, "Thou," which the Scripture oft applies to God, "Thou Lord," or "Thou Jehovah." Whence also the Grecians added to "*Attes, Hues.*" So Demosthenes, "*Hues Attes, Attes hues,*" which is taken "*Atta Jehovah,*" which so often occurs in the Psalms, and was so much used in the Hebrew devotions, and was thence taken by the Grecians, and applied to their idol Bacchus. But Bochart derives *Hues* from the Hebrew הוּא אֵשׁ, *hu-es*, "he is fire," as Deut. 4:24. "Thy God is a consuming fire." Bacchus was styled likewise Ζαγρεύς, i.e. "a mighty hunter," from the character given unto Nimrod (Gen. 10:9). And from "Hallelujah" sprang the famous Greek acclamation given to Bacchus, ἐλελεῦ. Bacchus was also called Adonis, *Adonai*, God's name. Bacchus was also styled *Eleleus*, from *El-Eloah*; and he was called *Evius* from Jehovah, and *Sabus* from Sabaoth. The Grecians make Bacchus to be the son of Jupiter, as Chus, the father of Nimrod, was the son of Ham. And they consecrated to Bacchus, amongst the birds κίσσαν, the pie, because he was κίσσιυς, Hebrew כּוּשִׁי, a Cushean, as Nimrod was. That Bacchus was Nimrod is further evident because his other name was *Nebrodes*. This is the very name of Nimrod among the Grecians. See the LXX,[2] Josephus, and others. By reason of the extent of his dominion, he was styled Belus. For that Belus, the head of the Assyrian monarchy, was the same with Nimrod (who had the first name given him from his dominion, the second from his rebellion), is proved by Bochart in his *Phaleg*; only the name Nimrod, because it was contumelious and odious, was obliterated, and that of Belus

---

2. I.e. the Septuagint.

only retained by the Chaldeans. To this name Belus, answers that of *Liber*, given to Bacchus, which Bochart makes the same for import with *Horim*, *Liberi*, free men, or princes, which is given to the Babylonian princes. Is. 34:12, "They shall call the nobles (*Horim*) thereof to the kingdom, but none shall be there, and all her princes." From this word comes "hero." The Chaldee[3] in this place in Isaiah reads, "*Bene Herin*," sons of *Liberi*, or heroes, whence Methodius calls Nimrod ἀδελφὸν τῶν ἡρώων, the brother of the heroes, i.e. in effect, *Liber*, "a prince." The Greek mythologists themselves, though they are ambitious of vindicating Bacchus for their countryman, yet they acknowledge that Staphylus, his son and successor, was king of Assyria; which is as much as if they had said, that Bacchus reigned in Assyria. Yea, in the epitaph of Ninus, Nimrod's son and successor, there is mention made of the Bacchae, as Athenae, Lib. 12. 7. Bacchus is said to be the God of wine, because he ruled over Babylon, where that most excellent wine, so much celebrated among the poets under the name of nectar, was found. So Atheneus *Deipnos.*, Lib. 1, "Chaereas (saith he) reports that there was a wine in Babylon, which the natives call nectar, which they called also the drink of the gods." Lastly, the expeditions of Bacchus into the East as far as India seem evident references unto Nimrod, and his successors' achievements in those parts, as Bochart, *Phaleg*, Lib. 1, ch. 2. That Bacchus was the same with Nimrod, and that the whole of his worship was transported out of the oriental parts into Greece by the Phoenicians, see Bochart, *Can.*, Lib. 1, ch. 18.

Many things also that the heathens attributed to their God Bacchus were taken from the history of Moses.

1. As Moses, so Bacchus was feigned to be born in Egypt. 2. Orpheus calls Bacchus *Miens*; so Sandford, *de descensu Christi*. There is extant in Orpheus a hymn, wherein he celebrates Mises, whom in the first verse he styles Dionysus, and in the third Jacchus. Now Mises differs not from Moses, save in the punctuation, etc. 3. Bacchus is said to be shut up in an ark, and imposed on the waters, as Moses was. Thus Sandford, *de descensu Christi*. Moses' ark, as also his danger in the waters, and deliverance thence, was known to divers nations; and that most fabulously, detorted unto Bacchus,

3. I.e. the Chaldee Paraphrast.

etc. 4. Bacchus is made to be beautiful in form, and διμήτωρ, one that had two mothers. Thus Sandford, *de descensu*, Lib. 1, §18. "Moses' adoption was also known: therefore the poets fable Bacchus to be *bimatrem*, which they call *Isidas*." "The Egyptians (saith Plutarch) affirm, that Isis, with a pensive mind, and weeping, was, by the maids, brought to the queen, to nurse the child." The names Thryambus, Lythirambus, and Dithyrambus given to Bacchus, which the Syrians express by דתרי אבהן, *dithere abhan*, which signifies διπατέρα, from the fiction of Bacchus's being twice born. 5. Plutarch makes mention of the flights of Bacchus, which answers to Moses' flying from Egypt, as Stillingfleet. So Sandford, *de descensu*. The banishment of Moses was known, whence Plutarch, *de Iside*, says, that Bacchus's banishment was a common song amongst the Grecians. Also Moses' flight was matter of common fame; unto which Bacchus's flight, so much celebrated by the poets, refers, as everyone ought to acknowledge, specially since those [things] they mention of Bacchus's flight towards the Red Sea, can be understood of none but Moses. [This flight may refer either to Moses' flight into the land of Midian, or to his flight from[4] Egypt with the congregation of Israel, when they went forth in haste, and his flight from Pharaoh through the Red Sea.][5] 7. Bacchus was called Dionysus, which (as Bochart observes) answers exactly to the inscription of Moses, on the altar by him erected (Ex. 17:15): "Jehovah Nissi," which posterity interpreted, "the God Nyseus," in Greek Διόνυσυς, Dionysus; or it may be taken from the mountain Nysa, sacred to Bacchus. Concerning Nysa, the city sacred to Bacchus, Homer, being taught by the Phoenicians, writes thus in his hymn of Bacchus. "Nysa, or Nyssa, is a mountain in Arabia near Egypt." This mountain Nysa, by a transposition of the letters, is the same with Syna. Thus Sandford. "Though some latter geographers seek Nysa among the Indians; yet the most ancient fix it in its proper place, so as it agrees well with the sacred history touching Syna. So Herodotus placeth Nysa above Egypt, and Diodorus Siculus between Egypt and Phoenicia."

8. Among the mysteries of Bacchus, serpents are reckoned, which answers to Moses' brazen serpent. According to the image whereof, a serpent was used among the sacreds of Bacchus, as

---

4. JE deleted "Pharaoh and his host."
5. JE's brackets.

Nonnus attests. [This may also be taken from Moses' rod being turned into a serpent.][6] 9. Bacchus is said to have a dog for his companion, which answers to Caleb, Moses' companion, whose name signifies a dog. So Sandford. "Caleb, who in Hebrew sounds a dog, gave rise to that fable of Bacchus' dog, which alone followed him wandering on the mountains." [This story seems to be taken from such expressions in sacred story, as those, Num. 14:24.][7] 10. Bacchus was famous for his passing the Red Sea, and wars; especially for that he had women in his army, as Moses in his march towards Canaan. 11. In Euripides, the Bacchae are said to draw water out of a rock, having struck it with their rod; and wherever they went, the land flowed with wine, milk, and honey. 12. Orpheus calls Bacchus the Legislator, and so attributes to him δίπλακα θεσμόν, as it were two tables of laws. 13. Bacchus was also called *bicornis*, two-horned, as Moses is usually pictured, from the mistake of that text, Ex. 34:29, "the skin of his face shone." 14. To which we may add what is mentioned in Nonnus' *Dionysiacis*, "That Bacchus, having touched the rivers Orontes and Hydaspes with his rod, and dried them up, he passed over; and his staff, being cast on the ground, it began to creep like a serpent, and to wind itself about an oak. Again, that the Indians continued in darkness, while the Bacchae enjoyed the light." 15. Farther, Moses learned on Mt. Sinai the rites of sacrifices, and thence taught them to the people. The same is sung of Bacchus by Ovid, *Fast.* "*Ante tuos ortus arae fine honore fuere.*" 16. Again, Moses was the first that brought in sacred music. Thus in like manner Strabo, *Lib.* 10, 453, informs us, that the Bacchic music was famous throughout Asia. 17. We find a fabulous mention of Bacchus' *Maira*, who is referred and seated among the stars, which probably was taken from Maria, or Miriam, sister to Moses and Aaron. 18. To which we may add that of Diodorus and Strabo, who affirm that Osiris (who was the Egyptian Bacchus), his sepulchre was unknown, agreeable to what is said of Moses (Deut. 34:6).

Gale's *Court of Gentiles*, Pt. 1, Bk. 2, ch. 3.[8]

The acts, both of Nimrod and Moses, came to be ascribed to Bacchus, probably this way.

6. Ibid.
7. Ibid.
8. Gale, *Court of the Gentiles* (2nd ed.), Pt. 1, Bk. 2, pp. 25–34. JE's citations do not follow the order of Gale's text.

The Phoenicians and other eastern nations, ascribing to Bacchus the honors of the true God, called him by many of the names of the God of Israel, as appears by what precedes, and hearing the Israelites calling that God that did such great acts in Egypt, and the Red Sea, and the wilderness, by the same names that they gave to Bacchus, supposed it was the same God; and also confounding Moses, that was but God's instrument in these things, with the God that wrought by him. Hence they ascribed those things that belonged to Moses unto their God Bacchus. It was very natural for the blind heathen, that saw or heard of the great things that God wrought by Moses, to attribute those things to Moses himself; and so, hearing that these things were done by the God *Iao*, and *Adonai*, and *El Eloah*, and Jehovah Sabaoth, etc., which were names by which they called Bacchus, as above, hence they gave Moses the same names with Bacchus. The Egyptians, when they saw so many and such great wonders wrought by the hand of Moses, and particularly after they saw what was done at the Red Sea, and heard of what was done in the wilderness, called Moses Bacchus (though Bacchus was a name they had before from Nimrod), as the men of Lystra called Barnabas, Jupiter, and Paul, Mercurius [Acts 14:12]. And possibly from hence came the fable among the heathen that Bacchus was twice born, once when Nimrod was born, and another time when Moses was born. See this further confirmed by what follows in the next note.

402. JOSHUA 10.[9] Concerning Joshua's war with the inhabitants of Canaan. The[1] things reported among the heathen concerning the giants' war with the gods seem to be taken from things from the story of Joshua, viz. 1. The war of the devils against God in heaven. These devils are in Scripture sometimes called Rephaim [Gen. 14:5], or giants. The giants among men in their wars were types of them.[2] 2. The notorious wickedness of the giants before the flood, mentioned Gen. 6:4, who probably were great persecutors of the church, and that the church was saved from utter ruin by them by the waters of the flood. And therefore we read of Noah and his family being saved by water [I Pet. 3:20]. 3. The building of Babel. 4. The war of the giants with the

9. JE wrote the following running heads on the pages of this entry: "War between the Gods & Giants," "Joshua's Parallel with Hercules," "Heathen Fables of Hercules taken from Joshua," and "Fables concerning Hercules taken from Joshua."
1. MS: "~~Many~~ ⟨The⟩."
2. JE interlined the last three sentences later and then renumbered the next two items.

four kings of the East, that we have account of, Gen. 14:5.[3] And, 5. The war of the race of giants in Canaan with the people of God, whom God was miraculously with in that war, and fought against the giants from heaven by the sun's standing still, and sending down great hailstones upon them, as well as by miraculously dividing Jordan, etc. Or thus. The fable of the famous war between the gods and giants seems to be taken from these four things. 1. From traditions handed down to the nations from the fathers of the ancient church of God that was after the flood, concerning the fall of the angels, or the war between the devil and God the Father, and the Son, and the holy angels. And Typhon, the chief of the giants, is the same with *Satan*, the grand apostate. The devils are sometimes in Scripture called Rephaim, which signifies giants. 2. The wickedness, and violence, and persecution of the giants before the flood, who were terribly destroyed by God,[4] struck probably with thunder and the artillery of heaven, and struck down to Tartarus, as is fabled of Typhon, and buried under the waters, as is also reported of him. 3. From the building of Babel, whence seems to arise the fable of the giants' heaping mountains on mountains. See No. 411 *-*.[5] 4. From the war between the true God and the race of giants in and about Canaan, that was carried on against them, first by the eastern monarchs that came against Sodom (Gen. 14), and afterwards by the posterity of Abraham, till the times of David, when the race was totally extirpated. See note on Gen. 14:5.[6] The war between the gods and giants, which the heathen speak of as only a particular battle or expedition, but a standing thing, a war of long continuance— see note on Num. 22:28.[7] The race of giants that was in and about Canaan was probably the only race of giants that was in the world; and it was wonderfully ordered so that there should be such a race there, that in the victory of Joshua and God's people over them might be

3. JE interlined this sentence later and then renumbered the next item.

4. JE crossed out with a large "X" the following: "into the water is agreeable has some agreement with Job 26:5, 'Dead things are formed under the waters,' which is translated by others, 'The giants groan under the waters.'"

5. This cross-reference is a later addition.

6. JE notes that the race of giants in Canaan was totally destroyed in the days of David ("Blank Bible").

7. JE suggests that the giants in Canaan "represent the devils who once were the inhabitants of heaven," who opposed God's people seeking to possess that land. They "were overcome by the spiritual Joshua, the Lord Jesus Christ, in their rebellion and war in heaven, and were cast out of that land." They continue to make war with God's people. "And 'tis all one to God's elect people, as if they were still dwelling in heaven, and fought there as once they did" ("Blank Bible").

typified the victory of Christ and God's people over the devils (see note on Gen. 14:5–6),[8] even as it was purposely ordered, that there should be many persons possessed with devils when Christ was on earth, that he, by dispossessing them, might represent the business he came into the world upon. "The fables agree that[9] the gods, which engaged against the giants, came up out of Egypt, and that they were twelve tribes; also that they constituted Bacchus, commander in chief of the whole army. (This Bacchus was Moses, agreeable to No. 401, the next preceding note.)[1] But because the main conduct of the war, after Moses' death, was incumbent on Joshua, therefore they attribute the chief management of the war unto him, under the disguise of Hercules. So Vossius, *de Idololat., Lib.* I, ch. 26, where he gives us a lively parallel betwixt Hercules and Joshua. 1. Whereas 'tis said that Hercules, as well as Bacchus, made an expedition into India, hereby he proves must be meant Arabia; for the Greeks esteemed all countries beyond the midland sea as parts of India. 'Tis true, some mythologists place this Nyssa, near which Hercules overcame the giant Typhon, in India; but 'tis evident that the ancient Grecians meant thereby no other than Arabia, for they styled all the oriental parts beyond the midland sea by this name of India, as appears by that of Ovid, *de Arte Amandi, 'Andromedam Perseus nigris portavit ab Indis.'*[2] Whereas Perseus brought not his wife Andromeda from India, but from Joppa, a town of Phoenicia, as Strabo, *Lib.* 1. So Dickinson and Vossius. As for Serbonis, the other place, near which the giant Typho was overcome by Hercules, Ptolemaeus tells us it, that Serbonis was betwixt Egypt and Palestine. And according to Plutarch, the Egyptians call the marshes of Serbonis, 'the expiration of Typho.' That his body should be cast into the water has some agreement with Job 26:5, 'Dead things are formed under the waters,' which is translated by others, 'the giants groan under the waters.' Thus also Sandford, *de descensu Christi,* 'That under Hercules must be understood Joshua, firstly, appears by commemorat-

---

8. JE writes, "That race of giants that was in and about Canaan was probably the only race of giants upon earth. God had long war with them, and they were all destroyed for the sake of his people. The race was entirely extirpated in the days of David. They seem to have been raised up for that end, that they might be types of the devils, and that their being destroyed before his people might be a type of the victory Christ obtains over the devils for the sake of his people" ("Blank Bible").

9. JE deleted "many things reported among the heathen of Hercules are taken from the story of Joshua."

1. JE inserted this parenthesis.

2. Perseus brought Andromeda from dark India.

ing that (which is the head of this affair) the Egyptian Hercules and Dionysus, by common counsel and consent, engaged against the Indians. The time exactly accordeth, according to Austin, who assigns to Hercules and Bacchus their times betwixt the departure of the Israelites out of Egypt and the death of Joshua.' 2. As for the persons which engaged in this expedition, Apolladorus, *biblioth.* 10, relates, that on the one side there were engaged Typhoeus, with the rest of the giants, and on the other part Jupiter, with Hercules and the rest of the gods. This oriental Hercules (says Vossius), for some ages, more ancient than the Theban, was by his true name called Joshua, who made war with the Canaanites, amongst whom were the sons of Anak, and other giants, as Num. 13:29, 33. But more particularly, the land of Bashan was called the 'land of giants,' as Deut. 3:13,[3] among whom Og was king. Now this Og is called by the Grecians Τυφῶν, Τυφώς, Τυφάων, or Τυφωεύς, which words, being derived from τύφω, which signifies to 'kindle' or 'burn,' have the same import with Og, which comes from עוג, i.e. burnt. So that Typho is the same with Og. Sandford, *de descensu Christi*, says 'that Typhoeus was the same with Og, king of Bashan. I am convinced by many indubitable arguments, the chief whereof is taken from his bed. For Homer (*Iliad* β) tells us, that the chief of the giants had his bed, εἰν Ἀρίμοις, in Arimis, which exactly answers to that of the sacred Scripture, Deut. 3:11. "For only Og, king of Bashan, remained of the remnant of the giants. Behold, his bedstead was a bedstead of iron. Is it not in Rabbath of the children of Ammon? Nine cubits was the length thereof, and four cubits the breadth of it."' See below, this mark ##. 'Tis possible that Hercules, from this name Og, was by the Phoenicians first, and then by the old Gauls, called Ogmius, as Lucian in *Hercul.* 'The Celti call Hercules Ogmius,' as the Grecians called Apollo, from the slain dolphin, Δελφίνιον. So peradventure Hercules, or Joshua, from the slain Og, was called Ogmius. The Grecians often insert μ in the middle of words, as Eustathius in *Il.* 2. 3rdly. Hercules seems parallel with Joshua in the mode of fighting. 'Tis said of Hercules, that whilst he was fighting with the giants, Jupiter rained down stones. This answers exactly to the story of Joshua, his strenuous achievement, and God's raining down stones, by which he slew great part of the giants. Josh. 10:11, 'The Lord cast down great stones from heaven upon them.' Thus Sandford, *descensu Christi*. Whence had Homer the tradition of this horrible earthquake, thundering, and

---

3. JE deleted "as Deut. 3:13" and interlined "Deut. 2:20." Both passages have the phrase, "land of giants," but the former is the correct association with Bashan and Og.

lightning in the giants' war?" Thundering and lightning attended that storm of hail (see No. 208), besides the thunders and lightnings that terrified the world from Mt. Sinai, and those at the Red Sea, and in Egypt. "Thus likewise, Dickinson, *Delphi Phoeniciz.*, ch. 4. Moreover as Joshua, so Hercules also was aided by stones sent from heaven, whence, I suppose, he received the name Saxanus, the origination whereof Lillius Gyraddus (in *Hercule*) confesseth he was ignorant. 4. There is also a very great agreement as to the place where this battle was fought. The place where Hercules and the great giant Typho fought seems, by Apollonius, to be Arabia near Nyssa and Serbonis, in *Argonaut* β, 'He (i.e. Typhoeus) came thus to the mountains and Nyssean field, where also he lies overwhelmed under the water of Serbonis.' That by Nyssa here is to be understood a mountain of Arabia, the Scholiast acknowledgeth."

See above, this mark ##. 5. "Homer in his *Iliad*, speaking of Jupiter's striking down this giant Typho with his thunderbolt, adds 'εἰν Ἀρίμοις, where they say Typhon's bed remains.' This is thus expressed by Virgil:

> *Durumque cubile*
> *Inarimes, Jovis imperiis imposita Typhoeo.*[4]

Where, what Homer expressed in two words, Virgil, upon a mistake, joins in one, *inarimes*. That this Arima, where Homer and Virgil place Typhon's bed, is the same with Syria, is evident from that of Strabo, *Lib.* 13. 'By the Arimi they understand the Syrians, who are now called Arami,' rightly indeed; for Aram, the son of Sem, was the father of the Syrians, whence Syria was also called Aram, and the Syrians Arameans, as Strabo, *Lib.* 16." The word in the Hebrew Bible for Syrian is *Aram*, and in the Syriac version of the New Testament it is *Armojo*. See Jones' *Canon of the New Testament*, Pt. 1, ch. 17.[5]

'Tis the more probable that the giant, so much famed under the name of Typhon, whom Hercules slew, was Og, the king of Bashan, because Og was the most noted giant of any that we have any account

---

4. And the hard bed in Arima, placed by command of Jupiter on Typhon.

5. This reference and the preceding sentence are a later interlineation. See Jeremiah Jones, *A New and Full Method of Settling the Canonical Authority of the New Testament. Wherein All the antient Testimonies concerning this Argument are produced; the several Apocryphal books, which have been thought canonical by any Writers, collected, with an English Translation of each of them; together with a particular Proof that none of them were ever admitted into the Canon, and a full Answer to those, who have endeavoured to recommend them as such* (3 vols. London, 1726–27), *1*, Pt. 1, 132. Ch. 17 attempts to prove that the Syriac version of the New Testament was "made in or near the Apostles Times" (p. 126).

of, and more likely to be taken notice [of], and his memory and fame upheld among the heathen nations, than any other. 1. Because of his prodigious stature. There is particular notice taken in Scripture of the dimensions of his bedstead, nine cubits the length thereof, and four cubits the breadth thereof (Deut. 3:11), which can be for no other reason but to represent the prodigious size of the man. If he was near nine cubits in height, as we must suppose, Goliath was a mere child to him. Og would be three[6] times so big as he. And 2. There was his being a king, added to his prodigious size, to make him famous in the world. A private man of such a stature would be much famed, but how much more a king. And besides, it is evident by the Scripture that he was actually much famed among the heathen on the account of his stature, and his bedstead was kept as a monument and memorial of it a long time in one of their great cities.[7]

Indeed, all that the Phoenicians reported of Hercules don't seem to be taken from the acts of Joshua, but some of them from some other person that traveled to the western parts of the Mediterranean Sea. But 'tis easy to be accounted for, that such ancient things that were taken originally from different persons, and handed down by tradition, and handed from one nation to another, should at length come to be understood of the same person. And 'tis likely that the way that the acts of Joshua, and some other warriors and great captains in war, famous among the Phoenicians and Egyptians, came to be looked upon as one and the same person among the Greeks, was this. Hercules, or Melicarthus, which was Hercules' name among the Phoenicians, was probably first not a proper name, but an appellative, a word that signified any great hero, or a general name for all mighty and valiant leaders in war, that in length of time might be taken for a proper name, and especially by the Grecians, that did not understand the signification of the word. "Thus the word Melicarthus, given to Hercules by Sanchoniathon, seems to be an appellative that signifies a 'terrible king' or 'valiant leader in war.' The word in the Hebrew, or Phoenician tongue, probably was עָרִיץ מֶלֶךְ, *Melek-arits*, the 'terrible' or 'valiant' king or captain. 'The Terrible' in the Old Testament is[8] put for those that are champions in war, where the word in the original is *Arits*. Hence Ἄρτης with the Egyptians was Mars, and of the same original

6. MS: "~~four~~ ⟨Three⟩."
7. This paragraph, written originally after No. 412 on the last page of the second manuscript, is a later addition.
8. JE deleted "frequently."

with Ἄρης, Mars's Greek name; and Mars and Hercules were promiscuously used in the oriental parts. The heroes used therefore to be called ἀρταῖοι. We find both joined together by Hesychius in his character of the Persian princes, or heroes, ἀρταῖοι οἱ ἥρωες ὠαρὰ Πέρσαις. Gale's *Court of Gentiles*, Pt. 1, Bk. 2, ch. 5.[9]

403. GENESIS 49:10. "Until Shiloh come." "Silenus, so famous among the poets, whom they place in the order of their gods, is derived from hence. Diadorus, Lib. 3, says, 'The first that ruled at Nysa was Silenus, whose genealogy is unknown to all, by reason of his antiquity,'" which is agreeable to what the Scriptures say of the Messiah. Is. 53:8, "Who shall declare his generation?" And elsewhere, "To us a child is born, to us a son is given, and his name shall be called Wonderful, Counselor, the Everlasting Father" [Is. 9:6]; and other places. "As for Nysa, where Silenus reigned, it seems to be the same with Sinai" (as was showed elsewhere; see No. 401). The Messiah dwelt there. It was he that dwelt there in the bush, and there he manifested himself, and spake with Moses and the children of Israel. And this is represented as his dwelling place several times in Scripture; and therefore, when God redeemed the children of Israel from Egypt, and brought 'em there, he is represented as bringing them to himself. Near this mountain was the altar called "Jehovah Nissi" [Ex. 17:15], which is a name Moses gave the Messiah. "Of Shiloh, it is said, 'And to him shall the יִקְּהַת, the gathering, or the obedience (as the word signifies), of the people be' [Gen. 49:10]. Thus Silenus is made by the poets to be the greatest doctor of his age, and he is called Bacchus's preceptor; i.e. according to Vossius's account, Bacchus was Moses. [See before, No. 401.][1] And Silenus, or Shiloh, or Christ,[2] instructed Moses on Mount Sinai, or Nysa, the place where Bacchus and Silenus were said to be. Bacchus and Silenus are made by the poets to be inseparable companions. Another attribute given to Silenus is, that he was carried for the most part on an ass, which Bochart refers to that, Gen. 49:11, 'Binding his ass's colt to the choice vine.' The mythologists fable Silenus, comrade of Bacchus, to be employed in treading out grapes. This Bochart refers to, Gen. 49:11, 'He washed his garments in wine, and his clothes in the blood of grapes'" (and is agreeable to what is said of the Messiah elsewhere in the Scripture: "I have trodden the wine press alone, and

9. Gale, *Court of the Gentiles* (2nd ed.), Pt. 1, Bk. 2, pp. 53–66.
1. JE's brackets.
2. JE deleted "at Mt. Sinai and in the wilderness was."

of the people was none with me" [Is. 63:3]). "They characterize Silenus, as 'one that was always drunk,' as 'tis supposed from what follows, Gen. 49:12. 'His eyes shall be red with wine,' which Solomon makes the character of one overcome with wine; Prov. 23:29–30, 'To whom redness of eyes,' etc. They ascribe to Silenus for his meat, cow's milk, which Bochart makes to be traduced from Gen. 49:12, 'And his teeth white with milk.' That Silenus is the same with Shiloh further appears from that of Pausanias, *Eliacon* 2. Ἐν γῇ τῇ Ἑβραίων χώρᾳ Σιληνῶ μνῆμα, 'The monument of Silenus remains in the country of the Hebrews.'" See Gale, *Court of Gentiles*, Pt. 1, Bk. 2, ch. 6, pp. 67–69.[3]

404. EXODUS 33:14–15. "And he said, My presence shall go with thee (in the original פָּנַי). And he said, If thy presence go not with us, carry us not up hence." Hence probably the heathen Pan and Faunus, the god of shepherds. The shepherds were the Israelites, that were by the Egyptians called "the shepherds," because a shepherd was a strange thing in their country. Hence "Pan is supposed to be one of Bacchus's principal commanders," because *God's presence* is here promised to [go] with Moses and the people, to help them in their wars. And Pan, going with Bacchus to war, is said to have sent "astonishing fears" on all their enemies, which arises from the great terrors with which the God of Israel (those shepherds) brought up the children of Israel out of Egypt, with which he terrified the Egyptians, and Israel themselves, and all nations, by what appeared when God gave the law, and the great terrors sent into the hearts of their enemies in Canaan, so very often spoken of. See Gen. 35:5, Ex. 15:14–16, 23:27, 34:10, and Deut. 2:25, 7:21, 10:17, 21, 11:25, 26:8, 34:12, and Josh. 2:9, and Ps. 106:22. God never manifested himself so much to the heathen nation in his awful terrors, as he did in that affair of leading Israel as their shepherd out of Egypt through the wilderness into Canaan, and settling them there. Those fears and terrors are spoken of as from the presence of the Lord. Ps. 68:7–8, "O God, when thou wentest forth before thy people, when thou didst march through the wilderness; Selah: the earth shook. The heavens also dropped at the presence (פָּנִים) of the Lord (the Pan or Faunus of the heathen); even Sinai itself was moved at the presence of the God of Israel (the shepherds)." And Ps. 97:4–5, "His lightnings enlightened the world; the earth saw and trembled.

3. Gale, *Court of the Gentiles* (2nd ed.), Pt. 1, Bk. 2, pp. 67–69.

The hills melted like wax at the *presence* of the Lord, at the *presence* of the Lord of the whole earth." For terror and trembling is often spoken of as what properly arises from the *presence* of the Lord. Is. 64:1–3, "Oh that thou wouldst rent the heavens, that thou wouldst come down, that the mountains might flow down at thy presence, as when the melting fire burneth, the fire causeth the waters to boil, to make thy name known to thine adversaries, that the nations might tremble at thy presence! When thou didst terrible things which we looked not for, thou camest down; the mountains flowed down at thy presence." So Is. 19:1, Jer. 5:22, and Ezek. 38:20. "Whence that proverbial speech, of 'Panic fears.'" Bochart says that "Faunus, among the Latins, is the same god, and of the same original with Pan. Pan is said to be an Egyptian god," to come up with Bacchus (i.e. Moses) to fight against the giants.[4] That which God promised Moses when he said, "My presence shall go with thee," was his Son, the same with the "angel of his presence," spoken of, Is. 63:9, and therefore when Christ was crucified. Hence that "relation of Plutarch, touching the mourning of the demoniac spirits, for the death of their great god Pan, and the ceasing of their oracles thereupon. Bochart says, the Hebrew פן, one that is struck, or strikes with astonishing fears." See Gale's *Court of Gentiles*, Pt. 1, Bk. 2, ch. 6, pp. 70–71.[5]

405. GENESIS 10:1–2. Concerning Japheth, the son of Noah. Neptune is the same with Japheth, who is called the "god of the sea," because maritime places, islands, and the great peninsulas of Asia Minor, Greece, Italy, and Spain were peopled[6] by his posterity.

The name Neptune is derived from the same radix that Japheth is, even from פָּתָה, "to enlarge," whence יֶפֶת, Japheth, and נִפְתָּה, *Niphtha*, in Niphal, according the allusion of Noah, *Japht Elohim Japhet*: Gen. 9:27, "God shall enlarge Japheth." Proportionable whereunto Neptune was called by the Greeks Ποσειδῶν, which grammarians in vain attempt to deduce from the Greek tongue, seeing as Herodotus in *Euterpe* asserts, the name Poseidon was at first used by none but the Libyans or Africans, who always honored this god. Poseidon is the same with the Punic word פשיטן *Pesitan*, which signifies "expanse" or "broad," from פָּשַׂט, *Pasat*, to "dilate"

4. JE deleted "So Diod. Sic."
5. Gale, *Court of the Gentiles* (2nd ed.), Pt. 1, Bk. 2, ch. 6, pp. 70–71.
6. MS: "people."

or "expand." Japheth's name, and what is said of him, "God shall enlarge Japheth," well suits with Neptune's character among the heathen, who is styled *Late imperans* and *Latisonans*, as also "one that has a large breast."

The genealogy of Neptune confirms that he is Japheth; he is the son of Saturn, i.e. Noah. See note on Gen. 1:27.[7] Gale's *Court of the Gentiles*, Pt. 1, Bk. 2, ch. 6, pp. 73–74.[8]

406. GENESIS 28:18–19. "And Jacob rose up early in the morning, and took the stone that he had put for his pillows, and set it up for a pillar, and poured oil upon the top of it. And he called the name of that place Bethel," etc. So Gen. 31:13, 45, and 35:14. "From hence the heathen *Baetylia*, mentioned by Philo Biblius, out of Sanchoniathon. The *god Uranus* excogitated *Baetylia*, having fashioned them into living stones. Bochart conceives that Sanchoniathon, instead of 'living stones,' writ 'anointed stones,' נְשֻׁפִים (from the radix *Shuph*,[9] which among the Syrians signifies 'to anoint'), which Philo Biblius read נְפָשִׁים, whence he changed 'anointed' into 'living stones.' So Damascius tells us, 'I saw a *Baetylus* moved in the air.' The Phoenicians, imitating Jacob at Bethel, first worshipped that very stone which the patriarch anointed. So Scaliger, in *Euseb.*, tells us, that 'the Jews relate so much, that although that *Cippus*, or stone, was at first beloved of God in the times of the patriarchs, yet afterwards he hated it because the Canaanites turned it into an idol.' Neither did the Phoenicians only worship this stone at Bethel, but also in imitation of this rite, erected several other *Baetylia* on the like occasion. As Jacob erected his pillar of stone as a memorial of God's apparition to him, so in like manner, both the Phoenicians and Grecians, upon some imaginary of some god (or devil rather), would erect their *Baetylia*, or pillars, in commemoration of such an apparition. So Photius, out of Damascius, tells us, 'That near Heliopolis in Syria, Asclepiades ascended the mountain Libanus, and saw many *Baetylia*, or *Baetyli*, concerning which he relates many miracles.' He relates also, 'That these *Baetylia* were consecrated, some to Saturn, some to Jupiter, and some to others.' So Phavorimus says,

---

7. In his entry on Gen. 1:27, JE cites Gale's judgment that the "heathen fables" concerning Saturn were drawn from the story of Noah. Gale links the three sons of Noah with three children of Saturn: Jupiter with Ham, Pluto with Shem, and Neptune with Japheth ("Blank Bible").

8. Gale, *Court of the Gentiles* (2nd ed.), Pt. 1, Bk. 2, pp. 73–74.

9. שׁוּף.

'*Baetylus* is a stone which stands at Heliopolis near Libanus.' This stone some also called στήλην, which is the same word by which the LXX[1] render Jacob's pillar." Gale's *Court of the Gentiles*, Pt. 1, Bk. 2, ch. 7, pp. 89–90.[2]

407. GENESIS 41. The history of Joseph's advancement in Egypt, etc. [That] the Apis and Serapis of the Egyptians seems to signify Joseph, is probable, because, "1. It was the mode of the Egyptians to preserve the memories of their noble benefactors by some significative hieroglyphics, or symbols. And the great benefits, which the Egyptians received from Joseph in supplying them with bread-corn, is aptly represented under the form of an ox, the symbol of an husbandman. Thus Suidas (in *Serapis*) tells us, 'That Apis, being dead, had a temple built for him, wherein was nourished a bullock, the symbol of an husbandman.' According to which resemblance also Minucius, in times past the prefect of provision at Rome, was in very like manner honored with the form of a golden ox or bull. 2. Joseph is compared to a bullock in Scripture (Deut. 33:17). 3. The same may be evinced from the names Apis and Serapis. For Apis seems evidently a derivative from אָב, father, as Joseph styles himself (Gen. 45:8). As for Serapis, it was the same with Apis, and also a symbol of Joseph, which Vossius collects from this. (1) That it had a bushel on its head, as a symbol of Joseph's providing corn for the Egyptians. (2) From the etymon of Serapis, which is derived either from שׁוֹר, an ox, or from שַׂר, a prince, and Apis, both of which are applicable to Joseph." Gale's *Court of Gentiles*, Pt. 1, Bk. 2, ch. 7, pp. 92–94.[3]

408. EXODUS 2. Moses is the same with the Egyptian Osiris, for, 1. Moses is the same with Bacchus, as has been showed before, No. 401. And "Diodorus tells us, that Osiris was called by the Greeks Dionysus, the name of Bacchus. 2. Diodorus tells us that Hercules was the chief captain of Osiris' army," who was Joshua, as has been shown, No. 402. 3. Diodorus tells us, "That Osiris had in his army Anubis, covered over with a dog's skin, which thence was pictured with a dog's head, and called the dog-keeper, etc. All which seems to refer to Caleb's name, which signifies a dog. 4. Pan is said to war under Osiris," which is the same with Christ, whom God promises should go with Moses when he

1. I.e. the Septuagint.
2. Gale, *Court of the Gentiles* (2nd ed.), Pt. 1, Bk. 2, pp. 89–90.
3. Ibid., pp. 92–94.

says, פָּנַי, "My presence shall go with" [Ex. 33:14], as has been shown,
No. 404. "5. Osiris is said to have horns, from the mistake of Moses'
character, who is thence pictured with horns," because of his beams of
light, the word in Hebrew for "horns" and "beams" being the same. "6.
Moses, with the princes of the tribes, carried up the bones of Joseph
unto Canaan; hence the poet's fable of Osiris' bones, etc." See Gale's
Court of Gentiles, Pt. 1, Bk. 2, ch. 7, p. 94.[4]

409. GENESIS 7. "Bochart, in the preface to his *Phaleg*, says, 'The
fame of the flood, wherein a few only remaining, the rest of men
perished, was diffused among all nations. The Hieropolitans (in Lucian's *dea Syra*) frame a large history thereof, and that drawn out of
their own archives, every way parallel with Moses' narration, excepting
that, instead of Noah, the name Deucalion is substituted. Plutarch
makes mention of the dove sent out of the ark, etc. The same Abydenus, from whom also we learn, that the ark rested in Armenia, and
that the relics thereof were extant there, which is also taught by Berosus and Polyhistor and Nicholas Damascenus. Epiphanius also affirms, that they were to be seen in his time.' And Grotius *de verit. Relig.
Christianae, Lib.* I, where we have many concurring testimonies of the
most ancient, touching the universal flood and its traditional notices
among the pagans. So Berosus makes mention of the flood and ark,
and Alexander the Polyhistorian of the preservation of animals in the
ark. Martinius *Hist. Sinic* (*Lib.* 1, p. 12) tells us, 'That there is great
mention of the flood among the Sinac writers.' Johan. *de Lact. de origin
Gent. American* (*Lib.* I, p. 115), acquaints us, 'That there is a constant
tradition of the flood amongst the Indians, both in New France, Peru,
etc.' Alexander Polyhistorian and Cyril in Josephus say, 'There was a
great flood, and that there was one Nisurus to whom Saturn revealed
it, and bid him make an ark; and he did so, and gathered some of all
beasts into it. And that the ark was in Armenia, and the fragments of it
are in Heliopolis.' Yea, we find some memory of the raven and the dove
sent forth by Noah, preserved in some fragments amongst pagan
writers. Thus Sandford *de descensu*, 'Plutarch, out of the ancient theology, makes mention of the dove sent out of Noah's ark.' So Bochart, in
his preface to *Hist. de animal. Sacris*, tells us, 'That peradventure the
raven sent forth by Noah belongs to the Greek fable of the raven sent
forth by Apollo, which returned not till after the figs were ripe.' But
more expressly, in the same preface, Bochart affirms, 'That of this

4. Ibid., p. 94.

history of the dove sent forth by Noah, there are evident vestigia or characters to be found in Abydenus, Plutarch, and the Arabians.' To conclude this discourse of the flood, we have a concise, yet clear hypotyposis, or adumbration, of it in Ovid, *Met., Lib.* 1, *Fab.* 7.

Fit fragor et densi funduntur ab aethere nimbi.[5]

See more in Seneca, *Lib.* 3, *Ques.*, ch. 27." See Gale's *Court of Gentiles*, Pt. 1, Bk. 3, ch. 6.[6] See No. 424.[7]

410. GENESIS 11:3–4, ff. Concerning the building of Babel and confusion of tongues. "Bochart, in his preface to *Phaleg*, about the middle; 'What follows, says he, concerning the tower of Babel, its structure, and the confusion of tongues ensuing thereon, also of its builders being dispersed throughout various parts of the earth, is related in express words by Abydenus, and Eupolemus, in Cyrillus, and Eusebius.' Bochart, in his *Phaleg*, gives us a description of the tower of Babel, out of Herodotus, parallel to that of the Scripture. And whereas 'tis said, Gen. 11:9, that it was called Babel, 'because the Lord confounded their language,' hence pagan writers called those of this dispersion, and their successors μέροπες, 'men of divided tongues.' So Homer's *Iliad*, αἱ γένεαι μερόπων ἀνθρόπων, 'generations of men having divided tongues.' Abydenus affirmeth that it was a common opinion, that the men, whom the earth brought forth, gathered themselves together, and builded a great tower, which was Babel; and the gods, being angry with it, threw it down." Gale's *Court of Gentiles*, Pt. 1, Bk. 3, ch. 8, pp. 83–84. See No. 430.[8]

411. JOSHUA 10. Add this to No. 402, at the place marked thus *-*, near the latter end. "Nimrod, the head of this faction, is called a 'mighty one' [Gen. 10:8], where the Hebrew גִּבּוֹר signifies a 'giant,' or 'mighty one.' The giants' war is thus described by Ovid, *Met., Lib.* 1, *Fab.* 5,

Affectasse ferunt regnum coeleste gigantes,
Altaque congestos struxisse ad sidera montes.[9]

Which is only a poetical adumbration of the design at Babel, of building a tower 'whose top might reach unto heaven' [Gen. 11:4]."

5. A great noise occurred, and heavy rains poured forth from the heavens.
6. Gale, *Court of the Gentiles* (2nd ed.), Pt. 1, Bk. 3, pp. 72–74.
7. This cross-reference is a later addition.
8. This cross-reference is a later addition.
9. The giants made an attempt on the heavenly kingdom, and built a pile of high mountains to the sky.

412. EXODUS 3:14. "I AM THAT I AM," etc. Some of the heathen philosophers seem to have derived notions that they had of the deity from hence. Plato and Pythagoras make the great object of philosophy to be "τὸ ὄν, 'that which is,' τὸ ὄντως ὄν, 'that which truly is,' and also τὸ αὐτοὸν, 'Being itself.' The LXX[1] renders this place in Exodus thus: ἐγὼ εἰμὶ ὁ ὤν. That the philosophers by their τὸ ὄν and τὸ ὄντως ὄν and τὸ αὐτοὸν meant God, appears by what Iamblichus saith of Pythagoras: 'By τῶν ὄντων, "Beings," he understood sole, and self agents, imma-terials, and eternals. Other beings indeed are not Beings, but yet are equivocally called such by participation with these eternals.' So Plato in his *Parmenides* (who was a Pythagorean), treating of τὸ ὄν καί ἕν, which he makes the first principle of all things, thereby understands God. So in his *Timaeus*, Locrus, he says, τὸ ὄν, 'Being is always; neither hath it beginning.' So again in his *Timaeus*, fol. 37–38, he proves 'nothing properly is but God, the eternal essence, to which, says he, we do very improperly attribute those distinctions of time, *was* and *shall be*.' Plu-tarch says, τὸ ὄντως ὄν: '*The True Being* is eternal, ingenerable, and incorruptible, unto which no time ever brings mutation.' Hence in the Delphic temple there was engraven, εἶ, 'Thou art.'" Gale's *Court of Gentiles*, Pt. 2, Bk. 2, ch. 8, pp. 173–76.[2]

That Plato by τὸ ὄντως ὄν meant God, appears by his own words, in his *Epist.* 6, fol. 323. "Let there be," says he, "a law constituted and confirmed by oath, calling to witness the God of all things, the Gover-nor of beings present and things to come, the Father of that governing cause, whom, according to our philosophy, we make to be the *true Being*," "ὄν, ὄντως," etc. This is the same with he that revealed himself to Moses by the name "I am that I am," out of the bush, that was the Son of God. Gale's *Court of Gentiles*, Pt. 1, Bk. 3, ch. 5, p. 64.[3] Plato seems evidently to have heard of this revelation that God made of himself to Moses by the name of I AM, etc., out of the burning bush on Mount Sinai, and to have a plain reference to it in his *Philebus*, fol. 17. "He confesseth, 'The knowledge of the τὸ ὄν, etc., was from the gods, who communicated this knowledge to us by a certain Prometheus, *together with a bright fire.*'" Gale's *Court of Gentiles*, Pt. 2, Bk. 3, ch. 2, p. 228.[4] See No. 457.[5]

---

1. I.e. the Septuagint.
2. Gale, *Court of the Gentiles* (Oxford, 1670), Pt. 2, Bk. 2, pp. 173–76.
3. Gale, *Court of the Gentiles*, Pt. 1, Bk. 3, p. 64.
4. Gale, *Court of the Gentiles*, Pt. 2, Bk. 3, p. 228.
5. This cross-reference is a later addition. Following this entry, on the back cover of Book

413. DANIEL 9:27. "And for the overspreading of abominations he shall make it desolate." It ought to have been translated, "*By* or *with* the overspreading of abominations he shall make it desolate." So the particle עַל sometimes is used (see Buxtorf).[6] 'Tis manifest that the abomination here mentioned is spoken of as the efficient, or instrument, of the desolation, by other scriptures that have a manifest reference to this, as Dan. 11:31. "And arms shall stand on his part, and they shall pollute the sanctuary of strength, and shall take away the daily sacrifice, and they *shall place the abomination that maketh desolate.*" And Dan. 12:11, "And from the time that the daily sacrifice shall be taken away, *and the abomination that maketh desolate set up,* there shall be a thousand two hundred and ninety days." And the expression is very much like those, concerning that which is spoken of, Dan. 8:11–13. "Yea, he magnified himself even to the prince of the host, and by him the daily sacrifice was taken away, and the place of his sanctuary was cast down. And an host was given him against the daily sacrifice by reason of transgression, and it cast down the truth to the ground; and it practiced and prospered. Then I heard one saint speaking, and another saint said unto that certain saint which spake, How long shall be the vision concerning the daily sacrifice, and the transgression of desolation, to give both the sanctuary and the host to be trodden underfoot?" And Matt. 24:15–16, "When ye therefore shall see *the abomination of desolation,* spoken of by Daniel the prophet, stand in the holy place (whoso readeth, let him understand). Then let them which be in Judea flee to the mountains." And the same words in Mark 13:14. The great difficulty of understanding these places seems to lie in these two things.

I. That the abomination of desolation spoken of in all these places seems to be the same. There are these following things that argue them to be the same. 1. In the manner of speaking of "the abomination that maketh desolate" in Dan. 11:31 and Dan. 12:11, seems to imply a reference to some such thing that there had been a revelation made of to Daniel, and that Daniel had already in his mind.[7] And that in Dan.

2, JE wrote: "If I live to make another book of this sort, to observe to cut the gashes for the stitching in deeper and not so near to the joinings of the stitch, that the book may open more freely and fully. And let the sheets be divided into twice so small divisions, and starch no paper in a paper cover, for that makes it crack. And if that don't do, try next stitching the backs of all the divisions of sheets to a slip of leather, and sew the cover over the leather."

6. Among the translations suggested by Johannis Buxtorf are *a* or *ab*, and *cum* (*Lexicon Hebraicum et Chaldaicum*, pp. 522–23).

7. JE deleted "But there had been no revelation of any such thing, even no abomination that maketh desolate before, but in Dan. 9:27."

9:27 seems to have a reference to that transgression of desolation in Dan. 8:11–12. It seems evidently to be the same thing spoken of several times. Here is something spoken of over and over, called by the same or a like name, called by way of eminency, the "abomination," or the transgression, described by the like property, "that it maketh desolate." All are spoken of with a special reference to the holy city and sanctuary, as appears by comparing the several places and contexts. All are spoken [of] in each place in Daniel, as attended with the ceasing of the sacrifice. 2. Christ, when he refers to the abomination of desolation spoken of by Daniel the prophet, seems to suppose but one abomination of desolation spoken of by Daniel the prophet. 3. Some things that Christ says of this abomination of desolation spoken of by Daniel the prophet seem to be especially taken from one place, others from another. He speaks of it as the abomination that makes desolate, that accompanies the destruction of Jerusalem by the Romans, and that seems to be taken from Dan. 9:27. He speaks of it as "standing," or "set up," in the holy place. This seems rather to be taken from Dan. 11:31, where it is said, "they shall pollute the *sanctuary*, or *holy place*, and *place* the abomination that maketh desolate." And Dan. 12:11, "And the abomination that maketh desolate *set up*"; and that manner of expression, "of desolation," seems to be taken from Dan. 8:13. And yet,

II. The prophecies of "the abomination that maketh desolate," in different places in Daniel, seem evidently to have respect to different seasons and events, as that in Dan. 8:11–13 and Dan. 11:31 have an evident reference to what came to pass in the days of Antiochus Epiphanes. And what is spoken of, Dan. 9:27, has an evident reference to what came to pass at the destruction of Jerusalem by the Romans; and that in Dan. 12 has a reference to what comes to pass in the days of Antichrist, as is manifest from the preceding part of the chapter.

But the reconciliation of the difficulty is in this, that they are all mystically one and the same, for they are lively types one of another. What is ultimately respected is that spoken of in the 12th of Daniel, which is accomplished in the days of Antichrist, of which the preceding are lively images. That setting up of the abomination that makes desolate in the sanctuary by Antiochus Epiphanes is typical of what is done by Antichrist, for he was a great type of Antichrist; and so was that which came to pass at the time of the destruction of Jerusalem by the Romans, spoken of, Dan. 9:27, and spoken of by Christ, Matt. 24:15. "Luke explains 'the abomination of desolation standing in the holy place,' by Jerusalem's being compassed with the Roman armies

(Luke 21:20–21). Jerusalem was the holy city, and so many furlongs about it were accounted holy. Now when the Roman army approached within the limits of the holy ground, then the 'abomination of desolation' might be said to 'stand in the holy place.' But the word 'abomination' seems particularly to refer to the Roman ensigns, upon which were the images of their emperors, which the Romans worshipped, as Suetonius expressly tells us, and Tacitus calls them, their *bellorum dei,* their 'gods of war.' Now it was an abomination to the Jews to see these idols set up within the limits of the holy city. To which may be added what Josephus tells us afterwards, that the Romans, after they had conquered the city, set up these ensigns in the ruins of the temple, and sacrificed to them." (Thus Archbishop Tillotson, Vol. 3 of his *Works,* Sermon 185, p. 533.)[8] This setting up the image of the emperor within the limits of the holy city, and afterwards in the ruins of the temple, and there sacrificing to it, is a lively[9] representation of setting up the Pope in the church of God, the spiritual Jerusalem, who is the emperor of the antichristian Roman Empire, and the image of the beast, an image of the heathen Roman emperors, who is set up as a god in the temple of God, where he exalts himself above all that is called God, or is worshipped, although it be in the temple in ruins. He first in effect destroys[1] the temple of God, and then sets himself up there as God, to be worshipped and sacrificed to. Here see Bishop Kidder's *Demonstration,* Pt. 2, pp. 11–13.[2]

414. MATTHEW 16:28. Add this to note on Matt. 16:28, No. 197. See No. 464.[3] There is this that argues that Christ did not suppose that the end of the world would be in that generation, that when he is discoursing of the destruction of Jerusalem and the end of the world (Matt. 24 and Luke 21), and says to his disciples, Luke 21:32, "Verily I say unto you, this generation shall not pass away till all be fulfilled," yet he says in the same discourse, v. 24, speaking of the terrible destruction of that land, "And they shall fall by the edge of the sword, and shall be led away captive into all nations, and Jerusalem shall be trodden down of

8. *The Works of the Most Reverend Dr. John Tillotson, Late Lord Archbishop of Canterbury* (3 vols. London, 1752), *3,* 533.
9. JE deleted "image."
1. MS: "~~Ruins~~ ⟨in Effect destroys⟩."
2. This reference is a later addition. Richard Kidder, *A Demonstration of the Messias. In which the truth of the Christian religion is proved, against all the enemies thereof; but especially against the Jews. In three parts.* (2nd ed., London, 1726), Pt. 2, pp. 11–13.
3. This cross-reference is a later addition.

the Gentiles, till the times of the Gentiles be fulfilled." From whence it seems evident, that Christ did not expect that the end of the world would be before many ages, for first all those things must be accomplished that had been spoken of by Christ as forerunners of the destruction of Jerusalem: wars, and rumors of wars, and earthquakes, and famines, and yet the destruction of Jerusalem not very near; and the gospel must be preached to all nations, which must be a work of time. And many other things are mentioned, as the rising of false Christs, and false prophets, and persecutions, etc., all which denote that considerable time was to pass before the destruction of Jerusalem. And then the whole land was to be destroyed by war, and great distress, and the people were to be dispersed into all nations, which also must be a work of time. And then "Jerusalem should be trodden down of the Gentiles, till the times of the Gentiles should be fulfilled," which at least intimates that Jerusalem was to [lie] a long time in ruins. Christ refers to the "time, times, and half" in the 12th of Daniel, which is there exceeding plainly spoken of as a long time. And then it is supposed in the words, that Jerusalem is to be again rebuilt after this, and rebuilt to some purpose, not just rebuilt and then immediately and eternally destroyed again, before the end of so great a work as the rebuilding could be answered, so as to answer the designs of the restoration of the state, the peace and prosperity of the people in their own land. For the words imply a restoration of the people from their miserable state as trodden down; and the times of the Gentiles in Daniel, which Christ refers to, are spoken of by that prophet, very plainly and abundantly, as ending in a comfortable restoration of God's people from a miserable ruined state. But to be rebuilt in a few years to be eternally destroyed, is not worth the name of a restoration, or end to their long-continued ruin. Besides, the mere rebuilding Jerusalem and restoring the state of the land after such a total and long-continued destruction, must be the work of a great deal of time; it was a work of considerable time when the people returned from their Babylonish captivity.

415. GENESIS 10:1. These things are evidences that all mankind are originally from one head or fountain, and "of one blood," viz. that all agreed in the same custom of sacrifices, which could be from nothing else than tradition from their progenitors. And their all agreeing in "counting by decads, or stopping at ten in their numerical computations, which Aristotle says, all men, both barbarians and Greeks, did use. Their having everywhere anciently the same number of letters,

and the same names, or little varied, of them [and the remarkable affinity of all ancient languages].[4] Their dividing time into weeks, or systems of seven days, of which practice to have been general there are many plain testimonies. Their beginning the day, or revolution of twenty-four hours, with the night. Yea perhaps, if one consider it, the whole business concerning matrimony." Thus Dr. Barrow, Vol. 2 of his *Works*, p. 93.[5]

416. Whether the PENTATEUCH was written by MOSES. That it was so is the voice of all antiquity, and it has been all along, even to this day, the received opinion, both of Jews and Christians, that Moses, being commanded and inspired by God, wrote those books that are called the Pentateuch, excepting only some particular passages that were inserted afterwards by a divine direction for the better understanding the history.

We read, Ex. 24:4, 7–8, that "Moses wrote all the words of the Lord," that before that had been delivered from Mt. Sinai, in a book that is there called "the book of the covenant." And afterwards, after God had added more precepts to [it], he again commands Moses to write those words. Ex. 34:27, "And the Lord said unto Moses, Write thou these words, for after the tenor of these words I have made a covenant with thee and with Israel." And near forty years afterwards, Moses was commanded to write all the commands that God had given the people, and the revelations that he had made of himself to them, in one [book], to be laid up by the side of the ark of the covenant, to be kept for a testimony against Israel. Deut. 31:24–26, "And it came to pass, when Moses had made an end of writing the words of this law in a book, until they were finished, that Moses commanded the Levites, which bare the ark of the covenant of the Lord, saying, Take this book of the law, and put it in the side of the ark of the covenant of the Lord your God, that it may be there for a witness against thee."

And the original of this book of the law was in being, as we read expressly, till the times of Josiah (II Kgs. 22 and II Chron. 34), and so doubtless till the captivity into Babylon. This book of the law, that Moses was thus commanded to lay up beside the ark, did not only comprehend those things which were contained in some of those pre-

4. JE's brackets and insertion.
5. Isaac Barrow, *The Works of the Learned Isaac Barrow, D.D.* (3 vols. London, 1716), 2, 93–94. This citation occurs in Barrow's sermon entitled "The Being of God Proved from Universal Consent."

ceding chapters of Deuteronomy, wherein some things of the law were repeated, but the whole system of divine laws which God gave to the children of Israel, expressing the whole of the duty which God expected of them. This appears by Josh. 1:7–8. "Only be thou strong and very courageous, that thou mayst observe and do according to all the law, which Moses my servant commanded thee. Turn not from it to the right hand or to the left, that thou mayst prosper whithersoever thou goest. This book of the law shall not depart out of thy mouth, but thou shalt meditate therein day and night, that thou mayst observe to do according to all that is written therein," etc. And therefore the Levites, that Jehoshaphat sent to teach the people their duty, did not do it any other way than out of the book of the law. II Chron. 17:9, "And they taught in Judah, and had the book of the law of the Lord with them, and went about throughout all the cities of Judah, and taught the people."

And then, 'tis further evident that the book of the law, which we have an account of his committing to the Levites, to be laid up in the side of the ark (Deut. 31), did not only contain what had been then lately delivered in some preceding chapters of Deuteronomy, because in this book of the law were contained the precepts concerning burnt offerings and sacrifices, and the office and business of the priesthood, which is not contained so much in Deuteronomy as in Leviticus and Numbers, as appears by II Chron. 23:18. "Also Jehoiada appointed the offices of the house of the Lord by the hands of the priests, the Levites, whom David had distributed in the house of the Lord, to offer the burnt offerings of the Lord, as it is written in the law of Moses" (II Chron. 30:5, 31:3, 35:12, Neh. 8:14–15, 10:34–36, Hag. 2:11 ff., Josh. 8:31, and Ezra 6:18).[6] And in that book of the law were contained not barely the precepts which God delivered to Moses, but the sanctions and enforcements of those laws, the promises and threatenings, as appears by Deut. 29:20–21. "The Lord will not spare him, but then the anger of the Lord and his jealousy shall smoke against that man, and all the curses that are written in this book shall lie upon him, and the Lord shall blot out his name from under heaven. And the Lord shall separate him unto evil out of all the tribes of Israel, according to all the curses of the covenant that are written in this book of the law." Also v. 27.[7] So Deut. 28:61, "Also every plague and every sickness, which is not written in the book of this law, will the Lord bring upon

6. These biblical references, entered at various times, are later interlineations.
7. This reference is a later interlineation.

thee, until thou be destroyed." See also II Kgs. 22:13, 16, 19, and parallel places in II Chron. 34 [and] Dan. 9:13.[8] And Josh. 8:34–35, "And afterward he read all the words of the law, the blessings and the cursings, according to all that is written in the book of the law. There was not a word of all that Moses commanded, which Joshua read not," etc. See Ps. 105:8–10.[9] Yea, not only the promises and threatenings were contained in that book of the law, but all the revelations that God [gave] that tended to enforce it, or any way related to it, and even the prophecies that were there contained of what should afterwards happen to the people on their sin or on their repentance. This appears by Neh. 1:8–9. "Remember, I beseech thee, the word that thou commandest thy servant Moses, saying, If ye transgress, I will scatter you abroad among the nations. But if ye turn unto me, and keep my commandments, and do them, though there were of you cast out unto the uttermost part of the heaven, yet will I gather them from thence, and will bring them unto the place that I have chosen to set my name there."

And besides, we read of Moses being expressly commanded to write histories of the acts of the Lord towards his people, as well as the revelations that he made to them. So he was commanded to write an account of the people's war with Amalek, with its circumstances, that posterity might see the reason of the perpetual war God had declared against Amalek. Ex. 17:14, "And the Lord said unto Moses, Write this for a memorial in a book, and rehearse it in the ears of Joshua; for I will utterly put out the remembrance of Amalek from under heaven." Now a full account could not be given of this affair without relating much of the history of Israel preceding of it; for an account must be given in the writing of the reason and occasion of the children of Israel's coming to the border of the Amalekites, and what was the cause of the discord and war that was between them and Israel, which would take up no small part of the history of the book of Exodus.

And besides, we are expressly told that Moses wrote the journeys of the children of Israel by God's command. Num. 33:2, "And Moses wrote their goings out according to their journeys by the commandment of the Lord." And is it reasonably to be supposed that he would write these for the use of the children of Israel in after generations, and not write the great and mighty acts of the Lord towards that people in Egypt, at the Red Sea, and Mt. Sinai, and the wilderness,

8. Ibid.
9. Ibid.

which were a thousand [times] more worthy of a record and of being delivered down to posterity, as a mere journal of the people's progress in the wilderness, without those mighty acts?

'Tis every way incredible that Moses, of whom we so often read expressly that he wrote God's commands, threatenings, promises, and revelations, and histories, that he should not write those great acts of the Lord, and leave a record of them with the congregation of Israel, especially when it is evident in fact that Moses was exceeding careful that they might not forget those great acts of the Lord in future generations. Deut. 4:9–12, "Only take heed to thyself, and keep thy soul diligently, lest thou forget the things which thine eyes have seen, and lest they depart from thine heart all the days of thy life; but teach them thy sons, and thy sons' sons, specially the day when thou stoodst before the Lord thy God in Horeb," etc. Here the very same orders are given for the keeping the acts of the Lord in the memory of posterity, as are given for the keeping up the memory of the precepts (Deut. 6:7, and 11:18–19). Job speaks of writing words in a book as a proper means to keep up the memory of them,[1] and so does God to Isaiah. Is. 30:8, "Now go, write it before them in a table, and note it in a book, that it may be for the time to come forever and ever." Moses did not trust the precepts of God only to oral tradition; he was sensible that way only was not sufficient, though he gave such a charge to the people to teach their children. And the memory of the war with Amalek, when God saw it needful that it should be transmitted to posterity, was not trusted to oral tradition, but Moses was commanded to write it, that other generations might know it. And so the travels of the children, when it was thought of importance to be remembered, was not trusted to tradition, but a record was written to be transmitted. Very great care was taken, that those acts should be remembered, in appointing monuments of them, as the passover was instituted as a perpetual monument, or memorial, of the redemption of the children of Israel out of Egypt, and the beginning of the year was appointed as a memorial of it. And the firstborn sons were consecrated to God in memory of God's slaying the firstborn of Egypt. Certain laws were appointed about strangers, and the poor, and bondmen (Deut. 15:15, 16:11–12, and 24:17–18, 22; Lev. 25:42, 55),[2] in remembrance of their peregrination and bondage in Egypt.[3] To suppose that such care should be taken, lest

---

1. The remainder of this and the following sentence are later interlineations.
2. These references are later interlineations.
3. JE deleted "There is something of an absurdity in supposing that."

the laws themselves should be forgotten that were appointed for that end, to keep up the memory of the facts, that those laws should be written, and yet not that care taken that the facts themselves should be remembered as to write them, the memory of which is supposed to be of the greatest importance, the very being and remembrance of those laws being by the supposition subordinate thereto, that being the end of the both, the being and memory of the laws, even the memory of the facts, [is absurd]. In Neh. 13:1–3, a precept is cited, with a part of the history annexed, as the reason of the law; and all together is said to be read in the book of Moses.[4] The manna was laid up as a monument of their manner of living in the wilderness, and God's miraculous sustaining of the people there. The feast of tabernacles was to keep in remembrance the manner of their sojourning in the wilderness, as in Lev. 23:43. Aaron's rod that budded was laid up as a memorial of the great things done by that rod in Egypt, at the Red Sea, and in the wilderness, and particularly of the contest with Korah and his company [Num. 16]. And the censers of the rebels were kept, and turned into broad plates for the covering of the altar, as a memorial of what happened in the matter of Korah. And the fire from heaven was kept, without ever going out, as a perpetual monument of its miraculous descent from heaven and the occasion of it. And the brazen serpent was kept as a memorial of the plague of fiery serpents, and the miraculous healing of those that were bitten. The tabernacle that was built in the wilderness was a monument of the great manifestations God made of himself there, and the many things that came to pass relating to the building of the tabernacle. The two tables of stone kept in the ark were a monument of those great things that happened when they were given. The rest of [the] Jewish sabbath was appointed as a memorial of the deliverance of the children of Israel out of bondage. So the laws concerning the Moabites and Ammonites are appointed as monuments; so the gold taken in the war with the Midianites was laid up for a monument of the war with them (Num. 31:54). A great many places were named only to keep in remembrance memorable facts in the wilderness. And who can think that all this care was taken to keep those things in memory, and yet no history be written to be annexed to those many monuments to explain them, by him by whose hand those monuments were appointed, and he so great a writer, and so careful to keep up the memory of events by writing, in those instances of the

4. This sentence is a later interlineation.

writing of which we have express mention? Another instance of Moses' great care that those great acts might not be forgotten, is his calling together the congregation to rehearse 'em over to them a little before his death, as we have an account in Deuteronomy. And besides, he left some precepts, wherein the children of Israel were required themselves, from time to time, to rehearse over something of the general history of their ancestors, the patriarchs, that we have an account of in Genesis, and so the history of the people from that time, as in the law of him that offered the first fruits (Deut. 26).

And we find that great care was taken to erect monuments of the great acts of God towards the people after Moses' death, as of their passing through Jordan, though less memorable than some of those. And that there was monuments expressly appointed to keep in memory of so many of God's acts in Moses' time, and not of some others more memorable, is an argument that they had a history of them instead of monuments, as particularly of the children of Israel's passing through the Red Sea, and the destruction of Pharaoh and his hosts there, than which no act of God towards that people is more celebrated through the Scripture; and yet we have no account of any monument or any ordinance expressly said to be appointed in memory of that, though there [was] a monument of their passing through Jordan, an event much like it, but less remarkable, and far less celebrated in Scripture. No account can be given of this, but the history and song that Moses wrote and left in the book of the law were [a] monument of it.

Such was the care that was taken, that some of the acts of God towards the people might be remembered, that in appointing the monuments for their remembrance, it is expressed that it was for that end, that they might have it perpetually in mind as a token on their hand and frontlets between their eyes, as particularly in appointing the law of consecrating the firstborn, to keep up the remembrance of God's slaying the firstborn of Egypt (Ex. 13:15–16). One of the laws or precepts themselves of the book of the law was that, that the people should take heed never by any means to forget the great acts of God which they had seen, and that they should not be forgotten by future generations (Deut. 4). How unreasonable then is it, to suppose that no history was annexed to those laws, and so, at the same time that such a strict injunction of great care to keep up the memory of those things in future generations, they should be left without the necessary means of it! Again, another precept is that they should not forget their own acts and behavior from time to time (Deut. 9:7 ff.). See also Deut. 8:14–16 ff., and 5:15. So they are strictly required to remember their bondage in the land of Egypt (Deut. 16:12, and 24:18, 22), and also to remember what God did to Pharaoh and all Egypt, all those great signs and wonders, and the manner of their deliverance out of Egypt (Deut. 7:18–19). And so they are strictly enjoined to remember all their travail, the way that they went, and the circumstances and events of their journey (Deut. 8:2–5, 14–20). And they are charged to know God's great acts in Egypt, and from time to time, in Deut. 11:1–7. They are commanded to remember what God did to Miriam (Deut. 24:9). Writing of those works of God that are worthy to be remembered and celebrated by praises to God, is spoken of as a proper way of conveying the memory of them to posterity for that end, in Ps. 102:18. "This shall be written for the generation to come, and the people which shall be created shall praise the Lord." And the importance of remembering these works of God related in the Pentateuch, is mentioned not only in the Pentateuch itself, but also in other parts of Scripture, as in Ps. 105:5. "Remember his marvelous works that he hath done, his wonders, and the judgments of his mouth." By the marvelous works which God has done and his wonders, is meant those marvelous works that he did to Abraham and his seed, from the calling of Abraham to the bringing in of the people into Canaan, as appears by the following part of the psalm. And 'tis observable here, that the Psalmist connects the wonderful works and the laws or judgments of God's mouth together, as in like manner worthy to be remembered. See also I Chron. 16:12, with the subsequent part of that song. The law, and covenant, and wonderful works, are in like manner connected, as not to be forgotten, in Ps. 78:10–11. And in the 111th psalm, the Psalmist intimates that God [had] taken some special care to keep up the memory of those works. V. 4, "He hath caused his wonderful works to be remembered," speaking of these works, as appears by what follows in the psalm. And what other way can we suppose it to be that God hath done this, than the same with that whereby he caused his covenant and commandments, spoken of in the following verses, viz. by causing them to be recorded? The works and commandments are joined together in v. 7. "The works of his hands are verity and judgment; all his commandments are sure." And again, in the 9th verse, "He hath sent redemption to his people; he hath commanded his covenant forever," as they are doubtless connected in the record. Compare Ps. 147:19 and 103:7.[5] In the 78th psalm, the Psalmist, speaking of this great care that Moses took, that the history of the great

5. Ibid.

works of God towards Israel in Egypt and the wilderness should be remembered, and delivered to future generations (vv. 4–7), then proceeds[6] to rehearse the principal things in that history in a great many particulars, so as to give us, in short, the scheme of the whole history, with many minute circumstances, in such a manner as to show plainly that what is there rehearsed is copied out of the history of the Pentateuch.

'Tis the more likely that the history of the Pentateuch should be a part of that which was called the law of Moses, because it is observable that the words law, doctrine, statute, ordinance, etc., as they were used of old, did not only intend precepts, but also promises, and threatenings, and prophecies, and monuments, and histories, or whatever was revealed, promulgated, and established, to direct men in or enforce their duty to God.[7] So the blessings and the curses that were written by Moses are included in that phrase, "the words that Moses commanded" (Josh. 8:34–35). So promises are called "law" and "the word which God commanded," in Ps. 105:9–10 [and] I Chron. 16:15. So promises and threatenings are called "the word which God commanded his servant Moses" (Neh. 1:8–9). Threatenings and promises are called "statutes and judgments," in Lev. 26:46. Thus we read, Ex. 15:25–26, that at Marah God made for the people "a statute and an ordinance," but that which is so called is only a promise. So we read in the last chapter of Joshua, 25th verse, that "Joshua made a covenant with the people, and set them a statute and an ordinance in Shechem," which was nothing else than only his establishing what had been there said by a record and a monument, as appears by the context. So when God, in the song of Moses (Deut. 32:1–2), calls upon heaven and earth to give ear to his doctrine, which, he says, shall distill as the rain, etc., therein is included both history and prophecy, as appears by what follows. And what in Ps. 78:1 is called a "law," is only a history, and the very same with the history in the Pentateuch in epitome, those dark sayings of old which the Psalmist there rehearses, as appears by what follows in the psalm, which makes it the more easily supposable that the original and more full history, of which this is an epitome, was also amongst them called a law. And 'tis probable that when we read of the great things of God's law (Hos. 8:12), and the wondrous things of God's law, that thereby is not only intended precepts and sanctions, but the

---

6. JE deleted "in a very particular manner."

7. The next four sentences are a later interlineation.

great and wondrous works of God recorded in the law. 'Tis evident that the history is as much of an enforcement of the precepts (and is so made use of), as the threatenings, promises, and prophecies; and why then should it not be included in the name of the law as well as they?[8] There is something of history, or a declaration of the great acts or works of God, in that [which] is by way of eminency called the "law," viz. the Decalogue, in that there is a declaration of the two greatest works that the history in the Pentateuch gives an account of, viz. the creation of the world and the redemption out of Egypt out of the house of bondage. The latter is mentioned in the preface, and both in the 4th commandment in Deuteronomy 5:6–15.

But that history was included in what was called "law" is so plain by nothing as by Moses' own words. Deut. 1:5, "On this side Jordan, in the land of Moab, began Moses to declare this law, saying." And then follows, in this and the ensuing chapters, that which is called this law, which consist in great part of history, being a rehearsal and recapitulation of the history in the preceding books of the Pentateuch. What follows next, in this and the two next chapters, is almost wholly history, which undoubtedly there is special reason to understand as intended[9] by those words, "Moses began to declare this law, saying." See also Deut. 4:44–45, 5:1, and 31:9, 24–26. And again, "the book of the law" and "the book of[1] the covenant" were synonymous expressions (among other places, see Ps. 105:8–10); but the word "covenant," as it was then used,[2] included history, as Deut 29:1. "These are the words of the covenant which the Lord commanded Moses," etc. And what next follows is history, such history as was introductory, or concomitant, or confirmatory to the precepts, and threatenings, and promises that follow. And of this nature is all the history of the Pentateuch. 'Tis abundantly manifest that the manner of inditing and writing laws in the wilderness, delivered by Moses, was to intermix history with precepts, counsels, warnings, threatenings, promises, and prophecies.

It may be noted, that it was very early the custom in Israel to keep records of the public transactions in Israel, and to look upon it of so great importance as to have men appointed to that, whose business and office it was. So we find it was in the days of Solomon and David;

8. This sentence is a later interlineation.
9. The last two words are a later interlineation followed by another interlineation that JE deleted: "(or included in the meaning of)."
1. The last three words are a later interlineation.
2. JE deleted "implied."

yea, and in the days of the judges, so early as the days of Deborah. Judg. 5:14, "Out of Zebulon they that handle the pen of the writer." It is probable by the context that these were their rulers, or some of the chief officers in the land, that kept records of public affairs. And before this, we have express account of Joshua and Moses making records of public transactions (as Josh. 24:26, and in the forementioned places, concerning Moses' writing records). And it is evident that those transactions that related to the bringing that nation into covenant state, and redeeming them out of Egypt, etc., were always by that nation chiefly celebrated and looked upon as the greatest and most memorable. Now therefore is it credible, that in a nation whose custom it was all along, even from the very times of those great transactions, to keep records of all the public affairs, that they should be without any written[3] records of those transactions? And,

There is no other way that would be natural of writing a divine law, or law given by God in an extraordinary manner, with wonderful and astonishing circumstances, and great manifestations of his presence and power, than that of writing it with this manner, and those extraordinary circumstances in which it was given, introducing it by giving an account that it was given by God, and declaring when and how, on what occasion, and in what manner; and this will bring in all the history, from the beginning of Exodus to the end of Deuteronomy. Who can believe that Moses wrote the law that God gave at Mt. Sinai, without giving an account how it was given there, when the manner of giving was so exceeding remarkable, and so affected Moses' mind, as appears by many things that Moses wrote in Deuteronomy, which are there expressly called by the name of "law," and which we are also expressly told that Moses wrote in the book of the law, and delivered to the priests to be laid up in the sanctuary?

There is such a dependence between many of the precepts and sanctions of the law and other parts of the Pentateuch, that are expressly called the law, and that we are expressly told were written in [the] book of the law and laid up in the sanctuary; I say, there is such a dependence between these and the history, that they can't be understood without the history. Many of the precepts, as were observed before (above p. 427), was appointed to that end, to keep up the remembrance of historical facts; and that is expressly mentioned in the words of those laws themselves. But such laws can't be understood

---

3. MS: "⟨written⟩ ~~publick~~."

without the history. Thus this is mentioned as the reason of the appointment of the feast of tabernacles, viz. that the children of Israel might remember how they dwelt in tabernacles in the wilderness (Lev. 23:43). Now this required the history of their travels and sojourning there. So the laws concerning the Amalekites, Moabites, and Ammonites, appointed in commemoration of what passed between the congregation in the wilderness in their travels there and them, can't be understood without the history of those facts; and those require the history of the travels of the children of Israel,[4] and of the things that led to those incidents, and the occasions of them. So that great law of the passover, that is said in the law to be in remembrance of their redemption out of Egypt, and the many particular rites and ceremonies of that feast, are said expressly in the law to be in remembrance of these and those circumstances of that redemption. Now 'tis impossible to understand all these particular precepts about the passover without an history of that affair; and this requires the history of their bondage in Egypt, and the manner how they came into that bondage; and this draws in the history of the patriarchs. The preface to the Ten Commandments can't be understood without the history of their redemption out of Egypt, and an account of their circumstances there in the house of bondage. Nor can what is given as one reason of the fourth commandment, in Deuteronomy, be understood without an account how they were servants in the land of Egypt, and how they were delivered from that servitude [Deut. 5:15]. We have very often this mentioned as an enforcement of one precept and another, viz. God's deliverance of the people out of the land of Egypt, out of the house of bondage, out of the iron furnace, etc., as Lev. 18:3, and 19:34, and 22:33, and 23:43, and 25:42, 55, and 26:13, 45; Num. 15:41; Deut. 4:20, and 6:12, and 7:8, and 8:14, and 13:10, [and] 20:1, which shows how necessary the history is to understand the law. And the many forementioned precepts about the poor bondmen and strangers, that are expressly enforced, from their circumstances in Egypt, absolutely require a history of their circumstances there. And there are, in the enforcement of the laws, frequent references to the plagues and diseases of Egypt, threatenings of inflicting those plagues, or promises of freedom from them, which can't be understood without the history of those plagues. The law of no more returning again into Egypt (Deut. 17:16) requires the history of their coming out from thence. The laws

---

4. The last two words are a later interlineation.

concerning not admitting the Moabites and Ammonites "into the congregation of the Lord" [Deut. 23:3], because they so treated them in their journey, could not be understood without the story of that treatment, and they required an account of their journey. In the law concerning sins of ignorance, Num. 15:22–24 ff., depends on the history for its being intelligible. "And if ye have erred, and not observed all these commandments, which the Lord hath spoken unto Moses, even all that the Lord hath commanded you by the hand of Moses, from the day that the Lord commanded Moses, and henceforward among your generations, then it shall be, if ought be committed by ignorance," etc. Here is a reference to God's revealing himself from time to time, in a long series unto Moses, that cannot be understood without the history.

The law was written as a covenant, or as a record of a covenant, between God and the people. And therefore the "tables of the law" and "the tables of the covenant," "the book of the law" and "the book of the covenant," are synonymous terms in Scripture. And the Psalmist, Ps. 105:9–10, speaking of the "covenant" that God made with the patriarchs, says that God "confirmed the same unto Jacob for a *law*, and unto Israel for an everlasting covenant." (It is to be noted that the promise to Abraham is what is there especially called the law and the word which God commanded.)[5] The threatenings are called "words of the covenant" God made by Moses, in Jer. 11:8. But if Moses wrote the book of the law as a record of the covenant that was made between God and the congregation of Israel, it was necessary to write the people's consent, or what was done on both sides, for there was a mutual transacting in this covenant. See Deut. 26:17–18, "Thou hast avouched the Lord this day to be thy God, and to walk in his ways," etc. "And the Lord hath avouched thee this day to be his peculiar people, as he hath promised thee, and that thou shouldst keep all his commandments." Agreeable hereto is the account we have, Ex. 19:8, and 24:3–8, and Deut. 5:27, and 26:17.

The discourse that we have in the 29th and 30th chapters of Deuteronomy are introduced thus: "These are the words of the covenant, which the Lord commanded Moses to make with the children of Israel in the land of Moab, beside the covenant which he made with them in Horeb" [Deut. 29:1]. But the following discourse, called "the words of the covenant," is made up of the following things, viz. a history of the

5. This and the following sentence are a later interlineation.

transaction, Moses' rehearsal of past transactions, and wonderful dealings of God with them, with reproofs for their insensibility and unaffectedness, as introducing what he had further to say. And then he proceeds to charge them to serve the true God, and to avoid idolatry, and then to enforce this charge with awful threatening and predictions of judgments that shall come upon them if they transgress, with the circumstances of these judgments, and promises of forgiveness, etc., on repentance, and the whole concluded with various arguments, pressing instances, solemn appeals, obtestations, exhortations, etc., to enforce their duty. If such a miscellany is called "the words of the covenant," we need not wonder if the whole book of the law, that is called "the book of the law," should be a similar miscellany.

It was necessary that a record of a covenant between God and the nation of Israel should contain[6] the story of the transaction. But this, if fully related, would bring in very much of the history of the Pentateuch, which is much made up with an account of those things that were done by God to bring the people into a covenant relation to him, and the way in which they became his covenant people. And therefore the Psalmist, in that 105th, having mentioned this covenant and law which God established with the people, proceeds in the ensuing part of the psalm, to rehearse the series of the events relating to this covenant transaction, from God's entering into covenant with the patriarchs, to the children of Israel's being brought into Canaan.

It was exceeding necessary, in particular when Moses was about to write a record of the covenant that God established with the people, and to give an account how he entered into covenant with and brought them into a covenant relation to him, to show the beginning of it with the patriarchs, with whom that covenant was first established, and with whom was laid the foundation of all that transaction, and that great dispensation of the Lord of heaven and earth with that people, in separating them from all the rest of the world to be his peculiar covenant people. The beginning and groundwork of the whole affair was mainly with them, and what was done afterwards by the hand of Moses was only in pursuance of what had [been] promised to them, and often established with them, and which God made way for by his acts and revelations towards them. What God said and did towards those patriarchs is often spoken of in the words of the law (those that are expressly called the "law"), as the foundation of the whole, and also in

6. The last fourteen words are a later interlineation.

other parts of the Old Testament, as most expressly in Ps. 105:8–10. See also Josh. 24:3 ff., and many other parallel places.

And there is very often in the law an express reference to the covenant that God had made with Abraham, Isaac, and Jacob, as in Lev. 26:42, Deut. 4:31, 37, 6:10, 18, and 7:8, 12, and 9:5, 27, and 10:11, 15, and 19:8, and 26:3, 15, and 30:20, which passages are unintelligible without the history of the patriarchs. And there are many other passages in the law, wherein there is an implicit reference to the same thing, as in those in which God speaks of the land which the Lord their God had given them, or had promised them, the land of the Amorites, the Hittites, the Canaanites, etc., referring to the promise made to Abraham (Gen. 15:18–20), where God promises to Abraham the land of those nations by name.[7]

Again, the forementioned considerations, many of them must at least induce us to believe that Moses wrote the history of the redemption of the children of Israel out of Egypt, so far at least as he himself was concerned in that affair, and was made the chief instrument of it, from his being first called and sent of God on that errand. But this naturally leads us back further still, even to what God said and did to the patriarchs, for the beginning of this history directly points and leads us to those things, as the foundation of this great affair, that God now called Moses to be the great instrument of. Thus when God first appeared to Moses, and spake to him in Mount Sinai out of the bush, and gave him his commission, it was with these words: "I am the God of Abraham, the God of Isaac, and the God of Jacob" (Ex. 3:6). So again, vv. 13–16,

> And Moses said unto God, Behold, when I come unto the children of Israel, and shall say unto them, The God of your fathers hath sent me unto you; and they shall say to me, What is his name? what shall I say unto them? And God said unto Moses, I AM THAT I AM. Thou shalt say unto the children of Israel, I AM hath sent me unto you. And God said moreover unto Moses, Thus shalt thou say unto the children of Israel, The Lord God of your fathers, the God of Abraham, the God of Isaac, and the God of Jacob, hath sent me unto you. This is my name forever, and this is my memorial unto all generations. Go and gather the elders of Israel together, and say unto them, The Lord God of your fathers, the God of Abraham,

7. JE deleted "These things lead us up in the history of the Pentateuch within about 10 chapters of the beginning of it."

and of Isaac, and of Jacob, appeared unto me, saying, I have surely visited you, and seen that which is done to you in Egypt.

So again, Ex. 4:5, "That they may believe that the Lord God of their fathers, the God of Abraham, the God of Isaac, and the God of Jacob, hath appeared unto thee." And Ex. 6:2–4, "And God spake unto Moses, and said unto him, I am the Lord. And I appeared unto Abraham, unto Isaac, and unto Jacob, by the name of God Almighty; but by my name JEHOVAH was I not known to them. And I have established my covenant with them, to give them the land of Canaan, the land of their pilgrimage, wherein they were strangers." It is unreasonable on many forementioned accounts, to believe any other than that Moses should write this history; and 'tis most credible that he did it on this account, that those first extraordinary appearances of God to him, as is natural to suppose, made most strong impressions on his mind, and if he wrote any history, 'tis like he wrote this. But by those things it appears that the history of the patriarchs, on which the history of the redemption of the children of Israel out of Egypt, and God's separating of 'em, and bringing them into covenant with himself, lays all the foundation of that affair, which can't be understood without the history of the patriarchs. Would it not therefore have been an essential defect in Moses, in writing this history, to leave the children of Israel without any record of that great foundation?

There is frequent mention in that part of the Pentateuch, which we are expressly told is the law, of several tribes of Israel, and their names of the patriarchs that were the heads of the tribes (Deut. 3:12–13, 15–16, 27:11, 13, and elsewhere). And Moses was commanded to engrave the names of the twelve patriarchs on the stones of the breastplate of the high priest. But these things are not intelligible without the history of Jacob's family. In Deut. 10:22 there is a reference to Jacob's going down into Egypt "with threescore and ten persons," which is not intelligible without the story.

The law, for him that brings the offering of the first fruits, can't be understood without the history of Jacob's difficulties and sufferings in Padan Aram, and the history of his going down into Egypt with its circumstances, and the history of the great increase of his posterity there, and the history of their oppression and hard bondage there, and the history and circumstances of their deliverance from [there], and the history of the great and wondrous works of God in Egypt, and the Red Sea, and the wilderness, till the people came to Canaan. And if

Moses left no record of these things, then, in the law, he enjoined him that offered the first fruits (i.e. of all the people, every individual householder, from generation to generation), to make an explicit confession and declaration of those things that he did not understand.

What is said in the law, of the Edomites as the children of Esau, and what God had given to him for his possession, and the favor God had showed Esau, in Deut. 2:4–8, 22, and the law concerning the Edomites (Deut. 23:7–8), how they should be treated because Esau was their brother, can't be understood without the history of the family of Isaac. And such a kind of mention as is made of Moab and Ammon, as the founders of the nations of the Moabites and Ammonites, and the favor showed them on their father Lot's account, in Deut. 2:9, seems to suppose the history of Lot and his family, and can't be understood without [it]. And the reference there is in the law, to the overthrow of Sodom and Gomorrah, Deut. 29:23, can't be understood without the history of that affair.

Those things that have been mentioned lead us up, in the history of the Pentateuch, within less than eleven chapters of the beginning of it, so that there is, by what has been said, but so small a part of the Pentateuch but what must have been delivered by Moses to the children of Israel; and it is unreasonable to suppose that that small part was not delivered by the same hand as part of the same record. The history of Abraham begins with the 26th verse of the 11th chapter of Genesis. And the beginning of that history there is so connected, and as it were grows upon the preceding history of Noah and his posterity, that to suppose any other than they were originally the same record, having the same author, is unreasonable; or that Moses' history began anywhere between that and the beginning of Genesis, or that that part of Genesis, from the beginning to the 26th verse of the 11th chapter, is to be divided, as having several writers, only a view of the history itself is enough to convince one. But it will appear the more unreasonable not to ascribe it to Moses, if we consider not only the connection of the beginning of the history of Abraham with it, but the dependence of many things in the following history upon it, and also in that part of the Pentateuch that is more plainly called the "law." There is frequent mention made, both in the law and history, of the posterity of those sons of Ham, Mizraim and Canaan, called by the names of those their ancestors, mentioned Gen. 10:6, and of those of the posterity of Mizraim called Caphtorim, mentioned v. 14, in Deut 2:23, and of the posterity of the sons of Canaan, mentioned vv. 15 ff., called by their names. And in the following history there is mention made of Ham, the son of Noah (Gen. 14:5); mention is made of Elam and Shinar (Gen. 14:1 ff.), that we have an account of, ch. 10. Frequent mention is made of the land of Cush (in our translation, "Ethiopia"), so named from the son of Ham we have account of, Gen. 10:6–8. So there is, in the following history, frequent mention of the land of Aram, the son of Shem. In Balaam's prophecy, that is mentioned in the law in Deut. 23:4–5, mention is made of Asshur, Chittim, and Eber (Num. 24: 22, 24).[8]

That great affair that Moses most evidently wrote the history of, and which takes up all the historical part of the Pentateuch, from Gen. 10:26 to the end of Deuteronomy, is God's separating the seed of Abraham and Israel from all nations, and bringing [them] near to himself to be his peculiar people; but to the well understanding of this, it was requisite to be informed of the origin of nations, the peopling of the world, and the Most High, his dividing the nations their inheritance. And therefore the 9th, 10th, and 11th chapters of Genesis are but a proper introduction to the history of this great affair. And in that song of Moses, of which there is mention made in the law, and which Moses in the law was required to write, and the people in the law were required to keep, and learn, and often rehearse, there is an express reference to the separating the sons of Adam, and God's dividing the earth among its inhabitants, which is unintelligible without the 10th and 11th chapters of Genesis. And in this place also is plainly supposed a connection between this affair and that great affair of separating the children of Israel from all nations to be his peculiar people, about which most of the history of the Pentateuch is taken up. The words are, and the people are there also called upon, to keep in remembrance both those events, that are so connected, which supposes an history of both. Deut. 32:7–9, "Remember the days of old, consider the years of many generations. Ask thy father, and he will show thee; thy elders, and they will tell thee. When the Most High divided to the nations their inheritance, when he separated the sons of Adam, he set the bounds of the people according to the number of the children of Israel. For the Lord's portion is his people; Jacob is the lot of his inheritance." And by the way, I would observe, that in the following words are also references to other historical facts of the Pentateuch that can't be understood without the history.

8. This sentence is a later interlineation.

In the 4th commandment, there is such a mention made of the creation of the heavens, and earth, and sea, and all that in them is, and resting the seventh [day], that is a kind of an epitome of the first chapter of Genesis and beginning of the 2nd, and is unintelligible without that history. And there is a reference, in Deut. 4:32, to God's creation of man; and there is mention, in the prophetical song of Moses, of the name of "Adam" as the grand progenitor of mankind (Deut. 32:8). And there is mention made of the garden of God, or paradise (Gen. 13:10).

And before I leave this argument from references to historical facts, I would observe that a very great part of the thirty-one first chapters of Deuteronomy (which are most evidently, as I observed before, part of the law of Moses laid up in the holy of holies), are made up of nothing but recapitulations, brief rehearsals, references, and hints of preceding historical facts, and counsels, and enforcements from history, that can't be understood without the foregoing history.

And not only does the law of Moses depend upon the history, and bear such a relation to it, and contain such references to it, that it can't be understood without it, but the manner of writing the law shows plainly that law and history were written together; they are so connected, interwoven, blended, inwrought, and incorporated[9] in the writing. The history is a part of the law, as its preamble from time to time,[1] often made an introduction to laws; and there are continually[2] such transitions, from history to law and from law to history,[3] and such a connection, and reference, and dependence, that all appears as it were to grow together as the several parts of a tree. The laws, as they stand, are parts of the continued history; and the history of the facts is only as an introduction and preamble, or reason and enforcement, of the laws, all flowing in a continued series, as the several parts of one uninterrupted stream, all as one body, that only a view of the writing, as it stands, may be enough to convince anyone that all has[4] the same author, and that both were written together. Such is the manner of writing the laws concerning the passover, the chief of all the ceremonial observances, in the 12th of Exodus, and the law concerning the

9. The last three words are a later interlineation.
1. The preceding twelve words are a later interlineation.
2. This word is a later interlineation.
3. The remainder of this sentence and most of the following sentence including "as one body" are a later interlineation.
4. The last two words are a later interlineation.

firstborn, in the 13th, and that statute and ordinance mentioned in the 15th of Exodus, vv. 25–26. Such also is the manner of writing that law, by which is made known to the children of Israel which particular day is the sabbath (Ex. 16:23). And such is the manner of writing the Decalogue itself, which in the highest sense is called the law of Moses, in Exodus 20. 'Tis unreasonable to think that it was recorded by Moses without any of the concomitant history, and those words in the law, Ex. 20:22–23. [Such are] the laws ordering the particular frame of the tabernacle, ark, anointing oil, incense, priests' garments, with the history of the consequent building, etc. The revelation made to Moses, when God proclaimed his name, Ex. 34:6–7, which is an important part of the law, together with vv. 10–11 ff., and vv. 30–31. The several laws given on occasion of Nadab and Abihu's being burnt (Lev. 10), and ch. 16, particularly vv. 1–2, taken with what follows, together with the last words in the chapter. See also Lev. 21:1, 24, and 22:1–3, 17–18. The law concerning blasphemy, with the story of the blasphemy of Shelomith's son (Lev. 24). The laws of the Levites' service, with the history of their being numbered, accepted instead of the firstborn, and consecrated (Num. 3–4, and 8). The law of putting the leper out of the camp (Num. 5:1–4). The law of polluted persons keeping the passover, with the history that gave occasion for it (Num. 9:6–12). The history of making the trumpets, with the laws concerning their use (Num. 10). The law constituting the seventy elders is only giving an history of their first appointment (Num. 11). The law of the presumptuous sinner, with the history of the sabbath-breaker (Num. 15:30–36). The law for the priests (Num. 18) supposes a foregoing history of the rebellion of Korah. See v. 5 and v. 27, compared with the 13th verse of the preceding chapter. The law of the inheritance of daughters, with the history of Zelophehad's daughters [Num. 27:1–5]. The law of the cities of refuge on the east side of Jordan, with the history of the taking of the country.

History and law are everywhere so grafted one into another, so mutually inwrought, and[5] do as it [were] grow one out of and into another, and flow one from another in a continued current, that there is all appearance of their originally growing together, and not in the least of their being artificially patched and compacted together afterwards. It seems impossible impartially and carefully to view the manner of their connection, and to judge otherwise.

---

5. The preceding four words are a later interlineation.

Another argument that the same care was taken to preserve the memory of the facts, as to preserve the precepts of the law, viz. by making a public record of them, to be preserved with the same care, and so in like manner laid up in the sanctuary, is that it is declared in the law, that the *whole law* was written, and the record of all the precepts of it transmitted to posterity as a monument of the historical facts, or to that end, that the memory of those facts might be kept up in future generations. Deut. 6:20–25,

> And when thy son asketh thee in time to come, saying, What mean the testimonies, and the statutes, and the judgments, which the Lord our God hath commanded you? Then thou shalt say unto thy son, We were Pharaoh's bondmen in Egypt; and the Lord brought us out of Egypt with a mighty hand. And the Lord showed signs and wonders, great and sore, upon Pharoah, and upon all his household, before our eyes. And he brought us out from thence, that he might bring us in, to give us the land which he sware unto our fathers. And the Lord commanded us to do all these statutes, to fear the Lord our God, for our good always, that he might preserve us alive, as it is at this day. And it shall be our righteousness, if we observe to do all these commandments before the Lord our God, as he hath commanded us.

It is a great argument that Moses was the penman of the history of the Pentateuch, and indeed[6] well nigh sufficient alone to determine the matter, that the historian, from time to time, speaks of himself as being on the eastern side of Jordan when he wrote, before[7] ever the children of Israel entered into Canaan. Num. 22:1, "And the children of Israel set forward, and pitched in the plains of Moab *on this side Jordan* by Jericho." And Deut. 1:1, "These be the words which Moses spake unto all Israel *on this side Jordan* in the wilderness, in the plain over against the Red Sea, between Paran and Tophel," etc. And v. 5, "*On this side Jordan*, in the land of Moab, began Moses to declare this law, saying." And Deut. 4:41, "Then Moses severed three cities *on this side Jordan toward the sun rising*." V. 46, "*On this side Jordan*, in the valley over against Beth-peor." V. 47, "And they possessed his land, and the land of Og, king of Bashan, two kings of the Amorites, which were *on this side Jordan toward the sun rising*." And v. 49, "And all the plain *on this*

---

6. MS: "~~almost enough~~ indeed ⟨well nigh⟩."
7. MS: "~~and not having~~ ⟨before ever the Children of Israel⟩."

side Jordan eastward," etc. This style is used nowhere else in any part of the history of the Old Testament; elsewhere the eastern side of Jordan is evermore called "the other side Jordan," and the western side, "*this side.*" The style is thus altered by the writer of the book of Joshua (Josh. 9:1).[8]

It is a plain and demonstrative evidence, that the Jews had all along some standing public record of the facts that we have an account of in the history of the Pentateuch, that these facts are so abundantly, and in such a manner mentioned or referred to all along in other books of the Old Testament. There is scarcely any part of the history, from the beginning of Genesis to the end of Deuteronomy, but what is mentioned or referred in other books of the Old Testament, that were the writings of after ages; and some of them are mentioned very often, and commonly with the names of persons and places, and many particular and minute circumstances, not only that part of the history which belongs more immediately to the redemption of Israel out of Egypt, and their journey through the wilderness, but the preceding introductory history, and not only that which concerns the Jewish patriarchs, but the first part of the history of Genesis, even from the very beginning. In these writings we have very often mention of God's creating the heavens and the earth: Is. 37:16, and 40:21–22, 28, and 42:5, and 44:24, and 45:12, and 51:13, and 65:17, and 66:1–2, 22, Jer. 10:11–12, and 14:22, and 32:17, and 51:15, II Kings 19:15, Ps. 89:11–12, and 102:25, and 115:15, and 121:2, and 124:8, and 134:3, and Zech. 12:1.

The manner of God's creating by speaking the word, Ps. 33:6, 9, 148:5.

The world's being at first "without form, and void," and covered with darkness, agreeable to Gen. 1:2, is referred to, Jer. 4:23.

God's creating the light, Ps. 74:16.

God's creating the light and darkness, Is. 45:7, agreeable to Gen. 1:3–4.

God's creating the firmament, Ps. 19:1.

God's creating the waters that are above the heavens, Ps. 148:4–5, agreeable to Gen. 1:7.

God's gathering together the waters, Ps. 33:7; his making the sea and the dry land, Ps. 95:5; stretching out the earth above the waters,

---

8. JE marked this paragraph with a vertical line approximately two inches from the left margin.

Ps. 136:6; appointing the sea its decreed place, Jer. 5:22, Prov. 8:29, Ps. 104:9.

God's creating the sun, Ps. 19:1, 4, 74:16.

God's creating the sun for a light by day, and the moon and the stars for a light by night, Jer. 31:35, Ps. 148:3, 6.

God's creating great lights, "the sun to rule by day," and "the moon and stars to rule by night," Ps. 136:7–9. See also Ps. 104:19, with v. 24.

God's creating the sea, and the many creatures that move therein, and the whale in particular, Ps. 104:25–26.

God's creating "the heavens, the earth, and the sea, and all that is therein," Ps. 146:6.

Many parts of the creation are mentioned, Prov. 8:22–29.

God's creating man and beast, Jer. 27:5.

God's creating man, Ps. 8:5.

Man's being made of the dust of the earth, Eccles. 12:7.

Man's having dominion given him in his creation over the fish of the sea, and the fowls of the air, and beasts of the earth, Ps. 8:6–8.

Man's having the herbs and plants of the earth given him for meat, Ps. 104:14–15, agreeable to Gen. 1:29, and 3:18.

The first marriage, or God's making Adam and Eve one, is referred to, Mal. 2:15.

Adam's name is mentioned, Hos. 6:7.

The garden of Eden is often mentioned by name, with its pleasures and delights, Is. 51:3, Ezek. 28:13, and 31:8–9, 16, 18, and 36:35, and Joel 2:3.

Adam's violating the covenant is referred to, Hos. 6:7.

The curse denounced against Adam, that as he was dust, so unto dust he should return, is referred to, Eccles. 12:7.

The curse denounced on the serpent, that he should eat dust all the days of his life, is referred to, Is. 65:25, Micah 7:17.

Mention is made of the flood of waters that stood above the mountains, and God's rebuking and removing the flood, Ps. 104:6–7.

Noah's name is mentioned, and his righteousness before God, and great acceptance with him, referred to, Is. 54:9, and Ezek. 14:14, 20.

The waters of Noah's flood, and their going over the earth, and God's covenant with Noah, that he would no more destroy the earth with a flood, are mentioned, Is. 54:9.

Many of the names of the descendants of Noah, that we have an account of (Gen. 10), are mentioned in other parts of the Old Testament, and some of them very often, and everywhere in an agreeableness with the account we have of them there: Ps. 78:51, 83:8, 105:23, 27, and 106:22, Is. 11:11, and 23:1–2, 12–13, Jer. 2:10, 25:20–25, 49:34–39, Ezek. 27:5–15, 20–25, 30:4–5, and 32:24, 26, and 38:2, 5–6, 13, Mic. 5:6, and in many other places.

The names of others also, that we have an account of as heads of nations in the history of the Pentateuch before Moses' birth, besides the patriarchs of the Jewish nation, are frequently mentioned, Ps. 83:6–7, Is. 11:14–15, 60:6–7, Jer. 2:10, 25:20, 25, 49 throughout, and in many other places, all in an agreeableness to the history of the Pentateuch.

The name "Babel" is often mentioned.

The Philistines coming forth out of Caphtor, Amos 9:7, Jer. 47:4, compared with Gen. 10:14, and Deut. 2:23.

There is particular mention of the ancestors of the Jews dwelling on the other side of the river Euphrates, and particularly "Terah, the father of Abraham, and the father of Nahor," as Josh. 24:2.

Abraham's being brought from thence of God, from the east, from the other side of the river, his coming at the call of God, and being led by him into the land of Canaan, Josh. 24:3, Is. 41:2.

His being called with Sarah his wife, Is. 51:1–2.

God's leading Abraham throughout the land of Canaan, Josh. 24:3, agreeable to Gen. 12:6, and 13:17.

God's blessing Abraham is mentioned, Is. 51:1–2.

Abraham is spoken of as a righteous man, and God's servant and friend, Is. 41:2, and v. 8, Ps. 105:42.

God's entering into covenant with Abraham, Isaac, and Jacob, promising to give them the land of Canaan, Ps. 105:8–11, 42.

The church of God in the families of those patriarchs, being very small, and their being strangers and sojourners in the land of Canaan, and their going "from one nation to another, and from one kingdom to another people," and God's wonderfully restraining men from hurting them, and his reproving kings for their sakes, and God's calling them prophets, Ps. 105:12–15.

God's giving Abraham an easy conquest over great kings and rulers of the principal nations of the world, as in Gen. 14:14 ff., mentioned in Is. 41:2–3.

Melchizedek is mentioned by name as being a great priest of the true God, and both a king and a priest, Ps. 110:4.

God's fixing the border of the seed of Abraham at the river Euphrates, as the history of the Pentateuch gives us an account that God did in his promise to Abraham, Gen. 15:18, and afterwards, from time to time, to the Israelites, is referred to, II Sam. 8:3.

The great plentifulness of the land of Sodom is spoken of, Ezek. 16:49.

The great wickedness of the people of Sodom and Gomorrah, Ezek. 16:46–56, Is. 1:10.

Their being guilty of notorious uncleanness, Ezek. 16:50, I Kings 14:24, and 15:12, and 22:46, II Kgs. 23:7.

Their being of a very proud and haughty spirit, Ezek. 16:49–50, agreeable to Gen. 19:5.[9]

Their being very open, and barefaced, and shameless in their wickedness, Is. 3:9.

Their being overthrown with a very great, and terrible, and utter destruction, Is. 1:9, 13:19, Jer. 49:18.

Their being the subjects of sudden destruction, Lam. 4:6.

God's overthrowing them with fire, Amos 4:11.

Their being overthrown with perpetual and everlasting desolation, without ever being rebuilt or inhabited anymore, Jer. 49:18, and 50:40, Ezek. 16:53, 55, Zeph. 2:9.

Their being overthrown together with neighbor cities, Jer. 49:18, and 50:40.

The birth of Isaac as a special gift of God to Abraham, Josh. 24:3.

The birth of Jacob and Esau, the sons of Isaac, by a special gift of God, Josh. 24:4.

Esau is mentioned under the names of both Esau and Edom, as Jacob's brother, in the book of Obadiah, and often elsewhere.

Jacob's taking hold of Esau's heel when they were born, is mentioned, Hos. 12:3.

Jacob's being preferred before his brother by God's election, Ps. 105:6, Is. 41:8, Mal. 1:2–3.

God's appearing to Jacob at Bethel, Hos. 12:4.

Jacob's fleeing into the country of Syria, and there serving for a wife, and particularly his serving there in doing the business of a shepherd, or keeping sheep, Hos. 12:12.

The two wives of Jacob, Rachel and Leah, are mentioned as those that did build the house of Israel, Ruth 4:11.

Jacob, by his strength having power with God, and having power over the angel, Hos. 12:3–4.

---

9. MS: "15.9." Gen. 13:13 and 18:20 are other possible corrections for JE's error.

The names of the twelve sons of Jacob are mentioned in Ezek. 48, and very often elsewhere.

Esau's having Mount Seir given to him, Josh. 24:4, agreeable to Gen. 36:8.

And the names of Ishmael, and his posterity, and of the sons of Abraham by Keturah, and the sons of Lot, and the sons of Esau, are often mentioned, agreeable to the account we have of them in Genesis.

Joseph's being sold into Egypt, and being a servant there, Ps. 105:17.

Joseph's being, by providence, [sold] into Egypt before the house of Israel, to preserve life, Ps. 105:16–17, agreeable to Gen. 45:5, and 50:20.

Tamar's bearing Pharez to Judah, Ruth 4:12.

Joseph's being bound in prison in Egypt, Ps. 105:18, as Gen. 39:20.

Joseph's having divine revelations in prison, and his thereby foretelling future events, and those predictions coming to pass, and that being the occasion of Pharaoh's taking him out of prison and setting him at liberty, Ps. 105:19–20.

And Joseph's being, upon this, exalted over all the land of Egypt, and being made lord of Pharaoh's house, and ruler of his substance, and being next to the king himself in power and dignity, and being Pharaoh's vicegerent, and so having power and authority over all the princes and nobles of Egypt, Ps. 105:21–22.

The famine that was at that time in the land of Canaan, that obliged Israel and his family to seek elsewhere for bread, is mentioned, Ps. 105:16.

Jacob's going down into Egypt with his family, Josh. 24:4, I Sam. 12:8, and Ps. 105:23.

Their multiplying exceedingly in Egypt, till they were become more and mightier than the Egyptians, and the Egyptians' dealing subtilely with them to diminish them, Ps. 105:24–25, agreeable to Ex. 1:9–10.

The Egyptians first loving the Israelites, and then afterwards being turned to hate them, Ps. 105:25.

Their being slaves in Egypt, Micah 6:4, Jer. 2:20, Judg. 6:8.

The cruelty of their bondage, its being as it were an iron furnace (as it is called, Deut. 4:20), is mentioned, I Kgs. 8:51, and Jer. 11:4, Judg. 6:9.

The particular kind of their service, in handling pots wherein they carried their mortar, and working in furnaces in which they burnt their brick, is referred to, I Kgs. 8:51, and Jer. 11:4, and Ps. 68:13, and 81:6.

God's taking notice of their cruel bondage and great affliction with compassion, and a fellow feeling of their calamity, Is. 63:9, agreeable to Ex. 2:23–25, and 3:7, 9, 16.

God's making known himself to 'em in Egypt, Ezek. 20:5, agreeable to Ex. 3:1–6, 13–16, 29–31, and 6:2–6.

God's making himself known to 'em by the name of JEHOVAH YOUR GOD, Ezek. 20:5, agreeable to Ex. 6:2–3, 6, especially v. 7.

God's promising and swearing to them in Egypt, to bring 'em forth out of the land of Egypt into "a land flowing with milk and honey," Ezek. 20:6, agreeable to Ex. 3:8, 10, 12, 14, 17, and 6:2–8, where we have an account of his swearing by his great name JEHOVAH, and I AM THAT I AM.

God's making use of Moses, a great prophet, as the main instrument of bringing the people out of Egypt, etc., Is. 63:11–12, Hos. 12:13.

Aaron's being joined with Moses in this affair, Josh. 24:5, I Sam. 12:6–8, Ps. 77:20, 105:26. Miriam's also being joined, Micah 6:4.

God's working very great wonders for his people in the time of Moses and Aaron, Ps. 77:11–14.

His working great wonders in Egypt, Ps. 78:12, 43, and 81:5, and 105:27, and 106:9, and 135:9, Josh. 24:5. Great tokens and wonders upon Pharaoh and all his servants, Ps. 135:9.

God's redeeming the people out of Egypt, Judg. 6:8–9, and 11:16, I Sam. 12:6–8, Ps. 74:2, and 77:15, and 78:42, and 81:10, and 111:9, and 114:1, Jer. 2:6, 20, and 11:4, and 16:14, I Kgs. 8:51, Ezek. 20:10, Hos. 12:13, Amos 9:7, Micah 6:4, and many other places.

God's turning the rivers and pools of Egypt into blood, so that the Egyptians could not drink the waters, and also thereby killing their fish, Ps. 78:44, and 105:29.

The land's bringing forth frogs in abundance, to fill even the chambers of Pharaoh, Ps. 78:45, and 105:30.

The plague of lice is mentioned, Ps. 105:31.

The plague of the swarms of flies, Ps. 105:31, and 78:45.

God's sending hail, and thunder, and lightning, and flaming fire with hail, to the breaking of the trees of the field, and destroying their cattle, Ps. 78:47–48, and 105:32–33, agreeable to Ex. 9:22–26.

God's sending locusts to eat up all the growth of the field, Ps. 78:46, and 105:34–35.

The plague of darkness, Ps. 105:28.

God's smiting and destroying all the firstborn of Egypt with the pestilence, the firstborn both of man and beast, Ps. 78:50–51, and 105:36, 135:8, and 136:10.

The children of Israel's going out of Egypt upon this last plague, Ps. 78:52, and 136:11, Josh. 24:5.

Their going out with silver and with gold, Ps. 105:37.

The Egyptians' being glad to be rid of them, Ps. 105:38, agreeable to Ex. 12:33.

Their being brought out with a strong hand, and an outstretched arm, Ps. 136:12.

Their being led by a pillar of cloud by day, and a pillar of fire to give 'em light by night, Ps. 78:14, and 105:39, and Is. 4:5.

Their being led into the wilderness, Ps. 68:7, 78:40, 52, 95:8, and 106:9, 14, and 136:16, Jer. 2:2, 6, Ezek. 20:10, Judg. 11:16.

The people's going to the Red Sea, Judg. 11:16.

The Egyptians' pursuing after the people with chariots and horsemen unto the Red Sea, Josh. 24:6.

The people's crying unto the Lord at the Red Sea, Josh. 24:7.

The perverseness of that generation, Ps. 106:6–7, 95:8–11, 78:8–11, Is. 63:10, Ps. 81:11.

Their provoking God at the Red Sea, Ps. 106:7, agreeable to Ex. 14:11–12.

God's putting darkness between Israel and the Egyptians, Josh. 24:7.

God's dividing the Red Sea, and causing the people to pass through, and causing the waters to stand as an heap; his turning the sea into dry land, so that the people went through on foot dry-shod, Ps. 66:6, and 74:13, and 77:10–20, 19–20, and 78:13, and 106:8–9, 114:3–4, and 136:13–14, Is. 10:26, 51:10, and 63:11–13, Hab. 3:8, 10, 15, Ps. 77:10–20.

God's destroying Pharaoh and his hosts, his chariots, and his horses, by the Red Sea, by bringing the waters upon them to cover them, so that there was not one of them left, Ps. 74:13–14, and 76:5–6, and 78:53, and 106:10–11, and 136:15, Is. 10:26, 51:9–10, and Josh. 24:7.

God's doing these things at the Red Sea by the lifting up [of] Moses' rod, Is. 10:26.

God's conquering and crushing Egypt in a forceable manner, and with mighty power, Ps. 89:10, Is. 51:9.

God's doing such great things for so perverse a people, for the glory of his own name, and to show his mighty power, Ps. 106:8, agreeable to Ex. 9:16.

The people's singing praises at the Red Sea, Ps. 106:12, Hos. 2:15, Ps. 66:6, and 105:43.

This destruction of Egyptians being reported and famed through the earth, Is. 23:5, agreeable to Ex. 9:16.

The people's murmuring in the wilderness for want of bread, Ps. 78:17–20, 106:14.

Their soon transgressing and provoking, after singing praises at the Red Sea, by lusting and tempting God, Ps. 106:13–15.

The people's dwelling in tents in the wilderness, Ps. 106:25.

The people's being encamped in the wilderness like an army, Ps. 78:28, and 106:16.

God's sending the people manna, and feeding with bread from heaven[1] that was rained down upon them, Ps. 78:23–25, 105:40.

God's revealing his holy sabbath to the people, as we have an account in the 16th of Exodus, Ezek. 20:12, Neh. 9:14.

God's giving the people waters plentifully, to supply the whole congregation out of the rock at Meribah, by smiting the rock and causing the waters to gush out, Ps. 78:15–16, 20, and 81:7, and 105:41, and 114:8.

Amalek's coming forth in a hostile manner against Israel "in the way, when he came up from Egypt," I Sam. 15:2.

What Jethro, the priest of Midian, said and did, that we have an account of, Ex. 18, is referred to, I Sam. 15:6.

God's entering into covenant with the people at Mt. Sinai, or Horeb, after they came out of Egypt, and giving[2] the law, and statutes, and judgments there, I Kgs. 8:9, Ps. 76:8, Ezek. 20:10–11, Mal. 4:4.

God's giving the law by a very terrible and awful voice from heaven, Ps. 76:8.

God's appearing there with extraordinary manifestations of his majesty and glory in the heavens and on the earth, with an exceeding shining brightness and beams of glory, attended with the utmost danger of being struck dead in a moment, as by a pestilence, to those that transgressed, Hab. 3:3–5.

The earth's trembling, and the mountains' quaking exceedingly, at that time, Judg. 5:4–5, Hab. 3:6–7, 10, Ps. 114:4, 68:8.

And particularly Mt. Sinai shaking, Judg. 5:5, Ps. 68:8.

The people's making a molten calf at Mt. Sinai, and worshiping

---

1. JE deleted "and causing it to fall round about their camp."
2. JE deleted "the law there in two tables Moses."

that as the representation of the God of Israel, Ps. 106:19–20, Ezek. 20:8.

God's saying on that occasion that he would destroy the people, but Moses' standing before him as an intercessor for them, to turn away God's [wrath], on which God spared them, Ps. 106:23.

Moses' putting the two tables of stone into the ark at Mt. Sinai, when he made a covenant with the children of Israel, when they came out of the land of Egypt, I Kgs. 8:9.

The people's lusting for flesh, and tempting God "by asking meat for their lust," Ps. 78:17–19.

God's wrath on that occasion, Ps. 78:21 ff.

God's giving the people quails in answer to their desire, in vast abundance, which were brought by a wind which God caused to blow, and let fall in the midst of their camp, round about their habitations, Ps. 78:26–28, 105:40, and 106:15.

The wrath of God coming upon them, while the meat was yet in their mouths, and suddenly slaying them with a great plague, Ps. 78:30–31, and 106:15.

The people's not believing, for all God's wondrous works that they had seen, despising the pleasant land, and not believing his promise that he would bring them into it, and murmuring at the report of the spies, and being for turning back again into Egypt, Ps. 78:32 ff., vv. 41 ff., 106:24–25.

God's appearing on that occasion as though he would pour out his fury, and consume the whole congregation, but yet sparing them for his name's sake, lest the Egyptians and other heathen nations should hear of it, and should take occasion from thence to reproach the name of God, Ezek. 20:13–14, 17.

God's swearing in wrath on that occasion, concerning that froward and perverse generation, that they should not enter into his rest, but that he would destroy them in the wilderness, because they had seen God's miracles, but yet exceedingly provoked him, and often tempted him, Ps. 95:8–11, and 106:26, Ezek. 20:15–16.

God's promising Caleb the land whereunto he went, Judg. 1:20.

Korah and his company envying Moses and Aaron in the camp, and the earth's opening her mouth and swallowing up Dathan, and Abiram, and their company, and a fire from the Lord consuming others of them, Ps. 106:16–18.

What Moses said to the Levites about their inheritance, Num. 18:20 ff., referred to, Josh. 13:33.

The people's angering Moses at the waters of strife, provoking his spirit "so that he spake unadvisedly with his lips," "so that it went ill with Moses for their sakes," Ps. 106:32–33, as Num. 20.

Israel's sending messengers to "the king of Edom, saying, Let me, I pray thee, pass through thy land," and the king of Edom's refusing to hearken thereto, Judg. 11:17.

The people's compassing or going round the land of Edom, going along through the wilderness, Judg. 11:18, agreeable to Num. 21:4, and Deut. 2:1–8.

The people's passing through a great and terrible wilderness, a land of pits, and of great drought, a waste and desolate country, Jer. 2:2, 6, Hos. 13:5.

The people's compassing the land of Moab, and coming by the east side of the land of Moab, and pitching on the other side of Arnon, because Arnon was the border of Moab, Judg. 11:18, exactly agreeable to the history of the Pentateuch, Num. 21:11, 13, and 22:36.

The people's not being suffered to pass through the land of Moab, Judg. 11:17–18.

Israel's sending messengers from their camp in the borders of Moab to Sihon, king of the Amorites, "saying, Let us pass, we pray thee, through thy land," and Sihon's refusing, but upon this, gathering all his people together, and coming to Jahaz to fight against Israel, Judg. 11:18–20.

God's delivering Sihon and all his people into the hand of Israel, and Israel's possessing their land, "from Arnon even unto Jabbok, and from the wilderness even unto Jordan," dwelling "in Heshbon and her towns, and in Aroer and her towns, and in all the cities" that belonged to Sihon, exactly agreeable to the history, Judg. 11:21–26, Josh. 24:8, Ps. 135:10–11, and 136:17–22.

And afterwards smiting Og, the king of Bashan, and possessing his land, Josh. 24:8, Ps. 135:10–11, and 136:17–22.

But that Balak, the king of Moab, durst not venture, after he had seen this, to go out against Israel, and never engaged them in battle, till Israel went against them, Judg. 11:25–26, agreeable to Num. 22:2, and the consequent history.

Balak's hiring Balaam, the son of Beor, to curse the people, and God's turning the curse into a blessing, while Israel abode in Shittim, Josh. 24:9–10, and Micah 6:5.

Israel's sinning[3] by joining themselves to Baal-peor, and eating the

3. JE deleted "in the matter of Peor."

sacrifices of their gods, and God's being provoked and executing wrath on the congregation for this sin, and Phinehas's executing judgment on this occasion, that was counted to him for righteousness unto all generations forevermore, Ps. 106:28–31.

The war of Israel with Balak, and their victory, Josh. 24:9–10.

The people's long sojourning in the wilderness, Josh. 24:7, Is. 63:9.

God's speaking from time to time to Moses and Aaron from a pillar of cloud, Ps. 99:6–7.

Moses' faithfulness in his office, Ps. 99:7, agreeable to Num. 12:7.

The great perverseness, hardness of heart, of that generation, and their frequent rebellions, and provoking and vexing God's Spirit, and tempting of him in the wilderness, even for forty years, Ps. 78 throughout, especially vv. 40–41, Ps. 81:11–12, and 95:8–11, Is. 63:10, Ezek. 20:13.

God's repeated and continual judgments against them, wasting them by a great mortality that pursued and destroyed, with great manifestations of divine wrath, Ps. 90, Is. 63:10.

God's often pardoning and sparing the people, so as to forbear to destroy the whole congregation at Moses' intercession, but yet not without giving great manifestations of his wrath towards their sins, taking vengeance of their inventions, as Moses ground their calf to powder, Ps. 78:38 ff., Ps. 99.

The people's seeming, time after time, to repent when smitten with terrible judgments, but yet turning again quickly to sin, not being steadfast in God's covenant, Ps. 78:31–37.

God's showing great favor to the young generation, Jer. 31:2.

God's entering covenant a second time with that young generation, Jer. 2:2–3, Ezek. 20:18–20.[4]

He that can[5] observe the facts of the history of the Pentateuch, after this manner mentioned and referred in the writings of the several ages of the Israelitish nation, and not believe that they had all along a great and standing record of these things, and this very history, can swallow the greatest absurdity. If they had not had this history among them, or one that exactly agrees with it, it would have [been] morally impossible but that, amongst this vast number of citations and references, with so great a multitude of particularities and circumstances mentioned by so many different writers in different ages, there must have been a great many inconsistences with the history, and a great many inconsis-

---

4. JE deleted "The Philistines coming from Caphtor, Amos 4:7, and Jer. 47."
5. JE deleted "believe."

tencies one with another. And it would have puzzled and confounded the skill of any writer that should have attempted to form an history afterwards, that should everywhere, without jarring, so harmonize with such various manifold citations, and rehearsals, and reference so interspersed in and dispersed through all those writings of several ages; and unless those writers had such a record to be their common guide, it could [not] have been otherwise than utterly impossible.

It was impossible that this vast number of events, with so many circumstances, with names of persons, and places, and minute incidents, should be so particularly and exactly known, and the knowledge of 'em so fully, and distinctly, and without confusion or loss, kept up for so many ages, and be so often mentioned in so particular a manner, without error or inconsistence, through so many ages without a written record. How soon does an oral tradition committed to a multitude vary, and put on a thousand shapes, and mix, and jumble, and grow into confusion! Here appears in fact to have been an exact consistent knowledge and memory of things kept up, and that shows that there [was] in fact a standing record; and the comparing the records of the Pentateuch with the innumerable citations and references, shows that this was in fact that record.

The facts of this history are very often rehearsed, just in the same order and manner as they are in the history of the Pentateuch; and in many places there is a rehearsal of the facts of very great parts, and sometimes a kind of abridgment of the bigger part of the history, as Josh. 24, Ps. 78, Ps. 105, and 106, and 136, Ezek. 20:5–23. And we sometimes find the facts of the former part of the history of Genesis joined with the story of the children of Israel's redemption out of Egypt, and travels in the wilderness, as introductory to it (and sometimes even beginning with the story of the creation, in like manner as it is in the Pentateuch),[6] and after the captivity, in Neh. 9.

These events are commonly mentioned after such a manner as plainly supposes that a full account of them was already in being, and well-known, and established, as in these words, "though Noah, Daniel, and Job stood before me" [Ezek. 14:14]. It supposes the history of those men was extant and well-known among the people. And so in these words, "we should have been like Sodom, and like unto Gomorrah" [Is. 1:9], it is supposed that the history of the destruction of those cities was what the people were well acquainted with. So these words,

---

6. The remainder of this sentence is a later addition.

Ps. 78:40, "How oft did they provoke him in the wilderness, and grieve him in the desert," plainly supposes an history extant that gives a particular account of those things. 'Tis after the manner of a reference to a history. So it is very often elsewhere, as Ruth 4:11. "The Lord make this woman that is come into thine house like Rachel and like Leah, which two did build the house of Israel." So Josh. 13:33, "But unto the tribe of Levi Moses gave not any inheritance; the Lord God of Israel was their inheritance, *as he said unto them*." The words are mentioned plainly after the manner of a citation. So Judg. 1:20, "And they gave Hebron unto Caleb, as Moses said." Ps. 110:4, "Thou art a priest forever after the order of Melchizedek"; it supposes an extant account of Melchizedek. See also II Sam. 8:3, Jer. 49:18, and 50:40, Ezek. 16:46–56, Amos 4:11, Zech. 2:9, Is. 13:19, and 41:1–8, and 51:1–2, 9–10, Micah 6:5; and very many other places there are that show the same thing, that it would be tedious to mention.

And sometimes these historical events are mentioned so much in the words of the history of the Pentateuch, as could not be without a written history to be a guide, as particularly Jephthah's rehearsal, Judg. 11:15–28.

That the children of Israel had a great standing record among them of these facts, that they looked upon sacred and holy, is evident by Ps. 111:4. The Psalmist there, speaking of these works, says that "God had made his wonderful works to be remembered." They are those works that we have an account of in the Pentateuch, as is manifest by vv. 7 and 9. The words in the original that are translated, "he hath made to be remembered," are זֵכֶר עָשָׂה, "he hath made a record." The word signifies "memorial" or "record." The word "recorder," II Sam. 8:16, and I Kgs. 4:3, II Kgs. 18:18, Is. 36:3, 22, and other places, is מַזְכִּיר, which is a word of the same root. The words *Zeker* and *Mazkir* are just in the same manner akin to one another, as the English words "recorder" and "record."

So the history of these facts is called "God's report" (as it is in the original). Hab. 3:2, "I have heard thy report, and was afraid." What that report was appears by what follows. It was the report of those works there mentioned, which works he, in this verse, prays God to revive. But in the 15th and 16th verses, the Prophet more plainly tells us what that report was that made him afraid, viz. the account of God's marching through the Red Sea, with the other great works of God, mentioned in the foregoing part of the chapter.

And that this great record, that the writers of the Old Testament

cited so often, was contained in the book of the law, may be argued
from the manner in which these facts are sometimes mentioned. The
Psalmist, in the introduction he makes to his rehearsal of the story of
the Pentateuch in the 78th psalm, calls that story by the name of "law"
(v. 1).[7] And the precepts and history are united in the notice he here
takes of them, and [he] mentions the history, as what God had commanded the memory of to be carefully kept up as the proper enforcement of the precepts, v. 7, with the foregoing verses. And being given
of God as an enforcement of the precepts of the law, [it] is as properly
looked upon as a part of the law as the prophecies and other arguments made use of in Deuteronomy and other parts of the law. So the
history is introduced in such a manner in the 105th psalm, speaking in
the introduction of the covenant and law which God established with
the people, vv. 5, 8–10, that makes it naturally to [be] supposed that
the history he rehearses is taken out of the book of the law. The wonderful works and precepts of the law are spoken of together, as in like
manner to be remembered. V. 5, "Remember his marvelous works that
he hath done, his wonders, and the judgments of his mouth." So these
wonderful works are repeated, mentioned, or referred to together, Ps.
111. And so again they are in the introduction to that rehearsal we
have of this history in the 106th psalm, as in vv. 2–3. So the law and the
historical facts are mentioned together, Ps. 103:7, as being both alike
of divine revelation: "He made known his ways unto Moses, and his
acts unto the children of Israel." We find the precepts and history cited
together, mixed, and blended, in the 81st psalm, as they are in the
Pentateuch.

It appears by profane history to have been the manner of the nations of old to keep the ancient histories of their nation, and their
genealogies, and the genealogies and acts of their gods in their tem-
ples, where they were committed to the care of their priests as sacred
things, which in all probability was in imitation of the example of the
Israelites in keeping the Mosaic history, which Moses committed to the
care of the priests, to be laid up in the sanctuary as a sacred thing. And
the ancient records of the neighboring heathen, particularly of the[8]
Phoenicians, show that the priests of the Jews had such a history in
keeping, giving an account of the creation of the world, etc., even so
long ago as the days of the judges. This appears by Sanchoniathon's

7. JE deleted "and speaks of what of himself as being about to rehearse ancient sayings or
history, and makes mention of the precepts and history together."
8. JE deleted "Tyrians."

history, wherein he mentions many of the same facts, and confesses that he had them from a certain priest of the god *Jao*.[9]

The ancient heathen writers do make mention of Moses as the writer of the things contained in the former part of the book of Genesis. See instances. See "Miscellanies," no. 1012, 3rd and 5th paragraphs, and no. 1014, 1st paragraph.[1] See also "Scripture," No. 429, the last sentence, and No. 432.[2]

Again, another argument that will invincibly prove that the history of the Pentateuch, as well as the precepts, was of old, from the beginning, contained in the book of the law, that sacred book which the children of Israel had among them laid up in the sanctuary from the days of Moses, is this, viz. that it is certain that the book which the Jews had among them when they first returned from the Babylonish captivity, which they called "the book of the law" and "the law of Moses," and made use of as their law, was the same book of the law that their nation had all along as their great and standing record and rule, and as such had kept in the sanctuary of old, was this very Pentateuch that we now have, containing both the history and precepts. This was the book of the law that Ezra made use of, and that Ezra and the Levites that were with him did so publicly and solemnly read and explain to the people, as we have account, Neh. 8, and which was laid up in the second temple in the same manner as the book of the law of Moses had been in the first. That this book was the same with the Pentateuch that we now have is exceeding manifest from the genealogies and historical references in the first book of Chronicles, that was written on occasion of all Israel's being reckoned by genealogies, after they came out of the captivity. See I Chron. 9:1. None that read those genealogies and historical references will make himself so ridiculous as to question whether these were not taken from the very history that we have in the Pentateuch, and an history that the Jews had among them as the ancient, great, and established records of their nation.

And again, if they had any other book of the law when they first came out of the captivity, it is impossible but that it must be preserved, for they must have a high regard to it as being the same with that

---

9. Bedford, *Scripture Chronology*, pp. 92–100, 512–13.

1. Based on his reading of Grotius's *De Veritate*, JE notes in no. 1012 that Numenius "affirms it was said by the prophet (meaning Moses) that the Spirit of God was moved upon the waters," and in no. 1014 that Cleodemus the Prophet, also called Malchus, "gives the same history as Moses" concerning Abraham's children by Keturah.

2. This paragraph is comprised of later additions.

sacred book that had been regarded in all former ages as the great and holy rule of their nation, and accordingly kept as most sacred by the priests in the sanctuary of God, in the holy of holies beside the ark of God. We find the writings of the prophet Jeremiah were preserved (Dan. 9:2); how much more would they preserve the law of Moses![3] But the Jews had no other book of the law preserved. They have none other now, and have had no other in all ages since. They had no other in Christ's time, and we have no account of any other in all the accounts we have of the nation, from Christ's time to the captivity, though in those accounts there be very much said about the book of the law, and though there were many controversies about it from time to time, and innumerable copies of it, and many that made it their business to study, to write, and to teach it, though there were synagogues established throughout Palestine, and through the world wherever the Jews were dispersed. The custom of synagogues in every city began near the first return from the captivity. See Prideaux, Part I, p. 534 ff.[4] Yet there is no mention made in any accounts we have of the Jews, of any other book of the law that was among 'em in any of those times, nor of any knowledge or thought that any of them had, that there had ever been any other book of the law in any former times. 'Tis evident that the book of the law that the Jews had in Ezra's time was very publicly known among the people, by the great pains that Ezra and others took thoroughly to acquaint them with it. And therefore it would have been impossible to make so great an alteration in that sacred book, that they were taught to pay such a regard to, and was laid up in the holy of holies in the temple, and that the people soon after the captivity became, in some respects, even superstitious in their regard to—I say, it would have been impossible to have made so great an alteration in it, that whereas formerly it had only a body of precepts, now it was turned into a large history, with precepts here and there mixed and blended, without some notice being taken of it, and some notable disputes and controversies, some remaining traces at least of the alteration, and some remaining knowledge of the former purer volume. It would be endless to reckon up the absurdities of such a supposition.

3. This sentence is a later interlineation.

4. Prideaux discussed the practical problems that led to the establishment of synagogues among the Jews "after the *Babylonish Captivity*," including the "inconvenience" of assembling to hear the law read, "especially in the winter and stormy seasons of the year" (*Old and New Testament Connected*, Pt. I, Vol. 1, pp. 534–36).

There were many sects among the Jews in Palestine, having many disputes and differences of opinion about the law of Moses, but there was no such dispute or difference as this, whether this was the genuine book of the law. And not only the Jews in Palestine, but all the Jews through the world, which were so vastly dispersed even in Esther's time, yet without controversy or any difference of opinion, all acknowledged this same book as the only book of the law. And this was the book of the law that was read in all synagogues through the world, and was owned by the Samaritans also (of which more afterwards), which would have been impossible, if this was so different from that book of the law that the Jews had, and was so publicly known in Ezra's time. The Sadducees, that were many of them learned men, and boasted of their freedom of thought, and taking liberty to differ from the rest of the Jews, and were a kind of infidels, and rejected most other writings that the Jews accounted sacred, yet acknowledged without dispute this book of the Pentateuch, as we now have it, as the genuine book of the law of Moses, and as the word of God. And so did the Samaritans, though they hated the Jews, and exceedingly differed from 'em in other things, and were such enemies to 'em after the captivity, that they would rather reject a thing for being one of their customs or principles. Yet they owned this Pentateuch as the genuine law of Moses, which it is exceeding absurd to suppose they would have done, if the book had been new made, with all the history foisted in sometime after Ezra. So that undoubtedly this was the book of the law that the Jews owned, and made use of, and regarded as the true law of Moses in Ezra's time.

Now, as to the consequence, if the Pentateuch, as we now have it with its history, was the book that the Jews had and used as the book of the law soon after the captivity, then it will follow that it was also the same book that was their book of the law before the captivity; for if such a great alteration was made in the book of the law, it was either done by Ezra, or by some of the Jews, before he came up to Jerusalem. It was not done by Ezra, for the priests[5] in Jerusalem had the book of the law among them before Ezra came, even when they first came out of the captivity, as appears by Hag. 2:11–13. "Thus saith the Lord of hosts, Ask now the priests concerning the law, saying, If one bear holy flesh in the skirt of his garment, and with his skirt do touch bread, or pottage,

5. MS: "~~People~~ ⟨Priests⟩."

or wine, or oil, or any meat, shall it be holy? And the priests answered and said, No. Then said Haggai, If one that is unclean by a dead body touch any of these, shall it be unclean? And the priests answered and said, It shall be unclean." See also Ezra 2:62–63, and 3:2–8, and 6:18. And therefore, if Ezra had made such an alteration, the Jews would all have known it, and could not have been imposed upon, and made to believe that this book was the same with the book of the law. The priests and Levites, nor any of the people, make the least opposition to Ezra's copy of the law, but all allow it, receiving it as an undoubted copy of the law of Moses. See Neh. 8. And then it is most apparent that the style of the history of the Pentateuch is very different from Ezra's style in the two books of Chronicles and the book of Ezra, whose style in history is very distinguishable from all the preceding histories of the Old Testament.

And besides, 'tis manifest that at the time that Ezra went up from Babylon to teach the Jews the law, the book of the law of Moses was not a thing that the Jews, that were then abroad in the world, were destitute of, as what was lost or secreted, that they were in quest of but had not the possession of, but was well-known by multitudes. And this was a thing at that time notorious and known to the heathen. 'Tis manifest by the copy of Artaxerxes' letter, Ezra 7:25. "And thou, Ezra, after the wisdom of thy God, that is in thine hand, set magistrates and judges, which may judge all the people which are beyond the river, *all such as know the laws of thy God*; and teach ye them that know them not." This made it impossible for Ezra to palm upon the people a book of his own contriving and writing, instead of the book of [the] law of Moses, the grand and ancient law of their God, which was the grand rule of their nation, and the foundation both of their civil and sacred constitution, and of all their privileges, and of their very being as a nation, separated from other nations.

'Tis very manifest, that soon after Ezra's coming first to Jerusalem, as 'tis thought about ten or a dozen [years], Nehemiah, the king's cupbearer in Shushan in Persia, was well acquainted with the book of the law of Moses, by Neh. 1:7–9, which clearly proves the falsity of the notion of the Jews having at that time no other book of the law of Moses, but that which was of Ezra's forging and publishing, as nothing would be more absurd than to suppose his new-forged book would in so short a time be published, and well-known, and received, and established, not only at Jerusalem and Judea, but among the Jews dispersed over the world as far as Shushan, in so short time.

And it could not be that any of the Jews in Judea should forge this book after the captivity, and impose it on the priests and the people before Ezra came, for this would have made no less jar between Ezra and the rest of the people than the other, for then Ezra would have known that this was not the true book of the law, for he was well acquainted with the law before he came out of the land of the captivity to Jerusalem. He was a noted scribe in the law of Moses in Babylon (Ezra 7:6), insomuch that he was famed for it among the heathen, and was noted for it by the king of Persia, who[6] over and over gives him that title as a name that he was known by, "Ezra, the scribe of the law of the God of heaven" (Ezra 7:11–12, 21). And Ezra went up with a design to teach the people in Jerusalem this law of Moses; that was his main errand, as appears by Ezra 7:6, 10, 14, 21, 23, 25–26. And the book of the law that he taught the people he did not receive at Jerusalem of any of the priests or others there, but carried it up with him in his hand, as appears by Ezra 7:14, 25, and Neh. 8:1–2.

This great forgery of such a book as the Pentateuch, instead of the book of the law of Moses (if that contained little besides precepts), could not be done and imposed on the Jews at any time soon after the return from the captivity, for from what has been said already, it appears that there was the same book of the law well-known by many, and received by all at that time, both by the Jews in Judea, and also by those that still remained in the land of their captivity, which it was impossible should be from any other cause than the tradition of this book from their forefathers that lived before the captivity. 'Tis impossible that such a forgery should so quickly, so easily, and universally, without dispute or difference of parties, obtain through so great a nation, so disunited in the places of their abode. A forgery, as nothing in the world, must be so difficult to be made so easily to obtain, as in the book of the law of Moses, their grand and sacred rule, and constitution, and foundation, that never any people did so much and in so many respects depend on any body of laws, as the Jewish nation depended on this book. It was for the sake of the laws commanded them, and the privileges given 'em in this book, that they forsook their habitations, and all their possessions in the land of their captivity, and bore the loss and trouble of their journey to Palestine, and the great difficulties of rebuilding their city and temple, and resettling again in the land, and reestablishing their state there. And therefore we may be

---

6. MS: "~~once and again~~ ⟨over & over⟩."

sure [they] would be, above all things, careful with regard to that book. In Haggai's and Zechariah's time, before the temple was finished, they had this book among them, as I observed before; but then many were living that had seen the former temple, and must know what kind of book that was that was called the law of Moses, that was amongst the people before the captivity, and was kept in that first temple. The highest ambition of the Jews that returned from the captivity, was to be like their forefathers in their religious privileges; and therefore they were for building a temple as near as they could like the former, and those that had seen the former temple wept bitterly that this new temple was no more like it, and doubtless they would be for having the same book of the law. The people that remembered the former temple must needs know what book that was, that was then called the book of the law, being so much and so severely reproved and threatened from time to time by the prophet Jeremiah, for not conforming themselves to it. See Jer. 2:8, the priests "that handle the law knew me not." Jer. 18:18, "Come, and let us devise devices against Jeremiah, for the law shall not perish from the priest." And Jer. 32:23, and 8:8, "How do ye say, We are wise, and the law of the Lord is with us. Lo, certainly in vain made he it; the pen of the scribes is in vain." Jer. 6:19, and 16:11, and 44:10, and 26:4, and 32:23. See also Lam. 2:9, and Ezek. 7:26, and 22:26. And indeed, the whole book of Jeremiah seems to suppose the book of the law extant and visible among the people. The people therefore that returned from the captivity would not easily have received any other book as the book of the law, to be their sacred rule, and to be laid up in the sanctuary, different from that which their forefathers had, and which had been laid up in the holy of holies in the former temple.

The book of the law of Moses was not lost in the time of the captivity, but was well-known amongst the Jews in Babylon (Dan. 9:10–13). That this was a fact very public and openly known among the heathen, that they had the law of their God among them in the time of the captivity, is a thing manifest by Dan. 6:5, and Ezra 7:12, 21, 25.[7] Yea, it was extant among [them] just before their return, as appears by Dan 9:10–13. "Yea, all Israel have transgressed thy law, even by departing, that they might not obey thy voice; therefore the curse is poured out upon us, and the oath that is written in the law of Moses, the servant of God." And several of the prophecies of Daniel suppose the book of the

---

7. This sentence and the preceding reference to Daniel are a later interlineation.

covenant to be extant (Dan. 11:22, 28, 30, 32),[8] which shows more plainly how impossible it was for another book so different to be so universally imposed on the nation in Babylon and Judea, instead of this book, so soon after the captivity. It appears that the Jews in the captivity kept the writings of the prophet Jeremiah among them, by Dan. 9:2. How much more would they keep copies of the law of Moses, which they esteemed as the foundation of all![9]

Again, 'tis most manifest that the Jews, on their first resettlement in Palestine, had those very records that we now have in the Pentateuch, as the records that had been constantly upheld in their nation as the ancient, established, and undoubted sacred records of their nation, insomuch that when they, on that occasion, reckoned the people by their genealogies, they founded their reckoning on those records, and run up their genealogies to the accounts given of their forefathers, and the first original of their families in them, making this record their standard and grand rule by which to judge who were true Israelites, and who not, and who were true priests, and who not; so that they refused so much as to admit those that could not prove themselves to be of the seed of the priests, or of the seed of Israel, according to the rule of this record, as appears by the genealogies in the first book of Chronicles, and particularly I Chron. 9:1, and Ezra 2:59, and 62–63. It was necessary for any, in order to prove themselves to be of the genuine seed of the priests, that they should be able to run up his genealogy to Aaron, for his proving that he was of the seed of some other person that lived since did not prove it, unless he also proved that that person was a descendant of Aaron. And so, for any to prove that he was of the seed of Israel, he must be able to run up his genealogy to Israel himself.

So that this[1] very record at that time were of such established reputation among them, that they all with one consent made it the very foundation of their reestablishment; they founded their nation and church in this, its restoration wholly on this foundation, and by this rule, which shows that this record was no new thing among [them], just then devised, that they before had never been acquainted with. It was a notorious fact in Esther's time, known to the heathen, that the Jews who remained dispersed all over the Persian Empire, from Judea to

8. This sentence, up to this point, is a later interlineation.
9. The last two sentences are a later interlineation.
1. MS: "~~these~~ (this)." JE wrote the entire paragraph in the plural and then changed to the singular.

Ethiopia, agreed in one established law which was very diverse from those of all other nations (Esther 3:8).[2]

Again, the *Zend-Avesta*, or book that Zoroastres wrote, shows that the history of the Pentateuch was extant, either in or before the time of the captivity of the Jews into Babylon, and was of great reputation then, because many things in that book of his are taken out of the history of the Pentateuch. He speaks of "Adam and Eve as the first parents of mankind, and gives in a manner the same history of the creation and deluge that Moses doth, and speaks therein of Abraham, Joseph, and Moses, in the same manner as the Scriptures do. And out of a particular veneration for Abraham, he called his book the Book of Abraham." See Prideaux, Pt. I, p. 318.[3] These things must have been taken from the Jews, either at or before the time of the captivity. See the preceding pages in Prideaux.[4]

Again, another argument that the Pentateuch with its history was the book that the Israelites anciently had among them as the book of the law of Moses, even before the captivity, is that the Samaritans had this Pentateuch, as it is with its history, under this name of the book of the law of Moses. One argument that the Samaritan Pentateuch was written before the captivity is that [it] is written in the ancient Phoenician or Hebrew character, whereas the Jewish copy is written in Chaldee letters, those letters becoming natural to them in their captivity. And therefore, if they had taken their Pentateuch from the Jews after the captivity, they would have doubtless taken it in the same characters in which they had [it]; but in that it is found among them, not in their characters, but in the characters that the Jews used before the captivity, 'tis a strong argument that they took it from the Jews before the captivity, and not afterwards. Whence should the Samaritans take those old Hebrew characters, if not from the Jews before the captivity? They were characters they were not used to in their own country, but were much more likely to be used to the Chaldean characters than them, living in the neighborhood of Chaldea. And if they took the Pentateuch from the Jews after the captivity, whence should they take

---

2. This sentence is a later interlineation.

3. Prideaux, *Old and New Testament Connected*, Pt. I, Vol. 1, pp. 318.

4. Ibid., pp. 299–301. Here Prideaux described Zoroaster as "the greatest Impostor, except *Mahomet*, that ever appeared in the world, and had all the craft and enterprising boldness of that *Arab*, but much more knowledge." He was well-versed in the writings of the Old Testament and in the Jewish religion which was for Prideaux "convincing proof" that he was a Jew by birth and possibly a servant of the prophet Ezra.

those characters, which were neither natural to themselves, nor in use among the Jews at that time?

Again, 'tis not at all likely that the Samaritans would be so fond of a conformity to the Jews after the captivity, as to adopt their laws and make the Jewish constitution their own, seeing there was always, even from the first return from the captivity, such a peculiar and inveterate enmity between them and the Jews.

And as such an alteration of the book of the law could not be made after the captivity without notice being taken, so neither could it at any time before; even in the most degenerate and ignorant times in Israel, yet there must be so much knowledge of this book as must render such a cheat impracticable, for the whole nation in all its constitution, both civil and sacred, and in the title they had to their inheritance, and in all their usages and innumerable peculiar customs, was so founded on this law, that it must unavoidably lead at least many in the nation to such a degree of knowledge of it, as to enable 'em to distinguish between that which is supposed to be so different from it, as such a book as the Pentateuch, and only the body of the Mosaic precepts. Though the law was commanded to be laid up in the sanctuary and kept there, yet it was not kept from the common use of the priests. The priests are called those "that handle the law" (Jer. 2:8). See also Jer. 18:18, and Ezek. 7:26, Hag. 2:11, Mal. 2:7. It was required of the priests that they should be thoroughly acquainted with the law, for they, in the law of Moses, are appointed to teach it to the people. The great number of ceremonies and minute circumstances with which their business was attended, and also the multitude of observances which they were to teach the people out of the law, made it necessary, in the nature of things, that they should be thoroughly acquainted with the law, even to the having it as it were by heart. Hence the priests and Levites, in all their cities and dwellings throughout the land, must be supposed to have copies of the law in their hands. And this being also the judicial or political law of their nation, the rule of the civil magistrate and judges in all civil and criminal matters, and the rule by which every man held his possession, and was defended in his civil and common rights, this made it necessary that the civil magistrates, and those that sat to judge in their gates, should have copies of the law in their hands. The king was, by an express statute of the law, required to write him out a copy of the law with his own hand. And the law was commanded to be read to the whole congregation of Israel once in seven years. And particular pious and devout persons were wont to have by them copies of the law, for 'tis mentioned as the character of the godly man, Ps. 1:2, and 37:31, that he meditates on God's law day and night. And all were commanded in the law to be continually meditating on the law, and make it as it were their constant companion day and night, that it might be for a sign on their hand, and as frontlets between their eyes, and that they should make it the continual subject of their conversation one with another, as they sat in the house, and as they walked by the way, etc. It was not to be shut up only in the holy of holies, and in any respect so disposed of as to be out of the reach of any, but to be nigh to everyone, in everyone's heart and mouth, as appears by Deut. 30:11–14. See also Deut. 6:6–9, and 11:18–20, and 4:9.

'Tis true the law, in times of great degeneracy, was much more neglected and less known; and copies of it were more rare than at other times, as in the reign of Manasseh [II Kgs. 21:1–18]. The original that Moses laid up in the sanctuary had been neglected and lost, being buried up in rubbish, as the temple of God itself was neglected; and the finding of it by the priest was a thing greatly taken notice of, and excited the observation and inquiry of the king and people into the nature of things contained in this book. And the Spirit of God set in on that occasion, greatly to impress the king's mind with the things contained in that book, and the finding and reading that very book, as written by Moses' own hand, had a natural tendency greatly to engage the attention of the king, and to affect him in the reading of it. But we are not [to] suppose that during that degenerate time there was no copy of the law extant and in use among any of the people. If in the most degenerate times in Israel, there were seven thousand devout worshipers of the true God left, though but little known, so undoubtedly in Manasseh's reign were many of the priests, and Levites, and others, that were devout worshipers of the true God, enough to keep many copies of the law for their use to direct 'em in God's service.

As to the passages in the Pentateuch wherein a later hand than Moses' are evident, they are very few, as Witsius, in his *Miscel. Sac.* observes.[5] Two of them are only a kind of translation of the names of places, as of the city of Hebron, and the place to which Abraham pursued the kings, where it is said, "he pursued them even unto Dan"

---

5. Herman Witsius devotes a section of the *Miscellaneorum Sacrorum Libri IV* (2nd ed., Lugduni Batavorum, 1695), pp. 102–30, to Moses' authorship of the Pentateuch which includes a discussion of the judgments of Jean Le Clerc on passages conflicting with Mosaic authorship.

[Gen. 14:14].[6] The history is exactly the same that Moses must be supposed to write,[7] and the place mentioned the same that Moses mentioned; but the alteration, that is made by some later hand, is rendering the name of the place by a word whose signification was known to the people. And these two are the only instances that appear manifest to me of all that Le Clerc mentions (see below, **),[8] excepting only the account of Moses' death and burial.[9] And it was not Ezra that made this addition, for the Samaritan Pentateuch, which was taken from the Jews before Ezra, has this addition and all other passages that have been supposed to be additions. This addition of Moses' death in all probability was made by Joshua, who, it is evident, was a divine writer, and a writer of divine records, and was Moses' successor, who alone was in the mount with him forty days and forty nights, and who succeeded in Moses' authority, and in most of his divine privileges and intercourse with heaven, on whom Moses laid his hand, and committed the care of the whole congregation, and of the law, and tabernacle into his hands. He succeeded Moses as the leader of the congregation, and as their judge, and as the person by whom they were to transact with God, as it was with Moses. He had the care of setting up the tabernacle, and therefore he took care to set it up in Shiloh. And he took the care of the settlement of the church of Israel, and the establishment of the worship of God in Canaan; and he was looked upon as having the care of the book of the law of Moses, even so as to have power to add words to it, as appears by Josh. 24:26.

+ The insertion, Deut. 3:14,[1] is the more probably put in by Joshua, because he, above all other persons, was concerned in the division of the land,[2] and therefore was the more likely to insert a passage that related to that division, declaring what part of the land was the inheritance of a particular family.[3]

** See above. Upon a further and more full consideration of the matter, with respect to the names of those two places, "Dan" and

6. JE deleted "The name Dan is used often of the place."

7. JE deleted "only the word varied."

8. This cross-reference is a later addition.

9. JE deleted the following interlineation: "two additions. The one addition is an insertion in Deut. 3:14 (+ next p.); the other is addition of the end v. 2."

1. JE deleted "(which looks altogether like an insertion independent of or parenthesis put in in the midst of Moses' continued discourse)." See above, n. 9.

2. JE deleted "and assigning to each family their inheritance and therefore."

3. JE marked this sentence with a vertical line approximately two inches from the left margin.

"Hebron," in the Pentateuch, it don't look to me at all likely that any later hand than Moses' was concerned in the matter. As to what is said, Gen. 14:14, of Abraham's pursuing the kings unto "Dan," 'tis pretty manifest that the Dan that is there intended is not the same place with Laish, that was afterwards called Dan from the children of Dan that took possession of it, but another Dan, somewhere in the eastern border of the land of Gilead, spoken of again, Deut. 34:1, "And the Lord showed him all the land of Gilead, unto Dan."[4]

As to the name "Hebron," so often used in the Pentateuch, it is very probable that there is in it no later hand in it than Moses', for though it was called Arbah at first [Gen. 35:27], yet it seems to have been named "Hebron,"[5] which signifies "fellowship," by his there entering into an association or covenant fellowship with Mamre, Eshcol, and Aner. See Gen. 13:18, with 14:13. 'Tis likely that Abraham might give a name to this place from his entering into this fellowship with those men here, as that he should name the place where he entered into covenant with Abimelech, Beersheba, from that covenant, as Gen. 21:31–32. Or possibly, this name Hebron, or "fellowship," might be given to the place from that wonderful communion and fellowship which Abraham there had with angels, whom he eat, and drank, and conversed most familiarly with under an oak, and where at the same time he familiarly conversed with God about the destruction of Sodom, which is much remarked by Abraham and God himself (Gen. 18:17, 27, 31). Or it might have been named so, at first from Abraham's fellowship with Mamre, Aner, and Eshcol, and afterwards confirmed from this his communion with God and the angels; as Beersheba was first so named, from Abraham's covenant with Abimelech, and afterwards confirmed from Isaac's covenant in the same place (Gen. 26:30–33). It seems that after this, when the posterity of Abraham left the land and sojourned in Egypt, this place went no more by that name of "Hebron" in the land of Canaan; but when the children of Israel returned, and Caleb took possession of the place, he restored the name which Abraham gave it.

See Dupin, at the beginning of the first volume of his *Ecclesiastical History*.[6]

---

4. JE marked this paragraph with a vertical line approximately two inches from the left margin.

5. JE deleted "by the patriarchs themselves."

6. Louis Ellies Dupin writes, "Of all those Paradoxes, that have been advanced in our Age, there is none, in my Judgment, more rash and dangerous than the Opinion of those, who

See concerning places inserted after Moses' death, SSS, on Num. 21:14.[7]

Places in the New Testament which[8] suppose Moses to be the penman of the Pentateuch: John 5:46–47, Mark 12:26 compared with Ex. 3:6, Acts 15:21, II Cor. 3:14–15, Heb. 12:21.[9]

417. GENESIS 33:1–7. As Jacob's family returned to the land of Canaan after Jacob had been long banished from thence, so 'tis probable will be the return of the spiritual Israel to God, its resting place, and as it were to the promised land, to the land flowing with milk and honey, to a state of glorious rest, plenty, prosperity, and spiritual joy, and delights, in the latter days, which is often represented by the prophets as a bringing God's people into the land of Israel, and recovering them from foreign lands where he had driven them.[1] Jacob, at his first entrance, meets with great opposition of Esau, his elder brother; so the true saints at that time will meet with great opposition from those professors who are often in Scripture represented by the elder brother, as Cain, and Ishmael, and Zarah, the son of Judah, who first

---

have presumed to deny, that *Moses* was the Author of the *Pentateuch*: For what can be more rash than to deny Matter of Fact, that has been established by express Texts of Holy Scripture, by the Authority of Jesus Christ, by the Consent of all Nations, and by the Authentick Testimonies of the most Ancient Authors? And what can be more dangerous, than to bid Defiance to Antiquity, and consequently destroy the Authority of those Books, which are, as it were, the very Foundations of our Religion?" Dupin allows that "some few Words, Names and Terms have been altered or added to render the Narrative more intelligible to those that lived in the following Ages," and yet that practice, common to ancient histories, is not ground for rejecting Moses' authorship. Nor is the account of his death, which was "necessary to finish the History of the *Pentateuch*," cause to deny the "certain Truth, That *Moses* was the Author of the first Five Books of the *Bible*" (*A New History of Ecclesiastical Writers: Containing an Account of the Authors of the several Books of the Old and New Testament; of the Lives and Writings of the Primitive Fathers; An Abridgment and Catalogue of their Works; Their Various Editions, and Censures Determining the Genuine and Spurious Together with a Judgment upon their Style and Doctrine. Also a Compendious History of the Councils; with Chronological Tables of the whole* [2nd ed., 13 vols., London, 1693], *1*, 1–2).

7. JE appears to have in mind Matthew Poole's discussion of the "book of the wars of the Lord" which, he states, was written before the Pentateuch, contained prophecies of future victories, and was woven into Moses' text. Poole asserted that it was not necessary to acknowledge the divine authority of this book simply because it was cited. Other profane authors were also cited in Scripture, he noted (*Synopsis Criticorum, 1* [London, 1669], Pt. 1, cols. 694–95).

8. JE deleted "evidently."

9. JE's interest in the Mosaic authorship of the Pentateuch was not confined to this entry. He also compiled a separate MS notebook of more than 100 pages in defense of Moses' authorship of the history, not simply the laws, contained in the Pentateuch. The notebook contains numerous references to No. 416 as a "treatise" on the same subject.

1. JE deleted "In the first place entered the provision of the family."

put forth his hand [Gen. 38:28–30], and David's eldest brother [I Sam. 17:28], and the elder brother of the prodigal [Luke 15:25–32]. But Jacob's meek and humble behavior towards his opposing brother, to soften and win his heart, teaches the duty of Christians. Jacob's family was divided into several companies, one going before another, with a space between; so the return of the church of God will be by several companies, that will come in one after another, by several seasons of pouring out of the Spirit of God, with a space between. In Jacob's family the lowest and meanest went first, and afterwards the more honorable, and most amiable, and best beloved; so in the spiritual return of the church of Christ, God will first bring in the inferior sort of people. He will "save the tents of Judah first," agreeable to the prophecy (Zech. 12:7). And the first outpouring of the Spirit will be the least glorious; and they that are first brought in are not only inferior among men, but the least pure, beautiful, and amiable as Christians in their experiences and practice. In Jacob's family went first the handmaids and their children; so this is the blemish of the first children of Christ that shall be brought in at the glorious day of the church, that though they will be true children of Jacob, yet shall be as it were children of the handmaids, with much of a legal spirit, i.e. spiritual pride and self-confidence. After these comes Leah and her children, who were more honorable and better beloved than the former; she was a true wife, but yet less beautiful and less beloved than his other wife. So after the first outpouring of the Spirit there will be a work of God that will break forth, that will be more glorious and more pure than the first. In Jacob's family came last of all the beautiful Rachel and Joseph, Jacob's best beloved and dearest child of all the family; so will it be in the church of God in days approaching. Jacob goes before them all, leads them all, and defends them all; so doth Christ go before his church as their leader and defense.

418. NUMBERS 24:17. "And shall smite the corners of Moab, and destroy all the children of SHETH." It would be unreasonable on many accounts to suppose that this Sheth is the same with Seth, the son of Adam [Gen. 4:25], and so that by the "children of Sheth" is meant all mankind. But the Sheth here mentioned is a founder of one of the chief families of the Moabites, probably one of the sons of Moab, the father of the people from him called *Shittim*, as the posterity of Heth [Gen. 10:15] are in Scripture from him called *Hittim*, which we trans-

late "Hittites." Whence that part of the land where those people dwelt was called Shittim, which was the part of that land in which the people now were, where Balaam beheld 'em when he blessed ['em]. He beheld 'em in the inheritance of the people of Sheth, or the land of the Shittim, or Shittites, as appears by the first verse of the next chapter, and Josh. 2:1 and 3:1, and Micah 6:5. All that renders this doubtful is, that the radical letters in *Sheth* and *Shittim* are not the same; in one is ת, and in the other ט.

419. GENESIS 10–11. THE DISPERSION AND FIRST SETTLEMENT OF THE NATIONS.[2] "By the descendants of Japheth 'were the isles of the Gentiles divided' (Gen. 10:5). By the 'isles,' the Hebrews [understood] not only such countries as were on all sides encompassed by sea, but also such countries as were so divided by the sea from them, as that they could not be well come unto, or at least used not to be gone unto, but by sea. In brief, they called 'islands,' all beyond-sea countries, and all people 'islanders,' which came by the sea to them and to the Egyptians, among whom the Jews lived a long time, and so called things by the same names," at least in Moses' time when the people were lately come out of Egypt. "Now, such are not only the island of Cyprus, Crete, and other islands of the Mediterranean, but also the countries of the Lesser Asia, and the countries of Europe.[3] And indeed those countries, so many of them as were then inhabited and known to the Jews, were not only beyond the sea, but peninsulas mostly encompassed by the sea, as the Lesser Asia, Greece, Italy, and Spain. And that not only Europe, but the countries of the Lesser Asia were called 'isles,' seems manifest by Is. 11:11. 'The Lord shall recover the remnant of his people from Assyria, Egypt, Pathros, Cush, Elam, Shinar, Hamath, and from the islands of the sea.'"[4] Lesser Asia is either here included under the term "islands of the sea," or wholly left out; but 'tis not likely the countries of Asia would be mentioned, so many of them to the south, east, and north of Judea, far and near, and the countries of Europe beyond the Lesser [Asia], and all countries of the Lesser Asia, wholly passed over.

2. JE wrote a variety of running heads in large letters across the pages of this entry.
3. JE deleted "especially those great peninsulas of Lesser Asia, Greece, and Italy."
4. Wells, *Historical Geography of the Old Testament, 1*, 112–13. This entry is drawn almost entirely from Wells, but JE often skipped pages or moved back and forth in the text as he quoted. The footnotes will identify the pages in clusters, as far as possible. At other times JE added his own reflections and commentary.

The sons of Japheth were seven: Gomer, Magog, Madai, Javan, Tubal, Meshech, and Tiras. The sons of Gomer were Ashkenaz, Riphath, and Togarmah. The sons of Javan were Elishah, Tarshish, Kittim, and Dodanim (Gen. 10:2–4).

To begin with Gomer and his sons, to whom we may assign the greatest part of the northern tract of the Lesser Asia for their first plantations. Josephus tells us expressly that the Galatians, who lived in this tract, were called Gomerites; and Herodotus tells us that a people called Cimmerii dwelt in these parts; and Pliny speaks of a town in Troas, a part of Phrygia, called Cimmeris. All the northern part of Lesser Asia was anciently called Phrygia by the Greeks, which is a word that in the Greek language signifies "torrid" or "burnt" country; as "Gomer" in Hebrew is from the radix *Gamar*,[5] which signifies to "consume," and its derivative, *Gumra* or *Gumro*, signifies a "coal." And 'tis certain there was a part of this country which was specially called by the Greeks, Φρυγία κεκαυμένη, "Burnt Phrygia."

Ashkenaz, who of the three sons of Gomer[6] is first named by Moses, was seated in the western part of the nation of Gomer, i.e. in the northwest part of the Lesser Asia, as is hardly to be questioned, there being so plain footsteps of his name to be found in these parts. For in Bithynia there is a bay, formerly called the Ascanian Bay, together with a river and lake of the same name. And in the Lesser Phrygia, or Troas, there was both a city and province anciently known by the name of Ascania, and there were isles lying on the coast called the Ascanian Isles. Nor is it any way unlikely but that in honor of this Ashkenaz, the kings and great men of these parts took the name of Ascanius. Of which name, besides Ascanius, the son of Aeneas, we find a king mentioned in the 2nd book of Homer's *Iliads*, which came to the aid of Priamus at the siege of Troy. And from hence probably came the name that the Greeks gave to the sea, the "Euxine Sea," from the family of Ashkenaz upon the coasts, along which lies the entrance into this sea, with some variation of the sound which length of time might naturally introduce. And the prophet Jeremiah, foretelling the taking of Babylon by Cyrus, has this expression, ch. 51, v. 27. "Call together against her the kingdoms of Ararat, and Minni, and Ashkenaz,"

5. גָּמַר.
6. MS: "Noah."

where, by the kingdom of Ashkenaz, may very well be understood the inhabitants of these parts we are speaking of. For Xenophon, as Bochart has well observed, tells us that Cyrus, having taken Sardes, sent Hystaspes with an army into the Phrygia that lies on the Hellespont; and that Hystaspes, having made himself master of the country, brought along with him from thence a great many of the horse and other soldiers of the Phrygians, whom Cyrus took along with the rest of his army to Babylon.

Riphath, the second son of Gomer, is probably supposed to have seated his [family] in the parts adjoining eastward to the plantation of his brother Ashkenaz. This opinion is confirmed by the testimony of Josephus, who expressly says that the Paphlagonians, a people inhabiting some portion of this tract, were originally called Riphateans, from Riphat. There are also some remainders of his name to be found here, among the writings of the ancient Greeks and Latins. For in Apollonius' *Argonautics*, there is mention made of the river called Rhebaeus, which rising in this tract, empties itself into the Euxine Sea. The same is called by Dionysius Periegetes and others, Rhebas. Stephanus does not only acquaint us with the river, but tells us also of a region of the same name, and whose inhabitants were called Rhebaei. And Pliny places here a people called Riphaei, and another called Arimphaei.

The third and last son of Gomer named by Moses is *Togarmah*, whose family was seated in the remaining, and consequently in the most easterly part of the nation of Gomer. And this situation of the family of Togarmah is agreeable both to sacred and common writers. For as to sacred Scripture, Ezekiel thus speaks, ch. 38, v. 6, "Gomer, and all his bands; the house of Togarmah of the north quarters, and all his bands." And again, ch. 27, v. 14, "They of the house of Togarmah traded in thy fairs (i.e. the fairs of Tyre) with horses, and horsemen, and mules." Now the situation that we assign to Togarmah makes it, in a manner, lie true north from Judea. And Cappadocia, by which name a considerable part of the lot of Togarmah was in process of time known to the Greeks, was very well stocked with an excellent breed of horses and mules, and that the inhabitants were esteemed good horsemen, as is well attested by several ancient heathen writers, as Solinus of Cappadocia, Dionysius Periegates, Claudian in Russin, and Strabo. And there are to be found footsteps of the very name of Togarmah in some of those names, whereby some of the inhabitants of this tract were known to old writers. Thus Strabo tells us, that the Trochmi dwelt in the confines of Pontus and Cappadocia; and several towns lying on the east of the river Halys, and so in Cappadocia, are assigned to them by Ptolemy. They are by Cicero called Trogmi, and Trochmeni by Stephanus; and in the Council[7] of Chalcedon they are called Trocmades, or Trogmades, there being frequent mention made in that council of Cyriacus, bishop of the Trogmades.

We next proceed to say something of the colonies which, coming from the nation of Gomer, in process of time spread themselves further and further, and settled themselves in several parts of Europe. Herodotus [tells] that a people called Cimmerii, formerly dwelt in that tract of Lesser Asia which we assign to Gomer; so he tells us withal, that these people sent out a colony to Palus Maeotis, on the north of the Euxine Sea, and so gave the name of Bosphorus Cimmerius to the strait betwixt the Euxine Sea and the Maeotick Lake, now commonly called the Strait of Caffa.

This colony of the Cimmerii, increasing in process of time, and so spreading themselves still by new colonies further westward, came along the Danube, and settled themselves in the country which from them has been called Germany. For as to the testimony of the ancients, Diodorus Siculus (as Mr. Mede observes) affirms, that the Germans had their original from the Cimmerians; and the Jews to this day (as the same learned person remarks) call them Ashkenazim, of Ashkenaz. Indeed they themselves retain plain marks enough of their descent, both in the name Cimbri, and also in their common name "Germans," or as they call themselves, *Germen*, which is but a small variation from *Gemran*, or *Gomren*; and this last is easily contracted from Gomeren, that is, Gomeraeans. For the termination "en" is a plural termination of the German language; and from the singular number, Gomer, is formed *Gemren*, by the same analogy that from "brother" is formed "brethren." The other name, Cimbri, is easily framed from Cimmerii; and by that name the inhabitants of the northwest peninsula of old Germany, now called Jutland, were known not only to ancient but later[8] writers; and from this name of the inhabitants, the said peninsula is called Cimbrica Chersonesus, and that frequently by modern authors.

Out of Germany the descendants of Gomer spread themselves into Gaul, or France. To prove this Mr. Camden quotes the testimony of Josephus, where he says, that those called by the Greeks "Galatae" were originally called "Gomerites," which words may be understood, either of the Asiatic Galatae, commonly called by us Galatians, or the European Galatae, commonly called by us Gauls. If it be taken in the former sense, then it is a testimony for the first seating of Gomer in that tract of the Lesser Asia we have assigned him, and on this account it is afore taken notice of by us. Mr. Camden also produces the testimony of other writers to prove the Gauls to be from Gomer, as of Appian, who in his *Illyrics* says expressly, that the Celtae, or Gauls, were otherwise called Cimbri. Those barbarians, whom Marius defeated, Cicero plainly terms Gauls. And all historians agree, that these were the Cimbri; and the coat armor of Beleus their king, digged up at Aix in Provence, where Marius routed them, does evince the same, for the words *"Beleos Cimbros"* were engraven upon it in a strange character. Again, Lucan calls that ruffian, that was hired to kill Marius, a Cimbrian, whereas Livy and others affirm him to have been a Gaul; and by Plutarch, the Cimbri are called Gallo-Scythians.

Hence we may conclude that the ancient inhabitants of Britain were descended from Gomer. For 'tis not to be questioned, but that this isle was first peopled from those countries of the European continent which lie next to it, and consequently from Germany or Gaul. The name by which the offspring of those ancient Britains, the Welsh, call them[9] to this very day, is Kumero, or Cymro, and Kumeri. And in like manner they call a Welsh woman, Kumeraes, and their language, Kumeraeg. And since the *Saxons* and *Angles* were Germans who, as was before observed, were descendants of Gomer, and were near neighbors to the people that were more especially called Cimbri, hence it follows that our ancestors, who succeeded the old Britains, were also descended from Gomer.

But now to proceed to the other sons of Japheth. As the nation of Gomer first seated itself in the northern tract of the Lesser Asia, so the nation of *Javan* seated itself in the southern tract of the same. And this appears, not only from the name of a country in this tract called Ionia, but also from the situation of the four families of

9. Wells reads "themselves."

Javan's sons within this tract, which are mentioned in this order by Moses: Elishah, Tarshish, Kittim, and Dodanim (Gen. 10:4).

Tarshish seated himself on the eastern part of this tract, as is probable on several considerations. For Tarsus is a chief town of Cilicia, and Josephus expressly affirms that Cilicia, and the country round it, was originally known by the name of Tarshish. 'Tis scarcely to be doubted, but this was the Tarshish to which the prophet Jonas thought to "flee from the presence of the Lord" [Jonah 1:3], as also that this principally was the Tarshish mentioned so often by the prophets, on account of its trading with Tyre.

To the west of Tarshish adjoined the portion appertaining to Kittim, or Cittim; which word, having a plural termination, does in all probability imply the "descendants of Keth," or the Ketians. Ptolemy tells us of a country here, called Cetis; and Homer in _Odyssey_, 4, mentions a people called Cetii, who were thought to take their name from a river Cetius, in the same quarter. But 'tis remarkable, that the seventy interpreters[1] render Kittim by Κήτιοι, Ketii, or Cetii, exactly agreeable to the name mentioned by Homer. Josephus will have the isle of Cyprus to have been the seat of the Cittim, because therein was a town called Citium, of good note. But 'tis not to be questioned, but the continent was peopled before the island, and consequently that Cittim first seated themselves on the continent, from which they might probably enough send, in process of time, some colony over into the neighboring island of Cyprus.

The two remaining families of Javan, viz. Elishah and Dodanim, seated themselves on the western coast of the southern tract of the Lesser Asia. Here upwards, or northwards, were anciently seated the Aeoles who, as they carry some marks of their pedigree in their name, so are expressly affirmed by Josephus to have been descended from Elishah, and from him to have taken their name. And since the country peculiarly called in after-ages Ionia, joined to the south of what was in said ages peculiarly called Aeolia, 'tis probable that the said Ionia (so peculiarly called, perhaps from Javan's living there with his son Elishah), was possessed originally by the sons of Elishah, or else partly by them, and partly by the Dodanim, of whom next.

On the same western coast, south of the family of Elishah, may the family of Dodanim be supposed to have first planted itself. For

---

1. Translators of the Septuagint.

there we find in ancient writers a country called Doris, which may not improbably be derived from Dodanim, especially if this be plural, as the termination seems to import; and so the singular was Dodan, which being softened into Doran, the Greeks might easily frame from thence Dorus, whom they assert to be the father of the Dorians. Certain it is from the Greek writers themselves, that the Dores, or Dorians, were a considerable body of the Greeks, insomuch that *Dorica Castra* is taken by Virgil to denote the whole Grecian camp. Wherefore 'tis very probable that they had their extraction from one of the sons of Javan, the father of the Greek nation, and distinguished themselves from the other families of Javan, by assuming to themselves the name of the father of their family, as the others did, and consequently called themselves Dodanim, which the Greeks in time molded into Dores. The Greeks say of Dorus, the father of the Dorians, that he was the son of Neptune, who evidently was the same with Japheth (see No. 405); and though Dodanim was the grandson of Japheth, yet according to the usual way of speaking among the Hebrews, he was called the son of Japheth. The change of Dodan into Dorus is the more likely, by reason of the great likeness there is between the Hebrew "D" and "R."[2] Hence (viz. from Doris) some might pass over to the isle of Rhodes, which might take its name from those Dodanim which, by reason of the likeness of letters, is sometimes writ Rodanim, which seems to have been the opinion of the seventy interpreters, by their rendering the Hebrew word *Dodanim* by ῾Ρόδιοι, *Rhodii*.

I proceed now to speak of the colonies of the posterity of Javan that, in process of time, were made from their first settlements, and I shall begin with the two last mentioned, Elishah and Dodanim. For these, lying on the western coast of the Lesser Asia, as they increased, peopled by degrees the many isles that lie in the adjoining sea, and so at length spread themselves into the European continent. The family of Elishah seem to have possessed themselves of most, or at least the most considerable, isles lying in the sea between Europe and Asia, forasmuch as they are called by the Prophet, Ezek. 27:7, "the isles of Elishah." What the Prophet there says, of the "blue and the purple from the isles of Elishah," is very applicable to the isles of this sea, forasmuch as they did abound in this commodity, and are on that account celebrated by common

2. ד and ר. Wells, *Historical Geography of the Old Testament*, *1*, 116–36.

authors, and some of them took their names from it. And the sea itself, on which these isles were, seems originally to have been called the sea of Elishah, which name, though it wore away in process of time in other parts, yet seems to have been all along preserved in that part, which to this day is frequently called the Hellespont, as if one should say Elishae-Pontus, the sea of Elishah. And this derivation of the word "Hellespont" will appear yet more likely, when we consider that the descendants of Elishah passing over into Europe, came afterwards to be termed Hellenes, and their country Hellas, a name which in process of time became common to all Greece, in which there were other footsteps of Elishah's name to be found formerly, as in the city and province of Elis in the Peloponnesus, in the city of Eleusis in Attica, and in the river Elissus, and Ilissus, in the same province. Some think the *Campi Elisii*, so much celebrated among the Greeks, to have been so called from Elishah.

As to Dodanim, or the Dorians, the Spartans, or Lacedaemonians, looked on themselves to be of Doric extraction; and there were formerly remainders of the name to be found in these parts of Greece. In the province of Messene in the Peloponnese, there was a town called Dorion; and of the other tract of Greece, lying above the isthmus of the Peloponnese, there was a considerable part called Doria, Dorica, or Doris, to say nothing of Dodona. And all the Greek nation is sometimes called Dores, as was before observed out of Virgil.

As to Kittim, or the Cittim, they probably sent their first colony to the neighboring isle of Cyprus,

which seems to be called the land of Chittim (Is. 23:1, and 12).

But in process of time wanting more room, and therefore seeking out further, and finding the lower parts of Greece already inhabited by the descendants of Elishah and Dodanim, they still proceeded on, coasting along the western shores of Greece, till they came to the upper and northern parts of it, which not being yet inhabited, some of them planted themselves there, whilst some others of them, descrying the coast of Italy, went and settled themselves in that country. Hence it comes to pass in probability, that both Macedonia in Greece and also Italy, are denoted in Scripture by the names of Cittim. The author of the Book of Maccabees plainly denotes Macedonia by the land of Chetiim, when he says that Alexander, the son of Philip the Macedonian, came out of the land of Chetiim (I Macc. 1:1). So also ch. 8, v. 5, the said author calls Perseus king of Macedonia, king of the Citims. The more ancient name of this country was Macetia, and the Macedonians themselves are otherwise termed Macetae.

The place of Scripture, where Chittim by the consent of almost all expositors denotes the Romans, is Dan. 11:29–30. For by "the ships of Chittim," there mentioned, is understood the Roman fleet, by the coming whereof Antiochus was obliged to desist from his designs against Egypt. There are also several footsteps of the name Chittim, or Cheth,[3] to be found in Italy among ancient writers, as a city of Latium called Cetia, mentioned by Dionysius Helicarnasseus; another city among the Volsci called Echetia, mentioned by Stephanus; also a river near Cumae called Cetus. Nay, there are not wanting authors, who expressly assert the Romans and Latins to have had their extraction from the Citii, or Cetii, as Eusebius, Cedrenus, Suidas, whose testimonies are produced by Bochart. And this learned person observes further, that the word Chetim does, in the Arabic tongue, denote a thing "hid," so that the name Latini might be originally only a translation of the old eastern name Chetim.

There remain now only the colonies of Tarshish to be spoken of. And wheresoever else they seated themselves, 'tis highly probable that Tartessus, a city and adjoining country in Spain, and much celebrated by the ancients for its wealth, was a colony of Tarshish. Bochart has observed that Polybius, reciting the words of a league between the Romans and Carthaginians, mentions a place under the name of Tarseium; and Stephanus expressly says that Tarseium was a city near Hercules' pillars, the situation whereof agrees well enough with that of Tartessus.

Again, what is said by Ezekiel, ch. 27, v. 12, agrees very well with this Tarshish, for the words of the Prophet run thus. "Tarshish was thy merchant, by reason of the multitude of all kinds of riches; with silver, iron, tin, and lead, they traded in thy fairs," i.e. the fairs of Tyre. Now, as has been before observed, Tartessus was celebrated among the ancients for its multitude of riches; and the metals mentioned by the Prophet were such as Spain did formerly abound with. Some also are of opinion, that the Etrusci in Italy, otherwise called Tyrrheni and Tusci, were a colony of Tarshish. The word

3. Wells reads "Chetim."

Etrusci, without the initial "E" (which was frequently added to derivatives), contains the radicals of Tarshish.

The descendants of Tarshish were the most expert seamen, and consequently the chief merchants of the early ages of the world. Hence the whole Mediterranean Sea seems to have been at length comprehended under the name of the sea of Tarshish. And because the descendants of Tarshish were wont to make longer voyages, and to adventure further into the open sea than others did in those days, 'tis not unlikely that they had ships built for this purpose, and so of somewhat a different make, both as to size and shape, from the vessels commonly used by others. And hence 'tis probable that all vessels built for longer voyages and greater burdens came to be called "ships of Tarshish," because they were built like the ships of Tarshish, properly so called.[4]

Having observed these things concerning the settlements and colonies of the four families of Javan, I would here add something with respect to Javan himself, the father of this whole nation. And I would observe that 'tis probable that the colonies that passed over in process of time into Europe, though they were distinguished in reference to their distinct families by their distinct names, yet were all at first comprehended under the name of Ionians. Indeed the Scholiast on Aristophanes (as Bochart hath observed) expressly says, that all the Greeks were by the barbarians called Iaones, i.e. Ionians. Hence the Ionian Sea came to be extended anciently quite to the western coast of Greece, and that northwards up as far as the western coast of Macedonia. Now 'tis plain that the name Ionians was derived from the founder of this nation, Javan, for the Hebrew word, setting aside the vowels which are of disputable authority, may be read "Ion," or "Iaon." But supposing the word to be all along pronounced with the same vowels it has in the Hebrew text at present, 'tis granted by the learned in the same language, that the true pronunciation of the Hebrew vowel, *Kametz*, carries in it a mixture of our vowel "O" as well as "A," so that the Hebrew יון is very regularly turned into the Greek 'Ιάων, whence by contraction may be made 'Ιων. Since therefore not only the forementioned Scholiast, but also Homer, styles those who were commonly called *Iones* by the name *Iaones*, 'tis not to be doubted but the Ionians were so called for Javan, the founder of their nation. Agreeably to what

4. Wells, *Historical Geography of the Old Testament*, *1*, 138–46.

has been said, we find the country of Greece denoted in the book of Daniel, from time to time, the country of Javan (Dan. 8:21, and 10:20, and 11:2), and also in Joel 3:6. And though the Athenians affirm that the Asiatic Ionians were a colony of theirs, yet Hecateus in Strabo affirms that the Athenians, or Ionians of Europe, came from those of Asia.

Having spoken something largely of the posterity of Gomer and Javan, because Europe appears to be chiefly peopled[5] by them, we now proceed to take notice of the other sons of Japheth, among whom I shall speak next of Tubal and Meshech, which are so mentioned together from time to time in Scripture, that 'tis evident that their settlements were adjoining one to the other.

Meshech joined onto the nation of Gomer eastward, and so settling at first in part of Cappadocia and Armenia. What, according to the present vowels in Hebrew, is Meshech, was by the seventy interpreters and others read Mosoch; and hence 'tis very probable that they are the same, called by the Greeks Μόσχος, Mosci, who were seated in these parts, and from whom no question but the neighboring ridge of hills took the name of *Montes Moschici*, mentioned by the old geographers.

To the north of Meshech adjoined the first plantation of Tubal, who by Josephus is expressly affirmed to be the father of the Asiatic Iberians. The same historian, asserting that whom the Greeks called Iberi were originally called *Thobeli* from Tubal, adds hereunto, that Ptolemy places in these parts a city called Thabilica. Mr. Bochart supposes the Tibareni, a people mentioned by old authors in this tract, to have been so called from Tubal, by the change of "L" into "R," which is very frequent. But that Meshech and Tubal seated themselves in these parts is in a manner put beyond dispute, by what is said of those two nations in Ezek. 27:13. "Tubal and Meshech were thy merchants; they traded in slaves and vessels of brass in thy market." For it is evident from the testimonies of heathen writers, that the Pontic regions, especially Cappadocia, was remarkable formerly for slaves, as also that in the country of the Tibareni and Iberia, there was the best sort of brass. Mr. Bochart observes, that the Hebrew word translated in this place "brass," is sometimes rendered "steel." And hence he remarks, that as a piece of iron or brass is in the Arabic tongue called "Tubal," probably

5. MS: "People."

from its coming out of the country of Tubal, so it is likely that from the excellent steel, that was made in this country, some of the inhabitants thereof were denominated by the name of Chalybes among the Greeks, the word *Chalybs* in the Greek language signifying "steel."

That the Muscovites, or Moscovites, in Europe were a colony originally of Meshech, or Mosoch, called by the Greeks *Moschi*, is very probable.[6]

Magog is, by the testimony of Josephus, Eustathius, St. Jerome, Theodoret, and (as Mr. Mede expresses it) by the consent of all men, placed north of Tubal, and esteemed the father of the Scythians, that dwelt on the east and northeast of the Euxine Sea. This situation is confirmed by the Scripture itself. Ezek. 38:2, "Set thy face against Gog, in *or* of the land of Magog, the chief prince of Meshech and Tubal." Bochart conjectures that the mountain called by the Greeks "Caucasus," took its name from Gog. But the name of Gog was entirely preserved in the name Gogarene, whereby was formerly denoted a country in those parts, as we learn both from Strabo and Stephanus. And from hence, perhaps in time, was fashioned[7] the name Georgia, whereby at this very day is denoted a considerable tract in this quarter. That Gog denotes the Scythians in the prophecy of Ezekiel, may be rationally inferred from Ezek. 39:3, where God speaks of Gog thus. "I will smite thy bow out of thy left hand, and will cause thine arrows to fall out of thy right hand." Now 'tis too well-known to the learned to need proof, that the Scythians were remarkably famous of old for their skill in the use of the bow and arrow, insomuch that some among them, for their winking with one eye when they shot, are said to have given them the name of *Arimaspi*, "one-eyed." Nay, 'tis thought by some, not without ground, that the very name of Scythians was derived from "shooting," forasmuch as in the German tongue shooters are called *Scutten*.

To say something of the colonies of Magog. In the panegyric of Tibullus to Messala, we find mention made by the poet of a people about the river Tanais, called Magini, which probably came from Magog. Yea, 'tis not improbable that the Maeotick Lake, into which the Tanais runs, took its name from the descendants of Magog; for

---

6. Wells, *Historical Geography of the Old Testament*, *1*, 151–58.
7. MS: "~~Greeks fashion by degrees~~ (in time was) fashioned."

Magogitis, or Magotis, the Greeks might naturally after their manner soften into Maiotis, which the Latins and we render Maeotis. We read in Pliny that the city in Syria called Hierapolis was by the Syrians called Magog, which name it is thought most likely to have taken from the Scythians, when they made an excursion into Syria, and took this city. On the like account, it is that the city in Judea called Bethsan was also called in after ages Scythopolis. Now Hierapolis, being thus called Magog, it is not improbable but the adjoining part of Syria might be from thence called Magogene, which afterwards might be molded into Gomagene, and so into Commagene, by which name the northern part of Syria was denoted among the Greeks and Latins.

The next son of Japheth is Madai, who is almost universally looked upon to be the father of the Medes, who are all along denoted by the name of Madai in the Hebrew text. Bochart thinks the Sarmatians a colony from these.[8] He conjectures that the name of the Sarmatians was originally *Sear-Madai*, which in the original languages, denotes the "remnant" or "posterity of the Medes."

See objections against this, and another region allotted to Madai, in Poole's *Synopsis*, Vol. 1, cols. 117–18.[9]

Tiras, or Thiras, the last son of Japheth, is by universal agreement esteemed the father of the Thracians. The name whereby the country of Thrace is called in oriental writers, plainly shows that the Greek name Thrace was originally derived from Thiras, the founder of the nation. Ancient writers also tell us that here was a river, a bay, and an haven, each called by the name of Athyras; and they mention a city on the peninsula of Thrace called Tyristasis, and a tract in this country called Thrasus, and a people called Trausi. We learn also from them that one of the names of Mars, the god of the Thracians, was Θοῦρος. Hence old Homer calls Mars by an epithet, Θοῦρος Ἄρης, "Mars Thurus." We read also in old authors of Tereus, the son of Mars, and first king of the Thracians, and of one Teres, king of the Odrysae, a people in Thrace. And the Odrysae themselves are said to take their name from one Odrysus, a great person among them, insomuch that in after-ages he was

---

8. Wells, *Historical Geography of the Old Testament*, *1*, 160–65.

9. This sentence is a later interlineation. Among the objections cited by Poole is the fact that this location would situate a son of Japheth among the sons of Shem (*Synopsis Criticorum*, *1* [London, 1669], Pt. 1, cols. 117–18).

worshiped by the Thracians as a god. As for the colonies of Tiras, it is hardly to be doubted, but some of them planted themselves in the country over against Thrace, on the north side of the Euxine Sea. For there is a considerable river in those parts called, in both Greek and Latin writers, "Tiras," the very same as the name of the father of the Thracian nation, which river is now called the Niester. There was also a city of the same name standing on this river. The inhabitants of these parts were also formerly known by the names of Tyritae, or Tyragetae. Though probably the Tyritae might denote the true descendants of Tyras, the Tyragetae might denote a mixed race, that arose out of the Tyritae mixing with the Getae, a bordering people descended of the Cetim, that settled in Macedonia.

'Tis not unlikely that Tyras might first sit down with his family in the Lesser Asia, in the country of Troy, which had nothing to part it from Thrace but the narrow strait of the Hellespont. And the ancient king named Tros, whence the country is denominated, was probably no other than Tyras.

'Tis the common opinion [and] tradition among Greek writers that the inhabitants on the east of the Hellespont and Propontis were originally, or anciently, Thracians.[1]

We proceed next to the first plantations of the sons of SHEM. There are five sons of Shem mentioned by Moses, viz. Elam, and Asshur, and Arphaxad, and Lud, and Aram [Gen. 10:22].

I shall begin with the settlements of Aram, as being the first nation of the branch of Shem, adjoining to the nations of the branch of Japheth already spoken of, for the portion that fell to the nation of Aram lay in the countries called by the Greeks Armenia, Mesopotamia, and Syria. 'Tis probable that Armenia took its present name from Aram. Mesopotamia, as it was so called by the Greeks, from its situation between the rivers Euphrates and Tigris, so it was called by the Hebrews *Aram-Naharaim*, i.e. "Aram of," or "between the two rivers." And whereas one part of this country, viz. that lying next to Armenia, was very fruitful, and the other to the south, very barren, and so of the like soil with Arabia Deserta, to which it adjoined, hence the former is in Scripture distinguished by the name of Padan-Aram, which denotes as much as "fruitful Aram."

1. Wells, *Historical Geography of the Old Testament, 1*, 168–72.

Aram's sons are four: Uz, Hul, Gether, and Mash. As for Uz, he is by a great agreement of the ancients said to be the builder of the city of Damascus,

and his posterity are supposed to have settled the country about it. Here see Poole's *Synopsis* on Gen. 10:23.[2]

The family of Hul, or as it is in the original, *Chul*, may with great probability be placed in Armenia, particularly the Greater Armenia, for there we find the names of several places, beginning with the radicals of *Chul*, as Cholua, Choluata, Cholimna, Colsa, Colura; and to mention but one more, Cholobetene, which last seems to have been formed from the oriental *Cholbeth*, which denotes the same as the "house" or "dwelling of Chol." Now this Cholobatene, being the name of a province in Armenia, from this especially we may gather, with great probability that Chul, with his family, seated himself in those parts.

Between Hul to the north and Uz to the south, their brother Mash seated himself, viz. about the mountain Masius. From this mountain issues out a river of Mesopotamia, called by Xenophon, "Masca," which probably comes from the name of this son of Aram, who otherwise is called in Scripture Meshech, the radicals whereof are plainly contained in the name Masca. The inhabitants of the tract adjoining to the mount Masius are by Stephanus called Masieni, or Masiani.

Gether probably seated himself east of his brother Hul, on the eastern borders of Armenia, where some in Ptolemy observe a city called formerly Getarae, and a river of the same country called Getras.

We now pass on to the nation of Asshur, which [lay] eastward of the nation of Aram, in the country called Asshur in the eastern tongues, which is the Assyria properly and originally so called, lying east of the Tigris, and wherein stood the city of Nineveh, which was afterwards called Adiabene, and also was sometimes, by a change of "S" into "T," formerly called Attyria. The most ancient king of Assyria was said to be the son of Zames, i.e. Shem, and is styled in Suidas and some others, "Thuras," corruptly for At-

2. This reference is a later interlineation. Poole's account of the four sons of Aram includes discussion of the traditional locations where they are said to have settled. In the case of Uz, he wrote, "*Is conditor Damasci. Ita veteres magno consensu*" (*Synopsis Criticorum, 1* [London, 1669], Pt. 1, col. 135).

thuras, i.e. Asshur; for Asshur, in the Chaldee tongue, is Atthur, or Atthura. This Thuras, the son of Zames, was worshiped by the Assyrians as their Mars, or god of war.

That Elam seated himself in the southern tract beyond the river Euphrates, is beyond dispute, not only from the authority of the Scripture, wherein the inhabitants of the said tract are plainly and frequently denoted by the name of Elam, but also from heathen writers, wherein we read of a country here called Elymais, and a city of the same name.

To the lot of Arphaxad is assigned, by learned men, the more southern part of Mesopotamia, where the plain or vale of Shinar lay on the river Tigris, together with the country of Eden, and the tract on the east side of the same river, called Arapachitis, a name plainly derived from *Arpachshad*, which is the name of Arphaxad in the Hebrew text. That the vale of Shinar, with the country of Eden, was part of the first plantation of Arphaxad, is supposed on these probabilities. 1. That Noah after the flood returned and settled himself again in these parts, as well knowing the goodness of the soil, and pleasantness of the country, which is confirmed by a town here called Zama, from "Shem." 2. That upon the dispersion of mankind and confusion of tongues, as the primitive or Hebrew tongue was preserved in the family of Arphaxad, so agreeably hereunto this family still continued in the same parts, where they then were, together with their grandsires, Noah and Shem. 3. This opinion may be confirmed from Gen. 10:30, "And their dwelling was from Mesha, as you go unto Sephar, a mount of the east." For the Mesha here mentioned is probably esteemed to be the same mountain as is before mentioned under the name of Mash, or Masius, in the western parts of Mesopotamia. So that if the fore-cited text is to be understood of the descendants of Arphaxad (as is thought by several learned men, and also by the historian Josephus), it will import thus much, that the southern part of Mesopotamia, lying on the east of the mount Mesha, or Masius, was first peopled by the descendants of Arphaxad (and accordingly we here find Phalga, a town probably named from Peleg, or Phaleg, settling there), and so on eastward as far as to Sephar, a mount in the east. Now this mount Sephar is probably thought to be the mountain adjoining to Siphare, a city in Aria, and which lies directly east from Mesha. And though this be a long tract of ground, yet it will be but proportional to the numerous descendants of Arphaxad, especially by Joktan, of which more by and by. 4. It is the tradition of the ancients, Eustathius Antiochenus and Eusebius, that Selah, the son of Arphaxad, seated himself in Susiana. And agreeably hereto, we read in old writers of a town called Sela. But now Susiana did contain part of the country of Eden, which adjoined to, or in probability was part of, the vale of Shinar, largely taken. 5. It is further confirmed, that Arphaxad seated himself in the vale of Shinar, because we find that Terah and Abraham his son came out of those parts. Gen. 11:31, "And Terah took Abraham his son, . . . and went forth with them from Ur of the Chaldees, to go into the land of Canaan." Now 'tis confessed, I think by all, that Chaldea comprehended at least a great part of the vale of Shinar; and 'tis certain that it comprehended as much of the country of Eden as lay west of the common channel of the Euphrates and Tigris. And on this text of Scripture seems to be grounded what Josephus saith of the Chaldeans being called the Arphaxadeans.

Having thus seen the first settlements of the descendants of Arphaxad, let us turn our eyes a little upon their after-colonies, particularly those that sprang from Joktan, of whom Moses reckons up no fewer than thirteen sons. And as Moses assigns their habitation from Mesha to Mount Sephar, so in this tract learned men have observed the names of several places, which by their likeness to the names of Joktan's sons, seem to tell their respective situations.

There is nothing certain concerning Lud, the remaining son of Shem, but that he did not seat himself in the country of Lesser Asia called Lydia.

HAM was the youngest of the three sons of Noah. He had four sons: Cush, Mizraim, Phut, and Canaan. We find Egypt twice or thrice, in the book of Psalms, called the land of Ham, whence it seems probable that Ham went thither himself, and there settled with his son Mizraim. And 'tis scarce to be doubted, but the person denoted by the Greeks under the name of Jupiter Ammon (in honor to whom there was a temple erected in the parts of Libya adjoining to Egypt, much celebrated for its oracles), was no other than Ham.

'Tis well-known that the nation of Canaan settled itself in the country so often called in Scripture the land of Canaan.[3] Upon the dispersion of mankind, the country lying on the east and southeast

3. Wells, *Historical Geography of the Old Testament, 1*, 175–91.

of the Mediterranean Sea fell to the share of Canaan, so that he was seated between the nation of Aram to the north and east, and the nation of Cush, his brother, to the south and southeast, and Mizraim, another of his brothers, to the southwest. His western boundary was the Mediterranean Sea.

His descendants are thus reckoned up by Moses. Gen. 10:15–18, "Canaan begat Sidon his firstborn, and Heth, and the Jebusite, and the Emorite,[4] and the Girgasite, and the Hivite, and the Arkite, and the Sinite, and the Arvadite, and the Zemarite, and the Hamathite."

Of Sidon were the inhabitants of the city Sidon, and the country about, which city, as is apparent both from sacred and old profane writers, in the more early ages of the world, was much more considerable than Tyre. Sidon is called "great Sidon" (Josh. 19:29), but Tyre don't seem to have become considerable till[5] about David's time. Homer never so much as once mentions Tyre, but often makes mention of the Sidonians; and Tyre is expressly called the "daughter of Zidon" (Is. 23:12).

The second family of Canaan mentioned by Moses is that of Heth,

whose posterity placed themselves in the southern parts of Canaan, about Hebron, as appears by Abraham's[6] concern with them there (Gen. 23). We also read that during Isaac's dwelling at Beersheba, Esau took him wives of the daughters of Heth (Gen. 26:34).

The Jebusites were seated about Jerusalem, which was originally called Jebus (I Chron. 11:4), so that the Jebusites joined onto the Hittites in the mountains towards the north.

As the Hittites and Jebusites, so also the Amorites dwelt in the mountainous or hilly part of the land of Canaan, as appears by Josh. 11:3. And the spies give this account, Num. 13:29. "And the Hittites, and the Jebusites, and the Amorites dwell in the mountains; and the Canaanites dwell by the sea, and the coast of Jordan." Now as the Hittites seem to have possessed the hill country to the west and southwest of Hebron, and the Jebusites to the north, so the Amorites might settle themselves at first in the hill country to the east and southeast of Hebron. This seems probable, because

4. I.e. Amorite.
5. JE deleted "the reign of."
6. MS: "Abrahams ⟨& Isaacs.⟩"

the mountainous tract lying next to Kadesh-barnea is called the "mount of the Amorites" (Deut. 1:7). And we are [told], Gen. 14:7, that Chedorlaomer smote the Amorites that were in Hazezon-Tamar, which was the same place with Engaddi (II Chron. 20:2), and so was seated in the hilly part of the land of Canaan to the east, or towards Jordan. And their neighborhood to the country beyond Jordan might be the occasion that the Moabites were in process of time dispossessed thereof by the Amorites, whence that tract beyond Jordan is called the "land of the Amorites," and Sihon, the king thereof, is always called king of the Amorites.

The Girgasite is the next family mentioned by Moses, who probably seated themselves at first along the upper part of the river of Jordan. Here, on the eastern side of the sea of Tiberias, or Galilee, we find in our Savior's time a city called Gergesa.

The Hivite we find was seated in the upper or northern parts of Canaan, and so adjoining to his brother Sidon. For we read, Judg. 3:3, that "the Hivites dwelt in Mount Lebanon, from Mount Baal-Hermon unto the entering in of Hamath."

In process of time, these families intermixed one with the other. Whence we read of some Hivites, Amorites, and Hittites, in some other places than we have assigned them for their first settlements, and also the Amorites becoming the most potent nation in process of time. Hence they are put to denote, frequently, any one or more of the other nations of Canaan.[7]

Many of the posterity of Canaan of different families, either originally or afterwards (possibly by being dispossessed of their original settlements by the Philistines, or by some other means), [seem] to have settled confusedly together, and so intermixed, that the names of their distinct families were not kept up, but they were called by the general name of Canaanites.

Hence we read in the forecited, Num. 13:29, that "Canaanites dwelt by the sea, and by the coast of Jordan."

As to the remaining families of Canaan mentioned by Moses, the first of them that occurs is the Arkite, which is probably thought to have settled himself about that part of Mount Libanus, where is placed by Ptolemy and others a city called Arce. Not far from this

---

7. JE deleted the following text from Wells, "As to the several of the remaining families of Canaan mentioned by Moses, they seem several of them," and substituted his own wording in what follows.

settlement of the Arkite did the Sinite likewise settle himself, for in the parts adjoining, St. Jerome tells us, was once a city called Sin. As for the Arvadite, the little isle of Aradus, lying up more north on the coast of Syria, is supposed to have taken its name from the founder of that family. In the neighborhood on the continent did the Zemarite probably fix, forasmuch as on the coast there we find a town called Simyra, not far from Orthosia. And Eusebius does expressly deduce the origin of the Orthosians from the Samareans.

The only remaining family is the Hamathite, or the inhabitants of the land of Hamath, often mentioned in sacred writ, and whose chief city was called Hamath. This country lay to the north of all the rest of the posterity of Canaan.[8]

The nation of CUSH had its first settlement in the country adjoining to his brother Canaan on the south, that is, in Arabia. That by "Cush" in Scripture is denoted Arabia, and not Ethiopia in Africa, is manifest everywhere in Scripture, particularly by Num. 12:1 compared with Ex. 2:15–21, and Hab. 3:7, II Kgs. 19:9, II Chron. 14:9, and Ezek. 29:10. "I will make the land of Egypt desolate, from the tower of Syene even unto the border of Cush." Now all that have any knowledge of old geography know that Syene was the border of Egypt towards Ethiopia in Africk. There[9] Cush, being the opposite boundary, can't be Ethiopia in Africk, but must be Arabia.

The sons of Cush are Seba, and Havilah, and Sabtah, and Raamah, and Sabtechah, to which Moses subjoins the two sons of Raamah, Sheba and Dedan, and then adds lastly, that "Cush begat Nimrod, who began to be a mighty one upon earth" (Gen. 10:7–8, ff.). Now we shall find all these, but the last, seated in Arabia. As for Seba, the first son of Cush, he probably seated himself in the southwest of Arabia, where we find a city called Sabe. On the southeast side we find another city called Sabana, where we may therefore place Sheba, the grandson of Cush by Raamah. And the reason why we choose this to be his situation, rather than the other side of the country, is because it is on the eastern side of Arabia that we find his father and his brother situated; and 'tis likely he seated himself in their neighborhood. On this account we find him always mentioned with his father and brother, as Ezek. 27:22, "The merchants of Sheba and Raamah were thy merchants"; and Ezek. 38:13,

8. Wells, *Historical Geography of the Old Testament, 1,* 255–56, 259–68.
9. Wells reads "Therefore."

"Sheba, and Dedan, and the merchants of Tarshish," etc. Now these two names, Sheba and Sebah, being so much alike, the two different families were confounded by the Greeks, and called promiscuously Sabaeans. Hence Pliny says that the Sabaean nation inhabited these parts, spreading themselves to both seas, i.e. from the Red Sea to the Gulf of Persia. But the sacred writers exactly distinguish them. Ps. 72:10, "The kings of Sheba and Sebah shall offer gifts."

On the same side of Arabia with Sheba were seated, as has been mentioned, both his father Raamah and his brother Dedan. For as to the former, we find on this shore of the Persian Gulf a city called Rhegma by Ptolemy, which, 'tis not to be doubted, was so called from this reason. For the Hebrew name, which in our translation is rendered Raamah, is in other translations, particularly the Septuagint, rendered (agreeably enough to the radicals) *Rhegma*. Not far from Rhegma, mentioned by Ptolemy, we find on the same coast eastward, another city called Dedan, nowadays Dadaen, from which the neighboring country also takes its name, as Bochart has observed from Barboza, an Italian writer, in his description of the kingdom of Ormuz.

On the same shore of the Persian Gulf, but higher northward, we find in Ptolemy the situation of a city called Saphtha, whence 'tis probable that Sabtah, the son of Cush, seated himself here.

Higher still to the northward was seated Havilah, or Chavilah, along the river Pison, or the western channel of the two, into which the common channel of the Tigris and Euphrates again is divided, before the waters thereof empty themselves into the Persian Gulf.[1]

That Havilah was seated here is confirmed, in that Moses tells us it was seated on a branch of that common channel, of which Euphrates and Hiddekel were a part. And in this country where we have placed Havilah, there was, agreeable to what Moses says of Havilah, plenty of gold, and that good gold [Gen. 2:11–12], which is agreeable to what ancient authors tell us of Arabia. Moses adds that in Havilah was *Bedolach*,[2] which some take to signify pearls, others the bdellium gum. 'Tis much the most likely that pearls are what are intended, for Moses, in describing the manna, says it was "like coriander seed, and the color thereof as the color of *Bedolach*" [Num. 11:7]. Now 'tis evident from another

1. Wells, *Historical Geography of the Old Testament, 1,* 191–97.
2. בְּדֹלַח.

description, that the color of manna was white (Ex. 16:14, and 31), which is apposite to pearls, as also is the roundness of the manna, but in no wise to the bdellium gum. Hence the Talmudists, mentioning this description of manna, instead of saying that 'tis like the color of bdellium, say 'tis like the color of pearls. "And 'tis certain that there is no place in the world that produceth so fine pearls, and in so great plenty," as the sea next to the shore of this country where we place Havilah, as is evident by the testimony of Nearchus, one of Alexander's captains, and Isidorus of Chorax, who lived a little after, and Pliny, and Aelian, and Origen, and Benjamin, a Navarrar, who lived five hundred and fifty years ago, and Teixeira a Portuguese, and Balby, Linscot, Vincent le Blanc, Tavernier, and Thevenot. And if we understood the *Beladoch* of the bdellium gum, this also abounded in Arabia, and particularly near the Persian Gulf, as appears by the testimony of many ancient writers. And as to the *Schoham*,[3] which Moses says was to be found in Havilah, which we render the "onyx stone," it is doubtless some precious stone is meant by this. And it is evident by the ancient writers, both sacred and profane, that Arabia formerly abounded with precious stones. See Ezek. 27:22–23.

And that this very country was the country of Havilah is manifest from Gen. 25:18, where we are told that the Ishmaelites "dwelt from Havilah unto Shur, that is before Egypt," and I Sam. 15:7, where we are told that "Saul smote the Amalekites from Havilah until thou comest to Shur, that is before Egypt." In both which places, by this expression, "from Havilah unto Shur," is probably meant the whole extent of that part of Arabia from east to west. And it is evident that Shur was the western boundary of Arabia, by those places, and also by Ex. 15:22, where we read that "Moses brought Israel from the Red Sea, and they went out into the wilderness of Shur." And therefore it seems no less evident that Havilah was in the eastern extremity of Arabia over against it, and consequently where we have placed it, where we find in common authors a people placed, whose name retains the visible footsteps of the name of their forefather Havilah, or *Chavilah*, as it is in the original.

> Thus by Eratosthenes are placed in these parts the Chaulothaei, by Festus Anienus the Chaulosii, by Dionysius Periegetes the Chablasii, and by Pliny the Chavelaei.

---

3. שֹׁהַם.

There remains now Sabtechah,[4] who, we need not doubt, placed himself among the rest of his brethren, especially since there is room enough left for him in the northern part of Arabia. His descendants might from him regularly enough be styled at first by the Greeks, "Sabtaceni," which name might afterwards be softened into Saraceni, by which name it is well-known, that the people of this tract were formerly denominated. And this is the more probable, because Stephanus mentions a country in those parts called Saruca. The reason why no mention is made in the Scripture of the Sabtaceni may be this, that these parts of Arabia lying next to the Holy Land are by the sacred writers denoted by the name of[5] the whole land of Cush, or Arabia, it being to them as it were *instar totius*, being the only part of the land of Cush they were usually concerned with; and they probably learnt it first in Egypt of the Egyptians, who after their father Mizraim, called the country the "land of Cush," it being natural to him to call it from the name of his brother rather than from one of his children.[6]

Moses,[7] having named the other sons and grandsons of Cush, he subjoins, Gen. 10:8, "And Cush begat Nimrod." By this distinct mention of Nimrod after the rest of his brethren, the sacred historian is supposed to intimate that Nimrod was indeed the youngest of the sons of Cush, but however the most remarkable of them. And accordingly, it immediately follows in the text, "He began to be a mighty one upon the earth."

By what method Nimrod became thus mighty, Moses seems to intimate by these words, "He was a mighty hunter before the Lord" [v. 9]. He probably applied himself to hunting, to destroy the wild beasts that began to grow very numerous, and very much to infest the parts adjoining to the nation of Cush; and by his great art and valor in destroying wild beasts, he inured himself and companions, to undergo fatigue and hardship, and withal to manage dexterously several sorts of offensive weapons, being thus occasionally trained up to the art of war, and perceiving at length his skill and strength sufficient to act offensively against men.

4. MS: "~~only~~ Sabteca ~~of Cush's Sons~~."

5. JE deleted "Cush the father of Sabtaca Sabteca, and who it is likely settled himself in those parts with his son Sabtechah," which is Wells' text.

6. Wells, *Historical Geography of the Old Testament*, *1*, 11, 13–19, 198–99. JE did less direct quoting from Wells in this section.

7. MS: "~~we proceed now~~ Moses."

The country at first assigned to Nimrod, the youngest son of Cush, was probably the country on the east of Gihon, the eastern branch of the common channel of Euphrates and Tigris, after its second division, before it emptied itself into the Persian Gulf, next to his brother Havilah, his brethren having possessed Arabia. This part next to Arabia was assigned to him, and so being the portion of one of the sons of Cush was called the land of Cush, as it is by Moses when speaking of the river Gihon. "The same is it which compasses the whole land of Cush" [Gen. 2:13], which country was formerly, by the Greeks and Latins, called by the name of Susiana, and is now called Chuzestan. The Nubian geographer and some other Arabians call it Churestan.

> The inhabitants of the land call it absolutely or plainly Chus, if we will believe Marius Niger. The same region is called Cushah (II Kgs. 17:24), speaking of the people transported thence into Samaria by Shalmaneser. The word Cuthah, or Cuth, undoubtedly came from the word Cush, or Cus, the last letter of which is often changed by the Chaldeans into a "T" or "Th," as Dion hath observed; so they called "Theor" for "Sor," and "Attyria" or "Assyria." There are yet many marks of the word "Cush" found in the same province. We find there the Cosseans, neighbors to the Uxians, according to the position of Pliny, Ptolemy, and Arrian. There is also a little province of Susiana, viz. Cissia, and the people Cissians. The poet Aeschylus takes notice of a city of that name situated in the same land; and, what is remarkable, he does distinguish it by its antiquity.

This country was probably named Cush before Nimrod was born, or at least while he was young, before he distinguished himself in the world from Cush, his father's living here in that part of the face of the earth that fell to the lot of him and his posterity, that was nearest to the original settlement of Noah and his sons, and was the pleasantest and most fruitful, like Eden that it bordered upon. While Cush sent forth his elder sons to settle Arabia, 'tis likely that he stayed here himself with his youngest son, that was probably very young when the earth was divided.

But Nimrod, when he found his strength and ability for war, and being grown famous for his extraordinary valor in destroying wild beasts, was not contented with the lot assigned him, but invades first the neighboring parts of the nation of Shem, which upon the division of the earth fell to the lot of the family of Arphaxad, and so makes himself master of the lower part of the land of Shinar (being a most fruitful and pleasant country), and pitches on that very place where the city and tower of Babel had been begun, to build the capital city of his kingdom. Moses says, "The beginning of his kingdom was Babel, and Erech, and Accad, and Calneh, in the land of Shinar" [Gen. 10:10]. As to Erech, 'tis probably the same that occurs in Ptolemy under the name of Arecca, and which is placed by him at the last or most southern turning of the common channel of the Tigris and Euphrates. The fields hereof are mentioned by Tibullus, on account of its springs of naphta. The Archevites, mentioned, Ezra 4:9, are thought to be some that were removed from Erech to Samaria. What in the Hebrew is *Achad*, is by the LXX interpreters writ Archad, whence some footsteps of this name are probably thought to be preserved in the river Argades, mentioned by Ctesias as a river near Sittace, lying at some distance from the river Tigris, and giving name formerly to Sittacene, a country lying between Babylon and Susa. And because it was very usual, particularly in these parts, to have rivers take their name from some considerable city they run by, hence it is not improbably conjectured, that the city Sittace was formerly called Argad, or Acchad, and took the name of Sittace from the plenty of *psittacias*, or pistachios, a sort of nut that grew in the country. Strabo mentions a region in those parts under the name of Artacene, which might be framed from Archad. As to the other city belonging to the beginning of Nimrod's kingdom, viz. Calneh, and which is called, Is. 10:9, "Calno," and Ezek. 27:23, "Canneh," it is mentioned as a considerable place. Amos 6:2, "Pass ye unto Calneh, and see." It is said by the Chaldee interpreters, as also by Eusebius and Jerome, to be the same with Ctesiphon, standing upon the Tigris, about three miles distant from Seleucia, and for some time the capital city of the Parthians. That this opinion concerning the situation of Calneh is true, is mightily confirmed from the country about Ctesiphon, being by the Greeks called Chalonitis. And since we are expressly told by Ammianus Marcellinus that Pacorus, a king of the Parthians, changed the name of the city Ctesiphon, when he gave it that name, we may reasonably suppose that its old name was Calneh, or Chalone, and that from it the adjacent country took the name of Chalonitis.

And whereas it is said, Gen. 10:11–12, in our translation,[8] "Out of that land went forth Asshur, and built Nineveh, and the city of Rehoboth, and Calah, and Resen between Nineveh and Calah; the same is a great city," it might have been rendered as agreeably to the original, and much more agreeably to the preceding verses and the drift of the historian, "Out of that land he went forth into Asshur, and built Nineveh," etc. For Moses, in the preceding verse, having told us what was the beginning of Nimrod's kingdom in the land of Shinar, then goes on to tell us how he extended it further afterwards to other cities beyond the land of Shinar into the land of Asshur.[9]

Nineveh was a city that lay on the river Tigris, somewhat above the mouth of the river Lycus, where it runs into the Tigris.

> *Rehoboth* is a word in the Hebrew tongue that signifies "streets." And there being a city or town called Birtha by Ptolemy, and the said name denoting in the Chaldee tongue the same as *Rehoboth* does in the Hebrew, hence 'tis thought to be the same city; and it is not to be doubted but the Birtha mentioned by Ptolemy is the same which Ammianus Marcellinus calls Virta. It was seated on the river Tigris about the mouth of the river Lycus.
>
> As for Calah, or Calach, since we find in Strabo a country about the head of the river Lycus, called Calachene, 'tis very probable the said country took this name from Calach, which was once its capital city. Ptolemy also mentions a country called Calacine in these parts. And whereas Pliny mentions a people called Classitae, through whose country the Lycus runs, it's likely that Classitae is a corruption for Calachitae. To this city and country in all probability it was that Shalmaneser transplanted some of the ten tribes. II Kgs. 17:6, "He placed them in *Chalach*," as it is in the original.

Resen, the other city mentioned by Moses [Gen. 10:12], is supposed to be the same with

> a city mentioned by Xenophon under the name of Larissa, lying on the Tigris, and being, as Moses says, "between Nineveh and Calah," and was also said by Xenophon to have been strong and great, but then ruinated, being two parasangs, that is, eight miles in compass, and its walls an hundred foot high and twenty-five foot broad,

---

8. I.e. the KJV.

9. Wells, *Historical Geography of the Old Testament*, *1*, 27–29, 219–21, 227–30, 232. In this section JE moved back and forth in his citations from Wells.

which agrees with what Moses says of Resen: "The same was a great city." *Larissa* was a Greek name; we find a city so called in Thessaly. There was another which the Greeks called by the same name in Syria, which the Syrians themselves called Sizara.

'Tis therefore easy to suppose that the Greeks might change Resen into *Larissa*.

'Tis likely that the Greeks asking, What city those were the ruins of, the Assyrians might answer, *Laresen*, i.e. "of Resen," which word Xenophon expressed by *Larissa*, like the names of several Greek cities.

We proceed now to MIZRAIM, who by Moses is named second among the sons of Ham. And where he at first settled himself, we need not doubt, since the Hebrew text generally denotes Egypt by the name of the "land of Mizraim," or simply "Mizraim." I proceed therefore to the descendants of Mizraim. The names whereby these are denoted by Moses are plurals. They are thus enumerated by Moses: "Mizraim begat *Ludim*, and *Anamim*, and *Lehabim*, and *Naphtuhim*, and *Pathrusim*, and *Casluhim* (out of whom came *Philistim*), and *Caphtorim*" [Gen. 10:13–14].

To begin with LUDIM, whereby are denoted the Ethiopians in Africk, and who alone are commonly so called, both in ancient and modern writers. That these Ethiopians are denoted in Scripture by the name of Ludim, and their country Ethiopia by the name of Lud, the learned Bochart has proved at large by no fewer than ten distinct arguments. I shall mention only those that are drawn from the sacred Scripture, as from Is. 66:19, and Jer. 46:9, where Lud, or Ludim, are said to be very skillful in drawing the bow, which agrees punctually to the character given to the Ethiopians by many ancient writers.[1]

As to Anamim, Bochart thinks the inhabitants of the country about Jupiter Ammon's temple might be denoted from this Anamim. The same learned person thinks Nazamones took their rise and name, as also the Amantes, and Garamantes, and Hammamientes, mentioned by old writers, in the adjacent parts.

The Lehabim come next, both in the text and in situation. For 'tis very probable that Lehabim and Lubim are one, and that from

---

1. JE deleted "Again, in the forecited place, we find Phut and Lud joined together, whence it may be probably inferred they denoted," which is Wells' text.

hence was derived originally the name of Libya, which, though at length extended to the whole African continent, yet at first belonged only to the country Cyrenaica. Now this country lying next over against Greece, hence the name of Lehab, or Lub, originally belonging to this tract only, was molded into Libya, and given to the whole continent over against them on the other side of the Mediterranean Sea, just as the name of Africa, properly pertaining only to that part of this continent which lies over against Italy, was therefore by the Latins extended to all the continent. Or, to come to our own times, much after the same manner as we extend the name of Holland to all the Dutch provinces, and the name of Flanders to all the Spanish provinces in the Netherlands, whereas they properly denote only the two particular provinces in the Spanish and Dutch Netherlands that lie next over against our island of Great Britain.

The Naphtuhim are probably enough placed by Bochart in the country adjoining to Cyrenaica, or Libya, properly so called, toward Egypt, viz. in Marmarica. For here we find in Ptolemy some remainder of the name in a place called Aptuchi Fanum. And in the heathen fables, Aptuchus, or Aphtuchus, or Autuchus, is said to be the son of Cyrene, from whom the city and country of Cyrene took its name.

The Pathrusim, or descendants of Pathros, are mentioned next by Moses [Gen. 10:14], whereby are to be understood the inhabitants of the upper Egypt, or Thebais, where Ptolemy places Pathyris, an inland town not far from Thebes. And agreeably hereto, the Septuagint translation renders the Hebrew *Pathros* by the Greek *Pathyris*.

The Casluhim are thought to have first settled in the country on the other side of Egypt, called Casiotis, where also is a mountain called Casius. And this situation of them is confirmed by what Moses says concerning them, viz. that from them sprang the Philistines [Gen. 10:14], who in process of time made themselves masters of the adjoining tract of the land of Canaan.

That the Caphtorim were situated near to the Casluhim is inferred not only from Moses' putting them next one to another in the forecited place of Gen. 10, but also from this, that the Philistines, who are, in Gen. 10:14, said to be descended of the Casluhim, are elsewhere denoted by the name of Caphtorim, as Deut. 2:23, Jer. 47:4, and Amos 9:7, which perhaps can't be better accounted for than by supposing the Casluhim and Caphtorim to be neighbors, and so in time to have been mutually intermixed, as to be looked upon as one and the same people.

Now the name Caphtor seems to be preserved in an old city of Egypt called Coptus. From which, as the name of Cophtes is still given to the Christians of Egypt (whence the translation of the Bible used by them is called also the Coptic translation), so 'tis not unlikely that the common name of Egypt was derived from it, it being called Aegyptus, for Aegoptus, as if one should say in Greek αἶα Κόπτου, the "land of Coptus." And 'tis a good remark of the learned Mede, that the Greek *Aia*, or *Aea*, is likely derived from the Hebrew **אי**, *Ai*, or *Ei*, to which may be very pertinently subjoined this remark, that, in Jer. 47:4, what we render "the country of Caphtor" is in the Hebrew text formed *Ai-Caphtor*, which are the two words which we suppose the Greeks to have molded the name Αἴγυπτος. Our translators observe, on the forementioned place in Jeremy, that the Hebrew word translated the "country" in the text denotes also an "isle," as 'tis rendered in the margin, agreeably to which it is observable that the city of Coptus stood on a small island. So that upon the whole, we need not doubt thereabout to fix the first settlement of the Caphtorim.

Of the four original nations descended from Ham, there remains now only that of PHUT to be spoken of. And the first settlement of this is with good reason supposed to be in the parts of the Libyan, or African, continent, which join on next to those possessed by the descendants of Mizraim. For in Africa properly so called, below Adrumetum was a city named Putea, mentioned by Pliny. And in Mauritania there is a river mentioned by Ptolemy called Phut. St. Jerome is very full to the point, telling us that there is a river in Mauritania, which was till his own time called Phut, and from which the adjacent country was called *Regio Phytensis*, the "country of Phut."[2]

Mr. Bedford supposes it was the river Niger [that] was called by this name, and that the posterity of Phut[3] settled themselves chiefly on that river (as the first inhabitants of the earth were wont to choose the neighborhood of rivers for their settlements), and from thence spread themselves into other parts.[4]

2. Wells, *Historical Geography of the Old Testament*, *1*, 199–207, 240–41, 243–44.
3. JE deleted "soon."
4. *Scripture Chronology*, p. 228.

420. GENESIS 25:12–18. Concerning the SONS OF ISHMAEL and their settlements in Arabia. The two firstborn sons of Ishmael are *Nebajoth* and *Kedar*. "The descendants of Nebajoth are the people called Nabathaei by heathen writers; and they seem to have been of better note among the Greeks and Latins than the rest, forasmuch as they are more frequently mentioned by their writers, whether historians or poets. But among the sacred writers, there is more frequent mention made of Kedar. These people are also mentioned by Pliny, under the name of Cedreni, or Cedareni, and are placed by him next to the Nabatheans."

The next sons of Ishmael are *Adbeel*, and *Mibsam*, and *Mishma*, and *Dumah*, and *Massa, Hadar*, and *Tema, Jetur, Naphish*, and *Kedemah*. "Stephanus the Geographer mentions a city in Arabia called Dumatha, probably from this Dumah. And there is a city named Teman, mentioned by Ptolemy, probably the same that is called Tamna by Strabo. As for Jetur and Nephish, two other sons of Ishmael, we read, I Chron. 5:19, that the Reubenites, and the Gadites, and the half-tribe of Manasseh made war with them, and overcame them, and 'dwelt in their stead (i.e. in their country) until the captivity' (v. 22), whereby is confirmed the opinion that Iturea, a country mentioned by St. Luke, being so called from Jetur, the son of Ishmael [Luke 3:1].

"It remains only to observe, that as these people were from their father called Ishmaelites, so from the mother of Ishmael they were also denominated Hagarens, or Hagarites. And under this last name they are mentioned by heathen writers, some calling them Agraei, others Agareni." Wells' *Sacred Geography*, Vol. 1, ch. 9.[5]

421. GALATIANS 3:16. "Now to Abraham and his seed were the promises made. He saith not, And to seeds, as of many, but as of one. And to thy seed, which is Christ." This Mr. Locke paraphrases thus. "God doth not say, 'And to seeds,' as if he spoke of more seeds than one, that were entitled to the promise on different accounts, but only of one sort of men, who upon one sole account were that seed of Abraham which was alone meant and concerned in the promise; so that 'unto thy seed' designed Christ and his mystical body, i.e. those that become members of him by faith." And Mr. Locke adds in his notes,

By "seeds" St. Paul here visibly means the οἱ ἐκ πίστεως, "those of faith," and the οἱ ἐκ ἔργων νόμου, "those of the works of the law,"

5. Wells, *Historical Geography of the Old Testament*, *1*, 341–43.

spoken of above, vv. 9–10, as two distinct seeds, or descendants, claiming from Abraham. St. Paul's argument to convince the Galatians, that they ought not to be circumcised, or submit to the law, from their having received the Spirit from him, upon their having received the gospel which he preached to them (vv. 2 and 5), stands thus. The blessing promised to Abraham, and to his seed, was wholly upon the account of faith (v. 7). There were not different seeds who should inherit the promise, the one by the works of the law, and the other by faith. For there was but one seed, which was Christ (v. 16), and those who should claim in and under him by faith. Among those there was no distinction of Jew and Gentile. They, and they only, who believed, were all one and the same true seed of Abraham, "and heirs according to the promise" (vv. 28–29). And therefore the promise made to the people of God, of giving them the Spirit under the gospel, was performed only to those who believed in Christ: a clear evidence that it was not by putting themselves under the law, but by faith in Jesus Christ, that they were the people of God, and heirs of the promise.[6]

422. GALATIANS 3:17–18. "And this I say, that the covenant, that was confirmed before of God in Christ, the law, which was four hundred and thirty years after, cannot disannul, that it should make the promise of none effect. For if the inheritance be of the law, 'tis no more of promise; but God gave it to Abraham by promise." Mr. Locke paraphrases it thus. "This therefore I say, that the law, which was not till 430 years after, cannot disannul the covenant, that was long before made and ratified to Christ by God, so as to set aside the promise. For if the right to the inheritance be from the works of the law, it is plain it is not founded in the promise to Abraham, as certainly it is. For the inheritance was a donation and free gift of God, settled on Abraham and his seed by promise."[7]

423. GALATIANS 3:19–20. "It was added because of transgressions, till the seed should come to whom the promise was made; and it was ordained by angels in the hand of a mediator. Now a mediator is not a mediator of one, but God is one." The Apostle's design in mentioning the law's being ordained "in the hand of a mediator," is to[8] show the

6. John Locke, *A Paraphrase and Notes on the Epistle of St. Paul to the Galatians* (3rd ed., London, 1708), p. 21.
7. Ibid., pp. 21–22.
8. JE deleted "convince."

contrary of what the Jews and Judaizing teachers supposed concerning that transaction of Mt. Sinai between God and the people when the
law was ordained. They supposed it to be a merely legal transaction,
that God acted therein merely as a sovereign righteous lawgiver in that
affair, prescribing to the people legal terms of life and death. This is
implied in their doctrine of justification by the works of the law. The
Apostle, in what he here mentions of the transaction's being by a
mediator, would show the contrary, viz. that it was not a mere legal
transaction, but a transaction of grace; for a mere legal transacting of
God with man don't admit of any mediator, but a transaction of grace
does. Indeed, in a mere legal transaction, a middle person may be
improved to act in the name of God, and appear for God to them; but
such a middle person don't answer the notion of a mediator, as the
Apostle would signify. A mediator acts for both parties: he don't only
appear for God to man, and so act for God, but he also appears for
man to God, and acts for man. For a mediator is not of one; he is not a
middle person to act only for one of the parties. "But God is one," i.e.
God is but one of the parties transacting. If he acts as a middle person
only on one side, he don't act as mediator. But a mediator appears for
both parties; he acts for each to the other. A legal transaction would
have admitted of a middle person to act for one side, viz. for God to
man, but not for man to God, to intercede and plead for him. So was
Moses. (Moses was the mediator here spoken of, as is confirmed by
Deut. 5:5.) God condescended, because the people could not bear the
terrors of the law, to admit Moses as a mediator for them, to stand
before him, and hear and bear those terrors for them, as well as to act
his messenger to them. This shows plainly that it was a transaction of
grace, wherein God was willing to admit a method to screen and save
the poor fearful people, to screen 'em from[9] the dreadful thing apprehended, as well as from the terrible apprehension they had by hearing
the dreadful voice, and seeing the raging fire. Therefore this is an
evidence of what the Apostle is arguing for, viz. that God in this transaction was not disannulling the transaction of grace, or that gracious
covenant that had before been established with Abraham. He was now
only building on that foundation that was then laid, and not setting it
aside by this transaction that seemed to have an appearance of a legal
transaction. This inference is made very much after the same manner
with many others that the Apostle makes, from transactions and pas-

9. JE deleted "that suffering."

sages of the Old Testament, in the epistle to the Hebrews, and here and there in other epistles. And this reasoning is not so farfetched, and the argument so much out of sight, as some may imagine. The words might be paraphrased thus. "In that transaction of Mt. Sinai, when the law was given, a mediator was made use of; and the notion of a mediator is one that appears and pleads for both parties with the other. This mediator therefore that was admitted did not only transact for God, who in the transaction was but one party, but also appeared and pleaded for the other party also with God, which shows that it was not a merely authoritative and legal, but a gracious transaction." The 20th verse comes in as a kind of a parenthesis, or a short exegetical digression, just to explain the meaning of the word "mediator" that the Apostle had used, because the argument the Apostle intended his readers should conceive from it depended on their understanding what a mediator was. And therefore he was willing to let 'em know that, by a mediator, he did not only mean a middle person to act for God towards the people, but also one to act and plead for the people towards God. The Apostle's words therefore may be otherwise paraphrased thus. "The law was ordained by angels in the hands of a mediator, i.e. in the hands of a middle person that appeared[1] and pleaded for each party with the other, and not only for God, who was but one party."[2]

424. GENESIS 7. THE FLOOD. Add this to No. 409. "Lucian's representation of this matter is almost parallel to that of Moses; he tells you, the first generation of men were destroyed, and Deucalion was the progenitor of a second generation. He ascribes their destruction to their wickedness, and makes the means of it to be a flood of water; that Deucalion and his family only were saved, and that in a great λάρναξ, or chest, into which he came with his children, and with several animals; and that the deluge of water sunk into a great hiatus or gap in the earth." Bennet's *Inspiration of the Scripture*, p. 98–99. And in the marginal notes in the same place, the publisher, Mr. L. Latham, adds as follows. "Berosus the Chaldean historian, Abydenus, and Alexander Polyhister describe it under the name of Xisuthrus's flood, and mention a great many particulars concerning it that have a surprising coincidence with the account given by Moses. As, that he was fore-

1. JE deleted "before God for men and."
2. Although he did not quote directly from it, in this entry JE was engaged with Locke's discussion of Gal. 3:19–20 in the *Paraphrase and Notes on Galatians*, pp. 22–23.

warned of it beforehand, was directed to build a sort of a ship for the preservation of himself and his kindred, eight persons in all, to take provision with him for their subsistence, together with beast and fowls; that accordingly he did so, and when the flood abated, sent out some birds which returned to the ship twice, but the third time came back no more, whereby he understood that the earth began to appear; upon which, taking off the cover, he found the ship rested upon a mountain, and after some time he went out and offered sacrifices. And no doubt Ogyges's flood, spoken of by other ancient writers, was only a corrupt tradition of the same event, that of Noah. Lucian says that all creatures went into the ark by couples. Plutarch mentions the very time when Noah (under the name of Deucalion) entered into the ark, and of his sending forth the dove to discover the state of the waters, whether they were decreased or no; and he adds, that it returned into the ark again."[3]

Again, Mr. Bennet in the same book, p. 210, speaking of the testimony of the most ancient heathen writers to the flood, says, "One of them, of great reputation, tells us that Osiris, or Noah, went into the ark on the seventeenth day of the Egyptian month Atbyr, when the sun passes the sign Scorpio, which is the very same day mentioned by Moses, the seventeenth day of the second month [Gen. 7:11], as some have shown from astronomical calculations."[4] See further No. 429.[5]

425. II CORINTHIANS 13:1. "In the mouth of two or three witnesses shall every word be established." "These words seem to be quoted from the law of our Savior (Matt. 18:16), and not from the law of Moses in Deuteronomy [17:6, 19:15], not only because the words are the same with those in St. Matthew, but from the likeness of the case. In Deuteronomy the law given concerns only judicial trials; in St. Matthew it is a rule given for the management of persuasion used to reclaim offenders, by fair means, before coming to the utmost extremity, which is the case of St. Paul here, the witnesses, which he means that he made use of to persuade them, being his two epistles. That by 'witnesses' he means his two epistles, is plain from his way of expressing himself here, where he carefully sets down his telling them twice, viz. before in his former epistle (I Cor. 4:19), and now a second time in his

---

3. Benjamin Bennet, *The Truth, Inspiration, and Usefulness of the Scripture Asserted and Proved in Several Discourses on 2 Tim. III. XVI*, ed. L. Latham (London, 1730), pp. 98–99.
4. Ibid., p. 210.
5. This cross-reference is a later addition.

second epistle, and also by these words, 'as if I were present with you a second time' [II Cor. 13:2]. By our Savior's rule, the offended person was to go twice to the offender, which the Apostle refers to." Mr. Locke's Exposition.[6]

426. ROMANS 4:12. "And the father of circumcision to them who are not of the circumcision only, but also walk in the steps of that faith of our father Abraham," etc. In the foregoing verse it is set forth how Abraham is the father of those that are *uncircumcised*, if they have the faith of Abraham. In this verse the Apostle declares that he also is the father of the *circumcised*, who han't only, or barely, circumcision, but also walk in the steps of the faith of their father Abraham. So that, put both verses together, this is what the Apostle declares: that Abraham received circumcision, a seal of the righteousness of faith, which he had being yet uncircumcised, whereby God sealed to him the promise he made to him, that he should be the father of all such as should believe as he had done, and only to such, whether they were circumcised or not, that he should be the father of the uncircumcised Gentiles that should believe as he had done, and the father of no more of the circumcised Jews than should believe as he had done.[7]

427. GENESIS 1:2. "And the Spirit of God moved upon the face of the waters." The word translated "moved" in the original is מְרַחֶפֶת, which, as Buxtorf says, the Hebrews note, properly signifies "to hover as a bird," or "to brood as a bird" over the young or her eggs when sitting on them,[8] and, both Grotius and Buxtorf observe from the writers of the Talmud, properly signifies the brooding of a dove upon her eggs. See Buxtorf on the radix רָחַף,[9] and Grotius, *De Veritate*, Bk. 1, sec. 16, notes, where Grotius also asserts more than once[1] that

6. John Locke, *A Paraphrase and Notes on the Second Epistle of St. Paul to the Corinthians* (London, 1706), pp. 55–56.

7. John Locke writes, "For he received the Sign of Circumcision a Seal of the Righteousness of the Faith, which he had being yet uncircumcised, that he might be the Father of all those who believe, being uncircumcised, that Righteousness might be reckon'd to them also; And the Father of the Circumcised, that Righteousness might be reckon'd not to those who were barely of the Circumcision, but to such of the Circumcision as did also walk in the steps of the Faith of our Father *Abraham*, which he had been uncircumcised" (*A Paraphrase and Notes on the Epistle of St. Paul to the Romans* [London, 1707], pp. 36–37).

8. JE deleted "and that the Talmudists."

9. Buxtorf describes the motion in these words: "*Quemadmodum columba incumbit pullis suis*," in *Lexicon Hebraicum et Chaldaicum*, pp. 695–96.

1. MS: "~~observes~~ ⟨asserts more than once⟩."

the word *Merachepheth* signifies "love." Hence the many fables among the heathen about the world's being formed[2] by love and by the brooding of a dove, etc. Sanchoniathon says, that the living creatures (that is, the constellations) were in that μώτ, as in an egg. Macrobius resembles the world to an egg, in the 7th book and 16th chapter of his *Saturnalia*.[3] And hence the Syrian gods are called by Arnobius "the offspring of eggs," by which gods he means the stars. Orpheus had his opinion from the Phoenicians, one of which was this in Athenagoras, "That *mud proceeded from water.*" After which he mentions a great egg split into two parts, heaven and earth.

"In the *Argonautics*, ascribed to Orpheus, we have these lines.

In verse he sang the origin of things, . . .
How love, the cause of all things, by his power
Creating everything, gave each his place.

And Aristophanes, in his play called *The Birds*, in a passage preserved by Lucian in his *Philopatris*, and [by] Suidas, 'First of all was chaos and night, dark Erebus and gloomy Tartarus. There was neither earth, nor air, nor heaven, till dusky night, by the wind's power, on the wide bosom of Erebus, brought forth an egg, of which was hatched the god of love (when time began); who with his golden wings, fixed to his shoulders, flew like a mighty whirlwind, and mixing with black chaos, in Tartarus, dark shades, produced mankind, and brought them into light. For, before love joined all things, the very gods themselves had no existence; but upon this conjunction, all things being mixed and blended, Aether arose, and sea, and earth, and the blessed abodes of the immortal gods.'" Grotius, *Ibid.*[4]

428. GENESIS 6:4. "And there were giants in the earth in those days," etc. "Pausanias, in his *Laconics*, mentions the bones of men of a more than ordinary bigness, which were shown in the temple of Aesculapius

2. MS: "~~brought forth~~ ⟨formed⟩"
3. JE deleted "The beginning of generation in the Orphic verses, mentioned by Plutarch, *Symposiack* 11, ch. 3, and Athenagores."
4. Hugo Grotius, *The Truth of the Christian Religion in Six Books by Hugo Grotius, Corrected and Illustrated by Mr. Le Clerc. To which is added a Seventh Book Concerning this Question, What Christian Church we ought to join our selves to; By the said Mr. Le Clerc. The Second Edition with Additions. Done into English by John Clarke, D.D. and Chaplain in Ordinary to His Majesty* (London, 1719), pp. 27–29, 32.

at the city of Asepus; and in the first of his *Eliacs*, of a bone taken out of the sea, which aforetime was kept at Pisa, and thought to have been one of Peleps'. Philostratus, in the beginning of his *Heroics*, [says] that many bodies of giants were discovered in Pallene, by showers of rain and earthquakes. Pliny, Bk. 7, ch. 16, says, 'That upon the bursting of a mountain in Crete, there was found a body standing upright, which was reported by some to have been the body of Orion, by others, the body of Eetion. Orestes' body, when it was commanded by the oracle to be digged up, is reported to have been seven cubits. And almost a thousand years ago, the poet Homer continually complained, that men's bodies were less than of old.' And Solinus, ch. I, 'Were not all that were born in that age, less than their parents?' And the story of Orestes' funeral testifies the bigness of the ancients, whose bones, when they were digged up, in the 58th Olympiad at Tegea, by the advice of the oracle, are related to have been seven cubits in length. And other writings, which give a credible relation of ancient matters, affirm this, that in the war of Crete, when the rivers had been so high as to overflow and break down their banks, after the flood was abated, upon the cleaving of the earth, there was found a human body of three and thirty foot long, which L. Flaccus, the legate, and Metellus himself, being very desirous of seeing, were much surprised to have the satisfaction of seeing, what they did not believe when they heard." Grotius, *De Veritate*, Bk. 1, sec. 16, notes.

"Josephus, Bk. 5, ch. 2, of his ancient history. 'There remains to this day some of the race of the giants, who by reason of the bulk and figure of their bodies, so different from other men, are wonderful to see, or hear of.' Their bones are now shown, far exceeding the belief of the vulgar.' Gabinius, in his history of Mauritania, said that Antaeus' bones were found by Sertorius, which, joined together, were sixty cubits long. Phlegon Trallianus, in his 9th chapter of *Wonders*, mentions the digging up [of] the head of Ida, which was three times as big as that of an ordinary woman. And he adds also, that there were many bodies found in Dalmatia, whose arms exceeded sixteen cubits. And the same man relates out of Theopompus, that there were found in the Cimmerian Bosphorus, a company of human bones twenty-four cubits in length." Le Clerc's notes on Grotius, *De Veritate*, Bk. 1, sec. 16.

"We almost everywhere in the Greek and Latin historians meet with the savage life of the giants, mentioned by Moses. In the Greek, as Homer, *Iliad* 9, and Hesiod in his *Labors*. To this may be referred the wars of the gods, mentioned by Plato in his *Second Republic*, and those distinct and separate governments, taken notice of by the same Plato, in his third book of *Laws*. And as to the Latin historians, see the first book of Ovid's *Metamorphosis*, and the 4th book of Lucan, and Seneca's third book of *Natural Questions*, Ques. 30, where he says concerning the deluge, 'That the beasts also perished, into whose nature men were degenerated.'" Grotius, *De Veritate*, Bk. 1, sec. 16.[5]

429. GENESIS 7. Concerning THE FLOOD. Add this to No. 424. "Sisuthrus, Ogyges, and Deucalion are all names signifying the same thing in other languages," says Grotius, in his notes on Book 1, *De Veritate*, sec. 16, where he cites several testimonies out of ancient heathen writers, that it was the manner of old for nations, when they wrote histories, that they took from other nations, to change names into words that had the same signification in their own language.

"Abydenus, in his book, where he inquires, 'Which have most cunning, water or land animals?' has these words, 'They say Deucalion's dove, which he sent out of the ark, discovered at its return, that the storms were abated, and the heavens clear.'" Ibid.

Lucian, in his book concerning the goddess of Syria, where having begun to treat of the very ancient temple of Hierapolis, he adds, "They say this temple was founded by Deucalion the Scythian, that Deucalion in whose days the flood of water happened. I have heard in Greece the story of this Deucalion from the Greeks themselves, which is thus. The present generation of men is not the original one, for all that generation perished; and the men which now are, come from a second stock, the whole multitude of them descending from Deucalion. Now concerning the first race of men, they relate thus. They were very obstinate, and did very wicked things, and had no regard to oaths, had no hospitality or charity in them, upon which account many calamities befell them. For on a sudden the earth sent forth abundance of water, great showers of rain fell, the rivers overflowed exceedingly, and the sea overspread the earth, so that all was turned into water, and every man perished. Deucalion was only saved alive, to raise up another generation, because of his prudence and piety. And he was preserved in this manner; he, and his wives, and his children entered into a large ark, which he had prepared, and after them went in bears, and horses, and lions, and serpents, and all other kinds of

5. Ibid., pp. 43–45.

living creatures that feed upon the earth, two and two. He received them all in; neither did they hurt him, but were very familiar with him, by a divine influence. Thus they all sailed in the same ark as long as the water remained on the earth. This is the account the Greeks give of Deucalion."

Lucian goes on, in the same place, to mention a ceremony performed by the Syrians twice every year in the temple of Hierapolis, by pouring water into an hiatus or gap in the earth, to commemorate the earth drinking in the water and drying up the flood.

"Eusebius, in his 9th book of the *Gospel Preparation*, ch. 19," cites a passage of Molo in these words,

"At the deluge, the man and his children that escaped, came out of Armenia, being driven from his own country by the inhabitants, and having passed through the country between, went into the mountainous part of Syria, which was then uninhabited." Josephus gives us these words of Nicolaus Damascenus, of the ninety-sixth book of his *Universal History*. "There is above the city of Minyas (which Strabo and Pliny call Milyas) a huge mountain in Armenia, called Batis, on which they say a great many were saved from the flood, particularly one who was carried to the top of it by an ark, the relics of the wood of which was preserved a great while. I believe it was the same man that Moses, the lawgiver of the Jews, mentions in his history." To these writers we may add Hieronymus the Egyptian, who wrote the affairs of Phoenicia, and Mnaseas, mentioned by Josephus, and perhaps Eupolemus, which Eusebius quotes out of Alexander the Historian, in his *Gospel Preparation*, Bk. 9, ch. 17.

Grotius, *De Veritate*, Bk. 1, sec. 16.[6] See further, No. 454.[7]

430. GENESIS 11:3–9. CONCERNING THE TOWER OF BABEL.[8] Add this to No. 410. "Cyril, Bk. 1, *Against Julian*, quotes these words out of Abydenus. 'Some say that the first men, who sprang out of the earth, grew proud upon their great strength and bulk, and boasted they could do more than the gods, and attempted to build a tower, where Babylon now stands. But when it came nigh the heavens, it was overthrown upon them by the gods, with the help of the winds; and the

6. Ibid., pp. 46–49.
7. This cross-reference is a later addition.
8. JE deleted "Eusebius, in his *Preparation*, Bk. 9, ch. 14."

ruins are called Babylon. Men till then had but one language, but the gods divided it, and then began the war between Saturn and Titan.'" Grotius, *De Veritate*, Bk. 1, sec. 16, notes.[9]

Dr. Winder supposes that crime of the builders of Babel to have been an obstinate renouncing the orders before given by Noah, and agreed to by his sons, under the divine direction, for a general dispersion and division of the earth among the various families of mankind, and that the builders of Babel were not the whole body of mankind, but that part of them that, according to the forementioned[1] orders and regulation, were to [be] settled in parts that were to the westward of the original settlement where Noah dwelt, and that after they had dwelt in Shinar, ambition might inspire some of their leaders with the thoughts of setting up a great empire. But that this supposes that there were at that time other tribes elsewhere, against which they might direct their ambitious projects. "There appears (says he) to have been something of ambition, either for power, or fame, or both, in their design. For they said, 'Let us make us a name'" [Gen. 11:4].[2]

There is (says Dr. Winder, p. 127) a most noble authentical confirmation of the Mosaic history. By that city or country retaining the name Babel, or "confusion," by which every age and nation called this great city, the supposed seat of the first empire, even according to heathen writers, which seems to be a name of infamy and reproach, which its own princes or inhabitants would not have given it without some such notorious, undeniable circumstance obliging them to it. "What a signal defeat (say he) was here given, by providence, to their ambitious plan, 'Let us make us a name.' For what they aimed to erect, as a monument of their grandeur and glory, God indeed suffered to stand long, but then it was as a monument of their own infamy and folly, the impotency of their rebellion, and their decisive defeat."[3]

431. GENESIS 19. Concerning the burning of Sodom, etc. "Diodorus Siculus, Bk. 19, where he describes the lake Asphaltitis, says, 'The neighboring country burns with fire, the ill smell of which makes the bodies of the inhabitants sickly, and not very long-lived.' Strabo, Bk.

9. Grotius, *Truth of the Christian Religion* (1719), p. 55.

1. MS: "foremention."

2. This paragraph and the following one are a later addition. Henry Winder, *A Critical and Chronological History of the Rise, Progress, Declension, and Revival of Knowledge, Chiefly Religious. In Two Periods. I. The Period of Tradition from Adam to Moses. II. The Period of Letters from Moses to Christ* (2 vols. London, 1745–46), *1*, 116–18.

3. Ibid., p. 127.

16, after the description of the lake Asphaltitis, says, 'There are many signs of this country's being on fire, for about Masada they show many cragged and burnt rocks, and in many places caverns eaten in, and the ground turned into ashes, drops of pitch falling from the rocks, and running waters stinking to a great distance, and their habitations overthrown, which give credit to a report amongst the inhabitants, that formerly there were thirteen cities inhabited there, the chief of which was Sodom, so large as to be sixty furlongs round; but by earthquakes, and fire breaking out, and by hot waters mixed with bitumen and brimstone, it became a lake as we now see it. The rocks took fire; some of the cities were swallowed up, and others forsaken by those inhabitants that could flee.' Tacitus, in the fifth book of his *History*, has these words. 'Not far from thence are those fields, which are reported to have been formerly very fruitful, and inhabited with a large city, but were burnt by lightning, the marks of which remain, in that the land is of a burning nature, and has lost its fruitfulness. For everything that is planted, or grows of itself, as soon as it comes to an herb or flower, or grown to its proper bigness, vanishes like dust into nothing.' Solinus, in the 36th chapter of Salmasius' edition, has these words. 'At a good distance from Jerusalem, a dismal lake extends itself, which was struck by lightning, as appears from the black earth, burnt to ashes. There were two towns there, one called Sodom, the other Gomorrah. The apples that grow there cannot be eaten, though they look as if they were ripe, for the outward skin encloses a kind of sooty ashes, which, pressed by the least touch, flies out into smoke, and vanishes into fine dust.'" Grotius, *De Veritate*, Bk. 1, sec. 16, notes.[4]

432. EXODUS 2.[5] CONCERNING MOSES. "Clemens Alexandrinus, *Strom.* 1, reports out of the books of the Egyptian priests, that an Egyptian was slain by the words of Moses; and *Strom.* 5, he relates some things belonging to Moses out of Artapanus, though not very truly. Justin, out of Trogus Pompeius, says of Moses, 'He was leader of those that were banished, and took away the sacred things of the Egyptians, which they, endeavoring to recover with arms, were forced by a tempest to return home; and Moses, being entered into his own country of Damascus, he took possession of Mount Sinah.'[6] And what follows is a mixture of truth and falsehood. Where we find 'Arvas' written in him,

4. Grotius, *Truth of the Christian Religion* (1719), pp. 55–56.
5. JE mistakenly entitled this entry "Genesis 2."
6. I.e. Sinai.

it should be read 'Arnas,' who is Aaron, not the son of Moses, as he imagines, but the brother, and a priest. The Orphic verses expressly mention his being taken out of the water, and the two tables that were given him by God. The verses are thus.

> So was it said of old, so he commands,
> Who's born of water, who received of God
> The double tables of the law.

The great Scaliger in these verses, instead of *hulogenes*, with a very little variation of the shape of a letter, reads *hudogenes*, 'born of the water.'

"The ancient writer of the Orphic verses, whoever he was, added these lines after he had said that[7] there was but one God to be worshiped, who was the Creator and Governor of the world.

"Polemon, who seems to have lived in the time of Antiochus Epiphanes, has these words. 'In the reign of Apis, the son of Phoroneus, part of the Egyptian army went out of Egypt, and dwelt in Syria, called Palestine, not far from Arabia.' Several things are related about his coming out of Egypt, from the Egyptian writers, Manetho, Lysimachus, Chaeremon. The places are in Josephus against *Appion*, with abundance of falsities, as coming from people who hated the Jews; and from hence Tacitus took his account of them. But it appears from all these compared together, that the Hebrews descended from the Assyrians, and possessing a great part of Egypt, led the life of shepherds; but afterwards, being burdened with hard labor, they came out of Egypt under the command of Moses, some of the Egyptians accompanying them, and went through the country of the Arabians unto Palestine Syria, and there set up rites contrary to those of the Egyptians.[8]

"Diodorus Siculus, in his first book, where he treats of those who made the gods to be the authors of their laws, says, 'Amongst the Jews was Moses, who called God by the name of Ἰάω,' i.e. Jehovah, which was so pronounced by the oracles, and in the Orphic verses mentioned by the ancients, and by the Tyrians.

"Strabo, in his sixteenth book, speaking of Moses as an Egyptian priest (which he had from the Egyptian writers, as appears in Josephus),[9] says, 'Many who worship the deity agreed with him (Moses),

7. Jonathan Edwards, Jr., inserted this word.
8. JE deleted "These things above written are taken out of Grotius, *De Veritate*, Bk. 1, sec. 16."
9. JE deleted "adds his own opinion."

for he both said and taught, that the Egyptians did not rightly conceive of God, when they likened him to wild beasts and cattle, nor the Libyans, nor the Greeks, in resembling him by a human shape; for God is no other than the universe which surrounds us, the earth, and the sea, and the heaven, and the world, and the nature of things, as they are called by us. Who, says he (i.e. Moses), that has any understanding, would presume to form any image like to those things that are about us? Wherefore we ought to lay aside all carved images, and worship him in the innermost part of a temple worthy of him, without any figure.' He adds, that this was the opinion of good men. He adds also, that sacred rites were instituted by him, which were not burdensome for their costliness, nor hateful, as proceeding from madness. He mentions circumcision, the meats that were forbidden, and the like; and after he had shown that man was naturally desirous of civil society, he tells us that it is promoted by divine and human precepts, but more effectually by divine.

"Pliny, book xxx, ch. 1, says, 'There is another party of magicians which sprang from Moses.' Juvenal has these lines.

> They learn, and keep, and fear the Jewish law,
> Which Moses in his secret volume gave.

Tacitus, *History* V, according [to] the Egyptian fables, calls Moses 'one of them that were banished.'

"Dionysius Longinus (that lived in the time of Aurelian the emperor, a favorite of Zenobia, queen of the Palmyrians), in his book of the lofty way of speaking,[1] after he had said that they who speak of God ought to take care to represent him as great, and pure, and without mixture, he[2] adds, 'Thus does he who gave laws to the Jews, who was an extraordinary man, who conceived and spoke worthily of the power of God, when he writes in the beginning of his laws, "God spake." What? "Let there be light, and there was light. Let there be earth, and it was so."'

"Chalcidius took many things out of Moses, of whom he speaks thus. 'Moses was the wisest of men, who, as they say, was enlivened, not by human eloquence, but by divine inspiration.'

"Numenius, as Eusebius quotes his words, Book 8, ch. 8, says, 'Afterwards Jamnes and Mambres, Egyptian scribes, were thought to be

1. Jonathan Edwards, Jr., deleted the previous four words and inserted in their place "sublime."
2. Jonathan Edwards, Jr., deleted this word.

famous for magical arts, about the time that the Jews were driven out
of Egypt, for these were they that were chosen out of the multitude of
the Egyptians to contend with Musaeus, the leader of the Jews, a man
very powerful with God by prayers; and they seemed to be able to repel
those sore calamities, which were brought upon Egypt by Musaeus.'
Origen, *Against Celsus*, refers us to the same place of Numenius.

"Artapanus, in the same Eusebius, Bk. 9, ch. 27, calls them the
priests of Memphis, who were commanded by the king to be put to
death, if they did not do things equal to Moses.

"Strabo, in his 14th book, after the history of *Moses*, says, 'That his
followers for a considerable time kept his precepts, and were truly
righteous and godly.' And a little after he says, 'that those who believed
in Moses, worshipped God and were lovers of equity.'"

These things concerning Moses are taken from Grotius, *De Veritate*,
Bk. 1, sec. 16.[3] See also SSS on Ex. 2:3, and on Ex. 12:12.[4]

433. EZEKIEL 38–39. Concerning GOG AND MAGOG. This prophecy
concerning Gog and Magog seems manifestly to have respect to two
things foretold in the book of Revelation.

FIRST, that great company or multitude of the enemies of Christ and
the church, that shall be gathered together to fight against them, after
religion has begun wonderfully to revive and prevail in the world, just
before the utter destruction of Antichrist and of the visible kingdom
of Satan upon the earth, that we read of, Rev. 16:13–21, and Rev.
19:17–21. And,

SECONDLY, that vast multitude that shall be gathered against the
church after the millennium, a little before the end of the world, that
we read of in the 20th chapter of Revelation, who are expressly called
Gog and Magog.

[FIRST.] That there is some respect to the former of these, though
they are not expressly called Gog and Magog, is evident by[5] the many
things wherein there is an agreement.

In Rev. 16:14, "the kings of the earth and of the whole world" are
represented as gathered together to war against the church of God. So
here the kings and nations of the world are represented as gathered
together against God's Israel, from the four quarters of the world, or

---

3. Grotius, *Truth of the Christian Religion* (1719), pp. 60–65.
4. These references are later additions. See Poole, *Synopsis Criticorum*, *1* (London [1669],
Pt. 1, cols. 322–23, 364).
5. JE deleted "several things in this prophecy."

the four winds of heaven: Magog, and Meshech, and Tubal, Gomer, and Togarmah, of the north quarters (Ezek. 38:2, 6); Persia from the east (v. 5); Ethiopia, or Cush, and Libya, or Phut, Sheba, and Dedan, from the east, and south, and southwest (vv. 5, 13); the merchants and young lions (i.e. princes) of Tarshish, and they that dwell in the isles, from the west (v. 13, and Ezek. 39:6).

The great occasion of the gathering of that innumerable host, spoken of in the 16th and 19th chapters of Revelation, to war against the church, is evidently her late great prosperity in a great revival, and restoration from her long continued, captivated, desolate state under Antichrist. So here Gog and his multitude are represented as excited to come and war against Israel, on occasion of her being brought back from a long continued, and as it were perpetual captivity and desolation (vv. 8–12). This long desolation and captivity of Israel in the latter days, which is expressed by an having been always waste, can agree to nothing but the lying waste either of Israel according to the flesh, or the Christian church, the spiritual Israel, which has been [waste] for many ages in these latter days, and both of them through the[6] devastations of Rome, or the mystical Babylon.

Rev. 16:18–20, it is said, "There was a great earthquake, such as was not since men were upon the earth, so mighty an earthquake, and so great. . . . And the cities of the nations fell. . . . And every island fled away, and the mountains were not found." And in Ezek. 38:19–20, it is said, "Surely in that day there shall be a great shaking in the land of Israel; so that the fishes of the sea, and the fowls of heaven, and the beasts of the field, and all creeping things that creep upon the earth, and all the men that are upon the face of the earth, shall shake at my presence, and the mountains shall be thrown down, and the steep places shall fall, and every wall shall fall to the ground." There seems to be a reference to this very place, in that in Revelation.

Rev. 19:21, it is said, "And the remnant were slain with the sword of him that sat upon the horse." And here, v. 21, it is said, "I will call for a sword against him throughout all my mountains."

Rev. 16:18, it is said, "And there were thunders, and lightnings." And v. 21, "And there fell upon men a great hail out of heaven, every stone about the weight of a talent; and men blasphemed God because of the plague of the hail, for the plague thereof was exceeding great." And here, Ezek. 38:22, it is said, "I will rain upon him, and upon his

6. JE deleted "oppressions."

bands, and upon the many people that are with him, an overflowing rain, and great hailstones, fire, and brimstone." There seems to be reference to this, in that in Revelation.

Rev. 19:17–18, John says, "And I saw an angel standing in the sun; and he cried with a loud voice, saying to all the fowls that fly in the midst of heaven," etc. And v. 21, "And all the fowls were filled with their flesh." And here, Ezek. 39:4–5, it is said, "Thou shalt fall upon the mountains of Israel, thou, and all thy bands, and the people that is with thee. I will give thee unto the ravenous birds of every sort, and to the beasts of the field, to be devoured. Thou shalt fall upon the open field, for I have spoken it, saith the Lord God." And vv. 17–20, it is said, "And thou son of man, thus saith the Lord, Speak unto every feathered fowl," etc., very much in the same manner as there in the Revelation, so that there is a most plain reference in one place to the other.

In Rev. 16:14, the day of that battle there spoken of, is called the "great day of God Almighty"; and in v. 17, it is said, "There came a great voice out of the temple of heaven, from the throne, saying, It is done." So here, Ezek. 39:8, it is said, "Behold, it is come, and it is done, saith the Lord God; this is the day whereof I have spoken." Here also seems to be a like reference.

SECONDLY. This prophecy has also respect to that innumerable multitude that should be gathered against the church after the millennium, a little before the end of the world, spoken of in the 20th chapter of Revelation, which is evident not only because they are expressly called Gog and Magog in Revelation, but there are many other things that argue it.

The church of God is represented as being in a state of peace, and quietness, and great visible prosperity, at the time that they are thus invaded, as vv. 8, 11–13. This better agrees with that invasion of the church of Christ in the 20th of Revelation, than that in the 16th and 19th [chapters].

The multitude of Gog is represented as being gathered from the four quarters of the earth. So it is said expressly in Rev. 20:8, that the devil should "go out to deceive the nations which are in the four quarters of the earth, Gog and Magog."

As it is said, Rev. 20:9, concerning the multitude there spoken of, that "fire came down from God out of heaven, and devoured them," so here, Ezek. 39: 6, it is said, "I will send a fire on Magog, and among them that dwell carelessly in the isles."

In Ezekiel 38:16, "Thou shalt come up against my people Israel, as a cloud to cover the land." This agrees with Rev. 20:9, "And they went up on the breadth of the earth, and compassed the camp of the saints, and the beloved city."

In Ezekiel [38], v. 8, "In the latter days thou shalt come into the land"; and v. 16, "And thou shalt come up against my people, as a cloud to cover the land, and it shall be in the latter days." This more eminently agrees with that in Rev. 20, which is just before the end of the world.

That invasion, Rev. 20, is spoken of as following the first resurrection, wherein[7] the martyrs, or God's people that had been oppressed and persecuted by their enemies, should live and reign with Christ, which is undoubtedly the same resurrection with that spoken of in the 37th chapter of Ezekiel, where we have an account how that God's Israel, that had been captivated and killed by their oppressing enemies, are brought out of their graves, and God's servant David should be king over them, which is represented as preceding this invasion of Gog and his multitude.

In Revelation, the vision of the New Jerusalem follows in ch. 21, and [in] 20:8–9, the account of the destruction of Gog and Magog; and it was represented to John from a great and high mountain. Rev. 21:10, "And he carried me away in the spirit to a great and high mountain, and he showed me that great city, the holy Jerusalem, descending out of heaven from God." So a vision of the city Jerusalem in its renewed state, after its glorious restoration, follows the prophecy of Gog in Ezekiel, and is represented to the Prophet in like manner. Ezek. 40:1–2, "The hand of the Lord was upon me, and he brought me thither. In the visions of God brought he me into the land of Israel, and set me upon a very high mountain, by which was as the frame of a city on the south." There is doubtless a reference in that in Revelation, to this in Ezekiel; and that, Rev. 21:3, "And I heard a great voice out of heaven saying, Behold, the tabernacle of God is with men, and he will dwell with them, and they shall be his people, and God himself shall be with them, and be their God," from Ezek. 37:26–27. "Moreover I will make a covenant of peace with them; it shall be an everlasting covenant with them. And I will place them, and multiply them, and I will set my sanctuary in the midst of them forevermore. My tabernacle also shall be with them. Yea, I will be their God, and they shall be my people."

7. JE deleted "the saints should live and."

434. Concerning the BOOK OF PSALMS. That the penmen of these psalms did pretend to speak and write by the inspiration of the Spirit of God, as much as the prophets when they wrote their prophecies, the following things do confirm.

1. Singing divine songs was of old one noted effect of the inspiration of the Spirit of God in the prophets, insomuch that such singing was called by the name of prophesying. I Sam. 10:5–6, "Thou shalt meet a company of prophets coming down from the high place with a psaltery, and a tabret, and a pipe, and a harp, before them; and they shall prophesy. And the Spirit of the Lord will come upon thee, and thou shalt prophesy with them." See also I Chron. 25:1–3.[8] This seems to have been the most ancient way of prophesying; inspired persons of old used to utter themselves in a parable, as sometimes it is called, or a kind of song. Thus it was that Miriam uttered herself, when she did the part of a prophetess. Ex. 15:20–21, "And Miriam the prophetess, the sister of Aaron, took a timbrel in her hand, and all the women went out after her with timbrels and with dances. And Miriam answered them, Sing ye to the Lord, for he hath triumphed gloriously; the horse and his rider hath he thrown into the sea." She, in the 12th chapter of Numbers, v. 2, boasts that God had spoken by her as well as by Moses. She seems to have reference to this time, for it does not appear that God ever had spoken by her at any other time; and it is probable that it was from her being inspired at that time (or at least chiefly), that she was called a prophetess. And this was the way that Moses delivered his chief and fullest prophecy concerning the future state of Israel, and the church of God, and the world of mankind, in that song in the 32nd of Deuteronomy. The words were all indited by God, as appears by Deut. 31:19–21. And Moses' blessing of the children of Israel, and his prophecy of their future state, in Deut. 3, is delivered song-wise, which especially appears in the beginning and ending; and so are Balaam's prophecies or parables. Jacob's blessing and prophecies concerning the future state of the posterity of his twelve sons (Gen. 49), is delivered in a like style, as may be plain to anyone that observes. Zacharias is said to prophesy in uttering a song (Luke 1:67).[9]

2. Singing these very psalms in the sanctuary by the musicians that David appointed is called prophesying (I Chron. 25:1–3). And Asaph

8. This reference is a later interlineation.
9. This sentence is a later interlineation.

is called a seer or prophet, and represented as speaking as such in uttering those psalms that he penned (II Chron. 29:30).[1]

3. We are expressly informed of David, in an eminent[2] instance, wherein he uttered himself in a remarkable manner as "the sweet psalmist of Israel," that he did profess himself to speak by the immediate inspiration of the Spirit of God. II Sam. 23:1–3, "Now these be the last words of David." (And then in what next follows, David's words begin, as may be confirmed by comparing them with Num. 24:3–4, 15–16.) "David, the son of Jesse, hath said, and the man who was raised up on high, the anointed of the God of Jacob, and the sweet psalmist of Israel, said, The Spirit of the Lord spake by me, and his word was in my tongue. The God of Israel said, the Rock of Israel spake to me." In its being said that "these are the last words of David," it[3] is implied that there had been many other words, that he as "the sweet psalmist of Israel" had uttered many things before. And when David, in these his last words, says, "The Spirit of the Lord spake by me," it must be understood[4] of all these words spoken of in this place, whether mentioned or referred to, all the words that he had uttered as "the sweet psalmist of Israel." And there can perhaps no other good reason be given, why he should be mentioned under that character of "the sweet psalmist of Israel" here, in the introduction of these his last words, rather than all other places of his history, but only because these were the last words that David had uttered as "the sweet psalmist of Israel," and as it were the sum of all those preceding words referred to, expressing the main drift and substance of those holy songs he had sung by the inspiration of the Spirit of God all his lifetime, and the *ultimum*, the chief thing he had in view in those psalms.

4. 'Tis evident that the penmen of the psalms did pretend to speak by a spirit of prophecy, because the psalms are full of prophecies of future events, as Ps. 11:6, 22:27–31, 37:9–11, 60:6–8, 64:7–10, 68:31, 69:34–36, 72, 86:9, 96:13, 102:13–22, 108, 138:4–5, 149:7–9. And many other things in the psalms are uttered in a prophetical manner and style.

---

1. JE interlined this second point after completing the entry and then renumbered the following sections.
2. MS: "~~Certain~~ ⟨Eminent⟩."
3. JE deleted "seems to be inti."
4. The preceding four words are a later interlineation.

5. 'Tis also most manifest that the penmen of the psalms did pretend to speak by the Spirit, and in the name of the Lord, as the prophets did, by this, that God in the psalms is very often represented as speaking, and the words are evidently represented as his words, in like manner as in the prophets,[5] as Ps. 2:6–12, 14:4, 32:8–11, 45:16–17, 50:7–14, 53:4, 60:6–8, 68:13, 75:2–3, 81, 82, 87, 89:3–4, 19–37, 91:14–16, 95:8–11, 108:7–9, 110:1, 4, 132:14–18. See further, Nos. 440 and 506.[6] See "Prophecies of the Messiah," "Miscellanies," no. 1067, sec. 87.[7]

435. CANTICLES 4:9. "Thou hast ravished my heart with one of thine eyes, with one chain of thy neck." What that one chain of the spouse's neck is, that does so peculiarly ravish the heart of Christ, we may learn by Ps. 45:10–11. "Forget thine own people, and thy father's house; so shall the king greatly desire thy beauty." The thing here recommended to the spouse, in order to the king's greatly desiring or being ravished with her beauty, is poverty of spirit. That this peculiarly delights and attracts the heart of Christ is agreeable to many scriptures. I Pet. 3:3–4, "Whose adorning let it not be that outward adorning of plaiting the hair, and wearing of gold, and putting on of apparel; but let it be the hidden man of the heart, in that which is not corruptible, even the ornament of a meek and quiet spirit, which is in the sight of God of great price." This is in a peculiar manner a sweet savor to God (Ps. 51:17). This in a peculiar manner draws the eye of God (Is. 60:2), and attracts his presence (Is. 57:15, and Ps. 34:18). Or perhaps it may be the eye of faith that includes poverty of spirit and love; these graces, being exercised in faith, are peculiarly acceptable. Faith derives beauty from Christ's righteousness, by which all mixture of deformity is hid.[8]

436. THE BOOK OF CANTICLES. The following places in the Psalms are a confirmation that by her, that the bridegroom in this book calls "my love," "my dove," "my sister," "my spouse," and the like, is meant the church, viz. Ps. 22:20, and 35:17, and 60:4–5, and 74:19, and 108:6, and 127:2.

5. The preceding seven words are a later interlineation.

6. These cross-references and the reference following are later additions.

7. In sec. 87, subtitled "The Book of Psalms in General in great Part Relates to the Messiah," JE argues that even in those psalms "where the speech is in the present or preter tense" (e.g. when speaking of "captivity and the temple, city, and land in desolation," or restoration from the same), the intention is prophetic of "the times of the Messiah" ("Miscellanies," no. 1067).

8. The last two sentences are a later addition.

437. ISAIAH 41:18–20. "I will make the wilderness pools of water. . . . I will plant in the wilderness the cedar . . . . That ye may see, and know, and consider, and understand together, that the hand of the Lord hath done this, and the Holy One of Israel hath created it." God will cause waters to flow in the dry desert, and[9] turn the barren wilderness into a pleasant garden, and bring forth these glorious things in such places that were most [un]likely and most distant from anything of this nature, and where was the least of any previous disposition, preparation, or foundation for anything of this, that his hand might be the more visible, and his power and efficacy the more apparent and undeniable, as of old when God furnished a table in the wilderness, and brought forth water out of flinty rock. Therefore here it is said, "The Holy One of Israel hath created it." To "create," as the word is used in Scripture, is either to make out [of] nothing, or which is equivalent, to make out of that which has in itself no natural fitness, disposition, or preparation, or foundation for such an effect.

438. ISAIAH 41:22. "Let them bring forth, and show us what shall happen. Let them show us former things, what they be, that we may consider them, and know the latter end of them, or declare us things for to come." See also vv. 4, and 23, 26, and 42:9, and 43:9–12, and 44:6–8, and 45:21–22, and 46:9–10, and 48:3–8, 14–16.

By "former things" in these passages of the Prophet is meant former predictions of future events, or former and ancient dispensations, or works that pointed at things future, either by representing and typifying them, or in preparing for them, and ordering things with an evident respect to future events. Or more briefly, by "former things" is meant such words or works that so pointed at things future, as to show plainly that they, whose words or works they were, had the foreknowledge and ordination of those future events. 'Tis evident that by "former things" are meant former signs of future events, by what is said here in Is. 41:22. "Let 'em show us former things, what they be, that we may consider them what they be, and know the latter end of them"; i.e. let 'em bring forth their ancient predictions or dispensations pointing at future events, that we may consider them, and compare 'em with the event, and see how they prove in the latter end, see how they come out in the event of things. This is confirmed by v. 26. "Who hath declared from the beginning, that we may know, and beforetime, that we may say, He is righteous?"; i.e. that we may acknowl-

9. JE deleted "cause these trees."

edge that his cause is good, and that he is to be justified in his pretenses. For here God is calling of them to come near together with him to judgment, that it may be tried who can best make out their pretenses to divinity and claims of divine honors. See vv. 1 and 21. This is further manifest by Is. 42:9. "Behold, the former things are come to pass, and new things do I declare; before they spring forth, I tell you of them." And Is. 43:9–10, "Let all nations be gathered together, and let the people be assembled. Who among them can declare this, and show us former things? Let 'em bring forth their witnesses"; i.e. let 'em bring forth their witnesses, that such and such things they foretold, or by some dispensations of theirs showed their foreknowledge of such and such events, and that the events exactly agreed with the prediction. Producing witnesses, that they may be justified, is a form of speech still alluding to a coming together in judgment. See also vv. 10–12, and 44:6–8, and 45:21–22, and 46:9–10, and 48:3–4 ff.

439. Exodus 2:6. "And, behold, the babe wept." As Moses in the water was a type of the church in affliction, so his weeping a little before he is taken out of the water, seems to be typical of the spirit of repentance, mourning, and supplications, often spoken [of] in the prophets, given to the church a little before her deliverance from adversity.

440. The Book of Psalms. Add this to No. 434. It is a further confirmation of those things, that we find that David very early was endowed with the spirit of prophecy and miracles. He wrought a miracle when he slew the lion and the bear, and acted and spake by that spirit of prophecy when he went forth against Goliath, as is very apparent by the story. See further, No. 506.[1]

441. Exodus 32–34. There are many of [the] things in the circumstances of this second giving of the law, that we have an account of in these chapters, that are arguments that these two transactions did represent the two great transactions of God with mankind in the covenant of works and covenant of grace. It was in this last covenanting of God with the people especially, that Moses appeared as a mediator, which the Apostle has respect to in Gal. 3:19. "It was ordained by

---

1. This cross-reference is a later addition.

angels in the hand of a mediator." When the people had broken the covenant given at first with thunder and lightning, the law then was made use of as a schoolmaster, to convince them of sin. God threatened to leave 'em, and not to go up with them; and when the people were awakened by it, and mourned when they heard the evil tidings, God then further awakened and terrified them, sending such a message as this to them. "Ye are a stiffnecked people; I will come up into the midst of thee in a moment, and consume thee. Therefore now put off thy ornaments from thee, that I may know what to do unto thee." Thus this awful threatening was given forth with some hope and encouragement, that peradventure they might live, given in that last clause, "that I may know what to do unto thee." By thus applying the terrors of the law, God brought the people to put off their ornaments, which were typical of their own righteousness (Ex. 33:5–6).

Moses now acted as a mediator, not only as an intermessenger as he did in the first giving of the law. He offers his life for theirs; he offers up himself to be accursed and blotted out of God's book for them, after he had told the people that they had sinned a great sin, and peradventure he should make atonement for their sin, which is to do the part of a mediator. See Ex. 32:30–32.

On this occasion [the] Lord speaks to Moses "face to face, as a man speaketh unto his friend," when he came to speak to God in behalf of the people, well representing the intercourse of our Mediator with the Father (Ex. 33:11). And on this occasion God made all his goodness pass before Moses, and proclaimed himself "the Lord, the Lord God, gracious and merciful," forgiving iniquity, etc. (Ex. 33:19, and 34:5–7).

The covenant the first time was written in tables that were the workmanship of God, as the soul or heart of man in innocency was, which workmanship of God was destroyed by man's apostasy, as upon the children of Israel's apostasy, Moses brake the tables that were the workmanship of God. The covenant now was written on tables that were the workmanship of Moses, the mediator, as the law of God after the Fall is written in the fleshly tables of the heart renewed by Christ.

God promises, that in fulfillment of the covenant he now (the last time) enters into with his people, he will do marvels, such as have not been done in all the earth, nor in any [time], and that all the people should see the work of the Lord. So God, in the way of the new covenant that he entered into with Christ, did those great things by Christ in the work of redemption, which are so often spoken of in Scripture as being so exceeding wonderful, and were infinitely the greatest wonders that ever were wrought.

God made this covenant with Moses, the typical mediator, as the head and representative of the people, and with the people in him or under him as his people, that he showed mercy to for his sake. Ex. 34:27, "And the Lord said unto Moses, Write these words, for after the tenor of these words I have made a covenant with THEE and with Israel." And v. 10, "Behold, I make a covenant; before all THY people I will do marvels."

Before, Moses came down from the mount in wrath, with the tables broken; so Christ comes as God's messenger, to execute wrath for the breach of the covenant of works. Now he comes down with the tables of the testimony in his hand, with his face shining, this being typical of the light of grace with which Christ's face shines on God's Israel. See note on Ex. 32:19, and Ex. 34:1.[2]

442. EXODUS 4:20. MOSES' ROD. See No. 195. One thing at least typified by this rod is faith, the same that was signified by Jacob's staff with which he passed over Jordan, and that he leaned upon in his last sickness, that the Apostle speaks of in Heb. 11:21, and Elisha's staff that he bid his servant lay on the dead child [II Kgs. 4:29], and the staves of the princes with which they digged the well [Num. 21:18], and David's staff he took in his hand when he went against Goliath [I Sam. 17:40]. The word properly signifies a staff as well as rod, such a staff as persons walk with, or lean upon; the word comes from a root, one signification of which is "to lean."[3] The word translated "bed,"[4] Gen. 47:31 ("Jacob bowed himself upon the bed's head."), comes from the same root, and therefore the Apostle renders it "staff" in Heb. 11. The word is not the same in the original with that used to signify Elisha's staff that was laid on the child, but it is a word of the same signification. And therefore both words are used to signify "the stay of

2. These references are a later addition. JE suggests that Moses' breaking the tables of the law in Ex. 32:19 signifies two things: "That sin breaks the law, and particularly that it breaks it as a covenant of works," and that God broke the covenant with his people because of their sin. JE explains God's command for Moses to make a second set of tables of stone in Ex. 34:1 as evidence that "after the Fall the heart needs to be first prepared . . . by the law of Moses, or by legal convictions." Yet the law can only be fulfilled by Christ. JE also contrasted the two occasions of the giving of the law, the first being accompanied by "thunder, and lightning, and earthquakes," but the second with a "gracious proclamation of mercy" ("Blank Bible").
3. מַקֵּל.
4. מִטָּה.

bread," the latter in Is. 3:1, and the former in Lev. 26:26. This word is used to signify Judah's staff that he gave to Tamar as a pledge (Gen. 38:18).

443. EXODUS 4:6–7. "And the Lord said furthermore unto him, Put now thine hand into thy bosom. And he put his hand into his bosom; and when he took it out, behold, his hand was leprous as snow. And he said, Put thine hand into thy bosom again. And he put his hand into his bosom again, and plucked it out of his bosom; and, behold, it was turned again as the other flesh." This sign is much like the foregoing, of casting the rod on the ground and its becoming a serpent [Ex. 4:3]; and much the same thing is signified, but only more is signified in this latter sign than in the former. By Moses' hand is represented the hand or arm of the Lord, which often in the Old Testament signifies the Messiah. By God's plucking his hand out of his bosom is meant his appearing for the salvation of his people. While God long forbears to appear for his church's salvation, while they are longing and waiting for him, he as it were hides his hand in his bosom. Ps. 74:11, "Why withdrawest thou thy hand, even thy right hand? Pluck it out of thy bosom." There are remarkable appearances of God in the world for the salvation of his people, which are both by the coming of the Messiah, both of which are long wished and waited for before they are accomplished. The first is God's appearing in the world[5] for the redemption of the church, by laying the foundation of her salvation in the first coming of the Messiah, after the church had long waited for him, while God had hid his hand in his bosom. At length the arm of the Lord is made bare. The Messiah appears, but [in] such a manner that it was to the surprise and astonishment of those that saw him. Many were astonied at him; his visage was so marred, more than any man, and his form more than the sons of men. They were offended in him. He had no form nor comeliness; and when they saw him, there was no beauty that they should desire him [Is. 53:2]. He appears in the form of sinful flesh. He was as it were diseased with the leprosy, because [he] himself took our infirmities and bore our sicknesses. He was made sin for us, as though he had been all over leprous or sinful. God's second remarkable appearance will be in the Messiah's second coming for the actual salvation of his people, when he will appear without sin unto salvation, without the leprosy of our sin, and will appear in that glory that he had

5. MS: "word."

with the Father before his humiliation, which he emptied himself of at his first coming, God having answered his prayer in glorifying him with his own self, with the glory he had with him before the world was, as Moses' hand, the second time he plucked it out of his bosom, was restored as it was at first.[6] This type of the redemption of the Messiah was fitly given on this occasion, and as a sign of the redemption of the children of Israel out of Egypt, and the carrying them through the Red Sea, the wilderness, and Jordan, into Canaan, because the redemption of the Messiah, both fundamental and actual, was various represented and presignified in that great work of God.

444. CANTICLES 2:14. "O my dove, that art in the clefts of the rock, in the secret places of the stairs, let me see thy countenance, let me hear thy voice." There is probably respect here to the rock of Mt. Zion, on which Solomon's house was built, or of the mountain of the temple, and to the stairs by which they ascended that high rock to go up to Solomon's palace (see Neh. 3:15, and 12:37),[7] or the stairs by which they ascended through the various courts into the temple. It comes much to the same thing, whether we suppose the rocks and stairs referred to, to be of the mountain of Solomon's palace or temple, for both were typical of the same thing; and both mountains seemed to have been called by the same name, "Mt. Zion."[8] The church in her low state, before that glorious spring spoken of in the foregoing verses, is not admitted to such high privileges, and such nearness to God, and intimacy with him as she shall be afterwards, is kept at a greater distance not only by God's providence, but through her own darkness and unbelief, and remains of a legal spirit whereby she falls more under the terrors of God's majesty manifested at Mt. Sinai, under that legal dispensation through which Moses, when God passed by, hid himself in the clefts of the rock. Her love to the spiritual Solomon causes her to remain near his house, about the mountain on which his palace stands, watching at his gates, and waiting at the posts of his doors, and by the stairs by which he ascends to his house, but yet hides herself as ashamed, and afraid, and unworthy to appear before him, like the woman that came behind Christ, to touch the hem of his garment [Matt. 9:20]. She has not yet obtained that glorious privilege spoken of, Ps. 45:14–15 and Rev 19:7–8, which she shall be admitted to in the

6. JE deleted "This sign was fitly given."
7. These references are a later interlineation.
8. JE deleted "These stairs were typical of."

glorious day approaching, when she shall enter into the king's palace. She remains now waiting at the foot of the stairs that go up to the house, as Jacob lay at the foot of the ladder, at the place of which he said, "This is the house of God; this is the gate of heaven" [Gen. 28:17]. And there she hides herself in the secret places of the stairs, but then she shall be made joyfully to ascend, and with boldness and open face to go to the king in his palace.

445. JOHN 19:14. "And it was the preparation of the passover, and about the sixth hour." Mark says, Mark 15:25, "It was the third hour, and they crucified him," which seems by the context to be manifestly the time of his being nailed to the cross at Golgotha, with which this place in John is reconciled thus. John is here as it were beginning a new paragraph, containing an account of that grand event of the last passion of our Savior, which he proceeds to do, from hence to the 38th verse. John had before been giving a large account of those things that went before this his last passion, and made way for it; but now, he being about to proceed directly to this event itself, the greatest and most astonishing of all events, he as it were makes a pause, and begins the account of it as [a] distinct story, worthy to be peculiarly taken notice of. These words in the 14th verse are the introduction to the story of this event, giving an account at what time it came to pass, viz. on the day of "the preparation of the passover, and about the sixth hour," that is, in the middle of the day; so that the words, "it was the preparation of the passover, and about the sixth hour," do not relate especially to the words immediately following, "and he saith unto the Jews, Behold your king," but rather to the whole story, beginning with these words and ending with the 37th verse, or the grand event related in the story, viz. Christ's last passion. For the words are an introduction to the story of this event, and not to that particular fact of Pilate's saying, "Behold your king"; and this is very manifest by John's now as it were interrupting the thread of his narrative, and standing to tell us that it was the preparation of the passover. If he only meant it was the preparation of the passover when Pilate said, "Behold your king," for if so, why should he stand in this place to tell us it was the preparation of the passover, and to tell us that this fact happened on this day, any more than any of the other many facts as important as this that[9] he had been giving an account of before, from the 28th verse of the preceding

9. The preceding five words are a later interlineation.

chapter, which all were on the same day? So that John's design is not to give us an account of the precise time when Pilate said these words, but of the time in general of that great event of Christ's last passion, the story of which he immediately introduces in this verse, and goes on with to the end of the 37th verse. He says it was "about the sixth hour," i.e. at the middle part of the day, it beginning at the third hour, or middle of the forenoon, and ending at the ninth hour, or middle of the afternoon; and if the time of this grand event be signified by mentioning any hour about which it was, it is most properly said to be "about the sixth hour," for that was the very center or middle of the time about which it was, it beginning three hours before it, and continuing three hours after it. The three preceding evangelists all agree that the darkness, by the sun's withdrawing his light, began[1] at the sixth hour; and as they all relate the story of crucifixion, it seems manifest that some considerable time passed after he was nailed to the cross before this darkness began. So that it seems on the whole beyond doubt, that Christ was[2] nailed to the cross about the third hour, and hung about six hours on the cross before he expired.

446. JOHN 1:31. "And I knew him not. But that he should be made manifest to Israel." This may seem strange that John did not know Jesus, seeing the families were so related, Elizabeth his mother being cousin to the Virgin Mary; and they were intimately acquainted one with another, and at the very time of their pregnancy, when the child of each had been already conceived in their wombs, and were both thoroughly acquainted with the miraculous circumstances of each other's conception, and what the children were that they had conceived, and to what end they were to come into the world, and conversed together of these things. Soon after Christ's birth, he was conveyed away privately by his parents into Egypt for fear of Herod, and probably nobody knew where they were gone, or what was become of them. There it is supposed that he remained, in Egypt, till the death of Herod; and Archelaus his son, reigning in his stead in the province of Judea, and manifesting by some bloody acts in the beginning of his reign the like tyrannical disposition with his father, Joseph and Mary returned from Egypt, we may suppose, as privately as they could, into Nazareth, an obscure city in Galilee, the province of Herod

---

1. JE deleted "about."
2. JE deleted "crucified."

Antipas. And as to John the Baptist, when Herod massacred the infants at Bethlehem, his malice proceeded as far as the hill country; for having heard great things of John, the son of Zachary,[3] he sent one of his messengers of death to dispatch him. The care of his mother prevented the design, by flying with him "into the wilderness, or unfrequented parts of the country, on the south side of the river Jordan. It is recorded by Nicephorus, Lib. 1, ch. 14, that he was about eighteen months old when he was conveyed into this sanctuary; that forty days after, his mother died; and near the same time his father Zachariah was killed in the court of the temple."[4] (There is an account of these things in Reading's *Evangelical History of Christ*, chs. 7–10.)[5] However, thus much seems manifest from the Scripture, that[6] John's parents were both old when he was born; and therefore we may well suppose that they died not long after, so that he could not be led by them into personal acquaintance with Jesus. And 'tis also manifest that John was from his infancy in the desert, in a hidden secret state of life, even unto the day when he began his public ministry (Luke 1:80); and that there he lived so much separated from the rest of the Jews, and from the society of mankind, that he lived on the spontaneous productions of the uncultivated desert, his meat being locusts and wild honey, and his garment nothing but camel's hair, girt about him with a girdle of skin (Matt. 3:4, Mark 1:6). And so when he began to preach, it was in the borders of the wilderness where he had lived all his days (Matt. 3:1, 3, Mark 1:4, Luke 3:2, 4). Therefore Christ says to the multitudes concerning John, "What went ye out into the wilderness for to see?" (Matt. 11:7, and Luke 7:24).

Things being thus, it is not to be wondered at that John had never seen Jesus, who lived obscurely so remote from him, and that he knew not where he was, or how to find [him], till God showed him to him.

447. THE GOSPEL OF JOHN. Arguments confirming that this gospel was written as a supplement to the other gospels,[7] from Dr. Doddridge's *Family Expositor*.

3. I.e. Zacharias.
4. William Reading, *The History of our Lord and Saviour Jesus Christ. In Three Parts with suitable Meditations and Prayers. To which are added the Lives of the Holy Apostles and Evangelists. To Which is Prefix'd the Life of the Blessed Virgin Mary, Mother of Our Lord* (2nd ed., London, 1717), p. 48.
5. Chs. 7–10 are pp. 29–57 in Reading, *History*.
6. JE deleted "John lived in the desert is."
7. JE deleted "collected."

1. This is the tradition of the ancients.

2. 'Tis confirmed from John 3:24, "For John was not yet cast into prison," where this evangelist speaks of John [the] Baptist's imprisonment as a thing known in the Christian church (probably having respect to the public records they had already in their hands), and yet says nothing himself in the course of his history of John's martyrdom. "We cannot suppose that he would have omitted so material a fact, had he not known that other evangelists had recorded it at large." Doddridge, *in loc.*[8]

448. GENESIS 1:2. "And the earth was without form, and void." *Tohu bohu,*[9] which both are words signifying "vanity" and "emptiness." Thus God was pleased in the first state of the creation to show what the creature is in itself; that in itself it is wholly empty and vain, that its fullness or goodness is not in itself, but in him and in the communications of his Spirit, animating, quickening, adorning, replenishing, and blessing all things. The emptiness and vanity here spoken of is set in opposition to that goodness spoken of afterwards. Through the incubation of the Spirit of God (as the word translated "moved" signifies), the Spirit of God is here represented as giving form, and life, and perfection to this empty void and unformed mass, as a dove that[1] sits, infuses life, and brings to form and perfection the unformed mass of the egg. Thus the fullness of the creature is from God's Spirit. If God withdraws from the creature, it immediately becomes empty and void of all good. The creature, as it is in itself, is a vessel, and has a capacity, but is empty; but that which fills that emptiness is the Spirit of God.

As the Spirit of God here is represented as hovering or brooding as a dove, so 'tis probable when the Spirit of God appeared in a bodily shape, descending on Christ like a dove, it was with a hovering motion on his head, signifying the manner not only he personally was filled with the fullness of God, but also Christ mystical, and every individual member of his mystical body. So that this that we have here an account of is one instance wherein the old creation was typical of the new. See note on Eph. 3:9.[2]

8. Doddridge, *Family Expositor, 1*, 159.
9. תֹהוּ וָבֹהוּ.
1. JE deleted "broods on e."
2. JE asserts that all the works of providence from the beginning of the world, including the creation of the world itself, are "subordinate to the great purposes of the work of redemption" ("Blank Bible").

449. JOHN 5:2 ff. Concerning the POOL OF BETHESDA. "I imagine this pool might have been remarkable for some mineral virtue attending the water, which is the more probable, as Jerome tells us it was of a very high color [and so the fitter type of the blood of Christ].³ This, together with its being so very near the temple (as travelers relate), where a bath was so much needed for religious purposes, may account for the building such stately cloisters round it, three of which remain to this day. (See Maundrel's *Travels*, p. 108.) Sometime before this passover, an extraordinary commotion was probably observed in the water; and providence so ordered, that the next person who accidentally bathed here, being under some great disorder, found an immediate and unexpected cure. The like phenomenon in some other desperate case, was probably observed on a second commotion. And those commotions and cures might happen periodically, perhaps every sabbath, some weeks, or months. This the Jews would naturally ascribe to some angelic power, as they did afterwards the voice from heaven (John 12:29), though no angel appeared. And they and St. John had reason to do it, as it was the Scripture scheme that those benevolent spirits had been, and frequently are, the invisible instruments of good to the children of men. (See Ps. 34:7, and 91:11, Dan. 3:28, and 6:22.) After Christ had wrought this miracle on the impotent man that lay at this pool, this celestial visitant probably returned no more, the Jews making so ungrateful a return to Christ for this miracle, [and on the antitype's being come, the type probably ceased].⁴ And therefore it may be observed, that though the Evangelist speaks of the pool as still at Jerusalem when he wrote (which was before the city was ruined by the Romans), yet he mentions the descent of the angel as a thing that had been, but not as still continuing (compare vv. 2 and 4). This may account for the surprising silence of Josephus in a story which made so much for the honor of his nation. He was himself not born when it happened; and though he might have heard the report of it, his dread of the marvelous, and fear of disgusting his pagan readers with it, might as well lead him to suppress this, as to disguise the passage through the Red Sea, and the divine voice from Mt. Sinai, in so cowardly and ridiculous a manner, as it is known he does. And the relation in which this fact stood to the history of Jesus would make him peculiarly cautious in touching upon it, as it would have been so difficult to

3. JE's brackets.
4. Ibid.

have handled it at once with decency and safety." Doddridge.[5] See note on the place in "Blank Bible."[6]

450. GENESIS 2:2. "And on the seventh day God ended all his *work*." The word translated "work" is מְלַאכְתּוֹ, which comes from מַלְאָךְ, "angel" or "messenger," and therefore most properly signifies a work done in the execution of some function to which the workman is appointed, as the angel, messenger, officer, or workman of another, and so is fitly used concerning the work of creation, which was performed by the Son of God, who is often called "the angel of the Lord," he being the Father's great officer and artificer, through whom he performs all his work, and executes his eternal counsels and purposes.

451. GENESIS 2:5. "And every plant of the field before it was in the earth, and every herb of the field before it grew; for the Lord God had not caused it to rain upon the earth, and there was not a man to till the ground." This seems to be observed to teach that all the life that is in the creation is immediately from God, and not from the creature itself, that in itself is wholly lifeless, and void, and empty of all perfection. The vegetable life that is in this lower world was immediately from God; of all the innumerable kinds of principles of life that now are manifest, every one were immediately from God. Though the earth, and the rain, and the cultivation and husbandry of men be now made use of, yet these living principles were not first owing to them, for they were before them. So is it as to all principles of spiritual life in the spiritual creation.

452. GENESIS 3:14. "Upon thy belly shalt thou go, and dust shalt thou eat all the days of thy life." This doubtless has respect not only to the beast that the devil made use of as his instrument, but to the devil, that old serpent, to whom God is speaking to chiefly, as is evident by the words immediately following. Those words, "on thy belly shalt thou go," as they respect the devil, have respect to the low and mean exer-

---

5. Doddridge, *Family Expositor*, *1*, 284–85.

6. JE suggests that the pool at Bethesda was "a type and representation of gospel ordinances and means of grace, and the way that persons are to seek spiritual healing by them." Such ordinances heal by "supernatural influence," not by any virtue inherent in them. God "gives the influences of his Spirit" when he pleases, so persons must be "diligent and constant" in their use of the "means of salvation." The story of Bethesda is therefore "encouragement for all sorts of sinners . . . to seek healing in the ways of God's appointment" ("Blank Bible").

cises and employments that the devil should pursue, and signify that he should be debased to the lowest and most sordid measures to compass his ends, so that nothing should be too mean and vile for him to do to reach his aims. Those words, "dust shalt thou eat all the days of thy life," have respect to the mean gratifications that Satan should hereafter have for his greatest good, instead of the high and glorious enjoyments that heretofore he was the subject of in heaven, and that even in those gratifications, he should find himself sorely disappointed. And so his gratifications should, from time to time, in all that he obtained as long as he lived, turn to his grief and vexation, agreeable to the use of a parallel phrase, Prov. 20:17, "Bread of deceit is sweet to a man, but afterwards his mouth shall be filled with gravel." When a man has eagerly taken into his mouth that which he accounted a sweet morsel, but finds it full of dirt, it moves him immediately to spit it out, and to endeavor to clear his mouth of what he had taken, as eagerly as he took it in. So Satan is, from time to time, made sick of his own morsels, and to spit them out again, and vomit up what he had swallowed down, as the whale vomited up Jonah [Jonah 2:10], and as the devil vomited up Christ, when he saw he had swallowed down that which, when within him, gave him a mortal wound at his vitals.

453. GENESIS 4:3–4. CAIN'S AND ABEL'S SACRIFICE. Abel, when he comes before God, is sensible of his own unworthiness and sinfulness, as the publican [Luke 18:13], and so is sensible of his need of an atonement, and therefore comes with bloody sacrifices, hereby testifying his faith in the promised great sacrifice. Cain comes with his own righteousness, like the Pharisee who put God in mind that he paid tithes of all that he possessed [Luke 18:12]. He comes without any propitiation, with the fruit of his ground, and produce of his own labors, as though he could add something to the Most High by gifts of his own substance. And therefore he was interested in no atonement, for he was not sensible of his need of any, nor did he trust in any. And so, being a sinner, and not having perfectly kept God's commands, sin lay at his door unremoved; and so his offering could not be accepted, for guilt remained to hinder. This reason God intimates, why his offering was not accepted, in what he says to him, v. 7. "If thou dost well, if thou keepest my commandments, you and your offerings shall be accepted. But seeing thou dost not well, as thy own conscience witnesses, that in many things thou hast offended, the guilt of sin remains to hinder thy being accepted. Without an atonement, your

righteousness can't be accepted, whatever offerings you bring to me."
See Bishop Sherlock's *Use and Intent of Prophecy*, pp. 74–75; and Owen
on Hebrews 11:4, p. 18.[7]

454. GENESIS 7. CONCERNING THE FLOOD. Add this to No. 429. "As to
the history of Berosus [who wrote the history of the Chaldeans],[8] the
substance of it, as it is given us from Abidenus, Apollodorus, and
Alexander Polyhister, is to this purpose, that there were ten kings
of Chaldea before the flood: Alorus, Alasparus, Amelon, Amenon,
Metalarus, Daorus, Aedorachus, Amphis, Oliartes, Xisuthrus. That
Xisuthrus was warned in a dream that mankind was to be destroyed by
a flood upon the 15th day of the month Daesius, and that he should
build a sort of ship, and go into it with his friends and kindred, and that
he should make provision of meat and drink, and take into his vessel
fowls and four-footed beasts. That Xisuthrus acted according to the
admonition, built a ship, and put into it all that he was commanded,
and went into it with his wife, and children, and dearest friends. When
the flood was come, and began to abate, Xisuthrus let out some birds,
which finding no food nor place to rest on, returned to the ship again.
After some days, he let out the birds again, but they came back with
their legs daubed with mud. Some days after, he let them go the third
time, but then they came to the ship no more. Xisuthrus understood
hereby that the earth appeared again above the waters; and taking
down some of the boards of the ship, he saw that it rested on a mountain. Sometime after, he, and his wife, and his pilot went out of the ship
to offer sacrifice to the gods, and they were never seen by those in the
ship more. But the persons in the ship, after seeking him in vain, went

7. These references are later additions. Thomas Sherlock writes, "*Abel* came a Petitioner
for Grace and Pardon, and brought the *Atonement* appointed for Sin; Cain appears before
God as a *just Person wanting no Repentance*, he brings an *Offering* in Acknowledgment of God's
Goodness and Bounty, but no *Atonement* in Acknowledgment of his own Wretchedness." *The
Use and Intent of Prophecy, in the Several Ages of the World. In Six Discourses Delivered at the Temple-
Church in April and May 1724* (3rd ed., London, 1732), pp. 74–75. John Owen's discussion of
Heb. 11:4 distinguishes between Abel's "justifying" faith and Cain's "common and tempor-
ary" faith. From that distinction he derives the warning for "all ages, that the Performance of
the outward Duties of Divine Worship is not the Rule of the Acceptance of Men's Persons
with God." On the contrary, the "inward Principle" from which those duties proceed accounts for the fact that they are "accepted in some, and rejected in others." *A Continuation of
the Exposition of the Epistle of Paul the Apostle to the Hebrews: (viz) On the Eleventh, Twelfth &
Thirteenth Chapters, Compleating that Elaborate Work* (London, 1684), p. 18. It is impossible to
determine the precise location JE intended by his added reference, the "place marked in the
margin" on p. 18.
8. JE's brackets.

to Babylon. Berosus supposes from Alorus to Xisuthrus ten generations, and so many Moses computes from Adam to Noah." Shuckford's *Connection*, Vol. 1, pp. 15–16.[9]

455. GENESIS 8:4. CONCERNING THE MOUNTAIN ON WHICH THE ARK
RESTED, AND FOHI, OF CHINESE, HIS BEING THE SAME WITH NOAH. See
No. 259.[1] "The common opinion is that the ark rested on one of the
Gordyaean hills, which separate Armenia from Mesopotamia; but
there are some reasons for receding from this opinion. 1. The jour-
neying of mankind from the place where the ark rested to Shinar, is
said to be from the east, but a journey from the Gordyaean hills to
Shinar would be from the north. 2. Noah is not once mentioned in all
the following part of Moses' history," an argument that he remained in
a place far different from those of his posterity, that came to Shinar
and thence dispersed abroad, which the history is taken up about.

Some authors, for these reasons, have supposed Mount Ararat to
be one of the mountains north of India. This is favored by old
heathen testimonies. "Two hundred and fifty years before Ninus
(says Portius Cato), the earth was overflowed with waters, and mankind began again in Saga Scythia." Now Saga Scythia is in the same
latitude with Bactria, between the Caspian Sea and Imaus, north to
Mount Paraponisus. And this agrees with the general notion, that
the Scythians might contend for primaevity of original with the
most ancient nations of the world. The original Scythians were
situate near Bactria. Herodotus places them as far east as Persia,
and says that the Persians called them Sacae, and supposes them
and the Bactrians to be near neighbors. 3. The notion of Noah's
settling in these parts, and not coming at all to Shinar, is agreeable
to the Chaldean traditions about the deluge, which inform us that
Xisuthrus (for so they called Noah) came out of the ark with his
wife, and daughter, and the pilot of the ark, and offered sacrifice to
God, and then both he and they disappeared, and never were seen
more. And that afterwards Xisuthurus's sons journeyed towards
Babylonia, and built Babylon and several other cities. 4. The language, learning, and history of the Chinese do all favor this ac-

9. Samuel Shuckford, *The Sacred and Prophane History of the World Connected, From the
Creation of the World to the Dissolution of the Assyrian Empire at the Death of Sardanapalus, and to the
Declension of the Kingdoms of Judah and Israel, under the Reigns of Ahaz and Pekah* (2nd ed., 4 vols.
London, 1731), *1*, 15–16.
1. MS: "⟨See No. ~~119~~ 259 B 1⟩."

count. Their language seems not to have been altered in the confusion of Babel. Their learning is reported to have been full as ancient as the learning of the more western nations. Their polity is of another sort, and their government established on very different maxims and foundations. And their history reaches up indisputably to the times of Noah, not falling short, like the histories of other nations, such a number of years as ought to be allowed, for their inhabitants removing from Shinar to their place of settlement. The first king of China was Fohi; and as I have before observed, that Fohi and Noah were contemporaries, at least, so there are many reasons from the Chinese traditions concerning Fohi to think him and Noah the same person. (1) They say Fohi had no father, i.e. Noah was the first man in the post-diluvian world. His ancestors perished in the flood; and no tradition hereof being preserved in the Chinese annals, Noah, or Fohi, stands there as if he had no father at all. (2) Fohi's mother is said to have conceived him encompassed with a rainbow, a conceit very probably arising from the rainbow's first appearing to Noah, and the Chinese being willing to give some account of his original. (3) Fohi is said carefully to have bred seven sorts of creatures, which he used to sacrifice to the supreme spirit of heaven and earth; and Moses tells us, that Noah took into the ark, of every clean beast by sevens, and of fowls of the air by sevens. And after the flood Noah built an altar unto the Lord, and took of every clean beast and every clean fowl, and offered burnt offerings.[2] (Lastly) The Chinese history supposes Fohi to have settled in the province of Xeusi, which is the northwest province of China, and near to Ararat where the ark rested. And the history of the world does necessarily suppose that these eastern parts of the world were soon peopled, and as populous as the land of Shinar. For in a few ages, in the days of Ninus and Semiramis, about three hundred years after the dispersion of mankind, the nations that came of that dispersion attacked the inhabitants of the East with their united force, but found the nations about Bactria, and the parts where we suppose Noah to settle, fully able to resist and repel all their armies. Noah therefore came out of the ark near Saga Scythia, on the hills beyond Bactria, north to India. Here he lived, and settled a numerous part of his posterity, by his counsels and advice. He himself planted a vineyard, lived a life of retire-

---

2. JE deleted "(4) The Chinese derived the name of Fohi."

ment, and having seen his offspring spread around him, died in a good old age. As they spread down to India south, and further east into China, so 'tis probable they also peopled Scythia, and afterwards the more northern continent; and if America be anywhere joined to it, perhaps all that part of the world came from these originals.

Shuckford's *Connection,* Vol. 1, pp. 98–104.[3]

456. GENESIS 3:14–15. "And the Lord said unto the serpent," etc. In this first prophecy that ever was uttered, we have a very plain instance of what is common in divine prophecies through the Scripture, viz. that one thing is more immediately respected in the words, and another that is the antitype principally intended, and so of some of the words being applicable only to the former, and others only to the latter, and of God's beginning to speak in language accommodated to the former, but then as it were presently forgetting the type, and being taken up wholly about the antitype. Here in the words in the 14th verse, the words that are choosed are properly applicable only to that serpent that was one of the beasts of the field, for here it is said, "Thou art cursed above all cattle," which shows that this prophecy has some respect to that beast that is a type of Satan. But, in the things spoken in the next verse, the beast called a serpent seems to be almost wholly forgotten, and the speech to be only about the devil; for the "enmity" that is there spoken of is between the seed of the woman and the serpent, and not the seed of the man and that "seed," a particular person, for the words in the original are, "He shall bruise thy head, and thou shalt bruise his heel." It is *Hu* in the Hebrew, and *autos* in the Septuagint, as is observed in Shuckford, Vol. 1, p. 286.[4] See also what Bedford says of this, in note in "Blank Bible."[5]

---

3. Shuckford, *Sacred and Prophane History* (2nd ed.), *1*, 98–104.

4. Shuckford writes, "If by the *Seed of the Woman,* had been meant the Descendants of *Eve,* in the Plural Number, it should have been, *they shall bruise thy Head, and thou shalt bruise their Heels.* The Septuagint took particular Care in their Translation to preserve the true Meaning of it, by not using a Pronoun that might refer to the Word *Seed,* but a Personal Pronoun, which best answers the *Hebrew* Word הוא, or *He* in *English*" (*Sacred and Prophane History* [2nd ed.), *1*, 286.

5. On the basis of his reading of Bedford's *Scripture Chronology,* JE notes that in Gen. 3:15, "the pronoun 'he,' the verb 'bruise,' and the affix 'his,' are all of the singular number, . . . which shows that by 'seed' is meant a particular person, and not her posterity in general" ("Blank Bible").

457. EXODUS 3:14. "And God said unto Moses, I AM THAT I AM. And he said, Thus shalt thou say to the children of Israel, I AM hath sent me unto you." See No. 412. "We are informed that there was an ancient inscription in the temple at Delphos, over the place where the image of Apollo was erected, consisting of these letters, '*EI*.' And Plutarch introduces his disputants querying, what might be the true signification of it. At length Ammonius, to whom he assigns the whole strength of the argumentation, concludes that the word *EI* was the most perfect title they could give the deity; that it signifies 'THOU ART,' and expresses the divine essential being, importing, that though our being is precarious, fluctuating, dependent, subject to mutation, and temporary, so that it would be improper to say to any of us, in the strict and absolute sense, 'Thou art,' yet we may with great propriety give the deity this appellation, because God is independent, uncreated, immutable, eternal, always and everywhere the same; and therefore he only can be said absolutely 'to be.' Plutarch would have called this Being, τὸ ὄντως ὄν; Plato would have named him, τὸ ὄν, which he would have explained to signify ὠσία, implying him to BE essentially or self-existent." Shuckford's *Connection*, Vol. 2, pp. 385–86.[6]

458. CANTICLES 1:5. "As the tents of Kedar, as the curtains of Solomon." That the spouse in this song is compared to a tent, and to the curtains of the tabernacle and temple, is an evidence that this song is no ordinary love song, and that by the spouse is not meant any particular woman, but a society, even that holy society, the church of God. 'Tis common in the writings of the Old Testament to represent[7] the church of God by a tent or tents, and an house and temple, but never a particular person. See Is. 54:2, Zech. 12:7, Is. 33:20, Lam. 2:4, 6, Is. 1:8. And the tabernacle and temple were known types of the church, and the curtains of both had palm trees embroidered on them, which are abundantly made use of to represent the church. The church of God is called an "house" in places too many to be mentioned. The church used to be called "the temple of the Lord," as appears by Jer. 7:4. The church is represented by the temple, as is evident by Zech. 4:2–9.

459. ROMANS 8:28. "And we know that all things work together for good to them that love God, to them who are the called according to his

---

6. Shuckford, *Sacred and Prophane History* (2nd ed.), 2, 385–86.
7. JE deleted "a people by a tent."

purpose." 'Tis a matter of some difficulty to understand[8] exactly how this is to be taken, and how far the temptations the saints meet with from Satan and an evil world, and their own declensions and sins, shall surely work for their good. In order therefore rightly to state this matter, there are these two things may be undoubtedly laid down[9] in the first place.

1. The meaning cannot be that God's dispensations and disposals towards them are the best for them, most for their happiness, of all that are[1] possible,[2] or that all things that [are] ordered for them, or done by God with respect to them, are in all respects better than anything else that could have been ordered for them, or the very best that God could have done for them, tending to and issuing in the highest good or happiness that it is possible they should be brought to; for that would be as much as to say, that God will bestow on every one of his elect as much happiness as he can in the utmost exercise of his omnipotence, and this sets aside all those different degrees of grace and holiness here, and glory hereafter, which he bestows according to his sovereign pleasure. If every dispensation of God towards every one of his elect, in ordering all the circumstances under which he is brought into the world, and all the circumstances that attend his state in the world, and all things God in his providence brings to pass concerning him, is better for him than any other possible dispensation, that is as much as to say that God will make everyone as happy as he can. All things may tend to and issue in some good to every saint, but not the utmost degree of good possible. The text and context speaks of God's eternal purpose of good to the elect, predestinating them to a conformity to the image of his Son in holiness and happiness. And as the elect are from eternity predestinated to holiness and happiness, so there is a certain measure of holiness and happiness that each one is eternally appointed to; and all things work together to bring to pass this appointed measure of good. The reasoning implied in the words of the Apostle leads us to suppose that all things will surely concur, to bring to effect God's eternal purpose. And therefore from his reasoning it may be inferred that all things will tend to, and work together to bring to pass that degree of good that God has purposed for them, and

8. MS: "~~determine~~ ⟨understand⟩."
9. JE deleted "as evident and certain truth."
1. The preceding ten words are a later interlineation.
2. JE deleted "i.e. or tending to and issuing in the greatest ~~p~~ degree of good, or highest degree of happiness, of all that is possible they should be brought to."

not any more. And indeed, it would be in itself unreasonable to suppose anything else but this, inasmuch as God is the Supreme Orderer of all things. Doubtless all things shall work together to bring to pass his aims, ends, and purposes; but surely they do not concur to bring to pass what he does not aim at and never intended. God, in his government of the world, is carrying on his own designs in everything, but he is not carrying on that which is not his design. And therefore there is no need of supposing that all the circumstances, means, and advantages of every saint are the best in every respect that God could have ordered for him, or that there are no circumstances possible that could have tended to an higher [degree] of happiness, and that there could have been no means that the saint could have been the subject of that would, with God's usual blessing on means, have issued in his greater good. Every saint is as it were a living stone that, in this present state of preparation, is fitting for the place appointed for him in the heavenly temple. And in this sense all things undoubtedly "work together for good to everyone that loves God, and is called according to his purpose." He is, all the while he lives in this world, by all the dispensations of God's providence towards him, a-fitting for the particular mansion in glory that is appointed and prepared for him, and a-hewing for his appointed place in the heavenly building.[3] And so God is always carrying on a design of love to him, carrying on one way or other the good work he has begun in his heart, and all things cooperate thereunto. All their trials and all the temptations of their enemies, though they may be an occasion for the present of great spiritual wounds, backslidings, and declensions, yet at last they shall be an occasion of their being more fitted for their place in glory by an increase of self-emptiness, experience, trust in God, and solidity and ripeness of grace. And therefore we may determine, that however the true saint may die in some respects under decays, under a decay of comfort and of the exercise of some religious affections, that yet undoubtedly every Christian dies at that time when his habitual fitness for his place in the heavenly temple is most complete, because otherwise all things that happen to him while he lives would not work together to fit him for that place.

2. Another thing no less certain and demonstrable than the position that has already been laid down, and indeed follows from it,[4] is this. When it is said, "All things work together for good," etc., thereby

3. JE marked the remainder of this paragraph with a large "X."
4. The last five words are a later interlineation.

cannot be intended all things both negative and positive, or that it is so universally that not only everything that is positive that the saints are the subjects of, or are concerned with, will work for their good, or also that when anything is absent or withheld from them by God in his providence, that absence or withholding is also for their good, or is better for them than the presence or bestowment would have been. For this would have the same absurd consequence that was mentioned before, viz. that God makes everyone as happy as possibly he can; and besides, if so, it would follow that God's withholding greater degrees of the sanctifying influences of his Spirit is for the saints' good, and that it is best for them to be so low in grace as they are, which would be as much as to say, that 'tis for their good to have no more good. If we take good notice of the Apostle's discourse in the eighth [chapter] of Romans, it will be apparent that his words by no means imply or intend so much. The context leads us to understand that God is for the saints, and works for them, each person of the Godhead: God the Father, who "spared not his own Son" (v. 32), and justifies the saints (v. 33), and is the Father of the saints (v. 14 ff.); and God the Son, who died for them, and rose again, and ascended to the right hand of God for them, and makes continual intercession for them (v. 34); and God the Holy Ghost, who bears witness with their spirits, that they are the children of God, and helps their infirmities, and leads and conducts them, etc. (vv. 14–16, 23, 26–27). And all God's creatures, the whole creation groaning and travailing in pain, waiting "for the manifestation of the sons of God" (vv. 19–22), and even their persecuting enemies (vv. 33–37), and not only things in this world, but also in the world to come, not only all mankind, but angels and devils (v. 38), and all dispensations of providence,[5] not only in bestowing prosperity, but in bringing adversity and chastisements (vv. 35–37), not only in giving life, but bringing death (v. 38)—all things shall befriend the saints and work for their good.[6] But there is nothing in all the context that leads us to suppose that all dispensations of providence that are merely negative, and their negative consequences in withholding grace, or withholding means and advantages, so that no possible advantages could have been greater, or tending to higher degrees of holiness and happiness [also do good].

5. MS: "(v. 38) & all Positive & dispensations of Providence ⟨all & those that are privative that causing proper Effects & real Changes and whatsoever may properly said to be an Event or a Thing real Event all positiv all positive consequences of privative & negative Causes⟩ bringing not only Po best."
6. MS: "Good ⟨or proper Effects⟩."

This would be to say, as was observed before, that God makes every saint as happy as he can. All that God does is for the good of the saint, but it will not thence follow that all his forbearing to do is also for his good, or that it is for his good that God does no more for him.

+ From these two positions[7] it will follow that not all that is truly called the sin of the saints works for their good, in such a manner as that in the issue it shall prove best for them that they have had sin, in that respect, rather than the contrary virtue or duty. For instance, their sinful defects, that they have so much failed of having and exercising a due love to God, that they been no more suitably humble, heavenly, etc., all the defects of the saints, whereby they fall short of perfect holiness in every particular, is sin. 'Tis sin in them that they love God and Christ no more, are no more thankful, etc. But to be thus sinful and deficient, in general, cannot be for their good; for if so, then it will follow, that 'tis for the saints' good and happiness to have no more grace here, and no more happiness hereafter, which is very absurd. It can't therefore be truly affirmed of the saints, that it is best for them[8] that they have so much sin and corruption, and of the exercises of it in general, and so little grace and of the exercises of that, for in proportion, as grace and its exercises are small, will corruption and its exercises be great, as certainly as that darkness will be in proportion to the want of light. The sins of the saints and their exercises of corruption, in particular instances, may through God's sovereign grace[9] be so for their good, that it may be better for them that they have been, than if instead of them the contrary exercises of grace had been at that time and under those circumstances, but this can't be affirmed of their being, in general, so defective and sinful in heart and practice. But then here one thing must be borne in mind, viz. that a thing may be for the good of the saints, that is, there may be some real benefit that may be the issue, and yet that thing may not be for the best, or better for them than anything else could have been. So all the exercises of corruption and acts of sin that are found in the saints may all be for the good of the saints; there may be some real benefit may accrue to them in the issue, and so it may be better for them than if the occasion and temptation never had been, and yet it may not be so well for them as if, on that occasion, instead of the exercise of corruption, there had

7. MS: "~~Hence~~ ⟨From these two Positions⟩."
8. MS: "~~for their Good~~ ⟨best for Them⟩."
9. The last eight words are a later interlineation. In addition to the specific changes noted, this entry reflects extensive reworking by JE.

[been] the contrary exercise of grace, or as if when the temptation arose, instead of yielding to it and committing the sinful act, they had resisted it and overcome it. The former may be ever true, but the latter cannot be so at all times; for if so, it will follow that it is better for the saints that they have so little of holiness and its exercises in general, and consequently so little glory hereafter, which was before observed to be absurd.[1] And in one sense their sin in general may be said to be for their good, viz. that it shall be better for them in the issue than if they never had had any sin, better than if man had never fallen, but not in that sense that it is better for them that their recovery and rectification of the corruption of nature is no greater.[2] Everyone's reward hereafter shall be according to his works. And therefore that saint that in the general course of his life don't do so well as another, whose works are not so good, or whose good works are not so many, shall hereafter not have so great a reward; and consequently it is not best for him that he did not do more good works. And he that in general does much ill, it is finally a loss to him; it is to his damage in the last day, when all things shall be as it were tried by fire, that he did [not] do well, where he did ill, though he himself be saved, as is apparent by I Cor. 3:12–15.

Another thing[3] may be noted, which is, that if the saying of the Apostle, Rom. 8:28, "All things shall work together for good to them that love God," holds true in this sense, that[4] while a man continues in the love of God, that love of God will be an occasion of everything's turning to his good all trials and opposition, this excellent and divine principle is of so wholesome and salutary a nature that it sucks sweetness and happiness out of everything, even those things that in their direct tendency are most against the saints.

The two foregoing positions being laid down, the things from thence inferred to be the truth, as they are more distinctly laid down in my letter to Mr. Gillespie,[5] are as follows. So that what is written above from this mark + may be omitted, the same things being here more distinctly expressed.[6]

1. JE deleted "The consequence of the sinful act may be good, in yielding to the temptation may be good, but yet if the."
2. JE deleted "'Tis manifest that if 'Tis apparent."
3. JE deleted "I suppose."
4. JE deleted "all things work together for the best."
5. The balance of this entry parallels JE's letter to Thomas Gillespie, 4 Sept. 1747, as printed in Dwight ed., *1*, 237–41.
6. This sentence is a later interlineation.

1. That all things whatsoever are for the good of the saints, things negative as well as positive, in that sense that God intends that some benefit to them shall arise from everything, so that something of the love and grace of God will hereafter be seen to have been exercised towards them in everything, although at the same time the sovereignty of God will also be to be seen with regard to the measure of the good or benefit aimed at, in that some other things, if God had seen cause to order them, would have produced an higher benefit. And with regard to negative disposals, consisting not in God's doing, but forbearing to do, not in giving, but withholding, some benefit, in some respect or other, will ever accrue to the saints even from these, though sometimes the benefit will not be equal to the benefit withheld, if it had been bestowed. As for instance, when a saint lives and dies comparatively low in grace, there is some good improvement shall be made, even of this, in the eternal state of the saint whereby he shall receive a real benefit, though the benefit shall not be equal to the benefit of an higher degree of holiness, if God had bestowed it.

2. God carries on a design of love to his people, and to each individual saint, not only in all things which they are the subjects of while they live, but also in all his works and disposals, and all his acts *ad extra*, from eternity to eternity.

3. That the sin in general of the saints is for their good and for the best, in this respect, that it is a thing that through the sovereign grace of God and his infinite wisdom will issue in a high advancement of their eternal happiness, that they have been sinful fallen creatures, and not from the beginning perfectly innocent and holy as the elect angels, and that they shall obtain some additional good on occasion of all the sin they have been the subjects of, or have committed, beyond what they would have had if they never had been fallen creatures.

4. The sin of the saints, in this sense, cannot be for their good, that it should finally be best for them, that while they lived in this world their restoration and recovery from the corruption they became subject to by the Fall was no greater, the mortification of sin and spiritual vivification of their souls carried on to no greater degree, that they remained so sinfully deficient as to love to God, Christian love to men, humility, heavenly-mindedness, etc., and that they were so barren, and did so few good works, and consequently that in general they had so much sin and of the exercises of it, and not more holiness and of the exercises and fruits of that (for in proportion, as one of these is more, the other will be less, as infallibly as darkness is more or less in proportion to the diminution or increase of light). It can't finally be best for the saints

that in general, while they lived, they had so much sin of heart and life, rather than more holiness of heart and life, because the reward of all at last will be according to their works. And he that has sowed sparingly, shall reap sparingly; and he that has sowed bountifully, shall reap also bountifully [II Cor. 9:6]. And he that builds wood, hay, and stubble, shall finally suffer loss, and have a less reward than if he had built gold, silver, and precious stones, though he himself shall be saved [I Cor. 3:12–15]. But notwithstanding this,

5. The sins and falls of the saints may be for their good and for the better, in this respect, that the issue may be better than if the temptation had not happened, and so the occasion not given, either for the sin of yielding to the temptation, or the virtue of overcoming it; and yet not in that respect (with regard to their sins and falls in general), that it should be better for them in the issue, that they have yielded to the temptations offered than if they had overcome. For the fewer victories they obtain over temptation, the fewer their good works, and particularly of that kind of good works to which a distinguished reward is promised, in Rev. 2 and 3, and in many other parts of Scripture. The Word of God represents the work of a Christian in this world as a warfare, and 'tis evident by the Scripture that he that acquits himself as the best soldier in this warfare shall win the greatest prize. Therefore when the saints are brought into backslidings and decays by being overcome by temptations, the issue of their backslidings may be some good to them; they may receive some benefit by occasion of it, beyond what they would have received if the temptation had never happened. And yet their backslidings in general may be a great loss to 'em, in that respect, that they shall have much less reward than if the temptation had been overcome, and they, notwithstanding, had persevered in spiritual vigor and diligence. But yet this don't hinder, but that

6. It may be so ordered by a sovereign and all-wise God, that the saints' falls and backslidings, through their being overcome by temptations in some particular instances, may prove best for them, not only that the issue may be greater good to them than they would have received if the temptation had not happened, but even greater in that instance than if the temptation had been overcome. It may be so ordered that their being overcome by that temptation shall be an occasion of their having greater strength, and in the whole of their obtaining more and greater victories, than if they had not fallen in that instance. But this is nowhere promised, nor can it be so, that in the general it should prove better for them that they are foiled so much,

and do overcome so little, in the course of their lives, and that finally their decay is so great, or their progress so small. From these things it appears,

7. That the saying of the Apostle, "All things work together for good to them that love God," though it be fulfilled in some respect to all saints, and at all times, and in all circumstances, yet is fulfilled more especially and eminently to the saints continuing in the exercise of love to God, not falling from the exercises or failing of the fruits of divine love in times of trial. Then temptations, enemies, and sufferings will be best; such as be will be best for them, working that which is most for their good every way. And they shall be more than conquerors over tribulation, distress, persecution, famine, nakedness, peril, and sword (Rom. 8:35–37).

8. As God is carrying on a design of love to each individual saint in all his works and disposals whatsoever, as was observed before, so the particular design of love to them that he is carrying on is to fit them for and bring them to their appointed place in the heavenly temple, or that individual precise happiness and glory in heaven, that his eternal love designed for them and no other (for God's design of love or of happiness to them is only just what it is, and is not different from itself). And to fulfill this particular design of love, everything that God does, or in any respect disposes, whether it be positive, privative, or negative, contributes, because doubtless everything that God does, or in any respect orders, tends to fulfill his aims and designs. Therefore, undoubtedly,

9. All the while the saint lives in the world, he is fitting for his appointed mansion in glory, and hewing for his place in the heavenly building; and all his temptations, though they may occasion for the present great spiritual wounds, yet at last they shall be an occasion of his being more fitted for his place in glory. And therefore we may determine that however the true saint may die in some respects under decays, under the decay of comfort and of the exercise of some religious affections, yet every saint dies at that time when his habitual fitness for his place in the heavenly temple is most complete, because otherwise all things that happen to him while he lives would not work together to fit him for that place.

10. God brings his saints at the end of their lives to this greatest fitness for their place in heaven, not by diminishing grace in their hearts, but by increasing it, and carrying on the work of grace in their souls. Otherwise, that cannot be true, that where God has begun a

good work, he will perform it, or carry it on to the day of Christ; for if they die with a less degree of grace than they had before, then it ceases to be carried on before the day of Christ comes. If grace is finally diminished, then Satan so far finally obtains the victory. He finally prevails to diminish the fire in the smoking flax, and then how is that promise verified, that God will not quench the smoking flax till he bring forth judgment unto victory [Is. 42:3]? So that it must needs be, that although saints may die under decays in some respects, yet they never die under a real habitual decay of the work of grace in general. If they fall, they shall rise again before they die, and rise higher than before, if not in joys and some other affections, yet in greater degrees of spiritual knowledge, self-emptiness, trust in God, and solidity and ripeness of grace.

From the things that have been observed, we may draw these corollaries.

1. That notwithstanding the truth of that of the Apostle in Rom. 8, the saint may have cause to lament his leanness and barrenness, and that he is guilty of so much sin, not only as that which is to the dishonor of God, but also as that which is like to prove to his own eternal loss and damage.[7]

2. Nothing can be inferred from that promise in Rom. 8:28, tending to set aside or abate the influence of motives to earnest endeavors to avoid all sin, and to increase in holiness, and abound in good works, from a view to an high and eminent degree of glory in the eternal world.

3. We may learn from the things that have been observed, how it may be to the eternal loss and damage of the saints when they yield to and [are] overcome by temptations; and yet Satan and other enemies of the saints, by whom the temptation come, are[8] wholly disappointed in the temptation, and baffled in their design to hurt the saints, in that it— the temptation and the saints' fall by it—may be for their good, and they may receive more good in the issue than if the temptation had not been, and yet less than if the temptation had been overcome.

460. THE BOOK OF SOLOMON'S SONG. No common love song, but a divine song, respecting the union between the Messiah and the church. It is an argument of it that such figures of speech are made use of, from

7. JE deleted "2. No argument can be drawn from that promise (Rom. 8)."
8. MS: "to."

time to time, in this song as are elsewhere used concerning the Messiah and the church. Cant. 1:3, Grace is elsewhere compared to "ointment."[9] That, Cant. 1:3–4, "Draw me," is parallel with Jer. 31:3. There the Lord, speaking to the church of Israel under the name of the virgin of Israel, says, "I have loved thee with an everlasting love; therefore with loving-kindness have I drawn thee." V. 4, "The king hath brought me into his chambers." Elsewhere the saints are represented as dwelling in "the secret place of the Most High" [Ps. 91:1]. Hos. 11:4, "I drew them . . . with the bonds of love." Representing the bridegroom as a shepherd, and [comparing] the spouse's children to kids and lambs, Cant. 1:7–8, is agreeable to frequent representations of the Messiah and the church in the Old Testament. The ornaments of the spouse are here represented as jewels and chains of silver and gold (Cant. 1:10–11, and 4:9); compare these with Ezek. 16:11–13. The excellencies, both of the bridegroom and bride, are compared to spices (Cant. 1:12–14, 4:6, 10, 13–14, 16, and 5:5, 13, and 8:2), and ointment perfumed with spices (Cant. 1:3, and 4:10). The same spices were made use of to represent the spiritual excellencies in the incense and anointing oil in the tabernacle and temple, and also in the oil for the light (Ex. 30:28). Cant. 1:16, "Our bed is green." This is agreeable to figures of speech often used concerning the church.[1] The comfort the spouse enjoyed in her bridegroom is compared to a shadow and the fruit of a tree (Cant. 2:3, 5). Cant. 2:2 is agreeable to Is. 35:1–2, and 55:13, and Hosea 14:5. Agreeable to Prov. 3:18, "She is a tree of life to them that lay hold upon her, and happy is everyone that retaineth her," and Prov. 8:19, "My fruit is better than gold," so the Messiah in the prophecies is often compared to a tree and branch. The comforts the bridegroom and bride have in each other are in this book often compared to wine (Cant. 1:2, 2:5, and 5:1). So wine was made use in the tabernacle and temple service to represent both the comforts the church has in Christ, and also the gracious exercises and good works of the saints offered to God. See also Prov. 9:2, Is. 27:2, Hos. 14:7, Zech. 9:15, and 10:7. The comforts the bridegroom and bride enjoy mutually in each other are in this song compared to wine and milk, agreeable to Is. 55:1, and also to the honey and honeycomb, agreeable to the frequent representations made of spiritual comforts in the Scripture. The spouse here is represented feasting with the bridegroom (Cant. 2:4, and 5:1); so the church of God

9. This sentence is a later interlineation. This entry shows extensive evidence of later reworking by JE.

1. The last two sentences are a later interlineation.

is represented as feasting with him, in the sacrifices and feasts appointed by Moses, and in the prophecies (Is. 25:6, 55:1). God's saints are all spoken of as "the priests of the Lord" (Is. 61:6), but the priests eat the bread of God. What the spouse entertains her lover with is called "fruits" (Cant. 4:16, 7:13, and 8:2), as the good works of the saints abundantly are represented elsewhere as fruit, which the church brings and offers to God. The spouse is here compared to fruitful trees (Cant. 4:13–16, 7:7–8); the saints are compared to the same[2] (Ps. 1:3, and Jer. 17:8, and Is. 27:6, and other places innumerable). The spouse is compared to a flourishing fruitful vine[3] (Cant. 2:13, 7:8); so is the church of God often compared to a vine. The spouse's excellency is compared to "the smell of Lebanon" (Cant. 4:11); so is the excellency of the church.[4] Hos. 14:6–7, "His branches shall spread, and his beauty shall be as the olive tree, *and his smell as Lebanon*. They that dwell under his shadow shall return; they shall revive as the corn, *and grow as the vine. The scent thereof shall be as the wine of Lebanon*." The fruits of the spouse are often compared to pomegranates in this song (Cant. 4:3, 13, 6:7, 8:2); so the spiritual fruits of the church of God are[5] represented by pomegranates in the tabernacle and temple. The spouse is in this song said to be like the palm tree (Cant. 7:7–8); so was the church of Israel, whose representatives were the seventy elders, typified by seventy palm trees (Ex. 15:27). So the temple was everywhere carved with cherubims and palm trees, representing saints and angels (I Kgs. 6:29, 32, 35, 7:36, II Chron. 3:5); so in Ezekiel's temple (Ezek. 40:16). The spouse in this song is compared to a garden and orchard, to a garden of spices, and of aloes in particular (Cant. 4:12–16, and 5:1, and 6:2), which is agreeable to the representations made of the church. Num. 24:5–6, "How goodly are thy tents, O Jacob, and thy tabernacles, O Israel! As the valleys are they spread forth, as the gardens by the river's side, as the trees of lign aloes which the Lord hath planted, as the cedar trees beside the waters." The spouse is compared to a fountain (Cant. 4:12); so is the church (Deut. 33:28,[6] Ps. 68:26). The twelve tribes of Israel are represented by twelve fountains of water (Ex. 15:27). The spouse is called "a fountain of gardens" (Cant. 4:15); so the church of God is represented

---

2. MS: "~~which is agreeable to~~ ⟨The Saints are Compared to the Same⟩."
3. JE deleted "with a pleasant smell."
4. MS: "~~Saints~~ ⟨Church⟩."
5. JE deleted "typified especially by."
6. JE deleted "Israel then shall dwell in safety alone; the fountain of Jacob shall be upon a land of corn."

as a fountain in the midst of "a land of corn and wine" (Deut. 33:28), and a stream amongst all trees of unfading leaves and living fruit [Ezek. 47:12], and as "a watered garden" (Is. 58:11, Jer. 31:12). The spouse is called "a well of living waters" (Cant. 4:15). The blessings granted to the church and by the church are represented by the same thing. Zech. 14:8, "Living waters shall go out of Jersualem." So Ezek. 47:1–12, where we read of waters going out of the temple and city of Jerusalem, that gave life to everything, and flowed in the midst of trees of life. Another thing that is a very great evidence that this song is mystical, and that the spouse signifies not a person, but a society, and the church of God in particular, is that she is compared to a city, and the city of Jerusalem in particular. Cant. 6:4, "Thou art beautiful, O my love, as Tirzah, comely as Jerusalem." And that particular parts of the spouse are compared to buildings, and strong buildings, as towers and walls. Cant. 4:4, "Thy neck is like the tower of David, builded for an armory, whereon they hang a thousand bucklers, all shields of mighty men." Cant. 7:4, "Thy neck is like a tower of ivory; . . . thy nose is the tower of Lebanon which looketh towards Damascus." Cant. 8:10, "I am a wall, and my breasts like towers." We find elsewhere peoples and societies of men represented by buildings, houses, and cities, but never particular persons. And the church of God is a society or people often represented in Scripture by such similitudes, and particularly is often compared to a city with strong towers and bulwarks, and to the city Jerusalem especially, and that on the account of her many fortifications and strong bulwarks.

Again, it greatly confirms that the spouse is a people, and the church of God in particular, that she is compared to an army, an army terrible with banners (Cant. 6:4, 10), and as a "company of two armies" [Cant. 6:13], or the company of Mahanaim.[7] So the church of God, when brought out of Egypt through the wilderness to Canaan, was by God's direction in the form of an army with banners. So the psalms and prophecies often represent the church of God as going forth to battle, fighting under an ensign, and gloriously conquering their enemies, and conquering the nations of the world. And the company of Jacob, that was as it were the church of Israel, with the host of angels that met them and joined them, to assist them against Esau's host, was the company of Mahanaim, or "company of two armies," so called by Jacob on that account (Gen. 32:2).

7. I.e. "two camps." See Gen 32:2.

So it is a great evidence of the same thing, that the spouse is compared to war horses[8] (Cant. 1:9), which it is not in the least likely would ever be a comparison used to represent the beauty of a bride in a common epithalamium, or love song. But this is exactly agreeable to a representation elsewhere made of the church of God. Zech. 10:3, "The Lord of hosts hath visited his flock, the house of Judah, and hath made them as his goodly horse in the battle." V. 5, "And they shall be as mighty men, which tread down their enemies as the mire of the streets in the battle; and they shall fight, because the Lord is with them." V. 7, "And they of Ephraim shall be like mighty men."

These expressions show this song to be mystical. Cant. 1:6, "My mother's children were angry with me," etc. If supposed to be used of the church, they are easily accounted for. They are agreeable to accounts in Scripture history of Cain's enmity against Abel,[9] Esau's against Jacob,[1] and their posterities' enmity against Israel, and [to] the prophecies that represent the future persecutions of the church by false brethren.

Another thing that shows this to be no common love song is that the spouse seeks company in her love to the bridegroom, endeavors to draw other women to join with her in loving him, and rejoices in their communion with her in the love and enjoyment of her beloved. Cant. 1:3–4, "Therefore the VIRGINS love thee. Draw me. WE will run after thee. The king hath brought me into his chambers. WE will be glad and rejoice in thee; WE will remember thy love more than wine. THE UPRIGHT love thee." Cant. 6:1–2, "Whither is thy beloved gone, O thou fairest among women? Whither is thy beloved turned aside, that we may seek him with thee? My beloved is gone down into his garden," etc. Cant. 8:13, "Thou that dwellest in the gardens, the companies hearken to thy voice."

The bridegroom in this song speaks of his willing people (Cant. 6:12),[2] which is agreeable to the language used concerning the people of the Messiah (Ps. 110:3).

461. ECCLESIASTES 1:9. "The thing that hath been is that which shall be, and that which is done is that which shall be done, and there is no new thing under the sun," etc. It appears by the connection of these

8. JE deleted "and chariots."
9. JE deleted "Ishmael's against Isaac."
1. JE deleted "David's brethren against him."
2. This is a puzzling reference. Perhaps JE intended Cant. 5:2.

words with what went before, that the design of the wise man is here to signify that the world, though it be so full of labor, mankind from generation to generation so constantly,[3] laboriously, and unweariedly pursuing after happiness and satisfaction, or some perfect good wherein they may rest, yet they never obtain it, nor make any progress towards it. Particular persons, while they live, though they spend their whole lives in pursuit, do but go round, round, and never obtain that satisfying good they seek after. "The eye is not satisfied with seeing, nor the ear with hearing" (v. 8). And as "one generation passes away, and another comes" (v. 4), the successive generations constantly laboring and pursuing after some good wherein satisfaction and rest may be obtained, not being discouraged by the disappointments of former generations, yet they make no progress. They attain to nothing new beyond their forefathers. They only go round in the same circle, as the sun restlessly repeats the same course that it used to do in former ages; and as the wind and water, after their running and flowing, have got no further than they were formerly, for to the place from whence they came, they constantly return again; and as the sea is no fuller now than it used to be in former ages, though the rivers have all the [while], with constant and indefatigable labor and continual expense of their waters, been striving to fill it up. That which goes round in a circle, let it continue moving never so swiftly and never so long, makes no progress, comes to nothing new.

462. PROVERBS 30:27. "The locusts have no king, yet go they forth all of them by bands." The following is taken from the *Evening-Post* of January 4, 1748. "Extract of a letter from Transylvania, August 23, concerning the locusts that had lately appeared there.

"These dreadful creatures, with which we are afflicted, move in two columns; the first places they invaded were the territories of Bellegisch and Banoize, where they passed the night. The next morning they directed their flight towards Peckska, Maradick, etc., and the day following towards Irriga, where they have eat the leaves, the grass, the cabbages, the melons, and cucumbers to the very roots. Yesterday they were in motion towards Schuliom, bending their flight manifestly towards Zealmo, and the parts thereabouts. They continue in the air, or, if one may use the expression, they march generally two hours and an half at a time. They form a close compact column, about fifteen yards

---

3. JE deleted "and earnestly."

deep, in breadth about four musket shot, and in length near four leagues; they move with such force, or rather precipitation, that the air trembles to such a degree as to shake the leaves upon the trees. They darken the sky in such a manner, that when they passed over us, I could not see my people at twenty foot distance.

"P.S. At this instant we have notice that two swarms more [are] approaching, which, after having settled in the neighborhood of Warosch, have returned back by Nerraden and Jasack, making a prodigious buzz or humming noise, as they passed."[4] The same account is also in the *Boston Gazette* of January 26, 1748.[5]

463. EXODUS 13:21. Concerning the pillar of cloud and fire, or the cloud of glory. This pillar of cloud and fire, and also the cloud of glory on Mt. Sinai, and in the tabernacle and temple, was a type of Christ in the human nature. The cloud was a fit representation of the human nature, being in itself a dark body, a vapor, a weak light thing, easily driven hither and thither by every wind, or the least breath of air, while it continues is a most mutable thing, sometimes bigger and sometimes less, constantly changing its form, puts on a thousand shapes; and it quickly vanishes away, is easily dispersed and brought to nought. A little change in the air destroys it; a little cold condenses it, and causes it to fall and sink into the earth (see II Sam. 14:14). A little increase of heat rarifies it, and causes it wholly to disappear. A cloud is a more fit resemblance of the human nature of Christ, because it is derived from the earth, but yet is an heavenly thing.

The bright, glorious, and inimitable fire or light that was in the midst of the cloud represented the divine nature united to the human. The cloud was as it were a veil to this fire, as Christ's flesh was a veil to the glory of the divinity. When Christ took the human nature upon him, he veiled his glory. The bright and strong light of the glory within, which otherwise would have been too strong for the feeble sight and frail eyes of men, was moderated, and as it were allayed and softened, to make it tolerable for mortals to behold. Thus the glory of God is exhibited in such a manner in our incarnate Savior, so as it were to moderate, soften, and sweeten the rays of divine glory, to give us a greater advantage for free access to God, and the full enjoyment of him. See further, No. 465.[6]

4. *The Boston Evening-Post*, Jan. 4, 1748, p. 4.
5. *The Boston Gazette, or Weekly Journal*, Jan. 26, 1748, p. 1.
6. This cross-reference is a later addition.

464. MATTHEW 16:28. Add this to No. 197. Christ's kingdom comes by various steps and degrees, and so the end of the world is brought to pass in like manner by various steps. One step was the abolishing the Jewish state and their ecclesiastical economy, the peculiarities of which the Apostle calls "the rudiments of the world" [Col. 2:20]. (See No. 197, p. 115.) Again, Christ's kingdom was set up, and the world came to an end in another step or degree, by the conversion of the Roman Empire, and so again at the destruction of Antichrist. In each of these is a degree of the accomplishment of the coming of Christ's kingdom, the resurrection, the judgment of the righteous and the wicked, and the end of the world. See note on Rev. 21–22, "Apocalypse," no. 73a.[7]

465. EXODUS 13:21. Add this to No. 463. Another [thing] signified by God's glorious appearing in a cloud was probably the mysteriousness of the divine essence and subsistence, and of the person of Christ, and of the divine operations. Thus it is said, Ps. 97:2, "Clouds and darkness are round about him; righteousness and judgment are the habitation of his throne." I Kgs. 8:12, "The Lord said that he would dwell in the thick darkness." Ps. 18:11, "He made darkness his secret place; his pavilion round about him were dark waters and thick clouds of the skies." Prov. 30:4, "What is his name, and what is his son's name, if thou canst tell?" Is. 9:6, "His name shall be called Wonderful." Judg. 13:18, "Why askest thou thus after my name, seeing it is secret?" God's nature is unsearchable. 'Tis high as heaven; what can we do? 'Tis deeper than hell; what can we know? His judgments are a great deep which we cannot fathom, and a cloud that we can't see through. "We cannot order our speech by reason of darkness" (Job 37:19). In the cloud of glory there was an excellent luster, but it was veiled with a cloud. There was a darting forth of[8] glorious light and an inimitable brightness. But if any over-curious eye pried into it, [it] would find itself lost in a cloud. God clothes himself with light as with a garment, but yet he makes darkness his pavilion. Thus the blessed and only Potentate dwells "in the light which no man can approach unto, and is he whom no man hath seen, nor can see" (I Tim. 6:16).

466. GENESIS 3:20. "And Adam called his wife's name Eve, because she is the mother of all living." Add this to No. 399. To suppose "the living" here to mean those that are restored to spiritual [life], and shall

---

7. Of the "new heavens and new earth," or New Jerusalem, JE writes, "This great and glorious work wrought, that is the effect of this new and spiritual creating, now appears perfect and complete at the end of the world" (*Works*, 5, 166–67).
8. JE deleted "light, unparalleled brightness."

be saved from death, and have everlasting life, is agreeable to the denomination the Apostle gives true Christians, II Cor. 4:11, οἱ ζῶντες "the living," or "the livers"; and again, II Cor. 5:15.

467. EZEKIEL 29:21. "In that day will I cause the horn of the house of Israel to bud forth, and I will give thee the opening of the mouth in the midst of them." "When the tide is at the highest it will turn, and so it will when it is at the lowest. Nebuchadnezzar was in the zenith of his glory when he had conquered Egypt. That conquest completed his dominion over the then-known world; in a manner, that was the last of the kingdoms he subdued. But within a year after, he run mad, was so seven years; and within a year or two after he recovered his senses, he resigned his life. When he was at the highest, Israel was at the lowest; then were they in the depth of their captivity. What the remains of that people who had taken refuge in Egypt suffered by him (agreeable to Jeremiah's prophecies) when he destroyed Egypt, was the last that this people suffered from him, and completed what he had to do against that nation. Then their interest began a little to revive, and their horn to bud forth. Then began to revive the honor of their princes, which were the horns of the house of Israel, the seat of their glory and power. These began to bud forth when Daniel and his fellows were highly preferred in Babylon. 'The king made Daniel a great man, and gave him many great gifts, and made him ruler over the whole province of Babylon, and chief of the governors over all the wise men of Babylon. And he sat in the gate of the king, and he set Shadrach, Meshach, and Abednego over the affairs of the province of Babylon' (Dan. 2:48–49). These all were 'of the king's seed, and of the princes' [Dan. 1:3]. And it was within a year after the conquest of Egypt that they were thus preferred. And soon after, three of 'em were made famous by the honor God put upon them, in bringing them alive out of the burning fiery furnace, on which occasion they were further promoted in the province of Babylon (Dan. 3:30). This very well might be called the budding forth of the horn of the house of Israel. Besides the great honor done them, their being in such honor and power over the whole province of Babylon, and having such great influence with the king, must needs have great influence for the benefit, protection, and comfort of the nation in general that were then in the power of Nebuchadnezzar, and mostly within that province of Babylon that they had committed to their inspection and care. And some years after, this promise had a further accomplishment in the enlargement

and elevation of Jehoiachin, king of Judah (Jer. 52:31–32). They were both tokens of God's favor to Israel, and happy omens." (See Henry.)[9]

Note the time of Daniel's advancement, according to Mr. Henry, is not agreeable to Prideaux's chronology.[1]

468. DEUTERONOMY 6:13. "Thou shalt fear the Lord thy God, and serve him, AND SWEAR BY HIS NAME."[2] It might have been rendered "swearing in the name," or "into the name," in the original, *Bishmo*.[3] And the thing chiefly intended here by it seems to be the making that public solemn profession of faith in the name of God of being the Lord's, and being devoted to his honor and glory, and that covenanting and vowing to be the Lord's, and serve him, that is very often in Scripture called by the name of swearing. A public profession of religion has respect to two things. It has respect to something present, viz. their belief of faith. This is the profession God's people make of their faith. And it has respect to something future, viz. their future behavior in the promises or vows that are made in a public profession. 'Tis evident the profession that is made in the latter, viz. in the promises and vows of the covenant, is often called "swearing"; but the profession that is made in the former, which relates to the former, is no less solemn. Professors, in the public profession they make of religion, profess what is present with the same solemnity as they promise what is future. They declare what[4] their[5] faith [is] with the same solemnity with which they declare their intentions. Both are declared with an oath, one an assertory oath, and the other a promissory oath; and the whole profession is called swearing in, or into, the name of the Lord.

9. Henry, *Exposition*, *4* (1725), 497–98.

1. Henry discusses the "great difficulty" with the date of Daniel's advancement to power and describes several options for resolving the problem. He prefers that it "be laid early in *Nebuchadnezzar's* reign" rather than late (*Exposition*, *4* [1725], 555). Prideaux summarizes his judgment as follows: "But in the second year of *Nebuchadnezzar's* reign at *Babylon* from his Father's Death (which was but the 4th year after his first taking of *Jerusalem*) *Daniel* had not only admission and freedom of access to the presence of the King, but we find him there interpreting of his dream, and immediately thereon advanced to be chief of the Governours of the wise men, and Ruler over all the Province of *Babylon*" (*Old and New Testament Connected*, Pt. I, Vol. 1 [10th ed.], p. 89).

2. JE used this entry in Pt. II of *An Humble Inquiry into the Rules of the Word of God, Concerning the Qualifications Requisite to a Complete Standing and Full Communion in the Visible Christian Church*, published in the summer of 1749. See *Works*, *12*, 199 ff.

3. בִּשְׁמוֹ.

4. JE deleted "they believe."

5. JE deleted "present belief."

In the former part of it, they swear their faith in the name of the Lord, and swear[6] that they are God's, that their hearts are his and for him. In the latter part, they swear to live to his honor and glory, which is often called his name. And by the whole, they appear by their profession to be God's people, which in Scripture is often expressed by being called by God's name. And so by this swearing, they come into the name of God, as persons, when they make profession of religion by baptism, are said to be baptized into the name of Father, Son, and Holy Ghost.

The former part of this profession of religion, viz. the profession of faith in God, is called saying or swearing, "The Lord liveth." Jer. 5:2, "And though they say, The Lord liveth, surely they swear falsely," have sworn by them that are no gods, i.e. had openly professed idol worship. Jer. 4:2, "And thou shalt swear, The Lord liveth, in truth, in judgment, and in righteousness; and the nations shall bless themselves in him, and in him shall they glory." That this saying, "The Lord liveth," was their profession [of] faith in the true God in the public profession they made of his name, is confirmed by Jer. 44:26. "Behold, I have sworn by my great name, saith the Lord, that my name shall no more be named in the mouth of any man of Judah in all the land of Egypt, saying, The Lord liveth," i.e. they shall never anymore make any profession of the true God and true religion, but shall be wholly given up to heathenism. And Jer. 12:16, "And it shall come to pass, if they will diligently learn the ways of my people, to swear by my name, The Lord liveth, as they taught my people to swear by Baal, then shall they be built in the midst of my people." Here is a promise to the heathen, that if they would forsake their heathenism, and turn to the true God and the true religion, and make an open and good profession of that, they should be received into the visible church of God. Jer. 16:14–15, "Therefore, behold, the days come, saith the Lord, that it shall no more be said, The Lord liveth, that brought up the children of Israel out of the land of Egypt; but, The Lord liveth, that brought up the children of Israel out of the land of the north," i.e. God's people, in their public profession of their faith, shall not so much insist on the redemption out of Egypt, as a much greater redemption that shall hereafter be accomplished. We have the same again, Jer. 23:7–8. Hos. 4:15, "Though thou, Israel, play the harlot, yet let not Judah offend; and come not ye unto Gilgal, neither go ye up to Beth-aven, nor swear, The Lord liveth."

6. JE deleted "devotedness to God."

This has respect to that public profession[7] of the religion which the ten tribes made at Bethel (here called Beth-aven), the place of their public worship before the calf that was set up there, by which they pretended to worship Jehovah. Amos. 8:14. "They that swear by the sin of Samaria, and say, Thy God, O Dan, liveth; and, The manner of Beersheba liveth." They had also places of public worship at Dan (where was one of their calves), and at Beersheba. See Amos 5:5.

These words,[8] "JEHOVAH LIVETH," summarily comprehended that faith which they professed in their public profession of religion. They signified hereby their belief of and dependence upon that all-sufficiency and faithfulness that is implied in the name Jehovah, which will appear by the consideration of the following places. Josh. 3:10, "Hereby ye shall know that the living God is among you." I Sam. 17:26, "Who is this uncircumcised Philistine, that he should defy the armies of the living God?" V. 36, "Seeing he hath defied the armies of the living God." II Kgs. 19:4, "It may be the Lord thy God will hear all the words of Rabshakeh, whom the king of Assyria hath sent to reproach the living God." Also v. 16, and Is. 37:4. Jer. 10:8–10, "The stock is a doctrine of vanities. . . . But the Lord is the true God (Hebrew, 'the God of truth');[9] he is the living God." Dan. 6:26, "He is the living God, and steadfast forever." Ps. 18:46, "The Lord liveth, and blessed be my rock; and let the God of my salvation be exalted." So II Sam. 22:47. Add here No. 477.[1]

The things professed in a public profession of religion are two, faith and obedience. The faith that was professed was called a believing in God, and believing in the name of God (*Beshem*, with the prefix *beth*). Gen. 15:6, "And he believed in the Lord, and he counted it to him for righteousness." Ex. 14:31, "And the people believed the Lord" (in the original, "believed in the Lord").[2] II Kgs. 17:14, "Did not believe in the Lord their God." II Chron. 20:20, "Believe in the Lord your God, so shall ye be established." Ps. 78:22, "They believed not in God." Dan. 6:23, "Because he believed in his God." The other thing professed is a believing obedience. This is called a walking in the name of God (still with the same prefix *beth*). Mic. 4:5, "All people will walk everyone in the name of his god, and we will walk in the name (*Besham*) of the Lord

7. JE deleted "and pretence of the nam."
8. JE deleted "THE LORD OR."
9. אֱלֹהִים אֱמֶת.
1. This cross-reference is a later addition.
2. יַאֲמִינוּ בַּיהוָה.

our God forever and ever." And that solemn professing or swearing, wherein both those were professed by a like idiom of speech, was called a "swearing in the name (*Beshem*) of the Lord."

Agreeable to this way of speaking, in the New Testament, when persons solemnly profess the name of God the Father, Son, and Holy Ghost, and are devoted to them in their baptism, they are said to be baptized in the name of the Father, and the Son, and the Holy Ghost.

Making a public profession of religion, or of faith in God, is often called "making mention" (*Zakar*)[3] of the Lord, or of the name of the Lord; and this in the original commonly is "making mention *in* the Lord," or "*in* the name of the Lord," with the prefix *beth*, as they are said to swear "*in* the name of the Lord." Thus Amos 6:10, "Hold thy tongue, for we may not make mention of the name of the Lord" (in the original, *Beshem*, "in the name"); i.e. we may not make profession of our God, being under the dominion of the heathen. Ps. 20:7, "Some trust in chariots, and some in horses; but we will remember the name of the Lord our God." In the original, "we will remember," or "make mention" (for the word is the same as before), "*in* the name of the Lord our God," with the prefix *beth*; i.e. we will openly profess and declare our faith, and trust in the Lord, etc. Is. 26:13, "O Lord, other lords besides thee have had dominion over us, but by thee (*Beka*, 'in thee') only will we make mention of thy name," i.e. we will forsake all other lords, and renounce our profession of idolatry, and profess and worship thee alone. They that professed the worship of false gods are said "to make mention *in* their name." Hos. 2:17, "I will take away the names of Baalim out of her mouth, and they shall no more be remembered (or mentioned, for still the word is the same) by their name," *Bishmam*,[4] "in their name"; i.e. their name and worship shall no more be professed. So Josh. 23:7, "Neither make mention of the name (in the original, 'IN the name') of their gods, nor swear by them." This abundantly confirms that swearing by or in a god signifies what was done in the public profession of his name and worship, which is signified by making mention in his name. This also very evidently appears in Is. 48:1–2. "Hear ye this, O house of Jacob, which are called by the name of Israel, and are come forth out of the waters of Judah, which SWEAR BY THE NAME (*Beshem*, 'in the name') of the Lord, and MAKE MENTION of the God (*Belohei*,[5] 'in the God') of Israel, but not in truth

3. זָכַר.
4. בִּשְׁמָם.
5. בְּשֵׁם and בֵּאלֹהֵי.

and in righteousness, for they call themselves of the holy city." By their profession they were visible of the church of God, were called by the name of Israel, and called themselves of the church.

That profession which in the law of Moses and many other places is called swearing "by the name" or "IN the name" of the Lord, with the prefix ב, is evidently the same with swearing "to" the Lord, with the prefix ל, spoken of, Is. 19:18. "In that day shall five cities in the land of Egypt speak the language of Canaan, and swear TO THE LORD OF HOSTS" (*Laihovah*).[6] In I Kgs. 18:32, 'tis said that Elijah "built an altar in the name of the Lord," *Beshem*, that is, "to the name of the Lord." Here the prefix *beth* is evidently of the same force with *lamed* in I Kings 8:44, "The house that I have built for thy name," or "to thy name." Here *Leshem* is plainly of the same signification, in speaking of building of a house to God, as with *Beshem* in the other place, that speaks of building an altar to God.

"In" and "to," or the prefixes *beth* and *lamed*, are manifestly used as of the same signification in the case of swearing to a god, or an object of religious worship, in the same sentence in Zeph. 1:5, "That swear by the Lord, and that swear by Malcham." The words are thus: "That swear *to* the Lord (*Laihovah*), and that swear *in* Malcham (*Bemalcam*)." In Gen. 23:8, "Entreat for me *to* Ephron, the son of Zohar." "To Ephron," in the original, is *Bengnephron*,[7] with the prefix *beth*.

What is meant by men's swearing "to the Lord" (*Laihovah*), we learn by II Chron. 15:12–14, with the context, viz. publicly and solemnly acknowledging God, and devoting themselves to God by covenant. "And they entered into a covenant to seek the Lord God of their fathers with all their heart and with all their soul. . . . And they sware unto the Lord with a loud voice." See Deut. 29:10–15. We also may learn what is meant by swearing to the Lord, by Is. 45:23–24, "Unto me every knee shall bow, and every tongue shall swear. Surely, shall one say, in the Lord have I righteousness and strength"; together with the Apostle's citation and explication of this place, which instead of the word "swear" uses "confess," in Rom. 14:11, and Phil. 2:10, which, in the Apostle's language, signifies the same as making open and solemn profession of Christianity. Rom. 10:9–10, "If thou shalt confess with thy mouth the Lord Jesus, and shalt believe with thine heart that God hath raised him from the dead, thou shalt be saved. For with the heart

6. לַיהֹוָה.
7. בְּעֶפְרוֹן.

man believeth unto righteousness, and with the mouth confession is made unto salvation." In that place, in the 45th of Isaiah, v. 24, 'tis said, "Surely shall one say, in the Lord have I righteousness and strength." This is the profession of their faith in Christ, and is the same with what is called "MAKING MENTION" of God's righteousness. Ps. 71:16, "I will go in the strength of the Lord God; I will make mention of thy righteousness, even of thine only." The phrase, "MAKE MENTION," as was observed before, is used for making a public profession. And here in this place in Isaiah, glorying in God and blessing themselves in him (or in his righteousness and strength), are joined with swearing to him, as they are in Jer. 4:2. "And thou shalt swear, The Lord liveth, in truth, in judgment, and in righteousness; and the nations shall bless themselves in him, and in him shall they glory." And Ps. 63:11, "The king shall rejoice in God; everyone that sweareth by him shall glory."

The prefix *beth* is put for "into" as well as "in." See innumerable instances of this in places directed to in the concordance under the words "enter," "put," "brought."[8] Judg. 9:26, "Went over to Shechem," in the Hebrew, *Beshechem*.[9]

To choose other gods is, in Judg. 10:14, expressed by "choosing in them," with a prefix "*beth.*" Agreeable to the manner of speaking among the Hebrews, confessing Christ before men, Matt. 10:32, in the original is "confessing in him." "He that shall confess in me (ὁμολογήσει ἐν ἐμοί), before [men], I will confess in him, before my Father, and before his angels."

Judg. 18:5, "Ask counsel now of God," *Bhelohim*,[1] with the prefix "*beth.*"[2]

469. GENESIS 2:9 and 3:22–24. On the TREE OF LIFE. Add this to No. 397, at the cross-reference. There is not the least probability that every fruit tree in the Garden of Eden was then loaden with ripe fruit all at one time. If so, there would have been no provision made for Adam's subsistence through the year, according to those laws which God had established concerning the trees when he created them. For according to those laws, the same fruit was not to be perpetually hanging; but

---

8. See Alexander Cruden, *A Complete Concordance to the Holy Scriptures of the Old and New Testament* (London, 1738), entries under "enter," "put," and "brought" (np).

9. This paragraph is a later addition.

1. בֵאלֹהִים.

2. The last two paragraphs, written originally on MS pages following No. 419, are a later addition.

when the fruit was ripe, the fruit was to be shed, otherwise the seed would not be shed upon the earth in order to a new production, according to Gen. 1:11–12. "And God said, Let the earth bring forth grass, the herb yielding seed after his kind, and the tree yielding fruit after his kind, whose seed is in itself upon the earth; and it was so," etc. 'Tis much more probable that it was with the trees of paradise as is represented of the trees that grew on the banks of Ezekiel's river of living waters [ch. 47]. 'Tis represented as though there were all sorts of fruit trees, and some yielding their fruit one month, and another another, so that there were ripe fruits newly produced every month of the year, and so a perpetual summer, and also a perpetual spring. Some trees were hung with ripe fruits, and others in the blossom in each month in the year. St. John's vision, Rev. 22, may be so understood, that each single tree bore "twelve manner of fruits" [v. 2] on different branches (and yet perhaps there is no necessity of so understanding it), and so one sort bore ripe fruit in one month, and another in another, so that the same tree was always in the blossom in some part, while some other part was loaden with ripe fruit. But in Ezekiel's vision, the variety of fruits seems to be on different trees, because it is said, there "shall grow *all* trees for meat" [Ezek. 47:12].

470. REVELATION 22:11. "He that is unjust, let him be unjust still," etc. That the thing which [is] intended by these words was, that now the revelation of the mind and will of God was finished, the great standing rule of faith and practice sealed, and that no[3] further means of grace were to be expected, no additions to the Word of God, no other revelations should be given, till his last coming; and that therefore they that would not well improve these means and this revelation, and were not made righteous and holy thereby, should continue in a state of sin forever—God would never provide any further means than this Word, these holy Scriptures, which were now completed and sealed: I say, that this is Christ's meaning is much confirmed by the words of the same glorious person with which is ended and sealed the visions of Daniel. Dan. 12:9–10, "Go thy way, Daniel, for the words are closed up and sealed till the time of the end. Many shall be purified, and made white, and tried; but the wicked shall do wickedly. And none of the wicked shall understand, but the wise shall understand." Daniel desired a further revelation to [be] given to him concerning those mat-

---

3. JE deleted "other revelations were to be expected til."

ters that had been represented to him, as in the preceding verses. But Christ here signifies to him that the vision and revelation, that was to be given concerning these matters unto the church of Israel, was now finished, completed, and sealed, and all the rest that he curiously desired to pry into was concealed, and should be so to the time of the end, and moreover signifies that this revelation of them, that already [had] been given, was sufficient for the ends that God designed it for, to give wisdom, and be a means of the sanctification of his own people. But as for the rest, they will not understand, nor will be reclaimed from their wickedness. If they would not make a good improvement of the revelation that is now given, neither would they if a further revelation should be given. Therefore they that will not be made wise and holy by what is revealed, shall have no further revelation; they shall have no further means to make 'em wise, or bring 'em to repentance. They that are wise and holy shall increase in wisdom, and be built up in holiness by this revelation; but they that are unwise, let 'em continue without understanding. They that are unholy and unrighteous, let 'em continue still to do wickedly.

471. EXODUS 12:2. "This month shall be unto you the beginning of months: it shall be the first month of the year unto you." Because in this month God wrought out for them that great typical redemption out of Egypt, representing the redemption by Jesus Christ, and also because he intended at the same time of year actually to complete the spiritual and eternal redemption of his church by the death, resurrection, and ascension of the great Redeemer, 'tis probable that the Israelites, as well as other nations, had till now began the year in autumn, about the autumnal equinox, about which time of year there is reason to think the world was created. But as now God at the time of the redemption changed the day of their sabbath (as Mr. Bedford in his *Scripture Chronology* makes probable),[4] so he changed the beginning of their year from the autumnal equinox, the time when the old creation was wrought, to the spring about the vernal equinox, the time of the new creation. The old creation was wrought in the fall of the year, the time when things are just going to decay, and to a kind of ruin, and winter approaching, that shuts up the whole face of the earth as it were in a state of death, the Orderer of all things probably this signifying, that the old creation was not to continue. The heavens and the earth

4. See *Scripture Chronology*, pp. 297–98.

that then were, should be shaken, and soon begin to decay, as it did by the sin of man. The curse which that brought, which was in effect its ruin, as it were brought all to its chaotic state again, and laid a foundation for its actual total destruction. But the work of redemption was wrought in the spring, signifying that as in the spring, the world as it were revives from a state of death, and all things are renewed, and all nature appears in blooming beauty, and as it were in a state of joy, so by the redemption of Christ a new world should be as it were created; and the spiritual world, the elect creation, should be restored from death, and brought to new, glorious, and happy life.

472. II KINGS 5:19. "And he said unto him, Go in peace."[5] These words don't at all imply that the Prophet approved of the design Naaman had just before declared, of bowing in the house of Rimmon. There indeed seems here to be some difficulty; at first view, it looks as if these words of the Prophet manifested an approbation of what he had expressed. But a particular consideration of the circumstances of the affair may serve wholly to remove the difficulty, and to make it manifest that they implied no such approbation, for 'tis to be considered that the Syrians were now at war with Israel. We have an account but a little before this, I Kgs. 22, of a great battle of the king of Syria, of his thirty-two captains, with both the kings of Israel; and we have no account of any peace made after this. But, on the contrary, it appears by the second and third verses of this chapter, and by what we have an account of in the next chapter, that the war still continued. And Naaman was the chief actor in the war, and had been the chief instrument of the mischief that the Syrians had done Israel, for he was the captain of the host of the king of Syria, or general of his army, and a very valiant, successful general, and he by whom the chief exploits had been done that had been accomplished by the Syrians in war, as is signified in the first verse of this chapter, and was probably, under the king, the chief general that led the Syrians in the battle forementioned, wherein Israel received that great defeat,[6] wherein their king was slain, which seems to be the thing aimed at in the first verse of this

5. JE wrote the following running head across two MS pages: "No. 472. Concerning Elisha's Saying to Naaman, 'Go in peace,' II Kings 5:19."

6. JE interlined the preceding 22 words sometime after he wrote and deleted the following: "probably ~~he it~~ he was doubtless in that battle that we have an account of forementioned wherein the Syrians obtained so and was the main instrument of that victory great victory the Syrians ~~ob~~ then obtained over Israel and the defeat they gave Israel."

chapter, when it is said that "by him the Lord had given deliverance," or "victory" (as it is [in] the margin) "unto Syria." And these things were now fresh in memory, being but two or three years before. So that Naaman must needs know that it would be a remarkable thing if so great and terrible an enemy to Israel[7] as he had been, and one that Israel had suffered so much from, and[8] an enemy that they had now cause to fear above all enemies on earth (the war between the two nations yet continuing), I say, he must be sensible that it would be a remarkable thing if he came into the midst of the land of Israel, and to that great prophet that was as it were the father of that people, and should be suffered to return again to his own country in peace. And there is reason to think that he did not come and go without a trembling fear, lest he should be troubled on this score. It was the manner among the heathen nations at that day, as the Syrians knew, for their augurs, diviners, magicians, and those who had immediate intercourse with their gods, which were their prophets, to interest themselves in affairs of their respective nations, and for the nations to have great dependence upon them in time of war. And they doubtless had heard the great things the prophets of Israel had done for them against their enemies—Moses, Samuel, and others—and how the prophets had assisted the Israelites against their nation, even in that generation. (See I Kgs. 20.) And the Syrians appear apt enough to discern how this very prophet Elisha assisted the king of Israel in war. (See the next chapter.) And doubtless Naaman now looked upon this prophet, who had healed him of his leprosy, as a man of great power, and judged that he could easily destroy him. And though as yet he had received no hurt from his power, but great good, yet he seems to be full of fear and jealousy, as appears by this, that although Elisha had bid him, "Go in peace," thereby signifying that no harm should be done him on the account of the war with Syria, and for his being so great an enemy to Israel, yet when he sees Gehazi coming after him, his fears are excited anew. He was afraid that the Prophet had a reckoning to require of him. And therefore as soon as Naaman sees him, he immediately lighted down from his chariot to meet him; and his first question is, "Is there peace?" (for so it is in the Hebrew,[9] v. 21). The Prophet was sensible what Naaman's fears were, and probably knew that, that he made him the offer of a large present partly for that end, to secure

7. JE deleted "and one that had been the instrument of so true."
8. JE deleted "one that above all others was."
9. הַשָׁלוֹם.

his favor and friendship, that he might not hurt him, and that his fears were increased by his refusing his present. He was afraid that this was a sign that he would not be friends with him, for accepting of presents was looked upon as a token and seal of friendship and peace. And therefore Manoah's wife says, "If the Lord had been pleased to kill us, he would not have accepted an offering at our hands" [Judg. 13:23]. And therefore Jacob urges Esau to accept his present, because he desired a seal of peace and friendship with Esau [Gen. 33:8]. And when, after the Prophet had utterly refused Naaman's present, Naaman professes a design of changing his religion, this probably still is one thing he has in view, thoroughly to reconcile this great prophet to him. The Prophet, fully knowing Naaman's circumstances and apprehensions, 'tis with respect to these things that he says to him, "Go in peace," signifying no more than that he bid him farewell, and that, though he had refused his present, yet he need not fear his troubling him, or taking the opportunity, now he was in the land of Israel, to do him any mischief on account of the war that was between Israel and Syria, or for his having been so terrible and destructive an enemy to his country. Designedly avoiding making any reply at all to those things he had been saying to him, either his request that he would give him "two mules' burthen of earth" [II Kgs. 5:17], that he might offer sacrifices to God, or his design, which he had taken occasion to signify to him, of bowing in the house of Rimmon, he neither answers his request by commanding that any earth should be given him, or giving him leave to take it. He says nothing at all about it; nor does he make any observations on his intimated design, but only takes leave of him, and let him understand that he may go in peace, without fear of any such mischief as he seemed to [be] guarding against. And Naaman seems to understand him. When the Prophet spake of peace, there is reason to think that he understood him to mean what he himself means, when presently after he speaks of peace, saying to Gehazi, "Is there peace?," fearing that the Prophet now intended to molest him as an enemy. And the words themselves, according to the common use of such phrases, did not carry any more in them. Thus when Judah, after the cup had been found in Benjamin's sack, says to Joseph, "Behold, we are my lord's servants, both we, and he also with whom the cup is found," Joseph answers, Gen. 44:17, "God forbid that I should do so. But the man in whose hand the cup is found, he shall be my servant; and as for you, get you up in peace unto your father"; as much as to say, "I have no quarrel with you for your brother's crime, but will dismiss you without doing you any harm." So Gen. 26:28–29. "Let us make a covenant with thee, that thou wilt do us no hurt, as we have not touched thee, and as we have done thee nothing but good, and have sent thee away in peace." And v. 31, "And Isaac sent them away, and they departed in peace." So 'tis noted of Abner, II Sam. 3:21, after he had [been] carrying on a war against David in favor of Ishbosheth, that he came and conversed with David. "And David sent him away, and he went in peace," i.e. David did not do him any hurt for his having acted before as his enemy. So, Josh. 10:20–21, 'tis noted of the people of Israel, that after they [had] been carrying on a successful war against the Amorites, and had slain them with a great slaughter, "the people returned to the camp in peace," and that "none moved his tongue against the children of Israel." Many other places might be mentioned where such phrases are used in the same manner, but I shall now mention but one more. In II Chron. 19:1, we are informed that after Jehoshaphat had been to war with the Syrians to assist Ahab, he "returned to his house in peace." The meaning is only, that he was not slain as Ahab was, and returned without receiving any hurt in the war, not that he returned under the divine smiles, and with his favor and approbation, for he did not so return; but, on the contrary, he in his return met with a severe rebuke from God, and denunciation of his wrath for the business he had been about.

Here perhaps it may be objected, that it is hardly credible that the Prophet should make no reply to what Naaman had said, the occasion so naturally leading him to it, and duty obliging him to manifest his disapprobation of it, if it was sinful.

As to his not replying when the occasion naturally led to it, it may be observed, that the former part of Naaman's speech seemed much more to lead to and require some reply, wherein he desires of the Prophet that he would give him "two mules' burthen of earth." What he there proposes is in the form of a request to Elisha. "Shall there not then, I pray thee, be given unto thy servant two mules' burden of earth?" etc. As to what he says concerning bowing in the house of Rimmon,[1] he therein indeed expresses his intention, but asks no request of the Prophet. He don't ask his leave, or his opinion, or advice,[2] nor does he ask him any question, propose anything to him for his opinion, or as though he expected any reply. But yet it is evident, in

---

1. JE deleted "it came in as it were incidentially."
2. JE deleted "in the matter."

fact, that he makes no reply at all to the former part of his speech, that was evidently proposed to him for that end, that he might have a reply. He consecrates no earth for altars for Naaman. He gives no orders to his servant to give him his "two mules' burthen of earth," nor does he say a word signifying that he consents he should take it, approving of his design of building an altar with [it], but bids him farewell, without any reply at all. And therefore it is not incredible that he should make no reply to that part of his speech which came in incidentally, that did in no wise so naturally lead the Prophet to answer.

As to the latter part of the forementioned objection, which relates to the Prophet's being bound in duty to forbid what Naaman declared to be his intention, or to have manifested his disapprobation of it, if it were unlawful, when so fair occasion was given him to express his mind concerning it, to this I would say,

1. The prophets spake under the immediate direction of heaven. They were to deliver God's messages, and were only the organs to utter his words. In this whole affair of Naaman, he[3] acted in his character of a prophet, and Naaman is now addressing him as such; and God was not pleased to put any reply into his mouth.

2. God herein dealt with Naaman as he commonly does with such hypocrites that pretend to be his servants, but are joined to idols. Hos. 4:17, "Ephraim is joined to idols; let him alone." Matt. 15:14, "Let 'em alone; they be blind leaders of the blind." It was just with Naaman as it was with the elders of Israel in Chaldea. They pretend to worship the God of Israel alone, but yet, living among idolaters and in subjection to them, they thought they might comply with the people of the land, who now were their masters, in some of their idolatrous customs, seeing they must render themselves very obnoxious by refusing. And they come to the prophet Ezekiel to inquire of him something concerning this affair, but God replies by the Prophet. Ezek. 14:3, "Son of man, these men have set up their idols in their heart, and put the stumbling block of their iniquity before their face. Should I be inquired of at all by them?" Again, Ezek. 20:1, "Certain of the elders of Israel came to inquire of the Lord, and sat before me." V. 3, "Thus saith the Lord God, Are ye come to inquire of me? As I live, saith the Lord, I will not be inquired of by you"; with v. 31, "For when ye offer your gifts, when ye make your sons to pass through the fire, ye pollute yourselves with all your idols, even unto this day. And shall I be in-

---

3. I.e. Elisha.

quired of by you, O house of Israel? As I live, saith the Lord God, I will not be inquired of by you." That what was the especial reason of God's treating them with such manifestations of abhorence, and refusing any intercourse with them, was that they[4] joined idolatry with a profession of his name and a pretense of worshiping him, or had a disposition so to do, is manifest by v. 39. "As for you, O house of Israel, thus saith the Lord God, Go ye, serve everyone his idols, and hereafter also, if ye will not hearken unto me. But pollute ye my holy name no more with your gifts and your idols." And that the thing that was in their mind, about which they came to Ezekiel to inquire, was whether they might not comply with the people they dwelt among in some of their idolatrous customs, though they professed in heart to serve the true God only, is pretty plain by v. 32. "And that which cometh into your mind shall not be at all, that ye say, We will be as the heathen, as the families of the countries, to serve wood and stone."

3. Though Elisha made no reply to what Naaman had said of bowing in the house of Rimmon, and so did not directly declare his dislike of it, yet his manner of treating Naaman on this occasion (though no other than friendly), if duly weighed and rationally reflected upon by Naaman, would sufficiently show him the Prophet's disapprobation of it, and in a manner tending more to convince and affect him than if he had directly forbid it. Naaman made a proposal to Elisha of taking "two mules' burthen of earth" of the land of Canaan (as though he highly valued the very dust of that land), to build an altar to Elisha's God, doubtless expecting that Elisha would show himself much pleased with it, and desires to have this earth as given and consecrated by Elisha. But Elisha don't grant his request; he takes no notice of it, intimating that he looked on his pretenses not worthy of any regard, and immediately, without saying one word to what he had said, sends him away, and takes his leave of him, as not thinking it worth his while to enter into any conversation with him about such a mongrel worship as he proposed, nor desiring any unnecessary communion with such an idolater.

473. EXODUS 17:9."I will stand on the top of the hill with the rod of God in my hand." Moses' rod, as has elsewhere been observed,[5] signifies three things, each of which it signifies in this case. 1. It signifies

4. JE deleted "mingled."
5. See Nos. 195, 385, and 442.

faith, by which God's people overcome their enemies; "for this is the victory that overcomes, even our faith" [I John 5:4].

Mr. Henry says this rod was held up "to God, by way of appeal to him. Is not the battle the Lord's? Is not he able to help, and engaged to help? Witness this rod, the voice of which, thus held up, was that, Is. 51:9–10, 'Put on thy strength, O arm of the Lord! Art thou not it that hath cut Rahab?'"[6]

2. It represents the word of God, the rod of his strength, which is the weapon by which Christ, the antitype of Moses, overcomes his church's enemies. This is the sword which proceeds out of his mouth [Rev. 19:15].

3. Christ himself lifted up as the banner of his militant church. Christ is prophesied of in Is. 11:1 as a "rod," "a rod out of the stem of Jesse." And in the same place, 'tis said, "He shall stand for an ensign of the people," and their ensign as an army brought out of Egypt, and fighting and conquering their enemies; the children of Edom in particular are mentioned (vv. 1, 10–12, 14–16). This ensign or banner is *Jehovah Nissi*, "Jehovah our banner," agreeable to the name of the altar Moses built on this occasion (Ex. 17:15). Moses stood on the top of an hill, and there lift up this ensign, the wonder-working rod, which had brought such plagues on their enemies, and such marvelous deliverance for them before, that the people at the sight of it might be animated in the battle. Christ himself, when he was lifted up on the cross, that he might draw all men to him [John 12:32–33], was lifted up on an hill. He stood and cried on the top of an hill, even the mountain of the temple, at the feast of tabernacles. God hath exalted him to heaven, set him on his holy hill of Zion, hath caused him to ascend an high hill, as the hill of Bashan, hath set this rod on the mountain of the height of Israel; and from thence his glory is manifested to gather men to him, and to animate his church to fight his battles. From thence his glory was manifested on the day of Pentecost after his ascension, and from thence it will be manifested to his church, when they shall go forth [to] their victory over Antichrist and all their enemies. He will shine forth on that mountain of the house of the Lord, from behind the veil, from between the cherubims; and all flesh shall behold it, and so all nations shall flow together to the mountain of the Lord, shall be gathered to this ensign, and then shall that be fulfilled in Is. 11:10. "At that day there shall be a root of Jesse, which shall stand for an ensign of the

6. Henry, *Exposition*, *1* (1725), 195.

people; to it shall the Gentiles seek." And v. 12, "And he shall set up an ensign for the nations, and shall assemble the outcasts of Israel, and gather together the dispersed of Judah from the four corners of the earth." See No. 205.

474. EXODUS 20:24–26. "An altar of earth thou shalt make unto me. . . . And if thou wilt make me an altar of stone, thou shalt not build it of hewn stone; for if thou lift up thy tool upon it, thou hast polluted it. Neither shalt thou go up by steps unto mine altar." These rules have respect to what was to be done now immediately, the altars they were to erect, and the sacrifices that were to be offered in the wilderness before the building of the tabernacle. God's altar was to be very plain and very low, so that they might have no occasion to go up to it by steps. The heathens greatly adorned their altars with the curious works of their own hands, and worshiped in high places, and built their altars very high, thinking hereby to put great honor on their gods, and made their services very acceptable to them. But God lets his people know that their seeming adorning, by their own art and handiwork, will be but polluting, and their recommending themselves by their high altars will be dishonoring themselves, and showing their own nakedness; perhaps typifying this, that whenever men ascend high, and exalt themselves in their own works or righteousness in God's service, they show their own nakedness, and pollute his worship, and render the services they offer abominable to God. Mr. Henry has this note on this rule for plain altars. "This rule, being prescribed before the ceremonial law was given, which appointed altars much more costly, intimates that after the period of that law, plainness should be accepted as the best ornament of the external services of religion, and that gospel worship should not be performed with external pomp and gaiety."[7]

475. EXODUS 25:23–40. Concerning the SHOWBREAD TABLE and the Golden CANDLESTICK.[8] These both were to stand continually in the holy place before the veil of the holy of holies, one on the north side and the other on the south. Each of these seems to represent both a divine person and also the church. Each represents a divine person. The showbread represents Christ, and was set on [the] south side at God's right hand, as Christ is often represented as being set at God's

7. Ibid., p. 205.
8. JE wrote the following running head on pages of this entry: "No. 475. The Showbread and Golden Candlestick (Exodus 25:23 to the End)."

right hand in heaven, being next to God the Father in his office, and above the Holy Spirit in the economy of the persons of the Trinity. The candlestick, or at least the oil and lamps of it, represent the Holy Spirit, and is set at the left hand of God's throne. Christ is as it were "the bread of God"; he is so called, John 6:33.[9] He is the portion of God the Father in whom is his infinite delight and happiness; and as our Mediator and sacrifice, he is as it were the bread of God, as the ancient sacrifices, that were only typical of Christ, are often called the "bread of God." This bread is called the showbread, in the Hebrew, *Lechem Panim*,[1] "the bread of God's face," or "presence." So Christ, in Is. 63:9, is called *Malak Panim*,[2] "the angel of God's face," or "presence." This bread had pure frankincense set on it, which undoubtedly signifies the merits of Christ, and so proves the bread that had this pure frankincense on it to be a type of Christ. And besides this, the bread and frankincense are called "an offering made by fire unto the Lord" (Lev. 24:7, 9), which is another proof that this bread and incense were a type of Christ offered in sacrifice to God. The bread was prepared to be as it were the food of God by being baked in the fire; and the frankincense, when removed for new to be set on, was probably burnt in the fire on the altar of incense. There were twelve cakes of showbread, according to the number of the tribes of Israel, to signify that Christ, as offered up in sacrifice to God, is offered as representing his people and church, and presenting himself to God in their name. This bread represents Christ, not only as presented in the presence of God as God's bread, but as proceeding from the presence of God as the bread of the saints, for this bread was eaten by the priests in the temple (Lev. 24:9). So Christ is often spoken of as the bread of the saints. He is the bread they will feed upon in heaven, which is the holy temple of God, where the saints are all kings and priests.

This bread also represents the church, who are spoken [of] not only as partaking of Christ, the divine bread, but as being themselves the bread of God (I Cor. 10:17). God's people are very often, in both Old Testament and New, spoken of [as] God's food, his fruit, his harvest, his good grain, his portion, etc. This seems to be one reason why the showbread was to be in twelve cakes, representing the twelve tribes of Israel, because the bread represented the church, as the twelve precious stones in the breastplate did [Ex. 28:21]. These loaves had frank-

---

9. MS: "~~in him is the life and infini~~ ⟨he is so called Joh. 6. 33⟩."
1. לֶחֶם פָּנִים.
2. מַלְאַךְ פָּנָיו.

incense set on them, to represent that God's people are not acceptable food to God, any otherwise than as rendered so by the incense of Christ's merits. The loaves of showbread were to be set on the table anew every sabbath, representing several things.

1. That in God's finishing the work of redemption, or in Christ's finishing of it, when he rested from it, Christ especially became the bread or sweet food of God, wherein he was refreshed, as God is said to have rested and to have been refreshed, when he finished the work of creation; so much more when Christ finished the work of redemption. 2. As the sabbath day especially is the day of the worship of Christ's church, so on that day especially does Christ present himself as their Mediator, and present his merits as the sweet food and incense of God, to recommend them and their worship to the Father. 3. Christ is, on the sabbath day, especially set forth as the bread of his church in the preaching of the Word and administration of the sacraments. On the sabbath day the disciples came together to break bread. And 'tis then especially that his saints do feed upon him in meditation, hearing his Word, and partaking of the sacrament of the Lord's Supper, as the priests eat the showbread on the sabbath. 4. The sabbath is that time wherein especially God's people do present themselves to God as his portion through Christ. 5. The time, wherein in a most eminent manner they shall be presented by Christ, and will present themselves to God as his portion, is in the time of that eternal[3] rest (the antitype of the sabbath) in heaven. 6. This is also the time wherein they will, in the highest degree, feed and feast on Christ as their bread, as the priests eat the showbread in the temple on the sabbath.

In the golden candlestick that stood before the throne on the left side was a representation both of the Holy Spirit and of the church. The pure oil olive that fed the lamps is indisputably a type of the Holy Ghost, and 'tis evident by Rev. 4:5, compared with Rev. 1:4, and 5:6, and Zech. 3:9, and 4:2, 6, 10. The burning of the lamps represents that divine, infinite, pure energy and ardor wherein the Holy Spirit consists. The light of the lamps filling the tabernacle with light, which had no windows and no light but of these lamps, represents the divine blessed communication and influence of the Spirit of God, replenishing the church, and filling heaven with the light of divine knowledge in opposition to the darkness of ignorance and delusion, the light of holiness in opposition to the darkness of sin, and the light of comfort

3. JE deleted "sabbath in heaven."

and joy in opposition to the darkness of sorrow and misery. This light's being communicated from a candlestick represents the way in which these benefits are communicated to the church, viz. the way of God's ordinances, which are called a "candlestick" (Rev. 2:5).

'Tis evident that the candlestick represents the church (the 4th chapter of Zechariah, and the 1st of Revelation, and Matt. 5:13–15, and I Tim. 3:15). The matter was gold, as the church is constituted of saints, God's precious ones. The candlestick was like a tree of many branches, and bearing flowers and fruit, agreeable to the very frequent representations of the church by a tree, an olive tree, a vine, a grain of mustard seed that becomes a tree, the branch of the Lord, a tree whose substance is in it, etc. The continuance and propagation of the church is compared to the propagation of branches from a common stock and root, and of plants from the seed. In this candlestick every flower is attended with a knop, apple, or pomegranate, representing the good profession attended with answerable fruit in the true saints. Here were rows of knops and flowers, one after another, beautifully representing the saints' progress in religious attainment, their going from strength to strength. Such is the nature of true grace and holy fruit, that it bears a flower, that promises a further degree of fruit, the flower having in it the principles of new fruit. And by this progress in holiness, the saint comes to shine as a light in the world. The fruit that succeeds the uppermost flower is the burning and shining lamp, representing several things.[4] 1. That the fruit of a[5] true saint, or his good works and holy life, is as it were a light by which he shines before men (Matt. 5:13–15). 2. That in a way of holy practice and by progress in holiness, the saints obtain the light of spiritual comfort. 3. That in the way of going from strength to strength, and making progress in holiness, they come at last to the light of glory. The lamps were fed wholly by oil constantly supplied from the olive tree, representing that the saints' holiness, good fruits, and comfort are wholly by the Spirit of God constantly flowing from Christ. The oil that was burnt in the lamps before God was an offering to God. So God is the prime object of the grace and holiness of the saints; their divine love flows out chiefly to him, as Mary's precious ointment was poured on the head of Christ, but ran "down to the skirts of his garments" [Ps. 133:2].[6] Their good works are acceptable sacrifices to God through Christ, and are

4. JE deleted "1. That a true Christian by his fruits or good."
5. JE deleted "good Christian."
6. The reference is from the New Testament, but the quotation is from Psalms.

not of the nature of Christian works, if not offered to God as if there be nothing of a gracious respect to God in them. The saints' light shines before God; their graces and holy practices are pleasant to him, and of great price in his sight, as the light is sweet. And the light shone around, and filled the temple, as the odors of Mary's box of ointment filled the house [John 12:3]. The inhabitants of the temple had the benefit of the light of the candlestick, as the saints of God have especially the benefit of the good works of the saints.

The propagation of the church through successive generations is sometimes represented in Scripture to the gradual growing of a tree and shooting forth branches. And when the church is represented as bringing forth fruit as a tree, by her fruit is sometimes meant her children, or converts. And therefore one thing that may be intended by fruit and flowers succeeding one another in this candlestick, may be the continuance of the church and gradual increase, her bringing forth fruit, and that in order to the bringing forth more fruit, till she hath reached the latter-day glory, when God [shall] bring forth her righteousness as the light, and her salvation as a lamp that burneth. Then shall she come to a state of glorious light, of truth, knowledge, holiness, and joy.

476. EXODUS 30:7–8. When the high priest lighted and dressed the lamps, then was he to burn incense on the golden altar of incense, signifying that the sweet and infinitely acceptable incense of Christ's merits was by the Holy Spirit signified by the lamps. (See the foregoing number.) It was by the eternal Spirit that Christ offered up himself without spot to God. It was by the Holy Spirit many ways. It was by the Holy Spirit that the human nature of Christ was united to the divine Logos, from which union arises the infinite value of his blood and righteousness. It was by the eternal Spirit that Christ performed righteousness. It was by the Spirit of God that Christ was perfectly holy and performed perfect righteousness. It was by the Holy Spirit not only that his obedience was perfect, but performed with such transcendent love. It was by this Spirit that his sacrifice of himself was sanctified, being an offering to God in the pure and fervent flame of divine love, which burnt in his heart as well as in the flame of God's vindictive justice and wrath into which he was cast. And it was this that his obedience and sacrifice were offered with such a love to his people that he died for, as implied a perfect union with them, whereby it was accepted for them.

477. DEUTERONOMY 6:13. Add this to No. 468, at the reference to this note. Other places showing that by Jehovah's "living," or being the "living God," is meant his being all-sufficient, and immutable, and faithful. Gen. 16:14, Deut. 5:26, Josh. 3:10 compared with Ex. 3:14 and 6:3, with the context, I Sam. 17:26, 36, II Kgs. 19:4, 16, Ps. 42:2, and 84:2, Is. 37:4, Jer. 10:10, with the context, Jer. 23:36, Hos. 1:10, II Sam. 22:47, Ps. 18:46, Job 19:25, Matt. 16:16, John 6:69, Acts 14:15, Rom. 9:26, II Cor. 3:3, and 6:16, I Tim. 3:15, and 4:10, and 6:17, Heb. 10:31, and 12:22.

478. JEREMIAH 2:2–3. Add this to No. 296. That there was a time of remarkable influence of God's Holy Spirit on the younger generation during the forty years' travel, is confirmed by comparing Neh. 9:20–21 and Deut. 32:10, and also Deut. 8:2–5, and v. 15. See also note on Num. 31:48–54 in "Blank Bible."[7] See Deut. 34:9.

479. ISAIAH 42:8. "I am the Lord [Jehovah],[8] that is my name; and my glory I will not give to another, neither my praise to graven images." Together with Is. 48:11, "For mine own sake, even for mine own sake, will I do it; for how should my name be polluted? And my glory I will not give unto another."[9] Concerning this text, these things may be remarked confirming the divinity of Christ. 1. The name "Jehovah" is a peculiar name of the true God; this is plain by the words. See also Ps. 83:18. [Quote the words.][1] 1. That the name "Jehovah" here spoken of is often undeniably given to him,[2] and it is not denied by Arians themselves. 'Tis given in this very book. See Is. 6:1 ff., compared with John 12:41.[3] 2. God says expressly concerning Christ, who is called the "angel of the Lord,"[4] "*my name* is in him"; and therefore he requires the children of Israel to obey his voice. 3. He is often called "the name

7. JE, citing Matthew Henry, holds up the officers of the army of Israel as "a great example of piety and devotion." Rather than taking pride in their victory and demanding "recompense for the good service they had done," they brought "an oblation to make atonement for their souls, being conscious . . . that they had been defective in their duty." This was "an instance of the piety" of the younger generation ("Blank Bible").

8. JE's brackets.

9. Jonathan Edwards, Jr., deleted this sentence.

1. Jonathan Edwards, Jr., inserted this item no. 1, including the brackets. He changed the following numbers to accommodate his insertion.

2. Jonathan Edwards, Jr., deleted "him" and inserted "Christ."

3. The two preceding sentences are a later interlineation.

4. Jonathan Edwards, Jr., inserted the last three words.

of God." (See papers on this subject.)[5] 4. The glory of the Lord was given to him, so that that glory with which the angel of the Lord was wont to appear, was in a peculiar manner called "the glory of the Lord." 5. He is himself often called the "glory of the Lord." The Apostle expressly says, he is "the brightness of God's glory" [Heb. 1:3].

480. I PETER 2:7–8. "Unto you therefore which believe he is precious; but unto them which be disobedient, the stone which the builders disallowed, the same is become the head of the corner, and a stone of stumbling, and a rock of offense," etc. There are several ways and respects that stones or rocks are valuable and of benefit to men, in each of which Christ in Scripture is compared to a stone or rock with regard to believers. 1. Some stones are highly valued for the preciousness of their nature and substance, and beauty of their form, and so are valued as a great treasure, and that which is prized because it enriches and adorns. So Christ is said to be a stone that is precious to believers. He is spoken of as a pearl of great price. So he was typified by the precious or costly stones that were brought for the foundation of the temple. 2. Stones or rocks are a great benefit to mankind as a sure foundation of a building; so is Christ to believers. 3. Rocks were commonly [made] use of for defense from enemies. Their fortresses were ordinarily built on high rocks or rocky mountains. So is Christ often spoken of in Scripture as the strong rock, high tower, refuge, and sure defense of believers. 4. Rocks were of great benefit to travelers in the hot parched deserts of Arabia near to Canaan, by their cool shadow. The benefit believers have by Christ is compared to this, Is. 32:2. 5. In a time of inundation, mountains or rocks would be the places to resort to for safety, to keep from being overwhelmed. The benefit believers have by Christ is compared to this. Ps. 61:2, "When my heart is overwhelmed, lead me to the rock that is higher than I."

On the contrary, there are several ways that stones or rocks are disesteemed among men, and hurtful to 'em, wherein Christ is compared to a stone or rock with regard to unbelievers. 1. Nothing is ordinarily looked upon and treated by men as more worthless than common stones. So is Christ disesteemed and rejected by unbelievers, as builders throw away misshapen stones as not for their purpose,

---

5. Separate papers on the name of God have not yet been identified or located. JE, however, indexed four entries in the "Table" of the "Miscellanies" under "Name of God": nos. 88, 1102, 1105, and 1114. The last three of these, entitled "TRINITY," discuss the use and implications of "Jehovah" and "Elohim" in the Old Testament.

and of no value. 2. Stones are offensive to travelers, and an occasion of their stumbling and falling; so is Christ to unbelievers "a stone of stumbling." 3. Rocks are very often fatal to sailors, and the occasion of their suffering shipwreck. So those that enjoy the gospel, and have the means of grace, but fail through unbelief, are in Scripture compared to them who suffer shipwreck at sea. I Tim. 1:19, "Concerning faith have made shipwreck." 4. Those high rocks that were most fit for places of defense had dreadful precipices, which if men fell over, they would be broken in pieces. Is. 8:14–15, "And he shall be for a sanctuary, but for a stone of stumbling and a rock of offense," etc., "And many among them shall stumble, and fall, and be broken, and snared, and taken."

481. EPHESIANS 1:23. "The fullness of him that filleth all in all." Add this to No. 235. The church is not only represented as Christ's ornament, but God's people are often spoken of in the Old Testament as God's portion, inheritance, his treasure, his jewels, his garden of pleasant fruits, "his pleasant plant" (Is. 5:7), the plant of his pleasures, his pleasant food as the first ripe figs (Jer. 24:2, Hos. 9:10), "the first fruits of all his increase" (Jer. 2:3), a garden and orchard of spices, his bed or field of lilies among which he feeds, his fountain of gardens as refreshing streams from Lebanon, a garden where he gathers his myrrh and his spice, and where he eats his honeycomb with his honey, and drinks his wine with his milk.

So the saints in the New Testament are spoken of as God's wheat and good grain, that he gathers into his garner.

482. JOHN 10:34–36. "Jesus answered them, Is it not written in your law, I have said, Ye are gods?" etc. "In the 82nd psalm, to which this refers, we see, v. 6, those who are called 'sons of the Highest,' by the word of God that came to them, are by that same word called 'gods'; so that in that passage, 'son of the Highest' is the same with 'God.' Jesus takes notice, that they are called 'gods,' and he says, 'The Scripture cannot be broken,' i.e. it must be verified. But verified it could not be in them, who died like men, and fell thereby, like other princes [who were not called gods][6] from that eminent station wherein they were called gods. It is not every prince or potentate among men that is called 'god' in this psalm. Those called 'gods' are plainly the princes of Israel, that

---

6. JE's brackets.

judged in God's land, who stood and judged among them in that theocracy. And they are manifestly distinguished from other princes on the very same account on which they are called gods. For in their office as rulers and judges of Israel, they prefigured him who was to rule the house of Jacob forever; and they stood in that office as his types, even as the priests prefigured him in his priesthood. Therefore they are called gods. And the Scripture calling them so is not broken, because what is said of these types holds fully true in their antitype, who is plainly enough pointed at in that same psalm, v. 8, 'Arise, O God, judge the earth, for thou shalt inherit all nations.' They 'shall *die* like men, and fall like one of the princes' [Ps. 82:7]; but he arises from the *dead* to judge and inherit the church of all nations. His resurrection manifests him to be truly God, the same God that stood in the congregation of these mighty, and judged among them, 'to whom the word of God [came]' [John 10:35], 'Ye are gods, and sons of the Highest.'" Mr. Glas's *Notes on Scripture-Texts*, No. 1, pp. 11–12.[7] They are called gods, as the manna is called the bread from heaven and angels' food, and as Cyrus is called God's Christ[8] and his beloved (Is. 45:1, and 48:14), and as Saul (whom the Psalmist has a special respect to in that psalm 82) is called the Lord's Christ (He fell like one of the other princes who were not called gods.), and as the rock in the wilderness is said to be Christ, and as many things are said of Solomon in the 72nd psalm that are verified only in Christ. That passage, I Kgs. 18:31, may serve to explain these words, "To whom the word of God came." "According to the number of the tribes of Jacob, unto whom the word of the Lord came, saying, Israel [i.e. the prince of God][9] shall be thy name." The word of God came to Jacob in his prevailing with God, two ways. 1. God said to him, I have called you Israel, "prince of God" [Gen. 35:10], as here, Ps. 82, he says to the princes of Israel, "I have called you gods"; and that word of God came to 'em in Ex. 22:28. 2. God, by a special designation, made Jacob, in what he ordered con-

---

7. No copy of John Glas, *Notes on Scripture-Texts, No. 1*, has been located, but that publication is printed in *The Works of Mr. John Glas* (2nd ed., 5 vols. Perth, 1782–83). The citation here appears in vol. 3, pp. 21–22. JE apparently received some of the separately issued numbers by Glas in the winter of 1749–1750 from John Erskine, one of his correspondents in Scotland. In a letter to Erskine written July 5, 1750, JE acknowledged receipt of the same and commented, "There were various things pleasing to me in Glass' [sic] Notes, tending to give some new light into the sense of Scripture. He seems to be a man of ability; though I cannot fall in with all his singularities" (Dwight ed., *1*, 405–06).

8. I.e. anointed.

9. JE's brackets.

cerning him, to be a type. Now types are a sort of word; they are a language, or signs of things, God would reveal, point forth, and teach as well as vocal or written words, and they are called "the word of the Lord," in Zech. 4:6, and 11:11. And thus also the word of the Lord came to the princes of Israel, i.e. that state and those[1] circumstances came to 'em, and were ordered to 'em, that were typical of the Son of God, and were as it were God's word, signifying the dignity and office of the Messiah. Such divine significations, when persons were made the inherent subjects of them, were generally of the Son of God, the eternal personal Word. And therefore when such a typification happened, or was ordered to a person, or any person became the inherent subject of such a divine signification, then the word of God was said to come to him. It was the signification or typification (if I may so speak), was the word of God, both as it was God's signification, and also as the thing signified was the personal Word of God.

483. HABAKKUK 3:2. "Revive thy work in the midst of the years; in the midst of the years make known, and in wrath remember mercy." There was a certain number of years that were as it were the appointed day of the church's trouble and calamity, and the day of God's wrath or anger. The Prophet prays that though God's anger were not wholly removed till the number of years was finished, and the day of wrath passed, yet that God would remember mercy in wrath, and grant some revival in the midst of the years, and not hide himself wholly from his people for so long a time, but make himself known to them in some measure before the expiring of this dark season. The Prophet here in his prayer, speaking of the appointed years, has respect to the same appointed time that he speaks of in the foregoing chapter, vv. 2–3. "And the Lord answered me, and said, Write the vision, and make it plain," etc. "For the vision is yet for an appointed time, but at the end it shall speak, and not lie," etc. What he has a more immediate respect to, is the appointed time of deliverance from the Babylonish captivity. This whole book seems to relate to that captivity and the deliverance from it. That was a time of sore trouble to the church, from the captivity till the restoration of Jerusalem. The appointed time was seventy years; but God remembered mercy, and gave some revival in the midst of the years by Daniel's advancement, which was doubtless greatly for the ease and relief of the Jews. And then the destruction of Babylon

1. JE deleted "divinely ordered."

and Cyrus's decree was before the end of seventy years from the destruction of Jerusalem, though the temple was not rebuilt till the seventy years was ended; and religion revived among the people in the younger generation in the midst of those years. So God is wont to remember mercy in the midst of the years, in the times of the church's oppression, as in the times of its sore distress by Antiochus's tyranny and cruelty. They were "holpen with a little help" by the Maccabees before the appointed time expired (Dan. 11:32–34). So God remembered mercy to his church during the reign of Antichrist, and granted a revival of his church before the time of his[2] reign and the church's captivity was expired, and made himself known in the midst of the years, in the time of the Reformation.

484. I JOHN 2:18. "Little children, it is the last time; and as ye have heard that Antichrist shall come, even now there are many antichrists, whereby we know that it is the last time." It is not reasonable to think that the Apostle supposed that this time was the latter part of the space that should be, from Christ's ascension to his second coming to the general judgment. For 'tis evident by what he here says, that he knew[3] that the great Antichrist should come before that. And if he supposed that this great Antichrist now appeared, 'tis not likely that he would have expressed himself as he does, "Even now are there may antichrists." He would rather [have] said, "Even now Antichrist is come," and would have deciphered him, and pointed him forth. We must therefore understand the Apostle thus. 'Tis now long since the apostles foretold the coming of Antichrist, which they told you in the first age of the Christian church, which reached from Christ's ascension to the destruction of Jerusalem. And now, since Jerusalem's destruction, has commenced the last state of things, the last age of the world, which is to continue from the destruction of Jerusalem and the perfect abolishing of the Old Testament dispensation, to the end of the world, which the apostles had been wont to call the "latter days" and "last times," during which last age they foretold that Antichrist would appear (II Thess. 2:3 ff., I Tim. 4:1 ff., II Tim. 3:1 ff.). And now the spirit of Antichrist doth very visibly appear. And there are many apostates and corrupters, that we may look upon as the forerunners of Antichrist, and are therefore an evidence that we are now come to that

2. I.e. Antichrist's.
3. MS: "know."

last age in which it has been foretold that Antichrist should arise, which should make you behave yourselves more circumspectly; for the apostles often told you that those last times, wherein Antichrist should appear, would be perilous times. See "Miscellanies," no. 842.[4]

485. ISAIAH 40:15. "He taketh up the isles as a very little thing." "'Tis a very fine remark, and a solid correction of the common translation, made by that learned, sagacious, and devout expositor Vitringa. He observes that the common translation is neither answerable to the import of the original, nor consonant to the structure of the discourse. The Prophet had no intention to inform mankind what the Almighty could do, with regard to the islands, if he pleased to exert his power. But his design was to show how insignificant, or rather what mere nothings they are, in his esteem, and before his majesty. The islands, says he, though so spacious as to afford room for the erection of kingdoms, and the abode of nations, though so strong as to withstand for many thousands of years the raging and reiterated assaults of the whole watery world, are yet, before the adored Jehovah, small as the minutest grain, which the eye can scarce discern, light as the feathered mote, which the least breath hurries away like a tempest. אִיִּים כְּדַק יִטּוֹל.[5] *Insulae sunt ut leve quid, quod avolat.*[6] The deep-rooted islands are as the volatile atom, which, by the gentlest undulations of the air, is wafted to and fro in perpetual agitations." Hervey's *Meditations*, Vol. 2, p. 130.[7]

486. CANTICLES 4:3.[8] "Thy lips are as like a thread of scarlet." There is probably a special respect to the speech of the saints in prayer, which is dyed in the blood of Christ, and by this means becomes pleasant, and acceptable, and of an attractive influence, like a scarlet cord, to draw

---

4. No. 842, entitled "CHRISTIAN RELIGION," deals with the potential challenge to the truth of Christianity posed by the apostles' speaking often of the day of judgment as though "they thought it near at hand." JE rejects the supposition of that objection and deals successively with a variety of New Testament passages frequently cited in support of that position, offering in each case alternative explanations to prove that the apostles did not intend so to be understood. On the contrary, the prophecies of Christ's coming to judgment were to be fulfilled "in several successive ages." No. 842 contains a reference to No. 484 added after its original composition.

5. He lifts up islands as a very thin thing.

6. The islands are like something light that flies away quickly.

7. James Hervey, *Meditations and Contemplations* (2 vols. London, 1748), 2, 130.

8. JE crossed out the following before writing this entry with the same number: "486. The Book of CANTICLES was no epithalamium on occasion of Solomon's marriage to Pharaoh's daughter, for there is great evidence that it was written many years after that marriage."

down blessings. The prayers of saints are lovely and prevalent only through the incense of Christ's merits. See SSS.[9]

487. CANTICLES 4:4. "Thy neck is like the tower of David builded for an armory, whereon there hang a thousand bucklers, all shields of mighty men." This probably represents faith, for it is that by which the church is united to her head, for Christ is her head. Or if we look at ministers as a subordinate head, yet they are so no otherwise than as they represent Christ, and act as his ministers. And the same that is the union of believers to Christ is their union to ministers, and in receiving them, they receive him. 'Tis by the same faith whereby they receive Christ and obey his word, that they receive and obey the instructions of ministers, for their instructions are no other than the word of Christ by them. Faith is the church's life, and strength, and constant support, and supply, as the neck is to the body. Faith is the church's shield (Eph. 6:16); it is the church's armory, furnishing her with shields, because it provides them out of Christ's fullness, which is contained in the promises. See SSS.[1]

488. CANTICLES 4:5. "Thy two breasts are like two young roes that are twins, which feed among the lilies." "Like two young roes," i.e. fair, loving, and pleasant (see Prov. 5:19). Roes "which feed among the lilies," not in a wilderness, but in a good pasture, or a pleasant garden, fair and flourishing. And by their having the white unspotted lilies for their nourishment may also represent her chastity and purity, that her breasts are not defiled by an impure love.[2] By the church's breasts are meant means of grace. See Cant. 8:1, 8, and Is. 66:11, [and] I Pet. 2:2. These two breasts may signify the same with the two olive trees with the two golden pipes emptying "the golden oil out of themselves," and the two anointed ones (Zech. 4:3, 11–12, 14), and the two witnesses in Revelation, and the two testaments, and two sacraments. Another thing meant is love. (See No. 495.) The two breasts are love to God and love to men.

9. Poole's discussion of Cant. 4:3 includes the following judgment which JE echoes in this entry: "*Rubicunda, vel, quia tincta sanguine Christi. . . . Labia sunt instrumenta ad osculandum & loquendum; & significant h.l. tum internam conversationem cum Deo, tum externam tractationem de Deo.*" See *Synopsis Criticorum*, 2 (London, 1671), Pt. 2, cols. 2006–2007.

1. Poole writes, "[P]*raecones Verbi, qui in Ecclesia eminent & conspicui sunt, & quasi in specula excubias agunt; & per quos spiritualis esca ad Ecclesiam, ut cibus per collum ad corpus, transmittitur; qui etiam Ecclesiae membra Christo, capiti suo, committunt, sicut collum caetera membra cùm capite conjungit,*" which JE's entry echoes (*Synopsis Criticorum*, 2 [London, 1671], Pt. 2, col. 2007).

2. The remainder of this entry is a later addition.

489. CANTICLES 5:14. "His belly is as bright ivory overlaid with sapphires." The word is the same in the original,[3] which in v. 4 is rendered "bowels," and wherever it [is] attributed to God, it is translated "bowels," as Is. 63:15 and Jer. 31:20. His belly, with regard to his bowels, or his affection, is said to be like "bright ivory overlaid with sapphires," representing the justice and mercy which are both so perfectly exercised and manifested in him in the work of redemption. The bright, or pure white, ivory represents his perfect justice. Solomon's throne of justice was ivory [I Kgs. 10:18], which substance was chosen to be the matter of his throne in all probability, because it fitly represented justice, as the throne of Christ at the day of judgment, Rev. 20:11, is represented as "a great white throne." His belly was "overlaid with sapphires," being a precious stone of a beautiful azure, or sky blue, the softest of all the colors, to represent mercy. Thus the throne of God had the appearance of sapphire (Ezek. 1:26), to signify that he sat on a throne of grace. See note in "Blank Bible."[4]

490. CANTICLES 7:1. "How beautiful are thy feet with shoes, O prince's daughter!" This is to signify the amiableness of her conversation, and that her conversation is not naturally amiable, but that this beauty of conversation is put upon her.[5] And another thing implied is that she was prepared for travel, as the people in Egypt were to have their shoes on their feet (Ex. 12:11). So the Apostle directs that Christians should have their "feet shod with the preparation of the gospel of peace" (Eph. 6:15),[6] i.e. a preparation for travel, according to the gospel, and by the gospel of peace. See note on the place.[7]

To the same scope is what follows. "The joints of thy thighs are like jewels, the work of the hands of a cunning workman" [Cant. 7:1]. The joints, the knees, and hips are especially the seat and means of motion

3. מֵעִים.

4. This reference is a later addition. JE's note on this passage in Canticles in the "Blank Bible" reinforces the association of the "belly" with Christ's mercy and love. His mercy is "perfectly pure and holy," represented by the bright ivory, and "exceeding sweet, mild, and gentle," represented by the sapphires, a stone the color of the sky, "one of the mildest of the colors."

5. JE deleted "She is created in Christ Jesus unto good works, which God hath foreordained that she should walk in them [Eph. 2:10]."

6. MS: "⟨Eph 6. 15.⟩ ~~Philip 1. 27.~~" The remainder of this paragraph is a later interlineation.

7. JE equates "the gospel of peace" in Eph. 6:15 with "a peaceable spirit, or a spirit of Christian meekness and calmness of mind" which equips persons well for Christian warfare and for the journey "through this world so full of enemies and injuries" ("Blank Bible").

in walking. When it is said, "The joints of thy thighs are the work of the hands of a cunning workman," this may be explained by that of the Apostle, Eph. 2:10. "We are his workmanship, created in Christ Jesus unto good works, which God hath foreordained that we should walk in them."8 The whole body of the church is fitly joined together "by joints and bands" [Col. 2:14]. The joints are kept firm and fit for their proper motion and operation by mutual charity, holy love, and union, and communion of saints. See SSS.9

491. CANTICLES 7:2. "Thy navel is like a round goblet, which wanteth not liquor." The navel, according to the ancient notion they had of things, was the seat of health. Prov. 3:8, "It shall be health to thy navel." Job 40:16, "His force is in the navel of his belly." So that the thing which is here most probably represented is the spiritual health of the church. Her navel is compared to a goblet "which wanteth not liquor," i.e. full of wine, that enlivening, invigorating liquor. The word signifies mixture, or temperament, or wine mixed or tempered, that is, wine that is so prepared as to make it the most agreeable and wholesome.1 See Prov. 23:30, and 9:2. Probably the same may be meant that is called "spiced wine," in Cant. 8:2. See SSS.2

492. CANTICLES 7:4. "Thine eyes like the fishpools in Heshbon, by the gate of Bath-rabbim." It seems there were two or more noted fishpools near to the city Heshbon, the chief city in the country of Moab, by one of the gates of that city, called the gate of Bath-rabbim, i.e. the gate of "the house of the multitude," probably so called because at that gate was an house for the resort of the multitudes, that resorted to those pools for the sake of the water of the pools, and fish which were caught there, and to wash themselves there.3 And perhaps those pools might be remarkable for the clearness of the water, and their fitness to exhibit a true and distinct image of the multitudes that resorted thither, wherein men might see themselves as they were, and might see the spots and filth which they would wash off, and wherein

8. The remainder of this entry is a later interlineation.
9. Poole, *Synopsis Criticorum*, 2 [London, 1671], Pt. 2, cols. 2030–2031.
1. The remainder of this entry is a later addition.
2. Poole takes note of the fact that it was common to mix or dilute wine with water in warm regions, a practice which produced what he called elsewhere, *vinum aromaticum*, "spiced wine" (*Synopsis Criticorum*, 2 [London, 1671], Pt. 2, cols. 2031–2032, 2042).
3. The last five words are a later interlineation. There are several other later interlineations in this entry relating to the use of the water for washing.

was a true representation of other things. So that the thing signified by the eyes of the spouse may be the spiritual knowledge and understanding of the church,[4] by which she has a true knowledge of her filth and her own pollutions, and also a true representation or idea of other things. And also hereby may be signified the benevolence and bountifulness of the eyes of a true saint, so that they as it were yield meat and drink[5] to a multitude, as it is probable those fishpools did (Prov. 22:9).

493. CANTICLES 7:4. "Thy nose is as the tower of Lebanon which looketh towards Damascus." The tower of Lebanon looking towards Damascus was probably some tower built in Lebanon on the frontier, next to the kingdom of Damascus, to watch over that country, and for the defense of Israel from its inhabitants. By the accounts which history give of Damascus, it was a magnificent city, and an exceeding pleasant, delightful place, like a mere garden of pleasure. And therefore it is called "the city of praise and joy" (Jer. 49:25), and in Amos 1:5 is called *Beth-eden*, or "the house of Eden." Men of carnal minds would prefer the land to the land of Israel, that God calls the pleasant land and the glory of all lands. Naaman the Syrian condemned the waters of Israel in comparison of Abana and Pharpar, rivers of Damascus [II Kgs. 5:12]. And it seems their religion and worship was exceeding pompous, tending much to please a vain carnal mind, that savors the things of men more than the things of God. King Ahaz was greatly taken with the curious fashion and workmanship of the altar he saw there, and he sent to Urijah the priest a pattern of it, that he might make one like it in the courts of God's house, and chose rather to offer his sacrifices on this new altar than on the altar of the Lord (II Kg. 16:10 ff.).

The nose is the organ of smelling. Therefore here the church is commended for her spiritual scent, which was a good defense to her from corrupt doctrines and false ways of worship of men's invention, however specious, and fair, and tending much more to please a carnal taste than the true religion of Jesus Christ.[6] Pomp, and magnificence, and the curious inventions of men, and the things which men's wisdom teaches, please men of corrupt mind; but a true saint, through a spiritual taste or scent, nauseates those things, and is defended from them.

4. MS: "⟨the Chh.⟩ ~~Believers~~."
5. MS: "⟨meat & drink⟩ ~~Food~~."
6. JE deleted "in its plainness."

This spiritual scent is the best defense from those things that would corrupt her mind from the simplicity that is in Christ. See SSS.[7]

494. CANTICLES 7:5. "Thine head upon thee is like Carmel (or 'crimson,' as it is in the margin),[8] and the hair of thine head like purple." If by "head" here be understood the eldership of the church, then her head is compared to Carmel, probably because Carmel was a very fruitful hill, and an high hill whose fruits were seen at a distance, as Christ compares his disciples to a city set on an hill, whose works could not be hid [Matt. 5:14]. (See note on Cant. 4:1.)[9] The hair is the fruit of the head,[1] and may represent both the doctrine and conversation of faithful ministers who know nothing and savor of nothing, either in their doctrine or life, but Jesus Christ and him crucified; and so their preaching and walk is as it were colored with his blood. And this also may be signified by it, that the[2] holy doctrine and conversation of ministers are a princely ornament to them, purple being the color of the robes of princes.

But perhaps by the head of the spouse here may be meant the doctrine which she holds, the doctrine of the gospel, which is represented as a glorious crown on her head, in Rev. 12:1.[3] This may be compared to Carmel, that fruitful hill, because 'tis the doctrine that is according to godliness, or to crimson, because Jesus Christ and him crucified, or Christ's shedding his blood, is the sum and substance of it.

495. CANTICLES 7:7. "And thy breasts to clusters of grapes." By her breasts here most probably is intended the grace of love, or spiritual complacence, affection to her husband and her children. The bosom

7. According to Matthew Poole, the comparison of the nose to a watchtower denotes several things, including ministers of the word who guard against dangers, the fortitude of the church against the enemies of truth, and the general spiritual perception that equips one to defend beforehand against hostile assaults and to discern virtue from corruption, truth from error (*Synopsis Criticorum*, 2 [London, 1671], Pt. 2, cols. 2033–2034).

8. I.e. the margin of the KJV.

9. JE suggests that the hair of the spouse being compared to a flock of goats on Mt. Gilead has reference to the good works of ministers and elders being open to public view from a great distance. They are to be "ensamples to the flock." JE also links the hair, or "fruit of the head," to the meditations or "the living fruits of ministers' studies" ("Blank Bible").

1. JE deleted "the good works of faithful ministers are."

2. JE deleted "good works of faithful min."

3. JE deleted "And this is is that which seems to be intended by that ~~salvat~~ salvation and hope of salvation which the Apostle speaks of as the Christian helmet or headpiece (Eph. 6:17)."

is put for love. So Christ is said to be "in the bosom of the Father" [John 1:18]. This agrees with that in Prov. 5:19, "Let her breasts satisfy thee at all times, and be thou ravished always with her love." Christ's love is compared to wine (Cant. 1:2), and so is the love of the spouse. Cant. 4:10, "How much better is thy love than wine!" And here her breasts are compared to "clusters of grapes." See No. 488.

496. CANTICLES 7:8. "And the smell of thy nose like apples." As by the roof of the mouth in the next verse is not simply [intended] the roof of the mouth itself, as though that were exceeding pleasant to the bridegroom, that being a part of the body that is hidden, but thereby is probably meant the speech which comes from the mouth; so here, by the nose, is not meant the nose itself, but the breath. So the bridegroom would hereby signify that the smell of her breath was sweet, her vitals and inwards being sound, and pure, and sweet, being made so by the food she eat, viz. apples, the food she, from time to time, desires to be refreshed with, it being the fruit that he yields, who is as the apple tree among the trees of the wood, whose fruit was sweet to her taste. Persons' breath commonly smells of the food which they eat; thus the breath of the spouse is represented as smelling like apples. See SSS.[4]

497. CANTICLES 7:9. "And the roof of thy mouth like the best wine for my beloved, that goeth down sweetly, causing the lips of those that are asleep to speak." By the "roof of the mouth" is here probably meant her discourse, which is like excellent wine that goes sweetly down, and so refreshes and enlivens other saints (whom here Christ calls his beloved), that it causes those of them that are asleep, and in the dullest frame, to speak. It enlivens their hearts and tongues in divine things.

498. JOHN 16:8–11. "And when he is come, he will convince the world of sin, of righteousness, and of judgment: of sin, because they believe not on me; of righteousness, because I go to my Father, and ye see me no more; of judgment, because the prince of this world is judged." In these words of our[5] Savior is a great manifestation of his divine knowledge and wisdom.[6]

The greatest SIN that is in the world is sin against the gospel, contempt of and opposition to Jesus Christ. And the greatest evidence of

4. Poole's exposition emphasizes the fact that "the smell of the nose" evidences not only the quality of outward activity, but also the inward condition of the person (*Synopsis Criticorum*, 2 [London, 1671], Pt. 2, cols. 2036–037).

5. MS: "a."

6. JE deleted "By righteousness ~~as though we~~ we may justly understand the righteousness chiefly."

the sin and wickedness of man is the world's ill treatment of Christ, and the gospel, and the followers of Christ. In this does most clearly appear the malignant nature of sin, and the true nature of it is fully manifest,[7] and particularly that violent opposition that appears on occasion of the pouring out of the Spirit of God. As the coming of the Spirit is the occasion of this, so his coming eventually holds forth matter of conviction to the world of its wickedness. And those that are savingly taught by the Spirit are, in the first place, convinced of sin, especially as appearing in their sinning against Christ, or against God, as revealing himself in the gospel. Thus we find that immediately after the pouring out of the Spirit of God on the day of Pentecost, the Jews that were awakened were reproved for this sin of rejecting and crucifying Christ; and for this they were pricked in their hearts and said, "Men and brethren, what shall we do?" (Acts 2:37). See also Acts 3:13–14 ff., 4:11 ff., 5:30 ff., 7:51 ff. And when Saul was converted, this especially was the sin which he was reproved for and convinced of (Act 9:4–5). In most places where the apostles preached, there first arose great opposition, and the gospel finally prevailed against that opposition, and opposers were converted. And in this case we may suppose the thing wherein chiefly they were convinced of their sinfulness was their opposition to Christ. This seems to have been the case with the jailor [Acts 16:27 ff.]. And so in all ages, they that [are] truly humbled by the Spirit of God, and brought to repentance, are wont to be convinced of their sins against the gospel.

The greatest and most glorious RIGHTEOUSNESS that ever was in the world is the righteousness of Christ. Indeed, it was infinitely the most excellent righteousness that ever was wrought out by any servant of God in heaven or earth. It was the only righteousness properly so called (i.e. agreeable to that grand and eternal rule of righteousness, the law of God) that ever was among mankind, and the only righteousness by which any of mankind are accepted as righteous. And the greatest, strongest, and most convincing evidence of the reality, excellency, sufficiency, and completeness of this righteousness was Christ's going to the Father, and his being seen here no more in such a state as he was in when the disciples saw him here. God's raising Christ from the dead was a great testimony of God to the sufficiency and completeness of Christ's righteousness. But his bestowing upon him so glorious a reward in heaven, God's exalting him at his own right hand, "far above all principality," etc. [Eph. 1:21], and there admitting this High

---

7. Up to this point the sentence is a later interlineation.

Priest into that holy of holies with his own blood, not meetly[8] to bow before the throne in humble posture as the high priests of old, but to sit down on the throne at the right hand of the Majesty on high, and so to be a priest on the throne, was a far[9] more striking evidence of it. And it was a greater evidence of the transcendent excellency of this righteousness, its acceptableness to the Father, and his exceeding delight in it. And it greatly heightens the strength and brightness of the evidence, that Christ did not only go to the Father, but that he went thither, to return no more to be seen on earth in a state of humiliation. He needed to suffer no more, to go through no more labors and self-denial, in order to complete his righteousness. He offered up himself; "by one offering he perfected forever them that are sanctified" [Heb. 10:14]. Having by his righteousness completed our redemption, he sat down forever on the right hand of God. He entered into the holiest of all, not as the high priests of old, to be there a little while and then to return, and go there again once a year; but he there enters to abide there. He is set down forever on the right hand of God. He ever lives[1] there to make continual intercession for us. See Heb. 10:12–13, and 9:11–12, 24–26.

Christ's ascension into heaven, everlastingly to live and reign there, was the greatest evidence of righteousness in all senses and respects. It was the greatest evidence of Christ's innocency, and that he suffered wrongfully. It was the greatest evidence of the righteousness and veracity in the words which he spake, the doctrines he taught concerning God and himself, and his design in coming into the world, and concerning life and immortality and a future state, and the greatest evidence and confirmation of the truth of his promises made to his disciples of eternal life and heavenly glory, and indeed of all his promises, especially taken with that consequence of his ascension, the coming of the Spirit, whereby his people are sealed to the day of redemption, the great promise of Christ, the sum of all his promises fulfilled in the earnest of it in their hearts. And this ascension, taken as the completing and crowning of the grand affair of redemption, and so taken with its antecedents, and the things manifested by it, particularly the divinity and infinite dignity of the person of Christ, I say, taken with these things, it was the greatest evidence of the righteousness and holiness of God in saving sinners, of his faithfulness in fulfilling the promises of

8. Or: "meekly."
9. JE deleted "higher testimony."
1. JE deleted "and reigns."

the Old Testament, and in general by far the greatest manifestation and the brightest effulgence of the moral perfection and glory of the divine Being that ever was.

The greatest instance of JUDGMENT that ever was, or ever will be in the world, is in Christ's judging Satan, the "prince of this world." God hath set Christ as king on his holy hill of Zion, having put all things under his feet, made him the head of all authority and power, and has committed all judgment to the Son; and this is the greatest instance of Christ's power of ruling and judging. Satan is the greatest and highest of all the enemies of God, and Christ, and his people. He [was] probably originally the highest and strongest of all creatures. He has usurped the throne, as he is called the "prince of this world." He has set up himself as God of this world. 'Tis the greatest evidence of Christ's kingly power, and his might as the captain of the salvation of his people, to overcome this enemy, dispossess him of his throne, cast him like lightning from heaven, and make him his footstool, and bruise his head under his feet. And 'tis the greatest manifestation of his high judicial authority to judge and condemn this grand rebel, and head and leader of all the rebellion in the universe, and to execute vengeance upon him.

By "judgment," as the word is used in the New Testament, as appears by the Greek concordance,[2] is most commonly meant the exercise of judicial authority, or the manifestation and effect of it, sometimes the exercise of rule and authority in general, because judging is a chief exercise of it, and sometimes particularly for a *righteous* exercise of such authority. And when the fruit or effect of judgment is meant in sentence or execution, commonly a sentence of condemnation, or the execution of such a sentence is meant. Sometimes, though rarely, the word is used to signify a judgment passed in the mind concerning moral matters, or the expression of it in words, and sometimes it means one's right in judgment, so that the use of the word in the New Testament will clearly justify the interpretation that has been given of it in this place.

---

2. JE's reference probably points to Erasmus Schmidius's concordance to the Greek testament, *Novi Testamenti Jesu Christi Graeci, hoc est, originalis linguae, ταμεῖον, aliis Concordantiae* (1638, 1716) which Alexander Cruden praised in his preface to *A Complete Concordance to the Scriptures of the Old and New Testament* as both "accurate" and "complete" [np]. JE, who took note of Cruden's positive judgment in the "Catalogue" (p. 14), later apparently owned Schmidius's volume which he lent to Samuel Hopkins on July 15, 1752 ("Diary or Account Book" [MS], p. 66).

Gospel light and knowledge consists in these three things, and the things implied in them.

A conviction of these three things is the sum of that conviction which is implied in saving faith. By the knowledge of these things, God's people say, "In the Lord have I righteousness and strength" [Is. 45:24].

In the knowledge of these things consists the true knowledge of ourselves, and the knowledge of God in Jesus Christ, or the sight of his glory in the face of Jesus Christ. The knowledge of these things is the foundation of all true compliance with the gospel in the heart, of repentance, faith, hope, charity, obedience, and joy.

The knowledge of them all is necessary to repentance, faith, hope, charity, and obedience, though in repentance is especially a conviction of sin, and a conviction of righteousness is especially the foundation of faith and charity, and a conviction of judgment especially the foundation of hope and obedience.[3]

God permitted the Fall that his elect people might know good and evil. The saving knowledge of good and evil consists in the spirit's conviction of these three things.

These three things are the most important objects of knowledge in the world, in order to sanctification and comfort, holiness and happiness.

499. JEREMIAH 2:2–3. Add this to Nos. 478, and 296, and 282. A considerable instance of the faith and obedience of that generation was their readily complying with God's command by Joshua in submitting to that painful rite of circumcision, which had been disused for above thirty-eight years, and that, just on their entering into the land of Canaan, full of their strong enemies, being now shut in by Jordan. It was not only a considerable thing for the whole congregation under forty years at once to submit to what was so painful and disagreeable, but so to expose themselves to their [enemies]; for, excepting the divine protection, they must in those circumstances have been an easy prey to their enemies, if their enemies had fallen upon them while sore, as the Shechemites were to Simeon and Levi [Gen. 34:20–31]. And having just entered the country of their gigantic and numerous enemies, that they had heard such formidable accounts of, not knowing what preparation their enemies [had made], nor how soon they

3. JE marked this paragraph with a large "X" on the left side of the page.

would fall upon them, tended to make 'em the more fearful and cautious; but they obeyed God and trusted in his protection, without murmuring against God or Joshua, as Zipporah did against Moses, saying, "Surely a bloody husband art thou to me" [Ex. 4:25]. See No. 500.[4]

500. JOSHUA 6. Concerning what the congregation of Israel were to do in order to the taking of Jericho. See No. 499. "It was to try the faith, and obedience, and patience of the people, to try whether they would obey a precept, which to human policy seemed foolish to obey, and believe a promise, which in human probability seemed impossible to be performed. They were also proved, whether they could patiently bear the reproaches of their enemies, and patiently wait for the salvation of the Lord. Thus 'by faith the walls of Jericho fell down' (Heb. 11:30). They were commanded to be silent, not to speak a word, 'nor make any noise' (v. 10), which intimates their reverent expectation of the event. Zech. 2:13, 'Be silent, O all flesh, before the Lord.' Ex. 14:14, 'God shall fight for you, and you shall hold your peace.'" They were to[5] go round the city, blowing the trumpet "for six days together, and did so, and seven times the seventh day (v. 14). God could have caused the walls of Jericho to fall upon the first surrounding them, but they must go round them thirteen times before they fall, that they may be kept waiting patiently for the Lord. Though they were newly come into Canaan, and their time was very precious, for they had a great deal of work before them, yet they must linger so many days about Jericho, seeming to do nothing, nor to make any progress in their business. He that believes does not make haste. Go yet seven times before anything appears (I Kgs. 15:43)." Henry.[6]

Their faith was further tried in that one of the seven days must needs be the sabbath, on which they were commanded to rest. A unbelieving mind would have objected on that account, as the unbelieving Jews objected against Christ's healing and commanding the man to carry his bed on the sabbath day. It is to be noted that it was the same person, even Jesus Christ, who now commanded the people to go round Jericho, and the priests all the while to blow the trumpets on the sabbath, which commanded the impotent man to carry his bed on the sabbath (John 5:11). Compare Josh. 5:13–15 and 6:2–5.

4. This cross-reference is a later addition.
5. JE deleted "compass."
6. Henry, *Exposition*, 2 (1725), 23–24.

A further trial of the people's faith was that all the men of war,[7] in going round the city, were obliged to leave their camp, and all their goods, and their wives and children, every day defenseless, as to any other guard but the divine protection.

This last observed is agreeable to God's proceedings in the course of his providence, in the revolutions of the natural world, and in the revolutions in the world of mankind. Things only seem to go round [and] round and return where they were before, as though no progress was made, till God's time comes. But this is through the narrowness of our views. He that looks only on the wheel of a chariot and sees nothing beyond it, won't see that it does anything but go round, the same spoke rising and falling alternately to the same place. But he that looks beyond the wheel to the world around, may see the progress that is made continually to an appointed journey's end.

This generation failed not of their duty under such temptations, as Saul failed under when he was sent to destroy Agag [I Sam. 15]. They destroy all the inhabitants, cattle, and goods of Jericho, the first city they took, when they were under the greatest temptation greedily to take 'em to themselves, being lately come out of the wilderness, where they had been destitute of all such things for so long a time. None transgressed but Achan; and when he was found out, none stood in his defense, but "all Israel stoned him with stones" [Josh. 7:25].

See how Joshua commands the soldiers of the two tribes and half (Josh. 22:1–3).

501a. Micah 5:2.[8] "But thou, Bethlehem Ephratah, though thou be little among the thousands of Judah, yet out of thee shall he *come forth* unto me that is to be ruler in Israel, *whose goings forth* have been from of old, from everlasting."

Here it may be noted[9] concerning these two expressions in the verse, "shall he come forth unto me," and that other, "whose goings forth have been from of old," etc., that the verb COME FORTH, in the former, and GOINGS FORTH, in the latter, are words of the same root in the Hebrew.[1]

Now in order to an understanding of this text, and a clear discerning of the great doctrines taught in it, it may be worth the while to observe

7. MS: "men."
8. JE failed to number this entry initially.
9. JE deleted "that when it is said."
1. יֵצֵא and מוֹצָאֹתָיו.

particularly how these words, and words of this root, are used in the Hebrew Bible.

These words are often used to signify the proceeding or flowing forth of water, as from a fountain. Gen. 2:10, "A river *went out* of Eden"; Deut. 8:7, "fountains that *spring out* of valleys"; Ezek. 47:1, "waters *issued out* from under the threshold"; v. 8, "waters issue"; so v. 12. Zech. 14:8, "Living waters shall *go out* of Jerusalem"; Num. 20:11, "and the waters *came out* abundantly"; Judg. 15:19, "and there *came* water *thereout*," i.e. out of the jawbone, or out of Lehi. Is. 58:11, "Like a *spring* of water," in the Hebrew, "a *going forth* of waters";[2] so Ps. 107:33, "*water springs*," Hebrew, "going forth of water"; so v. 35, "*water springs*"; Is. 41:18, "the dry land *springs* of water."

They are often used to signify the rising of the sun, or the rising of the light of the morning, or the proceeding of beams of light from a shining body or luminary. Gen. 19:23, "The sun was *risen* on the earth"; Ezek. 7:10, "the morning is *gone forth*"; Is. 13:10, "the sun shall be darkened in his *going forth*." Is. 62:1, "*Go forth* as brightness"; Hos. 6:5, "thy judgments are as the light that goeth forth." Ps. 19:6, "His *going forth* is from the end of heaven"; Ps. 65:8, "the *outgoings* of the morning."

They are often used [to signify] the springing or sprouting of plants, or something that grows like a plant. Job 14:2, "He *cometh forth* like a flower"; Is. 11:1, "and there *came forth* a rod out of the stem of Jesse"; I Kgs. 4:33, "the hyssop that *springeth out* of the wall." Deut. 14:22, "All that the field *bringeth forth*," Hebrew, "all that goeth forth out of the field";[3] Job 8:16, "his branch *shooteth forth* in his garden." Dan. 8:8, There *came forth* four notable horns; Ex. 25:32, "six branches shall *come out* of the sides of it"; so vv. 33, 35, and Ex. 37:18, 21. Is. 42:5, "He that spread forth the earth, and that which cometh out of it."

They are often used to express the proceeding [of] a word or voice from him whose word or voice it is. Gen. 24:50, "The word proceedeth from the Lord"; Judg. 11:36, "according to that which proceedeth out of thy mouth"; Esther 7:8, "as the word went out of the king's mouth"; Jer. 44:17, "whatsoever thing goeth forth from" my mouth; Dan. 9:23, "came forth" the word. Is. 48:3, "They went forth out of my mouth"; Num. 30:2, "do according to all that proceedeth out of his mouth"; Ezek. 33:30, "what is the word that cometh forth from the Lord." Num. 32:24, "Do that which proceedeth out of your mouth"; Josh.

2. וּכְמוֹצָא מָיִם.
3. הַיֹּצֵא הַשָּׂדֶה.

6:10, "neither shall any word proceed out of your mouth." I Sam. 2:3, "Let not arrogancy, or hard speech, come out of your mouth"; Job 37:2, "the sound that goeth out of his mouth"; Is. 55:11, "my word that goeth out of my mouth." Lam. 3:38, "Out of the mouth of the Most High proceedeth not evil and good"; Ps. 89:34, "nor alter the thing which is gone out of my lips," Hebrew, "alter the going forth of my lips."

They are very often used for proceeding by generation, both as from the father and the mother.

They are often used for proceeding from a father by generation. II Sam. 16:11, "My son, which came forth out of my bowels"; Gen. 10:14, "out of whom came Philistim"; so I Chron. 1:12. I Chron. 2:53, "Of them came the Zareathites"; Is. 48:1, "are come forth out of the waters of Judah." I Kgs. 8:19, "Thy son that cometh forth out of thy loins"; so II [Chron.] 6:9, the same words; Gen 46:26, "that came out of his loins"; so Ex. 1:5, "that came out of the loins of Jacob"; Judg. 8:30, "threescore and ten sons" going out of his thigh, so in the Hebrew. Gen. 15:4, "He that shall come forth out of thine own bowels"; II Sam. 7:12, "thy seed which shall proceed out of thy bowels"; II Kgs. 20:18, "and of thy sons which shall issue from thee." Is. 39:7, "Thy sons which shall issue from thee"; Gen. 17:6, "kings shall come out of thee"; Gen. 35:11, "kings shall come out of thy loins"; II Chron. 32:21, "they that came forth out of his bowels." Jer. 30:21, "Their nobles shall be of themselves, and their governor shall proceed from the midst of them." So commonly the word "offspring," in our translation, in the Hebrew is a word of this root, that signifies as much as "goings forth." Is. 22:24, "All the glory of his father's house, the *offspring*, and the issue"; Is. 48:19, "the offspring of thy bowels"; Is. 44:3, "my blessing upon thine offspring"; Is. 61:9, "their offspring among the people"; Is. 65:23, "and their offspring with them"; Job 21:8, "and their offspring before their eyes." Job 27:14, "His offspring shall not be satisfied"; Job 31:8, "yea, my offspring be rooted out."

They are often used to signify a being born, or that proceeding which there is in the birth from the mother. Gen. 25:26, "His brother came out"; Gen. 38:28, "this came out first"; v. 29, "his brother came out"; v. 30, "afterwards came out his brother." Job 38:29, "Out of whose womb came the ice?" Eccles. 5:15, "As he came forth out of his mother's womb"; Job 3:11, "when I came out of the belly"; Job 10:18, "wherefore came I forth out of the womb." Job 1:21, "Naked came I out of my mother's womb"; Ex. 21:22, "so that her fruit depart from her"; Deut. 28:57, "her young one that cometh out from between her feet"; Num. 12:12, "when he cometh forth out of his mother's womb"; Job 38:8, "as if it had issued out of the womb."

Now concerning these things, I would make the following observations.

1. The generation of mankind, their proceeding from their fathers, or ancestor, or of a particular stock and family, is often compared in the Old Testament to the issue of waters from a fountain; so Is. 48:1, Ps. 68:26, Deut. 33:28, and other places.

2. The generation of mankind is often compared to the springing or shooting forth of plants. Is. 44:3–4, "I will pour my blessing upon thine offspring, and they shall spring up as among the grass, and as the willows by the water courses." Ps. 72:16, "They of the city shall flourish as the grass of the earth." So Job 14:2, "He cometh forth as a flower"; and many other places. And particularly is the birth of the Messiah often compared to the springing of a plant or branch, as in Is. 11:1. "There came forth a rod out of the stem of Jesse." See many other places in my discourse on the "Prophecies of the Messiah."[4]

3. The birth of a prince is compared to the rising of a luminary, the birth of Christ in particular, in that prophecy of Balaam: "A star shall rise out of Jacob" [Num. 24:17].

4. It being thus, and the words used in this [passage], Micah 5:2, which express the Messiah's "coming forth" out of Bethlehem, and also his "goings forth" from everlasting, being the same, or from the same root, with those that are so often used to signify the issuing of waters from a fountain, and the sprouting forth of plants, and the going forth of a luminary, and not only so, but also abundantly used expressly to signify generation, or a being born, hence 'tis most reasonable and natural to understand the "coming forth" and "goings forth" of the Messiah, here spoken of, concerning his generation.

5. Considering these things, and that the word used, when it is said that the Messiah shall "come forth" out of Bethlehem, is so often used to signify a person's being born of his mother, and to be "born unto" such an one is a phrase used in the Scripture to signify that[5] the person to whom he is said to be born is his father, hence when God says, Out of

---

4. In "Miscellanies," no. 891, entitled "CHRISTIAN RELIGION. PROPHECIES OF THE MESSIAH," JE wrote extended expositions of such texts as Is. 11:1, Jer. 23:5–6, Jer. 33:15–16, Zech. 3:8–10, etc. In each of these texts he points to the coming of the Messiah being spoken of as a "branching forth" or "growing out."

5. JE deleted "such an one is his father."

Bethlehem shall the Messiah "come forth unto me," 'tis most natural to interpret it thus. "In Bethlehem shall the Messiah be born of a woman, who shall be his mother, but not as begotten of a man, or having any man for his father. But I only will be his Father. She shall not bear this child to any earthly father, but to me only."

6. And when then these words are subjoined, "whose *goings forth* were of old, of everlasting," and the word, "goings forth," are so very frequently used for generation of a father, hence it is most natural to interpret the text thus. "In Bethlehem shall the Messiah be born of his mother, who is begotten not by any man, but by me only as his Father. And this generation of him, by which I am his Father, won't be then a new thing. It is an eternal generation; it has been already 'of old, from everlasting.'"

7. It greatly confirms that the "goings forth," which are said to be "of old, of everlasting," intends his eternal generation, or proceeding from the Father; that Christ, with respect to his proceeding from the Father, is represented as the Father's glory and brightness, as though he proceeded from him, as brightness from a luminary, and as the Father's "word"; and that the original word used here is so,[6] from time to time, used to signify the going forth of light or brightness, and abundantly for the proceeding of a word from him whose word it is.

501b. HEBREWS 6:4–6. Concerning "those who were once enlightened," etc. 'Tis an argument that those here spoken of are such as were never regenerated, that they are compared to the thorny ground, which, however it may seem to receive the seed and to nourish it, so that it may spring up and appear flourishing a while, yet never brings forth any good fruit, but the fruit finally produced always is briars and thorns, because the ground is thorny, full of seeds and roots of thorns, which never [were] purged out to prepare the ground for the good seed. So that whatever showers descend upon it, how benign soever they are, yet only go to nourish the thorns, and make 'em grow the faster, v. 8, which representation certainly implies that the ground is naught. It was never so changed as to prepare it to bring forth good fruit. 'Tis a good rule in our endeavors to understand the mind of the Spirit of God, to compare spiritual things with spiritual, and to interpret Scripture by Scripture. Now 'tis manifest that Christ represents the thorny ground as different from the good ground. The ground

6. JE deleted "often used to."

itself is naught, and not fitted so to receive and nourish the seed as to bring good fruit to perfection. And they that are represented by the thorny ground are, in Christ's explanation of the parable [Luke 8:4–15], distinguished from those that have good and honest hearts. The fault of the wayside, of the stony ground, and the thorny ground, was, in each, the nature of the ground; and the good fruit in the good ground is ascribed to the better nature of the ground. And therefore they that are here represented as ground, which though often receiving refreshing benign showers, and yet always bringing forth briars and thorns, is ground that never has been purged, and changed, and made good, but is inveterately evil, and therefore fit for nothing but to be burnt. 'Tis not impossible that thorny ground may be brought to bring forth good fruit, but then it must be changed. The very roots of the thorns must be killed or rooted up. If this ben't done, let good seed be sown in it, and good and kindly showers of rain descend upon it never so often, it will bring forth briars and thorns. This killing or rooting up of the lusts of the heart, compared to thorns, is done by a work of regeneration, or circumcising the heart, as is represented, Jer. 4:3–4. "Break up your fallow ground; sow not among thorns. Circumcise yourselves to the Lord, and take away the foreskins of your heart, lest my fury come forth like fire, and burn that none can quench it." There the end of the ground that bears briars and thorns is represented as being to be burned, as here in the 6th chapter of Hebrews. This is the end of those whose hearts do as it were bring forth briars and thorns, and that, because their hearts were never circumcised, i.e. never regenerated.

In Luke 8:18, when Christ had ended the parable of the sower, he concludeth, "Take heed how you hear" (i.e. that you, in hearing the word, ben't like the wayside, the stony or thorny ground, on which the seed fell); for, says Christ, "Whosoever hath, to him shall be given; and whosoever hath not, from him shall be taken, even that which he seemeth to have," referring still to the parable, and the taking away, or the withering and perishing of the seed from the evil sorts of ground, implying that such have no true spiritual life, no real goodness, and that the seeming good they have, they shall lose.

502. EPHESIANS 1:19–22. "And what is the exceeding greatness of his power to us-ward," etc., "according to the working of his mighty power, which he wrought in Christ Jesus, when he raised him from the dead, and set him at his own right hand in heavenly places, far

above all principality, and power," etc., "and hath put all things under his feet," etc.

In the work that was wrought, and the alteration made in exalting Christ from the depth of his humiliation to his height of glory, two things are to be considered, viz. the relative and circumstantial change, or change of Christ's circumstances, and the real change made in the human nature, which was not only greatly exalting it from that low state, state of sorrow, weakness of body and mind, and comparative meanness of nature, and narrow capacity, to that high and as it were infinite degree of knowledge, power, holiness, joy, and real inherent glory (Here is to be considered the change made both in body and soul. Christ in his exaltation not only received power, riches, honor, and blessing, wherein the change of circumstances consisted, but also wisdom and strength, as in Rev. 5:12.), and exalting it to this from a far lower state, from a state of death, under which he descended into the lower parts of the earth, and as it were into hell, in raising him from which, we may conceive greater difficulty than in raising another from the dead, as we may suppose all the powers of hell engaged to their utmost to hinder his resurrection. This real change made in Christ in his resurrection and exaltation is an unspeakably greater power than the work of creation, not only considering the term from which was a state of death, and so a creation as it were from nothing, but as overcoming the greatest created power, but especially if we consider the term to which, or the thing finally extant, or the fruit of this work, which is as it were infinitely higher, greater, and more excellent than anything accomplished in the old creation.

But then Christ in this affair is not to be considered, nor is considered by the Apostle, singly and personally;[7] but all his church are considered as thus raised and exalted with him, and in him, he as the head, and they as partaking members. This power is manifested in raising them, in raising their dead souls from an infinite depth, infinitely lower than a state of nonentity, and from under as it were infinitely strong chains to hold 'em in that state, and the most mighty opposition to their restoration; and also raising their bodies from the dead, and from a state of corruption, and exalting them with Christ, making their bodies like his glorious body, and their souls like his glorious soul, giving them a participation of his elevation of nature, his exalted knowledge, strength, holiness, beauty, glory, and joy, according to their capacity and station. Herein, in this whole work of restora-

---

7. JE deleted "as though he only was thus raised."

tion and exaltation of Christ mystical, is above all things manifested the power of God in the new creation.

503. ISAIAH 11:10. "And in that day there shall be a root of Jesse, which shall stand for an ensign of the people; to it shall the Gentiles seek. And his rest shall be glorious," or as it is in the original, "his rest shall be glory."[8] There is an evident allusion in these words to the things which came to pass pertaining to the affair of God's redeeming the children of Israel out of Egypt, leading them through the wilderness, and bringing them [into Canaan]. This is very manifest by the words immediately following, and by all the succeeding context to the end of the chapter. This is a prophecy of a second, much greater work of salvation, wherein not only the Jews, but the Gentiles and all nations, shall partake. When God redeemed his people out of Egypt to lead 'em to Canaan, which was God's rest, they were gathered together under ensigns. They were the standards, or ensigns, of the four quarters of the army: those of Judah, Reuben, Ephraim, and Dan. And then the ensign for the whole army,[9] placed in the middle of the congregation, was the tabernacle and ark, where was Moses, the captain and leader of the whole host, with his rod, which was used from time to time as the banner, or ensign, of the congregation, as it was especially at the time when it was held up over Israel while they were fighting with Amalek, and obtained a signal victory under that ensign, on which occasion Moses built an altar and called it *Jehovah Nissi*, "the Lord my banner," or ensign [Ex. 17:15]. (The word is the same in the original[1] as here in this place in Isaiah.) And both the rod and altar were types of Christ (who is Jehovah),[2] who then was the ensign of his church, and would more especially and gloriously be exhibited as such in the days of the gospel, as is here foretold in Isaiah. As then it was a rod that was held up as an ensign of the people, so here in this 11th [chapter] of Isaiah, Christ is spoken of as a "rod," as in the first verse. "And there shall come forth a rod out of the stem of Jesse, and a branch shall grow out of his roots." So in this 10th verse. "And in that day there shall be a root of Jesse, which [shall] stand for an ensign," i.e. plainly a rod or plant from a root of Jesse (though something further may be aimed in using the phrase, "root of Jesse."

---

8. וְהָיְתָה מְנֻחָתוֹ כָּבוֹד.

9. JE deleted "or congregation."

1. נֵס.

2. JE deleted "which is the very thing plainly meant."

As the rod of Moses was occasionally used as an ensign of the people, so more constantly the tabernacle and ark. These were placed in the midst of the congregation, and the whole was to pitch in exact order round about it, at due distance from it, all having equal respect to it. And the ark is represented as going before the people in their marches (Num. 10:33), because, that however it was in the middle of the army, yet they had respect to [it] as their guide, their banner, that[3] all whose motions they were to attend. When they went through Jordan into Canaan, their "rest," the ark was remarkably made use of as the ensign of the people. It was to be carried before them at such a distance that it might be well seen by all the leaders of the people; and they were to take heed to its motions with the greatest care and exactness, and to follow when that went (Josh. 3:3–4).

But more especially was the pillar of cloud and fire the ensign of that congregation in their marches from Egypt to Canaan, their rest. A banner or ensign was lifted up on high, that it might be seen by the whole company. The ark and tabernacle could not be seen by the whole congregation, but the pillar of cloud and fire, which abode on the tabernacle and departed not from it, were lifted up to open sight, and displayed to the view of every individual person. That was the banner the people were listed under, that they were always to cleave to most strictly, and diligently to observe, [and] steadfastly to follow, and never to depart from, and were to be directed by it in every step they took. When that moved, they were to move; when that rested, they must rest. See Num. 9:15–23. This pillar of cloud and fire was the special symbol of Christ's presence, and in that's standing as an ensign, Christ stood as an ensign of the people. And 'tis moreover very manifest that that pillar of cloud and fire was a remarkable type of Christ incarnate, or the Son of God in the human [nature], concerning whom it is here prophesied that he should stand as an ensign of the people.

When it is said, "HIS REST SHALL BE GLORY," there is doubtless an allusion to Canaan, the promised rest that the ark and pillar of cloud and fire led the children of Israel [to]; and the thing intended is heaven. 'Tis said, Num. 10:33, that "the ark of the covenant of the Lord (over which was the pillar of cloud, as in the following verse) went before the people to search out a resting place for them." That was the use of their ensigns to which that people were gathered together. They were to lead 'em to their rest. The "rest," spoken of in the text under

---

3. JE deleted "that they were to follow and attend."

consideration, is called "Christ's rest," which is agreeable to the style used concerning the rest to which God was leading the congregation in the wilderness. Ps. 95:11, "To whom he sware in his wrath that they should never enter into MY REST."

Here the "rest" that Jesus Christ, God-man, or the rest to which he should bring the Gentiles as well as Jews after his incarnation, is spoken of as another rest, a different rest from that which God brought the Jews to[4] of old, agreeable to the observation of the Apostle, Heb. 4:8–10. "For if Jesus had given them rest, then would he not afterward [have] spoken of another day. There remaineth therefore a rest to the people of God. For he that is entered into his rest, he also hath ceased from his own works, as God did from his." Here 'tis remarkable that, take these words of the Apostle with the foregoing context, the Apostle seems to suppose that what is called "God's rest," or "Christ's rest," in the promises of the Old Testament, is so called not only because it was a rest of God's providing and promising, but because it was his personally. So here the rest which remains for the people of God, which Christ gives his people, is spoken of as Christ's own rest and happiness that he has entered into. And so the land of Canaan of old was represented as God's own dwelling place, his inheritance, etc., his "mountain in the field" [Jer. 17:3], etc.; and therefore, when God brought the people out of Egypt to Canaan, he is represented as having brought 'em to himself. But especially was that particular part of Canaan, which God chose to place his name there, represented as God's or Christ's rest, namely, Jerusalem, Mt. Zion, and the temple. Ps. 132:8, "Arise, O Lord, into thy rest; thou, and the ark of thy strength." Vv. 13–14, "The Lord hath chosen Zion; he hath desired it for his habitation. This is my rest forever; here will I dwell, for I have desired it." I Chron. 28:2, "It was in my heart to build an house of rest for the ark of the covenant of the Lord." The temple that Solomon built was the rest of the ark, and the rest of the cloud of glory that abode over the ark, which had before that wandered long in the wilderness, and had "walked in a tent and in a tabernacle" (II Sam. 7:6). But when the temple was built in the place which God chose, then the glory of the Lord had rest, took up its settled abode there as the place it delighted in. And Mt. Zion and the temple are in Scripture often represented as the dwelling place, and quiet and delightful abode, which they long after, and never can be at rest till they come to dwell, and which shall be

---

4. JE deleted "under Joshua."

their settled dwelling place. How often does the Psalmist, speaking not only in his own name, but the name of the church, express his longings and pantings after God's courts, his amiable tabernacles, his altars, etc., and make this place his rest, as the swallow and sparrow their nest did. And how often do the prophets foretell of a future redemption of God's people, and their coming from places of captivity and bondage, and from under the hand of their enemies, to dwell in Mt. Zion, and in God's holy mountain, etc.

But yet sometimes the prophets speak of no temple built by men as God's true rest, but represent heaven as God's true rest. Is. 66:1, "Thus saith the Lord, The heaven is my throne, and the earth is my footstool. Where is the house that ye build unto me, and where is the place of my rest?" And Is. 57:15, "For thus saith the high and lofty One that inhabiteth eternity, whose name is Holy, I dwell in the high and holy place," etc.

The "rest" of that root of Jesse, that should stand for an ensign, is said to be "glory"; so the land of Canaan, Zion, and the temple, the rest of him, who, as an ensign to the people, in the pillar of cloud and fire, are represented. The land of Canaan is called "the glory of all lands" (Ezek. 20:6, 15), and "the glorious land" (Dan. 11:16), and "the glorious holy mountain" (v. 45). Mt. Zion is said to be "beautiful for situation, the joy of the whole earth" [Ps. 48:2], and in another place, to be "the perfection of beauty" [Ps. 50:2]. So concerning the temple, it is spoken of as "exceeding magnificent, of fame, and of glory throughout all lands" (I Chron. 22:5). So in Ps. 29:2, as the words might have [been] (and probably better) translated, it is said, "Worship the Lord in his glorious sanctuary." Ps. 96:6, "Honor and majesty are before him; strength and beauty are in his sanctuary." Jer. 17:12, "A glorious high throne from the beginning is the place of our sanctuary." [The] temple was truly glorious in Solomon's time, when the people first began fully to enjoy the promised rest in Canaan, David having fully subdued the inhabitants of the land and their enemies round about; and then indeed the land was happy and glorious.

All these things show plainly that here is an allusion to God's salvation of Israel of old, when they were brought out of Egypt, and led through the wilderness to Canaan under Christ as their ensign, manifested by those types and symbols of his presence: Moses' rod, the tabernacle and ark, and especially the cloud of glory above them; and that the rod of Jesse, here spoken of, is that person there exhibited in those types [and] symbols. And they all manifestly show that the Messiah was to work out another redemption far greater than that of Egypt, of both Gentiles and Jews, and gather both into one great congregation, and lead 'em to another and far more glorious rest than that of Canaan, Jerusalem, and the temple, even in their greatest glory in Solomon's time, and a rest which should be his own land, and his own dwelling place, and temple, where his people should partake with him in his rest, happiness, and glory. And so that, as the Apostle says, there "remains a rest to the people of God" [Heb. 4:9], besides that which Joshua brought Israel into, and that heaven is that rest. Some description is given of the comfort and happiness of the rest, which this ensign guides God's[5] people to, in the next chapter.

504. EPHESIANS 2:7. "That in the ages to come he might show the exceeding riches of his grace in his kindness towards us in Christ Jesus." Dr. Goodwin's *Works*, Vol. 1, part 2, p. 237.

There are two interpretations of this.

I. Some say that what is intended is God's holding forth in that kindness which he had shown to the primitive Christians, whom he had converted out of so desperate and damnable a condition, an assurance of the communication of the like riches of his grace in all ages to come, to the end of the world, whereof they were the patterns and examples. I find most of the Protestant writers run this way, and the most judicious among the Papists.

II. Others say, that this showing forth the riches of his grace in ages to come, is to eternity, after the resurrection, which he had spoken of in the words immediately before, and that these words do contain the utmost accomplishment, the manifestation and breaking up of the hidden treasure, which shall be expended in the world to come, and requires an eternity to be spending in. And I find this latter to be the sense that all the ancient interpreters run upon, not one exempted, and some of our Protestant writers, and most of the Papists.

Ibid., p. 238. That of the Apostle, I Tim. 1:16, is alleged as parallel with those words in the former interpretation. "For this cause I obtained mercy, that in me first Jesus Christ might show forth all long-suffering, for a pattern to them which should hereafter believe on him to life everlasting."

5. MS: "Ensign that Guide Gods."

Pp. 240–244.

But to go on to the second interpretation, which I think to be as much the scope of the Apostle here, if not more than the other. And if both cannot stand together, I had rather cast it, to exclude the other and take this. To confirm this interpretation to you, I shall lead you along through these several reasons.

I will begin with the phrase, "in the ages to come," in opposition to "this present world," as the Apostle calleth this in Gal. 1:4. You have the very phrase in the first chapter of this epistle (to the Ephesians), v. 21, "Far above all principality," etc., "not only in this world, but that which is to come," ἐν τῷ αἰῶνι. The word translated there, "world to come," is the word which is used here for "ages." And in Heb. 6:5, they are said to have tasted of "the powers of the world to come"; it is the word that is here used for "ages."

But it will be objected, Are "ages" in the plural, taken for the times after the day of judgment to eternity, where there is no flux of time?

For that, my brethren, the Scripture often expresseth it in the plural also. You read of the phrase, "for ever and ever"; you have it in Revelation again and again. We shall reign with Christ "for ever and ever"; it is for ages and ages. You have the same in Rom. 16:27; and in the 3rd chapter of this epistle (to the Ephesians), v. 21, you shall find it is in the plural as well as here. "Unto him be glory in the church by Christ Jesus throughout all ages, world without end." He means not only this world, but the world that is to come too. And why? Because that to come is "the age of ages"; it is the *secula seculorum*.

And then it is to be considered that in these words, "That in the ages to come he might show the exceeding riches of his grace," is held forth God's ultimate and highest end that he hath in the salvation of man. He mentions it as the close of all, in the language of a final event. But this is accomplished in heaven, nowhere else. The gospel revealeth infinite grace to us, but the exceeding riches of grace shall be broken up in the world to come. There is a reserve of it for eternity, such as we cannot now comprehend. Therefore here is now intended the actual enjoyment that those saints, which God hath now quickened and set in heaven in Christ, shall have in ages to come, of those exceeding riches of grace which Christ hath taken possession of for them in heaven.

And then is to be observed the Apostle's order in discoursing of our salvation in this place. He sets out salvation in all the gradual accomplishments of it, till it is made fully perfect and complete. First, he shows what is begun in our own persons, in quickening of us. He tells us, secondly, how heaven and the resurrection is made sure to us, though we do not enjoy it. V. 6, "He hath raised us up together, and made us sit together in heavenly places in Christ Jesus." Now then here in the 7th verse, as the close of all, he shows how that God will spend to eternity the exceeding, the utmost riches of that grace; there he will show it, and then he will bring it forth. In the world to come, he will bring forth all his rich treasure, and then shall salvation be complete, and there shall be the utmost demonstration of it.

It answers the parallel that the Apostle did intend to make between Christ and us. He tells us, in the first chapter, that the same power works in us that believe, that "wrought in Christ when God raised him from the dead, and set him at his own right hand in heavenly places" [Eph. 1:20]. And here you see, in the 6th verse of this 2nd chapter, the verse next before the text, he brings in the parallel. He "hath quickened us," saith he, "and raised us up, and made us sit in heaven in him." There it is said of Christ, that in heaven he sits "far above all principality," etc., "not only in this world, but that which is to come" [Eph. 1:21]. To make up the reddition now on our parts, he shows us in this chapter. Saith he, "You have worlds to come" (for it is the same word, only in the plural number) "to sit with Christ, and you shall have all the riches of God's free grace, bringing in joys and happiness to you, to feast you with unto eternity."

Then again, the phrase, "show forth," will exceedingly fit this interpretation. For we do not see now otherwise than by faith the riches of the glory that Christ hath taken possession of for us in heaven. But, saith he, after the resurrection, in the world or ages to come, he will show them forth. And so it is a parallel place with that, Col. 3:3–4, where [the Apostle] had said, v. 1, "Ye are risen with Christ." As here he addeth, "Your life is hid with Christ in God, but when Christ, who is your life, shall appear, then shall ye also appear with him in glory."

That in Rom. 9:23 is a clear parallel to this in the text. The Apostle there, in v. 22, says, "What if God, willing to show his wrath" (it is the same word), "and to make his power known, and that he might make known the riches of his grace," which he there calls the "riches of his glory, on the vessels of mercy, before prepared unto glory."

The word likewise, "exceeding riches," agrees well with this sense. The Apostle useth the phrase, "the exceeding riches of his grace," nowhere that I know of, but here. And why? Because he speaks of the utmost manifestation and accomplishment of the height of the riches of grace, which shall not be till then.

And there is another confirmation also of this interpretation. We have here a continued discourse of the Apostle, which began with the 18th verse of the foregoing chapter, which ends with this verse of the second chapter. There he begins this discourse by praying that they might know what is "the riches of the glory of his inheritance in the saints," and then concludes his discourse in this verse by signifying that there is a world to come, wherein God will show forth "the exceeding riches of his grace" towards them. The Apostle begins and ends his discourse with those riches of grace and glory in this glorious circle, involving all things concerning our salvation.[6]

See No. 300.[7]

505. EXODUS 3:18. "And you shall say unto him, The Lord God of the Hebrews hath met with us; and now let us go, we beseech thee, three days' journey into the wilderness, that we may sacrifice to the Lord our God." That is, inform Pharaoh that your God, that hath met with you, has instructed you to ask this of him. In this Pharaoh was not treated with any falsehood or unjust deceit. The utmost that can be supposed by any objector is, that here is an implicit promise, that if he would let 'em go three days' journey into the wilderness, they would return again after they had there served their God, and received the revelation of his will, which he should there make to them. But if[8] there had not been not only an implicit but an express promise of this, it might have been so consistent with[9] God's real design, and the revelations of it that he had made to Moses, and by him to the people,

---

6. Thomas Goodwin, *An Exposition on the First Eleven Verses of the Second Chapter of the Epistle to the Ephesians*, in *The Works of Thomas Goodwin*, Vol. I, Pt. 2 (London, 1681), pp. 237–38, 240–44.

7. This cross-reference is a later addition.

8. JE deleted "we should suppose not only an."

9. JE deleted "the goals God had revealed of his real design."

without any false or unjust dealing. God knew that Pharaoh would not comply with the proposal, and that his refusal would be the very occasion of their final deliverance. He knew he would order it so, and therefore might reveal this as the event that should finally be brought to pass, and promise it to his people, though he revealed not to 'em the exact time and particular means and way of its accomplishment. Conditional promises or threatenings of that which God knows shall never come to pass, and which he decreed and revealed shall not come to pass, are not inconsistent with God's perfect justice and truth, as when God promised the prince and people of the Jews in Jeremiah's time that the city should surely be preserved, and never should be destroyed by its enemies, if they would repent, and turn to God, and cleave to him, though it has been often most expressly and absolutely foretold that Jerusalem should be destroyed by the Chaldeans, and as the apostle Paul denounced unto the mariners, that were about to flee out of the ship, that if they did, the ship's crew must perish, though he had before, in the name of God, foretold and promised that there should be the loss of no man's life, but only of the ship [Acts 27:22].

506. THE BOOK OF PSALMS. See Nos. 434 and 440. That this is divinely inspired may be further argued from this, that it is every way probable that what are called "the songs of Zion" and "the Lord's song," in Ps. 137:3–4, are songs contained in this book. It appears that Zion, or God's church, had sacred songs, fancied as such in the world, and that they were properly called "the Lord's songs," which argues that they had God for their author, and were consecrated by his authority as a "word." Being called the "word of the Lord" argues it to be a word that came from God; and as a house being called "the house of the Lord" signified its being an house consecrated to God by divine authority, so of the Lord's day, the city of God, the altar of God, etc.

When all the utensils of the temple were exactly, and even in the most minute circumstances, formed by divine direction, it would be strange if the songs of the temple, which are vastly more important and material in the worship of God, should not be formed by divine direction. These were not merely external circumstances of divine worship as the other, but the very matter of the worship. As David was divinely instructed in all the place, and form, and instruments of the temple, and all the new ordinances relating to the attendance and orders of the priests, and the new business of the Levites, and the circumstances of their ministration, and particularly of the singers, it would be strange if the songs that they were to sing, the most material and essential thing of all, should not be of divine appointment, but should be left wholly to human wisdom and invention. See I Chron. 6:31, and 16:4–7, 23:6, 25–32, and ch. 25, and 28:11–21, especially vv. 19 and 21.

We have an account that David and Samuel the seer acted jointly in appointing the order of the porters of the Levites (I Chron. 9:22), and much more the order of the Levites that were to be singers. 'Tis noted of some of those Levites themselves, that were appointed by David as chief musicians or singers, [that they] were seers or prophets; so of Heman (I Chron. 25:5). And the expressions there in that verse and the context lead us to suppose that he acted as prophet in that matter, in assisting David in composing psalms, and appointing the order of singers. Yea, 'tis expressly said that the order of the singers was appointed by David with the assistance of the prophets by the commandment of the Lord. II Chron. 29:25, "And he set the Levites in the house of the Lord with cymbals, with psalteries, and with harps, according to the commandment of David, and of Gad, the king's seer, and Nathan the prophet. For so was the commandment of the Lord by his prophets." And Asaph, another of the chief musicians, and penman of many of the psalms, is spoken [of] as acting as a seer or prophet in this matter. V. 30, "Hezekiah the king commanded the Levites to sing praise unto the Lord, with the words of David, and of Asaph the seer." See the like of Jeduthun (II Chron. 35:15).

507. The great agreement between the BOOK OF SOLOMON'S SONG and the 45th psalm, and the express and full testimonies of the New Testament for the authority and divine inspiration of that psalm in particular, and that the bridegroom there spoken of is Christ, whose bride, the New Testament abundantly teaches us, is the church, I say, this agreement with those full testimonies are a great confirmation of the constant tradition of the Jewish church, and the universal and continual suffrage of the Christian church for the divine authority and spiritual signification of this song, as representing the union and mutual love of Christ and his church, and enervates the main objections against it. They agree in all particulars that are considerable, so that there is no more reason to object against one than the other.

They are both love songs.

In both, the lovers spoken [of] are compared to a man and a woman, and their love to that which arises between the sexes among mankind.

Both these songs treat of these lovers with relation to their espousals one to another, representing their union to that of a bridegroom and bride.

In both the bridegroom is represented as a king, and in both the bride is spoken of as a king's daughter. Ps. 45:13, "The king's daughter is all glorious," etc. Cant. 7:1, "How beautiful are thy feet, O prince's daughter."

In each, both the bridegroom and bride are represented as very fair or beautiful. The bridegroom, Ps. 45:2, "Thou art fairer than the sons of men." Cant. 5:10, "My beloved is white and ruddy, the chiefest among ten thousands."

In both the bridegroom is represented as greatly delighted with the beauty of the bride. Ps. 45:11, "So shall the king greatly desire thy beauty." Cant. 4:9, "Thou hast ravished my heart, my sister, my spouse; thou hast ravished my heart with one of thine eyes, with one chain of thy neck."

In both the speech of the bridegroom is represented as exceeding excellent and pleasant. Ps. 45:2, "Grace is poured into thy lips." Cant. 5:16, "His mouth is most sweet."

In both the ornaments of the bride are represented by costly, beautiful, and splendid attire, and in both as adorned with gold. Ps. 45:9, "Upon thy right hand did stand the queen in gold of Ophir." Vv. 13–14, "Her clothing is of wrought gold. She shall be brought unto the king in raiment of needlework." Cant 1:10–11, "Thy cheeks are comely with rows of jewels, and thy neck with chains of gold. We will make thee borders of gold with studs of silver." Cant. 7:1, "How beautiful are thy feet with shoes, O prince's daughter!"

The excellencies, and amiable and honorable endowments, of the bridegroom in both are represented by perfumed ointment. Ps. 45:7, "Hath anointed thee with the oil of gladness above thy fellows." Cant. 1:3, "Because of the savor of thy good ointments, thy name is as ointment poured forth; therefore do the virgins love thee."

In both the excellent gifts or qualifications of these lovers, by which they are recommended to each other, and delighted in one another, are compared to such spices as myrrh, aloes, etc. And in both the sense these lovers have of this amiableness, and that sense by which they have comfort and joy, is represented by the sense of smelling. Ps. 45:8, "All thy garments smell of myrrh, and aloes, and cassia, whereby they have made thee glad." Cant. 1:13–14, "A bundle of myrrh is my well-beloved unto me; my beloved is unto me as a cluster of camphire." V. 12,

"While the king sitteth at his table, my spikenard sendeth forth the smell thereof." Cant 2:13, Let us see whether the vines "give a good smell." Cant. 3:6, "Who is this that cometh up out of the wilderness like pillars of smoke, perfumed with myrrh and frankincense, with all powders of the merchant?" Cant. 4:14, "Spikenard, saffron, calamus, and cinnamon, with all trees of frankincense, myrrh, aloes, with all the chief spices."

Indeed in some parts of Ps. 45, the Psalmist makes use of more magnificent representations of the bridegroom's excellency. Vv. 3–4, "And gird thy sword upon thy thigh, O most mighty, with thy glory and thy majesty; and in thy majesty, ride prosperously." So we find it also with respect to the bride. Cant. 6:10, "Who is this that looketh forth as the morning, fair as the moon, clear as the sun, and terrible as an army with banners?" And in both these representations the excellencies of these lovers are represented as martial excellency, or the glorious endowments of valiant warriors.

In both these songs the bride is represented as with a number of virgins that are her companions in her nuptial honors and joys. Ps. 45:14, "She shall be brought in unto the king; the virgins, her companions that follow her, shall be brought unto thee." So in many places of Solomon's Song, the spouse is represented as conversing with a number of the daughters of Jerusalem that sought the bridegroom with her, and therefore she speaks in the plural number. Cant. 1:4, "Draw me, we will run after thee; we will be glad and rejoice in thee. We will remember thy love more than wine."

The representation in both of the manner of the bride's being brought into the king with her companions, with great joy, is exactly alike. Ps. 45:14–15, "She shall be brought in unto the king in raiment of needlework. The virgins, her companions that follow her, shall be brought unto thee. With gladness and with rejoicing, shall they be brought unto thee; they shall enter into the king's palace." Compare this with Cant. 1:4, "The king hath brought me into his chambers; we will be glad and rejoice in thee."

Those who are the friends of the bridegroom, that are united to him and partake of his dear love, are in both these songs represented as gracious and holy persons. Ps. 45:4, "In thy majesty ride prosperously because of truth, meekness, and righteousness." Cant. 1:4, "We will remember thy love more than wine; the upright love thee."

To represent the excellency of the bridegroom's place of abode, in Ps. 45:8, the excellent materials that his palace is made of are mentioned. 'Tis represented as made of ivory. In like manner, as the excellent materials of his palace are spoken of, Cant. 1:17, "The beams of our house are cedar, and our rafters of fir," as elsewhere, the materials of his chariot are mentioned, viz. "the wood of Lebanon," gold, silver, and purple (Cant. 3:9–10).

'Tis objected by some against Solomon's Song, that some expressions seem to have reference to the conjugal embraces of the bridegroom. But perhaps there is nothing more directly supporting this than the 14th, 15th, and 16th verses of the 45th psalm, where seems to be a plain reference to the manner in Israel in which the bride at night used to be led into the bridegroom's bed chamber, her bridesmaids attending her, in the 14th and 15th verses; and then, immediately in the next verse, are we told of the happy fruit of the intercourse in the offspring which they have, "Instead of thy fathers shall be thy children."

'Tis supposed by many to be very liable to a bad construction that the beauty of the various parts of the body of the spouse is mentioned and described in Solomon's Song. But perhaps these are no more liable to a bad construction than the 13th verse of the 45th psalm, where there is mention of the beauty of the bride's clothes, and her being "glorious within," where setting aside the allegory, or mystical meaning of the song, what is most naturally understood as the most direct meaning would seem to be, that she had not only glorious clothing, but was yet more glorious in the parts of her body within her clothing, that were hid by her clothing.

GENERAL INDEX

The abbreviation JE has been used for Jonathan Edwards in this index.

615

INDEX OF BIBLICAL PASSAGES

NEW TESTAMENT

INDEX OF "NOTES ON SCRIPTURE" ENTRIES

Boldfaced page numbers refer to text of entry.

669